CONTEMPORARY POLITICAL THOUGHT

CONTEMPORARY POLITICAL THOUGHT

A READER AND GUIDE

Edited by
Alan Finlayson

EDINBURGH UNIVERSITY PRESS

Selection and editorial material © Alan Finlayson, 2003.
Copyright in the individual chapters is retained by the
contributors. Previously published material is reprinted
by permission of other publishers.

Transferred to Digital Print 2009

Edinburgh University Press Ltd
22 George Square, Edinburgh

Typeset in Sabon and Gill Sans
by Servis Filmsetting Ltd, Manchester, and
printed and bound in Great Britain by
CPI Antony Rowe, Chippenham and Eastbourne

A CIP Record for this book is available from
the British Library

ISBN 0 7486 1382 X (hardback)
ISBN 0 7486 1383 8 (paperback)

CONTENTS

ANALYTICAL TABLE OF CONTENTS

PREFACE

This book, like so many things, took longer than it was meant to. But the delay has been advantageous. It has turned a text that reflected on the state of political theory at the end of one century into a book that looks forward to the shape of things to come in a new one. In so doing, the book tries to remain introductory while refusing to pretend that the field (and world) it addresses is in anything other than a condition of considerable flux. It focuses on the immediacies of practical political life in the twenty-first century and endeavours to show how political theory has contributed to that life and what it might have to become if it is to continue to do so.

Acknowledgements must go to the authors of the individual chapters who responded so well to the challenge set them and to Nicola Carr, editor at Edinburgh University Press, who continues to impress with her patience as well as her skilfully subtle way of exerting pressure. I would also like to thank Holly Roberts (formerly at EUP) who provided invaluable administrative assistance at times when the labyrinth of contemporary publishing left me up the creek in search of a copyright holder. Naturally, the individual authors can take responsibility for the chapters they wrote, but it should be noted that I alone take responsibility for any naivety, callowness, stupidity, ugliness, arrogance or error found in any of the section introductions, questions for discussion, further reading and the glossary. Meanwhile, outside of publishing and academe, my family, as ever, bore the brunt of things. The computer is now available for the playing of games.

NOTES ON THE CONTRIBUTORS

Terrell Carver is Professor of Political Theory at the University of Bristol. He has written extensively on Marx, Engels and Marxism, most recently new translations of *Marx's Later Political Writings* (Cambridge University Press, 1996) and *The Postmodern Marx* (Manchester University Press, 1998). He has also co-edited a volume on poststructuralist methodologies and discourse analysis: *Interpreting the Political: New Methodologies* (Routledge, 1997).

Mark Evans is a Lecturer in the Department of Politics and International Relations in the University of Wales, Swansea, where he co-ordinates the 'Liberalism at the Millennium Project'. In addition to writing various articles on aspects of Liberal political thought, he has edited *The Edinburgh Companion to Contemporary Liberalism* (Edinburgh University Press, 2001).

Adrian Favell is Associate Professor of Sociology at UCLA. He is the author of *Philosophies of Integration: Immigration and the Idea of Citizenship in France and Britain* (2nd edn: Palgrave, 2001), and has written widely on migration in Western Europe, multiculturalism, the integration of immigrants, and EU immigration policy. He is currently undertaking research in various European cities for a book about the lives, experiences and impact of 'free-moving' foreign professionals within the EU.

Alan Finlayson is a Lecturer in the Department of Politics and International Relations in the University of Wales, Swansea. He is a co-author of *Contemporary Social and Political Theory: An Introduction* (Open University Press, 1998) and co-editor of *Politics and Post-structuralism: An Introduction* (Edinburgh University Press, 2002). His own book, *Making Sense of New Labour*, was published by Lawrence and Wishart in 2002.

Tim Hayward is Reader in Politics in the School of Social and Political Studies, University of Edinburgh. His publications include *Ecological Thought: An Introduction* (Polity Press, 1995) and *Political Theory and Ecological Values* (Polity Press, 1998).

Michael Kenny is Reader in Politics at the University of Sheffield. He is the author of *The First New Left: British Intellectuals after Stalin* (Lawrence and Wishart, 1995), and joint editor of *Planning Sustainability* (Routledge, 2000) and *Rethinking British Decline* (Macmillan, 2000). He is currently completing a study of *Liberal Citizenship and Identity Politics* (forthcoming with Polity Press), and is joint editor of *Political Ideologies: A Reader and Guide* (forthcoming with Oxford University Press).

Melissa Lane is University Lecturer in History and Fellow of King's College at Cambridge University. She is the author of *Method and Politics in Plato's Statesman* (Cambridge University Press, 1998) and *Plato's Progeny: How Socrates and Plato Still Captivate the Modern Mind* (Duckworth, 2001), and a contributor to the forthcoming *Cambridge History of Twentieth-century Political Thought*. She is currently writing about the relationship of democratic theory and values to non-electoral forms of political organisation.

Oliver Leaman is Professor of Philosophy at the University of Kentucky. He has written largely on Islamic, Jewish and Asian philosophy, and his recent books include *Averroes and his Philosophy* (Curzon, 1997), *Moses Maimonides* (Routledge, 1997), *Evil and Suffering in Jewish Philosophy* (Cambridge University Press, 1995), *Eastern Philosophy: Key Readings* (Routledge, 2000), *Key Concepts in Eastern Philosophy* (Cambridge University Press, 1999), *A Brief Introduction to Islamic Philosophy* (Polity Press, 1999) and *Introduction to Classical Islamic Philosophy* (Cambridge University Press, 2001). He is the editor of *Friendship East and West: Philosophical Perspectives* (Curzon, 1996) and *The Future of Philosophy* (Routledge, 1998), and co-editor of the *History of Islamic Philosophy* (1996) and the *History of Jewish Philosophy* (Routledge, 1996). He edited the section on Islamic philosophy in the *Routledge Encyclopedia of Philosophy* (1998) and has contributed to many other such works of reference. His latest work includes the *Companion Encyclopedia of Film in the Middle East and North Africa* (Routledge, 2001) and the co-editing of the *Encyclopedia of Death and Dying* (Routledge, 2001).

Iain MacKenzie is a Lecturer in Modern European Philosophy at Middlesex University. He is a co-author of *Contemporary Social and Political Theory: An Introduction* (Open University Press, 1999) and co-editor of *Reconstituting Social Criticism: Political Morality in an Age of Scepticism* (Macmillan, 1999). He has also written numerous articles on poststructuralism and philosophy in various journals including *The Journal of Political Ideologies*, *Critical Review of International Social and Political Philosophy*, *Angelaki* and *Radical Philosophy*.

Tariq Modood, an erstwhile political theorist, is Professor of Sociology, Politics and Public Policy and the founding Director of the Centre for the Study of

Ethnicity and Citizenship at the University of Bristol. His publications include (co-author) *Ethnic Minorities in Britain: Diversity and Disadvantage*, (ed.) *Church, State and Religious Minorities* (PSI, 1997), (joint ed.) *Debating Cultural Hybridity* (Zed Books, 1997) and (joint ed.) *The Politics of Multiculturalism in the New Europe* (Zed Books, 1997). He is a joint founding editor of the journal *Ethnicities* (Sage) and is currently working on several books on political multiculturalism.

Kate Nash is Lecturer in Sociology at Goldsmiths College, London. She is author of *Universal Difference: Feminism and the Liberal Undecidability of 'Women'* (Macmillan, 1998) and *Contemporary Political Sociology: Globalization, Politics and Power* (Blackwell, 2000), and is co-editor (with Alan Scott) of *The Blackwell Companion to Political Sociology* (Blackwell, 2001). She is currently working on issues of human rights and how the internationalising state might be gendered.

John Seery is Professor of Politics at Pomona College, California, where he teaches political theory. His publications include *America Goes to College: Political Theory for the Liberal Arts* (SUNY Press, 2002), *Political Theory for Mortals: Shades of Justice, Images of Death* (Cornell, 1996), *The Politics of Irony* (St Martin's and Macmillan, 1992) and *Political Returns* (Westview, 1990).

Anna Marie Smith is an Associate Professor in the Department of Government, Cornell University. She is the author of *New Right Discourse on Race and Sexuality: Britain 1968–1990* (Cambridge University Press, 1994) and *Laclau and Mouffe: The Radical Democratic Imaginary* (Routledge, 1998). She has had articles published in *New Formations*, *Feminist Review*, *Radical Philosophy*, *Diacritics*, *Constellations*, *Social Text* and the *Michigan Journal of Gender and Law*. She is currently writing a book, *Welfare Reform and Sexual Regulation*, to be published by Cambridge University Press.

GENERAL INTRODUCTION

Alan Finlayson

This book has a 'mission'. It wants to convince you that political theory *matters*; that the ideas, arguments and analyses of political theorists are of relevance and importance to the conduct of 'real-world' political life; that political theory has affected, and does affect, that world and that it can in turn help us to make sense of social life. To condense this 'message' into a short headline, let us declare that 'political theory is essential for life'.

But, unfortunately, that sounds like an advertising slogan – as if political theory were equivalent to bottled water, credit cards and vitamin-enriched breakfast cereal. But what is and is not 'essential for life'? Can we be sure how to answer that question when (for those of us in the rich parts of the world) everything is easily available to anyone with the means to pay for it, and everything is presented as 'essential' for someone, somewhere? Marketing is one of the most widespread of activities in the Western world and advertising one of the most ubiquitous forms of communication. Both have now become central aspects of politics in the Western democracies where debate about pressing social questions is increasingly being replaced by carefully designed strategies to sell potential leaders to passive publics. This book, with the purpose of making political thought available to you in an easily accessible form, of making you want more of it by demonstrating just how essential for life it is, thus runs the risk of becoming merely another exercise in marketing.

Yet politics and political thought cannot just be sold. They are not just one more commodity. Commodities (be they cars, skin moisturisers or religions) are usually presented as self-contained. They promise the answer to a problem (even if you didn't know you had that problem), suggesting that when you have whatever it is that is being sold you won't need anything else (until the next 'new' thing comes on the scene). A commodity takes care of things for you. Politics can't do that. If you approach it in search of an answer or in need of a system of thinking that, like a religious cult, you can just fit yourself into, then you will not 'get' politics or political theory.

Political thinking is thinking about how the world should be. That includes, among other things, thinking about what it means for us to have made a world where everything (including politics) is subject to being sold. Is it right for everything to be sellable? Are there limits to what should be freely available? Are there things that are so important (such as sex, religion or weapons of mass destruction) that they must not be sold? Only thinking (politically, ethically, philosophically) can help us properly address these sorts of question. We might say that political theory is a little like love. If you are paying for it (to save yourself the effort and anxiety of trying to create it), then it isn't the real thing. Loving and thinking are things we do despite the costs. Political thoughts help us find our place in the world, establishing the nature of our relationships with others, with ourselves and with the planet on which we live. Consequently, it is meaningless to declare that political theory is essential for life, that it is 'good' or 'bad' for you, simply because, inevitably, life includes thoughts about how it is to be lived. Political thinking is an unavoidable fact of life.

And yet it isn't. Most of us do not make political thinking a central aspect of our daily living. We are far too busy for that. If I ask what the place of political theory is in our world today, many of the readers of a book such as this will probably answer to themselves that the place of political theory is on introductory politics courses for undergraduates. This is where many of us first encounter systematic inquiry into the ways in which political life should be conceived and ordered or begin to engage in serious and informed debates around questions such as 'should a state embody a particular ethical standpoint?', 'what obligations do we owe to our community?' or 'what is power and who should have it?'

Outside of this learning environment, such debates may seem distant and arcane, perhaps even self-indulgent and almost certainly disconnected from 'the things that really matter'. In any case, 'real' political life (by which people usually mean the things our governments and politicians do) often appears to be little more than the activity of elites that were empowered long before they were elected. We may trust such people and their experts to get on with it, or we might consider them hopelessly corrupt; but either way we probably want to think hard about anything other than politics, for it seems a complicated, tedious business, and the problems it might aim to resolve look hopelessly intractable. Day-to-day tribulations with work, money, friendships and romances – the sheer challenge of finding our way in life – can easily seem far more immediate and pressing than politics.

Lack of interest in politics, as well as distrust of politicians, are widespread and regularly revealed by polling data. In the USA, ongoing polling conducted by the Harris organisation has been turned into an 'alienation index' measuring the extent to which people feel disaffected from the political system. Over the period from 1998 to 2001, this fluctuated between a low of 47 per cent and a high of 62 per cent. It is surely not much comfort to say that 'only' 47 per cent of the American population think that politics and politicians do not have the interests of the people at heart. Citizens of the USA consistently say they feel that their government favours the interests of big business and does not pay much attention to ordinary people.[1] It is no surprise, then, that two of the most used of current political clichés are 'they are all the same', said of politicians, and 'it never makes any difference', said of politics.

But none of this means that political theory is not important. There is, without doubt, too great a distance between our personal experiences, the practical challenges of life, the social problems that concern us and the world of official politics. This distance is one of the core problems of contemporary politics. It is also one to which political theory addresses itself. Many people lack faith in politics and feel that different political positions are really more or less the same. They believe that 'one lot is as bad as another' and that there is no way out of our present impasse: nobody can eradicate poverty, clean up the environment or stop people killing each other. But this is when political theory is needed most. When society feels disconnected, or social change confronts us with new problems, we need to stand back and take a long view; to think again about the underlying issues, the ways in which we analyse and evaluate them and the principles that shape our social values. We need to find ways to address each other clearly, establish the nature of our disputes and ways of resolving them, and we need a diagnosis of our political disaffection. All of this, and more, is what political theory is for.

POLITICAL THEORY IN A SPECIALISED WORLD

The varied chapters that make up this collection address themselves to the ways in which political thought can and does respond to the problems of the world. Certainly, political thought has links to governmental politics. But it is also a more general activity that can help us to understand and participate in society. Political theory does not demand that one withdraw from the world. At its best, it urges us to be part of a world which we all share. But, at a number of points, the authors of the chapters of this book find it necessary to remark on the ways in which political theory has been affected by its comfortable placing in universities, where it has become a specialist discipline composed of experts who mostly talk only to each other and lack connections to other forms of related endeavour.

This problem of specialisation and disconnection from general social life is not unique to political theory. One of the things that characterises contemporary Western societies is the seemingly endless refinement of the division of labour and with it the spread of ever more specialised forms of activity. One is not just a 'manager' but a personnel, financial or resource manager (probably specialising in work for a particular sort of company or organisation). A medical doctor isn't just a doctor but a psychiatrist, oncologist, paediatrician and so forth. As part of such specialisation, many professions have developed their own specialist, technical vocabulary or jargon. For biologists, personnel managers and philosophers, there are associations providing support and updates on the latest techniques and technologies. There are stars of the field, leading players and mavericks. There is your own team to support and rivals with whom to do battle.

In return for cultivating and protecting such areas of specialist knowledge, practitioners (be they psychologists, theologians or reflexologists) can charge a premium for their expertise. But the more they become so refined, the more these activities become cut off from the very people they are supposed to be for. Biologists, for example, examine life at such a high resolution that it seems to us non-specialists as if it has little to do with life as it is lived at all. I feel like a unified organism (most of the time) and not a collection of cells or genes. What seems obvious and clear to the scientist is not so straightforward for the rest of us who can become confused and maybe even anxious about what is being said and done. This can lead to panics (about animal diseases in the food chain, for example, or the risks of genetic experimentation) and to a turning away from science and the medical profession. We don't understand, and so don't trust, the experts. The price of sophistication may well be dislocation.

This is a very particular sort of problem for politics. It too has become specialised and self-referential. Politicians, though many pretend otherwise, are professionals. Most decided early on in life that politics would be their career of choice and then worked assiduously to make themselves successful. There are a whole host of techniques to help politicians get where they want, touching on everything from presentation to policy. Consequently, politicians live in an increasingly rarefied world of politics that isn't the same one we ordinary people with ordinary jobs and aspirations live in. Surrounded by subsidiary specialists (pollsters, defence analysts, economic gurus) and advisers on everything, from the healthcare of the population to the haircare of the President, political leaders come increasingly to see their society as something they must act on rather than be a part of. This not only makes most people *feel* distant from politics. It ensures that they *are*. Specialisation and disconnection are not only a problem *of* politics. They are a problem *for* politics. Specialisation makes society more disconnected and thus managing it or negotiating between its constituent parts ever more complex. Politics cannot be just one specialisation among others, since it is supposed to stand apart from (or above) all competing specialisations, providing a space or opportunity for negotiations between them to take place. This is what 'governing' is thought by many to mean. But it is exactly this sort of governing that the development of politics as a specialist activity makes problematic. After all, how can politics deal adequately with economics or health or the environment when each of these areas requires specialist understanding? But can we leave decisions about these matters simply to experts? We need someone to adjudicate between competing claims; but, if politics is itself an arcane and narrow specialisation, then how can politicians (let alone political theorists) play that role?

As governing becomes more complicated and specialised, the nature of politics itself changes. Government becomes a more purely bureaucratic and technocratic activity, and the intensification of the division of labour changes political society, leading not only to changes in the problems *for* politics but also to changes in the kinds of things that can be understood *as* politics: a proliferation of the types of places and relationships that are of political concern. Politics has stretched and spread 'vertically' and 'horizontally' throughout society: 'vertically' in the sense that there are more and more points where people feel that others are exercising an unaccountable, perhaps unjust, authority over them or find themselves able to exercise some authority over others; 'horizontally' because we also come into greater contact with people who are sufficiently different from us that we find our way of life challenged, questioned or threatened.

Let us consider the 'vertical' extension of politics first. Much political thought is shaped by the problem of the relationship between individuals and the state. It is concerned with how the individual can be protected from the undue interference of the state at the same time as allowing the state to be in a position to undertake the role of governing society as a whole. But this neglects the extent to which we may experience authority exercised over us not by the state but by other people in society. Whatever and wherever it is, politics is not simply a matter of the relationships between a citizen and the government. There are many more locations and forms of power than that. In a democratic society, politics is not only about what 'they' do to 'us'. It is about what we do to (and with) each other – at work, in our leisure time, in the street and even at home. Perhaps in the doctor's consulting room we feel that we are being judged, manipulated and assessed in ways that do not take full account of who we are. We may feel we are being sold medical care by people with an interest that is as much institutional or financial as it is medical, or that a medical 'establishment' is going to look after the interests of doctors more than it will care for patients. There are similar potential power relationships in schools, universities and most workplaces. Perhaps our professors or schoolteachers are not according us the respect or the rights we feel to be ours, or maybe our boss is acting towards us in a way we feel is excessive or unjust. But our doctors and professors may in turn feel that they are being imposed upon by senior figures in their profession who exercise managerial and intellectual authority over them. Then again, these professional leaders are put under pressure by state bureaucrats or institutional managers who don't necessarily understand the duties and needs of the profession. Even the politicians may think that they are no longer in charge of things since they are affected by the actions of other governments, global private companies or supranational organisations such as the **European Union** or the **World Bank** and **International Monetary Fund**.

Now let us briefly consider the 'horizontal' expansion of politics. It is easy to imagine that politics takes place within fairly homogeneous communities (usually called nations). But this view has been challenged repeatedly by those who point out that such communities are in fact divided on the basis of social class and gender. It is increasingly becoming clear that these are not the only instances of such division. Society in general is coming to consist of ever more diverse groups, each of which seems to have a distinct appeal to make and a culture of its own. In addition to being citizens and workers of a particular kind, we are also people with specific beliefs or values (religious or otherwise) and distinct cultural practices. We might experience discrimination because of our ethnic background, our sexuality or our gender. We might feel that our traditional way of life is being undermined and that we are continually forced to accept the ways which a majority (or a minority) demands be imposed upon us. We cannot always feel safe with 'our' ways. The pushing together of peoples in cities and workplaces, the exposure of each of us to the culture of others (through mass media and commodification as well as physical proximity) forces us to realise the differences between ourselves and others, making us feel less certain about the rightness of 'our' ways or ever more determined to defend them by any means necessary. The relationships we have to others thus become a matter of political concern because we have to work out how we will get along with each other (or not), and this raises in an intense way questions about how the law should treat us, of whether or not the state should try to represent the special interests of all, some or none.

This situation is a challenge for political theory, which needs to address these problems, to understand them and develop ways of helping us plot paths through the world. But, at the same time, political theory is subject to these kinds of changes and is part of these new problems. As a field of intellectual endeavour, it has become more and more specialised and cut off from the public at large. As a professional activity, it has become internally more diverse and hierarchical as well as pressurised to prove its relevance – its 'unique selling point' in a world that is not short of 'lifestyle' options.

But there is no consensus about how politics should be studied. Some think it should be a quasi-scientific endeavour focused on hypothesis-generation and empirical testing. Others continue to broaden the scope of what counts as a viable topic for political analysis or interpretation.[2] Within universities, political analyses are undertaken in departments of History, Literature, Sociology, Economics, Geography, Cultural Studies, Communication Studies and Leadership Studies (to mention just a few). At the same time as all these disciplines across the arts and sciences make claims that are political in nature, political theory over the twentieth century has come to be conceived as an endeavour related to but nevertheless distinct from them. It is not political science or International Relations (which have their own theories), and has its own divisions or departments in universities as well as professional associations, journals and prizes. Some of the people in departments of politics, research institutes or think-tanks study voting behaviour, policy-formation or political culture. Others look at defence, social security or education. Political theory is understood as just another subfield. As if this weren't enough differentiation, there are also greater and greater divisions within political theory itself. One might specialise in the history of political thought, moral theory or legal philosophy; European, American or African political thought; individual rights, group rights or international state's rights. This is before we even begin to account for divisions and differences on the basis of political or philosophical inclination (and these are legion). All of this, needless to say, is deeply problematic.

It was not always so. There was a time when the primary division of labour was that between mental and manual labour. Those fortunate enough to be in a position to think about things could think about whatever was in need of thinking: art or science, theology or cosmology.[3] Works of political theory were concerned with many aspects of social and spiritual life. For the philosophers of Ancient Greece, studying a regime didn't mean examining only the minute processes of government. It meant looking at the whole structure of the society and asking about the kind of people it produced or the virtues it promoted. To study and pronounce on politics was to study and pronounce on the best ways in which a life could be lived. Thinking about politics meant looking at the constitutions of existing states, studying theories and considering, in some detail, the best size for a state, the sort of land it should be on and the best geographical location. Political analysis involved thinking about religion, language, the cultural and the natural worlds. The whole was orientated towards establishing what the best way to live might be. **Aristotle**, for example, saw the purpose of his work as a consideration of 'what form of political community is best of all for those who are most able to realise their ideal of life'.

In this context, political theorists might (for a variety of reasons) imagine entire political societies. As part of a massive metaphysical argument, **Plato**, in *The Republic*, described an entire ideal city state and, later, enumerated all its laws. In more recent times, political thinkers have not only imagined or debated the best possible political structures but also participated in bringing them about. Thomas **More** (who made the idea of Utopia famous) was also a politician and, as Lord Chancellor, for a time the closest adviser of King Henry VIII (who later had him executed). **Rousseau**, who also described an ideal republic of presumed perfect freedom, was invited to write a constitution for Corsica. James **Madison** didn't only consider the best way to order a state but also helped design one and then became its President. For all these thinkers, political theories were inseparable from wide-ranging beliefs about human nature, the best to way to live and the commitment to make that life liveable through establishing an appropriate form of government.

Political theorists do not now think about the entirety of life in such an explicit way and are unlikely to be directly involved in the management of a state. It was once possible to imagine realistic alternatives to present ways of ordering things, since states were always forming and reforming and, because they were smaller and simpler in structure, a well-placed philosopher might, conceivably, bend the ear of the people (or person) in charge (or wanting to be in charge). Indeed, the political theorist might be considered an important part of a movement for political change with valuable skills in justifying outlandish courses of action. Today, even if a philosopher had the ear of a king or president (as some, on occasion, do), it is far from certain that such a ruler would have the power to act on whatever wise words might be whispered to them. Thousands of functionaries, business leaders and media opinion-formers would also have to be spoken to.

But this does not mean that there is no longer a possibility or a need for political theory, and it certainly is not a cue to lapse into nostalgia under the illusion that things were better in a bygone simpler age. Rather, it means that the doing and the thinking of politics have changed. It is something that cannot be done alone but is carried out as part of the collective labour of many people doing many different things. Political theory builds on the grand legacy that commits it to asking how life together can and should be lived. But it also has to face up to new problems, and that means finding new ways to think about things. It can only begin to do this because it has a past composed of thoughts and deeds that have shaped where we are now and because of the many acts of many thinkers in many fields. What looks today like esoteric specialisation is just the present end of an important activity that has been going on for millennia. In a fragmenting social universe, we need political theory (though not theory alone) more, not less.

THREE TYPES OF POLITICAL THEORY

Western intellectual culture is rooted in the philosophy and poetry of Ancient Greece and the theology and morality of Judaism and Christianity. It is aware of these roots thanks, in large part, to the efforts of preservation made by the Islamic world during Europe's 'Dark Age'. All contemporary Western thinkers share in this legacy and the more recent heritage of the European **Reformation** and **Enlightenment**. The former challenged the singular authority of the Church and its automatic relationship to political power and decision-making. When Protestantism split into many different sects, it generated a powerful force for the secularisation of politics and the separation of Church and state. Such is the basis of liberal neutrality and the non-doctrinal state, something definitive of Western political thinking (if not practice). Few in the West, whatever their religious beliefs, argue that our states should be theocracies, run by the same people who run the churches.

The separation of Church and state was part of the movement towards what was known as Enlightenment: the commitment to the use of reason in the analysis of human affairs rather than reliance on tradition or superstition. Thinkers of Enlightenment believed that we could reason out the best ways of managing our affairs and in so doing improve our conditions, emancipating ourselves from all forms of despotism. In the famous words of the eighteenth-century philosopher Immanuel Kant, Enlightenment was concerned with freeing humanity from 'self-incurred immaturity'. Its motto, he said, was 'have the courage to use your own understanding' (Kant, 1996b: 54). All political theory, even now, stands in the shadow cast by such ambitions.

But what is emancipation? What does it mean to be free? Enlightenment Liberalism was in large measure defined by opposition to the absolute power of monarchs and demands for accountability and legitimacy. Its principles emphasised restrictions on the power of the state as, for example, in the US Constitution. But, by the nineteenth century, the power taken away from the monarch had reappeared elsewhere in society, and it seemed to some radicals that the state was simply serving the interests of the few who controlled the wealth and productive capacity of capitalist industrial economies. For those well-off people, their situation was the welcome result of the freedom of people from their rulers. But, for the rest, it was a new form of domination, even enslavement. It came to seem that emancipation from the state was not enough and that we also needed to be freed from domination by each other, especially those who could monopolise state power. Where some saw the promise of Enlightenment fulfilled by liberal capitalism, socialists and Marxists saw it as an emancipation yet to be achieved. Western political thought can still be understood as consisting of a variety of responses to the ways of thinking and doing inaugurated by Enlightenment.

Firstly, what we might call the mainstream tradition of Enlightenment Liberalism has produced a political thought that is interested in rational solutions to certain sorts of problem. Methodologically individualist, such theorising aims to develop defensible norms by which we can act or justify our political actions (or challenge those of others). This sort of political theory has a lot in common with moral philosophy in general. It is concerned to test out the rightness of our opinions and principles; to see how they can be justified and thus to consider the basis to such claims. But this tradition starts from certain premises: that when talking about political society we are talking about the interrelationship of rational and free individuals who take priority over society. Rational, normative principles make it possible to adjudicate in the sorts of disputes that arise between these individuals and to provide principles to which all can assent. Such theory sees itself as a kind of guide to the conduct of political life and may often see the state as a body that should be neutral with regard to the particular interests of groups in society since its function is, essentially, to mediate and adjudicate between them. For these reasons, it tends to be legalistic in form and is often closely linked to **jurisprudence** or legal philosophy. Indeed, one might say that the archetypal form of such theorising is the deliberations of the US Supreme Court.

But abstract principles, however well constructed, don't always easily apply in concrete conditions. We also need political theory that explains the very

nature of politics and political activity or explicates certain political phenomena. We need to know what a state is and how states come to be the way they
are. We might also want to reflect further on the needs, wants and overall
nature of individuals. What if it is a mistake to think of people as removed from
the social contexts which give meaning and purpose to their lives? Addressing
such questions is the task of what we can call explanatory political theory. But
there are two sides to this. On the one hand, there is what we might call the
ontological aspect – that concerned with specifying the essential nature or
source of things. That might include specifications regarding human nature and
the constitution of societies or even the universe itself. Such ontological thinking may be, in a way, opposed to political thinking. Politics is concerned with
how we can remake the world. Ontology tells us the way things are and have
to be. If you believe that God created man and the world and that man is inherently sinful, then this ontology will lead you to conclude that society should be
run according to God's law, and in it the Church must have a central place.
Political dispute often turns on rival ontologies, the clash of different beliefs
about the way things are (which is why normative theory tries to push such
commitments to the background). At this level, politics has most in common
with metaphysical philosophy in general. But there is a second level to explanatory theory. Marxist theory, for example, provided a framework for the analysis and explanation of the capitalist economy and state. Feminism, in
advancing the case for the equitable treatment of women, had to show how the
inequality of women had come about and been maintained. In both cases, political theory turned its attention to explaining the workings of various state or
social institutions; and, although ontologies may have been implied in their
thinking, such a focus was not always a central part of their analytical procedure. In this aspect, political theory is quite close to fields such as political sociology and social theory.

Such explanatory political theories reveal the workings of political phenomena not simply out of disinterested curiosity but because this can assist in any
normative project. But, as well as being a handmaid to normative projects,
explanatory political theory may also want to explain the creation of those very
norms. It may therefore take a focus that is much broader than normative
theory, looking at how and why political systems develop, notions of the political itself arise and people believe what they do. At such moments, political
theory may become linked to what we will here call **critical theory**.[4] This is
explicitly motivated by the desire to criticise the present state of things. Critical
political theory can come in a variety of different forms, but the central thread
is that it seeks not only to explain or to justify but also to be engaged with political events. Critical political theory wants to find a way to criticise things that
are wrong *and* develop a strategy for making things better. When we undertake
critical political theory, we are not only *thinking* about politics – we are trying
to *do* it. After all, what is the good of the best normative principles and the most
clear-headed explanation of the social world if we do not have a clue about how

to effect change? In its critical moment, political theory is focused on such change. It may even become strategic in orientation, helping us to be sure about what is achievable in the here and now and then generating some courses of action to go about achieving it.

Naturally, this division of the field (into normative, explanatory and critical) would be contested by other political theorists. Certainly, they would be right to say that these are not completely distinct areas of endeavour. Normative theorising must have its explanatory and critical moments. An explanatory theory without a normative or critical aspect runs the risk of turning into empty scholasticism, while an explicitly critical political theory, speaking from a particular political viewpoint, will also need to clarify its own normative basis and certainly be in need of arguments about how and why societies work in the ways they do. These are all parts of the activity of political theory. Our judgements about the world and our ways of acting within it are dependent on our beliefs about how that world works. By the same token, these are linked to the way we act on and understand the world. This is why political theory cannot take for granted any assumptions about the way things are. It does not build uncritically on the findings of social or natural science, accepting without query their statements about the way the world is made. Political theory always involves a combination of intellectual moments. Explanation, critique and judgement combine and fold back on each other. Political theory is always aware that this is a world we have made (at least to a degree) and that central to that world is power. Viewed from the political angle, society looks like a way of organising and exercising power, and this means that political theory must develop an unwillingness to let anything go by uncontested. We cannot let the claims of theologians be free from criticism. We cannot even let reason itself walk in the world free and unquestioned. Always, we want to know the powers at work in a situation, the reasons why people come to make their claims and whose interests may be served by them.

Political thinking is burdensome because it never has a place to rest and never finds a secure ground on which to stand and pronounce. Its duty in the world is to ensure that things can always be questioned and disputed (even as it tries to ensure that the dispute doesn't get too out of hand). This too is part of the legacy of Enlightenment. Our commitment to reason means that we must question reason itself, however, whenever and wherever it manifests itself. The specialised task of political theory is therefore to challenge all specialisation including its own. Political thought is not at all arcane or abstract for, fundamentally, it is concerned to establish how we ought to live, how we do live and how we may come to live as we might.

POLITICAL THEORY OF THE PRESENT

Social change has always thrown up new things for societies to deal with; but today certain sorts of problems are particularly intense, and we seem to find them on a larger scale and of greater complexity than ever before. The chapters in this book, and the forms of thought they examine, all touch on (and are shaped by) these contemporary political problems. However, the political complexity of these social changes is doubled because claims regarding social change (its extent, nature and causes) are themselves political in character. Political dispute does not centre only on rival arguments about how to deal with particular problems. It also concerns arguments about what those problems are and even whether or not they are problems at all. Medical doctors may disagree with each other over the best form of treatment for a particular illness but can (to a significant degree) objectively assess the nature of the disease itself. But diagnoses of social problems are never so objective or disinterested. We disagree not only about what should done to 'improve' society but also about the need for such improvements and the causes of problems. For example, people may agree that poverty is a problem. But they will probably disagree over the extent to which there is poverty (disputing statistics, for example) and certainly disagree over definitions of poverty and its causes. One side may identify the problem as the moral weakness and idleness of the poor (leading them to advocate some sort of programme of moralisation). Others, however, might argue that poverty is caused by the structure of wealth-creation and distribution and so advocate changes to governmental taxation and investment priorities. Still others might argue that poverty is not a political problem at all; that we should simply accept the fact that some will be richer than others and not make it an object of public policy. It is easy to forget this 'higher' level of political debate, but it is one of the most important since the definition of a problem often determines the sorts of things that can be considered as solutions.

In this next section, we will remind ourselves (in a very general way) of some issues and problems that appear to be specific to our time and which are preoccupying political thinkers of all sorts. But we need to be aware that it is possible (and perhaps necessary) to contest the ways in which these problems are presented.

Global instability

Internationally, everything about politics is in upheaval. From the end of the Second World War until 1989, international politics was conducted in the shadow of the Cold War: the face-off between the two superpowers of the USA and the Soviet Union. With the collapse of the Soviet Union, the 'world system' has completely altered. Rather than initiate an era of peace and security, the ending of the Cold War has created numerous fractures in world politics and engendered more uncertainty than we could have imagined. During the Cold War, the superpowers held potential conflicts in minor regions of the world in check. Without this, many regions of the world are highly unstable. This is manifested in the outbreak of numerous civil wars and, of course, in the spread of global terrorism. As the only superpower, the USA is in the position of being able to dominate others militarily, economically and (to a considerable degree) culturally. That puts great strain on, and induces great pressures within, the countries subject to that power and places a frighteningly intense burden of power and responsibility on the government and citizens of the USA.

This situation demands an effort to redefine and reshape the way in which the world is ordered. But to what end should those efforts be directed? How are we to decide? Some advocate the consolidation of international institutions that can order the world: international courts of justice reinforcing human rights; more international agreements that limit the stockpiles of weapons countries keep; organisations to oversee many aspects of international inter-action. Such a view is shared by the liberal left across the USA and Europe. Others, however, see such moves as a dangerous threat to national sovereignty and an attempt to impose the way of life of one part of the world onto others. This latter view, perhaps ironically, is shared by the political right in the USA, Europe and the Middle East.

In the past, the establishment of peace and justice *within* states was a central concern of political thought. Now we must focus on peace and justice *between* states, devising principles to guide us in our judgements of disputes between sovereign authorities. There is precedent for this in the work of Immanuel Kant, and it has been notably pursued by the leading contemporary exponent of polit-ical thought in a Kantian style (Rawls, 1999). But in its explanatory and criti-cal aspects there is also a job of work for political theory (in collaboration with other forms of investigation and analysis) to undertake. We need to understand as best we can the nature of global politics, the forces that influence it and the ways in which actions taken at the global level come from and have a recipro-cal influence upon the local.

This means that political theory has to be critical of itself, assessing its own attachment to the nation state as the privileged unit of politics in the modern world and challenging the ways in which a traditional focus on political com-munity may have led to a neglect of intercommunal relations or at least their abandonment to proponents of a hard-faced and usually militaristic 'realism'. Our most venerable political concepts, from sovereignty to justice, were built alongside notions of territorially defined states that were presumed to be con-gruent with culturally homogeneous communities. In a world where territori-alism, nationhood and cultural homogeneity are all phenomena and concepts under intense scrutiny and revision (thanks to forces that are economic and cul-tural as much as they are governmental), our political ideas are stretched to breaking point.

Economic globalisation

Instability and restructuring in world politics are just a part of what is now usually referred to as 'globalisation'. This is an ambiguous term, and there is much debate as to its validity, but generally the idea of globalisation suggests that the world is far more interconnected than it used to be (see Giddens, 1999; Held and McGrew, 2000; Held, 1999; Baylis and Smith, 2001). Economically, pro-duction and exchange take place in an international arena. Huge multinational corporations, with annual turnovers larger than the entire economies of many of the countries in the world, are engaged in business that is far from limited to one country. Machine parts can be made in a number of different countries then shipped to another place where they are assembled into a finished product before being moved on again to the many countries in which they will be sold. This represents more than a change in economic or productive relationships. It is a change in social relationships in general, and as such it poses new kinds of moral and political questions. The clothes I wear may have been made by people in a country far from mine. They may have been made by children working for a pittance. In buying and wearing such clothes, am I colluding in their exploitation or assisting them in their overall economic development? Perhaps the reason why textile manufacturers are sourcing their product in distant countries is that the regulation of employment is less strict there. Could it be that the privileges and protections of workers in my country are bought at the expense of the rights of those in others? But then, workers in my country lose their jobs when companies relocate. What can be done about this?

The sorts of political movements and political relationships we were used to in the twentieth century, when a nationally based working class might be organised through national trade unions to negotiate with nationally based employers and governments, are no longer with us (or at least not in the same form). The rights enjoyed or lost by people in one part of the world are now inextricably linked to the rights of those elsewhere, and the multinational corporations cannot be regulated by single national governments. As a result, economic actions are increasingly presented to us as inevitable, necessary and unavailable for challenge. Our states, it seems, have no choice but to satisfy the demands of the global market or face terminal decline. Once again, the arguments and proposals of political theory need to be revised in ways that acknowledge and respond to these developments. Perhaps it is the duty of political theory to raise uncomfortable questions about the global accumulation of wealth and the current primacy of economics over other aspects of social life such as community, religion, family, justice and freedom. At the same time, we need to think about the extent to which such problems are really new.

Political globalisation

Just as economics and culture become globalised, so too does politics (see Baylis and Smith, 2001). There are many political phenomena that can't be dealt with at the national level. For example, air pollution caused by factories in the UK falls as acid rain in Scandanavia. No single country can stop the causes of ozone-depletion and global warming. Security crises in one part of the world rebound on others (perhaps in the form of population-displacement), and economic collapse in one region will inevitably affect others. Consequently, there are more and more international bodies designed to oversee these and with the power to shape the politics of individual nations, and these too have become part of political disputes.

At the same time, there seems to be an increasing demand from many people that their own nations should not stand by while other people's suffer, and the newer communications technologies allowing the fast movement of information from one place to another have supported the growth of global networks of political organisation. As political problems and issues become global in scale, those involved in them begin to organise globally. So it is that we have seen the global co-ordination of oppositional campaigns to match the globalisation of economic power. Some argue that we need to develop a form of global civil society capable of responding to such phenomena (see Walzer, 1995). What is for certain is that there is a growing trend towards the reconfiguration of international political, economic and cultural space and a backlash against it. Political thought has no choice but to address this, not only by providing evaluative frameworks that sanction and legitimise international organisations or international actions (humanitarian and other military interventions) but also by facilitating contact between the varied political traditions of the world, not the least of which is that between the West, the Far East and the Middle East.

Cultural globalisation

In addition to its economic aspect, there are definite cultural dimensions to globalisation. It is unlikely that the people within a single nation will partake in the same forms of cultural experience all of the time or that they will even share in their own national culture. Some may live very 'traditional' lives, but others may experience a highly variable and cosmopolitan existence, regularly travelling to other countries, perhaps with jobs that necessitate them developing a 'postnational' perspective. Because we can travel more than we used to, we are more exposed than ever before to the lifestyles and cultures of many different places and peoples. Internet technology has changed the relationship of individuals to the world around them, allowing people in distant locations but with similar interests to meet and share ideas. Such processes place new stresses on traditional social formations but also create opportunities for new kinds of political alliance and new forms of cultural expression and even identity-formation.

If the people of a given political community really are varied in their tastes, habits and affiliations, then the state has to adjust to this. It may not be able to represent the interests of all and may have to act as a different sort of broker in new kinds of political dispute that are primarily cultural in nature. But political theory, again, has to ask some of the tricky normative questions. Is it good that our societies are now so diverse? Should politics be concerned with shoring up and defending traditional ways of being and doing, or does this amount to advocating a kind of communal purity that can only be achieved at the expense of hard-won rights and that might, as it has done in the past, end in terror? The end of the Cold War has led to conflicts that have displaced many millions of people, and the globe is full of refugees seeking a place to settle or at least to be safe until they can return to their homes. Such massive population-movement has become a political problem across Europe and in Australasia because people appear to experience such immigration as some sort of threat. In the USA too (a nation founded by migrants), immigration, particularly from Latin America, has become a fraught and contentious issue. Political thought needs to be aware that its own traditions of thinking, from the Ancient Greeks to the Romantics of the eighteenth and nineteenth centuries and the nationalists of the twentieth, have caused us to think of citizenship in terms of stable communities united around a unique tradition or spirit. Rights have been given to people on the basis of their membership of these communities from which they take in as much as they also contribute to them. The movement of many peoples in and out of these communities makes such notions problematic. Can we think of ways to give people rights regardless of their location at any particular time? What are the duties of nations to those who come into them seeking sanctuary or greater opportunities to prosper? Can we reconceive ideas developed at the 'national' level so that they are fit for the conditions of an international world? Should governments accept that their populations just don't like new ethnic minorities coming to live with them, or is it their role to encourage and foster more tolerance?

Cultural differentiation

These global-level developments are partly cause and partly effect of a range of social changes happening across the Western world. As we have seen, much political thought has proceeded on the basis that political communities would always be fairly homogeneous and that they would be made up of people who were mostly alike. For example, **Aristotle** believed that the ideal political community would be composed of people who would know each other, and even advocated that it was a bad thing for any one person in the state to be too good or great, as he might unbalance it. Such a view is perhaps no longer possible, if it ever was.

The ancients did recognise (even if they did not value) certain differences. They knew there was a division of labour of some sort. They believed there would always be slaves, and they appreciated certain distinctions between women and men. Now, just as these sorts of prejudicial differentiation have been systematically challenged across the globe, we find a whole host of further differentiations developing and affecting the organisation of polities. For example, we increasingly live in multi-cultural societies. On the one hand, this is because of population change and movement. Immigration has changed the shape of populations and means that we live in countries of many faiths and many cultural practices. In politics, this means we have to think about whether states should try to treat peoples in ways that acknowledge and respect these differences or endeavour to produce homogeneity. In some places where there has been ethnic conflict, legislatures or assemblies are explicitly organised so as to mirror the division of the population. Should political thought continue to think in terms of homogeneity, or should it try to start from the position that such unity is not possible and perhaps even undesirable? Should it aim to valorise difference, to respect and protect it, or should it seek to re-establish the basis for a more universal commonality?

Individuation

Just as this differentiation of polities into more and more discrete groups intensifies, we also seem to be seeing what the sociologists call 'individuation'. In contemporary Western culture, the individual is sovereign. We experience any attempt to limit the scope of individual action as an affront against our very humanity. In a sense, this is another side to the process of specialisation, for people increasingly conceive of themselves as individuals free from the general constraints of tradition or habit. Where once we might have grown up expecting to become the same sort of adult as our parents (following in a father's footsteps by taking on the same job, or learning to be like the mother who trained us for a life of domestic labour), this is ceasing to be the most common pattern of life. Instead, we expect to 'make our own way' in the world and to live lives that are markedly different to those of our family. Rather than being 'like them', we expect to 'be ourselves', unconstrained by traditions that define us in terms of our class, occupation or gender. This is sometimes explained by sociologists as the result of modernisation uprooting traditional forms of life (see Giddens, 1990, 1996). The local contexts within which life used to be lived and that provided us with a map directing our choices in certain directions have become 'disembedded', detached from their grounding in social life. We inhabit 'post-traditional' societies and can't rely on old routines or habits. Instead, 'we have no choice but to choose how to be and how to act [to cope with] the multiplicity of possibilities which almost every aspect of daily life . . . offers' (Giddens, 1996: 28). For some sociologists, this is a concrete situation to which politics must adapt. It means that people are suspicious of arrangements or institutions that perpetuate 'outdated' forms of identity and organisation. Pollsters and 'focus-group' analysts claim that people's aspirations are now much greater than they once were and that people value, above all, choice. They do not want states to manage society and do not want to be treated as simply members of large social categories. If true, this poses a considerable challenge to habits of political thinking. But scepticism towards the arguments of pollsters, pundits and would-be sociological gurus is usually a good default starting position. It is quite possible to construct the opposite argument – that the world is becoming more culturally homogeneous thanks to the dominance of a consumer and media culture that makes available the same products to countries across the world.

The argument about individuation is closely related to very particular political and ideological claims. For much of the twentieth century, there appeared to be a consensus across Europe, and to some extent in America also, that it was the responsibility of states to ensure the presence of mechanisms that could care for those who had fallen on hard times. The British welfare state, and in the USA Lyndon Johnson's 'Great Society', conceived of nations as collectives that owed protection to each of their members. Welfare states treated people as aggregates of social groups and intervened into social life in order to reshape and even redefine the lives of individuals. The corollary of arguments about individuation is that individuals resented this since they felt they were being treated as passive parts of a larger social organism and now want to be responsible for themselves and their families. The task of the state is therefore to minimise the barriers to individual choice or, at most, to ensure that we all have the skills to be responsible individuals. This is not merely an 'objective' piece of sociological analysis. It is also an ethical prescription deriving from a description of how things are presumed to be, a claim about how they ought to be. For the most bold of the theorists of **rational choice** individualism, it is good if people regard themselves as disconnected from tradition and habit since this prevents attachment to prejudicial or bigoted ways of thinking, freeing them to be active and entrepreneurial (see Chong, 2000). Political theory has to examine this sort of assumption at all levels (normative, explanatory and critical), taking on the responsibility of asking if this sort of 'individualism' is a good thing or if it is indeed a real trend. It may be that individuation goes along with a kind of depoliticisation of life and too exclusive a focus on our private lives to the detriment of public need. Indeed, it may be that excessive individualism only increases personal anxiety. Freed from tradition and expectation, we find ourselves buffeted by the cold winds of unprotected social life. But, if individuation is a real trend to be welcomed, then we require the development of new sorts of politics and new forms of political organisation to fit with this aspiration. Certainly, individualism is current orthodoxy; and, as a product, in part, of Enlightenment forms of political thought, it is the obligation of that political thought to reflect on what it has created.

Identity politics

The growth, or extension, of individuation links with increasing cultural differentiation within polities to produce the most notable phenomenon of the end of the twentieth century and the beginning of the twenty-first: an obsession with what are called '**identity politics**'. By this is meant the organisation of political demands around issues related to identity. A good example of this, but by no means the only one, is feminism. Strictly speaking, not all forms of feminism should be understood as **identity politics**. Much feminist political action and thinking has been orientated towards the removal of inequality, prejudice, exploitation and oppression. But some feminisms have also been concerned with asserting the place in society of women specifically as women and with demanding a public realisation of the difference of women and their different needs. Other forms of political action also turn on this sort of demand, such as the gay-rights movement and groups organised around a range of cultural, racial and ethnic identities. What is specific about these is that they constitute a demand not simply for equal treatment or full inclusion in the universal category of human or citizen but for acceptance of particular differences as a necessary requirement for the health and well-being of individuals. In the jargon, they demand 'recognition' (see Taylor, 1994). Out of this, we see a range of groups active in the name of particular identities. To those already mentioned, we might add a whole host of religious and regional 'identities' (not merely the 'emancipatory' movements of the liberal left), all of which draw on claims about group identity in shaping political constituencies that are markedly different to those, such as social class, that appeared to dominate politics in the twentieth century. Political thought has built up a battery of concepts and methods for thinking about equality and civil, political and social rights. Generally, this has been associated with the expansion of the numbers of people afforded these rights, of those recognised as part of the universal category of citizen. But **identity politics**, at its most interesting, seems to want something else – respect and protection from forms of oppression other than the strictly economic/exploitative (Young, 1990). In concrete political terms, this takes the form of policies that are certainly orientated towards equality (such as affirmative action or positive discrimination) but also to special sorts of support for groups understood as minorities whose distinct way of life may be undermined by the dominance of a majority culture. The long revolution in political society whereby democracy was extended to all seems to have evolved into a process of increasing fragmentation and a proliferation of particular identities[5] (now including those who are overweight or simply fat),[5] each of which demands the right to be unique and free from criticism. In some arguments, this is a natural step in the growth of democratic freedom, but for others it undermines the core principles of liberty. Only political theory can help clarify this debate.

New technologies

Alongside, or rather inside, all these social, cultural, economic and political changes is the impact of a variety of new technologies. Human innovations and inventions have always had immense, usually unintended and mostly unpredictable effects upon social life. This is not simply a matter of the potential dangers or risks of technologies such as nuclear power, nor only of the uses to which they might be put (such as building yet more destructive weapons). Technologies can transform the ways in which social life is conducted. Think, for example, of what is made possible thanks to Edison's invention of the electric lightbulb. Without it there would be no, or at least very little, night life. The working day could not extend much past sunset for most people, and, as in times past, every philosopher would wear glasses due to eye-strain thanks to reading by candlelight. The electric lightbulb gave humanity a little more mastery over nature and transformed our relationship to time. In so doing, it made possible drastic alterations in the way we relate to each other and changed our visions of what the good life might be.

Political theorists have not usually been the first to notice the importance of technological innovation. In his landmark work of political thought, *Leviathan*, Thomas **Hobbes**, in a passage that with hindsight seems foolish, remarked that the invention of the printing press, while ingenious, was of no great significance. But in our time it is clear that communications technologies, like the printing press, are of particular significance for politics, which is so deeply related to the flow and control of information and ideas and which can only take place in polities that are themselves made possible by networks of communication. The growth of mass media, then global media and now international one-to-one communication achieved through mobile phones and the Internet has changed the size, scale and type of communities that can be formed into political constituencies. But also of importance to and for politics are the technologies that can in themselves raise new political problems. This is most obvious in the case of environmental degradation caused by polluting industries. But we also have to consider the ways in which technologies, as with the electric lightbulb, have changed the way we experience our world and even our own bodies. Not only do we use machines with our bodies, but we can put machines inside our bodies or treat our body as a machine and, when it doesn't work, 're-engineer' it. With artificially produced chemicals, we can alter the perception of the brain, its moods and experiences. The ability of medicine to extend life has already meant that an increasing proportion of the population of the most advanced states are in old age, which leads them to make particular demands. The scientific capacity to affect the plant, animal and human genome raises new moral and political problems and changes our relationship to the very stuff of life. Should private corporations be allowed to retain patent rights on parts of the human genome? What should be our attitude to experimentation on human embryos? These are not simply new issues for political or moral theory to address – for, in changing the way we think about what it is to be human, they can affect our conceptions at their very root and transform what we understand about being alive.

The end of 'grand narratives' and the end of ideology

Combined, all these new trends and pressures have led many to declare the collapse of 'grand narratives'. By grand narratives is meant those large-scale totalising theories that offered explanations of society, even history as a whole, and so provided a framework for the adjudication or understanding of all political matters. The most obvious example would be Marxism, which, in the crude form too often deployed by supposed advocates, believed it could explain society through the prism of class struggle and which, understood correctly, could entirely liberate humankind. But one should also include in the list of grand narratives all the Enlightenment philosophies of human progress and improvement that sought to unite society under this or that universally applicable framework. Many now feel that even the argument that we should recognise a universally shared 'humanity', of which all people formed a part, has been too insensitive to particularity and individuality. It has been 'difference-blind' and so, in the name of extending liberty, has inadvertently imposed a particular framework on all.

In part, this sort of argument forms a critique of Western traditions of philosophy and political thought. A good case can be made that Enlightenment thought was closely tied to the colonial expansion of Europe and that the assertion of Western civilisation necessitated the subjugation of the non-Western and its confinement within labels such as 'uncivilised' and 'primitive'. European scholars and adventurers have tended to treat other regions of the world as if they were homogeneous units of more or less exotic 'others' to be understood in terms of their deviation from the Western 'norm' (see Said, 1978; 1994). For such critics, the universal principles of Western Enlightenment were in fact the product of a particular configuration of power relations which they helped to legitimate. But now the West can no longer be imagined as a separate cultural bloc of the world. Our social and political ideas must consequently be revised to take account of the experience of the non-Western world.

Naturally, such arguments are not uncontroversial, receiving heavy criticism from the political 'right', which sees them as an attempt to undermine all that is good and true about Western liberal democracy. But they have also received criticism from those on the radical left who see them as just another way in which the West extends its particular, and repressive, notion of tolerance over the globe (see Žižek, 1997). Such critics see the argument that all values are merely the expression of particular interests as emerging from the same sources that have produced an avowedly right-wing argument about the 'end of ideology', most famously advanced by Francis Fukuyama (1992). Fukuyama argued that, with the collapse of the Soviet Union and the triumph of liberal democratic capitalism, history in the sense of a continual process of development to a better and more rational world had come to an end. There were no more challenges to the way of the West: its values and political arrangements had been accepted by the rest of the world, and all that was left was to consolidate the dominion of liberal democracy in those parts of the world still in need of catching up. There were no more large-scale ideological conflicts to be had, only minor arguments about the best procedures. In a sense, for such a view there is no more for political theory to do, since all we now need is good administration.

This, undoubtedly, is the greatest of the challenges faced by political theory, for in it all that we have discussed is united. Now, in a way that has not been the case before, the very possibility of politics has to be a core preoccupation of political theory. It may be tempting to welcome a world in which politics becomes a thing of the past; one in which there is no need for ideological or social antagonism. We imagine such a world to be a utopia of perpetual peace. But then again, a world without politics presupposes a world in which there is no change, in which all routines and practices are settled and placed beyond question and where the state has only to ensure that a natural order is protected from any external threat. This would be a world in which each pursues their own specialised activity (opaque to everyone else), and experts take care of everything that matters. We have heard such dreams recounted before, and they have all led to totalitarianism. But if, as political theorists, we do believe that politics will persist, then we have to address the question of what politics is and can be and of what it means to be political in a world transformed by economic, political and cultural globalisation; cultural differentiation, individuation and **identity politics**; the end of 'grand narratives', the end of ideology and the rapid spread of new technologies.

But, alongside all these new problems, the old ones still persist. There is still competition over scarce resources and hence inequality and a need to decide how goods should be distributed. There is still a need to clarify the rights we do and don't have and to ensure a balance between protections and demands made by and placed on citizens and their states. There is still prejudice and intolerance, warfare and violence. Perhaps those things that look like new problems will turn out to be, on inspection, variations of the old ones. Political thought, at its best and truest, addresses itself directly to a world of which it is a part in both thought and action and which it has played a part in creating. In laying out and explaining the ways in which people have thought about politics, the chapters in this book show the points where this connects to pressing problems of public life. They show how political thought always has been and always will be more than just a specialism. It follows that it must be for more people than just specialists. It is hoped that you will be able to use this book as a starting point for considering your own political thinking, which in turn is part of your doing political things. You may even find that political theory really is essential for life.

HOW TO USE THIS BOOK

This book includes a number of features to assist you in getting to grips with political theory, and it is worth taking some time to get familiar with them.

Section introductions

It is worth paying attention to the section introductions. Often, I suspect, these are skipped by readers understandably eager to go direct to the chapter that covers the topic they want (or have) to find out about. But these short introductions try to be more than just a summary of what is in the chapters and readings. They attempt three things. Firstly, they provide context for the debates within and around political theory discussed in the various chapters. This should help you get a sense of where these ideas and arguments are coming from. Secondly, they relate the chapters to each other in terms of common themes or approaches and, importantly, in terms of their differences. Thirdly, they relate each section to the others so that you can build up a broader picture of this diverse but always interconnected field.

Glossary

The next item to assist you as you go along is the glossary. As we have seen, political theory has become a specialised practice and, like all specialised fields from physics to plumbing, has created its own vocabulary and pantheon of key figures around whom we mere mortals position ourselves. For those of us working within the framework of political theory, it is easy to forget that we are speaking within a kind of shorthand that is not always familiar to others. The glossary aims to remedy this by providing a quick point of reference for various terms that readers may be unfamiliar with or that are used in a special way that might not be immediately understood. I also felt that an extensive glossary would be necessary given the transatlantic nature of the book. Despite the closeness of Britain and the USA there are a few points of reference that are everyday for one culture yet not for the other. The glossary might go some way to preventing any confusion arising from this. There are entries for many of the proper names that appear in the main text (though not for those that appear only as references or those mentioned in the extracts). There are also entries for many other terms or cultural/historical references. If a term or name is highlighted in the main text, that means it appears in the glossary. However, in some cases where the word or name appears frequently (as in 'subject', 'difference', 'Enlightenment' or 'Kant'), it has not been highlighted. There are some other general terms also listed in the glossary that may be of help or interest. Information on those whose work appears as an extract in the book is provided at the front of that extract.

Readings

Next, as you will have seen, this book combines original essays with material reprinted from elsewhere. The precise relationship between an essay and a reading varies. In some cases, authors have chosen to structure their essays as direct commentaries on the texts they have selected. This is particularly the case in those chapters where the readings are most likely to be highly unfamiliar. Others have structured their essays so as to fill in the gaps between the selected readings, while others have very much designed essays the reading of which should be punctuated by reference to the reprints. You too have to make a choice about how to read these. The thing to realise is that no essay is a definitive comment on any reading. There is always a complex interplay between a 'classic' text or a useful source and the contemporary commentator who will inevitably be drawing out some things while neglecting others. You should be aware of this interplay and that you are participating in it.

Questions

Questions are asked at the end of the various sections. These are there to assist readers in focusing on the topics they have encountered and to help them continue thinking about them. They have been placed not at the ends of the chapters but at the ends of the sections so that they encourage reflection on the relationships between things in an open and general way. This is much better than questions that may be taken to be a kind of test of understanding of what has gone before.

Further reading

Finally, suggestions for further reading are made at the end of each section. Readers could simply refer to the texts cited within the various chapters (details of which can be found in the bibliography); but particular texts are suggested in the further reading. This too should foster the impression that political theory is always an ongoing activity where arguments and perspectives relate to others and where the debate is always continuing. Political theory is not like science. There are few problems that have been given definitive solutions to which everyone assents. Certainly there is movement within the field, and it is not just endless pontificating about the same questions. But there is also movement in social life, and political theory is in part about the provision, refinement, invention and reinvention of tools that help us make sense of that social movement.

These features are all indicative of the fact that political theory is extremely diverse. There are different perspectives not only on how to do it but on what it is, on what counts as a proper subject of discussion and even on how it should be discussed. Each of these different approaches is itself likely to be based on presumptions that are eminently political in nature. This books tries not to deny that diversity but to allow it some expression. At the same time, in order to prevent the book from becoming too sprawling and incomprehensible, we have included these features so that we can compensate for the diversity by showing the interlinked nature of different forms of political theory.

The book is divided into four sections. In the first section, 'Histories, Interpretations and Precursors', John Seery lays out the twentieth-century context that has shaped political theory as we enter a new millennium, showing how political theory can stand aside from the scientism and specialisation that so mark our age. Melissa Lane considers the importance of the history of political thought and the ethical as well as intellectual challenges it presents. The second section, 'Traditions and their Discontents', examines the current state of play in three of the core theoretical and ideological traditions of Western political thought. Mark Evans examines Liberalism and the varied forms it now takes; Alan Finlayson looks at Conservatism, stressing its philosophical critique of the place of reason in political life; and Terrell Carver compares differing routes taken by contemporary thinkers influenced by the Marxist tradition. Section 3, 'Alternative Visions and Revisions', examines forms of political thought that, in varying ways, challenge the mainstream traditions. Mike Kenny looks at the communitarian critique of Liberalism but questions the originality and newness of the former. Kate Nash reviews the differing strands that make up feminist political theory, considering in particular the different ways in which these challenge key tenets of mainstream political thinking. Tim

Hayward asks what is distinctive about political theory concerned to take proper account of the environment and of the place of human beings within a particular natural ecology. Finally, Iain MacKenzie introduces the forms of thought associated with poststructuralism, a recent philosophical movement that has challenged many of the ways in which we habitually think about politics and ideas. In the final section, we look at new directions for political theory. Tariq Modood and Adrian Favell consider political theory relating to multiculturalism and the practical challenge of developing ideas that can be applied in a world that is always more complex than we might like. Oliver Leaman introduces some examples of political thought beyond the narrow Western tradition and that will surely become ever more important for the West as bodies of ideas we need to understand and appreciate as well as sources for reviewing our own traditions. Finally, Anna Marie Smith presents an argument for a radicalised conception of democracy and of political thought, showing how we need to focus on hard, real-world problems of discrimination and exclusion.

All that is left by way of introduction is the expression of the hope that readers will find this book readable, useful and, above all, interesting.

NOTES

1. See the data collected at http://www.policyattitudes.org/ems.htm
2. There has been considerable dispute within political science about the ways in which the subject should be studied. In the United States, this caused great tension in the American Political Science Association, culminating in the formation of a group advocating 'perestroika' or restructuring. For background on this, consult back issues (especially that for December 2000) of the online journal of APSA (PS Online) which can be found at www.apsanet.org. For a British-based dispute on related grounds, see Dowding (2001); Marsh and Smith (2001).
3. Though such a life of leisure (as experienced by the philosophers of Ancient Greece) was only possible because of a major division of labour between the free and slaves.
4. There is a particular school of Critical Theory, and this is explained in the glossary. Here, we are certainly alluding to this methodology but also using the term in a more general way.
5. See, for example, the National Association to Advance Fat Acceptance: http://naafa.org/

SECTION I
HISTORIES, INTERPRETATIONS AND PRECURSORS

INTRODUCTION

Theory, of whatever sort, is never simply an abstraction from the world. There is a common stereotype of the philosopher or theorist that imagines her or him to be someone who withdraws from the world in order to live in a more perfect realm of the intellect. It is not an entirely unjustified picture. The philosophical life may entail a partial distance from the world, but this is taken up only in order to attain a better view of that world.

Political theory in particular is always situated in the world about which it speaks and to which it addresses itself. As John Seery points out in Chapter 1, it is only recently that political theory has become something primarily practised by and for academics. In previous eras, the political theorist might also have been an activist, a government official or an artist. They may even have been artisans, peasants or proletarians. Such people wrote for a wide audience of interested people and not only for each other or for a student market in desperate need of simplifying textbooks. Indeed, many of those whose work has been reproduced in this volume have been much more than cloistered academics. They have also been active in public political life and read as people with something important to say. Hannah Arendt (whose work appears in this section) was an energetic campaigner in relation to anti-Semitism. Michel Foucault (who also appears in this section) was similarly a recognised public commentator and led campaigns in France on issues such as penal reform. Sir Isaiah Berlin (whose work appears in Section 2) was not only an Oxford academic but also, during the Second World War, served in the British Information Service in New York and later as First Secretary of the British Embassy in Washington. John Gray (another writer whose work can be found in Section 2) has advised a number of British governments, while Roger Scruton (also in Section 2) is no longer a full-time academic and is more widely known in Britain as a public commentator, journalist and broadcaster. He too has been associated with particular British governments. The communitarian writer Michael Sandel is a popular writer and commentator in the USA addressing the ills (as he sees them) of his country, while Amitai Etzioni is extremely well known as a campaigner in both the UK and the USA. He is perhaps now more active in his public organisation The Communitarian Network than in the academy. Work by both can be found in Section 3, where you will also find Geoff Mulgan, an adviser to the British Prime Minister Tony Blair. Bhikhu Parekh (whose work is considered in Section 4) is a member of the British House of Lords, one of the two houses of the parliament (the British legislature), and recently chaired an important public commission on multi-ethnic Britain.

Others in this book are equally active but not so closely associated with governmental authority. Vandana Shiva is an activist and campaigner for the rights of oppressed peoples, writing powerfully about the environment, the impact of Western technologies and on feminism. She organises an important campaign group and has a global standing (her work appears in Section 3). Gwendolyn Mink (who can be found in Section 4) has been a prominent campaigner around the issue of welfare in the USA. Note also the presence in Section 4 of a leading Buddhist spiritual figure, D. T. Suzuki, and two deceased world leaders, Ayatollah Khomeini and Mao Tze Tung.

All these writers and thinkers have pursued their ideas not only for their own sake but because they believe these ideas to be of public political or ethical importance and as indispensable in developing a view about the ways in which the polity should be organised and understood. They have been motivated in their thinking and writing by the very concrete political situations in which they have found themselves or in some cases which they have helped to create. The history of political thought includes many such figures confronted by the contradictions and the tensions of their time (often manifested in bloodshed, conflict and even warfare), forced to question the assumptions on which otherwise accepted principles and practices rested. In response, they invented and developed new ideas that they believed were better suited to making sense of their present and getting a grip on the future. We in our turn start from where they left off, taking their projects further or pointing out their errors. Political theory, in a sense, always takes off because of a failure of some sort and a conviction that things are not as they could or should be, and hence with the need to resolve something. As such, it is always motivated by the world around it.

Because of this, we have to be aware when examining political theory that it is not at all produced in a vacuum or only in relation to the large body of texts that constitute the history of political thought. Political theory is always defined at first by the specific situations and problems political thinkers have witnessed. To understand political theory, we need to understand both the history of ideas on which thinkers draw and the problems they considered themselves to be facing and to which their work was addressed. This may also be a valuable exercise because the ways in which we now think about the how and why of our social universe are the product (to a considerable degree) of the things that have happened in the past and the things that were thought by people who came before us. Knowing about them can give us a sense of why we have the values, norms and moral expectations that we do have: of how we got here. From this position, we can see if these values still work for our present-day situation, understand the contexts they were originally intended to help with or even critically assess whose particular interests they may have been devised to serve. That is why we begin this book with two chapters that, in different ways, deal with the historical background of present political theory. Studying that history can help us find out how and why we think the way we do.

John Seery reminds us of this social and historical context by situating political thought today in the background of the twentieth century from which we have only just emerged, not as unscathed as we might like. In discussing the experiences of himself and his family, Seery causes us to think about the enormity of the transformation experienced by Western civilisations in just three generations. From working with their hands, living off the land, the Seery family passed through war, social unrest, racial conflict and disease until, entering the twenty-first century, Seery himself is a professor in a university. In moving along this route, the Seerys, like everyone else, haven't escaped but have participated in the major political events Western civilisation has faced over the last 100 years.

In addition to war, genocide and totalitarianism, the West in the twentieth century has been subject to what Seery calls 'massification'. Things became faster, larger in scale, industrialised and mechanised. With this there came new forms of political organisation, including the mass organisation of terror. Political thinking had to respond to this, yet it often found itself uncertain as to how. Debates about how political theory should be done were also debates about how we might respond to the new phenomena and patterns of life around us. By the century's end, as Seery shows, some theorists had rejected political theory for something called political science. Others had found different reasons to demote political theory from its position as legislator, and still others began to focus on the politics of hitherto neglected phenomena such as the body and sexuality.

As the world turns, so must political thinking. It is not enough just to respond to events as they occur, to reserve judgement until the day of the vote and then hammer out an ill-conceived compromise. Political thinking has to address the causes of these conditions and establish the principles by which we can not only think about them but also find their place and think beyond them. Yet, despite the massive alterations in the scale and scope of social (and therefore political) life, we are still human beings who, perhaps, want for the same things as our ancestors. There is a tradition from which we have come and to which we can turn. In her discussion of that tradition, Melissa Lane explores the ways in which we may view the texts of the past. Are they a part of history alongside any other (say the history of warfare or the history of medicine), or is there something special about the history of ideas? And how are we to go about making sense of the political thought of the past? Indeed, if it was formed out of a context that is no more, can we really make sense of it all? What can it say to us, or do for us, now that the world is seemingly so different?

It is always tempting to think of our own time as unique, faced by such new kinds of problem that the works of the past must be more of a hindrance than a help, wedding us to outmoded ideas from outmoded ages. Perhaps the past can teach us not to be so sure of our own originality. Just because we live in the present and imagine ourselves to be at the forefront, the cutting edge, of whatever Western civilisation may have to offer or to face, it does not mean that we aren't part of a context that we come from and speak to. Lane introduces us to a number of reasons why the history of political thought matters to us: it can demonstrate that it is possible to think in ways other than those currently dominant or fashionable; it can illuminate the sources of our ideas and help us know them better. But we still face the problem of how to make sense of the political ideas of the past, given that they were conceived in circumstances that are not the same as ours. This methodological question has been the source of much research. Lane shows how, in the twentieth century, those concerned with the history of political thought came in particular to focus on language. It is easy for us to imagine that language is a relatively unproblematic mechanism by which we express our ideas or feelings. But, when we look at the things written in the past, it is immediately apparent that words can change their meanings, and things that could once be thought and expressed in a certain way cannot be any longer. What is more, one of the things that major works of philosophy (or indeed literature) do is challenge or redescribe the meanings of words. The use of language is a creative activity, and sometimes intellectual endeavour is concerned to create the words that help us to understand our situation.

Some historians of political thought have, for these reasons, argued that we should examine the language of historic texts, put that language into context and attempt to understand what sort of 'language game' writers of the past were involved in. But, in so doing, they have shown with clarity the problems that arise in trying to understand each other and our ancestors. This does not mean that the effort to make sense of the past is futile. As Lane points out through her discussion of thinkers such as Collingwood or Gadamer, each generation must write their own history. We do this so that we can be clearer on the causes of our thinking but also because it is a way of thinking. We do not simply canonise the past and think that all great wisdom is buried there. We see what previous questions and answers have been offered and use this as a way of thinking differently about our problems now.

It is notable that both Lane and Seery choose to conclude their discussions with reference to the philosopher Michel Foucault. One of the things Foucault sometimes appeared to be doing (though he wouldn't have put it like this) was trying to develop the self-understanding of us Westerners. He described himself as a 'historian of the present', a conceptual archaeologist uncovering the ways in which we, without noticing, came to think and feel the way we do. In considering the history of events and ideas that has shaped political theory, we too are being historians of the present, establishing what is new and what is old about 'the now'. As such, this is an indispensable starting point for understanding, and practising, contemporary political theory.

I

POLITICAL THEORY IN THE TWENTIETH CENTURY

John Seery

Introduction

My task in this opening chapter is to write about the enterprise of political theory in the twentieth century. I shall present the broadest and barest of overviews, a cartoon-like sketch, albeit bereft of any animated Hollywood-style special effects. Even summoning forth all of my faculties for theoretical abstraction, I simply know not how to serve as an adequate tour guide to an entire century, or even the latter half to which I personally stood witness. A few family anecdotes through the years are perhaps telling for starters, in order to get some kind of preliminary grasp on the century as a century.

My grandparents were farmers who farmed in the manner of their day in middle America, namely, with horse-drawn plows and pitchforks (while also making do without electricity, running water, telephone service, or regular mail delivery), although after the Depression they bought both a tractor and their first automobile, a second-hand Model T, with crankshaft still intact. Counting backward from 1920, I realize that my grandmothers could not vote in the United States when they came of age. My father as a very young man was a machine gunner on a navy destroyer during the Second World War, but he professed not to know whether he actually shot down any of those enemy dive-bombers amid all of the ratta-tat-tat rumble. My older cousin, Donny, marched in the **civil-rights movement** in Alabama, where we watched him back home on our fuzzy black-and-white television screens, and thereafter he scandalized the neighbors by marrying an African American woman and, after she died of sickle-cell complications, scandalized everyone a second time by becoming a gay activist in the 1970s in Chicago, where he eventually died of AIDS. For my own part, I was too young to become a hippie or to be drafted into the **Vietnam War**, but when I was 12 I did compose the following sign-o'-the-times poem (in longhand, because I did not learn how to type until the ninth grade, at which time I pecked away on a clanky manual typewriter):

Do Something!

Do something,
Before it's too late.
This world needs more love,
Not more hate.
There's a war going on,
Mud in our shoes,
Poverty in the mouth,
Crime makes the news.
Pollution is a word
Constantly used.
Come on, people,
Let's get united, joined, fused!
President Nix
Is in one hell of a fix.
Economy's down
And some whites won't mix.
Long-haired kids
Run away from their homes.
People sit on their asses
Reading God damn poems.

My proud if perplexed parents tried to channel those early wayward tendencies of mine into an upwardly mobile law career – and so, during my freshman year in college, I sought a **résumé**-padding internship in the nation's capital with the upstart senator from my state, Dick Clark, whose report on US corporate involvement in South Africa I helped distribute to the national press at its first release. Later in that fateful internship, all of us Iowans on staff in DC were invited to the White House for dinner and dancing to celebrate President Jimmy **Carter**'s first year in office. Wearing my tan corduroy bell-bottomed three-piece suit and gum-soled shoes (the **Reagan** black-tie years were yet to come), I was the first on the dance floor when the US Marine big band started playing *In the Mood*. Upon my return to campus, after watching my fellow students march in a protest calling for college divestment in those companies doing business in South Africa, companies named in Senator Clark's report, I switched my major from pre-law to a specially designed course of studies called political theory, which seemed to emulate a Nelson **Mandela**-like outlook on political possibility, wistful *and* realistic yet compelled onward seeking greater justice.

Having graduated into an oil-shocked, arms-escalating, downwardly mobilizing economy, I jumped coasts to California for postgraduate study in political theory. On my first day in Berkeley, Wavy Gravy (the clownish emcee of Woodstock and former merry prankster roadster) gave me a personal tour of his house after I knocked unassumingly on the door, having recognized his 'Nobody for President' campaign bus parked outside. Increasingly keen to the theatrical politics around me, I started attending select street demonstrations, for instance against US involvement in Nicaragua or against nuclear weapons build-up. Soon after President **Reagan** announced his Project Democracy initiative, a graduate professor networked me into a modestly gainful position in San Francisco, where I eventually discovered that I was now working for a CIA front organization, funded by that same **Reagan–Thatcher** initiative, which apparently wanted a political theorist to reformulate plans for covert operations in South East Asia (my boss, however, kept rejecting my above-board recommendations to challenge the Marcos regime in the Philippines). Back on the streets, I became impressed by the millions of people marching, worldwide, against nuclear madness, and I noticed in particular that the anti-nuclear movement attracted great numbers of women, and that most of its leaders were women – Helen Caldicott, Randall Forsberg, Petra Kelly, Mary Kaldor, Pam Solo, Christa Wolf, Katya Komisaruk, the Women's Action for Nuclear Disarmament (WAND), and the Greenham Common Camp. Eventually, I wrote my laser-printed dissertation on such matters. By 1989, a bunch of men were crediting nuclear weapons with bringing down the Berlin Wall, but I remembered a different post-Soviet history altogether. For the remainder of the century, my own theoretical efforts correlated inversely with the rise of the stock market: in the greedy 1980s, I invested heavily in irony, trying to sell it as the trope of that decade; in the millennialist rush toward riches in the 1990s, I wrote about death instead, another self-mocking master trope that never quite caught on with my professional colleagues.

In Britain, by the end of the century, a sheep was cloned. In Japan, the toilet-paperless turbo-toilet was introduced. Back home, my elderly father never found a hearing aid that would stop the background ringing in his ears, and we await even further miniaturization of the digital revolution.

THE END AND THE BEGINNING OF POLITICAL THEORY

Political theorists seldom agree these days about the proper nature and uses to which political theory ought to be put. Nonetheless, it is probably fair to say that most political theorists attempt to look at politics, at least part of the time, from broad, large-scale, long-range points of view – informed by history, comparative analysis, textual exegesis, philosophical reflection, and imaginative projection. The word *theory* derives from an ancient Greek practice whereby city officials sent emissaries to neighboring cities to observe their rival religious practices. Reportedly, such information was not put to any immediate, urgent use but was considered illuminating nonetheless.

For my present purposes, if I may assume some generous license based on the example of the ancient theorist's spectatorial wanderings and musings, I suggest that the century we just concluded was one of *massification*. It was a century featuring fast-paced change and monumental events. These events and changes conspired to bring people's fates colliding together, so that large human population blocs would be *massed* together and their destinies increasingly intertwined. It was a century of world wars, both hot and cold; of major revolutions and sweeping social movements; of assembly-line production, economic expansion, and widespread consumption; of breathtaking technological advances in travel, communication, and destruction. Human institutions had to adapt on large scales to these massive changes. It was a century wherein we witnessed the spread of communism, the spread of Islam, the spread of democracy; of nationalism and multinationalism; of imperialism and postcolonialism; of the population explosion; of space travel and exploration; of natural-resource depletion and global pollution; of scientific and medical breakthrough and discovery.

From afar or in retrospective repose, one would think that political theory's general knack for breadth would have been especially helpful in comprehending twentieth-century major trends toward massification; but it is as yet unclear how well political theory fared along these lines. Some notable theorists surveyed below – Hannah Arendt, Sheldon Wolin, and Michel Foucault – examined this issue in various ways and drew troubling conclusions that may shed some light on the overall topic of this opening chapter: the role of political theory in the twentieth century. All three questioned whether political theory was at all *useful* in the twentieth century, and yet their disparately skeptical appraisals of theory's uneven role may lead to the unexpected conclusion that theory's perverse benefit after all was to call into tacit question, to hold such a question at least in reserve, whether 'usefulness' under terms of societal massification should be championed as a standard for critical evaluation at all.

By almost any measure, the Second World War represented nothing less than a watershed event in human affairs. It introduced the world to totalitarianism – the practice whereby an organised state attempts to exert total control over the thought and behavior of its subjects – and featured atrocities the likes of which the world hitherto had not experienced on the scale now exhibited: national fascism, Stalinism, concentration camps, systematic genocide, firebombs, nuclear bombs. Hannah Arendt, the German-educated émigré who fled to America, saw the war as signifying a profound turn in human affairs, a crisis of consciousness for which there could be no turning back nor any easy repair for the future. As she wrote in the final passage of the preface to her book *The Origins of Totalitarianism* (first published in 1951):

> We can no longer afford to take that which was good in the past and simply call it our heritage, to discard the bad and simply think of it as a dead load which by itself time will bury in oblivion. The subterranean stream of Western history has finally come to the surface and usurped the

> dignity of our tradition. This is the reality in which we live. And this is why all efforts to escape from the grimness of the present into nostalgia for a still intact past, or into the anticipated oblivion of a better future, are vain. (Arendt, 1973: ix)

The war revealed a dirty secret about our Western civilization.[1] For all of our vaunted progress, for all of our enlightened practices and democratic institutions, for all of our material comforts and technological gizmos, we found that we could commit calculated acts of cruelty unto one another – and somehow not be utterly shaken at the horror of it all. That we prided ourselves on our advanced techniques and rational science of large-scale social organization – our constitutions and our cars – should have made it even worse; but the world moved on, as if with a click of the remote control. For Arendt, the Holocaust was symptomatic of a much larger malaise potentially afflicting the entire Western world, spilling beyond totalitarian movements into the 'non-totalitarian' world (Arendt, 1953). People could now commit atrocities, or rather participate in bureaucratic structures that waged cruelties on their behalf, and yet such complicit participants could no longer quite recognize themselves or their actions or the effects of their actions as cruel. Surely they were intelligent enough people, yet apparently they were not *thinking* about the evil they were effecting. How could this be?

In her 1953 essay, 'Understanding and Politics' (reproduced below), Arendt approaches this question by asking whether we can understand totalitarianism when it, in practice and by definition, robs us of our independent critical resources. Earlier forms of radical state evil, she notes, were lumped together under the term 'imperialism'. Totalitarian government, on the other hand, is a *new* phenomenon, historically unprecedented, and so maybe we cannot understand it by making empirical recourse to past historical models. In fact, it may be, she suggests, that our methods of 'political science' are inadequate to grasp the uniqueness of modern totalitarian government. This is because totalitarian dynamics may continue to operate *sub rosa* or may have their functional equivalents elsewhere. Totalitarian logic, for instance, characteristically appeals to the dictates of scientific causality, the ostensibly absolute authority of which essentially pre-empts and eliminates dissent. Similar appeals to the authority of science in non-totalitarian venues may not violently rob us of our independent critical faculties, but they can provide all-too-convenient excuses for letting our vigilance lapse. Or, Arendt submits, reliance on the magic of the market and the concomitant appeal to 'self-interest' for organizing almost all of our collective affairs, making ourselves gullible to the advertising industry's manipulations, has made us more 'stupid' in the twentieth century. It was a century, according to Arendt, marked by 'the growth of meaninglessness', accompanied by 'the loss of common sense' and 'the increasing stupidity' of nearly everybody, intellectuals and non-intellectuals alike.

A remedy to this unhappy or vicious condition, if an internal diagnosis is even still possible, may spring from the evidently ineradicable and ever-recurring human tendency toward creative initiative and new beginnings – which may in turn inspire the lesson that we must always try to understand the world anew. At the least, Arendt suggests, we must remind ourselves that science, for all of its insights and accomplishments, cannot provide us with adequate self-under-standing, because science can never truly apprehend unprecedented newness. Arendt seems to recommend the classical theorist's occasional stepping away from the prevailing norms, practices, and categories of the day in order to gain a 'distanced' perspective on things. Theory *means* thinking, as a separation from worldliness. She ends her essay by appealing, strangely enough, to a faculty of 'imagination' whose distance from reality might actually afford greater clarity on reality than straight empiricism can ever offer. But she warns that if we humans ever want to be at home on this earth, the price might involve never being 'at home' in the twentieth century. Clearly, in Arendt's eyes, the twentieth century was a misbegotten one, and perhaps her theoretical follow-ers should not be too disheartened over political theory's alleged shortcomings and failures in that context.

AGAINST THEORY

Arendt's sweeping analysis of totalitarianism in the twentieth century, along with its backhanded estimation of the role of theory as foil, did not win the day. Instead, reflections on the significance of the Second World War grew into a chorus that actually blamed theory for the ills and evils of that period. Hitler supposedly had read **Nietzsche,** and the Nazis took other cues from German **idealism.** Communism owed its intellectual origins to **Marx,** whose dictates had been put into practice by **Lenin**'s theoretical vanguard. America, in contrast, had achieved its stability and success supposedly by eclipsing theory's promi-nence in favor of 'can-do' pragmatism and a checks-and-balances procedural-ism. **Madison**ian America had stayed above the fray of old-world tumult, because it did not seek to reinvent human nature but instead accommodated people's foibles and interests.

The post-war suspicion toward theory grew into an animus. During the 1950s and 1960s, a general movement developed that not only decried theory's earlier collaborative role in fostering communism and fascism but also proclaimed that theory would be and should be forever discredited. Theory was pronounced dead or dying.[2] Let the people choose their fates for themselves instead of having some high-minded, monomaniacal egghead ponder the universe on their behalf. Governments and officials should follow suit. Theory on this view was asso-ciated with idealism, ideology, abstraction, metaphysics, utopianism, romanti-cism, normative thinking, and social engineering. Even some political theorists during this time, apparently swept up into the mood of the day, publicly advo-cated that political theorizing should come to an end. Theory, they told their fellows, should cease and desist all operations, because it had become danger-ous or at least presumptuous or simply irrelevant and thus unnecessary.

Many of these anti-theory theorists were outspoken advocates of political liberalism, a system that supposedly does not require much theoretical intervention or oversight. Liberalism as a governmental system observes a strict, practical distinction between the public and private realm. The point of respecting and enforcing that distinction, for many of these anti-theory liberals, is to give the private sector its due and to restrict public regulation of private activities as much as possible. The underlying assumption of anti-theory Liberalism is that private **autonomy** does not require theoretical articulation. It runs more or less by itself. Accordingly, state regulatory influence should be limited. Private rights should be protected, and private interests should be freely expressed and pursued. Liberalism, its advocates assert, does not aspire to deliver perfect societies or heroic individuals, but it certainly does better than fascism or communism in avoiding outright cruelty.

Before the Second World War, writers whom we now have canonized as professional political theorists (**Machiavelli, Locke, Rousseau, Burke, Mill, Du Bois, de Beauvoir,** and so on) often occupied non-scholarly positions of note. Many of them were employed as diplomats, envoys, court officials, social rebels, pamphleteers, poets, preachers, or journalists. After the war, however, almost all political theorizing receded to university settings. Political theory increasingly became a delimited, specialized branch of academic discourse, to be housed in a discipline called 'political science'. But such a place offered little sanctuary from a hostile or an unappreciative world. Even here, political scientists did not entirely welcome their war-torn colleagues, for they not so secretly shared much of the suspicion leveled at large against political theory. In fact, in the decades following the war, in political science departments almost everywhere, political scientists and political theorists retreated into separate camps and defined themselves in opposition to one another. Political scientists, as their name would suggest, largely emulated the methods of natural science now applied to political phenomena: observation, hypothesis-testing, empiricism, data-collection, objectivity. Wary of becoming political partisans or advocates, political scientists often labored to limit their analytic purview to human 'behavior' as they saw it. New battle lines were thus drawn: political theory versus behaviorism. Political theory in the latter part of the twentieth century again found itself on the defensive.

Sheldon Wolin's 1969 essay 'Political Theory as a Vocation' (reproduced below) emerged out of this context. Political theory had become almost entirely a species of academic inquiry, now situated within the discipline of political science, and political theorists found that on a daily basis they had to contend with the methodism of their science-minded departmental colleagues. Since Wolin's essay harks back to the work of German sociologist Max Weber, a brief digression on Weber's writing would be helpful to provide some background to Wolin's piece.

In 1904, Weber predicted that the twentieth century would likely become 'disenchanted'. By 'disenchantment' Weber meant that the magic of religiosity and the mysteries of spirit, so influential in earlier epochs, would now be subjected to strictly secular scrutiny. Rationality, in turn, would eventually dominate all aspects of human life. A newly modern economic order of machine production would 'determine the lives of all the individuals who are born into this mechanism, not only those directly concerned with economic acquisition, with irresistible force' (Weber, 1958: 181). Such individuals would be capable of calculating only the means, not the ends, of life. They would know not where they were going (nor would they think much about it any more), but they would attempt to get there fast. 'Material goods', Weber warned, would gain an 'increasing and finally an inexorable power' (ibid.: 181) over the lives of such blindly ambitious people. They would become materialists and consumers. They would become careerists and bureaucrats: 'specialists without spirit, sensualists without heart' (ibid.: 182). In the United States, the place with the highest development of capitalism, according to Weber, the pursuit of wealth would assume the character of sport. Such sportive individuals simply abandon any attempt to justify their competitive activity by relating it to higher spiritual and cultural values. They are simply carried along by the momentum of their wealth-getting activity, and little else seems to matter in life. A 'mechanized petrification' thus goes hand in hand with 'convulsive self-importance' (ibid.: 182). Weber's prophetic work, *The Protestant Ethic and the Spirit of Capitalism*, provided an early analysis that capitalism eventually would win – but at a spiritual cost.

Weber's dark outlook for the future of the twentieth century contained a few bright notes. Withstanding the century's tendencies toward secularization, rationalization, **utilitarianism**, technicism, scientism, bureaucratization, and materialism would be a kind of epic individual who still regarded his or her work as if it were a religious calling – a vocation – even though such a person would no longer be a believer in old-time faith. Against the backdrop of the forces of disenchantment, such a person would stand up to the times and attempt to reinvest his ordinary work with, as it were, greater meaning and larger purpose, or at least with plain and simple integrity. Scholars who pursue scholarship as a vocation would attempt to bring a kind of moral clarity to their workaday academic strivings, even though modern science largely eschews such reflective broodings (Weber, 1946b). Weber suggested that there might even be a kind of person who pursues latter-day politics as a vocation, even though modern politics requires at times cold calculation and ruthless manipulation (Weber, 1946a). Indeed, Weber explicitly recommends that only a person who can combine ethics and pragmatism, pursuing politics with both the heart and the head – someone who is not altogether 'spiritually dead' – has a genuine 'calling for politics' in the modern world (ibid.: 127).

Taking his main cue from Weber, Wolin issued a similar call for political theory to be pursued as a vocation – one that would somehow conjoin the roles of scholar and citizen that Weber had kept functionally separate. Vocational political theory would engage the hearts and minds of its practitioners, abandoning the pretense of disinterest that informed the methodism of political science in the post-war/Cold War period. Wolin in fact saw the triumph of methodism as presenting a 'crisis' in political education. Political theory as a vocation furnishes and preserves *tacit* political knowledge, based on deep historical understanding and sharp awareness of the complexities of political experience – and only such an enlarged view of the political condition provides discriminating judgement adequate to our contemporary predicaments. Scientific methods alone do not and cannot provide sufficient grounds for making informed political decisions.

Political scientists, when they do venture forth with something like a theory about the proper role of political theory, often attempt to contain its influence to 'normative' affairs – as if theory's one comparative occupational advantage is to sermonize about remotely utopian fantasies. Or, political scientists will see theory's proper role as generating 'hypotheses' and 'models' for quasi-scientific testing and falsification. Wolin shifts the burden of explanation back to theory's detractors and trivializers. Methodism, he contends, cannot offer a well-rounded perspective on itself, especially one that is critical. The behaviorist boasts that his methods are not theory-driven or value-laden, but that braggadocio lacks the resources to prove itself, even empirically. By default, according to Wolin, the methodist's purview remains ensconced within, and therefore tethered to, and in the service of, the status quo. Small wonder that, under century-wide terms of massification, political scientists should observe patterned regularities of human conduct; but they lack the historical and cultural resources to be able to assess whether such regularities are indeed lawful or merely law-like because of mass mimicry or other humanistic variables.

Especially in times of crisis – or even in times of wide-scale mediocrity or collective dumbing down – Wolin claims that there is a need for 'epic' political theorists who can break radically with the paradigms of the day. Such theory is 'epic' because of the magnitude of its scope and claims. It has the audacity but also the intellectual reach to challenge society's fundamental assumptions, if need be. It has the vision to suggest alternatives that may be available, even if such possibilities appear distant and foreclosed under current conditions. Epic theory is 'extraordinary', Wolin says, borrowing from Thomas **Kuhn**, because it 'inaugurate[s] a new way of looking at the world, which includes a new set of concepts, as well as new cognitive *and* normative standards'. The methodist can hardly postulate beyond observable facts and trends, and such a modest outlook can hardly keep pace with the shifting realities of politics over the long run. (Latter-day case in point: few, if any, political scientists predicted the 1989 collapse of the Soviet empire, whereas theorists familiar with Marx were saying all along that the Soviet Union had been operating on precarious theoretical grounds.) The epic theorist, on the other hand, steeped in the contingencies of the human condition, 'aims to grasp present structures and interrelationships, and to re-present them in a new way'. But even as he outlines the need for epic theory in today's world, Wolin invokes Weber's nightmare scenario and suggests that it has come true:

In a fundamental sense, our world has become as perhaps no previous world has, the product of design, the product of theories about human structures deliberately created rather than historically articulated. But in another sense, the embodiment of theory in the world has resulted in a world impervious to theory. The giant, routinized structures defy fundamental alteration and, at the same time, display an unchallengeable legitimacy, for the rational, scientific, and technological principles on which they are based seem in perfect accord with an age committed to science, rationalism and technology. Above all, it is a world which appears to have rendered epic theory superfluous. (Wolin, 1969: 108)

For some contemporary students of political theory, Wolin's cry for epic theory was soon heeded. In 1971, John Rawls wrote *A Theory of Justice*, which some admirers hailed as restoring the moribund field of political theory to some level of respectability and currency. Artfully conjoining a **Hobbes**-like **state of nature** with a Kantian overlay, Rawls concocted a grand thought experiment about politics that captured the imagination of many of his readers. His 'original position' provided a way to connect 'normative' philosophical gambits with real-world concerns about distributive economics, and thus spoke to generational anxieties about the welfare state. At bottom, the book seemed to answer the tricky question about how a liberal state could be 'just' without being socialist, and an entire publishing industry devoted to Rawlsian analysis and explication grew in the decades following.

Yet at the same time, Rawls's book failed to reflect and address many of the political realities of his day. Feminism was enjoying tremendous waves of resurgence during the 1960s, 1970s, and 1980s. The **civil-rights movement** and the growing matter of racial politics were similarly not well covered in his lengthy volume. The protracted antagonisms of the **Vietnam** War; the pressures on the liberal state due to nationalist postcolonial uprisings; the international threats of nuclear conflagration and arms escalation; sexual and cultural revolutions and the coming-out of the gay and lesbian movement; assassinations, high crimes and misdemeanors, and other political corruptions – all of these realities that formed the living context for Rawls's work somehow did not find their way into his vision and at best became relegated in the book to the 'non-ideal' world. While many academics argued at length about his abstract designs for achieving justice, Rawls's actual influence on electoral politics or judicial decision-making was nugatory. *A Theory of Justice* owed its eventual popularity more to political thinkers residing in philosophy departments than to political theorists operating in political science departments. Although its scope was clearly 'epic' in Wolin's general sense of the term, the book failed to provide the 'tacit knowledge' based on historical experience and empirical understanding that Wolin claimed was central to the crafty insights of political theorizing.

While analytic, mostly American political philosophers reveled in Rawls's rhapsody, a counter-movement was gaining ground within European continental circles. In the late 1960s, structuralist theory – the idea that social systems follow regular patterns of development issuing from constant cultural, historical, psychological, anthropological, linguistic, or economic determinants – confronted a serious challenge by a movement later known as poststructuralism. Poststructuralists rejected the investigative assumption that societies or individuals necessarily follow fixed rules or patterns of behavior and instead shifted focus to the specific workings of power within particular societies. One of the leading figures of this movement was Michel Foucault, whose own work over the course of his career migrated from structuralism to poststructuralism.

It may be a bit awkward to include Foucault in this brief survey of epic contributions to twentieth-century political theory, if only because he explicitly disclaimed that his aim was ever to construct a general 'theory'. He repeatedly voiced a suspicion about the Enlightenment project of seeking universal truths about human nature, and he associated most Western political philosophy with that universalistic aspiration. For Foucault, the hallmark of such political theory has been its devotion to idealist abstractions, first principles, and utopias (see Rabinow, 1984: 5). But Foucault's contention was precisely that the attempt to achieve foundational clarity and theoretical elegance deflected attention away from the way power actually operates. He thus shifts the focus away from the traditional concerns of theory and toward specific historical studies of particular institutional practices that seem to reveal an alternative view of how power functions.

Yet Foucault's avid readers could scarcely resist the temptation to take from his many investigations what might be called a 'new theory of power'. The old theory of power saw it as located within specific sites, issuing outward from centralized states or from strong intentional subjects, such as kings or governmental officials, and the power of such centered authorities derived from their right to threaten their subjects with violence and death. But power in the modern world does not operate very often in this crudely coercive way. Instead, it is dispersed throughout society, not vested in one body. People are slowly disciplined over time into the prevailing order of things, until they become self-disciplining. No cold-blooded commander-in-chief need threaten them with bodily injury for them to become civilly compliant. Modern power, for Foucault, is thus 'decentered' and hails from multiple sources. In fact, it often is invisible or 'masked', to the extent that the modern exercise of power passes as normal and normalizing for all parties involved. Now taken for granted, power stakes a claim over our entire *living* existence. According to Foucault, modern power is organised around the management of life, not the menace of death. As he argues in *The History of Sexuality*, the study of power must therefore shift from an 'analytics of blood' to an 'analytics of sexuality' (Foucault, 1978: 148). Power in the modern world, operating on live bodies, not just dead or soon-to-be dead ones, exercises itself primarily through the administration of sexuality. Contemporary political theorists, following Foucault, must therefore study *sex* as the royal road toward understanding power.

In the 1970s and 1980s, a number of sexualized studies indeed followed Foucault's lead. **Queer studies** became a mainstay in academic circles. Feminism experienced what some called a 'third wave' of resurgence. **Identity politics**, focusing on the intersecting dynamics of race, class, sex, and gender, became extremely influential. Poststructuralists in general were concerned with the capacity of power to construct identities and to erect boundaries within specific contexts, and they applied most of their efforts toward exposing and deconstructing the hold that particular disciplinary practices have over concrete lives – stopping short, à la Foucault, of generating any unified field theory of power.

Postmodernism, as opposed to poststructuralism, was an amorphous term that many associated with any reaction against modernity. 'Modernity' was understood as the project of seeking rational progress for the good of humanity everywhere, but in-the-know postmodernists also associated modernity with a tendency to periodize history, especially according to a linear trajectory that defines 'modernity' as having escaped the forces of 'tradition'. All 'moderns', the beneficiaries of such progress, see themselves as having graduated from an earlier dark period – thus the postmodern pronouncement of entering into a new phase beyond modernity was itself ironic. The term 'postmodern' was therefore deviously self-subverting. That is where the fun begins.

Jean-François **Lyotard** defined postmodernism – too baldly, as he knew – as 'incredulity toward metanarratives' (Lyotard, 1984: xxiv). The main metanarratives informing the modernist period would probably be those of historical progress, liberation, universalism, legitimacy, coherence, individualism, democracy, nationalism, Enlightenment, science, and utility. Unrelenting incredulity over these tropes and metanarratives probably yields various reactive tendencies that subsequently have been associated with various postmodern moods: playfulness, eclecticism, polyvocality, **incommensurability**, **hybridity**, instability, and contestation. Characteristically, the postmodern practitioner would not assume that rival discourses could be reconciled via a mediating third term, thus the clash of differences must be allowed to play itself out. Difference would be showcased. In general, then, postmodernism applied to political analysis seemed to foster a growing sensitivity toward pluralized practices and manifold, protean, transgressive identities. It helped prepare the way for new multicultural and globalized investigations while bracketing the assumption that such pursuits are necessarily leading toward a humane future. Critics of postmodernism, in turn, complained that it led to political listlessness and playful paralysis.

Although postmodernism attracted few zealous devotees, its lingering influence probably will continue to inform political theory's future. Political theory at the *fin de siècle* was left without a unifying mission, direction, or mandate. Today it is marked by robust diversity or 'fragmentation'. Political theorists, now operating almost exclusively as academicians, go about their separate projects wherever and however they see fit, to whatever end as well. They pursue a wide variety of topics, texts, methods, manners, periods, and people. Given such scattershot efforts, political theory's overall usefulness to the rest of society is doubtful, a question that probably should remain open and unsettled. Whether the field's diversity is, on balance, a good thing is subject to ongoing debate. Therewith, such debates can now occur in numerous contexts, not simply one, all-confining public arena. New voices are finding creative expression in political theory, whereas in the ancient world only white male citizens could speak. For pestering his fellows, Socrates was executed, whereas political theorists today surely need not worry about reaching that dire conclusion. Nevertheless, gadflies can be swatted or one can shoo them away, but they also can be simply ignored by the slumbering beast that they attempt to sting.

NOTES

1. I have benefited in this section by reading Tracy B. Strong's 'Nihilism and Political Theory', in John S. Nelson (ed.), *What Should Political Theory Be Now?* (Albany: State University of New York Press, 1983), pp. 243–63.
2. David Easton, *The Political System* (New York: Alfred A. Knopf, 1953); Alfred Cobban, 'The Decline of Political Theory', *Political Science Quarterly* 68: 2 (September 1953): 321–37; T. D. Weldon, 'Political Principles', in Peter Laslett (ed.), *Philosophy, Politics and Society*, first series (Oxford: Basil Blackwell, 1956), pp. 22–34; Leo Strauss, 'What Is Political Philosophy?', *Journal of Politics* 19 (August 1957): 343–68; Judith N. Shklar, *After Utopia: The Decline of Political Faith* (Princeton: Princeton University Press, 1957); Robert A. Dahl, 'Political Theory: Truth or Consequences', *World Politics* 11 (October 1958): 89–102; Daniel Bell, *The End of Ideology: On the Exhaustion of Political Ideas in the Fifties* (New York: Free Press, 1960); Isaiah Berlin, 'Does Political Theory Still Exist?', in Peter Laslett and W. G. Runciman (eds), *Philosophy, Politics and Society*, second series (Oxford: Basil Blackwell, 1962), pp. 1–33.

'UNDERSTANDING AND POLITICS' BY HANNAH ARENDT

The German-born political theorist Hannah Arendt (1906–75) became a US citizen in 1951. Her work combined social and political philosophy with public activism, especially in relation to the Nazi Holocaust. Her account of the trial of Adolf Eichmann, the man who designed the plans for the 'final solution', has been very widely read. Arendt's importance for political theory lies in her real-isation that the study of politics should focus on the nature (and experience) of political life itself and not only on the construction of purely analytical and logical theorisations. Her key works include *The Origins of Totalitarianism* (Harcourt Brace and Company, 1973), *On Revolution* (Faber, 1963), *The Human Condition* (Cambridge University Press, 1958), *Eichmann in Jerusalem: A Report on the Banality of Evil* (Penguin, 1977) and *Between Past and Future: Six Exercises in Political Thought* (Faber, 1961). In this extract, Arendt focuses on the role of 'understanding' in political theory, analysis and action. She con-trasts this with the 'scientific' modes of political thought beginning to predom-inate in the USA at the time and which she links, as a form of thought, to the problem of totalitarianism. For Arendt, politics is one of the central realms of human existence in and through which we make sense of the strangeness of exis-tence and the strangeness of the others with whom we share it. As such, the essay can be read as a plea for recognition of the distinctive 'sense' of politics as opposed to its reduction to mere technocratic method. These are timely thoughts indeed. Arendt's focus on the importance of the experience of the polit-ical can usefully be linked by the reader to the arguments of other writers whose work is presented elsewhere in this volume. These include Wolin and Connolly but also Gadamer, who writes out of the phenomenological tradition to which Arendt (through her 'mentor' Heidegger) can be linked.

'UNDERSTANDING AND POLITICS' (1953)*

Hannah Arendt

Many people say that one cannot fight totalitarianism without understanding it. Fortunately this is not true; if it were, our case would be hopeless. Under-standing, as distinguished from correct information and scientific knowledge,

---

* Hannah Arendt, 'Understanding and Politics', *Partisan Review*, 20:4 (1953).

is a complicated process which never produces unequivocal results. It is an unending activity by which, in constant change and variation, we come to terms with, reconcile ourselves to reality, that is, try to be at home in the world.

Understanding is unending and therefore cannot produce end results; it is the specifically human way of being alive, for every single person needs to be reconciled to a world into which he was born a stranger and in which, to the extent of his distinct uniqueness, he always remains a stranger. Understanding begins with birth and ends with death. To the extent that the rise of totalitarian governments is the central event of our world, to understand totalitarianism is not to condone anything, but to reconcile ourselves to a world in which these things are possible at all.

Everything we know of totalitarianism demonstrates a horrible originality which no far-fetched historical parallels can alleviate. The originality of totalitarianism is horrible, not because some new 'idea' came into the world, but because its very actions constitute a break with all our traditions; they have dearly exploded our categories of political thought and our standards for moral judgment.

Understanding, while it cannot be expected to provide results which are specifically helpful or inspiring in the fight against totalitarianism, must accompany this fight if it is to be more than a mere fight for survival. Insofar as totalitarian movements have sprung up in the non-totalitarian world (crystallizing elements found in that world, for totalitarian governments have not been imported from the moon), the process of understanding is clearly, and perhaps primarily, also a process of self-understanding. For while we merely know, but do not yet understand, what we are fighting against, we know and understand even less what we are fighting for.

Understanding precedes and succeeds knowledge. Preliminary understanding, which is at the basis of all knowledge, and true understanding, which transcends it, have this in common: they make knowledge meaningful. Historical description and political analysis can never prove that there is such a thing as the *nature* or the *essence* of totalitarian government, simply because there is a *nature* to monarchical, republican, tyrannical or despotic government. This specific nature is taken for granted by the preliminary understanding on which the sciences base themselves, and this preliminary understanding permeates as a matter of course, but not with critical insight, their whole terminology and vocabulary. True understanding always returns to the judgments and prejudices which preceded and guided the strictly scientific inquiry. The sciences can only illuminate, but neither prove nor disprove, the uncritical preliminary understanding from which they start. If the scientist, misguided by the very labor of his inquiry, begins to pose as an expert in politics and to despise the popular understanding from which he started, he loses immediately the Ariadne thread of common sense which alone will guide him securely through the labyrinth of his own results.

Yet, has not the task of understanding become hopeless if it is true that we arc confronted with something which has destroyed our categories of thought and standards of judgment? How can we measure length if we do not have a yardstick, how could we count things without the notion of numbers? Maybe it is preposterous even to think that anything can ever happen which our categories are not equipped to understand. Maybe we should resign ourselves to the preliminary understanding, which at once ranges the new among the old, and with the scientific approach, which follows it and deduces methodically the unprecedented from precedents, even though such a description of the new phenomena may be demonstrably at variance with the reality. Is not understanding so closely related to and interrelated with judging that one must describe both as the subsumption (of something particular under a universal rule) which according to Kant is the very definition of judgment, whose absence he so magnificently defined as 'stupidity', an 'infirmity beyond remedy'?

These questions are all the more pertinent as they are not restricted to our perplexity in understanding totalitarianism. The paradox of the modern situation seems to be that our need to transcend preliminary understanding and the strictly scientific approach springs from the fact that we have lost our tools of understanding. Our quest for meaning is at the same time prompted and frustrated by our inability to originate meaning. Kant's definition of stupidity is by no means beside the point. Since the beginning of this century, the growth of meaninglessness has been accompanied by loss of common sense. In many respects, this has appeared simply as an increasing stupidity. We know of no civilization before ours in which people were gullible enough to form their buying habits in accordance with the maxim that 'self-praise is the highest recommendation', the assumption of all advertising. Nor is it likely that any century before ours could have been persuaded to take seriously a therapy which is said to help only if the patients pay a lot of money to those who administer it – except there exists a primitive society where the handing over of money itself possesses magical power.

What has happened to the clever little rules of self-interest has happened on a much larger scale to all the spheres of ordinary life which, because they are ordinary, need to be regulated by customs. Totalitarian phenomena which can no longer be understood in terms of common sense and which defy all rules of 'normal', that is chiefly utilitarian judgment, are only the most spectacular instances of the breakdown of our common inherited wisdom. From the point of view of common sense, we did not need the rise of totalitarianism to show us that we are living in a topsy-turvy world, a world where we cannot find our way by abiding by the rules of what once was common sense. In this situation, stupidity in the Kantian sense has become the infirmity of everybody, and therefore can no longer be regarded as 'beyond remedy'. Stupidity has become as common as common sense was before; and this does not mean that it is a symptom of mass society or that 'intelligent' people are exempt from it. The only difference is that stupidity remains blissfully inarticulate among the non-intellectuals and becomes unbearably offensive among 'intelligent' people.

Within the intelligentsia, one may even say that the more intelligent an individual happens to be, the more irritating is the stupidity which he has in common with all.

In our context, the peculiar and ingenious replacement of common sense with stringent logicality which is characteristic of totalitarian thinking is particularly noteworthy. Logicality is not identical with ideological reasoning, but indicates the totalitarian transformation of the respective ideologies. If it was the peculiarity of the ideologies to treat a scientific hypothesis, like the survival of the fittest in biology or the survival of the most progressive class in history, as an 'idea' which could be applied to the whole course of events, then it is the peculiarity of their totalitarian transformation to pervert the 'idea' into a premise in the logical sense, that is into some self-evident statement from which everything else can be deduced in stringent logical consistency. (Here truth becomes indeed what some logicians pretend it is, namely consistency, except that this equation actually implies the negation of the existence of truth insofar as truth is always supposed to reveal something, whereas consistency is only a mode of fitting statements together, and as such lacks the power of revelation. The new logical movement in philosophy, which grew out of pragmatism, has a frightening affinity with the totalitarian transformation of the pragmatic elements, inherent in all ideologies, into logicality, which severs its ties to reality and experience altogether. Of course, totalitarianism proceeds in a cruder fashion, which unfortunately, by the same token, is also more effective.) The chief political distinction between common sense and logic is that common sense presupposes a common world into which we all fit and where we can live together because we possess one sense which controls and adjusts all strictly particular sense data to those of all others, whereas logic and all self-evidence from which logical reasoning proceeds can claim a reliability altogether independent of the world and the existence of other people. It has often been observed that the validity of the statement $2 + 2 = 4$ is independent of the human condition, that it is equally valid for God and man. In other words, wherever common sense, the political sense par excellence, fails us in our need for understanding, we are all too likely to accept logicality as its substitute, because the capacity for logical reasoning itself is also common to us all. But this common human capacity which functions even under conditions of complete separation from world and experience and which is strictly 'within' us, without any bond to something 'given', is unable to understand anything and, left to itself, utterly sterile. Only under conditions where the common realm *between* men is destroyed and the only reliability left consists in the meaningless tautologies of the self-evident, can this capacity become 'productive', develop its own lines of thought whose chief political characteristic is that they always carry with them a compulsory power of persuasion. To equate thought and understanding with these logical operations means to level down the capacity for thought, which for thousands of years has been deemed to be the highest capacity of man, to its lowest common denominator where no differences in actual existence count any longer, not even the qualitative difference between the essence of God and men.

For those engaged in the quest for meaning and understanding, what is frightening in the rise of totalitarianism is not that it is something new, but that it has brought to light the ruin of our categories of thought and standards of judgment. Newness is the realm of the historian who, unlike the natural scientist concerned with ever-recurring happenings, deals with events which always occur only once. This newness can be manipulated if the historian insists on causality and pretends to be able to explain events by a chain of causes which eventually led up to it. He then, indeed, poses as the 'prophet turned backward', and all that separates him from the gifts of real prophecy seems to be the deplorable physical limitations of the human brain, which unfortunately cannot contain and combine correctly all causes operating at the same time.

Fortunately the situation of the political sciences, which in the highest sense are called upon to pursue the quest for meaning and to answer the need for true understanding of political data, is quite different. The great consequence which the concept of beginning and origin has for all strictly political questions comes from the simple fact that political action, like all action, is essentially always the beginning of something new; as such, it is, in terms of political science, the very essence of human freedom. The central position which the concept of beginning and origin must have in all political thought has been lost only since the historical sciences have been permitted to supply their methods and categories to the field of politics.

Just as in our personal lives our worst fears and best hopes will never adequately prepare us for what actually happens, because the moment even a foreseen event takes place, everything changes, and we can never be prepared for the inexhaustible literalness of this 'everything', so each event in human history reveals an unexpected landscape of human deeds, sufferings and new possibilities which together transcend the sum total of all willed intentions and the significance of all origins. It is the task of the historian to detect this unexpected *new* with all its implications in any given period and to bring out the full power of its significance. He must know that though his story has a beginning and an end, it occurs within a larger frame, history itself. And History is a story which has many beginnings but no end. The end, in any strict and final sense of the word, could only be the disappearance of man from the earth. For whatever the historian calls an end, the end of a period or a tradition or a whole civilization, is a new beginning for those who are alive. The fallacy of all prophecies of doom lies in the disregard of this simple but fundamental fact.

In the light of these reflections, our endeavoring to understand something which has ruined our categories of thought and our standards of judgment appears less frightening. Even though we have lost yardsticks by which to measure, and rules under which to subsume the particular, a being whose essence is beginning may have enough of origin within himself to understand without preconceived categories and to judge without the set of customary rules which is morality. If the essence of all, and in particular of political, action is to make a new beginning, then understanding becomes the other side of action, namely that form of cognition, in distinction from many others, by which acting men (and not men who are engaged in contemplating some progressive or doomed course of history) eventually can come to terms with what irrevocably happened and be reconciled with what unavoidably exists.

As such, understanding is a strange enterprise. In the end, it may do no more than articulate and confirm what preliminary understanding, which always consciously or unconsciously is directly engaged in action, sensed to begin with. It will not shy away from this circle but on the contrary be aware that any other results would be so far removed from action, of which it is only the other side, that they could not possibly be true. Nor will it in the process itself avoid the circle which the logicians call 'vicious' and may in this respect even somewhat resemble philosophy whose great thoughts always turn around in circles, engaging the human mind in nothing less than an interminable dialogue between itself and the essence of everything that is.

In this sense, the old prayer which King Solomon, who certainly knew something of political action, addressed to God for the gift of an 'understanding heart' as the greatest gift a man could receive and desire, might still hold for us. As far removed from sentimentality as it is from paperwork, the human heart is the only thing in the world that will take upon itself the burden which the divine gift of action, of being a beginning and therefore being able to make a beginning, has placed upon us. Solomon prayed for this particular gift because he was a King and knew that only an 'understanding heart', and not mere reflection nor mere feeling, makes it bearable for us to live with other people, strangers forever, in the same world, and makes it possible for them to bear with us.

If we wish to translate the biblical language into terms that are closer to our speech (though hardly more accurate), we may call the gift of an 'understanding heart' the faculty of imagination. In distinction from fantasy which dreams up something, imagination is concerned with the particular darkness of the human heart and the peculiar density which surrounds everything that is real. Whenever we talk of the 'nature' or the 'essence' of a thing, we actually mean this innermost kernel of whose existence we can never be so sure as we are of darkness and density. True understanding does not tire of interminable dialogue and 'vicious circles' because it trusts that imagination eventually will catch at least a glimpse of the always frightening light of truth. To distinguish imagination from fancy and to mobilize its power does not mean that understanding of human affairs becomes 'irrational'. Imagination, on the contrary, as Wordsworth said, 'is but another name for . . . clearest insight, amplitude of mind,/And Reason in her most exalted mood'.

Imagination alone enables us to see things in their proper perspective, to put that which is too close at a certain distance so that we can see and understand it without bias and prejudice, to bridge abysses of remoteness until we can see and understand everything that is too far away from us as though it were our own affair. This 'distancing' of some things and bridging the abysses to others is part of the dialogue of understanding for whose purposes direct experience establishes too close a contact and mere knowledge erects artificial barriers.

Without this kind of imagination, which actually is understanding, we would never be able to take our bearings in the world. It is the only inner compass we have. We are contemporaries only so far as our understanding reaches. If we want to be at home on this earth, even at the price of being at home in this century, we must try to take part in the interminable dialogue with its essence.

'POLITICAL THEORY AS A VOCATION' BY SHELDON S. WOLIN

At the time of writing, Sheldon Wolin is Emeritus Professor of Politics at Princeton University. In North America, he has been one of the most influential political theorists of his generation, breathing new life into the field at a time of atrophy. The focus of Wolin's work can be understood as the nature of politics itself and thus of political theory also. This in turn has required a sustained consideration of the meaning and experience of democracy, particularly in the USA (see *The Presence of the Past: Essays On the State and the Constitution*, Johns Hopkins University Press, 1989), and of the links between theory and political life itself (see *Tocqueville: Between Two Worlds: The Making of a Political and Theoretical Life*, Princeton University Press, 2001). Though out of print now, his early book *Politics and Vision: Continuity and Innovation in Western Political Thought* (Allen and Unwin, 1961) is still important and notable for its arguments concerning the fate of politics in modern, highly organised and complex, liberal states: that it becomes 'sublimated' into diverse areas of society, and the 'politicalness' of politics depreciates in the eyes of analysts. Recently, a volume has been published that discusses, assesses and develops Wolin's work (see *Democracy and Vision: Sheldon Wolin and the Vicissitudes of the Political*, edited by Aryeh Botwinick and William Connolly, Princeton University Press, 2001).

This extract neatly demonstrates Wolin's commitment to the practice of politics and to theorising about it. In a way not dissimilar to that of Arendt, he stresses the importance of a specifically political form of understanding that is different in form to the abstracted 'science' of politics and which depends on a 'tacit political knowledge' that is more allusive and imaginative. The 'epic' political theorist seeks to grasp something about the nature of the world and even to change the way we, the readers of political theory, perceive it. Wolin too is critical of the increasingly bureaucratic nature of political thinking. However, it is probably true to say that the 'methodism' of which Wolin is critical has extended its power even further in the thirty or so years since this essay was written.

'POLITICAL THEORY AS A VOCATION' (1969)*

Sheldon S. Wolin

The purpose of this paper is to sketch some of the implications, prospective and retrospective, of the primacy of method in the present study of politics and to do it by way of a contrast, which is deliberately heightened, but hopefully not caricatured, between the vocation of the 'methodist'[1] and the vocation of the theorist.

In compiling its recent *Biographical Directory*, the American Political Science Association distributed a questionnaire which in its own way helped raise the present question, 'What is the vocation of the political theorist?' Political theorists were invited to identify themselves by choosing among 'Political Theory and Philosophy (Empirical)', 'Political Theory and Philosophy (Historical)' and 'Political Theory and Philosophy (Normative)'. Although the choices offered may signify vitality and diversity, they may also testify to considerable confusion about the nature of political theory. For their part, political theorists may think of it as an identity crisis induced by finding themselves officially assigned a classification which others have defined, a classification traceable to a set of assumptions about the nature of the theoretical life perhaps uncongenial to many theorists.

American political scientists, for the most part, have not only generally supported the traditional American diffidence toward theories, but they have elevated it to scientific status. The suspicion of theories is alleged to be a powerful contributor to the political stability of America and to its genius for pragmatic rather than ideological politics.

The extent of this transformation is such as to suggest that the study of politics is now dominated by the belief that the main objective – acquiring scientific knowledge about politics – depends upon the adoption and refinement of specific techniques and that to be qualified or certified as a political scientist is tantamount to possessing prescribed techniques. Concurrent with this development there has been an effort to imbue political scientists with what is understood to be the ethic of science: objectivity, detachment, fidelity to fact, and deference to intersubjective verification by a community of practitioners. These changes add up to a vocation, a *vita methodica*, which includes a specified set

* Sheldon S. Wolin, 'Political Theory as a Vocation', *American Political Science Review*, 63 (December 1969), 1,062–82.

of skills, a mode of practice, and an informing ethic. This vocation, and the education which it requires, may mark the significance of the behavioral revolution.

Although one might be troubled by the kind of human concern which would provoke a confrontation between 'political wisdom' and 'political *science*', the antithesis has the merit of opening the question, What is political wisdom? Put in this vague form, the question is unanswerable, but it may be reformulated so as to be fruitful. The antithesis between political wisdom and political science basically concerns two different forms of knowledge. The scientific form represents the search for rigorous formulations which are logically consistent and empirically testable. As a form, it has the qualities of compactness, manipulability, and relative independence of context. Political wisdom is an unfortunate phrase, for, as the quotation suggested, the question is not *what* it is but in *what* does it inhere. History, knowledge of institutions, and legal analysis were mentioned. Without violating the spirit of the quotation, knowledge of past political theories might also be added. Taken as a whole, this composite type of knowledge presents a contrast with the scientific type. Its mode of activity is not so much the style of the search as of reflection. It is mindful of logic, but more so of the incoherence and contradictoriness of experience. And for the same reason, it is distrustful of rigor. Political life does not yield its significance to terse hypotheses, but is elusive and hence meaningful statements about it often have to be allusive and intimative. Context becomes supremely important, for actions and events occur in no other setting. Knowledge of this type tends, therefore, to be suggestive and illuminative rather than explicit and determinate. Borrowing from Polanyi, we shall call it 'tacit political knowledge'.[2]

The acquisition of tacit political knowledge is pre-eminently a matter of education of a particular kind, and it is on this ground that the issue needs to be joined with the political methodist. The mentality which is impatient with the past and with traditional political theory is equally curt with the requirements of tacit political knowledge which is rooted in knowledge of the past and of the tradition of theory. The knowledge which the methodist seeks is fairly characterized in his own language as composing a 'kit of tools' or a 'bag of tricks'. To acquire knowledge of techniques is no small matter, for they are often difficult and require considerable 'retooling', which is to say that they imply a particular kind of program of instruction in specific methods.

The impoverishment of education by the demands of methodism poses a threat not only to so-called normative or traditional political theory, but to the scientific imagination as well. It threatens the meditative culture which nourishes all creativity. That culture is the source of the qualities crucial to theorizing: playfulness, concern, the juxtaposition of contraries, and astonishment at the variety and subtle interconnection of things. These same qualities are not confined to the creation of theories, but are at work when the mind is playing over the factual world as well. An impoverished mind, no matter how resolutely empirical in spirit, sees an impoverished world. Such a mind is not disabled from theorizing, but it is tempted into remote abstractions which, when applied to the factual world, end by torturing it. Think of what must be ignored in, or done to, the factual world before an assertion like the following can be made: 'Theoretical models should be tested primarily by the accuracy of their prediction rather than the reality of their assumptions'.[3] No doubt one might object by pointing out that all theorizing does some violence to the empirical world. To which one might reply, that while amputations are necessary, it is still better to have surgeons rather than butchers.

Vision, as I have tried to emphasize, depends for its richness on the resources from which it can draw. These extra-scientific considerations may be identified more explicitly as the stock of ideas which an intellectually curious and broadly educated person accumulates and which come to govern his intuitions, feelings, and perceptions. They constitute the sources of his creativity, yet rarely find explicit expression in formal theory. Lying beyond the boundaries circumscribed by method, technique, and the official definition of a discipline, they can be summarized as cultural resources and itemized as metaphysics, faith, historical sensibility, or, more broadly, as tacit knowledge. Because these matters bear a family resemblance to 'bias', they become sacrificial victims to the quest for objectivity in the social sciences. If scientists have freely acknowledged the importance of many of these items,[4] how much more significant are these human creations for the form of knowledge, political science, which centers on the perplexities of collective life, on objects which are all too animate in expressing their needs, hopes, and fears.

THE VOCATION OF THE POLITICAL THEORIST

If the preceding analysis has any merit, it will have suggested that the triumph of methodism constitutes a crisis in political education and that the main victim is the tacit political knowledge which is so vital to making judgments, not only judgments about the adequacy and value of theories and methods, but about the nature and perplexities of politics as well. Here lies the vocation of these who preserve our understanding of past theories, who sharpen our sense of the subtle, complex interplay between political experience and thought, and who preserve our memory of the agonizing efforts of intellect to restate the possibilities and threats posed by political dilemmas of the past. In teaching about past theories, the historically-minded theorist is engaged in the task of political initiation; that is, of introducing new generations of students to the complexities of politics and to the efforts of theorists to confront its predicaments; of developing the capacity for discriminating judgments discussed earlier; and of cultivating that sense of 'significance' which, as Weber understood so well, is vital to scientific inquiry but cannot be furnished by scientific methods; and of exploring the ways in which new theoretical vistas are opened.

What we should expect from a reading of Aristotle is an increase in political understanding. What we should expect from the study of the history of political theories is an appreciation of the historical dimension of politics. The cultivation of political understanding means that one becomes sensitized to the enormous complexities and drama of saying that the political order is the most comprehensive association and ultimately responsible as no other grouping is for sustaining the physical, material, cultural, and moral life of its members. Political understanding also teaches that the political order is articulated through its history; the past weighs on the present, shaping alternatives and pressing with a force of its own. At the present time, the historical mode is largely ignored in favor of modes of understanding which are inherently incapable of building upon historical knowledge. One of the most striking features of game theory, communications models, and mechanical systems is that in each case the organizing notion is essentially history-less.

But what of the vocation by which political theories are created rather than transmitted? Testimony that such a vocation has existed is to be found in the ancient notion of the *bios theoretikos* as well as in the actual achievements of the long line of writers extending from Plato to Marx. How shall we understand this tradition as containing an idea of vocation which is relevant both to the challenge raised by the prestige of science and to the contemporary state of political life?

In what follows, I shall develop the thesis that the traditional idea of political theory displays some features which resemble forms of scientific theory, but which, by virtue of their political bearing, are uniquely the properties of political theory. As a way of bringing out the distinctive nature of this vocation, I shall call it the vocation of 'epic theorist', a characterization which probably seems pretentious or precious, but which has been selected in order to call attention both to the unusual 'magnitudes' of this form of theorizing and to its distinguishing purpose and style.

Perhaps the pretentiousness of the phrase may be lessened by briefly recalling a comparable conception of theory in Kuhn's work. He employs the phrase 'extraordinary' science to describe the contributions of the great scientific innovators. Kuhn's main point is that these theories mark a break with previous ones; that is, they inaugurate a new way of looking at the world, which includes a new set of concepts, as well as new cognitive *and* normative standards. Taking this as a suggestion of how to think about great theories, the first feature shared by epic theorists has to do with magnitudes. By an act of thought, the theorist seeks to reassemble the whole political world. He aims to grasp present structures and interrelationships, and to re-present them in a new way. Like the extraordinary scientific theory, such efforts involve a new way of looking at the familiar world, a new way with its own cognitive and normative standards.[5]

Because history suggests that all political societies have both endured and employed violence, cruelty, and injustice, and known the defeat of human aspirations, it is not surprising that the theorist's concern for *res publicae* and the commonweal has issued in theories which, for the most part, have been critical and, in the literal sense, radical.

There is one setting, however, in which specific arrangements, decisions, and beliefs become theoretically interesting. That is when they are 'systematically mistaken': when arrangements or decisions appear not as random consequences of a system which otherwise works tolerably well or as the result of the personal foibles of a particular office-holder but as the necessary result of a more extensive set of evils which can confidently be expected to continue producing similar results. Such a system would be systematically deranged.

This concept of the *systematically* mistaken explains why most political theories contain radical critiques. Their authors have tried to get at the basic principles (in the sense of starting points) which produce mistaken arrangements and wrong actions. This same impulse determines why a political theory takes the form of a symbolic picture of an ordered whole. That it is a whole is dictated by its function, which is to be complementary to, or a substitute for, the systematically disordered whole which the theory seeks to displace. The possibility that the factual world is the outcome of a systematically disordered whole produces still another major difference between the epic political theorist and the scientific theorist. Although each attempts to change men's views of the world, only the former attempts to change the world itself. Although the scientist surely may claim for his theories the daring, beauty, and imaginativeness that are claimed for other forms of endeavor, he will concede that at some point his theory must submit to confirmation by the world. T. H. Huxley spoke sadly of 'beautiful' theories tragically murdered by 'an ugly little fact'. Plato, in contrast, had asked defiantly, 'Is our theory any the worse, if we cannot prove it possible that a state so organized should be actually founded?' Epic theory, if it has not strictly attempted to use theory to murder the ugly facts of the world, has taken a very different view of them, refusing to yield to facts the role of arbiter. Facts could never prove the validity of a true theory, because facts, in the form of practices or actions, were 'less close to truth than [is] thought'.[6] Thus for Plato the political facts of Athenian democracy were perfectly consistent with the theory of democracy, but the theory itself was systematically mistaken in its organizing principles, that is, deranged.

When we turn our attention to political life in the modern states, its appearance seems more suitable to methodical inquiry and mechanical models or theories. Our political and social landscape is dominated by large structures whose premeditated design embodies many of the presuppositions and principles of methodism. They are deliberately fabricated, their processes are composed of defined 'steps', and their work is accomplished by a division of specialized labor whose aggregate effect seems marvelously disproportionate to the modest talents which are combined. Not only do these organizations impart regularity and predictability to the major realms of our existence, thereby furnishing the conditions whereby methodical inquiry can pursue its goal of scientifically verifiable knowledge with reasonable hopes of success – for what could be more hopeful than to know that the political and social world is deliberately fashioned to produce regular and predictable behavior? – but also, since these organizations are uniquely the product of mind, rather than of mysterious historical forces, we are able to say with far greater confidence than Hobbes and Vico, who first announced the principle, 'we can know it, because we made it'.

Yet this is the state of affairs which the greatest modern philosopher of method, Max Weber, foresaw and despaired of, a world of bleak, forbidding, almost sterile reality, dominated by large and impersonal bureaucratic structures which nullified the strivings of those political heroes evoked in 'Politics as a Vocation'. 'A polar night of icy darkness and hardness' was his description of the world to come.[7] In a fundamental sense, our world has become as perhaps no previous world has, the product of design, the product of theories about human structures deliberately created rather than historically articulated. But in another sense, the embodiment of theory in the world has resulted in a world impervious to theory. The giant, routinized structures defy fundamental alteration and, at the same time, display an unchallengeable legitimacy, for the rational, scientific, and technological principles on which they are based seem in perfect accord with an age committed to science, rationalism and technology. Above all, it is a world which appears to have rendered epic theory superfluous. Theory, as Hegel had foreseen, must take the form of 'explanation'. Truly it seems to be the age where Minerva's owl has taken flight.

It would seem, then, that the world affirms what the leaders of the behavioral revolution claim, the irrelevance of epic theory. The only trouble is that the world shows increasing signs of coming apart; our political systems are sputtering, our communication networks invaded by cacophony. American society has reached a point where its cities are uninhabitable, its youth disaffected, its races at war with each other, and its hope, its treasure, and the lives of its young men dribbled away in interminable foreign ventures. Our whole world threatens to become anomalous.

Amid all this, a political scientist approvingly quotes the following from a social scientist: 'To argue that an existing order is "imperfect" in comparison with an alternative order of affairs that turns out upon careful inspection to be unobtainable may not be different from saying that the existing order is "perfect"'.[8]

This assertion poses squarely the issue between political theory on the one side and the alliance between the methodist and the empirical theorist on the other. The issue is not between theories which are normative and those which are not; nor is it between those political scientists who are theoretical and those who are not. Rather, it is between those who would restrict the 'reach' of theory by dwelling on facts which are selected by what are assumed to be the functional requisites of the existing paradigm, and those who believe that because facts are richer than theories, it is the task of the theoretical imagination to restate new possibilities. In terms of theory, the basic thrust of contemporary political science is not anti-theoretical so much as it is deflationary of theory. This is most frequently expressed in the anxiety of the behaviorist who discovers that the philosophy of democracy places excessive demands on the 'real world', and hence it is the task of political science to suggest a more realistic version of democratic theory.

Is it possible that in this genial, Panglossian twilight, Minerva's owl is beginning to falter as it speeds over a real world that is increasingly discordant and is beginning to voice demands and hopes that are 'unreasonably high'? Perhaps it is possible, especially if we remember that, according to Greek statuary, Minerva's pet was a screech owl, for a screech is the noise both of warning and of pain.

NOTES

1. *'Methodist*. One who is skilled in, or attaches great importance to, method; one who follows a (specified) method' (*Oxford Universal Dictionary*).

    Although most social scientists would contend that actual research rarely conforms to a step-by-step procedure, it remains the case that such procedure stands as a model for what they aim at. Thus, in a section of a textbook on research methods entitled 'Major Steps in Research', the authors insert the qualification above but acknowledge that 'published research strongly suggests the existence of a prescribed sequence of procedures, each step presupposing the completion of the preceding one'. See Claire Selltiz et al., *Research Methods in Social Relations*, rev. edn (New York: Holt, Rinehart & Winston, 1963), pp. 8–9.
2. M. Polanyi, *Personal Knowledge* (New York: Harper & Row, 1964), passim.
3. A. Downs, *An Economic Theory of Democracy* (New York: Harper & Row, 1957), p. 21.
4. For example K. Popper, *The Logic of Scientific Discovery* (New York: Science Editions, 1961), pp. 19, 38.
5. Here it is only necessary to recall Plato's long discussion of cognition or Hobbes' effort to place political philosophy upon a new and more scientific basis.
6. Plato, *Republic* 473 (Conford tr.).
7. H. Gerth and C. W. Mills, *From Max Weber: Essays in Sociology* (New York: Oxford University Press, 1946), p. 128.
8. Cited by A. Wilkausky, *The Politics of the Budgetary Process* (Boston: Little, Brown, 1964), p. 179.

'RIGHT OF DEATH AND POWER OVER LIFE' BY MICHEL FOUCAULT

The work of the French philosopher Michel Foucault (1926–84) has been hugely influential, and controversial, across many fields. One of the aspects of most interest to political theory is his argument that we should not be so focused on questions of sovereignty, the singular and central location of power, since this is inadequate for understanding modern societies. Power, Foucault argues, is spread throughout society and does not simply repress actions but constitutes them. One of the most important things power does is shape the ways in which we understand ourselves as particular sorts of subject or self. Foucault explored the way in which forms of knowledge (especially the social sciences) define and categorise humanity, informing the minute procedures that are carried out by, for example, doctors, teachers, psychologists and ourselves on our bodies and minds. His major works include those that investigated the methodology and epistemology of social science, such as *The Order of Things: An Archaeology of the Human Sciences* (Tavistock Publications, 1970) and *The Archaeology of Knowledge* (Tavistock Publications, 1972), and those examining specific phenomena, including *Discipline and Punish: The Birth of the Prison* (Penguin, 1977). His final completed works examined the discourses and power regimes of sexuality: *The History of Sexuality, Vol. 1: An Introduction* (Penguin, 1978), *The History of Sexuality, Vol. 2: The Use of Pleasure* (Penguin, 1987) and *The History of Sexuality, Vol. 3: The Care of the Self* (Penguin, 1990). A lot of excellent essays and comments on numerous issues are to be found in *Power/Knowledge: Selected Interviews and Other Writings 1972–1977*, edited by Colin Gordon (Harvester Press, 1980).

The extract here is from the introductory book of his three-volume study of *The History of Sexuality* and amply demonstrates the dazzling way in which Foucault can reorder our thinking about the exercise of power. He draws attention to what he terms 'bio-power' in order to mark the shift from a form of brutal monarchical sovereignty to the exercise of governmental power that focuses upon the management and control of the core processes of human life – regulation supplants the sharp application of law. The way Foucault's approach affects our understanding of what politics is (and of how it can take place) has stimulated much reflection, and readers may wish to compare the implications of his work with the arguments of other authors whose work is presented in this volume such as Wolin, Arendt, Laclau, Mouffe, Butler and Connolly.

'RIGHT OF DEATH AND POWER OVER LIFE' (1978)*

Michel Foucault

For a long time, one of the characteristic privileges of sovereign power was the right to decide life and death. In a formal sense, it derived no doubt from the ancient *patria potestas* that granted the father of the Roman family the right to 'dispose' of the lives of his children and his slaves; just as he had given them life, so he could take it away. By the time the right of life and death was framed by the classical theoreticians, it was in a considerably diminished form. It was no longer considered that this power of the sovereign over his subjects could be exercised in an absolute and unconditional way, but only in cases where the sovereign's very existence was in jeopardy: a sort of right of rejoinder. If he were threatened by external enemies who sought to overthrow him or contest his rights, he could then legitimately wage war, and require his subjects to take part in the defence of the state; without 'directly proposing their death', he was empowered to 'expose their life': in this sense, he wielded an 'indirect' power over them of life and death.[1] But if someone dared to rise up against him and transgress his laws, then he could exercise a direct power over the offender's life: as punishment, the latter would be put to death. Viewed in this way, the power of life and death was not an absolute privilege: it was conditioned by the defence of the sovereign, and his own survival. . . .

. . . Since the classical age, the West has undergone a very profound transformation of these mechanisms of power . . . Wars are no longer waged in the name of a sovereign who must be defended; they are waged on behalf of the existence of everyone; entire populations are mobilized for the purpose of wholesale slaughter in the name of life necessity: massacres have become vital. It is as managers of life and survival, of bodies and the race, that so many regimes have been able to wage so many wars, causing so many men to be killed. And through a turn that closes the circle, as the technology of wars has caused them to tend increasingly towards all-out destruction, the decision that initiates them and the one that terminates them are in fact increasingly informed by the naked question of survival. The atomic situation is now at the end point of this process: the power to expose a whole population to death is the underside of the power to guarantee an individual's continued existence. The principle

---

* Michel Foucault, 'Right of Death and Power over Life', from *The History of Sexuality, Vol. 1: An Introduction*, trans. Robert Hurley (London: Penguin Books, 1978).

underlying the tactics of battle – that one has to be capable of killing in order to go on living – has become the principle that defines the strategy of states. But the existence in question is no longer the juridical existence of sovereignty; at stake is the biological existence of a population. If genocide is indeed the dream of modern powers, this is not because of a recent return of the ancient right to kill; it is because power is situated and exercised at the level of life, the species, the race and the large-scale phenomena of population.

One might say that the ancient right to *take* life or *let* live was replaced by a power to *foster* life or *disallow* it to the point of death. This is perhaps what explains that disqualification of death which marks the recent wane of the rituals that accompanied it. That death is so carefully evaded is linked less to a new anxiety which makes death unbearable for our societies than to the fact that the procedures of power have not ceased to turn away from death. In the passage from this world to the other, death was the manner in which a terrestrial sovereignty was relieved by another, singularly more powerful sovereignty; the pageantry that surrounded it was in the category of political ceremony. Now it is over life, throughout its unfolding, that power establishes its dominion; death is power's limit, the moment that escapes it; death becomes the most secret aspect of existence, the most 'private'.

The old power of death that symbolized sovereign power was now carefully supplanted by the administration of bodies and the calculated management of life. During the classical period, there was a rapid development of various disciplines – universities, secondary schools, barracks, workshops; there was also the emergence, in the field of political practices and economic observation, of the problems of birth rate, longevity, public health, housing and migration. Hence there was an explosion of numerous and diverse techniques for achieving the subjugation of bodies and the control of populations, marking the beginning of an era of 'bio-power'.

For the first time in history, no doubt, biological existence was reflected in political existence; the fact of living was no longer an inaccessible substrate that only *emerged* from time to time, amid the randomness of death and its fatality; part of it passed into knowledge's field of control and power's sphere of intervention. Power would no longer be dealing simply with legal subjects over whom the ultimate dominion was death, but with living beings, and the mastery it would be able to exercise over them would have to be applied at the level of life itself; it was the taking charge of life, more than the threat of death, that gave power its access even to the body. If one can apply the term *bio-history* to the pressures through which the movements of life and the processes of history interfere with one another, one would have to speak of *bio-power* to designate what brought life and its mechanisms into the realm of explicit calculations and made knowledge-power an agent of transformation of human life. It is not that life has been totally integrated into techniques that govern and administer it; it constantly escapes them. Outside the Western world, famine exists, on a greater scale than ever; and the biological risks confronting the species are perhaps greater, and certainly more serious, than before the birth of microbiology. But what might be called a society's 'threshold of modernity' has been reached when the life of the species is wagered on its own political strategies. For millennia, man remained what he was for Aristotle: a living animal with the additional capacity for a political existence; modern man is an animal whose politics places his existence as a living being in question.

Another consequence of this development of bio-power was the growing importance assumed by the action of the norm, at the expense of the juridical system of the law. Law cannot help but be armed, and its arm, par excellence, is death; to those who transgress it, it replies, at least as a last resort, with that absolute menace. The law always refers to the sword. But a power whose task is to take charge of life needs continuous regulatory and corrective mechanisms. It is no longer a matter of bringing death into play in the field of sovereignty, but of distributing the living in the domain of value and utility. Such a power has to qualify, measure, appraise and hierarchise, rather than display itself in its murderous splendour; it does not have to draw the line that separates the enemies of the sovereign from his obedient subjects; it effects distributions around the norm. I do not mean to say that the law fades into the background or that the institutions of justice tend to disappear, but rather that the law operates more and more as a norm, and that the judicial institution is increasingly incorporated into a continuum of apparatuses (medical, administrative and so on) whose functions are for the most part regulatory. A normalising society is the historical outcome of a technology of power centred on life. We have entered a phase of juridical regression in comparison with the pre-seventeenth-century societies we are acquainted with; we should not be deceived by all the constitutions framed throughout the world since the French Revolution, the codes written and revised, a whole continual and clamorous legislative activity: these were the forms that made an essentially normalising power acceptable.

Moreover, against this power that was still new in the nineteenth century, the forces that resisted relied for support on the very thing it invested, that is, on life and man as a living being. Since the last century, the great struggles that have challenged the general system of power were not guided by the belief in a return to former rights, or by the age-old dream of a cycle of time or a Golden Age. One no longer aspired towards the coming of the emperor of the poor, or the kingdom of the latter days, or even the restoration of our imagined ancestral rights; what was demanded and what served as an objective was life, understood as the basic needs, man's concrete essence, the realisation of his potential, a plenitude of the possible. Whether or not it was Utopia that was wanted is of little importance; what we have seen has been a very real process of struggle; life as a political object was in a sense taken at face value and turned back against the system that was bent on controlling it. It was life more than the law that became the issue of political struggles, even if the latter were formulated through affirmations concerning rights. The 'right' to life, to one's body, to health, to happiness, to the satisfaction of needs, and beyond all the oppressions or 'alienations', the 'right' to rediscover what one is and all that one can be – this 'right' which the classical juridical system was utterly incapable of comprehending was the political response to all these new procedures of power which did not derive, either, from the traditional right of sovereignty.

This is the background that enables us to understand the importance assumed by sex as a political issue. It was at the pivot of the two axes along which developed the entire political technology of life. On the one hand, it was tied to the disciplines of the body: the harnessing, intensification and distribution of forces, the adjustment and economy of energies. On the other hand, it was applied to the regulation of populations, through all the far-reaching effects of its activity. It fitted in both categories at once, giving rise to infinitesimal surveillances, permanent controls, extremely meticulous orderings of space, indeterminate medical or psychological examinations, to an entire micro-power concerned with the body. But it gave rise as well to comprehensive measures, statistical assessments, and interventions aimed at the entire social body or at groups taken as a whole. Sex was a means of access both to the life of the body and the life of the species. It was employed as a standard for the disciplines and as a basis for regulations. This is why in the nineteenth century sexuality was sought out in the smallest details of individual existences; it was tracked down in behaviour, pursued in dreams; it was suspected of underlying the least follies, it was traced back into the earliest years of childhood; it became the stamp of individuality – at the same time what enabled one to analyse the latter and what made it possible to master it. But one also sees it becoming the theme of political operations, economic interventions (through incitements to or curbs on procreation), and ideological campaigns for raising standards of morality and responsibility: it was put forward as the index of a society's strength, revealing of both its political energy and its biological vigour. Spread out from one pole to the other of this technology of sex was a whole series of different tactics that combined in varying proportions the objective of disciplining the body and that of regulating populations.

The blood relation long remained an important element in the mechanisms of power, its manifestations and its rituals. For a society in which the systems of alliance, the political form of the sovereign, the differentiation into orders and castes, and the value of descent lines were predominant; for a society in which famine, epidemics and violence made death imminent, blood constituted one of the fundamental values. It owed its high value at the same time to its instrumental role (the ability to shed blood), to the way it functioned in the order of signs (to have a certain blood, to be of the same blood, to be prepared to risk one's blood), and also to its precariousness (easily spilled, subject to drying up, too readily mixed, capable of being quickly corrupted). A society of blood – I was tempted to say, of 'sanguinity' – where power spoke *through* blood: the honour of war, the fear of famine, the triumph of death, the sovereign with his sword, executioners, and tortures; blood was *a reality with a symbolic function*. We, on the other hand, are in a society of 'sex', or rather a society 'with a sexuality': the mechanisms of power are addressed to the body, to life, to what causes it to proliferate, to what reinforces the species, its stamina, its ability to dominate, or its capacity for being used. Through the themes of health, progeny, race, the future of the species, the vitality of the social body, power spoke of sexuality and to sexuality; the latter was not a mark or a symbol, it was an object and a target. Moreover, its importance was due less to its rarity or its precariousness than to its insistence, its insidious presence, the fact that it was everywhere an object of excitement and fear at the same time. Power delineated it, aroused it and employed it as the proliferating meaning that had always to be taken control of again lest it escape; it was *an effect with a meaning-value*. I do not mean to say that a substitution of sex for blood was by itself responsible for all the transformations that marked the threshold of our modernity. It is not the soul of two civilisations or the organising principle of two cultural forms that I am attempting to express; I am looking for the reasons for which sexuality, far from being repressed in the society of that period, on the contrary was constantly aroused. The new procedures of power that were devised during the classical age and employed in the nineteenth century were what caused our societies to go from *a symbolics of blood* to *an analytics of sexuality*. Clearly, nothing was more on the side of the law, death, transgression, the symbolic and sovereignty than blood – just as sexuality was on the side of the norm, knowledge, life, meaning, the disciplines and regulations.

It might be added that 'sex' performs yet another function that runs through and sustains the ones we have just examined. Its role in this instance is more practical than theoretical. It is through sex – in fact, an imaginary point determined by the deployment of sexuality – that each individual has to pass in order to have access to his own intelligibility (seeing that it is both the hidden aspect and the generative principle of meaning), to the whole of his body (since it is a real and threatened part of it, while symbolically constituting the whole), to his identity (since it joins the force of a drive to the singularity of a history). Through a reversal that doubtless had its surreptitious beginnings long ago – it was already making itself felt at the time of the Christian pastoral of the flesh – we have arrived at the point where we expect our intelligibility to come from what was for many centuries thought of as madness; the plenitude of our body from what was long considered its stigma and likened to a wound; our identity from what was perceived as an obscure and nameless urge. Hence the importance we ascribe to it, the reverential fear with which we surround it, the care we take to know it. Hence the fact that over the centuries it has become more important than our soul, more important almost than our life; and so it is that all the world's enigmas appear frivolous to us compared to this secret, minuscule in each of us, but of a density that makes it more serious than any other. The Faustian pact, whose temptation has been instilled in us by the deployment of sexuality, is now as follows: to exchange life in its entirety for sex itself, for the truth and the sovereignty of sex. Sex is worth dying for. It is in this (strictly historical) sense that sex is indeed imbued with the death instinct. When a long while ago the West discovered love, it bestowed on it a value high enough to make death acceptable; nowadays it is sex that claims this equivalence, the highest of all. And while the deployment of sexuality permits the techniques of power to invest life, the fictitious point of sex, itself marked by that deployment, exerts enough charm on everyone for them to accept hearing the grumble of death within it.

NOTE

1. Samuel von Pufendorf, *Le Droit de la nature* (French trans., 1734), p. 445.

2

INTERPRETING POLITICAL THOUGHT

Melissa Lane

INTRODUCTION

In many departments of government or political science, and in some of history or philosophy, the study of the history of political thought flourishes. Students read their way through the canon 'from Plato to NATO', taking in **Plato, Aristotle, Machiavelli, Hobbes, Locke, Rousseau** and **Marx**, perhaps alongside **Cicero, Wollstonecraft** or **Hegel**. Leaving aside the cynical view that 'political thought' must be an oxymoron, a reflective student of the subject will ask two questions. First, how is it possible to interpret the history of political thought? And second, why should we bother to do so? The two parts of this chapter correspond to these two questions: the how, and the why, of interpreting the history of political thought. The readings bear, as will be shown, on both.

HOW IS IT POSSIBLE TO INTERPRET THE HISTORY OF POLITICAL THOUGHT?

Until the eighteenth century, few people would have considered that this question raised any special difficulties. The idea that 'to interpret the history of political thought' poses any particular challenge – that it might not even be possible – is the fruit of three developments in what one may broadly call the Enlightenment. This term refers to a wide-ranging transformation in intellectual culture that spread across Europe in the eighteenth and nineteenth centuries, reconfiguring the way in which science, philosophy and, of course, politics were conceived.

Among these developments, one might mention first a renewed concern with history as such and with its effects. This promoted a sense of the economic, social and political differences between the classical past and the present, which came to override the previous acceptance of authority of the one over the other. Second, there was a concern with language and the interpretation of texts: an awareness that language may be opaque and contextual, that the meaning of something in the past may not be self-evident to readers in the present. And third, there was a concern with the notion of science. To ask whether there can be a science of politics, or a science of values, is potentially to alter the purpose for which the history of political thought might be interpreted.

To explain how each of these three concerns originated and developed is beyond the scope of this chapter. We can summarise them by noting that the question as expressed in the heading of this section, the question of 'how something is possible', bears the stamp of the eighteenth-century Prussian Enlightenment philosopher, Immanuel Kant. Kant inquired into the conditions of possibility of human knowledge and its concomitant limits. By distinguishing between causes (studied by the natural sciences) and intentions (the subject of ethics), Kant made the study of history into a problem which involved philosophical debate about the status of language and science alike. To ask how to interpret 'the history of political thought' thus involves asking how to interpret 'the history of thought' in general. This will be the focus of this section of the chapter. Why one might wish to interpret *political* thought in particular will be considered in the next.

'The history of thought' sounds like a specialised subfield of history, set apart from the general concern with battles and ploughs. But in the early nineteenth century G. W. F. Hegel proclaimed, against Kant, that all history is, in a sense, thought – the operation of the 'world-mind'. On this view, the history of thought is the essence of history itself. Hegel thus declared a new and absolute form of **idealism**, challenged in the same era by the declarations of **positivism**. For the absolute idealist, to study history is to understand with one's own mind the operation of mind in the past, establishing a distinct kind of moral science (if it be a science at all). For the positivist, to study history is to accumulate empirical facts which will eventually be explained by being brought under a framework of laws like those of natural science.

What **idealism** meant for the actual day-to-day practice of historians was best brought out in the early twentieth century by the Oxford don R. G. Collingwood (1889–1943), a professor of philosophy and enthusiastic avocational archaeologist of Roman Britain, whose great unfinished work *The Idea of History* (1946) was published posthumously. The selection reproduced below is taken from his *Autobiography*, where Collingwood recounts the way in which he came to understand the force of **idealism** against the realist tenets of his teachers. Reflecting on his own practice of archaeology, he realised that one learns nothing from an excavation simply by apprehending or contemplating it. Rather, one has to pose a question, and what one is able to learn or understand depends entirely on the question posed. Collingwood generalised this point from his own knowledge of the Roman past to the knowledge of objects and features of any kind of human practice.

According to Collingwood, to understand what someone means, it is not enough simply to read his statements; 'you must also know what the question was . . . to which the thing he has said or written was meant as an answer' (1939: 31). To understand what **Plato** wrote, or indeed even to understand what our neighbour meant by what she said a moment ago, involves a kind of historical skill in discovering the question which the writer or speaker intended to answer in saying what he or she did. And this is all the more necessary, and difficult, when the statement in question was made in the distant past. Most people, when writing, assume that their contemporaries share their interests and concerns, and 'consequently a writer very seldom explains what the question is that he is trying to answer' (ibid.: 39), and this question may well have since been forgotten. The interpretation of a writer who has become a 'classic' is the most difficult of all, since his or her answer to the question may have succeeded in reorientating subsequent generations to ask new questions, so that the original question answered by the 'classic text' becomes difficult to uncover. In the excerpt below, Collingwood states that nothing but thought can be the object of historical knowledge, so that the history of politics is itself the history of political thought.

Two points follow from Collingwood's thesis. The first is that the past can never be studied in total detachment from the present. To study the past must be to understand it; to understand it is to rethink the thoughts of the past. So history becomes part of our self-knowledge and is pursued for the sake of our own present questions, even though the particular elements of historical understanding may remain insulated from present concerns (ibid.: 113–15). The second is that people use language to do things. Language is not severed from human action, it is part of the story of human deeds used to perform actions as well as merely to describe or reflect on them. Collingwood concluded that this means that one cannot interpret the history of political thought as a history of subsequent theories of the same linguistic concept. 'Plato's *Republic* is an attempt at a theory of one thing; Hobbes's *Leviathan* an attempt at a theory of something else' (ibid.: 62).

In the 1960s, the historians Peter **Laslett**, John **Pocock**, Quentin **Skinner** and John Dunn – who became known as inspirers or founders of the 'Cambridge School' advocating the study of political thought in its historical context – took up Collingwood's second point but rejected his first. One reason for the rejection of the thesis of rethinking someone's thought was the emergence of a new paradigm in the philosophy of language. Collingwood's **idealism** had rested on the ability of one mind perfectly to understand another mind, as it were by private communion. But Ludwig **Wittgenstein**, the iconoclastic Cambridge philosopher, in his *Philosophical Investigations* (published posthumously in 1953), challenged the very notion of private meanings. Meaning, he suggested, was essentially public; we have no access into others' minds, indeed we cannot know that they do have minds except by observing their actions. A complementary perspective was advanced by the Oxford philosopher John **Austin**, whose short book *How to Do Things with Words* (given as lectures in 1955 and published posthumously in 1962) explained that language could be used not simply to describe or affirm, but also to have effects on others (e.g. to persuade) and to perform actions (e.g. to marry by saying 'I do'). The immediate impact of Austin, against the background of Wittgenstein, was (in effect) to affirm Collingwood's point about studying texts as forms of action (answering questions or, more generally, trying to depose kings or the like) while rejecting his thesis about mental union.

As the selection from John Dunn explains, a key principle of interpretation championed by Quentin **Skinner** is this: one must seek to identify the intention of the author to do something in, or by, saying what she says. **Skinner** disavows the notion of intention as something private in the author's mind, arguing against Collingwood that the author's thoughts as she thought them can never be accessible to the historian. But since her performative intentions must have been publicly manifested to her contemporaries in order to (have the chance to) achieve her aims, so they must be publicly available to the historian who is skilled and sensitive enough to understand them in light of the political and intellectual contexts in which they would have made sense. John **Pocock**, associated with the Cambridge School in the 1960s, focused less on the performative intentions of writers, and more on the vocabulary and associations afforded them by the 'languages' or, later, the 'paradigms' (borrowing the term from the philosopher of science Thomas **Kuhn**) which writers, in making their points, argue through, within and with (Pocock, 1989).

It has been observed that these approaches assimilate the question of how to interpret the history of political thought to the question of how to do history at all; indeed, according to David Wootton, they 'represent merely the application of the methods and values of professional history to the history of ideas' (1984: 12). Herbert **Butterfield**'s fusillade against *The Whig Interpretation of History* (1931) would represent an early sally in the same war. If one is sceptical about the possibility of understanding the past *tout court*, one will be sceptical about the notion of a history of political thought. Conversely, if one accepts that it is possible to write history (though also always possible to write it badly), one should accept that it is no less possible to write a history of ideas. The history of political thought just is part of history, not because (as for the absolute idealists) history is pure thought, but because all history is a record of intentional activity.

On the continent, as Richard Tuck (1991: 202) has observed, the link between thought and action had long been acknowledged, though the problem of interpretation tended to be approached in general terms rather than in terms of the special demands of the history of ideas. The philosopher Martin **Heidegger** had emphasised that all thought arose out of the inevitable forms of human practical engagement with the world. And he preoccupied himself with the history of philosophy on the grounds that a crucial 'forgetting of Being' had occurred in that tradition, which needed to be rethought in order that the 'question of Being' could once again be acknowledged, instead of being constantly reduced to the question of the nature of this or that particular being. His student Hans-Georg Gadamer saw Heidegger's work as decisive for the future development of **hermeneutics** (the technical name for the theory of interpretation).

Heidegger showed that, in Gadamer's words, 'a person who understands, understands himself, projecting himself according to his possibilities' (1975: 231). But this self-understanding is not of the idealist sort. It comes rather from the practical aspect of understanding as knowing one's way around, and from the fact that human existence has no essence but its temporal projection. To gain historical understanding is not to understand the essence of one's self but to gain an understanding of one's existence in time. As Gadamer puts it: 'The general structure of understanding acquires its concrete form in historical understanding, in that the commitments of custom and tradition and the corresponding potentialities of one's own future become effective in understanding itself' (ibid.: 234). Such understanding must take the form of a circle. The hermeneutic circle expresses the fact that each interpreter must begin not only with his or her own questions but with his or her own prejudices, and within his or her tradition, in engaging with a text. Such engagement will often provide 'the experience of being pulled up short by the text' (ibid.: 237), and so invite the interpreter to learn something from the text, making the circle a dynamic spiral of understanding rather than a barren stand-off. This conception led Gadamer to criticise what he took to be the Enlightenment ideal of pure rationality free from tradition and prejudice, which would make it (in his view) logically impossible for us to learn anything from the past at all.

The selection from Gadamer reproduced below shows him, like Skinner, drawing on Collingwood, though criticising the latter's stance in two notable ways. First, he envisages the perfect end-state of interpretation not as 'the immediate fusing of one person into another' (ibid.: 345) à la Collingwood, but as the 'fusion of horizons' between interpreter and text. This means that each generation must write its own history; there is no pure ideal history out there waiting to be found. Second, as mentioned at the end of the selection, he develops a picture of language very different from that of Collingwood or Skinner, and indebted to the later work of Heidegger. Whereas Collingwood emphasised the question being asked by use of language, and Skinner the intention expressed in or by it, Gadamer (following his teacher Heidegger) accords language a life of its own. We speak in a language, but that language also speaks (as it were) through us:

> The way in which one word follows another, with the conversation taking its own turnings and reaching its own conclusions, may well be conducted in some way, but the people conversing are far less the leaders of it than

the led . . . All this shows that a conversation has a spirit of its own, and that the language used in it bears its own truth within it, i.e. that it reveals something which henceforth exists'. (Gadamer, 1975: 345)

We see here in Gadamer what we saw in Skinner, and what, I would suggest, is a general phenomenon: a theorist's view of language shapes his or her judgement about how to interpret past political thought. An extreme instance of this link can be found in the **deconstruction**ist challenge, in which a view of the intrinsic instability of linguistic texts is used to suggest that there can be no stable interpretation of past political thought or indeed of anything at all. On the other extreme, it could be said that Marxists treat the link between language and political thought as of no fundamental significance in itself, the explanatory key to political thought being rather its role as ideology in relation to class struggle. But for those who hold that language is stable enough to bear interpretation and significant enough to deserve it, the view of language adopted will inevitably shape the account of interpretation.

Linguistic interactions constitute the history of political thought conceived simultaneously as an act of political reflection, as reflection on political activity, and as reflective political activity. It can be distinguished but not severed from the history of politics itself. As the editors of a study of changes in political concepts put it, 'Insofar as the political world is linguistically and communicatively constructed, then, conceptual change must be understood politically, and political change conceptually' (Ball et al. (eds), 1989: ix). To interpret the history of political thought is to interpret the way that language is used to constitute, imagine and interpret the phenomena of politics and their location in the human world.

WHY (BOTHER TO) INTERPRET THE HISTORY OF POLITICAL THOUGHT?

The attempt to celebrate the history of political thought as offering perennial values arose, as Richard Tuck has suggested, as a counterpoint to the value-free ambitions of American political science in the 1950s and before. Ironically, although Peter **Laslett** and Leo **Strauss** in their different ways proclaimed political philosophy to be dead in the early 1960s, killed off by positivistic political science, appeal to the history of political thought persisted. This was because, while most political scientists blithely assumed that values to guide public policy would be generated by citizens themselves, a few thought it prudent to appeal to the canonical texts as well. If these could be treated as valuable answers to perennial questions, they could provide the values which political science required to complement itself but could not rationally underwrite.

This was the ambition which was attacked in Skinner's 1969 manifesto, 'Meaning and Understanding in the History of Ideas'. His position was that if political science was incapable of prescribing policy or values, so too was the history of political thought, once the latter was rightly understood in terms of the specific intentional contexts in which it arose. Because it was history and had to be understood as history, Skinner proclaimed, the history of political thought could not be taken to constitute what other writers had hailed as 'timeless elements' in a 'dateless wisdom' with 'universal application' (1988a: 30, quoting from works by Merkl, Catlin and Hacker). What should step into the breach instead was political philosophy, which was being reborn in the 1960s with the reaffirmation of the significance of meaning and intention, and the development of a method of ethical argument by John Rawls. As Skinner concluded, rather than looking (say) to **Plato**, whose ideas about democracy are completely irrelevant to the modern context, 'we must learn to do our own thinking for ourselves' (ibid.: 66). History can remind us of the variety of questions and answers which have been posed previously, and so can help to free us from the straitjackets of present pieties. But since our own questions will necessarily differ from those asked in the past, history has no self-certifying answers for *us*.

That this is the inescapable implication of Cambridge School contextualism is, however, open to doubt. In a lecture given in 1986 and published in 1990, John Dunn explicitly retracted a provocative sentence from the preface to his 1969 book on **Locke**. The 'offending' sentence was this: 'I simply cannot conceive of constructing an analysis of any issue in contemporary political theory around the affirmation or negation of anything which Locke says about political matters' (1969: x, quoted and glossed in 1990: 9). The key to Dunn's change of heart was his change of mind about the significance of Locke's understanding of the secular predicament of politics, even given the theological context in which he had in 1969 insisted that Locke's thought must be understood. The repentant Dunn wrote that we 'have good reason to nerve ourselves for the full unfamiliarity of his [Locke's] vision – its unblinking historical distance – and to use it in all its integrity and imaginative force to help us to think again' (1990: 25). Cambridge contextualism in this case embraced the thought that one could still learn something from Locke.

Let us consider the general question. How, and how far, can understanding the history of political thought inform our present practice or understanding of politics? Or, to return to the original formulation, why bother to study it at all?

There are at least four ways that the history of political thought *could* matter to us. On one extreme, it could be a matter of purely antiquarian interest, which the historian studies for the sake of the integrity of the past, eschewing any form of relevance to present action at all. This was the conception defended by the Cambridge philosopher Michael Oakeshott in his sequence of essays 'On History' (1983). Secondly, the relevance to present action might be initially negative but still productive. The multiplicity and contingency of ideas in the past could serve to challenge the self-evidence of our current assumptions. On this view, the past would not prescribe how to think, but would prove that it is possible in principle to think differently. Thirdly, the history of political thought may serve to connect our own current concepts and ideas to their sources in the past, recognising that they arose contingently but illuminating them in light of their genealogy. This is especially significant with those concepts which may be found to be of relatively *longue durée*, such as the idea of the impact of global markets on national politics, or what is now called 'globalisation', which has been a concern since at least the eighteenth century. Finally, at the other extreme from Oakeshott, positions taken by past political thinkers might be invoked directly to bolster or undermine current philosophical or political positions (the American Founders on the importance of militias used to oppose current proposals for handgun control, for example).

Oakeshott himself would agree that the first position cannot logically exclude the others; he insisted only that the first alone deserved to be called 'historical'. The fourth position, on the other hand, would be logically ruled out by Skinner's arguments. Even if the American Founders would have opposed handgun control – something which can only be inferred, and only from a proper understanding of the context of their writings – this does not, without the additional premise of a constitutional theory of one's own, prescribe anything to the present world. On the other hand, on the methodological positions described in the previous section, appealing to a classic author is not really different from appealing to the authority of one's own contemporary. So long as the authority provided by someone else's writing rests on the validity of their arguments, not the other way round, we may be as justified in invoking James **Madison** as John Rawls, or any current commentator.

But the real issue at present is between the two positions in the middle. Can the history of political thought only enlighten us negatively, by showing us alternatives which are no longer ours? Or can there be meaningful histories of 'our' concepts, such that Adam **Smith**, for example, may be talking on some level about the same problem of global trade as we are today? Skinner has often been read as holding the former view, but I believe that he is better understood to hold (as I do) that the choice between them is a matter for the judgement of the historian herself. How far the history of one idea extends before being extinguished, or before merging into the history of another, is one of the things that only the historian can decide. There is an ideal type here, which F. H. **Bradley** called 'the historian as he should be' (1968: 78); but no method or doctrine can guarantee that the historian as she is will be in all respects the historian that she should be. Historians will make mistakes, and will disagree about whether they were mistakes, and no method or hermeneutic theory can stop them from doing so. So the history of some ideas will teach contingency, while the history of other ideas will teach continuity, and if that were not so then the piecemeal emergence of the present from the past could not have been possible, as it was.

On a more abstract level, what binds all four aims together is perhaps a hostility to oversimplification. The great left-wing historian E. P. **Thompson** hoped to rescue the poor workers of the past from 'the enormous condescension of posterity'. The temptation in every age is to take one's own understanding to be self-evidently adequate, and so to see much of the past (which did not share it) as self-evidently deluded. But elements of our present views were rejected by past thinkers for complicated reasons which they believed to be good ones. And we can be reasonably confident that elements of our present views will be rejected by future thinkers on similar grounds. This should not, and need not, license a general scepticism. But it can rightly license the historian's curiosity. Historical understanding is stimulated by apparent contrasts between the present and the past as much as by apparent similarities.

On general terms, then, one can justify the interpretation of political thought as a form of historical understanding. Yet what of politics? How, and how far, is the history of political thought relevant to modern politics? It is (or should be) obvious that such relevance cannot consist in the discovery of blueprints which are self-evidently desirable and unproblematically applicable to present problems. The history of political thought is a reflection on reflection, even where that reflection involved activity, and as such it is better suited to contribute to the reflective component in our own action than to direct that action in its entirety. In brief, the history of political thought is a form of (historical) understanding which can also contribute to a form of political understanding. And it can do so by playing at least two important roles: that of articulating traditions and that of facilitating imagination.

The notion of a 'great tradition' in the history of political thought with which this chapter began, the one which structures syllabi around the globe, is a distinct and modern one (and the question of who belongs in that tradition is highly contested). But the notion that present-day political practitioners see and justify their doings in light of past political ideas and practices is much older, and difficult to imagine eradicating altogether. Modern politics in particular is full of claims to legitimacy on the basis either of continuity with the past or (as in New Labour) of a novel break from it. Insofar as such claims are pressed, often with only a sketchy or faulty grasp of what the past involved, the historian of political thought has an evident role to play in evaluating them. And insofar as that historian is also able to identify which features of the past were crucial in evoking the words and deeds of a given political theory, she will be able to judge whether features of the present may felicitously evoke similar words and deeds, or whether they require different ones, though this is a judgement which can be proved only when put to the test.

Placing questions and ideas in a tradition is an important part of understanding politics (if not, with Gadamer, a necessary one of understanding anything at all). So too is being able to see that politics involves imaginative visions of what humans and the world are like, and being able to entertain as well as to assess these. Past political theories are, among other things, pools of the imagination, and studying them is an excellent way to learn the depths and the contours that having a political understanding requires. If understanding, as Wittgenstein said, involves throwing away the ladder, one still needs a ladder to begin.

Imagination might in principle be stimulated by studying any tradition, not necessarily the canonical history of political thought, although the scope and substance required by an adequate political imagination is shown by that latter history quite well. But the most ambitious claim made on behalf of studying the history of political thought is that it can help us to gain knowledge of ourselves. This is something on which Collingwood and Gadamer agreed. For Gadamer, such knowledge of self comes from the enlarged and altered horizons achieved by the encounter with a past text. For Collingwood, such knowledge comes from the enlarged experience which the historian gleans by thinking his way into the mind of someone in the past. As stated in the selection from his *Autobiography*:

> If he is able to understand, by rethinking them, the thoughts of a great many different kinds of people, it follows that he must be a great many kinds of man. He must be, in fact, a microcosm of all the history he can know. Thus his own self-knowledge is at the same time a knowledge of the world of human affairs. (1939: 115)

In the sixty-odd years since Collingwood wrote, we have learned to be sceptical of such statements, not least because the reference to 'man' jars with contemporary awareness of the habitual historical exclusion of women from the scope of political thought. To say too quickly that the traditional canon provides 'our' history or enriches 'our' 'self-understanding' overlooks the fact that the relations of the colonised or the excluded to the canon will be more complicated than that. Nevertheless, the history of political thought as taught today – the great procession – does include ideas and interventions, engagement with which has shaped the self-understanding of modern politics in most places on the globe, whether through a direct lineage or through importation and cross-fertilisation. In this sense, the colonised and the excluded cannot afford to ignore it. And with a sophisticated view of identity in relation to otherness (in fashionable jargon, '**alterity**'), one may yet rescue something in the aim of self-understanding which Collingwood proclaimed.

Consider the stance taken by the French theorist Michel Foucault (1926–84), whose works grew out of a different (Nietzschean) tradition from those discussed above, but whose approach to the study of past thought has inspired many historians of political thought (not least Quentin **Skinner** and his former student James **Tully**). Foucault saw power and liberty, power and knowledge, power and resistance, not as antithetical extremes, but as mutually constituting forms of interaction. There is no power without resistance, but there is also no idyll of liberty free from power. Many left-wing thinkers have therefore criticised his work for slamming a door on the possibility of action for political change. But, as David Halperin has urged, queer theorists and gay and lesbian activists are among those who have found political inspiration in Foucault's emphasis on strategic forms of resistance. Such resistance can engender the kind of self-knowledge which consists in exploration of one's limits and of new forms of creative action and interaction. As Foucault put it: 'I aim at having an experience myself – by passing through a determinate historical content . . . And

I invite others to share the experience, that is, an experience of our modernity that might permit us to emerge from it transformed' (remarks by Foucault reported by Pierre Hadot and quoted in Halperin, 1995: 104). Historical understanding reveals, in Halperin's words, 'our own otherness to ourselves' and, by showing us ourselves as 'sites of difference', therefore shows us ourselves as sites of 'possible transformation' (ibid.: 105).

History, and the history of political thought in particular, will sometimes appear as radically other in relation to the present, sometimes as the germ of what 'we' have become. Both, despite appearances, are forms of **alterity**; both can help to constitute a richer form of self-understanding. And while changed understanding does not always or only inform changes in action, it is a creative and – importantly – an unpredictable way to do so. On a suitably broad account of self and of understanding, self-understanding may indeed be one rich fruit of the interpretation of political thought.

'HISTORY AS THE SELF-KNOWLEDGE OF MIND' BY R. G. COLLINGWOOD

The British philosopher Robin George Collingwood (1889–1943) was an all-round polymath, achieving success not only in philosophy but also in history and archaeology. One of his central intellectual endeavours was the reconciliation of philosophy and history, and he argued that historical inquiry is not concerned only with the past or with what historians think about the past but with these two in relation. Among his many works are *The New Leviathan: or, Man, Society, Civilization and Barbarism* (Oxford University Press, 1992) and *Essays in Political Philosophy* (Clarendon, 1989). His most influential work concerns the philosophy of history, and there are a number of editions of his book *The Idea of History*. The 1993 edition published by Clarendon Press includes a number of interesting lectures. The extract here is taken from his autobiography, and in it he explains how and why he came to develop his approach to history which he saw as the basis for a science of human affairs. Crucial here is his explanation of the way in which historical study entails thinking the thoughts of those we are studying. Such arguments have been most influential, particularly upon British historiography, but they have taken on renewed resonance in the context of the growth of so-called 'postmodern' historiography. Readers could usefully compare Collingwood to the differing approach to the history of ideas presented by Foucault or to the approach taken to the theory (if not philosophy) of history discussed by Callinicos.

'HISTORY AS THE SELF-KNOWLEDGE OF MIND' (1939)*

R. G. Collingwood

I expressed this new conception of history in the phrase: 'all history is the history of thought'. You are thinking historically, I meant, when you say about anything, 'I see what the person who made this (wrote this, used this, designed this, etc.) was thinking'. Until you can say that, you may be trying to think historically but you are not succeeding. And there is nothing else except thought that can be the object of historical knowledge. Political history is the history of political thought: not 'political theory', but the thought which occupies the

---

* From R. G. Collingwood, *An Autobiography* (Oxford: Oxford University Press, 1939), pp. 110–16.

mind of a man engaged in political work: the formation of a policy, the planning of means to execute it, the attempt to carry it into effect, the discovery that others are hostile to it, the devising of ways to overcome their hostility, and so forth. Consider how the historian describes a famous speech. He does not concern himself with any sensuous elements in it such as the pitch of the statesman's voice, the hardness of the benches, the deafness of the old gentleman in the third row: he concentrates his attention on what the man was trying to say (the thought, that is, expressed in his words) and how his audience received it (the thoughts in their minds, and how these conditioned the impact upon them of the statesman's thought). Military history, again, is not a description of weary marches in heat or cold, or the thrills and chills of battle or the long agony of wounded men. It is a description of plans and counter-plans: of thinking about strategy and thinking about tactics, and in the last resort of what the men in the ranks thought about the battle.

On what conditions was it possible to know the history of a thought? First, the thought must be expressed: either in what we call language, or in one of the many other forms of expressive activity. Historical painters seem to regard an outstretched arm and a pointing hand as the characteristic gesture expressing the thought of a commanding officer. Running away expresses the thought that all hope of victory is gone. Second, the historian must be able to think over again for himself the thought whose expression he is trying to interpret. If for any reason he is such a kind of man that he cannot do this, he had better leave that problem alone. The important point here is that the historian of a certain thought must think for himself that very same thought, not another like it. If someone, hereinafter called the mathematician, has written that twice two is four, and if someone else, hereinafter called the historian, wants to know what he was thinking when he made those marks on paper, the historian will never be able to answer this question unless he is mathematician enough to think exactly what the mathematician thought, and expressed by writing that twice two is four. When he interprets the marks on paper, and says, 'by these marks the mathematician meant that twice two is four', he is thinking simultaneously: (1) that twice two is four, (2) that the mathematician thought this, too; and (3) that he expressed this thought by making these marks on paper. I will not offer to help a reader who replies, 'ah, you are making it easy for yourself by taking an example where history really is the history of thought; you couldn't explain the history of a battle or a political campaign in that way'. I could, and so could you, Reader, if you tried.

This gave me a second proposition: 'historical knowledge is the re-enactment in the historian's mind of the thought whose history he is studying'.

When I understand what Nelson meant by saying, 'in honour I won them, in honour I will die with them', what I am doing is to think myself into the position of being all covered with decorations and exposed at short range to the musketeers in the enemy's tops, and being advised to make myself a less conspicuous target. I ask myself the question, shall I change my coat? and reply in those words. Understanding the words means thinking for myself what Nelson thought when he spoke them: that this is not a time to take off my ornaments of honour for the sake of saving my life. Unless I were capable – perhaps only transiently – of thinking that for myself, Nelson's words would remain meaningless to me; I could only weave a net of verbiage round them like a psychologist, and talk about masochism and guilt-sense, or introversion and extraversion, or some such foolery.

But this re-enactment of Nelson's thought is a re-enactment with a difference. Nelson's thought, as Nelson thought it and as I rethink it, is certainly one and the same thought; and yet in some way there is not one thought, there are two different thoughts. What was the difference? No question in my study of historical method ever gave me so much trouble; and the answer was not complete until some years later. The difference is one of context. To Nelson, that thought was a present thought; to me, it is a past thought living in the present but (as I have elsewhere put it) incapsulated, not free. What is an incapsulated thought? It is a thought which, though perfectly alive, forms no part of the question–answer complex which constitutes what people call the 'real' life, the superficial or obvious present, of the mind in question. For myself, or for that which at first sight I regard as myself, the question 'shall I take off my decorations?' does not arise. The questions that arise are, for example, 'shall I go on reading this book?' and later, 'what did the *Victory*'s deck look like to a person thinking about his chances of surviving the battle?' and later again, 'what should I have done if I had been in Nelson's place?' No question that arises in this primary series, the series constituting my 'real' life, ever requires the answer 'in honour I won them, in honour I will die with them'. But a question arising in that primary series may act as a switch into another dimension. I plunge beneath the surface of my mind, and there live a life in which I not merely think about Nelson but am Nelson, and thus in thinking about Nelson think about myself. But this secondary life is prevented from overflowing into my primary life by being what I call incapsulated, that is, existing in a context of primary or surface knowledge which keeps it in its place and prevents it from thus overflowing. Such knowledge, I mean, as that Trafalgar happened ninety years ago: I am a little boy in a jersey: this is my father's study carpet, not the Atlantic, and that the study fender, not the coast of Spain.

So I reached my third proposition: 'Historical knowledge is the re-enactment of a past thought incapsulated in a context of present thoughts which, by contradicting it, confine it to a plane different from theirs'.

How is one to know which of these planes is 'real' life, and which mere 'history'? By watching the way in which historical problems arise. Every historical problem ultimately arises out of 'real' life. The scissors-and-paste men think differently: they think that first of all people get into the habit of reading books, and then the books put questions into their heads. But I am not talking about scissors-and-paste history. In the kind of history that I am thinking of, the kind I have been practising all my life, historical problems arise out of practical problems. We study history in order to see more clearly into the situation in which we are called upon to act. Hence the plane on which, ultimately, all problems arise is the plane of 'real' life: that to which they are referred for their solution is history.

If what the historian knows is past thoughts, and if he knows them by rethinking them himself, it follows that the knowledge he achieves by historical inquiry is not knowledge of his situation as opposed to knowledge of himself, it is a knowledge of his situation which is at the same time knowledge of himself. In rethinking what somebody else thought, he thinks it himself. In knowing that somebody else thought it, he knows that he himself is able to think it. And finding out what he is able to do is finding out what kind of man he is. If he is able to understand, by rethinking them, the thoughts of a great many different kinds of people, it follows that he must be a great many kinds of man. He must be, in fact, a microcosm of all the history he can know. Thus his own self-knowledge is at the same time his knowledge of the world of human affairs.

This train of thought was not complete until about 1930. By completing it, I completed my answer to the question that had haunted me ever since the War. How could we construct a science of human affairs, so to call it, from which men could learn to deal with human situations as skilfully as natural science had taught them to deal with situations in the world of Nature? The answer was now clear and certain. The science of human affairs was history. This was a discovery which could not have been made before the late nineteenth century, for it was not until then that history began to undergo a Baconian revolution, to emerge from the chrysalis of its scissors-and-paste stage, and thus to become, in the proper sense of that word, a science. It was because history was still in the chrysalis stage in the eighteenth century, that eighteenth-century thinkers, when they saw the need for a science of human affairs, could not identify it with history but tried to realise it in the shape of a 'science of human nature'; which, as men like Hume conceived it, with its strictly empirical methods, was in effect an historical study of the contemporary European mind, falsified by the assumption that human minds had everywhere and at all times worked like those of eighteenth-century Europeans. The nineteenth century, likewise in search of a science of human affairs, tried to realise it in the shape of a 'psychology' in which the mental was reduced to the psychical, the distinction between truth and falsehood thrown overboard, and the very idea of a science negated, psychology itself being involved in the resulting bankruptcy. But the revolution in historical method which had superseded scissors-and-paste history by what I called history proper had swept away these sham sciences and had brought into existence a genuine, actual, visibly and rapidly progressing form of knowledge which now for the first time was putting man in a position to obey the oracular precept 'know thyself', and to reap the benefits that only such obedience could confer.

'THE HISTORY OF POLITICAL THEORY' BY JOHN DUNN

At the time of writing, the British political philosopher John Dunn is Professor in the Faculty of Social and Political Sciences at the University of Cambridge. Dunn was a part of the intellectual movement associated with Quentin Skinner advocating the analysis of the historical texts of political thought as linguistic acts undertaken in particular contexts. He is particularly well known for his work on early modern political thought, as shown in *The Political Thought of John Locke: An Historical Account of the Argument of the 'Two Treatises of Government'* (Cambridge University Press, 1969), and on a number of other aspects of the history of political thought (see *Political Obligation in its Historical Context: Essays in Political Theory* (Cambridge University Press, 1980) and *Interpreting Political Responsibility: Essays 1981–1989* (Polity, 1990)). He has also, especially recently, brought his scholarship to bear on contemporary political concerns and on the ways in which we understand the nature of politics; see *The Cunning of Unreason: Making Sense of Politics* (HarperCollins, 2001). The essay extracted here comes from *The History of Political Theory and Other Essays* (Cambridge University Press, 1996). In it, Dunn reviews currents in the study of the history of political thought and gently argues for the importance of the work he and his Cambridge colleagues adopted, laying out the sorts of questions we can ask of a text from the history of political thought.

'THE HISTORY OF POLITICAL THEORY' (1996)*

[. . .]

METHOD

In contrast with sacred scriptures like the Koran, the Pentateuch or the New Testament, no one is likely to deny that the great texts of political theory, whether secular or devout, are essentially human artefacts: products of concentrated intellectual labour and imaginative exploration by palpably human agents (Dunn 1980, chapter 1). It is over the significance to be attached to this banal perception that the principal intellectual disputes about how best to

---

* From John Dunn, 'The History of Political Theory', *The History of Political Theory and Other Essays* (Cambridge: Cambridge University Press, 1996), pp. 18–26.

approach the history of political theory have been fought out. The range of viewpoints adopted in these disputes has by now become very large; and much of the disagreement, predictably enough, has not proved especially instructive. But the extent and animus of the quarrelling has served by now to underline the continuing appeal of three very different approaches.

One of these, strongly associated with one of the most distinguished contemporary historians of political theory, Quentin Skinner of Cambridge University (Tully 1988; Viroli 1987), takes the historical character of the texts as fundamental, and understands these, in the last instance, as highly complex human actions, emphasising especially the constitutive role of intention in human agency (though always firmly refusing to reduce the content of any human act to the agent's self-conscious intention). It treats, in effect, as the key to understanding every such text, the fact that it was the product of a human author (or set of authors) and focuses accordingly on the preoccupations and purposes that led that author to compose it at all and to do so just as they did. The second approach, best exemplified by scholars (like the late C. B. Macpherson) strongly influenced by one variety or another of Marxism, takes the historical character of the texts in question just as seriously as the first. But, unlike the first, it pays only the most perfunctory (or insincere) attention to the concerns of the author, and stresses instead the aspects of the historical society in which the text was composed, of which its author might well have been imperfectly aware but which, nevertheless, prompted him or her to think and express themselves as they did. By contrast, the third approach views the historical character of the texts with massive indifference, treating them, with varying degrees of attention and patience, simply as repositories of potential intellectual stimulation for a contemporary reader, and permitting themselves to respond, accordingly, just as the fancy takes them.

It does not take close intellectual attention to recognise that these three approaches involve no necessary intellectual disagreement with one another, but reflect, rather, more or less sharp divergences of taste and interest. (This point is well developed in Skinner's magisterial defence (1988) of the coherence of his pursuit of his own intellectual tastes and interests.) The three approaches plainly address different questions and, unsurprisingly, tend to offer different sorts of answers to these questions. But none need deny (and none would in fact be well advised to deny) the potential value of the others. Of the three approaches, however, it is the first, the self-consciously historical focus on authorial experience, intention and context, that has been pursued with most intellectual energy and panache over the last three decades. The ruling insight of this approach is that it is of profound intellectual and political (Tully 1988, Introduction; Ashcraft 1986; Dunn 1979) importance that political theory itself has a history. At first this judgement was expressed with relative caution, stressing the imaginative space opened up by a recognition of historical distance (Dunn 1969, Preface), and the resulting opportunities for more or less ironical self-detachment in political understanding (Skinner 1984, 1988). But more recently it has been pressed with more aggression and distinctly less caution (Hont and Ignatieff 1983; Dunn 1979, 1985, 1990a, 1990b; Pocock 1989). The potential force of this more intrepid phase in the historicist interpretation of the history of political theory depends as much on the degree of scepticism about the adequacy of contemporary political understanding that happens now to be apposite, as it does on the purely historical cogency of its analyses of past texts. Its evident temerity, therefore, may be charitably judged less absurd in the face of the effective collapse, both intellectually and practically, of Marxist understanding of a practical alternative to the capitalist world order (or disorder).

The historicist approach has beneath it the deep intellectual roots of the German historical movement (Herder, Ranke, Dilthey: Reill 1975; Meinecke 1972) and of German idealist philosophy. But its practical impact on the history of political theory probably owes more to the post-war professional standards of British historiography (Wootton 1986: 11–12), as interpreted, particularly in Cambridge, by Peter Laslett, Duncan Forbes, John Pocock and Quentin Skinner. Skinner's own philosophical inspiration came principally from the Oxford idealist philosopher (and historian) R. G. Collingwood. But over the last quarter of a century he has defended the relevance and philosophical cogency of Collingwood's approach (Collingwood 1939) and of modern professional historiographical practice, with increasing rigour and assurance, in the terms set by Oxford linguistic philosophy and American pragmatism (Tully 1988). At least as much to the point, he has also practised what he has preached in a series of dazzlingly exemplary studies of the development of Western political thinking (Skinner 1966, 1978, 1981, 1984, 1989).

This impressive oeuvre is neither offered nor advisedly received as a model for how all other students of the history of political theory should approach their subject. But its sheer force and brio has had the singular merit of sharpening the question of just what they suppose themselves to be doing, inviting thereby not merely abundant casual abuse, but also, if more intermittently, extended and relatively strenuous reflexive thought. The most prominent respondent over the last two decades has been an older scholar, from New Zealand, himself already far from averse to reflexive thought, J. G. A. Pocock, at present professor at Johns Hopkins University in Baltimore, USA. He shares, too, many tastes and concerns with Skinner – notably, like any true historian, a love of the past for its own interminable sake. But in some ways his key interests have always had a rather different ultimate focus. Like his scintillating first book, *The Ancient Constitution and the Feudal Law* (1957), his most famous and influential work, *The Machiavellian Moment* (1975), is centrally preoccupied with understanding the human significance of time. Both works, too, consider continuity and change in political belief and perception over a lengthy period, and in no way privilege the more searching or intellectually economical of the authors whose works they discuss. In contrast to Skinner's practise (but cf. Tully (1988) on his methodological precepts), Pocock is very much a historian of political thought, belief and language, rather than a historian of political theory: of highly self-conscious and energetic analytical argument, recoverable only by the closest analysis of given texts. For him, political thought is above all an aspect of the experience of a society in time; and the task of its historian is to recover that aspect of its experience as fully and faithfully as they can. This does not, of course, render him indifferent to contemporary political concerns. Both *The Ancient Constitution* and *The Machiavellian Moment* express a vivid scepticism about the historical trustworthiness of a Marxist approach towards the intellectual experience of past societies; and his subsequent writings have indicated an increasing dismay at many aspects of the American society and polity in which he has made his home and of the liberal ideology which, in his view, so distorts the understanding of its weaknesses and misdeeds.

Taken on its own, the principal impact of Skinner's work would probably have been to extend greatly the range of past thinkers whom historians of political theory chose to study with any intimacy, and to underline the indispensability of considering each of these with the utmost care in the dense and always somewhat opaque context which prompted their writings. Even Skinner's own more specific concern with the history of vocabulary focuses more upon the deployment of particular words and phrases in political dispute and on the constraints (ideological and political, as well as purely verbal) faced by a given historical disputant in defending their favoured line of conduct (Tully 1988). But authorial intentionality plays a far less prominent and structural role in Pocock's analyses; and the joint impact of their own oeuvres has now extended far beyond the history of what can aptly be described as political theory, into the history of political consciousness, expression and experience more generally.

There is no question of the historiographical value of this expansion. But it is less clear quite how important some of it is for the history of political theory itself. The constitutive role of language in human agency, and the fact that politics itself simply consists in human agency under constraints, together serve to guarantee that the history of political vocabulary must always be of great political importance: still more so, plainly, the history of the deployment and interrogation of the political concepts which that vocabulary is used to refer to and to convey. There has been much valuable work in the post-war decades on the history of the more analytically central terms in the modern vocabulary of social and political understanding, notably in Germany, under the editorial leadership of Reinhart Koselleck of the University of Bielefeld, in the preparation of the *Geschichtliche Grundbegriffe* (Koselleck et al. 1972–; Koselleck 1985). In ethics, the continuing importance of the historical mutation of concepts has long been effectively stressed for British and North American philosophers by Alasdair MacIntyre (1967, 1981, 1988), Charles Taylor (1975), 1989) and Bernard Williams (1985). But only relatively recently has this approach been reapplied to the history of specifically political concepts, and applied in a way which reflects not merely the historiographical scruples of the new history of political thought, but also its vivid sense of the intensely political career of all concepts that feature prominently in political understanding (Ball et al. 1989; Ball 1988).

What is already clear, however, is that a history of political concepts or political vocabulary, which both succeeds in meeting the epistemic standards set by the historicist school and also fully engages with the political importance of the vicissitudes of the words or concepts that it studies, will be an extraordinarily demanding intellectual genre. In relation to this new (and as yet almost wholly unwritten) history, the history of political theory will be at least as much a grateful consumer as it will a proud contributor. What is certain, however, is that whether or not this new genre does make rapid headway, it could not under any circumstances serve as an effective alternative to, or replacement for, the distinctive forms of understanding provided by the history of political theory.

QUESTIONS AND ANSWERS

To fathom the meaning of the canon of classic texts of the history of political theory cannot reasonably be thought of as a finite enterprise – as perhaps physicists, for example, might still hope will prove apt in the end with the project of identifying the fundamental particles (cf. Gadamer 1975; Collingwood 1939). But this absence of a reassuring cognitive destination does not mean either that the history of political theory cannot hope to be in some degree intellectually cumulative or that it cannot and should not be conducted by formulating clear and demanding questions and seeking to discover accurate and compelling answers to these questions. The historicist recognition of the heterogeneity of human purposes over time, and the sheer practical difficulty of identifying these purposes with any precision across great historical or cultural distances, is in no sense a sanction for intellectual licence: more a challenge to intellectual labour and imaginative energy than an excuse for indolence or complacency.

It is useful to distinguish four different types of questions that appropriately arise in attempts to understand the history of political theory. Three of these are unequivocally historical questions (which is not to say, of course, that they are unaffected by current human concerns). Only the fourth is asked not just from the present and for the present, but explicitly *about* the present. All four questions focus in the first instance on texts: but they do so with rather different purposes in mind. The first question asks simply what an author means by and in his or her text. (Only one woman, the late eighteenth-century English radical, Mary Wollstonecraft, author of *A Vindication of the Rights of Women* (1792), has yet staked at all an effective claim for inclusion in the canon. But if the history of political theory endures for long enough to make this relevant, the same is most unlikely to prove true in another century's time.) As we have seen, this first question has been the central concern of the new history of political thought. Perhaps the main lasting intellectual contribution of that historical movement has been to show why the question itself cannot reliably be answered without the most intimate and searching exploration of the context within which the author in question lived, experienced and chose to express themselves as they did.

The idea of a context of authorship has proved, on closer consideration, remarkably elusive: less a cheap recipe for secure comprehension than a mockery of the hope ever to win through to an understanding that is at all complete. But the idea that authorship itself is a form of agency, despite the challenges of Michel Foucault, has proved comparatively robust. Once a text is conceived as an extraordinarily complex form of action, the issue of authorial intention forces itself intractably forward; and the full context of agency becomes, inescapably, of at least potential relevance. Not all historical studies of what an author means by and in their text disclose anything important that would not be apparent to a casual and historically ignorant, but mentally alert, reader. But any such study *may* well do so. It is hard to defend the view that, if you really want to understand what someone else far away and long ago has said, there is little point in bothering to ascertain who they were or what they were talking about. For anyone who has the slightest interest in the human beings whose strenuous lives made possible these great texts, and who condescends to consider them at any point as what they initially were and in the light of why they ever came to be at all, there is no possible case against a strictly historical approach to this first question. This is as much true for those, like the late Leo Strauss and his followers, who stress the slyness and secretiveness of some of the greatest theorists of politics, as it is for those scholars who think of themselves merely as professional historians practising their modern craft on a more or less arbitrarily chosen subject matter.

The second question may be treated more tersely, since it casts the light away from the texts of political theory themselves and towards the historical societies within which these texts were composed. What does the composition of a given text by an author (or authors) in a particular historical setting show us about that setting itself, or about the broader historical context within which it subsisted? This question is an invitation to read the history of political theory not directly but symptomatically: not for its own sake, but for what it can disclose about the historical milieu within which it was first enacted. Marxist scholars have laboured harder and more imaginatively at this genre than any other comparably determinate intellectual grouping (Goldmann 1970; Hill 1972; in some degree Macpherson 1962). But here, unlike in their efforts to explain aspects of authorial intention by features of the historical context of authorship not necessarily (or necessarily not) apparent to the authors themselves (Macpherson 1962), while the object of their study is plainly the history of political theory, its products are scarcely in themselves contributions to understanding that history.

The first question is perhaps best formulated as: 'What did its author mean by his (or her) text?'; the second, perhaps, as: 'What does that text show us about its author's own society?' Both of these queries have a clear initial focus, however much the field of view may eventually have to be widened out, if they are to be answered at all adequately. But the third question is more obviously centrifugal, even in the first instance: 'What has that text meant to others, reading it then or subsequently, and why has it meant that and not something else?' Every great text (like any other human action) has an occasion – something which prompted it. But, unlike most human actions, great texts also have a protracted and wildly differentiated fate. That fate often stands (indeed perhaps always stands) in a somewhat ironical relation to its author's original intentions. But its very scope and variety are themselves a tribute to the unsteady but urgent power of the text itself. Studies of the fate of great texts could be immensely fascinating, as well as exceptionally illuminating. But they are also dismayingly demanding, not simply for the range of imaginative sympathy and the degree of intellectual control for which they call, but also for the sheer quantity of grubby and often unrewarding archival labour which they necessarily require (cf. Dunn 1980, chapter 3; Kelly 1989). It is an unsurprising index of human frailty that there should be so few studies of real ambition on the historical fate of the great texts of the history of political theory, and perhaps none, as yet, which fully realise the intellectual promise of the genre. From the viewpoint of professional historiography, it has to be said, this is probably the most intimidating – the most brutally labour-intensive – of all three of the genres which we have considered.

Only the last of these four questions is not a question about the past (though it is certainly a question about the present and future relevance of a set of human creations fashioned in the past): 'What do the great texts of the history of political theory mean today, and mean for us?' ('And what will they mean *tomorrow*, or for human generations to come?') That question has been waiting for us at the end of the corridor throughout. If it does not have an answer, none of the other questions could even refer to anything very definite, let alone arise with any urgency. It is that question, effectively, which has constituted the history of political theory as a subject for university education in Europe and North America, from the seventeenth or eighteenth centuries up to the present day, and since extended it, not just to the remainder of the European diaspora or the former colonial or imperial territories of European powers, but to those few world societies which were never really subjugated by the West.

The great scholars of the history of political theory since the Second World War have mostly not thought of themselves as essentially historians, though they have all perforce had to get to know a great deal of history and many have had considerable respect for history as a form of knowledge: in North America, Carl Friedrich and Judith Shklar at Harvard University, Sheldon Wolin at Berkeley or Princeton, Leo Strauss at Chicago, Charles Taylor at McGill; in Britain, John Plamenatz at Oxford, even Michael Oakeshott at the London School of Economics; in Italy, Norberto Bobbio at Turin; in France, Robert Derathé at Nancy, and Raymond Polin at Lille. True, in Oxford, Isaiah Berlin had deserted philosophy purposefully for the history of ideas by the time that he took up the Chichele chair of social and political theory; and in the dizzily prestigious law faculty of the University of Tokyo, Maruyama Masao and Fukuda Kan'ichi both saw themselves in part as intellectual historians. But it was only in Cambridge that the emphasis on the historicity of the history of political theory became overwhelmingly dominant. It would be nice to believe that Cambridge has been simply right, and everywhere else has been wrong. But it would be a shade ingenuous.

What is more likely to be true is that one aspect of the Cambridge emphasis of historicity, language and authorial intention does possess a real prudential force even when it comes to considering solely the current or future significance of the great works of political theory. It is not a necessary truth that a lengthy text can be best understood by reading it the right way up. But it remains an eminently sound practical judgement. By the same token, and however ironical the relation between the fate of a text and its author's own initial intentions may sometimes prove to be, it would be very odd if a great work of analytical argument were not in general best understood by considering in the first instance what the person who composed it intended it to convey. In their justifiably rising intellectual excitement at the discovery of how complicated and difficult it can often be to answer that question at all adequately, the new historians of political theory have sometimes allowed their attention to wander a little far from the blunt force of this simple admonitory commonplace. To understand what its author meant could never be sufficient for assessing the current significance of a great text's arguments. But it is both impertinent and ludicrous to assume that it is not in general a wise preliminary to trying to do so. As theorists of literature have shown us so amply over the last few decades, it is possible to use any text whatsoever as the equivalent of a sort of imaginative Rorschach test, on to which to project the interpreter's fancies. But, since the great texts of political theory are, among other characteristics, works of urgent analytical thought, and since their being so is a substantial part of the grounds for continuing to study them, the Rorschach blot approach to these texts, however assiduously applied, is not a promising recipe for fathoming their current significance.

[. . .]

REFERENCES

Ashcraft, R. 1986. *Revolutionary Politics and Locke's Two Treatises of Government*. Princeton: Princeton University Press.

Ball, T. 1988. *Transforming Political Discourse*. Oxford: Blackwell.

Ball, T., J. Farr and R. Hanson (eds 1989). *Political Innovation and Conceptual Change*. Cambridge: Cambridge University Press.

Collingwood, R. G. 1939. *An Autobiography*. Oxford: Clarendon Press.

Dunn, J. 1969. *The Political Thought of John Locke*. Cambridge: Cambridge University Press.

——1979. *Western Political Theory in the Face of the Future*. Cambridge: Cambridge University Press.

——1980. *Political Obligation in its Historical Context*. Cambridge: Cambridge University Press.
——1985. *Rethinking Modern Political Theory*. Cambridge: Cambridge University Press.
——(ed.) 1990a. *The Economic Limits to Modern Politics*. Cambridge: Cambridge University Press.
——1990b. *Interpreting Political Responsibility*. Cambridge: Polity Press.
Gadamer, H.-G. 1975. *Truth and Method*. London: Sheed and Ward.
Goldmann, L. 1970. *The Hidden God*, trans. P. Thody. London: Routledge and Kegan Paul.
Hill, C. 1972. *The World Turned Upside Down*. London: Temple Smith.
Hont, I. and M. Ignatieff (eds) 1983. *Wealth and Virtue*. Cambridge: Cambridge University Press.
Kelly, P. 1989. 'Perceptions of Locke in Eighteenth-century Ireland'. *Proceedings of the Royal Irish Academy* 89 (2): 17–35.
Koselleck, R. 1985. *Futures Past: On the Semantics of Historical Time*, trans. K. Tribe. Cambridge, MA: MIT Press.
Koselleck, R., O. Brunner and W. Conze (eds) 1972–. *Geschichtliche Grundbegriffe: Historisches Lexicon zur Sprache in Deutschland*, 5 vols (to date). Stuttgart: Klett-Cotta.
MacIntyre, A. 1967. *A Short History of Ethics*. London: Routledge and Kegan Paul.
——1981. *After Virtue: A Study in Moral Theory*. London: Duckworth.
——1988. *Whose Justice? Which Rationality?* London: Duckworth.
Macpherson, C. B. 1962. *The Political Theory of Possessive Individualism*. Oxford: Clarendon Press.
Meinecke, F. 1972. *Historism: The Rise of a New Historical Outlook*, trans. J. E. Anderson, London: Routledge and Kegan Paul.
Pocock, J. G. A. 1957. *The Ancient Constitution and the Feudal Law*. Cambridge: Cambridge University Press.
——1975. *The Machiavellian Moment*. Princeton: Princeton University Press.
——1989. 'Edmund Burke and the Redefinition of Enthusiasm: The Context as Counter-revolution'. In *The French Revolution and the Transformation of Political Culture 1789–1848*, ed. F. Furet and M. Ozouf, pp. 19–43. Oxford, Pergamon Press.
Reill, P. H. 1975. *The German Enlightenment and the Rise of Historicism*. Berkeley: University of California Press.
Skinner, Q. 1966. 'The Ideological Context of Hobbes's Political Thought'. *Historical Journal* 9 (3): 286–317.
——1978. *The Foundations of Modern Political Thought*, 2 vols. Cambridge: Cambridge University Press.
——1981. *Machiavelli*. Oxford: Oxford University Press.
——1984. 'The Idea of Negative Liberty'. In *Philosophy in History*, ed. R. Rorty, J. Schneewind and Q. Skinner, pp. 193–221. Cambridge: Cambridge University Press.
——1988. 'A Reply to my Critics'. In *Meaning and Context: Quentin Skinner and his Critics*, ed. J. Tully, pp. 231–88. Cambridge: Polity Press.
——1989. 'The State'. In *Political Innovation and Conceptual Change*, ed. T. Ball, J. Farr and R. Hanson, pp. 90–131. Cambridge: Cambridge University Press.
Taylor, C. 1975. *Hegel*. Cambridge: Cambridge University Press.
——1989. *Sources of the Self*. Cambridge: Cambridge University Press.
Tully, J. (ed.) 1988. *Meaning and Context: Quentin Skinner and his Critics*. Cambridge: Polity Press.
Viroli, M. 1987. ' "Revisionisti" e "ortodossi" nella storia delle idee politiche'. *Rivista di Filosofia* 78: 121–36.
Williams, B. 1985. *Ethics and the Limits of Philosophy*. London: Fontana.
Wootton, D. 1986 (ed.). *Divine Right and Democracy*. Harmondsworth: Penguin.

'THE LOGIC OF QUESTION AND ANSWER' BY HANS-GEORG GADAMER

Hans-Georg Gadamer (1900–2002) was one of the most influential of twentieth-century philosophers. He is best known as a leading theorist of hermeneutics, the 'science' of interpretation or understanding. Hermeneutics represents a challenge to those theories of social science that liken inquiry into human affairs to natural science. Hermeneutic inquiry into culture, language, texts and history requires a kind of ongoing dialogue between a scholar and that which they are trying to understand; a reconstruction of the questions behind a text and the development of an affinity with it. It does not proceed on the basis that there are exact laws and fully objective truths to be found, but emphasises the ongoing process of understanding. The hermeneutic method is a central one in social science. Readers can usefully compare Gadamer's presentation with the arguments of Foucault and to the interpretive strategies implied by Rorty (both of whose work is reproduced elsewhere in this volume).

This extract is from Gadamer's major work *Truth and Method*. In it, we can see the affinities between the work of Collingwood, the Cambridge School and the wider enterprise of hermeneutics. Gadamer reviews Collingwood's argument concerning establishing the question a text sought to answer and extends it into reflection on the nature of 'understanding', an ongoing, never-ending 'conversation'.

'THE LOGIC OF QUESTION AND ANSWER' (1989)*

Hans-Georg Gadamer

[T]he hermeneutic phenomenon also contains within itself the original meaning of conversation and the structure of question and answer. For a historical text to be made the object of interpretation means that it asks a question of the interpreter. Thus interpretation always involves a relation to the question that is asked of the interpreter. To understand a text means to understand this question. But this takes place by our achieving the hermeneutical horizon. We now

---

* From Hans-Georg Gadamer, *Truth and Method*, English translation edited by Garrett Barden and John Cumming from the 2nd edn (1965) of *Wahrheit und Methode*; revised translation by Joel Weinsheimer and Donald G. Marshall in 2nd rev. edn (New York: Crossroad, 1989).

recognise this as the horizon of the question within which the sense of the text is determined.

Thus a person who seeks to understand must question what lies behind what is said. He must understand it as an answer to a question. If we go back behind what is said, then we inevitably ask questions beyond what is said. We understand the sense of the text only by acquiring the horizon of the question that, as such, necessarily includes other possible answers. Thus the meaning of a sentence is relative to the question to which it is a reply, that is, it necessarily goes beyond what is said in it. The logic of the human sciences is, then, as appears from what we have said, a logic of the question.

Despite Plato, we are not very ready for such a logic. Almost the only person I find a link with here is R. G. Collingwood. In a brilliant and cogent critique of the 'realist' Oxford school, he developed the idea of a logic of question and answer, but unfortunately never developed it systematically. He clearly saw what was missing in naive hermeneutics founded on the prevailing philosophical critique. In particular, the practice that Collingwood found in English universities of discussing 'statements', though perhaps a good training of intelligence, obviously failed to take account of the historicality that is part of all understanding. Collingwood argues thus: we can understand a text only when we have understood the question to which it is an answer. But since this question can be derived solely from the text and accordingly the appropriateness of the reply is the methodological presupposition for the reconstruction of the question, any criticism of this reply from some other quarter is pure mock-fighting. It is like the understanding of works of art. A work of art can be understood only if we assume its adequacy as an expression of the artistic idea. Here also we have to discover the question which it answers, if we are to understand it as an answer. This is, in fact, an axiom of all hermeneutics which we described as the 'fore-conception of completion'.

This is, for Collingwood, the nerve of all historical knowledge. The historical method requires that the logic of question and answer be applied to historical tradition. We shall understand historical events only if we reconstruct the question to which the historical actions of the persons concerned were the answer. As an example, Collingwood cites the Battle of Trafalgar and Nelson's plan on which it was based. The example is intended to show that the course of the battle helps us to understand Nelson's real plan, because it was successfully carried out. The plan of his opponent, however, because it failed, cannot be reconstructed from the events. Thus, understanding the course of the battle and understanding the plan that Nelson carried out in it are one and the same process.

In fact, we cannot avoid the discovery that the logic of question and answer has to reconstruct two different questions that have also two different answers: the question of meaning in the course of a great event and the question of whether this event went according to plan. Clearly, the two questions coincide only when the plan coincides with the course of events. But this is a presupposition that, as men involved in history, we cannot maintain as a methodological principle when concerned with a historical tradition which deals with such men. Tolstoy's celebrated description of the council of war before the battle, in which all the strategic possibilities are calculated and all the plans considered, thoroughly and perceptively, while the general sits there and sleeps, but in the night before the battle goes round all the sentry-posts, is obviously a more accurate account of what we call history. Kutusov gets nearer to the reality and the forces that determine it than the strategists of the war council. The conclusion to be drawn from this example is that the interpreter of history always runs the risk of hypostasising the sequence of events when he sees their significance as that intended by actors and planners.

This is a legitimate undertaking only if Hegel's conditions hold good, namely that the philosophy of history is made party to the plans of the world spirit and on the basis of this esoteric knowledge is able to mark out certain individuals as of world-historical importance, there being a real co-ordination between their particular ideas and the world-historical meaning of events. But it is impossible to derive a hermeneutical principle for the knowledge of history from these cases that are characterised by the coming together of the subjective and objective in history. In regard to historical tradition, Hegel's theory has, clearly, only a limited truth. The infinite web of motivations that constitutes history only occasionally and for a short period acquires in a single individual the clarity of what has been planned. Thus what Hegel describes as an outstanding case rests on the general basis of the disproportion that exists between the subjective thoughts of an individual and the meaning of the whole course of history. As a rule, we experience the course of events as something that continually changes our plans and expectations. Someone who tries to stick to his plans discovers precisely how powerless his reason is. There are odd occasions when everything happens, as it were, of its own accord – that is, events seem to be automatically in accord with our plans and wishes. On these occasions, we can say that everything is going according to plan. But to apply this experience to the whole of history is to undertake a great extrapolation that entirely contradicts our experience.

The use that Collingwood makes of the logic of question and answer in hermeneutical theory is now made ambiguous by this extrapolation. Our understanding of written tradition as such is not of a kind that we can simply presuppose that the meaning that we discover in it agrees with that which its author intended. Just as the events of history do not in general manifest any agreement with the subjective ideas of the person who stands and acts within history, so the sense of a text in general reaches far beyond what its author originally intended. But the task of understanding is concerned in the first place with the meaning of the text itself.

This is clearly what Collingwood had in mind when he denied that there is any difference between the historical question and the philosophical question to which the text is supposed to be an answer. Nevertheless, we must hold on to the point that the question that we are concerned to reconstruct has to do not with the mental experiences of the author, but simply with the meaning of the text itself. Thus it must be possible, if we have understood the meaning of a sentence (i.e. have reconstructed the question to which it is really the answer), to inquire also about the questioner and his meaning, to which the text is, perhaps, only the imagined answer. Collingwood is wrong when he finds it methodologically unsound to differentiate between the question to which the text is imagined to be an answer and the question to which it really is an answer. He is right only insofar as the understanding of a text does not generally involve such a distinction, if we are concerned with the object of which the text speaks. The reconstruction of the ideas of an author is a quite different task.

We shall have to ask what are the conditions that apply to this different task. For it is undoubtedly true that, compared with the genuine hermeneutical experience that understands the meaning of the text, the reconstruction of what the author really had in mind is a limited undertaking. It is the seduction of historicism to see in this kind of reduction a scientific virtue and to regard understanding as a kind of reconstruction which in effect repeats the process of how the text came into being. Hence it follows the ideal familiar to us from our knowledge of nature, where we understand a process only when we are able to reproduce it artificially.

I have shown [earlier in the book] how questionable is Vico's statement that this ideal finds its purest fulfilment in history, because it is there that man encounters his own human historical reality. I have asserted, against this, that every historian and literary critic must reckon with the fundamental non-definitiveness of the horizon in which his understanding moves. Historical tradition can be understood only by being considered in its further determinations resulting from the progress of events. Similarly, the literary critic, who is dealing with poetic or philosophical texts, knows that they are inexhaustible. In both cases, it is the progress of events that brings out new aspects of meaning in historical material. Through being reactualised in understanding, the texts are drawn into a genuine process in exactly the same way as are the events themselves through their continuance. This is what we described as the effective-historical element within the hermeneutical experience. Every actualisation in understanding can be regarded as a historical potentiality of what is understood. It is part of the historical finiteness of our being that we are aware that after us others will understand in a different way. And yet it is a fact equally well established that it remains the same work, the fullness of whose meaning is proved in the changing process of understanding, just as it is the same history whose meaning is constantly being further determined. The hermeneutical reduction to the author's meaning is just as inappropriate as the reduction of historical events to the intentions of their protagonists.

We cannot, however, take the reconstruction of the question to which a given text is an answer simply as an achievement of historical method. The first thing is the question that the text presents us with, our response to the word handed down to us, so that its understanding must already include the work of historical self-mediation of present and tradition. Thus the relation of question and answer is, in fact, reversed. The voice that speaks to us from the past – be it text, work, trace – itself poses a question and places our meaning in openness. In order to answer this question, we, of whom the question is asked, must ourselves begin to ask questions. We must attempt to reconstruct the question to which the transmitted text is the answer. But we shall not be able to do this without going beyond the historical horizon it presents us with. The reconstruction of the question to which the text is presumed to be the answer takes place itself within a process of questioning through which we seek the answer to the question that the text asks us. A reconstructed question can never stand within its original horizon: for the historical horizon that is outlined in the reconstruction is not a truly comprehensive one. It is, rather, included within the horizon that embraces us as the questioners who have responded to the word that has been handed down.

Hence it is a hermeneutical necessity always to go beyond mere reconstruction. We cannot avoid thinking about that which was unquestionably accepted, and hence not thought about, by an author, and bringing it into the openness of the question. This is not to open the door to arbitrariness in interpretation, but to reveal what always takes place. The understanding of the word of the tradition always requires that the reconstructed question be set within the openness of its questionableness – that it merge with the question that tradition is for us. If the 'historical' question emerges by itself, this means that it no longer raises itself as a question. It results from the coming to an end of understanding – a wrong turning at which we get stuck. It is part of real understanding, however, that we regain the concepts of a historical past in such a way that they also include our own comprehension of them. I called this [earlier in the book] 'the fusing of horizons'. We can say, with Collingwood, that we understand only when we understand the question to which something is the answer, and it is true that what is understood in this way does not remain detached in its meaning from our own meaning. Rather, the reconstruction of the question, from which the meaning of a text is to be understood as an answer, passes into our own questioning. For the text must be understood as an answer to a real question.

The close relation that exists between question and understanding is what gives the hermeneutic experience its true dimension. However much a person seeking understanding may leave open the truth of what is said, however much he may turn away from the immediate meaning of the object and consider, rather, its deeper significance, and take the latter not as true but merely as meaningful, so that the possibility of its truth remains unsettled, this is the real and basic nature of a question, namely to make things indeterminate. Questions always bring out the undetermined possibilities of a thing. That is why there cannot be an understanding of the questionableness of an object that turns away from real questions, in the same way that there can be the understanding of a meaning that turns away from meaning. To understand the questionableness of something is always to question it. There can be no testing or potential attitude to questioning, for questioning is not the positing, but the testing of possibilities. Here, the nature of questioning indicates what it is demonstrated by the operation of the Platonic dialogue. A person who thinks must ask himself questions. Even when a person says that at such and such a point a question might arise, this is already a real questioning that simply masks itself, out of either caution or politeness.

This is the reason that all understanding is always more than the mere recreation of someone else's meaning. Asking it opens up possibilities of meaning, and thus what is meaningful passes into one's own thinking on the subject. Questions that we do not ourselves ask, such as those that we regard as out of date or pointless, are understood in a curious fashion. We understand how certain questions came to be asked in particular historical circumstances. Understanding such questions means, then, understanding the particular presuppositions whose demise makes the question no longer relevant. An example is perpetual motion. The horizon of meaning of such questions is only apparently still open. They are no longer understood as questions. For what we understand, in such cases, is precisely that there is no question.

To understand a question means to ask it. To understand an opinion is to understand it as the answer to a question.

The logic of question and answer that Collingwood elaborated does away with talk of the permanent problem that underlay the relation of the 'Oxford realists' to the classics of philosophy, and hence with the problem of the history of problems developed by neo-Kantianism. History of problems would be truly history only if it acknowledged the identity of the problem as a pure abstraction and permitted itself a transformation into questioning. There is no such thing, in fact, as a point outside history from which the identity of a problem can be conceived within the vicissitudes of the various attempts to solve it. It is true that all understanding of the texts of philosophy requires the recognition of the knowledge that they contain. Without this, we would understand nothing at all. But this does not mean that we in any way step outside the historical conditions in which we find ourselves and in which we understand. The problem that we recognise is not in fact simply the same if it is to be understood in a genuine question. We can regard it as the same only because of our historical short-sightedness. The standpoint that is beyond any standpoint, a standpoint from which we could conceive its true identity, is a pure illusion.

We can understand the reason for this now. The concept of the problem is clearly the formulation of an abstraction, namely the detachment of the content of the question from the question that in fact first reveals it. It refers to the abstract schema to which real and really motivated questions can be reduced and under which they can be subsumed. This kind of 'problem' has fallen out of the motivated context of questioning, from which it receives the clarity of its sense. Hence it is insoluble, like every question that has no clear unambiguous sense, because it is not properly motivated and asked.

This confirms also the origin of the concept of the problem. It does not belong in the sphere of those 'honestly motivated refutations' in which the truth of the object is advanced, but in the sphere of dialectic as a weapon to amaze or make a fool of one's opponent. In Aristotle, the word *problema* refers to those questions that appear as open alternatives because there is evidence for both views and we think that they cannot be decided by reasons, since the questions involved are too great. Hence problems are not real questions that present themselves and hence acquire the pattern of their answer from the genesis of their meaning, but are alternatives that can only be accepted as themselves and thus can only be treated in a dialectical way. This dialectical sense of the 'problem' has its place in thetoric, not in philosophy. It is part of the concept that there can be no clear decision on the basis of reasons. That is why Kant sees the rise of the concept of the problem as limited to the dialectic of pure reason. Problems are 'tasks that emerge entirely from its own womb', that is, products of reason itself, the complete solution of which it cannot hope to achieve. It is interesting that in the nineteenth century, with the collapse of the direct tradition of philosophical questioning and the rise of historicism, the concept of the problem acquires a universal validity – a sign of the fact that the direct relation to the questions of philosophy no longer exists. It is typical of the embarrassment of the philosophical consciousness that, when faced with historicism, it took flight into the abstraction of the concept of the problem and saw no problem about the manner in which problems actually 'exist'. The history of problems in neo-Kantianism is a bastard of historicism. The critique of the concept of the problem that is conducted with the means of a logic of question and answer must destroy the illusion that there are problems as there are stars in the sky. Reflection on the hermeneutical experience transforms problems back to questions that arise and that derive their sense from their motivation.

The dialectic of question and answer, that was disclosed in the structure of the hermeneutical experience, now permits us to state in more detail the type of consciousness that effective-historical consciousness is. For the dialectic of question and answer that we demonstrated makes understanding appear as a reciprocal relationship of the same kind as conversation. It is true that a text does not speak to us in the same way as does another person. We, who are attempting to understand, must ourselves make it speak. But we found that this kind of understanding, 'Making the text speak', is not an arbitrary procedure that we undertake on our own initiative but that, as a question, it is related to the answer that is expected in the text. The anticipation of an answer itself presumes that the person asking is part of the tradition and regards himself as addressed by it. This is the truth of the effective-historical consciousness. It is the historically experienced consciousness that, by renouncing the chimera of perfect enlightenment, is open to the experience of history. We described its realisation as the fusion of the horizons of understanding, which is what mediates between the text and its interpreter.

The guiding idea of the following discussion is that the fusion of the horizons that takes place in understanding is the proper achievement of language. Admittedly, the nature of language is one of the most mysterious questions that exist for man to ponder on. Language is so uncannily near to our thinking, and when it functions it is so little an object that it seems to conceal its own being from us. In our analysis of the thinking of the human sciences, however, we came so close to this universal mystery of language that is prior to everything else, that we can entrust ourselves to the object that we are investigating to guide us safely in the quest. In other words, we are seeking to approach the mystery of language from the conversation that we ourselves are.

If we seek to examine the hermeneutical phenomenon according to the model of the conversation between two persons, the chief thing that these apparently so different situations have in common – the understanding of a text and the understanding that occurs in conversation – is that both are concerned with an object that is placed before them. Just as one person seeks to reach agreement with his partner concerning an object, so the interpreter understands the object of which the text speaks. This understanding of the object must take place in a linguistic form; not that the understanding is subsequently put into words, but in the way in which the understanding comes about – whether in the case of a text or a conversation with another person who presents us with the object – lies the coming-into-language of the thing itself. Thus we shall first consider the structure of conversation proper, in order to bring out the specific character of that other form of conversation that is the understanding of texts. Whereas up to now we have emphasised the constitutive significance of the question for the hermeneutical phenomenon, in terms of the conversation, we must now demonstrate the linguistic nature of conversation, which is the basis of the question, as an element of hermeneutics.

Our first point is that language, in which something comes to be language, is not a possession at the disposal of one or the other of the interlocutors. Every conversation presupposes a common language, or, it creates a common language. Something is placed in the centre, as the Greeks said, which the partners to the dialogue both share, and concerning which they can exchange ideas with one another. Hence agreement concerning the object, which it is the purpose of the conversation to bring about, necessarily means that a common language must first be worked out in the conversation. This is not an external matter of simply adjusting our tools, nor is it even right to say that the partners adapt themselves to one another but, rather, in the successful conversation they both come under the influence of the truth of the object and are thus bound to one another in a new community. To reach an understanding with one's partner in a dialogue is not merely a matter of total self-expression and the successful assertion of one's own point of view, but a transformation into a communion, in which we do not remain what we were.

SECTION 1: QUESTIONS FOR DISCUSSION

- What do you think political theory is for? What do you think it can do for you?
- Chapters 1 and 2 mention arguments, popular in the middle of the twentieth century, that declared the death of political theory. Why might this have been a popular view at that time? Is political theory dead?
- What do you think are the central events or phenomena to which political theory has had to respond over the last 100 years? Has it done so creditably?
- What do you understand by the notion of 'massification'? What has been the importance of this development for the conduct of politics? Can political theory written in an age before 'massification' still be of use to us?
- What is the relation of politics to the past? Should politics be concerned to learn from the past or to transcend it?
- Marx famously wrote that 'Men make their own history, but they do not make it just as they please; they do not make it under circumstances chosen by themselves, but under circumstances directly encountered, given, and transmitted from the past. The tradition of all the dead generations weights like a nightmare on the brain of the living' (Marx, 1977: 300). Do you think this is true? How might this affect the way we go about understanding politics and political theory?
- To what extent should any work of political theory be understood in terms of the intentions of those writing it?

- Should there be a canon of 'great' works that all students of politics (and perhaps all politicians) should read? How should such a canon be selected? What would you include?
- Do you think it is possible truly to understand the minds of the past? Can things be learned from the effort so to do?

SECTION 1: FURTHER READING

The issues covered in this opening section are vast in both scope and scale, and, as might be expected, there is a wealth of literature relating to them. On the history of political thought in general, the reader new to the field can't do a lot better than look at Iain Hampsher-Monk, *A History of Modern Political Thought: Major Political Thinkers from Hobbes to Marx* (Blackwell, 1992) or the two volumes by Janet Coleman, *A History of Political Thought: From Ancient Greece to Early Christianity* (Blackwell, 2000) and *A History of Political Thought: From the Middle Ages to the Renaissance* (Blackwell, 2000). Both of these leading scholars are involved with the journal *History of Political Thought*, which is well worth consulting and will give the reader a good over-view of the field and its methods.

To find out more about Hannah Arendt, it is recommended that readers go directly to her own works, many of which are surprisingly accessible. A recent revival of interest in Arendt has also produced some good introductions and overviews of her work. See, for example, Maurizio Passerin d'Entrèves, *The Political Philosophy of Hannah Arendt* (Routledge, 1994), Phillip Hansen, *Hannah Arendt: Politics, History and Citizenship* (Polity Press, 1993) and Margaret Canovan, *Hannah Arendt: A Reinterpretation of Her Political Thought* (Cambridge University Press, 1992).

Foucault has sparked quite an industry and a variety of both interpretations and applications. For works or comments by the man himself that are perhaps easier to get into than the core works themselves (which are beautiful in their own right), readers could try the collection edited by Colin Gordon, *Power/Knowledge: Selected Interviews and Other Writings 1972–1977* (Harvester Wheatsheaf, 1980). Of the numerous introductory textbooks, Lois McNay's *Foucault: A Critical Introduction* (Polity, 1994) is useful and gives the perspective of a sociologist. Jon Simons, *Foucault and the Political* (Routledge, 1995) is very good and accessible, while Barry Hindess, *Discourses of Power: From Hobbes to Foucault* (Blackwell, 1996) gives an overview of broader debates. For applications of Foucault (which are legion and cross most fields), try Lois McNay, *Foucault and Feminism: Power, Gender and the Self* (Polity Press, 1992), or investigate the growing field of studies of 'governmentality', the application of Foucauldian methods to political analysis, demonstrated in *The*

Foucault Effect: Studies in Governmentality (edited by Graham Burchell, Colin Gordon and Peter Miller, published by Chicago University Press in 1991) or *Foucault and Political Reason: Liberalism, Neo-Liberalism and Rationalities of Government* (edited by Andrew Barry, Thomas Osborne and Nikolas Rose, published by UCL Press in 1996). For a full and original application, see Nikolas Rose, *Powers of Freedom: Reframing Political Thought* (Cambridge University Press, 1999).

For those interested in pursuing methodological and philosophical debates about what the past might mean to us, the anthology *The Philosophy of History in Our Time* edited by Hans Meyerhoff (Doubleday, 1959) is still a really useful place to start. A more recent text dealing with contemporary debates is *Philosophies of History: From Enlightenment to Postmodernity* (edited by Robert M. Burns and Hugh Rayment-Pickard, published by Blackwell in 2000). An older but still relevant and readable comment, including a criticism of Collingwood, is E. H. Carr's classic *The Idea of History*, a new edition of which was published in 2001 by Palgrave. For a good introduction to Collingwood himself, see David Boucher, *The Social and Political Thought of R. G. Collingwood* (Cambridge University Press, 1989). The best starting place to find out about the Cambridge School is the collection of writings by Quentin Skinner (and critical responses) edited by James Tully as *Meaning and Context* and published by Polity in 1988.

Gadamer scholarship is also a vast field. A useful introduction is Georgia Warnke, *Gadamer: Hermeneutics, Tradition and Reason* (Polity Press, 1987), while Hugh J. Silverman (ed.), *Gadamer and Hermeneutics* (Routledge, 1991), is also useful. For broader applications of hermeneutics, there are good articles such as Charles Taylor, 'Interpretation and the Science of Man', in P. Rabinow and W. M. Sullivan (eds), *Interpretive Social Science: A Second Look* (University of California Press, 1987), pp. 33–81, and Mark Neufeld, 'Interpretation and the 'Science' of International Relations', *Review of International Studies*, 19 (1993): 39–61.

SECTION 2
TRADITIONS AND THEIR DISCONTENTS

INTRODUCTION

Encapsulating the varieties of political thought in a single introductory volume always entails a kind of violence; a forcing of the square into the round. By its nature, political thinking cannot easily be neatly contained or limited, and the streams that feed into contemporary modes of conceiving of political life are many, varied and rich. Characterising Conservatism, Liberalism and Marxism as the 'most important' traditions of political thought is, from the start, an unhappy and unsatisfactory delineation. It is a simplification, to say the least, and runs the dual risk of freezing complex, diverse and mobile forms of thought (full of disputation within themselves) into too broadly defined 'traditions' and of excluding from account alternative forms of thought which may, precisely because of the difficulty of easily classifying and categorising them, be worthy of our attention. There is also a problem with taking as traditions of political thought ways of thinking that can also be characterised as dominant 'ideologies' or political movements. Political thought, while inseparable from such political movements, is more subtle and complex than activist dogma can ever be, even though there can be no activism without the theories that animate it. However, there are good reasons (and not only pedagogical ones) for approaching our topic in this way. Liberalism, Conservatism and Marxism are broad schools of thought that have shaped, and continue to shape, actual political communities and many of the judgements of policy that political representatives take. Those representatives may not always identify themselves as 'Liberals', 'Conservatives' or 'Marxists', and may not have paid much close attention to works of political thought (though, to be sure, many have); and, even when they do so identify, it is likely that the politicians' understanding of these political approaches differs greatly from that of philosophers. Nevertheless, this is a good reason to pay them close attention and to acknowledge the extent of their influence.

As we will see in Section 3, each of these strands of political philosophy has come in for much criticism by those concerned to advance alternative approaches; but even such would-be opponents have had no choice but to develop their positions using concepts animated by Liberalism, Conservatism or Marxism or in opposition to them. And, as we will see in Section 2, they have not at all been static movements and have undergone considerable revision and refinement in the light of criticism and changing historical circumstances.

In the general introduction to this volume, it was suggested that we could understand Western political thought as a set of differing responses to Enlightenment with some schools of thought celebrating it, others decrying it and still others arguing that its promise is yet to be fulfilled. We can now add a little more to that claim and suggest that we understand the mainstream traditions of Western political philosophy as a set of responses not only to Enlightenment rationalism but to the modernity of which it was a manifestation.

By modernity is meant the form of society and economy that emerged from feudalism (predominantly organised around land and agricultural labour), establishing itself on the basis of industrial production and commerce. This was the basis of a range of major social transformations: from rural to urban living and the concomitant growth of a 'mass' population; the development of new communications technology in the form of printing and the slow spread of literacy making possible something like a 'reading public'; and the spread of industrial forms of labour leading to the formation of a mass working class sharply differentiated from the bourgeois class and with some sort of direct relation of dependence between the two (how that relationship is conceived is a major point of difference between political philosophies). Allied to these transformations was the development of nation states in which political participation was extended to representatives of the new class of industrially wealthy people and, eventually, to the population as a whole (though it took a long time for political rights to be granted to the entire population of working men, let alone to women).

This massive social and cultural upheaval was matched, naturally, by intellectual transformation, particularly the development and extension of scientific knowledge and the related shift away from theocratic models of thought, action and political organisation and towards 'rational' ones. Much of the philosophy of the late medieval period is concerned with establishing what place there might be for God and religion in a world increasingly understood (by the intellectuals at least) as essentially mechanical and animated by physical laws that determine the flow of cause and effect that we experience as events. It was also concerned to establish, in the context of this notion of an ordered and determined universe, what the nature of free will might be. These considerations were not merely abstract philosophical or methodological concerns relating to the understanding and analysis of the universe. They were thoroughly political. Despite the often clear theological intentions of thinkers such as **Spinoza**, **Leibniz** or **Descartes**, their thoughts were themselves evidence of a move away from automatic deference to scriptural authority (in the case of **Spinoza** a sustained attempt to demolish it) and to make the matter of understanding the world a proper subject for independent reasoning rather than passive acceptance of the word of God and Church. Such arguments laid the ground for the political demand that individuals, being capable of reasoning with their own mind, were also deserving of the liberty to do so.

This is nowhere clearer than in the philosophy of Immanuel Kant. He is often read as a philosopher with a very 'academic' and formal mindset and style of reasoning, whose primary concern was to establish a solid foundation for metaphysical enquiry (the study of that which exceeds our experience of the world such as religious and moral questions). He does so by marking out the limits of metaphysics, the things which we can and cannot know about through the exercise of our reason. Reason independent of experience is given space by Kant only through a radical reversal of prior philosophical presumptions. He argues that the world necessarily conforms to our experience and that we can know things about the world with certainty because we perceive it through categories that are, as we might now say, 'hard-wired' within us. This meant that there were truths about the world, as we experience it, that could be established as both necessary and universal simply through the reasoning of our own minds. Presented as such, this may not seem like an obviously political claim. But, by clear implication, it establishes a basis for the equality of human beings. Each is capable of reasoning about the world and of establishing truths that are in fact common to the experience of all. What is more, this reason alone provides the basis for justifying any particular action or state of affairs. We cannot simply accept automatically the claims to authority made by those who do not proceed on this rational basis. In the preface to the first edition of his *Critique of Pure Reason*, Kant describes his age as having a 'ripened power of judgement'. In the face of the anxiety that underlay eighteenth-century Europe (born of political turmoil, social upheaval and sceptical philosophies), Kant declares:

> doubt, and finally strict criticism . . . [are] . . . proofs of a well-grounded way of thinking. Our age is the genuine age of criticism, to which everything must submit. Religion through its holiness and legislation through its majesty commonly seek to exempt themselves from it. But in this way they excite a just suspicion against themselves, and cannot lay claim to that unfeigned respect that reason grants only to that which has been able to withstand its free and public examination. (A xi)

Kant's philosophical project, then, can be understood (to a degree) as to provide the basis by which a rational society of free individuals can come to open agreements as to how to proceed about any particular matter: the public use of their reason. Kant was self-conscious about the age in which he lived, seeing it as one in which the capacity for humanity to reason about its affairs could be fulfilled through the efforts of a reasoning and reasonable public subjecting things to rigorous criticism and argument. This self-consciousness is itself evidence of a broader historical self-consciousness that enabled people to think of themselves as 'modern', as living at a particular time and at the present end of a progressive history. This went along with a new sense of self, of people not only as particular bearers of social rank or performers of well-defined social functions but as autonomous, unique selves in possession of a singular and coherent individuality, relating to an external world via the faculty of reason. That self or agent, because of these unique faculties, could be held to require sovereignty over itself and its private affairs as well as freedom to determine, with other such subjects, the rules of conduct that govern public affairs. It could form a 'social contract' with others and establish the framework, and limits, of public, political life.

This conception made possible revolutionary political ideas and practices. It is hard to think of concepts such as human rights (to liberty, free speech and political participation, for example) without assuming a singular, coherent and rational will to claim and exercise them. For Kant, if people were to become enlightened to use their own understanding, there had to be freedom 'to make public use of one's reason in all matters' (see Kant, 1996b: 54–60). This is a quintessentially liberal vision of the subject, and many would argue that this was the conception that helped make possible the modern forms of state and democratic politics. But it can also be argued that modern forms of state, democracy and social organisation presupposed the Enlightenment individual and were driven to bring about its invention and formalisation. As such, it may be claimed that the free, rational, liberal individual was a myth of Enlightenment: one that served to maintain and justify a particular sort of social system and that was a political/cultural imposition rather than a purely natural historical development. This is a charge one can find made against Enlightenment Liberalism by the political left and the political right, in the name of freedom and against it.

For a conservative such as **Burke**, specifically taking on the claims of the French Revolution to have founded a new order of liberty, equality and fraternity, the capacity for the individual to reason freely was severely curtailed by passions and prejudices. Burke saw the individual as foolish and argued that only the species, through the evolutionary interaction of history, experience and learning, could be wise. The application of abstract principles to the social order was an illegitimate intrusion bound to end in despotism and destruction. As such, the individual had to be limited in its freedom and held in place through a strong sense of tradition that orientated it in the world and gave it a firm sense of its place in society. For Burke (and this became a hallmark of subsequent conservative thinking), the attempt to model society in accordance with social laws or principles abstractly conceived by 'intellectuals' would always end in failure. Society, to put it simply, was not a 'rational' phenomenon. In this sense, Conservatism opposed Enlightenment and modernity on the grounds that it threatened to destroy, in the name of society, society itself.

Enlightenment modernity also came in for criticism from the left, but here the charge was that it was not, in fact, enlightened at all and that the freedom it promised was but a fiction supporting the ideological claims of bourgeois society. Marx and Engels declared in *The Communist Manifesto* of 1848: 'In bourgeois society capital is independent and has individuality, while the living person is dependent and has no individuality . . . By freedom is meant, under the present bourgeois conditions of production, free trade, free selling and free buying' (Marx, 1977: 233). In other words, the promise made by Enlightenment, that society could be rational and individuals emancipated and free, was a dubious fiction. Capitalist society was itself irrational, granting freedom to capital but not persons, treating commodities as living entities and people as mere things to serve them. The free subjectivity of modernity belonged only to the ruling classes and was denied to the alienated labourer. If true **autonomy** was to flourish, the class system had to be destroyed and a communist society of equals allowed to develop.

These three traditions (Liberalism, Conservatism and Marxist socialism) were thus formed in a context that constituted the legacy of Enlightenment as their battleground. In turn, they shaped the political movements that have forged the modern world as we know it and still define political dispute in most Western nations. While few today adhere exactly to the Conservatism of **Burke**, the Communism of Marx or the entirety of Kantian Liberalism, most 'real-world' political positions draw on them in varying measures. For the broad, liberal left in Europe and the USA, an unfettered capitalist market will have irrational outcomes. The endless search for profit will not bring about an equitable distribution of resources and will lead to irresponsible behaviour bringing about crisis or collapse in the economy. It is thus necessary that the state take a hand in, at the least, regulating the behaviour of capitalists or trying to manage the market. The state has a purpose to fulfil, namely that of spreading Enlightenment reason, making people better. This is still a major basis for dispute in Western politics, with Conservatism rejecting the idea that the state can have such a substantive purpose and attacking state intervention into the economy as an illegitimate attack on freedom: people should be left to be as they are and not interfered with by the state. For its part, Liberalism recognises that leaving people alone in this way can in itself generate problems (social conflicts of all kinds and inequalities that bring about social instability) but is generally unwilling to impose any particular framework on the whole of society, so it tries to manage the state as an intermediary body that represents no particular will other than that of Liberalism itself (which, as we have seen, may itself be a powerful and imposed will).

As society has changed, these perspectives have all had to change also. In Chapter 3, Mark Evans focuses on 'justification' and the question of how liberals might respond to the diversity of the world as it is today. He examines four such responses ranging from attempts to devise a logical, analytical justification for human rights to those deriving from pragmatism and agonistic Liberalism; but he pays particular attention, as one must, to John Rawls' landmark attempt to construct a justifiable and agreeable theory of justice and, latterly, to spell out the nature of a (limited) political liberalism that takes account of the presence within the polity of rival comprehensive doctrines.

In the twentieth century, the traditional Conservative emphasis on hierarchy and commitment to nationhood mutated into fascist authoritarianism. Consequently, Conservatism was forced to stress its vision of a limited state designed to protect individuals living in the context of a civil association based on natural, traditional and even non-rational values. It increasingly defined itself against the cold rationalism of Liberalism and Socialism, both of which, it would insist, sought to employ the state to carry out a task of social engineering, creating the population rather than being the organic expression of their communal being. As I show in Chapter 4, Conservative philosophy is a highly mobile formation ever ready to adapt to circumstances it finds itself in. As society has become more individualised, Conservatism has returned to its roots in opposition to a state that extends itself too far into society and has done so in particular by stressing the organic, natural and spontaneous nature of social organisation as embodied in traditions.

In Chapter 5, Terrell Carver considers the relationship between Liberalism and Marxism, going back to the journalism of the young Marx and interpreting him in his historical context (thereby touching on issues raised in Chapter 2). He argues that Marx's thinking was altogether more subtle than its characterisation as crudely opposing class politics to liberal tolerance would suggest. He stresses the importance of a theory of history for Marxism, one that shows how liberals are in error if they treat human nature as a timeless phenomenon. But this very theorisation of history may have contributed to a lack of sensitivity on the part of Marxists to the finer processes of human being and development. Such would certainly be the criticism of conservatives. But it has also been a charge made within Marxism itself. Post-Marxists seek to develop a form of theorising that may still be Marxist in origin but which moves beyond the deterministic streaks within traditional Marxism and becomes more attuned to the variety of forms of political subject that are contending for existence in the polity. As such, they may be returning to certain tenets of liberal political thinking.

In all three cases, we can see how the mainstream traditions of political thinking have found themselves forced to adapt to changing social circumstances and the new demands it appears to have caused to be made within the realm of practical politics. Just as modernity formed them, 'postmodernity' necessitates their revision. Whether that revision goes far enough is a question addressed by Section 3.

3

LIBERALISMS

Mark Evans

If we were to assume that a volume on contemporary political thought should reflect, precisely and exclusively, the current strength of doctrines in the 'real world' of politics, then we might be forgiven for expecting Liberalism to dominate its contents, casting a long shadow over its rivals. 'Liberal democracy', the institutionalised form of Liberalism, is the form of government many of the world's states profess to adhere to, including some of the most powerful, populous and prosperous. Many more, perhaps hypocritically, commit themselves, both to their own citizens and on the international stage, to liberal principles whose moral force they tacitly concede when they take pains to hide, or otherwise explain away, their violation. Liberalism is political 'common sense' for vast numbers of people: accepted almost automatically by those able to take it for granted in their social worlds, passionately fought for by those resisting the anti-liberalisms that have stubbornly and often bloodily refused to let it write the 'end of history' in its own name (see Fukuyama, 1992). Why, then, does Liberalism appear to be the object of such rigorous and impassioned philosophical hostility, the standpoint in opposition to which many of the alternative positions presented in this book explicitly define themselves?

We should straightaway acknowledge that its institutional predominance does not guarantee Liberalism immunity from valid philosophical critique. As a political theory, it may indeed be deeply flawed despite its remarkable historical achievements, and resistance to the liberal present may therefore be warranted. But we should also note that what the term 'Liberalism' actually refers to can vary enormously from context to context. Contemporary academic liberal political theorising has been conducted largely through the medium of Anglo-American analytic philosophy. This has yielded a highly distinctive version of the doctrine, usually elaborated as a set of abstract, ahistorically postulated principles and propositions said to model the form that 'justice' could take in society's fundamental institutions. Its philosophical technique typically presumes a **methodological individualism** and proceeds by isolating and clarifying the doctrine's individual elements before conjoining them according to criteria of rationality, logical progression and coherence. As for the kind of politics it suggests, the resulting theory often looks like a centre-leftist reading of the legalistic, rights-based constitutional politics practised in American capitalist democracy (see Freeden, 1996: Chapter 6).

It is specifically these types of politics and philosophy that contemporary philosophical critics of Liberalism tend to target. But it is vital to remember that throughout its history the liberal tradition has been populated by many more diverse styles of theory and practice, at least some of which could be congenial to those who today say they oppose 'Liberalism'. Further, even if we define Liberalism only in terms of its contemporary analytic-philosophical variant, it is hardly clear that its critics wish to reject *everything* it stands for. Their anti-Liberalism may be a protest only against its way of 'doing' theory, the assumptions about the relationship between individual and society, its beliefs about the nature of moral values or its recommended ideals and institutions: all features which may be detachable from each other. We should be clear, then, that contemporary theoretical assaults on Liberalism often have a rather more ambivalent relationship to their target than might be thought. And yet it is a key feature of much contemporary liberal thought that its own *justification* – the reasons it can offer as to why we should support its claims as opposed to any of its rivals – has become a matter for the most serious investigation by liberal theorists themselves.

LIBERALISM AND JUSTIFICATION

Far from assuming its theoretical superiority to be self-evident, many liberals have regarded it as necessary to strip their own doctrine back to its fundamental ideas in order to marshal what arguments they can to support them. This is not to deny that there has also been much important work that takes these fundamentals for granted in order to explore the liberal approach to specific policy issues. But the volume of theory struggling with the question of why we should take a liberal approach on anything in the first place is striking. So a survey of representative perspectives in what we can call *justificatory Liberalism* is a good guide to current liberal preoccupations.

But, before we proceed, we might ask why Liberalism has taken such an introspective turn. Part of the explanation lies with the analytic-philosophical method itself, which *tries* to offer independent reasons for accepting as many as possible of liberalism's separate, constituent ideas. Its exposition of the liberal position is thus premised upon a certain initial suspension of outright or immediate commitment to it. Although, as we shall see, there are limits to the independence that any such reason-giving can have from its objects, the liberal analytic-philosophical mindset is in some sense characterised by a degree of at least official initial uncertainty about its own tenets.

But, in a way, Liberalism has always been about reason-giving. By treating individuals with equal respect as free, rational, moral beings, it takes seriously the idea that they are owed 'good' reasons for accepting liberal beliefs: reasons that it is, in some sense, reasonable to expect others to accept. Further, there has also always been a sense in which Liberalism has been aware and respectful of the *differences* among people's outlooks and ways of life, which stiffen the challenge of demonstrating the possibility of agreement on its beliefs. Today, Liberalism's sensitivity to human diversity is typified by its acknowledgement of multi-culturalism as a normatively positive fact of modern society which liberal politics must embrace. When its audience is so variegated, it is hardly surprising if justificatory Liberalism acquires a certain humility about the beliefs it is asking them to embrace and finds itself testing a variety of strategies in pursuit of this goal.

Liberals pay close attention to the relevance of different forms of reason-giving, distinguished by who is giving reasons to whom and for what purposes. In particular, they often consider whether *public moral justification* – giving reasons to others as to why they could or, more strongly, should accept X for themselves – must differ from purely *personal moral justification*. Are the reasons that I, as a liberal (or we as a group in society), give to myself to justify my commitment to X also the reasons that are appropriate to give to everyone else as to why they should share it? More specifically, they focus on what they treat as the specifically 'political' dimension: they want to identify those principles that can be said to be legitimately enforceable by the state. And reasons given in such *public political justification* may not necessarily be those given in moral justification, where we may be talking about non-enforced acceptance. To add one final complication: liberals do not all assume that 'political justification' thus understood is the same as the venerable concern to *justify political authority*, which asks how the state might obtain the *right* to be the body to exercise power over others. These questions play important roles in structuring the four justificatory liberalisms discussed below.

Kantian Liberalism

Examining Kantian Liberalism first will help us to mark out some key terrain in present justificatory debates because it is a direct product of the Enlightenment, the eighteenth-century intellectual revolution that not only helped to generate Liberalism itself but framed, through its successive followers and opponents, a distinctively modern version of justification as the philosophical pursuit of justified belief by a secularised reason that *all* humans, by virtue of their essential rationality, can share. The so-called 'Enlightenment

Project', which has become a *leitmotif* of contemporary political thought, refers to what Alasdair **MacIntyre** calls 'the independent rational justification of morality' (1985: 43). If this is an overly restrictive description of the various intellectual currents set in train during the historical period we call the Enlightenment, it is nevertheless a useful term to group those theories that purport to show how reason can yield determinate moral principles to govern the behaviour of all rational (i.e. human) beings. Immanuel Kant is its most famous original exemplar, arguing in his *Groundwork of the Metaphysics of Morals* that universally valid moral imperatives could be established on rational grounds that were entirely independent of contingent, changeable human desires, agreements and conventions. For his present-day intellectual descendants, the Kantian liberals, this universal, rationally compelling, 'ultimate' characteristic – which is taken to be definitive of what is today often called **foundationalism** – characteristically leads them to present liberal political principles as 'neutral' or 'impartial' with respect to the various beliefs, tastes and lifestyles they think humans may legitimately choose. This is because the principles of political morality are (1) those to which all can agree and (2) therefore not to be based on grounds which some could reasonably reject. That which is unreasonable to reject is, for Kantians, to be found in the dictates of a universal reason, accessible by all human beings regardless of their contingent differences.

Alan Gewirth's *The Epistemology of Human Rights* (an extract from which is reproduced below) epitomises modern Kantianism in its claim that reason can morally and publicly justify the ascription of an unmistakably liberal set of rights to all human beings. It typifies an analytic-philosophical approach, assembling its case from logical inferences connecting a set of premises and proceeding from a foundational starting point that is presented as utterly uncontroversial: whoever we are, whatever we believe, we can all say to ourselves that 'I am an *agent*' in that we posit for ourselves specific purposes which we treat as worth pursuing in some thin sense, and we consequently choose to act accordingly. From these 'generic' features of human 'being' in this bare sense, it is deduced that 'freedom' and 'well-being' are necessary goods to facilitate our actions, which Gewirth believes logically commits agents to regard themselves as having *rights* to such goods. The argument moves from personal to public moral justification by universalising this ascription of rights: if I must logically regard myself as having rights to the goods that I need to exercise agency, then the principle of universalisability requires me to ascribe rights to the same, generic goods for all who have the same basic needs of agency.

Central to Gewirth's case is the claim that his argument exhibits a 'dialectically necessary' method: it proceeds solely from within the perspective of the agent, with statements that can be readily accepted, and then demonstrates what the agent is *logically* committed to, given that starting point (notice the quotation marks around each statement). Hence the argument is not designed to assert the existence of human rights as a fact that holds objectively, independently of the agent's beliefs. Rather, it shows what the agent – and every agent – is logically committed to believing once they embrace the barest proposition concerning their own agency and its necessary prerequisites.

Given the tons of ink spilt over the justification of morality throughout the ages, the self-confident brevity of Gewirth's argument is audacious. Critics have naturally sought to uncover sleights of hand in the argument to break the logical chains which hasten the reader towards its apparently unshakeable conclusion. Some, for example, might challenge the universalisability criterion: why would it be illogical to say that it is *my* need for goods that leads me to ascribe myself rights and thereby deny any moral entailment for other people's needs on the grounds that they are not mine and that I therefore have no reason to grant them any moral priority (a position of universal egoism)?

More powerfully, we might query whether every agent would necessarily accept the apparently impartial, innocent starting point and consequent assumptions built into Gewirth's logic. Note the presumption that it is 'I' who is the relevant agent. Although there is of course a sense in which every human being has, or could have, a purely individual, first-personal sense of self, it is unclear that this individualised form of identification is always the kind of starting point from which facts about human agency are necessarily contemplated. For it is also true that human beings are inherently social creatures: the very language with which one would frame one's very sense of self is a social, not a private construct that *immediately* implicates one in a (language) community. It is thus odd to set this basic fact aside straightaway in beginning the argument with an asocial 'I'. If this reflects the individualism of modern Western cultures, and it can be contrasted with numerous cultures in which the individual is conceptually indivisible from a wider social context, we can see how Gewirth's starting point may not be as universal as he thinks. It could be unrecognisable to some. The communitarians argue that no such abstraction of the individual from social context is *anywhere* conceptually coherent; for them, the 'reason' exhibited by Gewirth's agent is 'disengaged' from everything that could make it recognisably human (see Chapter 6).

Gewirth is not ignorant of such reservations. He would insist that his argument does not deny the essential sociality of human being or conflict with the beliefs of highly communitarian societies. Starting with 'I' implies nothing about the **ontological** relationship of the individual over society, or their respective priorities in agents' particular world views. Even those who prioritise 'we' have only demoted, not lost altogether, the purely individual sense of self; as long as it is still there, Gewirth would claim his argument remains accessible. However, these reservations may be enough at least to rob Gewirth's theory of its blithe certitude.

PRAGMATIST LIBERALISM

To fix the boundaries of the justificatory debate, we can examine a view which diametrically opposes Gewirth's ambitions for philosophical justification. Richard Rorty's **pragmatism** can be thought of as initially posing two questions for liberals to ask themselves. First: 'why do we actually engage in justificatory argument, the attempt to underwrite our principles with reference to some foundationalist feature about human beings and/or the universe?' Rorty thinks liberals would answer that they want to urge non- or anti-liberals to change their ways and share their liberal convictions instead; they wish to convert them. **Foundationalism** is supposed to furnish these convictions with an unimpeachable validity – the facts of nature – that ultimately only fools could ignore. And it is indeed difficult to resist the feeling that moral beliefs must have such foundations if they are to have real obligatory force. But Rorty's next question is: 'does the goal of moral conversion proceed at all effectively by the kind of search for foundations that philosophy has traditionally carried out?' as epitomised in modern times by the Enlightenment Project. His answer is a resounding no – and, in support of this, his work asks us to reflect upon (1) the long history of failed philosophical attempts to vindicate the faith that there are such foundations and (2) the fact that liberals nevertheless do not discard their convictions in the face of such failures.

'Pragmatism', then, denotes a strategy by which 'we liberals' (Rorty and those who share his liberal convictions) seek to spread a liberal creed – at the heart of which is the 'human-rights culture' – without foundations. His argument is that we do not need them to hold these convictions: we might well ask ourselves whether we really suspend our belief in, say, rights not to be killed or raped or tortured until we have proof, that all other rational beings could accept, that human reason yields them. We need only treat our convictions as 'the way people like us would prefer everyone to live' based upon our experience of 'the way we do things here': precisely the kind of non-universal, contingent or 'accidental' grounds that Kantians regard as too weak to undergird morality. And if this position implies that it is more useful to regard our convictions' origins as being relative to specific cultures, Rorty does not believe that this commits us to the idea that we must treat every cultural tradition as of equal value. In our desire that those who reject our human-rights culture should change their ways, we proclaim our feeling that this culture is a morally superior way of life without implying that this denotes some foundational fact that our opponents have failed to perceive.

Although our moral convictions 'stand alone', so to speak, Rorty does think that we can make some provisional statements about the nature of human beings, morality and so forth. Of course, he says, his position implies that we are interpretive beings: we make assumptions about the nature of ourselves and the world we live in. What he wishes us to do is simply to drop the idea that such interpretations are anything other than pragmatic conceptual constructs designed to facilitate our actions in the world, rather than being accounts of the way the world is outside of our descriptions of it. He thus comes close to the paradigmatic communitarian view of the socially located self, embedded in particular linguistic and other cultural conventions, although he ultimately wants to reject the claim, which many communitarians wish to make, that this is the objectively correct way of seeing the self. It may be a useful view with which to operate, and we can call it 'true' if we have a pragmatist's understanding of what it means for a statement to be 'true', but that is as far as he wishes to go.

Rorty's alternative to **foundationalism** proceeds on another provisional assumption that moral beliefs are rooted in empathy and sympathy, revolving around the feeling that cruelty is the worst thing that people can suffer. His conversion strategy is captured in the rather playful phrase 'the telling of long, sad, sentimental stories': moral reformation among non-liberals, he thinks, will come about ultimately through the manipulation of their sentiments, to get them to care about other human beings by establishing an empathetic identification, not to treat groups of them as 'Other' by, for example, discriminating between them on grounds of race. We describe and redescribe our way of looking at things in order to redescribe the views of our opponents and as a means of getting them to feel about such matters in different ways. This is not justification in the sense of providing independent reasons for adopting principles; the adoption is taken for granted in the sense that redescription ('storytelling') does not suspend commitment in the search for such reasons. And Rorty suggests that philosophical writing is ill-suited to this task; hence he has suggested that philosophy might best be superseded by literature as the means by which moral educators conduct the task of such sentimental manipulation.

Rorty's own beguiling writing style, in turn eloquent and ironic, playful and committed, helps to illuminate the possibilities for this strategy. But it can carry one far too rapidly towards conclusions that are, on more careful consideration, perplexing and contentious. We might, for example, suspect that **foundationalism** surreptitiously lingers on in his thought, for the provisional assumptions that he avowedly makes might seem to operate in much the same way as those he derides. Conversely, we might contest the claim that morality can do without the rational, universalised support that foundations can give it: what authority can it have over others if it is simply relative to how I and my fellow liberals feel about things? Isn't Rorty simply wrong to think he has sufficient resources to resist normative relativism and the forces of immoral barbarism against which it leaves itself nothing to say?

For a political theory, another crucial issue for liberals is whether Rorty's work helps us to theorise the 'political' at all. Recall that for liberals the 'political' refers primarily to the exercise of power by some over others, and it was their paramount concern to demonstrate how those with power acquired the authority to exercise it. The passages reproduced below typify Rorty's almost complete indifference to this question, which surely becomes serious when we consider how we deal with people who are not swayed to the human-rights culture by sad and sentimental stories (and history demonstrates how numerous they are). 'Storytelling' in whatever form would seem to be a quintessentially persuasive, consensual business, and any account of politics must tell us how to handle social problems which are not resolved by such means. Surely Rorty would not be happy to leave the unpersuaded rights-abusers be? But would he be able to describe the imposition of human rights in any other than culturally imperialistic terms? That 'we liberals are imposing our way of life on you non-liberals' seems to betray all the arrogance the liberal justificatory project seeks, by reasoned public-justificatory argument, to dispel.

RAWLSIAN POLITICAL LIBERALISM

This third form of Liberalism may be regarded as a way of mediating the differences between the first two: rejecting the Enlightenment **foundationalism** of Gewirth without jettisoning the practice of philosophical justification and, interestingly, addressing the problem of political justification much more plainly. Rawls's *political liberalism*, definitively laid out in the book of the same name, critically engages with his own *A Theory of Justice*. This argued that the principles of justice we should affirm are those which would be chosen in a hypothetical **'original position'** by rational moral agents who know nothing of their own particular identity, abilities and tastes so that their choices are unaffected by any particular personal inclinations leading them away from a concern with the interests of all as equals (Rawls, 1971). He dubs the central concern of his later work the problem of 'stability': how to present arguments for principles of justice, crystallised in devices such as the **original position**, without relying upon beliefs and ideas that might *reasonably* be rejected, namely, those over which we should expect free-thinking rational people living in democratic societies to disagree (see Rawls, 1996: Introduction).

In such a world, Rawls thinks that philosophy has a crucial role to play in illuminating the possibility of agreement on the principles that govern the fundamental social institutions, which is what for him politics is centrally about. The first extract (reproduced below) is a succinct defence of the abstractive analytic method: when we are unable to find agreement from the perspective of our legitimately conflicting overall beliefs and commitments, which Rawls calls 'comprehensive doctrines' (such as religions), we need to step back from them in order to discover other grounds upon which we might after all agree. By setting comprehensive doctrines aside, it seeks to *abstain* from passing judgement on them. Avoiding religious arguments in politics is not to regard their claims as wrong, merely inappropriate or unreasonable to expect everyone freely to accept. What he calls 'reasonable justification' thus conducted is a practical search for consensus. But it is also fired by an urgent moral conviction, as Rawls makes plain: for the belief that consensual justice is possible cannot be discarded if we are to care at all about how we are governed. 'Abstract' the theory may be in its method, but it claims to address the most urgent of 'real-world' concerns.

The interview with Rawls (reproduced here also) neatly summarises the essence of his political liberalism. Recalling that, when arguing about a fundamental political question, we are debating an issue whose resolution will be backed up by the use of political power, political Liberalism insists that its solution should be one that it is reasonable for all the subjects of the political power in question to accept. Hence the justification cannot be personal in the sense of drawing upon one's personally justified moral convictions which are in turn drawn from one's comprehensive doctrine. It must exemplify *public reason*: addressing only fundamental political questions, drawing upon ideas implicit in the political culture of a constitutional democracy. Its key idea is that, whatever moral beliefs and ideals we regard as true by virtue of our comprehensive doctrines, we would consider it unreasonable to offer these as justifications for coercively enforced laws to other citizens who might reasonably reject them. For political justification, we should set these beliefs aside and say that, as citizens, we can all accept as 'reasonable' (as opposed to 'true') the ideas implicit in the constitutional culture of the system which constitutes us as citizens. The argument about physician-assisted suicide illustrates this well. My religion tells me suicide is wrong, but because others may reasonably disagree with my religion I ought not to use it in arguments about whether it should be permitted by law. 'Public reason' enjoins me to address this question using ideas all citizens could accept: our shared constitutionally agreed right to liberty, say. So I may be led to conclude that it is reasonable to allow people the right to choose euthanasia on this basis, even though I don't regard it as 'true' in any metaphysical sense.

Now, it has become clear for Rawls that the public-reason ideal is more of a regulative, aspirational aim than a hard-and-fast rule on how politics should be conducted. He is not committed to the view that there is actual consensus on the kind of issue he broaches (hence the use of the phrase 'what it is reasonable to expect people to accept'). He knows that even this kind of consensus will be unavailable on many issues, in which case he considers a constitutionally regulated majoritarianism to be the most publicly acceptable way of resolving such disputes. He is also aware that more than one position could be plausibly articulated from a fund of public ideas, and his 'proviso' concedes that a blanket exclusion of comprehensive-doctrine argument from the **public sphere** might be an unacceptable limit on free speech.

Nevertheless, despite these qualifications and the specific localisation of his concerns to constitutional democracies, although Rawls does apply the same method to international law (Rawls, 1999), it is apposite to wonder whether political Liberalism aspires to a level of agreement on certain political questions that it is in fact *unreasonable* to expect in such societies. Does it have to suppress an appropriate sensitivity to diversity in hoping that citizens could set aside their differences to reason politically on the basis of ostensibly shareable commitments *qua* citizens of the same polity? Aren't there many fervent religious believers, for example, who simply can't put aside their faith in the way Rawls suggests without directly undermining it, particularly if public-reason arguments would draw them to opposing conclusions?

One way that some critics have expressed this reservation is to query the purely consensualist understanding of the 'political' in Rawls's theory. They suggest that, by believing or hoping that disputes over political fundamentals have been settled in the shareable understanding of what it means to be a citizen of a constitutional democracy, his 'political' Liberalism *begins* at a point *beyond* the processes by which such settlement is achieved. Surely, they say, politics must also be about what takes us to that point – if ever we can get there in the first place – and this leads them to regard the Rawlsian account as paradoxically 'anti-political'. Further, if such consensus is chimerical in modern society, then politics will have to be much more overtly and exclusively about coping with differences and conflicts. We might still do what we can to reason publicly in a Rawlsian way, but it has become too utopian an aspiration upon which to base our account of how politics should be conducted.

AGONISTIC LIBERALISM: A POLITICS OF CIVIL ASSOCIATION

The final version of Liberalism we will examine suggests one way to conceptualise a liberal justification in the much more radically pluralistic context implied in these criticisms of Rawls. Rather eclectic in its sources, it rejects the idea that the Rawlsian way of thinking politically is the way to resist barbarism (as is implied in the extract from *Political Liberalism*), but it steadfastly insists that the foundationalist aspirations of Enlightenment justifications are to be avoided. Following John Gray, we may dub it 'agonistic liberalism' (Gray, 1995b), derived from the Greek term *agon* to denote a potentially ceaseless conflict of values. It is a Liberalism which is designed not to settle the conflict generated by value pluralism but to accommodate, contain and live with it as a permanent feature of social life.

The extract from Isaiah Berlin's 'The Pursuit of the Ideal' renders vivid its conception of pluralism. Recall that Gewirth discerns a universal rational core of liberal morality at the heart of our conception of agency, Rorty glosses over any pluralism with which 'we liberals' have to live among 'ourselves', and Rawls thinks that pluralism is something that it is 'reasonable' to expect in comprehensive doctrines beyond the monistic, shareable commitments of citizenship. For Berlin, pluralism is clearly a much more profound and ineradicable fact of life, and he emphasises that we are thus 'doomed' to choose between the conflicting, **incommensurable** (unrankable) values that confront us.

Berlin's Liberalism therefore rejects the ideas that liberal principles are foundationally universal and that they can be shared as part of citizens' otherwise diverse moral outlooks within particular societies. It is based instead on two distinctive claims. The first is rather surprising given the apparently fundamental nature of Berlin's pluralist thesis: it turns out that we *can* actually postulate a 'universal minimum morality', ostensibly much thinner than Liberalism itself but enough to specify the very bare conditions that would make a form of life one that is fit for humans to live by. In general form, it is premised upon the avoidance of extremes of suffering and thus acts as a bar to outright normative relativism: evils such as Nazism have no place in the panoply of acceptable plural values.

Although this universal morality is not itself enough to mount an irresistible case for Liberalism, Berlin argues that it sets the terms which specify morally acceptable ways of life – and that 'managing' pluralism rather than trying to overcome it with a 'politics of perfection' is likely to make social life go better simply because this is a reconciliation with our pluralist reality, not an attempt to overcome it. But the liberal solution, with its politics of equal freedom and toleration, has no necessary universal authority: some societies have developed it as their way of life and it deserves support on those grounds, but others may proceed on different lines.

The localised, provisional, contingent nature of the liberal order is a feature of the justification for Liberalism that Gray discerns in the work of Michael Oakeshott, a philosopher often regarded as a conservative (and treated as such elsewhere in this volume). The Oakeshottian idea of Liberalism as a civil association may not be the only way in which an agonistic Liberalism may be conceptualised, but it has garnered attention in recent years because of the perceived attractiveness of the idea (particularly to those in postcommunist states who suffered under the 'enterprise-association' politics of Marxism-Leninism) that the liberal order is one that has no ends of its own but exists simply to 'facilitate' the mutual activities of its members as they pursue their own specific, diverse purposes. This *alone* is its justification, as the way in which certain societies have learned to cope with pluralism. For Oakeshott, there is no metaphysical foundation to demonstrate the universal authority of this politics; only historical experience and practice give rise and hence 'justify' it in the specific contexts where it has arisen. Gray thinks the contingent facts of pluralist life in many modern societies mean that civil-associationist forms of politics may have much to recommend them. But 'recommendation' here is really no more than suggestive advice which others may justifiably decline. Further, Oakeshottian politics is akin to a Hobbesian *modus vivendi*, as societies never overcome the need for adaptive techniques to cope with pluralism, meaning that we must always recognise the essential contingency and hence revisability of any political settlement. No 'hallucinatory' liberal philosophy, universalising and freezing the authority of the liberal order, and no perfectionist aspirations to overcome pluralism, often voiced in contemporary democracy, should lead us astray from this fact.

Constructed thus, agonistic Liberalism seems an unambitious form of politics and uninspiring in what it purports to achieve. But, for its supporters, this is one of its very great virtues. Resting the justification of Liberalism on its ability to accommodate and facilitate diversity alone suggests that we need only expect a 'patchwork' of reasons to hold in the personal justifications citizens give themselves as to why they support it, or at least are prepared to put up with it, with the state itself having to identify itself with none of them.

A central question, however, must be whether liberals could be happy with the essentially contingent nature of the defence it offers for liberalism. The Hobbesianism in its veins issues the warning: the constantly shifting forces in society that a *modus vivendi* approach seeks to balance may not always lead us towards a liberal solution. Keeping powerful anti-liberal forces 'on side', so to speak, might require significant compromises of liberal values. Could a liberal really be happy with this? Is there necessarily anything sinister in a liberal state resisting those under its auspices who would challenge the liberal order with justificatory arguments which are based upon the specific purpose of maintaining a liberal society as something which is worthwhile in itself regardless of any contingent trends to the contrary? Could a liberal state ever avoid having to commit itself to very specific liberal purposes? To say that civil association could or should ever be impartial with respect to such liberal goals may be a dangerous chimera if one truly wishes to resist those barbaric forces that may threaten existing political settlements.

CONCLUSION

The questions that have been raised about the four justificatory liberalisms presented here suggest that their plausibility rests at least in part upon their ability to avoid the following two problems:

1. the justification beginning with certain assumptions that effectively beg the question – assuming from the start what the justificatory process is meant to establish and hence surreptitiously guaranteeing its outcome in advance.
2. the justification employing arguments which do not guarantee a liberal outcome.

We must consider the possibility that the implied ideal scenario – a justification which does not proceed from assumptions that embody part of its intended outcome and yet which guarantees a liberal result – is actually unavailable. Many would argue that justificatory argument is an inevitably limited enterprise in the sense that (1) is always to some degree unavoidable. Perhaps we have to take certain beliefs for granted in asking ourselves whether a certain belief is justified. All of what you believe you know, for example, depends upon its justification that you are not just a disembodied brain in a vat of fluid being electronically stimulated to have the identity, experiences and memory that 'you' think 'you' have. But do we have to infer from this absolutely unverifiable possibility that in fact nothing of what we believe can be justified? Is it not better to say that the demand to justify our beliefs, though appropriate, invariably proceeds from certain substantive 'start-up' assumptions that cannot themselves be subjected to that demand; that moral and political justificatory arguments cannot begin from nothing, and some moral assumptions must already be in place for them to develop?

Given that, as we noted above, liberals will typically *not* suspend their commitment to their principles prior to the discovery of a suitable philosophical justification for them, the degree of question-begging in justificatory argument should not surprise us. It may in fact suggest that one function of justificatory argument is to clarify, refine and tease out the implications of the moral ideas from which we proceed – a process perhaps as much of self-clarification or self-disclosure (expressing and illuminating our basic commitments) as of leading others towards the sharing of our beliefs. Such 'confessional' interpretations of the justificatory project may explain the increasing interest in genealogical analyses of liberal morality, seeking to think afresh about the causes and effects of such commitments in our self-understandings.

This somewhat introverted account of 'justification' is, however, likely to be inadequate when thinking about reason-giving to others who do not share sufficiently similar 'start-up' assumptions. Whatever the level of support for Liberalism today, there are disturbing grounds for thinking that this problem will not diminish in the foreseeable future. Indeed, it may increase given that it is hardly obvious (*contra* Francis Fukuyama) that liberal-democratic principles and politics will prove to be optimal for dealing with the ever more urgent problems of the environment, sustainable development and international justice. Liberals may rightly suspect that the need for robust liberal justifications will grow as the liberal order strains to cope with these issues.

But reaching out to those whose beliefs are too dissimilar for the 'question-begging' forms of argument to work may instead require arguments that, because they lack initial pro-liberal assumptions, may not guarantee a permanent advocacy of liberalism. The kind of historicised, contingent defence of Liberalism offered by agonistic Liberalism might become the doctrine's best line of defence. If this deflates the hubris of those liberals who never think that their beliefs and practices need to be justified, then this modest attitude might serve as a useful reminder of the fragility and potential impermanence of the liberal achievement – suggesting that the liberal justificatory project may only ever be provisionally satisfied, never permanently settled.

'THE EPISTEMOLOGY OF HUMAN RIGHTS' BY ALAN GEWIRTH

At the time of writing, Alan Gewirth is Edward Carson Waller Distinguished Service Professor of Philosophy in the Human Rights Program at the University of Chicago. His work focuses on the philosophical and (as here) epistemological basis to human rights. Key books include *Reason and Morality* (University of Chicago Press, 1978), *The Community of Rights* (University of Chicago Press, 1996) and *Self-fulfilment* (Princeton University Press, 1998). In the extract reproduced here, we can see how Gewirth tries to provide a logical and consistent basis for arguments about human rights. Starting from basic claims concerning the nature of human action, Gewirth derives a general principle that must be accepted if we are not to fall into irrationality and inconsistency. Compare this sort of foundationalist approach with that of Rorty, also included in this section.

'THE EPISTEMOLOGY OF HUMAN RIGHTS' (1984)*

Alan Gewirth

Moral and other practical precepts . . . tell persons to *act* in many different ways. But amid these differences, the precepts all assume that the persons addressed by them can control their behaviour by their unforced choice with a view to achieving whatever the precepts require. All actions as envisaged by moral and other practical precepts, then, have two *generic features*. One is *voluntariness* or *freedom*, in that the agents control or can control their behaviour by their unforced choice while having knowledge of relevant circumstances. The other generic feature is *purposiveness* or *intentionality*, in that the agents aim to attain some end or goal which constitutes their reason for acting; this goal may consist either in the action itself or in something to be achieved by the action.

Now, let us take any agent A, defined as an actual or prospective performer of actions in the sense just indicated. When he performs an action, he can be described as saying or thinking:

(1) 'I do X for end or purpose E'.

---

* From Alan Gewirth, 'The Epistemology of Human Rights', *Social Philosophy and Policy*, 1:2 (1984).

Since E is something he unforcedly chooses to attain, he thinks E has sufficient value to merit his moving from quiescence to action in order to attain it. Hence, from his standpoint, (1) entails

(2) 'E is good'.

Note that (2) is here presented in quotation marks, as something said or thought by the agent A. The kind of goodness he here attributes to E need not be moral goodness; its criterion varies with whatever purpose E the agent may have in doing X. But what it shows already is that, in the context of action, the 'fact–value gap' is already bridged, for by the very *fact* of engaging in action, every agent must implicitly accept for himself a certain *value* judgement about the value or goodness of the purposes for which he acts.

Now, in order to act for E, which he regards as good, the agent A must have the proximate necessary conditions of action. These conditions are closely related to the generic features of action[:] . . . voluntariness or freedom, and purposiveness or intentionality. But when purposiveness is extended to the general conditions required for success in achieving one's purposes, it becomes a more extensive condition which I shall call *well-being*. Viewed from the standpoint of action, then, well-being consists in having the various substantive conditions and abilities, ranging from life and physical integrity to self-esteem and education, that are required if a person is to act either at all or with general chances of success in achieving the purposes for which he acts. So freedom and well-being are the necessary conditions of action and of successful action in general. Hence, from the agent's standpoint, from (2) 'E is good', there follows

(3) 'My freedom and well-being are necessary goods'.

This may also be put as

(4) 'I must have freedom and well-being',

where this 'must' is a practical-prescriptive requirement, expressed by the agent, as to his having the necessary conditions of his action.

Now, from (4) there follows

(5) 'I have rights to freedom and well-being'.

To show that (5) follows from (4), let us suppose that the agent were to deny (5). In that case, because of the correlativity of rights and strict 'oughts', he would also have to deny

(6) 'All other persons ought at least to refrain from removing or interfering with my freedom and well-being'.

By denying (6), he must accept

(7) 'It is not the case that all other persons ought at least to refrain from removing or interfering with my freedom and well-being'.

By accepting (7), he must also accept

> (8) 'Other persons may (i.e. it is permissible that other persons) remove or interfere with my freedom and well-being'.

And by accepting (8), he must accept

> (9) 'I may not (i.e. it is permissible that I not) have freedom and well-being'.

But (9) contradicts (4), which said 'I must have freedom and well-being'. Since every agent must accept (4), he must reject (9). And since (9) follows from the denial of (5), 'I have rights to freedom and well-being', every agent must also reject that denial. Hence, every agent logically must accept (5).

[. . .]

What I have shown so far . . . is that the concept of a right, as a justified claim or entitlement, is logically involved in all action as a concept that signifies for every agent his claim and requirement that he have, and at least not be prevented from having, the necessary conditions that enable him to act in pursuit of his purposes. I shall . . . refer to these rights as *generic rights* . . .

[. . .]

It must be noted, however, that, so far, the criterion of these rights that every agent must claim for himself is only prudential, not moral, in that the criterion consists for each agent in his own needs of agency in pursuit of his own purposes. Even though the right-claim is addressed to all other persons as a correlative 'ought'-judgement, still its justifying criterion for each agent consists in the necessary conditions of his own action.

To see how this prudential right-claim also becomes a moral right, we must go through some further steps. Now, the sufficient as well as necessary reason or justifying condition for which every agent must hold that he has rights to freedom and well-being is that he is a prospective purposive agent. Hence, he must accept

> (10) 'I have rights to freedom and well-being because I am a prospective purposive agent',

where this 'because' signifies a sufficient as well as a necessary justifying condition.

Suppose some agent were to reject (10), and were to insist, instead, that the only reason he has the generic rights is that he has some more restrictive characteristic R. Examples of R would include: being an American, being a professor, being an *Übermensch*, being male, being a capitalist or a proletarian, being white, being named 'Wordsworth Donisthorpe', and so forth. Thus, the agent would be saying

(11) 'I have rights to freedom and well-being *only* because I am R',

where 'R' is something more restrictive than being a prospective purposive agent.

Such an agent, however, would contradict himself. For he would then be in the position of saying that if he did *not* have R, he would *not* have the generic rights, so that he would have to accept

(12) 'I do not have rights to freedom and well-being'.

But we saw before that, as an agent, he *must* hold that he has rights to freedom and well-being. Hence, he must drop his view that R alone is the sufficient justifying condition of his having the generic rights, so that he must accept that simply being a prospective purposive agent is a sufficient as well as a necessary justifying condition of his having rights to freedom and well-being. Hence, he must accept (10).

Now by virtue of accepting (10), the agent must also accept

(13) 'All prospective purposive agents have rights to freedom and well-being'.

(13) follows from (10) because of the principle of universalisation. If some predicate P belongs to some subject S because that subject has some general quality Q (where this 'because' signifies a sufficient reason), then that predicate logically must belong to every subject that has Q. Hence, since the predicate of having the generic rights belongs to the original agent because he is a prospective purposive agent, he logically must admit that every purposive agent has the generic rights.

At this point the rights become moral ones, and not only prudential, on that meaning of 'moral' where it has both the formal component of setting forth practical requirements that are categorically obligatory, and the material component that those requirements involve taking favourable account of the interests of persons other than or in addition to the agent or the speaker. When the original agent now says that *all* prospective purposive agents have rights to freedom and well-being, he is logically committed to respecting and hence taking favourable account of the interests of all other persons with regard to their also having the necessary good or conditions of action.

Since all other persons are actual or potential recipients of his action, every agent is logically committed to accepting

(14) 'I ought to act in accord with the generic rights of my recipients as well as of myself'.

This requirement can also be expressed as the general moral principle:

(15) 'Act in accord with the generic rights of your recipients as well as of yourself'.

I shall call this the Principle of Generic Consistency (PGC), since it combines the formal consideration of consistency with the material consideration of the generic features and rights of action. As we have seen, every agent, on pain of contradiction and hence of irrationality, must accept this principle as governing all his interpersonal actions.

'HUMAN RIGHTS, RATIONALITY, AND SENTIMENTALITY' BY RICHARD RORTY

At the time of writing, Rorty is Professor of Comparative Literature and, by courtesy, of Philosophy at Stanford University. He is a very well-known and influential philosopher working within the tradition of American Pragmatism. Pragmatism, broadly speaking, rejects metaphysical speculation and turns attention to the empirical experience of the world. Rather than insist that our ideas and practices match up to some abstract notion of truth, the pragmatist emphasises the usefulness of our conceptions and asks us to consider what it is we want to do with our ideas, what they are for, and how well they work. Rorty's most important books include *Philosophy and the Mirror of Nature* (Blackwell, 1980) in which he systematically challenges the notion that philosophy should be concerned with matching up to a true picture of the world, and *Contingency, Irony and Solidarity* (Cambridge University Press, 1989) in which he develops a pragmatist theory of language in a political and philosophical direction, redescribing liberalism in terms of solidarity. He has also produced notable collections of essays such as *Consequences of Pragmatism: Essays 1972–1980* (Harvester Wheatsheaf, 1982) and three volumes of papers and writings published by Cambridge University Press: *Objectivity, Relativism, and Truth* (1991), *Essays on Heidegger and Others* (1991) and *Truth and Moral Progress* (1998). See also *Philosophy and Social Hope* (Penguin, 1999). It is worth comparing his approach to those of others presented in this volume such as Collingwood, Gadamer and Foucault and thinking about the ways in which his version of political pluralism differs from or overlaps with that advanced by Laclau, Mouffe or Connolly.

In the extract reproduced here, we can see how much Rorty's form of Liberalism differs from that of Gewirth. Where the latter began from a basic principle about the way in which all human beings act, Rorty rejects such a foundationalist procedure, embracing instead (and in marked contrast) an approach to rights based on appreciating their historical and contingent emergence. Instead of the search for a timeless human essence or an ultimate rational foundation, he advocates what he regards as a more efficacious approach based on emotional stories that encourage our identification with, and so sympathy for, others. For Rorty, the political question is not why should we accept human rights but how we can come to appreciate them better.

'HUMAN RIGHTS, RATIONALITY, AND SENTIMENTALITY' (1993)*

Richard Rorty

Philosophers have tried to . . . [explain] what is essential to being human. Plato suggested that there is a big difference between us and animals, a difference worthy of respect and cultivation. He thought that human beings have a special added ingredient that puts them in a different ontological category from brutes. Respect for this ingredient provides a reason for people to be nice to each other. Anti-Platonists like Nietzsche reply that attempts to get people to stop murdering, raping, and castrating one another are, in the long run, doomed to failure – for the real truth about human nature is that we are a uniquely nasty and dangerous kind of animal.

[. . .]

As I see it, one important intellectual advance that has been made in [the last] century is the steady decline in interest in this quarrel between Plato and Nietzsche about what we are really like. There is a growing willingness to neglect the question 'What is our nature?' and to substitute the question 'What can we make of ourselves?' We are much less inclined than our ancestors were to take 'theories of human nature' seriously, much less inclined to take ontology or history or ethology as a guide to life. We are much less inclined to pose the ontological question 'What *are* we?' because we have come to see that the main lesson of both history and anthropology is our extraordinary malleability. We are coming to think of ourselves as the flexible, protean, self-shaping animal rather than as the rational animal or the cruel animal.

One of the shapes we have recently assumed is that of a human-rights culture. I borrow the term 'human-rights culture' from the Argentinian jurist and philosopher Eduardo Rabossi. . . . [He] argues that philosophers should think of this culture as a new, welcome fact of the post-Holocaust world. Rabossi wants them to stop trying to get behind or beneath this fact, stop trying to detect and defend its so-called philosophical presuppositions. On Rabossi's view, philosophers like Alan Gewirth are wrong to argue that human rights cannot depend upon historical facts.

[. . .]

---

* From Richard Rorty, 'Human Rights, Rationality, and Sentimentality', Stephen Shute and Susan Hurley (eds), *On Human Rights: Oxford Amnesty Lectures 1993* (New York: Basic Books, 1993).

Human-rights foundationalism is the continuing attempt by quasi-Platonists to win, at last, a final victory over their opponents. Rabossi's claim that this attempt is *outmoded* seems to me both true and important . . . [here] I shall enlarge upon, and defend, Rabossi's claim that the question of whether human beings really *have* the rights enumerated in the Helsinki Declaration is not worth raising. In particular I shall defend the claim that nothing relevant to moral choice separates human beings from animals except historically contingent facts of the world, cultural facts.

This claim is sometimes called 'cultural relativism' by those who indignantly reject it. One reason they reject it is that such relativism seems to them incompatible with the fact that our human-rights culture is superior to other cultures. I quite agree that ours is morally superior, but I do not think that this superiority counts in favor of the existence of a universal human nature. It would only do so if we assumed that a claim of moral superiority entails a claim to superior knowledge – assumed that such a claim is ill-founded if not backed up by knowledge of a distinctively human attribute. But it is not clear why 'respect for human dignity' – our sense that the differences between Serbs and Muslim, Christian and infidel, gay and straight, male and female should not matter – must presuppose the existence of any such attribute.

Traditionally, the name of the shared human attribute that supposedly 'grounds' morality is 'rationality'. Cultural relativism is associated with irrationalism because it denies the existence of morally relevant transcultural facts. To agree with Rabossi one must, indeed, be irrationalist in that sense. But one need not be irrationalist in the sense of ceasing to make one's web of belief as coherent, and as perspicuously structured, as possible. . . . We [philosophers] see our task as a matter of making our own culture – the human-rights culture – more self-conscious and more powerful, rather than of demonstrating its superiority to other cultures by an appeal to something transcultural.

We think that the most philosophy can hope to do is to summarise our culturally influenced intuitions about the right thing to do in various situations. The summary is effected by formulating a generalization from which these intuitions can be deduced . . . We see the point of formulating such summarizing generalizations as increasing the predictability, and thus the power and efficiency, of our institutions, thereby heightening the sense of shared moral identity that brings us together in a moral community.

Foundationalist philosophers . . . have hoped to provide independent support for such summarizing generalizations. They would like to infer these generalizations from further premises, premises capable of being known to be true independently of the truth of the moral intuitions that have been summarized. Such premises *are* supposed to justify our intuitions, by providing premises from which the content of those intuitions can be deduced. I shall lump all such premises together under the label 'claims to knowledge about the nature of human beings'. . . . To claim such knowledge is to claim to know something that, though not itself a moral intuition, can *correct* moral intuitions. It is essential to this idea of moral knowledge that a whole community might come to *know* that most of its salient intuitions about the right thing to do were wrong.

But now suppose we ask: *is* there this sort of knowledge? What kind of question is *that*? On the traditional view, it is a philosophical question, belonging to a branch of epistemology known as 'meta-ethics'. But on the pragmatist view I favor, it is a question of efficiency: a question about how best to grab hold of history – how best to bring about the utopia sketched by Enlightenment. If the activities of those who attempt to achieve this sort of knowledge seem of little use in actualizing this utopia, that is a reason to think there is no such knowledge. If it seems that most of the work of changing moral intuitions is being done by manipulating our feelings rather than by increasing our knowledge, that is a reason to think there is no knowledge of the sort that [foundationalist] philosophers . . . hoped to get.

[. . .]

We pragmatists argue from the fact that the emergence of the human-rights culture seems to owe nothing to increased moral knowledge, and everything to hearing sad and sentimental stories, to the conclusion that there is probably no knowledge of the sort Plato envisaged. We go on to argue that since no useful work seems to be done by insisting on a purportedly ahistorical human nature, there probably is no such nature, or at least nothing in that nature that is relevant to our moral choices.

In short, my doubts about the effectiveness of appeals to moral knowledge are doubts about causal efficacy, not about epistemic status.

[. . .]

The best, and probably the only, argument for putting foundationalism behind us is . . . it would be more efficient to do so, because it would let us concentrate our energies on manipulating sentiments, on sentimental education. That sort of education gets people of different kinds sufficiently well acquainted with one another that they are less tempted to think of those different from themselves as only quasi-human. The goal of this sort of manipulation of sentiment is to expand the reference of the terms 'our kind of people' and 'people like us'.

Plato thought that the philosopher's task was to answer questions like 'Why should I be moral? Why is it rational to be moral? Why is it in my interest to be moral? Why is it in the interest of human beings as such to be moral?' He thought this because he thought that the best way to deal with people like Thrasymachus and Gorgias was to demonstrate to them that they had an interest of which they were unaware, an interest in being rational, in acquiring self-knowledge. Plato thereby saddled us with a distinction between the true and the false self.

[. . .]

By insisting that he could re-educate people who had matured without acquiring appropriate moral sentiments by invoking a higher power than sentiment, the power of reason, Plato got moral philosophy off on the wrong foot. He led moral philosophers to concentrate on the rather rare figure of the psychopath, the person who has no concern for any human being other than himself. Moral philosophy has systematically neglected the much more common case: the person whose treatment of a rather narrow range of featherless bipeds is morally impeccable, but who remains indifferent to the suffering of those outside this range, the ones he thinks of as pseudo-humans.

Plato set things up so that moral philosophers think they have failed unless they convince the rational egotist that he should not be an egotist – convince him by telling him about his true, unfortunately neglected self. But the rational egotist is not the problem. The problem is the gallant and honorable Serb who sees Muslims as circumcised dogs. It is the brave soldier and good comrade who loves and is loved by his mates, but who thinks of women as dangerous, malevolent whores and bitches.

Plato thought that the way to get people to be nicer to each other was to point out what they all had in common – rationality. But it does little good to point out, to the people I have just described, that many Muslims and women are good at mathematics or engineering or jurisprudence. Resentful young Nazi toughs were quite aware that many Jews were clever and learned, but this only added to the pleasure they took in beating such Jews. Nor does it do much good to get such people to read Kant and agree that one should not treat rational agents simply as means. For everything turns on who counts as a fellow human being, as a rational agent in the only relevant sense – the sense in which rational agency is synonymous with membership in *our* moral community.

[. . .]

[O]ne will [come to] see it as the moral educator's task not to answer the rational egotist's question 'Why should I be moral?' but rather to answer the much more frequently posed question 'Why should I care about a stranger, a person who is no kin to me, a person whose habits I find disgusting?' The traditional answer to the latter question is 'Because kinship and custom are morally irrelevant, irrelevant to the obligations imposed by the recognition of membership in the same species'. This has never been very convincing, since it begs the question at issue: whether mere species membership *is*, in fact, a sufficient surrogate for closer kinship.

[. . .]

A better sort of answer is the sort of long, sad, sentimental story that begins: 'Because this is what it is like to be in her situation – to be far from home, among strangers', or 'Because she might become your daughter-in-law', or 'Because her mother would grieve for her'. Such stories, repeated and varied over the centuries, have induced us, the rich, safe, powerful people, to tolerate and even to cherish powerless people – people whose appearance or habits or beliefs at first seemed an insult to our own moral identity, our sense of the limits of permissible human variation.

'POLITICAL PHILOSOPHY AND ABSTRACTION' BY JOHN RAWLS: AN INTERVIEW
WITH BERNARD PRUSAK

Before his death in 2002, the American political philosopher John Rawls (b. 1921) was James Bryant Conant University Professor, Emeritus, at Harvard University. With the publication of *A Theory of Justice* in 1971 (available in various editions), he became one of the most influential living political philosophers in the English-speaking world, and the book has defined debates in Northern American political thought. Subsequently, and particularly in the light of communitarian critiques, in *Political Liberalism* (Columbia University Press, 1993) Rawls revised and adapted his theory into an explanation and defence of Liberalism in general. Of late, a number of collections of papers, essays and lectures as well as some restatements have appeared. These include: *Liberty, Equality and Law: Selected Tanner Lectures on Moral Philosophy* (Cambridge University Press, 1987), *John Rawls: Collected Papers* (Harvard University Press, 1999), *The Law of Peoples* (Harvard University Press, 1999) and *Lectures on the History of Moral Philosophy* (Harvard University Press, 2000). The first of the extracts from Rawls is from *Political Liberalism*. In it, Rawls explains that the purpose of abstraction in political theory is to help in the resolution of the disputes we fall into. We need to establish the basic ideas of a political culture and from there establish how something like justice may reasonably be conceived. Not as dryly analytic as Gewirth but much less playful and poetic than Rorty, Rawls seeks a reasonable level of agreement and avers that without the hope of its attainment we automatically consign ourselves to miscry. This means, as shown in the second extract, an interview, that we need to distinguish between a fully comprehensive doctrine and the specifically political liberalism he advocates. The latter deals only with the basic structure of society that allows people to, reasonably, pursue their lives in line with their own comprehensive doctrines. In this way, Rawls responds to the charge that his Liberalism would be intolerant of strong value systems such as those deriving from religious belief. Such can co-exist in a liberal state but must accept that they should put forward arguments that all reasonable citizens could assent to and that in this way their own liberty, their right to pursue their 'good', is protected.

'POLITICAL PHILOSOPHY AND ABSTRACTION' (1996)*

John Rawls

In political philosophy, the work of abstraction is set in motion by deep political conflicts. Only ideologues and visionaries fail to experience deep conflicts of political values and conflicts between these and non-political values. Profound and long-lasting controversies set the stage for the idea of reasonable justification as a practical and not as an epistemological or metaphysical problem. We turn to political philosophy when our shared political understandings . . . break down and equally when we are torn within ourselves.

[. . .]

Political philosophy does not, as some have thought, withdraw from society and the world. Nor does it claim to discover what is true by its own distinctive methods of reason apart from any tradition of political thought and practice. No political conception of justice could have weight with us unless it helped to put in order our considered convictions of justice at all levels of generality, from the most general to the most particular.

[. . .]

Political philosophy cannot coerce our considered convictions any more than the principles of logic can. If we feel coerced, it may be because, when we reflect on the matter at hand, values, principles, and standards are so formulated and arranged that they are freely recognized as ones we do, or should, accept. Our feeling coerced is perhaps our being surprised at the consequences of those principles and standards, at the implications of our free recognition. Still, we may reaffirm our more particular judgments and decide instead to modify the proposed conception of justice with its principles and ideals until judgments at all levels of generality are at last in line on due reflection. It is a mistake to think of abstract conceptions and general principles as always overriding our more particular judgments. These two sides of our practical thought . . . are complementary, and to be adjusted to one another so as to fit into a coherent view.

The work of abstraction, then, is not gratuitous: not abstraction for abstraction's sake. Rather, it is a way of continuing public discussion when shared

* From John Rawls, *Political Liberalism*, 2nd edn (New York: Columbia University Press, 1996), pp. 44–6, lxi–lxii.

understandings of lesser generality have broken down. We should be prepared to find that the deeper the conflict, the higher the level of abstraction to which we ascend to get a clear and uncluttered view of its roots. Since the conflicts in the democratic tradition about the nature of toleration and the basis of co-operation for a footing of equality have been persistent, we may suppose they are deep. Therefore, to connect these conflicts with the familiar and the basic, we look to the fundamental ideas in the public political culture and seek to uncover how citizens themselves might, on due reflection, want to conceive of their society as a fair system of co-operation over time. Seen in this context, formulating idealized, which is to say abstract, conceptions of society and person connected with those fundamental ideas is essential to finding a reasonable political conception of justice.

[. . .]

Philosophy . . . may ask whether a just and well-ordered constitutional democracy is possible and what makes it so. . . . The answer we give . . . affects our background thoughts and attitudes about the world as a whole. And it affects these thoughts and attitudes before we come to actual politics, and limits or inspires how we take part in it. Debates about general philosophical questions cannot be the daily stuff of politics, but that does not make these questions without significance, since what we think their answers are will shape the underlying attitudes of the public culture and the conduct of politics. If we take for granted as common knowledge that a just and well-ordered democratic society is impossible, then the quality and tone of those attitudes will reflect that knowledge. A cause of the fall of Weimar's constitutional regime was that none of the traditional elites of Germany supported its constitution or were willing to co-operate to make it work. They no longer believed a decent liberal parliamentary regime was possible. Its time had passed.

[. . .]

The wars of [the twentieth] century with their extreme violence and increasing destructiveness, culminating in the manic evil of the Holocaust, raise in an acute way the question whether political relations must be governed by power and coercion alone. If a reasonably just society that subordinates power to its aim is not possible and people are largely amoral, if not incurably cynical and self-centred, one might ask with Kant whether it is worthwhile for human beings to live on the earth? We must start with the assumption that a reasonably just political society is possible, and for it to be possible, human beings must have a moral nature, not of course a perfect such nature, yet one that can understand, act on, and be sufficiently moved by a reasonable political conception of right and justice to support a society guided by its ideals and principles.

'INTERVIEW WITH BERNARD PRUSAK' (1998)*

John Rawls

BP: [I]n your recent work, *Political Liberalism* and 'The Idea of Public Reason Revisited', religion has become, if not the central theme, at least a major focus. You've had a turn in your interests. Where is this coming from? What's the motivation for this new focus?

JR: Well, that's a good question. I think the basic explanation is that I'm concerned about the survival, historically, of constitutional democracy. I live in a country where 95 or 90 per cent of the people profess to be religious, and maybe they are religious, though my experience of religion suggests that very few people are actually religious in more than a conventional sense. Still, religious faith is an important aspect of American culture and a fact of American political life. So the question is: in a constitutional democracy, how can religious and secular doctrines of all kinds get on together and co-operate in running a reasonably just and effective government? What assumptions would you have to make about religious and secular doctrines, and the political sphere, for these to work together?

BP: Your problem in your recent work, then, is very different from your problem in *A Theory of Justice*.

JR: Yes, I think it is. *A Theory of Justice* was a comprehensive doctrine of liberalism designed to set out a certain classical theory of justice – the theory of the social contract – so as to make it immune to various traditional objections. The difference is that, in *Political Liberalism*, the problem is how do you see religion and comprehensive secular doctrines as compatible with and supportive of the basic institutions of a constitutional regime.

BP: Keep to this new problem, to this question of how to make a liberal constitutional democracy not only receptive, but attractive to religious believers, people who wouldn't call themselves first and foremost liberals, people who live according to a comprehensive doctrine. Now the distinction between a comprehensive doctrine

---

* From John Rawls, Interview with Bernard Prusak, *Commonweal* (January 1998), reprinted in *John Rawls: Collected Papers*, ed. S. Freeman (Cambridge, MA: Harvard University Press, 1999).

and a political conception, in your language, has been difficult for many people to understand. Could you clarify it?

JR: A comprehensive doctrine, either religious or secular, aspires to cover all of life. I mean, if it's a religious doctrine, it talks about our relation to God and the universe; it has an ordering of all the virtues, not only political virtues but moral virtues as well, including the virtues of private life, and the rest. Now we may feel philosophically that it doesn't really cover everything, but it aims to cover everything, and a secular doctrine does also. But a political conception, as I use that term, has a narrower range: it just applies to the basic structure of a society, its institutions, constitutional essentials, matters of basic justice and property, and so on. It covers the right to vote, the political virtues, and the good of political life, but it doesn't intend to cover anything else. I try to show how a political conception can be seen as self-standing, as being able to fit, as a part, into many different comprehensive doctrines.

Now the good of political life is a great political good. It is not a secular good specified by a comprehensive doctrine like those of Kant or J. S. Mill. You could characterize this political good as the good of free and equal citizens recognizing the duty of civility to one another: the duty to give citizens *public reasons* for one's political actions.

BP: To make the distinction clearer and perhaps more concrete, could you discuss a particular example, like physician-assisted suicide? You co-signed the Philosophers' Brief, submitted to the Supreme Court [in 1997]. In the brief, you argue that people have different ways of understanding suffering and that, in a constitutional democracy, no philosophical or religious authority should be able to say how a person should live his or her last days. How, on the question of physician-assisted suicide, does your argument play out?

JR: We wanted the Court to decide the case in terms of what we thought was a basic constitutional right. That's not a matter of religious right, one way or another; it's a constitutional principle. It's said to be part of American liberties that you should be able to decide these fundamental questions as a free citizen. Of course, we know that not everyone agrees with assisted suicide, but people might agree that one has the right to it, even if they're not themselves going to exercise it.

Now, I think that a good argument against this view would be one like Cass Sunstein's. What he says is that it would be very unwise for the Court to establish a right like this which is so controversial. The Court's decision would depend on a philosophical argument of constitutional law and allow a right that a lot of people would object to. This would be my candidate for a good political argument against the Philosophers' Brief. The way to argue against the brief is that the Supreme Court should not, at this stage, take sides either way. It should say – as I think the Court can be interpreted as saying – that, no, we're not going to decide this question, it's being discussed, it may be tried in the states, different states can take different views, and we ought not to pre-empt the constitutional question when we don't have to.

[. . .]

BP: Your overall argument, then, has to do really with the kinds of arguments that should be made within a constitutional democracy. So 'public reason' – your technical term for these kinds of arguments – is not monolithic.

JR: Exactly: the idea of public reason has to do with how questions should be decided, but it doesn't tell you what are the good reasons or correct decisions. You see, the argument in the Philosophers' Brief, as I understand it, was a political argument. The argument by Sunstein is also a political argument.

[. . .]

BP: Now another argument against physician-assisted suicide would be like Michael Walzer's: that the vulnerable population – the elderly, the poor, the abandoned – would be too large, at least at this time, for this right to be granted. This right is fine and well for people with the means to use the law as an instrument of freedom, but for other people it would actually be quite dangerous. Now that would be yet another example of an argument within public reason.

JR: Absolutely. I'm not sure that it's a good argument, but that's another question. Public-reason arguments can be good or bad, just like other arguments. There are many arguments within public reason, and that's the thing to emphasize.

[. . .]

I want to say something here about what in ['The Idea of Public Reason Revisited'] I call the 'proviso', because I think it's important. It's this: any comprehensive doctrine, religious or secular, can be introduced into any political argument at any time, but I argue that people who do this should also present what they believe are public reasons for their argument. So their opinion is no longer just that of one particular party, but an opinion that all members of a society might reasonably agree to, not necessarily that they would agree to. What's important is that people give the kinds of reasons that can be understood and appraised apart from their particular comprehensive doctrines. So the idea of public reason isn't about the right answers to all those questions, but about the kinds of reasons that they ought to be answered by.

BP: A critique of your work is that, really, even though you're open to religiously grounded arguments that could be translated, let's say, into public terms, terms all people could understand, nonetheless you're making a veiled argument for secularism. Now this is something you deny.

JR: Yes, I emphatically deny it. Suppose I said that it is not a veiled argument for secularism any more than it is a veiled argument for religion. Consider: there are two kinds of comprehensive doctrines, religious and secular. Those of religious faith will say I give a veiled argument for secularism, and the latter will say I give a veiled argument for religion. I deny both. Each side presumes the basic ideas of constitutional democracy, so my suggestion is that we can make our political arguments in terms of public reason. Then we stand on common ground. That's how we can understand each other and co-operate.

BP: Let me restate this: the question would be who determines the terms of public reason. A religious believer might say, well, revelation isn't only private – it's here in this book. How come I can't make an argument from this background? Or more to the point, how come I have to argue in terms everybody agrees with, or might agree with? Given who I have to argue with, it seems that those terms slide into secularism. Take the argument for the sacredness of life. The believer might say that this has been revealed. But by having to make arguments in terms everybody recognizes, I'm being asked to renounce the truth as I know it.

[. . .]

JR: No, you're not being asked to renounce it! Of course not. The question is, we have a particular problem. How many religions are there in the United States? How are they going to get on together? One way, which has been the usual way historically, is to fight it out, as in France in the sixteenth century. That's a possibility. But how do you avoid that?

See, what I should do is to turn around and say, what's the better suggestion, what is your solution to it? And I can't see any other solution.

[. . .]

People can make arguments from the Bible if they want to. But I want them to see that they should also give arguments that all reasonable citizens might agree to. Again, what's the alternative? How are you going to get along in a constitutional regime with all these other comprehensive doctrines?

[. . .]

BP: You say, well, what's your alternative, what do you want? In a way, it almost sounds like what you're saying is, look, this is the best way of getting along, this is the best *modus vivendi*. But you want to argue for more than that as well: you want 'stability for the right reasons'. Well, what would those reasons be besides peace – which I think would be a very good reason?

JR: Peace surely is a good reason, yes. But there are other reasons too. I already mentioned the good of political life: the good of free and equal citizens recognizing the duty of civility to one another and supporting the institutions of a constitutional regime. I assume that, in line with Vatican II, Roman Catholics affirm these political institutions. So do many Protestants, Jews, and Muslims.

[. . .]

BP: So the common good would be the good that is common to each citizen, each citizen's good, rather than an overarching good.

JR: The point I would stress is this. You hear that liberalism lacks an idea of the common good, but I think that's a mistake. For example, you might say that, if citizens are acting for the right reasons in a constitutional regime, then regardless of their comprehensive doctrines they want every other citizen to have justice. So you might say they're all working together to do one thing, namely to make sure every citizen has justice. Now that's not the only interest they all have, but it's the single thing they're all trying to do. In my language, they're striving toward one single end, the end of justice for all citizens.

'THE PURSUIT OF THE IDEAL' BY SIR ISAIAH BERLIN

Sir Isaiah Berlin (1909–97), born in Riga, Latvia, was a widely known intellectual, historian, philosopher and essayist holding the Chichele Chair in Social and Political Theory at Oxford University. During the Second World War, he served in the British Information Service in New York and later as First Secretary of the British Embassy in Washington. He was a much-admired philosopher of Liberalism and historian of ideas. Most known for his approach to pluralism, that there are different, incompatible yet still valid conceptions of how to live (and that political life should be based around this irreducible pluralism) and for a famous argument on concepts of liberty, particularly the distinction between negative and positive conceptions of liberty, where the former understands freedom as the absence of restraint and the latter as the provision of the capacity to act in ways of one's own choosing, Berlin did not write long books of political theory but rather essays on a variety of topics. Of the numerous collections, the best and most useful are probably *Four Essays on Liberty* (Oxford University Press, 1969), *The Crooked Timber of Humanity: Chapters in the History of Ideas* (Fontana, 1991) and *Against the Current: Essays in the History of Ideas* (Hogarth Press, 1979). Given Berlin's conjoined interests in historical analysis and pluralism, readers might get a lot out of comparing him to other thinkers whose work has found its way into this text. See, for example, the historical approaches of Collingwood, Gadamer or Foucault and the pluralism of Mouffe or Connolly.

The extract below is typical of Berlin's general political attitude and explains the reasons for his pluralism. A clash of values, he argues, is an irreducible, perhaps essential, element of human existence. To seek a single and final way to resolve all of the conflicts of humanity is bound to end in disaster, and all we can seek is a reasonable equilibrium between competing desires in the hope that we can avoid the worst forms of calamity.

'THE PURSUIT OF THE IDEAL' (1991)*

Sir Isaiah Berlin

What is clear is that values can clash – that is why civilisations are incompatible. They can be incompatible between cultures, or groups in the same culture,

---

* From Sir Isaiah Berlin, 'The Pursuit of the Ideal', *The Crooked Timber of Humanity* (London: Fontana, 1991), pp. 12–19.

or between you and me. You believe in always telling the truth, no matter what; I do not, because I believe that it can sometimes be too painful and too destructive. We can discuss each other's point of view, we can try to reach common ground, but in the end what you pursue may not be reconcilable with the ends to which I find that I have dedicated my life. Values may easily clash within the breast of a single individual; and it does not follow that, if they do, some must be true and others false. Justice, rigorous justice, is for some people an absolute value, but it is not compatible with what may be no less ultimate values for them – mercy, compassion – as arises in concrete cases.

Both liberty and equality are among the primary goals pursued by human beings through many centuries; but total liberty for wolves is death to the lambs, total liberty of the powerful, the gifted, is not compatible with the rights to a decent existence of the weak and the less gifted. . . . Equality may demand the restraint of the liberty of those who wish to dominate; liberty – without some modicum of which there is no choice and therefore no possibility of remaining human as we understand the word – may have to be curtailed in order to make room for social welfare, to feed the hungry, to clothe the naked, to shelter the homeless, to leave room for the liberty of others, to allow justice or fairness to be exercised.

[. . .]

These collisions of values are of the essence of what they are and what we are. If we are told that these contradictions will be solved in some perfect world in which all good things can be harmonised in principle, then we must answer, to those who say this, that the meanings they attach to the names which for us denote the conflicting values are not ours. We must say that the world in which what we see as incompatible values are not in conflict is a world altogether beyond our ken; that principles which are harmonised in this other world are not the principles with which, in our daily lives, we are acquainted; if they are transformed, it is into conceptions not known to us on earth. But it is on earth that we live, and it is here that we must believe and act.

The notion of the perfect whole, the ultimate solution, in which all good things co-exist, seems to me to be not merely unattainable – that is a truism – but conceptually incoherent; I do not know what is meant by a harmony of this kind. Some among the Great Goods cannot live together. That is a conceptual truth. We are doomed to choose, and every choice may entail an irreparable loss. Happy are those who live under a discipline which they accept without question, who freely obey the orders of leaders, spiritual or temporal, whose word is fully accepted as unbreakable law; or those who have, by their own methods, arrived at clear and unshakeable convictions about what to do and what to be that brook no possible doubt. I can only say that those who rest on such comfortable beds of dogma are victims of forms of self-induced myopia, blinkers that may make for contentment, but not for understanding of what it is to be human.

[. . .]

So much for the theoretical objection, a fatal one, it seems to me, to the notion of the perfect state as the proper goal of our endeavours. But there is in addition a more practical socio-psychological obstacle to this, an obstacle that may be put to those whose simple faith, by which humanity has been nourished for so long, is resistant to philosophical arguments of any kind. It is true that some problems can be solved, some ills cured, in both the individual and social life. . . . The children have obtained what their parents and grandparents longed for – greater freedom, greater material welfare, a juster society; but the old ills are forgotten, and the children face new problems, brought about by the very solutions of the old ones, and these, even if they can in turn be solved, generate new situations, and with them new requirements – and so on, for ever – and unpredictably.

We cannot legislate for the unknown consequences of consequences of consequences. Marxists tell us that once the fight is won . . . the new problems that may arise will generate their own solutions, which can be peacefully realised by the united powers of harmonious, classless society. This seems to me to be a piece of metaphysical optimism for which there is no evidence in historical experience. In a society in which the same goals are universally accepted, problems can only be of means, all soluble by technological methods. That is a society in which the inner life of man, the moral and spiritual and aesthetic imagination, no longer speaks at all. Is it for this that men and women should be destroyed or societies enslaved? Utopias have their value – nothing so wonderfully expands the imaginative horizons of human potentialities – but as guides to conduct they can prove literally fatal.

[. . .]

So I conclude that the very notion of a final solution is not only impracticable but, if I am right, and some values cannot but clash, incoherent also. The possibility of a final solution – even if we forget the terrible sense that these words acquired in Hitler's day – turns out to be an illusion; and a very dangerous one. For if one really believes that such a solution is possible, then surely no cost would be too high to obtain it: to make mankind just and happy and creative and harmonious for ever – what could be too high a price to pay for that? To make such an omelette, there is surely no limit to the number of eggs that should be broken – that was the faith of Lenin, of Trotsky, of Mao, for all I know of Pol Pot. Since I know the only true path to the ultimate solution to the problems of society, I know which way to drive the human caravan; and since you are ignorant of what I know, you cannot be allowed to have liberty of choice even within the narrowest limits, if the goal is to be reached. You declare that a given policy will make you happier, or freer, or give you room to breathe, but I know you are mistaken, I know what you need, what all men need; and if there is resistance based on ignorance or malevolence, then it must be broken and hundreds of thousands may have to perish to make millions happy for all time. What choice have we, who have the knowledge, but to be willing to sacrifice them all?

[. . .]

[I]f we allow that Great Goods can collide, that some of them cannot live together . . . and if human creativity may depend upon a variety of mutually exclusive choices, then [we must ask], 'What is to be done?' How do we choose between possibilities? What and how much must we sacrifice to what? There is, it seems to me, no clear reply. But the collisions, even if they cannot be avoided, can be softened. Claims can be balanced, compromises can be reached: in concrete situations not every claim is of equal force – so much liberty and so much equality; so much for sharp moral condemnation, and so much for understanding a given human situation; so much for the full force of the law, and so much for the prerogative of mercy; for feeding the hungry, clothing the naked, healing the sick, sheltering the homeless. Priorities, never final and absolute, must be established.

The first public obligation is to avoid extremes of suffering. Revolutions, wars, assassinations, extreme measures may in desperate situations be required. But history teaches us that their consequences are seldom what is anticipated; there is no guarantee, not even, at times, a high enough probability, that such acts will lead to improvement. We may take the risk of drastic action, in personal life or in public policy, but we must always be aware, never forget, that we may be mistaken, that certainty about the effect of such measures invariably leads to avoidable suffering of the innocent. So we must engage in what are called trade-offs – rules, values, principles must yield to each other in varying degrees in specific situations. Utilitarian solutions are sometimes wrong, but, I suspect, more often beneficent. The best that can be done, as a general rule, is to maintain a precarious equilibrium that will prevent the occurrence of desperate situations, of intolerable choices – that is the first requirement for a decent society; one that we can always strive for, in the light of the limited range of our knowledge, and even of our imperfect understanding of individuals and societies. A certain humility in these matters is very necessary.

This may seem a very flat answer, not the kind of thing that the idealistic young would wish, if need be, to fight and suffer for, in the cause of a new and nobler society. And of course, we must not dramatise the incomparability of values – there is a great deal of broad agreement among people in different societies over long stretches of time about what is right and wrong, good and evil. Of course traditions, outlooks, attitudes may legitimately differ; general principles may cut across too much human need. The concrete situation is almost everything. There is no escape; we must decide as we decide; moral risk cannot, at times, be avoided. All we can ask for is that none of the relevant factors be ignored, that the purposes we seek to realise should be seen as elements in a total form of life, which can be enhanced or damaged by decisions.

But, in the end, it is not a matter of purely subjective judgement; it is dictated by the forms of life of the society to which one belongs, a society among other societies, with values held in common, whether or not they are in conflict, by the majority of mankind throughout recorded history. There are, if not universal values, at any rate a minimum without which societies could scarcely survive. Few today would wish to defend slavery or ritual murder or Nazi gas chambers or the torture of human beings for the sake of pleasure or even political profit – or the duty of children to denounce their parents, which the French and Russian revolutions demanded, or mindless killing. There is no justification for compromise on this. But on the other hand, the search for perfection does seem to me a recipe for bloodshed, no better even if it is demanded by the sincerest of idealists, the purest of heart. No more rigorous moralist than Immanuel Kant has ever lived, but even he said, in a moment of illumination, 'Out of the crooked timber of humanity no straight thing was ever made'.

[. . .]

Of course social or political collisions will take place; the mere conflict of positive values alone makes this unavoidable. Yet they can, I believe, be minimised by promoting and preserving an uneasy equilibrium, which is constantly threatened and in constant need of repair – that alone, I repeat, is the precondition for decent societies and morally acceptable behaviour, otherwise we are bound to lose our way.

'OAKESHOTT ON LAW, LIBERTY AND CIVIL ASSOCIATION' BY JOHN GRAY

At the time of writing, John Gray is Professor of European Thought in the Government Department at the London School of Economics. In the 1980s, Gray was well known in the UK as a philosopher in sympathy with the Conservatism associated with Margaret Thatcher. However, he shifted from this position, developing a critique of the unfettered market on the grounds that it corrodes the cultural, civil basis of the very liberties it is supposed to embody. Since then, he has developed a kind of communitarian position and advanced a rigorous critique of excessive support for neo-liberalism. See *Beyond the New Right: Markets, Government and the Common Environment* (Routledge, 1993), *Enlightenment's Wake: Politics and Culture at the Close of the Modern Age* (Routledge, 1995), *False Dawn: The Delusions of Global Capitalism* (Granta, 1998) and *Two Faces of Liberalism* (Polity Press, 2000). Gray's work can usefully be read alongside other authors included in this volume who also deal with the theme of how a common culture is necessary for politics (such as the communitarians, and especially Sandel), and it is worth comparing his kind of agonism to that found in Mouffe.

The extract considers Oakeshott (whose work appears in the section on Conservatism) and outlines his views on the distinction between civil and enterprise association. In common with other liberal thinkers discussed in this section, Gray, through Oakeshott, endorses a limited view of what is possible in political and social life and advocates (not unlike Rawls but for different reasons) acceptance of a *modus vivendi*, a way of jostling alongside one another (which is surely better than being forced to march in tune).

'OAKESHOTT ON LAW, LIBERTY AND CIVIL ASSOCIATION' (1983)*

John Gray

Oakeshott . . . [characterises] morality . . . as a non-instrumental practice. This is to say that moral life has no end, goal or *telos* outside itself, and it does not stand in need of any external justification. Further, Oakeshott avers, there is not a single or ideal form of ethical life of which the variety of forms of life

---

* John Gray, 'Oakeshott on Law, Liberty and Civil Association', *Liberalisms* (London: Routledge, 1983).

that we find among us are approximations. Rather, moralities are akin to vernacular languages, in that it is the nature of them to be several and diverse. If moral life is in this way non-instrumental, and so in one sense purposeless, so also are law and the form of civil association which is created by the union of law with morality, independent of any specific purpose. We come here to one of the key concepts in Oakeshott's later work – the conception . . . of society as a *civil association* – an association among persons who, having no ends or purposes held necessarily in common, nevertheless co-exist in peace under the rule of law. On this account, the office of law is not typically to impose any particular duty or goal on men, but instead seeks principally to facilitate their dealings with one another. . . . [T]he rule of law in a civil society is not [designed to promote] general welfare or any other similar abstraction (such as fundamental rights), but rather [to secure] the conditions in which persons may themselves contract into mutually chosen activities. Thus, law seeks not to impose on society any preferred pattern of ends, but simply to facilitate individuals in their pursuit of their own ends. Law has itself, for this reason, no purpose.

In modern societies, a powerful rival has emerged to this conception of civil association – . . . *enterprise association*. In this latter conception, . . . the State is understood as an organization for the attainment of a definite end, or hierarchy of ends. . . . This collectivist conception of society and government, while it has never completely extirpated the inheritance of civil association, has been dominant in our times – most clearly and widely in Soviet Communism and National Socialism, but also in the New Deal, the mixed or managed economy, Corporatism, and 'welfare capitalism'. The idea of the state as an enterprise association . . . is an idea inimical to any notion of a civil association among persons linked only by their common subscription to a non-instrumental rule of law.

[. . .]

What, then, is the alternative to collectivism? . . . What is needed, for Oakeshott, is in the first place a return to a tradition of limited government, in which we expect of the State no more than it can give. For this to be achieved, however, we must acquire in respect of government a conservative disposition which . . . has its spring in:

> The acceptance of the current condition of human circumstances . . . the propensity to make our own choices and to find happiness in doing so, the variety of enterprises each pursued with passion, the diversity of beliefs each held with the conviction of its exclusive truth; the excess, the over-activity and the informal compromise. And the office of government is not to impose other beliefs and activities upon its subjects nor to tutor or to educate them, not to make them better or happier in another way, not to direct them, to galvanize them into action, to lead them or to

co-ordinate their activities so that no occasion of conflict shall occur; the office of government is merely to rule. This is a specific and limited activity, easily corrupted when it is combined with any other, and in the circumstances, indispensable. The image of the ruler is the umpire whose business is to administer the rules of the game, or the chairman who governs the debate according to known rules but does not himself participate in it. (Michael Oakeshott, *Rationalism in Politics* (London: Methuen, 1962), p. 186)

In Oakeshott's paradoxical contention . . . this conservative conception of government as a limited activity involving the making and enforcing of general rules is, in fact, peculiarly appropriate to a culture and an epoch which is prone to restless individualism in virtually every aspect of life.

[. . .]

In its moral aspect, civil association is that mode of association which exemplifies individuality – the condition in which human beings accept and celebrate their autonomy, separateness and mortality. In its political dimension, civil association is characterized by the diffusion of power throughout society – by a complex structure of countervailing institutions of precisely the sort that is threatened by contemporary collectivist projects (of the Right and Left) of transforming government into an enterprise association.

[. . .]

Oakeshott does not pretend that civil association embodies any sort of universal prescription for political conduct, since he is concerned to stress the historical singularity of the circumstances which . . . made civil association a reality. If his account has a clear normative implication, it is that civil association is the expression in the context of the modern European state of the individualist morality which is the most distinctive achievement of our civilization. We may go further than Oakeshott himself does, and argue that the conception of civil association may be an appropriate and compelling one for those societies throughout the world which under the shocks of modernity are discovering the necessity of forging a civil society where none had existed, or of repairing it where (as in the Marxist states) it had been repressed or nearly destroyed. The idea of civil association, though it rightly repudiates . . . pretension to universal authority, at the same time has reference far beyond the cultural traditions which gave issue to it.

[. . .]

The [Hobbesian] image . . . of a restless band of castaways, among whom order is ever at risk, and who have little in common but aversion to violent death and a passion for self-assertion, is hardly an inapt metaphor of our condition; it is, whether we know it or not, the way we live. In this predicament, the

Hobbesian search for a *modus vivendi*, reached and renewed through dialogue, rhetoric, bargaining, force and all the devices of the political arts, is for us an historical fate, from which we are distracted as much by the hallucinatory perspectives of liberal philosophy as by the inordinate demands of mass democracy.

4

CONSERVATISMS

Alan Finlayson

INTRODUCTION

Seemingly the most pervasive and electorally successful of all political outlooks, Conservatism is one of the hardest to describe philosophically. It is relatively easy (though not uncontroversial) to use the 'methods' of social and political science to locate the sources of its popular support, their motivations or 'interests', but to examine and explain Conservatism in terms of principle or theoretical formulation is an activity for which things appear altogether more opaque.

A number of features can be identified as regular occurrences in the arguments of those who declare themselves conservative: a commitment to the principle of social order as embedded in tradition; disapproval of any form of large-scale or 'rational' societal planning; support for hierarchy sometimes extending into a defence of natural aristocracy; strong religious affiliations and a particular attachment to the role of Christian morality in the shaping of society; the belief that responsibilities should outweigh rights; private property as a positive value; the placing of liberty above equality in the system of political values; support for the free market. But the ways in which these concepts are related to each other by Conservatives are highly variable. At one end of the scale, we might place the deep commitment to tradition and the duties it places upon us found in a thinker such as F. H. **Bradley** (see Scruton, 1991: 40–58); at the other, the apparent individualism of more recent Conservatives associated with thinkers such as **Nozick** or politicians like Margaret **Thatcher** who emphasise the need to 'free' people from the state. The former perspective sees the individual as embedded in a web of social relationships whereas the latter appears to want to abstract him or her from it, yet both can accurately be called conservative. This, however, causes problems for any attempt to delineate a singular body of thought to be defined as conservative.

In contrast to socialists and liberals who strive to establish internal coherence for their philosophical arguments, and the descriptions of political systems that derive from them, Conservatives seem to advance arguments that vary widely from time to time and place to place, sometimes appearing positively opportunistic in the claims they make. But Conservatives make a virtue out of such variability, openly eschewing 'abstract' systems of thought, describing their outlook as anything other than a philosophy, preferring terms such as 'attitude' or 'disposition'. Thus, for the conservative philosopher Michael Oakeshott, while conservative 'conduct' *could* be elucidated through general explanatory principles, he preferred only to 'construe this disposition as it appears in contemporary character', famously concluding that to be conservative is 'to prefer the familiar to the unknown, to prefer the tried to the untried, fact to mystery, the actual to the possible, the limited to the unbounded, the near to the distant, the sufficient to the superabundant, the convenient to the perfect, present laughter to utopian bliss' (Oakeshott, 1981: 168–99). But even this very general statement seems to conflict with the absolute commitment of many, particularly American, conservatives to the principle of the free-market economy.

Clearly, Conservatism is not a rigidly unified or doctrinaire body of thought. To seek a singular essence of conservatism would be to misunderstand it from the start. For this very lack of essential unity is central to conservatism, affording it considerable leeway and enabling it to appear as a widespread, easily shared ideology encompassing different political persuasions within its very imprecision. That it can do so is evidence that, in addition to whatever else it may be, Conservatism is a particular form of skilled political intelligence, perhaps even a philosophy of exactly that.

Michael Freeden, in a careful and detailed analysis, has identified four features that are common to Conservative ideology and philosophy. Two of these he regards as substantive core concepts: resistance to change that is not 'organic' or 'natural', and the connected belief that 'the laws and forces guiding human behaviour have extra-human origins and therefore cannot and ought not to be subject to human wills and whims' (Freeden, 1996: 344). Two further features, he argues, take the form of underlying attributes derived from these core concepts. Firstly, conservatism creates its specific beliefs and values in reaction to challenges from progressive ideologies while, secondly, it defines and mobilises political concepts in relation to them. That is to say, in opposing Liberalism and socialism, Conservatives will treat certain core concepts in a highly flexible and even fluid manner, shifting ground the better to attack their enemies and defend themselves.

This may make conservatism appear merely opportunistic, even ad hoc and unstable. For example, since at least the 1970s the Conservative Party in Britain has embraced an economic agenda that is substantively derived from the principles of classical Liberalism (see Gamble, 1988), while in the USA many of those who call themselves Conservatives and actively decry the baneful influence of 'liberals' preach a particularly aggressive version of liberal individualism sometimes mixed with hard-line Christianity. Conservative political philosophy and ideology is easily capable of co-opting elements of other, seemingly antithetical doctrines and then pretending they were always its own.

Such is the paradox of conservatism: a mere 'disposition' that presents fundamental claims about the ontology of social life; a movement opposed to ideology that is one of the most successful ideologies in both Britain and America; an anti-liberal philosophy that draws extensively on liberal political thought; a movement that asserts the importance of timeless wisdom yet which varies (sometimes considerably) in all its manifestations. This chapter will examine this paradoxical Conservative 'attitude', focusing on the way in which conservatism is best understood not so much as a political philosophy but as a philosophy of politics: of how it should be done; of what it is for and, crucially, of its limits. In particular, we will consider the approach conservatives take to the role of rationality in politics and the importance they afford to tradition. We will then briefly reflect upon some of the recent history of conservatism and the formation of what has been called the New Right in order to investigate the present state of Conservative political thought.

THE CONSERVATIVE OUTLOOK

For the philosophical conservative, reflection must begin with the realisation that there is an aspect of human existence and experience that cannot be subordinated to human will or whim, eludes the understanding and yet with which we may learn to develop an affinity. If properly rooted in and attentive to the traditional world around us, we can intuit the best courses of action to take in maintaining the stability and prosperity of the state. This perspective has many roots, but they are particularly to be found in eighteenth- and nineteenth-century romanticism. As Mannheim notes, historically 'conservatism is characterised by the fact that it is aware of that irrational realm in the life of the state which cannot be managed by administration. It recognises that there is an unorganised and incalculable realm which is the proper sphere of politics' (Mannheim, 1976: 106). The only guide for political action is the slowly evolving 'spirit' of the people as manifested in its tradition and culture. Civil life, for the conservative, is ultimately contingent and non-rational in nature. The ideal Conservative ruler (if one can speak of conservative 'ideals') is there to steer the populous, to protect them and their popular ways from incursions be they from without (a rival populous perhaps) or within (the intellectuals with their fancy abstractions about equality or rights or rationality).

Conservatism thus presents a theory of social order achieved and protected through tradition which in turn requires deference to those who properly understand that tradition. Exactly who in society has such knowledge varies across different types of conservatism, but it is always an elite of some sort. For **Burke**, a conservative thinker of the latter part of the eighteenth century, that elite was the monarchy and the aristocracy. He argued that for men to become a properly constituted social body, a people, they must be 'in that state of habitual discipline, in which the wiser, the more expert, and the more opulent conduct, and by conducting enlighten and protect the weaker, the less knowing, and the less provided with the goods of fortune'. In other words the cleverer, stronger and richer among us must bring order to the stupider, weaker and poorer, for 'When the multitude are not under this discipline, they can scarcely be said to be in civil society . . . A true natural aristocracy is . . . an essential integrant part of any large body rightly constituted' (Burke, 1990 [1791]: 73–4). This inegalitarianism, found in early conservatism, is maintained in differing forms in later incarnations and is regarded by some as essential to the philosophy (ibid.). But the extent to which a commitment to inequality is central to conservatism is debatable. It may be that inequality is advocated only as a means to the end of social order and stability rather than an end in itself. Where liberals and socialists often speak of an essential equality between human beings and of the possibility of perfecting all individuals if the right social conditions are met and opportunities made available, the conservative understands human nature as fallible and imperfectible. Indeed, one notable conservative thinker has defined conservatism as a philosophy of imperfection which in turn advocates a limited style of politics (O'Sullivan, 1976: 13). In this sense, a rejection of equality on the part of a conservative may in fact be a rejection not of equality as such but of the politics of equality, for (based on an untenable presumption about humanity) they must lead to an unwarranted extension of political power and activity into domains that are none of its business (though of course this argument may well serve some particular inegalitarian interests).

If for Liberals Kant is the central modern philosophical source, then for Conservatism this role belongs to Hegel. In devising a moral system grounded in the **autonomy** of the individual alone, Kant proposed an ethic of duty without content, pursued for its own sake. What mattered was that an individual adhere only to the dictates of a moral law derived from his own reason (see the sharp critique offered by **Bradley**, in Scruton, 1991: 45–52). Scruton (in the reading reproduced below) criticises Liberalism by taking on just this principle of freedom for the individual. He argues that the perspective of the individual cannot in itself generate a political order or a criterion for evaluating the justness of society. Kant made **autonomy** central to his theory (as the essential condition of man), regarding man as inherently reasonable. To conform with reason, that individual must be autonomous and so able to will the right course of action. From this, there is derived a theory of rights and equality. Scruton tries to show that this position is untenable, not least because it forces us to abstract away from the very contingencies of social life that make moral reasoning and judgement necessary and because the 'first-person perspective' cannot generate anything other than a damaging scepticism. Instead, Scruton argues that we should regard individualism as an illusion but a welcome one, the operation of which in society can be justified by reference to the 'third-person perspective'. Thinking of ourselves as rational and autonomous agents helps us find values and to integrate our basic desires into a wider and shared picture of the good. In short, the **autonomy** of the individual can only be sustained if we conserve the social institutions that give it meaning and support even if those institutions appear to curtail that individualism. According to Scruton, Liberalism corrodes the very conditions which nurture it; only conservatism can offer true protection.

This perspective is connected to Hegel's original challenge to Kant. Hegel located ethical life within the context of the political community, regarding the person as always a part of something greater and as finding freedom only in assuming a place within that larger whole. That whole is itself composed of interrelated parts or moments taking a concrete form as the family (from which we learn ethical relations in a natural or immediate form), civil society (in which self-interested individuals find satisfaction of their needs in a 'system of complete interdependence, wherein the livelihood, happiness and legal status of one man is interwoven with the livelihood, happiness and rights of all . . . and only in this system are they actualised and secured' (Hegel, 1991: 183)) and the synthesis of these public and private realms in the state which is 'the actuality of the ethical idea', the expression in concrete, institutional form of the ethical life of the community.

This schema is rooted in Hegel's wider metaphysics, which has also shaped conservative thinking, giving it a certain sort of romantic attitude which (with all its mystical implications) is best expressed in the attitude of the greatest of all conservative literary artists, T. S. Eliot: 'Every experience is a paradox in that it means to be absolute, and yet is relative; in that it somehow always goes beyond itself and yet never escapes itself' (1964). The Conservative philosopher reflects on this paradoxical nature of experience, aware that it always exceeds his rational capacities because such experience is itself derivative of the greater rationality at work in the world. For Hegel, the 'true' doesn't lie in the abstractions of the understanding but is found in the world, manifesting itself in concrete history. Human culture is an objectification of reason. This contrasts greatly with the formalist Liberalism of Kant. The conservative 'utopia' is not an abstraction to be devised by reason and imposed on the world but, in Mannheim's words, 'is from the very beginning, embedded in existing reality' (1976: 209). The tools for social administration are thus forged through attentiveness to the now, and the last things needed are abstractions invented by enlightened philosophers.

For these reasons, despite a capacity for theoretical reflection, the Conservative philosopher feels such activity to be a mistake. Thought and experience are always immanent, rooted in the present. They are of the here and now and not transcendent. The point of reflection is simply to find ways of being in the world as it is, perhaps to commune with it and on occasion to experience something more, granted us by the poetic voice: 'a sort of truancy, a dream within the dream of life, a wild flower planted among our wheat' (Oakeshott, 1981: 247). Theoretical labour is forced on us as a kind of bereavement. To have to reflect on what one is doing is already to have lost touch with it. All that is left is the possibility of recuperating the loss through accepting and exploring it rather than trying to find illusions that may fool us into thinking it never happened. We are always already subjects of a fallen and frail humanity and must embed ourselves in the practices, rituals and myths of this everyday world if we are to see beyond it and find the strength to endure and act ethically within it.

For these reasons, Scruton opens his text on the idea of Conservatism by declaring: 'Its essence is inarticulate, and its expression, when compelled, sceptical' (Scruton, 1984: 15), closing it with the remark that a conservative 'having struggled for articulacy . . . must recommend silence' (ibid.: 191). It may appear odd to open and close a book on the philosophy of conservatism with statements suggesting that there is no such thing and that if there were it should keep its mouth shut. But this sensibility neatly marks the distinction between conservative political 'art' and liberal or socialist political 'science'. Appearing as a defence of that which already is, of that which is obvious, Conservatism presents itself as incapable of systematic exposition. Conservative writers, Scruton claims (1991:3),

> approach the matter of politics as living matter, which cannot be carelessly torn apart in the service of pseudo-scientific categories . . . those who seek for a comprehensive theory of man's nature, together with an enunciation of his goals, will always be impatient with conservative thinking . . . it lacks the attempt at system, and its careful language will rarely be persuasive to those for whom the only reasonable answers are those which are conveyed in systematic terms.

This refusal is not merely pragmatic or politic. It is intrinsic to the conservative attitude. Where the liberal or socialist enunciates great principles such as 'freedom' or 'social justice', the conservative speaks of authority, allegiance and tradition (Scruton, 1984: 27–46). Authority should be of a natural sort (such as that found within families) and have nothing to do with the sort of 'contract' associated with Liberalism, which is an 'artefact' that 'exists only in so far as men exercise, understand and submit to it'. Similarly, allegiance is born of a mythic attachment to one's particular homeland because one understands one's self and place in the world through 'concepts and perceptions embodied in the social organism, practices (such as that of marriage) which it does not make sense to think of as the products of individual will' (Scruton, 1984: 37). Traditions matter more than anything, for they can (if they are the right traditions) engage 'the loyalty of their participants . . . moulding their idea of what they are and what they should be', indicating 'something which survives and gives meaning to the acts that emerge from it' (ibid.: 42).

Such sentiments are found in different but related forms across varieties of Conservative thought which are all opposed to unwarranted abstraction and the attempt on the part of rationalists to treat society as if they had devised a truth or method independent of it. Thus, in a representative essay, the influential American Conservative philosopher Leo **Strauss**, attacking the generalising tendencies of the political science of his day, criticised the search for unifying concepts and contrasted the reductive 'sociological' approach with the careful and nuanced language of politics built up over time and through experience. Where the scientists complain of the vagueness of political language, Strauss counters that it is the attempt to produce a clear, neutral and scientific language that leads to vagueness precisely because it is not rooted in any understanding of actual political life as it is lived. For this reason, it cannot recognise real truths and simply legitimates the vagueness of liberal democracy which Strauss, in typical Platonic mode, condemns since 'by teaching in effect the equality of literally all desires, it teaches in effect that there is nothing that a man ought to be ashamed of . . . denying that there are things which are intrinsically high and others which are intrinsically low' (Strauss, 1970: 426). His target is a certain sort of social-science rationalism (by no means exclusively a 'left-wing' one) that, with its interest in surveys and the study of political 'groups', political psychology and comparative analysis, leaves behind the proper, and properly philosophical, concerns of classical political science – to understand regimes and their moral purposes. The new political science is blind to such nuance: 'All peculiarities of political societies and still more of the political societies with which we are concerned as citizens, become unrecognisable if treated in terms of the vague generalities which hold of every conceivable group' (ibid.: 416). But it is precisely this nuance to which the Conservative philosopher seeks to be attuned.

A classic statement of the Conservative opposition to a rationalist treatment of the political sphere is found in Oakeshott's well-known essay 'Rationalism in Politics' (reproduced in part below) in which he contrasts the disconnected and abstract technocratic attitude to political 'management' with a 'concrete knowledge of the permanent interests and direction of movement of a society'. He characterises the rationalist character as dry, rather dull and isolated. Always looking for problems to solve, the rationalist thinks of political practice as like a kind of engineering and stands outside of society, aiming not merely to repair it but to redesign it. This view is echoed by Scruton when he says of society's traditions: 'The detail of conservative theory lies in the attempt to understand such institutions, not from outside but from within, from the standpoint of their own life and purposes' (Scruton, 1991: 8). Both Scruton and Oakeshott display the conservative tendency to embrace politics as a very particular sort of activity: one that requires a careful probing intelligence that is as much artistic as it is 'intellectual'.

However, in evaluating Oakeshott's arguments, a couple of things are worth noting. Firstly, he does not really present arguments for his case, preferring instead simply to present it. His essay, which has a literary flair and style sadly lacking in most political studies, seeks primarily to paint an ugly picture of the rationalist that is its target. This is quite different from the high theorising common to most contemporary variants of Marxism or the 'logical' (and usually very lengthy) deductions prominent in contemporary Liberalism. As such, the style of the essay rather complements its claims but also exposes itself to the charge that it is nothing more than rhetoric.

Secondly, we should take note of the circumstances of the production of this essay. It was written in 1947 when Britain was into the third year of a landmark Labour Party government elected after the Second World War on a platform of nationalisation and the extension of a welfare state central to which was the National Health Service. This was Britain's 'New Deal', and we can safely surmise that this is what Oakeshott is attacking. His examples of rootless rationalism are William **Godwin** and Robert **Owen**, leading socialists of the eighteenth and nineteenth centuries, campaigners, advocates and practitioners of social reform (and, incidentally, both criticised by Marx, a different sort of Hegelian, for an approach to politics insufficiently rooted in an understanding of the concrete movement of history). When attacking rationalism in politics, then, Oakeshott is really attacking socialism. More specifically, he is attacking egalitarianism: notice that he is particularly critical of the idea that things can be learnt by just anybody (through 'correspondence courses' for example), stressing that they can only be learnt through patient experience alongside a master. But once again this attack on equality (on the possibility that anyone can learn anything) is motivated by a concern to protect social order which must, for the conservative, be embedded in slowly evolving tradition rather than abstract rationality. It is the fear that such widespread learning might undermine the traditions that give shape to social life that motivates the criticism of equality and leads to advocacy of a kind of mythology that the philosopher himself cannot truly legitimate (because it lies beyond reason).

Convinced that human reason is limited and its nature fallible, and that the world is greater than our understanding, the conservative intellectual is in a difficult position since he is a sceptic who is, apparently unsceptically, developing a philosophy of that which (according to his philosophy) cannot have a philosophy. Thus Scruton declares the need for silence since 'the pursuit of truth leads one to doubt the myths that reinforce society' (Scruton, 1984: 190), adding that

> the conservative who has risen above the fragments of his inheritance and reflected on the desolation that has been wrought in it, cannot return to an innocence which his own thinking has destroyed . . . He knows what he wants, and knows the social order that would correspond to it. But in becoming self-conscious he has to set himself apart from things. The reasons that he observes for sustaining the myths of society are reasons which he cannot propagate; to propagate his reasons is to instil the world with doubt. (ibid.: 191)

The conservative attitude is deeply rooted in this sensibility. It is a theory of order, or rather of how order is maintained through a sensitivity to something called tradition. In turn, this requires that people show deference to those who understand tradition or embody it. These might be those writers and pedagogues who see their duty as faithfully recording and expressing the history and feeling of the people, or the specially cultivated civil servants who safeguard the inner workings of the state. It can often mean the clerics who, by definition, are the representatives of a religious tradition and non-rational faith. For the Conservative, the Church is not simply a set of theological doctrines or beliefs (though these are of crucial importance). It is also an institution, a structure embedded in history and which in turn weaves into and gives shape to the lives of the members of that church, who are thus not inside or outside of the church but an integral part of it.

We might go so far as to say (though perhaps Conservatives would not like it) that there is in all this a mystical streak. Conservative philosophers and the writers or artists they often admire attempt to, as it were, commune with the spirit of the people where that spirit is expressed in the concrete traditions and institutions of that people. We can certainly see this in conservative artists like Coleridge, Arnold or Eliot, but it is there too in someone like Leo **Strauss**, who (although an altogether more abstract thinker than most English conservatives) certainly regarded himself as one protecting and interpreting a special tradition that required veneration and demanded that those who could, immerse themselves within it. This mysticism leads, in England, to support for institutions such as monarchy and aristocracy – that which Bagehot (1905) famously called the 'dignified' parts of the constitution. Things must, of necessity, be different in the American Republic, which lacks not just monarchy but also the range of very historic institutions that might produce quite such a dignified aristocracy. It is hard to imagine the American 'spirit of liberty' accepting anything like the hierarchical and entrenched British Civil Service. But we only have to think of the reverence afforded to the US Constitution and the peculiar form of ancestor-worship lavished on the **'founding fathers'** to see that the Conservative philosophy has its mystical manifestations in the USA as elsewhere.

Conservatism, it seems, consists of an anti-rationalist outlook on social life derived from a strong belief that human beings are frail, fallible and imperfectible. Tradition, custom, habit and prejudice are thus to be protected, not overthrown, since they alone permit the maintenance of social order, which is a prime good. In turn, there must be people able to understand and interpret that tradition (be they clerics, supreme court judges, civil servants, politicians, artists or writers) and who can thus make the necessary fine judgements about what course of political action may be required at any particular time. This outlook is intended not to undermine individuality and individualism but to make it possible by subordinating it to the necessity of maintaining a limited style of politics (for unlimited politics would undermine individualism and overthrow order).

The Conservative defence of tradition and its opposition to the full-scale employment of rationalism give rise to a very particular sense of what politics is and is for. We might even regard it as an attempt to define a particular sort of political wisdom. This is well characterised by Arthur Aughey as 'the inner vision of the life of the state' (Aughey, 1992: 14). But this is not to be confused with a simple attachment to 'statecraft' (though this is an important part of it), with the placing of reason of state above all principle. Rather, it is the recognition that principles only have value and meaning because they are embodied in a particular time and place from which they must not be displaced:

> It has always been conservative wisdom that the human world is too complex to conform to the neat categories and principles of radical idealism . . . an attempt to arrest political argument within the confines of the familiar and the known and to suggest that the only constructive possibilities for reform in a state are to be found in the particular potentials of that state. (ibid.: 15)

We have to be careful here. An ideology that advocates the control of the state by an elite with special knowledge of the will of the community and who operate the state in order to extend and defend that people is, essentially, a fascist ideology. But Conservatism is not Fascism. The difference lies in the fact that conservatives do not identify the state with the political community and fundamentally regard politics as something to be limited. Its purpose is only to maintain that form of non-state civil association in which individuals can thrive. This can be contrasted to the kind of state that takes on an overall purpose, regarding itself as the main agent directing society. Civil association, Oakeshott argued, does not exist for a particular purpose. Any ends it may attain are not the point of society but merely a means for its continuance. However noble it may sound, we must not impose a purpose on society. As Scruton puts it:

> The longed-for-release of the self from all restraint, from customary usage and authoritative guidance, may seem to be the fullest flowering of human freedom . . . Conservative politics does not aim to generate ever wider and more comprehensive liberties, but to 'care for institutions' – to maintain and invigorate what has been established for the common good. Because they impede the boisterous appetite for novelty, institutions are increasingly mistaken for obstacles to the free flowering of the self: It is institutions, and not individuals, which have always been the prime object of conservative concern . . . congenial authority is one of the goals of conservative politics. (1991: 9)

CONSERVATISM VS. LIBERALISM AND SOCIALISM

So far, we have looked at conservatism as a philosophy of order rooted in opposition to rationalist explanations of society and as generating the idea of a particular political wisdom. But this is perhaps not how Conservatism appears to many who observe only the contemporary political scene. Since the 1970s, Europe and America have been reshaped to a considerable extent by policies enacted by the New Right, which in many respects appears, ideologically, to be deeply embedded in the liberal philosophy of **laissez-faire**. Two critics have even described the political 'revolution' represented by **Reagan** in the USA and **Thatcher** in the UK as 'conservative capitalism' (Hoover and Plant, 1989). Centred on particularly aggressive claims in favour of the free market, these governments introduced large cuts in taxation, drastically reduced budgets for welfare and promoted the market over government as the key institution of social life (Hoover and Plant, 1989: Chapter 1).

Mobilising a rhetoric of freedom in opposition to the alleged slavery of the active state, the rhetoricians of the New Right gave their programme a distinctly moral tone. Economic policy was based on the notion that the primary cause of economic crises and of unemployment is inflation. Attempts by the interventionist state to reduce unemployment, it was argued, necessarily caused increases in inflation, which in turn caused crises and generated yet more unemployment. The answer was to focus economic policy on control of the money supply so that it would be strictly limited in line with overall growth and, in the absence of a gold standard or fixed exchange rates, would ensure the stability or 'soundness' of money. This was the policy known as monetarism, and it was complemented by a general focus on what are known as supply-side economics. The post-war welfare states in Europe (and, to a lesser degree, in the USA) practised what was called demand management. This meant, to simplify grossly, that crises of the economy were understood to come about because potential consumers were not spending enough. Because employers sought profits, they tended to raise prices at the same time as seeking to squeeze wages. But if wages are squeezed, people have less money to buy goods. This precipitates a squeeze on profits to which firms respond by laying off workers, thus exacerbating the situation even further. The task of government was to inject money into the economy through public spending and to redistribute wealth via taxation and benefits so that people would have the money to buy things. The state would also seek to invest in the economy directly since it controlled companies that were nationally owned or, as in the classic case of the New Deal in the USA, by sponsoring large-scale projects.

Supply-side economics effectively reverses this arrangement by concentrating policy effort on the producers and not the consumers of wealth. A dynamic economy, it was argued, depends on the dynamic individuals or entrepreneurs who create it. People with talent and commitment become such entrepreneurs because they have an incentive, namely to get rich. High taxation, however, is a disincentive and so should be cut. Similarly, state regulation of the economy interferes with the decisions of investors who alone know where it is best to put their money. Welfare can also be conceived as a disincentive to action because it gives people a safety net or cushion on which to rest. Furthermore, welfare spending is not limited by the mechanisms of the market and will induce dependency in claimants and ultimately corrupt government, which will hog resources that should be in the private sector. This represents what appears to be a return to the classical Liberalism of the eighteenth century commonly associated with Adam **Smith**. The market is praised as the locus of free individual actions in which redistribution occurs naturally. It may lead to poverty, but this is not important so long as there is no state distorting the preference expression of individuals. Poverty is not understood, as it may be by social liberals and socialists, as a hindrance on human freedom. Perhaps oddly, this aggressive neo-Liberalism (now the dominant ideology of most of the globe) combined, in Reaganism and Thatcherism, with a radical conservatism that, especially in the USA, was influenced greatly by renascent evangelical Christianity.

But this seems, on the surface, to be a rather unstable mix. The freedom of the market is also the freedom to undermine traditional ways of life if they are not profitable. What is more, the market may well function by encouraging the sort of individual desire that the conservative might prefer to limit and to encourage an individualism that is pitted against the state in a distinctly un-Hegelian fashion. Some libertarians argue, quite logically given their premises, that there should be no laws that prescribe individual morality. Thus prohibitions on drugs should be ended, prostitution legalised and so forth.

The question arises then of how it is that today conservatism appears as a philosophy wedded to neo-liberal conceptions of politics that, just as Scruton argued, seem to undermine their very own basis. Indeed, one prominent advocate of New Right policies has significantly recanted and returned to a gentler Hegelian social liberalism, mixed with an Oakeshottian sensibility, and has condemned the 'delusions' of global capitalism (see Gray, 1996, 1998).

Three possible answers perhaps immediately present themselves. The first of these is that those claiming to be conservative are lying: that politicians are venal and the electorate stupid. Unpleasant as this explanation sounds, it does appear to have some merit. The scaling-back of state involvement in the economy and consequent reduction in the social demands made on corporations and businessmen has enabled them to make vast amounts of money for themselves. The policies that have allowed this have been justified with a rhetoric that suggests this conforms with traditional values and respects the organic nature of the national community as well as individual rights. But this is a partisan political charge and not a philosophical one. Even if it were proven that cynicism had motivated politicians to pretend one thing while doing another, this would not actually invalidate either the philosophical claims or, of itself, justify the charge that the practical effects of such policies have been bad ones.

The second possible explanation is that, despite some differences, there is a significant overlap between the principles associated with Reaganism and those of traditional conservatism, and even that the contemporary neo-liberal agenda is the true core of conservatism. The philosopher Robert **Nozick**, often described as a **libertarian**, opposed state intervention into economic life partly on the grounds that for it to do so was to engage in a kind of 'end-state' politics where action is undertaken to achieve a specific state of affairs when politics ought to be concerned only with managing process and not specifying outcomes. At a wider level, the form of reasoning ideally associated with market activity fits very well with the conservative opposition to abstract reason. The individual acting in a market employs forms of knowledge that are practical, tacit and dependent on a social context outside of which they make no sense (Scruton, 1991: 4). Of particular importance to this line of thought is the work of the Austrian economist and philosopher Friedrich von **Hayek**, who has been a major influence, inspiration even, for many figures in the so-called 'New Right'. His important book *The Road to Serfdom* (1944) presented totalitarianism as the necessary but unintended outcome of all attempts to institute state planning of the economy.

But this leads us onto a third explanation for the nature of contemporary conservatism – that it has simply changed and adapted to new circumstances. Oakeshott, in the essay reproduced here, worried that the tradition of resistance to the abstraction and rigidity of rationalism has itself become a rigid and abstract ideology, noting that the significance of the work of **Hayek** may be

> not the cogency of his doctrine but the fact that it is a doctrine. A plan to resist all planning may be better than its opposite, but it belongs to the same style of politics . . . only in a society already deeply infected with rationalism will the conversion of the traditional resources of resistance to the tyranny of rationalism into a self-conscious ideology be considered a strengthening of those resources. (1981: 21–2)

There would seem to be, then, a clear conflict within conservative thinking of the present day. But to declare that there is an absolute contradiction would require us to define conservatism as a fixed ideology to which we can compare the equally fixed ideology of the New Right in search of complement or contradiction. But, as we have seen, this is exactly what conservatism is not. It is a varied and intrinsically variable philosophy of political reason. It is always defined by that which it opposes at any particular instance. As Freeden argues, Conservatism is 'an ideology predominantly concerned with the problem of change: not necessarily proposing to eliminate it, but to render it safe' (1996: 332). It does not persist in advocating the same things at all times but rather resists whatever represents a current danger to it. This leads conservatism, in Freeden's phrase, to develop a kind of 'mirror-image' of whatever ideology is prominent and which it wishes to oppose, what Mannheim saw as a counterutopia, a 'means of self-orientation and defence' when the 'as is' is disrupted by opposing forces. In the twentieth century, this has been socialism and welfarism. While libertarianism may appear to advocate a number of positions at odds with conservative sensibility, it also represents a solid challenge to socialist or liberal interventionism and, while it stresses a universal right that applies to all equally, it does not endorse the substantive claims of equality found in socialism or moderate liberalism. It thus defends the civil sphere of association that is so prized by the conservative.

CONCLUSION

In this chapter, we have tried to treat the philosophy of conservatism in simple and easily distinguishable terms. This, however, is something of a false activity. Conservatism itself points out the problems caused by trying to categorise too neatly, and we have probably demonstrated them here. Conservatism (like most political theories) is a fluid and varied movement of thought. In concentrating on Scruton and Oakeshott, we have been examining a very particular brand of conservatism (notably an English one), and we have done so in order to draw out an approach to the doing of philosophy and the doing of politics that is distinctly conservative. The cost of this has been a downplaying of the variety of this tradition. We have also considered the apparent shift in political conservatism that has so shaped the last thirty years of 'new right' government. But perhaps we should also emphasise the national differences of conservatism, as this may in fact provide the best explanation for recent changes to conservatism thinking. Clinton Rossiter pointed out some time ago that 'American conservatism never had the need or opportunity to be as gloomy, apprehensive, elitist, anti-progressive, or anti-liberal as European Conservatism' (1962: 201). He saw the US brand as more optimistic, materialistic and individualistic. Perhaps, then, we have witnessed not the wholesale transformation of conservatism but rather its Americanisation.

Recently, some figures from the social democratic left and even the radical left have appeared to embrace something a little like conservatism. Anthony Giddens, the sociologist who has advised the Blair government in Britain, has called for a 'philosophic conservatism' concerned with redeveloping or repairing social cohesion and solidarity (1994: 27–30). For Giddens, the normative and moral character of traditions has been lost to a 'de-traditionalising' world, and we need to find something to put in its place. A rather different sort of left-wing thinker has pointed out that 'It is now the Right which believes it has the right to shortcut political process because it benefits from the indisputable laws of one science, economics, that explains everything else' (Latour, 1999: 19). Furthermore, large sections of the British and American liberal and left intellectual communities have turned to the insights of postmodernism and post-structuralism in order to develop a social and political philosophy that is sensitive to historical and cultural context and to the contingency of social life. They have come to oppose the abstract rationalism of Liberalism and traditional Marxism. Perhaps, today, 'we' peoples of the West all live in irredeemably secular and disenchanted times. As a result, we lack anything that might console our frail selves, exposed as they are to the valueless brutality of natural life. Faced with this, we are easily tempted to find things in this world that enable us to imagine that human action and acts are the true centre of our universe. Then we make ourselves the object of worship, even our 'rational' utility-maximising and acquisitive selves. In so doing, we make the project of organising society into one that will redeem us as a species. This is exactly what the conservative cautions against, and the strangest paradox of our time may be that it is self-proclaimed conservatives who are doing it while radicals and liberals demand the defence of 'tradition'.

'RATIONALISM IN POLITICS' BY MICHAEL OAKESHOTT

While the English philosopher Michael Oakeshott (1901–90) should certainly be regarded as politically a conservative, he is probably better understood (philosophically) as Oakeshottian. As conservatives will, he objected to both empiricism and rationalism on the grounds that they failed to recognise the importance of history and tradition in organising the experience of a community and transmitting practical morality. Later, he developed insights into the nature of civil association and the need for properly constituted authorities to rule it. Civil association can be either 'moral' or 'enterprise' association, where the latter is created for the attainment of some specific purpose (an enterprise of some sort) and is rejected by Oakeshott since, for him, the state has no specific purpose to fulfil (such as the establishment of social justice). His most important work can be found in *Rationalism in Politics and Other Essays* (Methuen, 1962), *On Human Conduct* (Clarendon, 1990) and *Experience and its Modes* (Cambridge University Press, 1933). The extract is from the well-known essay 'Rationalism in Politics' and should serve to spell out what it is Oakeshott found reprehensible in the conduct of politics in the twentieth century. His arguments can helpfully be considered alongside other forms of 'anti-rationalism', particularly that advanced by the 'postmodern' left and 'postmodern' liberals such as Laclau, Mouffe and Connolly (for the former) and Rorty (an example of the latter).

'RATIONALISM IN POLITICS' (1962)*

Michael Oakeshott

Les grands hommes, en apprenant aux faibles à réfléchir, les ont mis sur la route de l'erreur (Vauvenargues, *Maxims et Réflexions*, 221)

1

The object of this essay is to consider the character and pedigree of the most remarkable intellectual fashion of post-Renaissance Europe. The Rationalism with which I am concerned is modern Rationalism. No doubt its surface reflects the light of rationalisms of a more distant past, but in its depth there is a quality

---

* From Michael Oakeshott, 'Rationalism in Politics', *Rationalism in Politics and Other Essays* (London: Methuen, 1962), pp. 1–38.

exclusively its own, and it is this quality that I propose to consider, and to consider mainly in its impact upon European politics. What I call Rationalism in politics is not, of course, the only (and it is certainly not the most fruitful) fashion in modern European political thinking. But it is a strong and a lively manner of thinking which, finding support in its filiation with so much else that is strong in the intellectual composition of contemporary Europe, has come to colour the ideas, not merely of one, but of all political persuasions, and to flow over every party line. By one road or another, by conviction, by its supposed inevitability, by its alleged success, or even quite unreflectively, almost all politics today have become Rationalist or near-Rationalist.

The general character and disposition of the Rationalist are, I think, not difficult to identify. At bottom he stands (he always *stands*) for independence of mind on all occasions, for thought free from obligation to any authority save the authority of 'reason'. His circumstances in the modern world have made him contentious: he is the *enemy* of authority, of prejudice, of the merely traditional, customary or habitual. His mental attitude is at once sceptical and optimistic: sceptical, because there is no opinion, no habit, no belief, nothing so firmly rooted or so widely held that he hesitates to question it and to judge it by what he calls his 'reason'; optimistic, because the Rationalist never doubts the power of his 'reason' (when properly applied) to determine the worth of a thing, the truth of an opinion or the propriety of an action. Moreover, he is fortified by a belief in a 'reason' common to all mankind, a common power of rational consideration, which is the ground and inspiration of argument: set up on his door is the precept of Parmenides – judge by rational argument. But besides this, which gives the Rationalist a touch of intellectual equalitarianism, he is something also of an individualist, finding it difficult to believe that anyone who can think honestly and clearly will think differently from himself.

But it is an error to attribute to him an excessive concern with *a priori* argument. He does not neglect experience, but he often appears to do so because he insists always upon it being his own experience (wanting to begin everything *de novo*), and because of the rapidity with which he reduces the tangle and variety of experience to a set of principles which he will then attack or defend only upon rational grounds. He has no sense of the cumulation of experience, only of the readiness of experience when it has been converted into a formula: the past is significant to him only as an encumbrance. He has none of that *negative capability* (which Keats attributed to Shakespeare), the power of accepting the mysteries and uncertainties of experience without any irritable search for order and distinctness, only the capability of subjugating experience; he has no aptitude for that close and detailed appreciation of what actually presents itself which Lichtenberg called *negative enthusiasm*, but only the power of recognizing the large outline which a general theory imposes upon events. His cast of mind is gnostic, and the sagacity of Ruhnken's rule, *Oportet quaedam nescire*, is lost upon him. There are some minds which give us the sense that they have passed through an elaborate education which was designed to initiate them into the traditions and achievements of their civilization; the immediate impression we have of them is an impression of cultivation, of the enjoyment of an inheritance. But this is not so with the mind of the Rationalist, which impresses us as, at best, a finely-tempered, neutral instrument, as a well-trained rather than as an educated mind. Intellectually, his ambition is not so much to share the experience of the race as to be demonstrably a self-made man. And this gives to his intellectual and practical activities an almost preternatural deliberateness and self-consciousness, depriving them of any element of passivity, removing from them all sense of rhythm and continuity and dissolving them into a succession of climacterics, each to be surmounted by a *tour de raison*. His mind has no atmosphere, no changes of season and temperature; his intellectual processes so far as possible, are insulated from all external influence and go on in the void. And having cut himself off from the traditional knowledge of his society, and denied the value of any education more extensive than a training in a technique of analysis, he is apt to attribute to mankind a necessary inexperience in all the critical moments of life, and if he were more self-critical he might begin to wonder how the race had ever succeeded in surviving. With an almost poetic fancy, he strives to live each day as if it were his first, and he believes that to form a habit is to fail. And if, with as yet no thought of analysis, we glance below the surface, we may, perhaps, see in the temperament, if not in the character, of the Rationalist, a deep distrust of time, an impatient hunger for eternity and an irritable nervousness in the face of everything topical and transitory.

Now, of all worlds, the world of politics might seem the least amenable to rationalist treatment – politics, always so deeply veined with both the traditional, the circumstantial and the transitory. And, indeed, some convinced Rationalists have admitted defeat here: Clemenceau, intellectually a child of the modern Rationalist tradition (in his treatment of morals and religion, for example), was anything but a Rationalist in politics. But not all have admitted defeat. If we except religion, the greatest apparent victories of Rationalism have been in politics: it is not to be expected that whoever is prepared to carry his rationalism into the conduct of life will hesitate to carry it into the conduct of public affairs.[1]

But what is important to observe in such a man (for it is characteristic) is not the decisions and actions he is inspired to make, but the source of his inspiration, his idea (and with him it will be a deliberate and conscious idea) of political activity. He believes, of course, in the open mind, the mind free from prejudice and its relic, habit. He believes that the unhindered human 'reason' (if only it can be brought to bear) is an infallible guide in political activity. Further, he believes in argument as the technique and operation of 'reason'; the truth of an opinion and the 'rational' ground (not the use) of an institution is all that matters to him. Consequently, much of his political activity consists in bringing the social, political, legal and institutional inheritance of his society before the tribunal of his intellect; and the rest is rational administration, 'reason' exercising an uncontrolled jurisdiction over the circumstances of the case. To the Rationalist, nothing is of value merely because it exists (and certainly not because it has existed for many generations), familiarity has no worth, and nothing is to be left standing for want of scrutiny. And his disposition makes both destruction and creation easier for him to understand and engage in than acceptance or reform. To patch up, to repair (that is, to do anything which requires a patient knowledge of the material), he regards as waste of time; and he always prefers the invention of a new device to making use of a current and well-tried expedient. He does not recognize change unless it is a self-consciously induced change, and consequently he falls easily into the error of identifying the customary and the traditional with the changeless. This is aptly illustrated by the rationalist attitude towards a tradition of ideas. There is, of course, no question either of retaining or improving such a tradition, for both these involve an attitude of submission. It must be destroyed. And to fill its place the Rationalist puts something of his own making – an ideology, the formalized abridgement of the supposed substratum of rational truth contained in the tradition.

The conduct of affairs, for the Rationalist, is a matter of solving problems, and in this no man can hope to be successful whose reason has become inflexible by surrender to habit or is clouded by the fumes of tradition. In this activity the character which the Rationalist claims for himself is the character of the engineer, whose mind (it is supposed) is controlled throughout by the appropriate technique and whose first step is to dismiss from his attention everything not directly related to his specific intentions. This assimilation of politics to engineering is, indeed, what may be called the myth of rationalist politics. And it is, of course, a recurring theme in the literature of Rationalism. The politics it inspires may be called the politics of the felt need; for the Rationalist, politics are always charged with the feeling of the moment. He waits upon circumstance to provide him with his problems, but rejects its aid in their solution. That anything should be allowed to stand between a society and the satisfaction of the felt needs of each moment in its history must appear to the Rationalist a piece of mysticism and nonsense. And his politics are, in fact, the rational solution of those practical conundrums which the recognition of the sovereignty of the felt need perpetually creates in the life of a society. Thus, political life is resolved into a succession of crises, each to be surmounted by the application of 'reason'. Each generation, indeed, each administration, should see unrolled before it the blank sheet of infinite possibility. And if by chance this *tabula rasa* has been defaced by the irrational scribblings of tradition-ridden ancestors, then the first task of the Rationalist must be to scrub it clean; as Voltaire remarked, the only way to have good laws is to burn all existing laws and to start afresh.[2]

Two other general characteristics of rationalist politics may be observed. They are the politics of perfection, and they are the politics of uniformity; either of these characteristics without the other denotes a different style of politics, the essence of rationalism is their combination. The evanescence of imperfection may be said to be the first item of the creed of the Rationalist. He is not devoid of humility; he can imagine a problem which would remain impervious to the onslaught of his own reason. But what he cannot imagine is politics which do not consist in solving problems, or a political problem of which there is no 'rational' solution at all. Such a problem must be counterfeit. And the 'rational' solution of any problem is, in its nature, the perfect solution. There is no place in his scheme for a 'best in the circumstances', only a place for 'the best'; because the function of reason is precisely to surmount circumstances. Of course, the Rationalist is not always a perfectionist in general, his mind governed in each occasion by a comprehensive Utopia; but invariably he is a perfectionist in detail. And from this politics of perfection springs the politics of uniformity; a scheme which does not recognize circumstance can have no place for variety. 'There must in the nature of things be one best form of government which all intellects, sufficiently roused from the slumber of savage ignorance, will be irresistibly incited to approve', writes Godwin. This intrepid Rationalist states in general what a more modest believer might prefer to assert only in detail; but the principle holds – there may not be one universal remedy for all political ills, but the remedy for any particular ill is as universal in its application as it is rational in its conception. If the rational solution for one of the problems of a society has been determined, to permit any relevant part of the society to escape from the solution is, *ex hypothesi*, to countenance irrationality. There can be no place for preference that is not rational preference, and all rational preferences necessarily coincide. Political activity is recognized as the imposition of a uniform condition of perfection upon human conduct.

The modern history of Europe is littered with the projects of the politics of Rationalism. The most sublime of these is, perhaps, that of Robert Owen for 'a world convention to emancipate the human race from ignorance, poverty, division, sin and misery' – so sublime that even a Rationalist (but without much justification) might think it eccentric. But not less characteristic are the diligent search of the present generation for an innocuous power which may safely be made so great as to be able to control all other powers in the human world, and the common disposition to believe that political machinery can take the place of moral and political education. The notion of founding a society, whether of individuals or of States, upon a Declaration of the Rights of Man is a creature of the rationalist brain, so also are 'national' or racial self-determination when elevated into universal principles. The project of the so-called Re-union of the Christian Churches, of open diplomacy, of a single tax, of a civil service whose members 'have no qualifications other than their personal abilities', of a self-consciously planned society, the Beveridge Report, the Education Act of 1944, Federalism, Nationalism, Votes for Women, the Catering Wages Act, the destruction of the Austro-Hungarian Empire, the World State (of H. G. Wells or anyone else), and the revival of Gaelic as the official language of Eire, are alike the progeny of Rationalism. The odd generation of rationalism in politics is by sovereign power out of romanticism.

2

The placid lake of Rationalism lies before us in the character and disposition of the Rationalist, its surface familiar and not unconvincing, its waters fed by many visible tributaries. But in its depths there flows a hidden spring, which, though it was not the original fountain from which the lake grew, is perhaps the pre-eminent source of its endurance. This spring is a doctrine about human knowledge. That some such fountain lies at the heart of Rationalism will not surprise even those who know only its surface; the superiority of the unencumbered intellect lay precisely in the fact that it could reach more, and more certain, knowledge about man and society than was otherwise possible; the superiority of the ideology over the tradition lay in its greater precision and its alleged demonstrability. Nevertheless, it is not, properly speaking, a philosophical theory of knowledge, and it can be explained with agreeable informality.

Every science, every art, every practical activity requiring skill of any sort, indeed every human activity whatsoever, involves knowledge. And, universally, this knowledge is of two sorts, both of which are always involved in any actual activity. It is not, I think, making too much of it to call them two sorts of knowledge, because (though in fact they do not exist separately) there are certain important differences between them. The first sort of knowledge I will call technical knowledge or knowledge of technique. In every art and science, and in every practical activity, a technique is involved. In many activities this technical knowledge is formulated into rules which are, or may be, deliberately learned, remembered, and, as we say, put into practice; but whether or not it is, or has been, precisely formulated, its chief characteristic is that it is susceptible of precise formulation, although special skill and insight may be required to give it that formulation.[3] The technique (or part of it) of driving a motor car on English roads is to be found in the Highway Code, the technique of cookery is contained in the cookery book, and the technique of discovery in natural science or in history is in their rules of research, of observation and verification. The second sort of knowledge I will call practical, because it exists only in use, is not reflective and (unlike technique) cannot be formulated in rules. This does not mean, however, that it is an esoteric sort of knowledge. It means only that the method by which it may be shared and becomes common knowledge is not the method of formulated doctrine. And if we consider it from this point of view, it would not, I think, be misleading to speak of it as traditional knowledge. In every activity this sort of knowledge is also involved; the mastery of any skill, the pursuit of any concrete activity is impossible without it.

These two sorts of knowledge, then, distinguishable but inseparable, are the twin components of the knowledge involved in every concrete human activity. In a practical art, such as cookery, nobody supposes that the knowledge that belongs to the good cook is confined to what is or may be written down in the cookery book; technique and what I have called practical knowledge combine to make skill in cookery wherever it exists. And the same is true of the fine arts, of painting, of music, of poetry; a high degree of technical knowledge, even where it is both subtle and ready, is one thing; the ability to create a work of art, the ability to compose something with real musical qualities, the ability to write a great sonnet, is another, and requires, in addition to technique, this other sort of knowledge. Again, these two sorts of knowledge are involved in any genuinely scientific activity.[4] The natural scientist will certainly make use of the rules of observation and verification that belong to his technique, but these rules remain only one of the components of his knowledge; advance in scientific discovery was never achieved merely by following the rules.[5] The same situation may be observed also in religion. It would, I think, be excessively liberal to call a man a Christian who was wholly ignorant of the technical side of Christianity, who knew nothing of creed or formulary, but it would be even more absurd to maintain that even the readiest knowledge of creed and catechism ever constituted the whole of the knowledge that belongs to a Christian. And what is true of cookery, of painting, of natural science and of religion, is no less true of politics: the knowledge involved in political activity is both technical and practical.[6] Indeed, as in all arts which have men as their plastic material, arts such as medicine, industrial management, diplomacy, and the art of military command, the knowledge involved in political activity is pre-eminently of this dual character. Nor, in these arts, is it correct to say that whereas technique will tell a man (for example, a doctor) *what* to do, it is practice which tells him *how* to do it – the 'bed-side manner', the appreciation of the individual with whom he has to deal. Even in the *what*, and above all in diagnosis, there lies already this dualism of technique and practice: there is no knowledge which is not 'know how'. Nor, again, does the distinction between technical and practical knowledge coincide with the distinction between a knowledge of means and a knowledge of ends, though on occasion it may appear to do so. In short, nowhere, and pre-eminently not in political activity, can technical knowledge be separated from practical knowledge, and nowhere can they be considered identical with one another or able to take the place of one another.[7]

Now, what concerns us are the differences between these two sorts of knowledge; and the important differences are those which manifest themselves in the divergent ways in which these sorts of knowledge can be expressed and in the divergent ways in which they can be learned or acquired.

Technical knowledge, we have seen, is susceptible of formulation in rules, principles, directions, maxims – comprehensively, in propositions. It is possible to write down technical knowledge in a book. Consequently, it does not surprise us that when an artist writes about his art, he writes only about the technique of his art. This is so, not because he is ignorant of what may be called the aesthetic element, or thinks it unimportant, but because what he has to say about *that* he has said already (if he is a painter) in his pictures, and he knows no other way of saying it. And the same is true when a religious man writes about his religion[8] or a cook about cookery. And it may be observed that this character of being susceptible of precise formulation gives to technical knowledge at least the appearance of certainty: it appears to be possible to be certain about a technique. On the other hand, it is a characteristic of practical knowledge that it is not susceptible of formulation of this kind. Its normal expression is in a customary or traditional way of doing things, or, simply, in practice. And this gives it the appearance of imprecision and consequently of uncertainty, of being a matter of opinion, of probability rather than truth. It is, indeed, a knowledge that is expressed in taste or connoisseurship, lacking rigidity and ready for the impress of the mind of the learner.

Technical knowledge can be learned from a book; it can be learned in a correspondence course. Moreover, much of it can be learned by heart, repeated by rote, and applied mechanically: the logic of the syllogism is a technique of this kind. Technical knowledge, in short, can be both taught and learned in the simplest meanings of these words. On the other hand, practical knowledge can neither be taught nor learned, but only imparted and acquired. It exists only in practice, and the only way to acquire it is by apprenticeship to a master – not because the master can teach it (he cannot), but because it can be acquired only by continuous contact with one who is perpetually practising it. In the arts and in natural science what normally happens is that the pupil, in being taught and in learning the technique from his master, discovers himself to have acquired also another sort of knowledge than merely technical knowledge, without it ever having been precisely imparted and often without being able to say precisely what it is. Thus a pianist acquires artistry as well as technique, a chess-player style and insight into the game as well as a knowledge of the moves, and a scientist acquires (among other things) the sort of judgement which tells him when his technique is leading him astray and the connoisseurship which enables him to distinguish the profitable from the unprofitable directions to explore.

Now, as I understand it, Rationalism is the assertion that what I have called practical knowledge is not knowledge at all, the assertion that, properly speaking, there is no knowledge which is not technical knowledge. The Rationalist holds that the only element of *knowledge* involved in any human activity is technical knowledge, and that what I have called practical knowledge is really only a sort of nescience which would be negligible if it were not positively mischievous. The sovereignty of 'reason', for the Rationalist, means the sovereignty of technique.

The heart of the matter is the pre-occupation of the Rationalist with certainty. Technique and certainty are, for him, inseparably joined because certain knowledge is, for him, knowledge which does not require to look beyond itself for its certainty; knowledge, that is, which not only ends with certainty but begins with certainty and is certain throughout. And this is precisely what technical knowledge appears to be. It seems to be a self-complete sort of knowledge because it seems to range between an identifiable initial point (where it breaks in upon sheer ignorance) and an identifiable terminal point, where it is complete, as in learning the rules of a new game. It has the aspect of knowledge that can be contained wholly between the two covers of a book, whose application is, as nearly as possible, purely mechanical, and which does not assume a knowledge not itself provided in the technique. For example, the superiority of an ideology over a tradition of thought lies in its appearance of being self-contained. It can be taught best to those whose minds are empty; and if it is to be taught to one who already believes something, the first step of the teacher must be to administer a purge, to make certain that all prejudices and preconceptions are removed, to lay his foundation upon the unshakeable rock of absolute ignorance. In short, technical knowledge appears to be the only kind of knowledge which satisfies the standard of certainty which the Rationalist has chosen.

Now, I have suggested that the knowledge involved in every concrete activity is never solely technical knowledge. If this is true, it would appear that the error of the Rationalist is of a simple sort – the error of mistaking a part for the whole, of endowing a part with the qualities of the whole. But the error of the Rationalist does not stop there. If his great illusion is the sovereignty of technique, he is no less deceived by the apparent certainty of technical knowledge. The superiority of technical knowledge lay in its appearance of springing from pure ignorance and ending in certain and complete knowledge, its appearance of both beginning and ending with certainty. But, in fact, this is an illusion. As with every other sort of knowledge, learning a technique does not consist in getting rid of pure ignorance, but in reforming knowledge which is already there. Nothing, not even the most nearly self-contained technique (the rules of a game), can in fact be imparted to an empty mind; and what is imparted is nourished by what is already there. A man who knows the rules of one game will, on this account, rapidly learn the rules of another game; and a man altogether unfamiliar with 'rules' of any kind (if such can be imagined) would be a most unpromising pupil. And just as the self-made man is never literally *self-made*, but depends upon a certain kind of society and upon a large unrecognized inheritance, so technical knowledge is never, in fact, self-complete, and can be made to appear so only if we forget the hypotheses with which it begins. And if its self-completeness is illusory, the certainty which was attributed to it on account of its self-completeness is also an illusion.

But my object is not to refute Rationalism; its errors are interesting only in so far as they reveal its character. We are considering not merely the truth of a doctrine, but the significance of an intellectual fashion in the history of post-Renaissance Europe.

[. . .]

3

Neither religion, nor natural science, nor education, nor the conduct of life itself escaped from the influence of the new Rationalism; no activity was immune, no society untouched.[9]

The slowly mediated changes by which the Rationalist of the seventeenth century became the Rationalist as we know him today, are a long and complicated story which I do not propose even to abridge. It is important only to observe that, with every step it has taken away from the true sources of its inspiration, the Rationalist character has become cruder and more vulgar. What in the seventeenth century was '*L'art de penser*' has now become *Your mind and how to use it, a plan by world-famous experts for developing a trained mind at a fraction of the usual cost*. What was the *Art of Living* has become the *Technique of Success*, and the early and more modest incursions of the sovereignty of technique into education have blossomed into *Pelmanism*.

The deeper motivations which encouraged and developed this intellectual fashion are, not unnaturally, obscure; they are hidden in the recesses of European society. But among its other connections, it is certainly closely allied with a decline in the belief in Providence: a beneficient and infallible technique replaced a beneficient and infallible God; and where Providence was not available to correct the mistakes of men it was all the more necessary to prevent such mistakes. Certainly, also, its provenance is a society or a generation which thinks what it has discovered for itself is more important than what it has inherited,[10] an age over-impressed with its own accomplishment and liable to those illusions of intellectual grandeur which are the characteristic lunacy of post-Renaissance Europe, an age never mentally at peace with itself because never reconciled with its past. And the vision of a technique which puts all minds on the same level provided just that short cut which would attract men in a hurry to appear educated but incapable of appreciating the concrete detail of their total inheritance. And, partly under the influence of Rationalism itself, the number of such men has been steadily growing since the seventeenth century.[11] Indeed it may be said that all, or almost all, the influences which in its early days served to encourage the emergence of the Rationalist character have subsequently become more influential in our civilization.

[. . .]

4

That all contemporary politics are deeply infected with Rationalism will be denied only by those who choose to give the infection another name. Not only are our political vices rationalistic, but so also are our political virtues. Our projects are, in the main, rationalist in purpose and character; but, what is more significant, our whole attitude of mind in politics is similarly determined. And those traditional elements, particularly in English politics, which might have been expected to continue some resistance to the pressure of Rationalism, have now almost completely conformed to the prevailing intellectual temper, and even represent this conformity to be a sign of their vitality, their ability to move with the times. Rationalism has ceased to be merely one style in politics and has become the stylistic criterion of all respectable politics.

How deeply the rationalist disposition of mind has invaded our political thought and practice is illustrated by the extent to which traditions of behaviour have given place to ideologies, the extent to which the politics of destruction and creation have been substituted for the politics of repair, the consciously planned and deliberately executed being considered (for that reason) better than what has grown up and established itself unselfconsciously over a period of time. This conversion of habits of behaviour, adaptable and never quite fixed or finished, into comparatively rigid systems of abstract ideas is not, of course, new; so far as England is concerned it was begun in the seventeenth century, in the dawn of rationalist politics. But, while formerly it was tacitly resisted and retarded by, for example, the informality of English politics (which enabled us to escape, for a long time, putting too high a value on political action and placing too high a hope in political achievement – to escape, in politics at least, the illusion of the evanescence of imperfection), that resistance has now itself been converted into an ideology.[12] This is, perhaps, the main significance of Hayek's *Road to Serfdom* – not the cogency of his doctrine, but the fact that it is a doctrine. A plan to resist all planning may be better than its opposite, but it belongs to the same style of politics. And only in a society already deeply infected with Rationalism will the conversion of the traditional resources of resistance to the tyranny of Rationalism into a self-conscious ideology be considered a strengthening of those resources. It seems that now, in order to participate in politics and expect a hearing, it is necessary to have, in the strict sense, a doctrine; not to have a doctrine appears frivolous, even disreputable. And the sanctity, which in some societies was the property of a politics piously attached to traditional ways, has now come to belong exclusively to rationalist politics.

Rationalist politics, I have said, are the politics of the felt need, the felt need not qualified by a genuine, concrete knowledge of the permanent interests and direction of movement of a society, but interpreted by 'reason' and satisfied according to the technique of an ideology: they are the politics of the book. And this also is characteristic of almost all contemporary politics: not to have a book is to be without the one thing necessary, and not to observe meticulously what is written in the book is to be a disreputable politician. Indeed, so necessary is it to have a book, that those who have hitherto thought it possible to get on without one, have had, rather late in the day, to set about composing one for their own use. This is a symptom of the triumph of technique which we have seen to be the root of modern Rationalism; for what the book contains is only what it is possible to put into a book – rules of a technique. And, book in hand (because, though a technique can be learned by rote, they have not always learned their lesson well), the politicians of Europe pore over the simmering banquet they are preparing for the future; but, like jumped-up kitchen-porters deputizing for an absent cook, their knowledge does not extend beyond the written word which they read mechanically – it generates ideas in their heads but no tastes in their mouths.

Among the other evidences of Rationalism in contemporary politics may be counted the commonly admitted claim of the 'scientist' as such (the chemist, the physicist, the economist or the psychologist) to be heard in politics; because, though the knowledge involved in a science is always more than technical knowledge, what it has to offer to politics is never more than a technique. And under this influence, the intellect in politics ceases to be the critic of political habit and becomes a substitute for habit, and the life of a society loses its rhythm and continuity and is resolved into a succession of problems and crises. Folk-lore, because it is not technique, is identified with nescience, and all sense of what Burke called the partnership between present and past is lost.

[. . .]

What are the circumstances that promoted this state of affairs? For the significance of the triumph lies not merely in itself, but in its context.

Briefly, the answer to this question is that the politics of Rationalism are the politics of the politically inexperienced, and that the outstanding characteristic of European politics in the last four centuries is that they have suffered the incursion of at least three types of political inexperience – that of the new ruler, of the new ruling class, and of the new political society – to say nothing of the incursion of a new sex. How appropriate rationalist politics are to the man who, not brought up or educated to their exercise, finds himself in a position to exert political initiative and authority, requires no emphasis. His need of it is so great that he will have no incentive to be sceptical about the possibility of a magic technique of politics which will remove the handicap of his lack of political education. The offer of such a technique will seem to him the offer of salvation itself; to be told that the necessary knowledge is to be found, complete and self-contained, in a book, and to be told that this knowledge is of a sort that can be learned by heart quickly and applied mechanically, will seem, like salvation, something almost too good to be true.

The new and politically inexperienced social classes which, during the last four centuries, have risen to the exercise of political initiative and authority have been provided for in the same sort of way as Machiavelli provided for the new prince of the sixteenth century. None of these classes had time to acquire a political education before it came to power; each needed a crib, a political doctrine, to take the place of a habit of political behaviour. Some of these writings are genuine works of political vulgarization; they do not altogether deny the existence or worth of a political tradition (they are written by men of real political education), but they are abridgements of a tradition, rationalizations purporting to elicit the 'truth' of a tradition and to exhibit it in a set of abstract principles, but from which, nevertheless, the full significance of the tradition inevitably escapes. This is pre-eminently so of Locke's *Second Treatise of Civil Government*, which was as popular, as long-lived and as valuable a political crib as that greatest of all cribs to a religion, Paley's *Evidences of Christianity*. But there are other writers, like Bentham or Godwin, who, pursuing the common project of providing for the political inexperience of succeeding generations, cover up all trace of the political habit and tradition of their society with a purely speculative idea: these belong to the strictest sect of Rationalism. But, so far as authority is concerned, nothing in this field can compare with the work of Marx and Engels. European politics without these writers would still have been deeply involved in Rationalism, but beyond question they are the authors of the most stupendous of our political rationalisms – as well they might be, for it was composed for the instruction of a less politically educated class than any other that has ever come to have the illusion of exercising political power. And no fault can be found with the mechanical manner in which this greatest of all political cribs has been learned and used by those for whom it was written. No other technique has so imposed itself upon the world as if it were concrete knowledge; none has created so vast an intellectual proletariat, with nothing but its technique to lose.[13]

The early history of the United States of America is an instructive chapter in the history of the politics of Rationalism. The situation of a society called upon without much notice to exercise political initiative on its own account is similar to that of an individual or a social class rising not fully prepared to the exercise of political power; in general, its needs are the same as theirs. And the similarity is even closer when the independence of the society concerned begins with an admitted illegality, a specific and express rejection of a tradition, which consequently can be defended only by an appeal to something which is itself thought not to depend upon tradition. Nor, in the case of the American colonists, was this the whole of the pressure which forced their revolution into the pattern of Rationalism. The founders of American independence had both a tradition of European thought and a native political habit and experience to draw upon. But, as it happened, the intellectual gifts of Europe to America (both in philosophy and religion) had, from the beginning, been predominantly rationalistic: and the native political habit, the product of the circumstances of colonisation, was what may be called a kind of natural and unsophisticated rationalism. A plain and unpretending people, not given over-much to reflection upon the habits of behaviour they had in fact inherited, who, in frontier communities, had constantly the experience of setting up law and order for themselves by mutual agreement, were not likely to think of their arrangements except as the creation of their own unaided initiative; they seemed to begin with nothing, and to owe to themselves all that they had come to possess. A civilization of pioneers is, almost unavoidably, a civilization of self-consciously self-made men, Rationalists by circumstance and not by reflection, who need no persuasion that knowledge begins with a *tabula rasa* and who regard the free mind, not even as the result of some artificial Cartesian purge, but as the gift of Almighty God, as Jefferson said.

Long before the Revolution, then, the disposition of mind of the American colonists, the prevailing intellectual character and habit of politics, were rationalistic. And this is clearly reflected in the constitutional documents and history of the individual colonies. And when these colonies came 'to dissolve the political bands which had connected them with one another', and to declare their independence, the only fresh inspiration that this habit of politics received from the outside was one which confirmed its native character in every particular. For the inspiration of Jefferson and the other founders of American independence was the ideology which Locke had distilled from the English political tradition. They were disposed to believe, and they believed more fully than was possible for an inhabitant of the Old World, that the proper organization of a society and the conduct of its affairs were based upon abstract principles, and not upon a tradition which, as Hamilton said, had 'to be rummaged for among old parchments and musty records'. These principles were not the product of civilization; they were natural, 'written in the whole volume of human nature'.[14] They were to be discovered in nature by human reason, by a technique of inquiry available alike to all men and requiring no extraordinary intelligence in its use. Moreover, the age had the advantage of all earlier ages because, by the application of this technique of inquiry, these abstract principles had, for the most part recently, been discovered and written down in books. And by using these books, a newly made political society was not only not handicapped by the lack of a tradition, but had a positive superiority over older societies not yet fully emancipated from the chains of custom. What Descartes had already perceived, 'que souvent il n'y a pas tant de perfection dans les ouvrages composés de plusieurs pièces et faits de la main de divers maîtres qu'en ceux anquels un seul a travaillé', was freshly observed in 1777 by John Jay – 'The Americans are the first people whom Heaven has favoured with an opportunity of deliberating upon, and choosing the forms of government under which they should live. All other constitutions have derived their existence from violence or accidental circumstances, and are therefore probably more distant from their perfection.'[15] The Declaration of Independence is a characteristic product of the *saeculum rationalisticum*. It represents the politics of the felt need interpreted with the aid of an ideology. And it is not surprising that it should have become one of the sacred documents of the politics of Rationalism, and, together with the similar documents of the French Revolution, the inspiration and pattern of many later adventures in the rationalist reconstruction of society.

[. . .]

5

Without alarming ourselves with imaginary evils, it may, I think, be said that there are two characteristics, in particular, of political Rationalism which make it exceptionally dangerous to a society. No sensible man will worry greatly because he cannot at once hit upon a cure for what he believes to be a crippling complaint; but if he sees the complaint to be of a kind which the passage of time must make more rather than less severe, he will have a more substantial cause for anxiety. And this unfortunately appears to be so with the disease of Rationalism.

First, Rationalism in politics, as I have interpreted it, involves an identifiable error, a misconception with regard to the nature of human knowledge, which amounts to a corruption of the mind. And consequently it is without the power to correct its own shortcomings; it has no homoeopathic quality; you cannot escape its errors by becoming more sincerely or more profoundly rationalistic. This, it may be observed, is one of the penalties of living by the book; it leads not only to specific mistakes, but it also dries up the mind itself: living by precept in the end generates intellectual dishonesty. And further, the Rationalist has rejected in advance the only external inspiration capable of correcting his error; he does not merely neglect the kind of knowledge which would save him, he begins by destroying it. First he turns out the light and then complains that he cannot see, that he is 'comme un homme qui marche seul et dans les ténèbres'. In short, the Rationalist is essentially ineducable; and he could be educated *out* of his Rationalism only by an inspiration which he regards as the great enemy of mankind. All the Rationalist can do when left to himself is to replace one rationalist project in which he has failed by another in which he hopes to succeed. Indeed, this is what contemporary politics are fast degenerating into: the political habit and tradition, which, not long ago, was the common possession of even extreme opponents in English politics, has been replaced by merely a common rationalist disposition of mind.

But, secondly, a society which has embraced a rationalist idiom of politics will soon find itself either being steered or drifting towards an exclusively rationalist form of education. I do not mean the crude purpose of National Socialism or Communism of allowing no education except a training in the dominant rationalist doctrine, I mean the more plausible project of offering no place to any form of education which is not generally rationalistic in character.[16] And when an exclusively rationalist form of education is fully established, the only hope of deliverance lies in the discovery by some neglected pedant, 'rummaging among old parchments and musty records', of what the world was like before the millennium overtook it.

[. . .]

The morality of the Rationalist is the morality of the self-made man and of the self-made society: it is what other peoples have recognized as 'idolatry'. And it is of no consequence that the moral ideology which inspires him today (and which, if he is a politician, he preaches) is, in fact, the desiccated relic of what was once the unselfconscious moral tradition of an aristocracy who, ignorant of ideals, had acquired a habit of behaviour in relation to one another and had handed it on in a true moral education. For the Rationalist, all that matters is that he has at last separated the ore of the ideal from the dross of the habit of behaviour; and, for us, the deplorable consequences of his success. Moral ideals are a sediment; they have significance only so long as they are suspended in a religious or social tradition, so long as they belong to a religious or a social life.[17] The predicament of our time is that the Rationalists have been at work so long on their project of drawing off the liquid in which our moral ideals were suspended (and pouring it away as worthless) that we are left only with the dry and gritty residue which chokes us as we try to take it down. First, we do our best to destroy parental authority (because of its alleged abuse), then we sentimentally deplore the scarcity of 'good homes', and we end by creating substitutes which complete the work of destruction. And it is for this reason that, among much else that is corrupt and unhealthy, we have the spectacle of a set of sanctimonious, rationalist politicians, preaching an ideology of unselfishness and social service to a population in which they and their predecessors have done their best to destroy the only living root of moral behaviour; and opposed by another set of politicians dabbling with the project of converting us from Rationalism under the inspiration of a fresh rationalization of our political tradition.

NOTES

1. A faithful account of the politics of rationalism (with all its confusions and ambivalences) is to be found in J. H. Blackham, *Political Discipline in a Free Society*.
2. Cf. Plato, *Republic*, 501A. The idea that you can get rid of a law by burning it is characteristic of the Rationalist, who can think of a law only as something written down.
3. G. Polya, *How to Solve It*.
4. Some excellent observations on this topic are to be found in M. Polanyi, *Science, Faith and Society*.
5. Polya, for example, in spite of the fact that his book is concerned with heuristic, suggests that the root conditions of success in scientific research are, first, 'to have brains and good luck', and secondly, 'to sit tight and wait till you get a bright idea', neither of which are technical rules.
6. Thucydides puts an appreciation of this truth into the mouth of Pericles. To be a politician and to refuse the guidance of technical knowledge is, for Pericles, a piece of folly. And yet the main theme of the Funeral Oration is not the value of technique in politics, but the value of practical and traditional knowledge (ii, 40).
7. Duke Huan of Ch'i was reading a book at the upper end of the hall; the wheelwright was making a wheel at the lower end. Putting aside his mallet and chisel, he called to the Duke and asked him what book he was reading. 'One that records the words of the Sages', answered the Duke. 'Are those Sages alive?' asked the wheelwright. 'Oh, no,' said the Duke, 'they are dead.' 'In that case,' said the wheelwright, 'what you are reading can be nothing but the lees and scum of bygone men.' 'How dare you, a wheelwright, find fault with the book I am reading. If you can explain your statement, I will let it pass. If not, you shall die.' 'Speaking as a wheelwright,' he replied, 'I look at the matter in this way; when I am making a wheel, if my stroke is too slow, then it bites deep but is not steady; if my stroke is too fast, then it is steady, but it does not go deep. The right pace, neither slow nor fast, cannot get into the hand unless it comes from the heart. It is a thing that cannot be put into words [rules]; there is an art in it that I cannot explain to my son. That is why it is impossible for me to let him take over my work, and here I am at the age of seventy still making wheels. In my opinion it must have been the same with the men of old. All that was worth handing on, died with them; the rest, they put in their books. That is why I said that what you were reading was the lees and scum of bygone men' (*Chuang Tzu*).
8. St François de Sales was a devout man, but when he writes it is about the technique of piety.

9. One important aspect of the history of the emergence of Rationalism is the changing connotation of the word 'reason'. The 'reason' to which the Rationalist appeals is not, for example, the Reason of Hooker, which belongs still to the tradition of Stoicism and of Aquinas. It is a faculty of calculation by which men conclude one thing from another and discover fit means of attaining given ends not themselves subject to the criticism of reason, a faculty by which a world believed to be a machine could be disclosed. Much of the plausibility of Rationalism lies in the tacit attribution to the new 'reason' of the qualities which belong properly to the Reason of the older intellectual tradition. And this ambiguity, the emergence of the new connotation out of the old, may be observed in many of the writers of the early seventeenth century – in, for example, the poetry of Malherbe, an older contemporary of Descartes, and one of the great progenitors of the sovereignty of technique in literature.

10. This was certainly true of the age of Bacon. And Professor Bernal now tells us that more has been found out at large and in detail about nature and man in the thirty years after 1915 than in the whole of history.

11. Not so very long ago, I suppose, the spectators at horse-races were mostly men and women who knew something at first-hand about horses, and who (in this respect) were genuinely educated people. This has ceased to be so, except perhaps in Ireland. And the ignorant spectator, with no ability, inclination or opportunity to educate himself, and seeking a short cut out of his predicament, demands *a book*. (The twentieth-century vogue in cookery books derives, no doubt, from a similar situation.) The authors of one such book, *A Guide to the Classics, or how to Pick the Derby winner*, aware of the difference between technical and complete knowledge, were at pains to point out that there was a limit beyond which there were no precise rules for picking the winner, and that some intelligence (not supplied by the rules themselves) was necessary. But some of its greedy, rationalistic readers, on the look-out for an infallible method, which (like Bacon's) would place their small wits on a level with men of genuine education, thought they had been sold a pup – which only goes to show how much better they would have spent their time if they had read St Augustine or Hegel instead of Descartes: *je ne puis pardonner à Descartes*.

12. A tentative, and therefore not a fundamentally damaging, conversion of this sort was attempted by the first Lord Halifax.

13. By casting his technique in the form of a view of the course of events (past, present and future), and not of 'human nature', Marx thought he had escaped from Rationalism; but since he had taken the precaution of first turning the course of events into a doctrine, the escape was an illusion. Like Midas, the Rationalist is always in the unfortunate position of not being able to touch anything without transforming it into an abstraction; he can never get a square meal of experience.

14. There is no space here to elucidate the exceedingly complicated connections between the politics of 'reason' and the politics of 'nature'. But it may be observed that, since both reason and nature were opposed to civilization, they began with a common ground; and the 'rational' man, the man freed from the idols and prejudices of a tradition, could, alternatively, be called the 'natural' man. Modern Rationalism and modern Naturalism in politics, in religion and in education, are alike expressions of a general presumption against all human achievement more than about a generation old.

15. Of course both 'violence' and 'accidental circumstances' were there, but being present in an unfamiliar form they were unrecognized.

16. Something of this sort happened in France after the Revolution; but it was not long before sanity began to break in.

17. When Confucius visited Lao Tzu, he talked of goodness and duty. 'Chaff from the winnower's fan', said Lao Tzu, 'can so blear the eyes that we do not know if we are looking north, south, east or west; at heaven or at earth. . . . All this talk of goodness and duty, these perpetual pin-pricks, unnerve and irritate the hearer; nothing, indeed, could be more destructive of inner tranquillity' (*Chuang Tzu*).

'LIBERALISM VERSUS CONSERVATISM' BY ROGER SCRUTON

On his homepage (rogerscruton.com), Scruton describes himself as a 'writer, philosopher, publisher, journalist, composer, editor, businessman and broad-caster'. He holds a visiting professorship in Philosophy at Birkbeck College, London, but is largely independent of institutionalised academia. A controversial figure, a keen fox-hunter and sometime advocate of tobacco companies (see *WHO, What and Why: Trans-national Government, Legitimacy and the World Health Organisation*, Institute of Economic Affairs, 2000), he is not afraid to offend. In the 1970s, he helped found the *Salisbury Review* (at the time a controversial journal of right-wing thought) and was broadly associated with the movement that brought Margaret Thatcher to power in the British Conservative Party. His philosophical work is as much (perhaps more) concerned with questions of aesthetics and culture in general as it is with politics, and he has written widely on architecture and music; see, for example, *The Aesthetics of Music* (Clarendon, 1997) and *An Intelligent Person's Guide to Modern Culture* (Duckworth, 1998). He writes for numerous popular periodicals and newspapers, and many of his books are aimed at a wider, non-specialist audience and to provoke opponents as well as promote his brand of political thinking. See *England: An Elegy* (Pimlico, 2001) and *Animal Rights and Wrongs* (Metro, 2000).

The extract reproduced here is taken from *The Meaning of Conservatism* (first published in 1980 but recently reprinted by Palgrave in 2001). A redevelopment of 'traditional' conservatism, it was probably as provocative to the right as it was to those who did not consider themselves conservative. The sections below specify quite neatly the differences, as Scruton sees them, between Liberalism and conservatism, stressing the need of the individual to form his sense of his purposes within the context of a wider community. Compare this argument with the criticism of Liberalism put forward by communitarians.

'LIBERALISM VERSUS CONSERVATISM' (1989)*

Roger Scruton

'Liberalism' is a term with many overlapping senses. In one use it denotes an attitude towards (and also a theory of) the state and its functions; in another use it denotes a moral outlook, which sometimes rises to the level of theory, but which for the most part remains hidden in the crannies of everyday existence. Its guiding principle is tolerance – although, as its critics do not fail to say, its tolerance towards non-liberals is quickly exhausted. In all its forms, liberalism incorporates an attitude of respect towards the individual existence – an attempt to leave as much moral and political space around every person as is compatible with the demands of social life. As such it has often been thought to imply a kind of egalitarianism. For by its very nature, the respect which liberalism shows to the individual, it shows to each individual equally. Partiality is itself a form of intolerance; by enlarging the space around one person, it diminishes the space enjoyed by his neighbour. In the perfect liberal suburb, the gardens are of equal size, even though decked out with the greatest possible variety of plastic gnomes.

Clearly, such an outlook – which could fairly be described as the official ideology of the Western world – is not without far-reaching assumptions concerning human nature and human fulfilment. In particular, the freedom of the individual is proposed as unquestionably valuable, and as the sole or principal criterion against which the legitimacy of social custom and political institutions is to be tested. As is well known, the criterion proves complex, and perhaps even contradictory, in its application. The very instinct which leads us to respect the freedom of an individual leads us also to curtail it, for the sake of the freedom of his neighbour. Moreover, the demand for 'equal treatment' often seems to be so pressing a requirement of the liberal outlook as to justify the most massive interference in the spontaneous projects of normal capitalist man – the 'possessive individualist' whose ideology this supposedly is. It should not go unremarked that the same emphasis on the free, self-fulfilling individual underlies both Milton Friedman's vision of a spontaneous order of private property, and Karl Marx's spectre of 'full communism', in which the freedom of all is guaranteed by the simultaneous disappearance of private property and

---

* From Roger Scruton, *The Meaning of Conservatism* (Basingstoke: Macmillan, 1989), pp. 192–203.

the institutions of the 'bourgeois' (which is to say, liberal) state. I shall argue that this tension in liberalism – which can be readily observed between the two principles of justice proposed by Rawls – is inevitable, and derives from an imperfect philosophical anthropology; the defects of this anthropology cannot be remedied without abandoning some of the fundamental tenets of the liberal outlook.

What, then, is meant, by the 'freedom of the individual'? I shall distinguish two kinds of liberal answer to this question, which I shall call, respectively, 'desire-based', and 'autonomy-based' liberalism. The first argues that a man is free to the extent that he can satisfy his desires. The modality of this 'can' is, of course, a major problem. More importantly, however, such an answer implies nothing about the value of freedom, and to take it as the basis for political theory is to risk the most absurd conclusions. By this criterion, the citizens of *Brave New World* offer a paradigm of freedom, for they live in a world designed expressly for the gratification of their every wish. A desire-based liberalism could justify the most abject slavery – provided only that the slave is induced, by whatever method, to desire his own condition. The defect of desire-based liberalism lies in its caricature of human nature – a caricature that may have appealed to Hobbes, but which ought to be accepted by a post-Kantian philosopher only with the greatest reluctance. Clearly, if freedom is to be a self-evident value, something more needs to be said about the kind of agency which requires it. This 'something more' is what I shall summarise with the word 'autonomy'. Autonomy-based liberalism argues that we are not the simple creatures of Hobbes, propelled by desires as by electrical impulses, but the more complex creatures of Kant, whose motives are shaped and reshaped by the ubiquitous operation of practical reason. We have choices and intentions, as well as desires. We act from a sense of value – and in pursuing what we value, we find a reason which both compels and justifies our conduct. Such conduct seems to issue, not from the arbitrary compulsion of a transient desire, but from the self, as the ultimate origin and final beneficiary of rational conduct.

In saying that the liberal wishes each individual, in Dworkin's words, to 'work out and live according to his own conception of the good' (the idea which is in fact common to the liberalism of Rawls and Dworkin), we are saying that it is not desire, but autonomy – the peculiar structure of motivation which characterises the Kantian rational agent – that the liberal wishes to fulfil.

Autonomy-based liberalism argues, then, that we are rational agents, or selves, and that this feature defines our predicament. Fulfilment of the individual is fulfilment of the autonomy through which he finds expression. In order to respect the individual, we must, therefore, leave room for the exercise of his autonomy. Not to do so is quite simply to deny his existence – for it is to impede the flourishing of that rational centre in which his self, or essence, resides.

It is clear at once that autonomy-based liberalism has no difficulty in explaining the value of freedom, or in finding the reason for elevating individual freedom into the ultimate test of political order. Not to respect freedom, indeed, is to threaten the very existence of those individuals for the sake of whom political order exists, and in the eyes of whom it must be made to appear in the fair colours of legitimacy.

We can also see how the concept of a right becomes central to the theory of liberalism. Rights define that sphere of privacy within which the individual resides – the sphere which must be safeguarded if his autonomy is to be preserved. His freedom may be curtailed in every particular, except this: for to curtail his rights is to diminish his existence. This is what is meant by the idea (to use Dworkin's words) that 'rights are trumps': by invoking his rights, an individual invokes his autonomy, and places in the balance of deliberation the absolute value of his own existence.

A vast gloss is required if the theory of autonomy-based liberalism is to be made cogent. For present purposes, I must assume that its broad outlines are intelligible, and that its basic vision of the human agent – as a creature motivated by rational choice – is understood.

I wish now to make, in my own terms, a familiar contrast: that between the first-person and the third-person view of human actions – between the view that *I* have upon my voluntary activities, and the view which another might also have upon them. Connected with each point of view is a mode of justification: some justifications of my action may be reasons for doing it; some may be simply reasons why it should be done. To take an example: a primitive tribesman may be dancing so as to worship the god of war. To the observing anthropologist (one persuaded by the tenets of functionalism), the dance has quite a different meaning: it exists so as to raise the spirits, and increase the cohesion of the tribe, at a time of danger.

In this example, the third-person justification could not be part of the first-person reasoning of the dancer. To think of his dance in *that* way is at once to be alienated from it, to lose the immediate and imperative quality of the motive. Hence it is to lose the spirit of the dance. The first-person reason ('Because the god demands it') is here opaque to the third-person perspective: by shutting the dancer within his dance, it abolishes the distance between agent and action. In general, it could be said, many of our actions have quite separate justifications from the first- and the third-points of view, and what may seem rational from one of those perspectives may seem quite incomprehensible from the other.

The much-canvassed opposition between liberalism and utilitarianism has, I believe, its origin in this contrast. The liberal view of human freedom is simply a generalisation of the first-person viewpoint: its idea of justification is circumscribed by the idea of a first-person reason. The justification of any constraint must consist in reasons that can be offered to the agent: reasons for *me* to obey it. And the value of freedom lies precisely in the fact that it is presupposed in every first-personal point of view.

Utilitarianism, by contrast, sees the world as it is, and not just as it seems to the agent (although, of course, how it seems to the agent is a very important part of how it is). The utilitarian rises above the individual's predicament and sees the meaning of his actions in their long-term success or disaster. Actions that are justified from this perspective may naturally seem irrational or impermissible to the agent. For the utilitarian, justification may identify no motive to action – it may even identify a motive to refrain. And a consideration that provides no motive provides no reason for *me*. It is because the first-person perspective is at least partly impermeable to third-person reasons that utilitarianism fails as an account of practical reason. And its clash with liberal values derives from the fact that, for the liberal, the first-person perspective is sovereign, and also sufficiently equipped in itself to generate the measure of political order, and the criterion of a just society.

It seems to be that the liberal is profoundly wrong in believing that the first-person perspective can generate such a measure and such a criterion. He is right, however, in believing that the perspective of the autonomous agent is inescapable, and that it is one of the first tasks of political existence to ensure that it may flourish as best it can.

The point may perhaps most clearly emerge through the contrast between liberalism and another political outlook which, like utilitarianism, is, or ought to be, wedded to the third-person perspective: the outlook of conservatism. The typical conservative resembles the functionalist anthropologist, in his concern for the long-term effects of social customs and political institutions. He sees wisdom in those immediate and consoling prejudices whereby people conduct their lives, and is reluctant to countenance the reform of institutions that seem to nurture the happiness of those who submit to them as well as any that might be offered in their place.

Liberalism, however, is essentially revisionary of existing institutions, seeking always to align them with the universal requirements of the first-person perspective – this, I believe, is the true meaning of Rawls's 'hypothetical' contract, designed to identify a point of view outside present arrangements, from which they may be surveyed and, where necessary, amended or condemned. This revisionism pertains not only to liberal political *theory*, but also to the individualistic emphasis that guides the daily conduct of the liberal-minded person. In all its variants, and at every level, liberalism embodies the question: 'Why should *I* do *that*?' The question is asked of political institutions, of legal codes, of social customs – even of morality. And to the extent that no answer is forthcoming which proves satisfactory to the first-person perspective, to that extent are we licensed to initiate change.

There are, broadly, two kinds of answer which the liberal will tolerate: an answer in terms of a first-person reason for action, and an answer in terms of a human right. In respective rights, you respect the first-person reasons of others, by conceding to them the autonomy within which those reasons prevail. The inevitable tendency of liberal theory towards an idea of natural rights can be seen to reside in this – that I can give you no reason to restrain your conduct, unless I can show that there is an objectively binding reason for you to respect the rights of others. If there can be no such reason, then no rights are 'natural' – none have greater sway in the deliberation of the autonomous agent than is provided by his own contingent willingness to accept them.

It is on this assumption that the liberal is able to assault the conservative's position. His argument is – and in the first instance must be – 'onus-shifting'. 'Why should I do that'?, he asks; and the conservative must show either (1) that the liberal has a first-person reason to do what is in question – in other words, that he can be brought rationally to *consent* to it, or (2) that he is bound to do it by his obligation to respect the objective rights of others. Without recourse to (2), the onus-shifting argument, which has proved so powerful a weapon in liberalism's war of extermination against natural intolerant humanity, reduces merely to a form of radical scepticism, to a self-centred rejection of servility, and the renunciation of all truly political existence. With the help of (2), however, the liberal is able to erect, from that very first-person perspective which is the premise of his outlook, the picture of an alternative political condition, of laws and institutions that are something more than the arbitrary legacy of custom and prejudice, and of the contingent circumstance of human history. But since I do not believe that the liberal is entitled to (2), I do not believe that he can succeed in shifting the onus of proof in quite the simple way that he supposes.

It is difficult to show this. But I shall consider a representative liberal theory, and hope that my argument will suggest its own generalisation. This theory derives originally from Kant, and puts forward a succinct but seemingly inescapable description of the first-person perspective, which is held to be definitive of our condition. I shall argue that the theory embodies a contradiction, that this contradiction is integral to the liberal idea of autonomy, and that it is also responsible for the tensions which emerge in the *application* of liberal theory. I shall defend a modified conservatism, as the alternative, and more reasonable outlook on the human condition – on the condition from which the first-person perspective grows.

According to the Kantian theory, there can be first-person reasons for action only if there are reasons which motivate action. It is because it motivates me that a reason is *my* reason. In choosing to act, I suppose myself to be inspired by reason, and also constrained by it, so that reason alone may set limits to my choice. But the heart of this supposition is the thought of my *self* as an initiating cause of action. I act, not simply because acted upon by this or that desire, but because I have chosen. In this very thought, according to the Kantian, lies the constraint of obligation: not just, what shall I do, but what ought I to do, or what would be the good course of action? If a Kantian believes that an autonomous being should be allowed to work out his 'own conception' of the good, it is because this exercise is precisely what his autonomy requires.

The exercise is held to generate real objective constraints. The autonomous being, the Kantian argues, is constrained by the thought of his own autonomy – of himself as motivated by reasons – to accept the guiding principle of practical reason, which is the categorical imperative that circumscribes his ends. This categorical imperative has three compelling variants, forced upon us by our self-conception as rational agents, and each variant seems to capture some separate strand in the outlook that has since become known as 'liberal universalism': we must act only on those considerations which we would also impose upon our fellows; we must treat rational beings not as means only but as ends; we must conduct ourselves so as to realise in our actions that 'Kingdom of Ends' in which free and equal rational beings are alike subjects and sovereigns under the law of reason.

These three ideas can be paraphrased thus: we cannot make exceptions in our own favour; we must acknowledge the universal right to autonomy; and we must endeavour to realise the ideal of equal freedom. In other words, for the Kantian, the desired liberal conclusion emerges from the premise of autonomy: the first-person viewpoint constrains the agent to recognise objective rights, and to recognise also the equal entitlement of all agents who are, like himself, blessed with a first-person perspective. Kant's résumé of this idea – the theoretical cornerstone of liberalism – is, I believe, more persuasive than anything that has since been said in support of it. Hence serious difficulties may be projected for the liberal position, should Kant's exposition be involved in a self-contradiction.

Already we can see emerging some of the *practical* contradictions of liberalism: the 'as if' of the Kingdom of Ends, which points towards a world of real equality, encounters obstinate resistance from the individual right – from the injunction that others are to be treated as ends. This, I believe, has been shown by Nozick, who incautiously believes that he can sever the second categorical imperative from the countervailing claims of the other two. In fact, it seems to me, a proper study of the three formulations will show us not only that socialism and liberalism issue equally from a single idea – that of the first-person perspective – but also that the conflict between them can never be resolved. The history of 'actually existing socialism' shows this, I believe, as well as it is shown by the history of 'actually existing liberalism'.

The major problem, as I see it, is this: Kant wishes to derive, from the premise that we are, or at least think ourselves to be, motivated by reason, the conclusion that we are also constrained by an objective principle of equal rights. In order to do this, he proceeds by a method of abstraction. He supposes that I *advance* to the standpoint of reason, by discounting my 'empirical conditions' – by removing from my thought every consideration which ties me to the 'here and now' of lived existence. Only in this way, he supposes, can I reach that standpoint 'outside nature' in which I respond to the call of reason alone. It is from this standpoint that the universal, equalising law of reason is apparent. However, as Kant acknowledges, in so abstracting from my 'contingent', or 'historical' condition, I abstract also from the circumstances of my act – and in particular from the desires and interests which initially raised, for me, the question of action. I posit my own existence as a 'transcendental self', and indeed, insofar as there is 'motivation by reason alone', only such a transcendental self could exhibit it.

But now the paradox is obvious. Clearly, a transcendental self, outside nature and outside the 'empirical conditions' of the human agent, has no capacity to act *here* and *now*. It responds to reason, but only because the world of action, having been abstracted away, no longer resists the demands of reason. The transcendental self is not an agent of change in the actual world, in which case how can the reasons which affect it also motivate it to do *this*, *here*, *now*? If I think of myself as a transcendental self, therefore, I think of myself as without a coherent motive. On the other hand, if I retain the thought of myself as an 'empirical self' – one subject to the demands of circumstance and the promptings of desire – then I can no longer reach an appreciation of my predicament by the process of abstracting away from it. This process – which may indeed take me to the point where I recognise the rights of others – deprives me of the very motive which would make it necessary. Insofar as I remain *within* my predicament, then, I must accept the historical givenness of my aims and projects, and refrain from removing myself to the point where their significance dwindles into nothing.

In short, the Kantian abstraction invites me to think of myself as the subject of an irresoluble dilemma: either I am a transcendental self, obedient to reason, in which case I cannot act; or else I am able to act, in which case my motives are part of my circumstance and history, and remain unresponsive to the voice of reason, which calls always from beyond the horizon of my present condition. The supposition that I am a concrete, historical agent of change, and at the same time bound to recognise the rights of others, becomes contradictory.

It will be said that, even if such considerations show that a contradiction arises from the Kantian attempt to justify rights from the first-person perspective, they show no more than that. They do not provide any general reason for thinking that autonomy-based liberalism *must* fail to justify natural rights.

However, it seems to me that the considerations that I have presented are generally applicable. For – while I have, for clarity's sake, presented them in the form of a familiar objection to Kant's ethical theory – they do not depend upon the detail of that theory for their force. They derive, rather, from a conflict contained in the very idea of a valid first-person reason for action. To be objectively valid, such a reason must be divorced from the conditions which distinguish *me*. It must derive its rational force from considerations which abstract from my present predicament. At the same time, it can have no *motivational* force – and hence can form no part of my first-person reasoning – unless it derives directly from the circumstances which prompt me to act. It must refer to a motive for *me*, *here*, *now*. It is the contradiction between those two requirements that I have described, and it is a contradiction that may equally be discerned in the 'Kantian constructivism' of Rawls. In Rawl's case, it takes the following form: granted that, when choosing from behind the veil of ignorance, I choose the abstract principles of justice, what then binds me to that choice when the veil is removed? Either I *am* bound, in which case I cannot emerge into the real world of agency; or else I enter that world, in which case these merely 'hypothetical considerations' cannot bind my action. Once again, the first-person perspective, which casts this shadow of natural justice in the world, remains unhampered by its shadowy demands.

Although Hume never expressed himself in the terms that I have chosen, we can see his insistence that 'reason is, and ought only to be, the slave of the passions', and his attack on the idea of practical reason generally, as a rejection of the first-person perspective, on the ground that it is fraught with illusion. For Hume, the correct outlook upon the human world must adopt the third-person point of view, in which people are seen to be immersed in the contingencies of social life, acting from passions which arise in response to the changing circumstances of existence.

The first-person perspective, which flatters me with a picture of my rationality, misrepresents my condition. The only justification that can be found for the virtuous stance that it recommends to me – the stance of justice, in which I extend towards others an active recognition of their rights – is to be found in the long-term benefit conferred upon humanity, by man's desire to deal equably with his kind. But this justification is not a first-person reason for action.

Even if we accept my conclusion, however (and I realise that much more needs to be said before we are compelled to do so), this will not require the total rejection of liberalism. Indeed, we cannot reject liberalism entirely without also abandoning the first-person perspective – something that it is neither possible nor desirable to do. I believe that Kant is right in thinking that the argument which takes him to the categorical imperative, and to the postulation of a 'transcendental self', is not *just* a piece of philosophy. It is, rather, the continuation of a thought experiment that haunts the actions of the rational being. Each of us is compelled to think in this way whenever he asks himself not, what shall I do?, but, what ought I to do? And he cannot cease to ask that question without losing all conception of the good. To safeguard his autonomy, therefore, we must safeguard the perspective from which the question of duty can be asked. The Kantian thought-experiment is, in one form or another, integral to our condition as autonomous beings – as beings who have values and intentions in addition to desires.

The argument suggests, however, that this necessary perspective is also a systematic illusion. It is necessary to sustain the illusion in everyday life. But in an important sense, it cannot sustain itself. Kant sought to validate the first-person perspective internally, so as to derive from it an abstract system of natural law. In doing so – as he repeatedly acknowledges – he came up against an insuperable barrier. It seems that the first-person perspective cannot validate itself. The best it can do is to remain innocently unaware of this, to continue peaceably *as if* it were a member of a Kingdom of Ends, and to conceal from itself the mighty, Humean, fact – that its only reason for respecting the rights of others is that this is what it wants. The first person must hide his own benevolence from himself in order to think of himself as bound. For it is the thought that I am bound by duty, Kant rightly argues, which awakens the idea that I am free.

The liberal, therefore, who rightly respects the first-person perspective as definitive of our condition, must ask himself the question: how can this perspective be sustained? If his onus-shifting argument is too often repeated, it will inevitably defeat itself. At some point, the person who asks 'why should I do that'? of every custom and every law must force upon himself the more devastating question, 'why should I do anything?' For as long as he can sustain the first-person view of action, he may comfort himself with a kind of answer: the answer in terms of Kantian natural law, which enjoins him to respect the rights of others. But, in these ultimate reaches to which the liberal pushes us, the illusion of such a law is on the point of vanishing. It needs only one further question, one more 'why?', for the edifice to collapse in ruins, and for the liberal to confront the spectre of an intransigent scepticism.

Nor can the problem be solved by moving to the third-person perspective – for to make this move is to leave motivation behind. While there may be very good reasons why I *should* be motivated by a concern of others' rights – reasons which even relate to my own happiness – they will not generate that motive. For they will not be reasons for *me*.

Nevertheless, the third-person point of view is able to give us some purchase on this problem. There is something inescapable in the Kantian theory of autonomy. It is impossible that I should *be* a transcendental self; but it is necessary that I should suffer the *illusion* that I am. Indeed, as a rational agent, I am *essentially* subject to this illusion. If I am to be fulfilled at all, I must belong to a world in which this illusion can be sustained, so that my projects are also values for me, and my desires are integrated into a vision of the good. There is, therefore, a third-person justification for the first-person perspective – a justification which, because it recognises the illusoriness of that perspective, cannot cross the barrier into the first-person point of view. Hence the conservative anthropologist will smile indulgently on the liberal; his only concern will be lest the liberal's disposition to question every given fact of community might not leave him entirely disinherited. And it is a real concern. If there is no point at which the liberal can rest with what is given, and find value immanent in the world, without recourse to transcendental illusions, then the liberal will never rest – not, at least, until he has torn down every law and every institution with his exterminating 'why?' He who shifts the onus will have to shift everything; he will confront, then, a world bereft of social artifacts, principal among which is morality itself.

I can do no more than hint at the vision which this third-person perspective proposes. But that it should be a conservative vision, in the sense outlined in these pages, is, I believe, inescapable. For consider what it is that leads people to see the world in terms of value, and so to develop that transcendental perspective which the liberal requires. Men are born into a web of attachments;

they are nurtured and protected by forces the operation of which they could neither consent to nor intend. Their very existence is burdened with a debt of love and gratitude, and it is in responding to that burden that they begin to recognise the power of 'ought'. This is not the abstract, universal 'ought' of liberal theory – or at least, not yet – but the concrete, immediate 'ought' of family attachments. It is the 'ought' of piety, which recognises the unquestionable rightness of local, transitory and historically conditioned social bonds. Such an 'ought' is essentially discriminatory; it recognises neither equality nor freedom, but only the absolute claim of the locally given.

Until he has felt that claim, the rational being has no motive to find value in the human world. Gradually, however, as he recognises the incommensurability between the demands of love, and the imperfection of the object of love, the shadow world of transcendental illusion begins to grow. Liberalism is the salve with which he attempts to heal a primal disappointment. It is the expiation of an original sin: the sin of love.

It seems to me, therefore, that if there are arguments for liberalism, there are stronger arguments for conservatism. For we must conserve the institutions, customs and, in particular, the local attachments through which the first-person perspective of the liberal is nurtured. At the same time, these attachments, being founded not in abstract justice but in Wordsworth's 'natural piety', are corroded by the very liberal conscience which they generate. They can no more resist the why?' of reason than a parent can resist the withering reproaches of his child.

The Hegelian defence of the family at which I have just hinted requires much more elaboration than I have provided. But, by way of illustrating the paradox of liberalism – that it is doomed to corrode the conditions which nurture it – I should like to give a political illustration: the institution of monarchy.

There is no doubt in my mind that, from the third-person point of view, monarchy is the most reasonable form of government. By embodying the state in a fragile human person, it captures the arbitrariness and the givenness of political allegiance, and so transforms allegiance into affection. The attachment to a monarch is a natural response and the simplest possible way of discharging the debt of obligation into which every political being is born. And what more reasonable way to govern people than by their affections?

At the same time, from the first-person perspective, the loyalty to the monarch is mysterious. It is an immediate, unthinking prejudice, which has no reason beside itself. To look for reasons – in the character of the sovereign, for example – is to open the way to irony and doubt. Once the liberal asks his question, therefore, the institution begins to suffer from the shock. At the same time, *that* he asks this question is inevitable.

When the medieval jurists such as Fortescue advocated the *constitutio libertatis*, it was in order to bind the monarch by his own laws – in other words, in order to subject the absolute attachment to the will of the sovereign to the equalizing discipline of an abstract right. By a series of compromises, both the attachment and the discipline have survived. And there is no doubt that the result has been beneficial. But whether either could survive, when liberalism finally triumphs, is a matter of doubt. The best we can hope for, I believe, is that liberals will begin to take their own ideology seriously, and so compromise with conservatism. They may call this compromise 'reflective equilibrium', and thereby imagine that it is reasonable, in just the way that the first-person singular is always reasonable. But of course, it will not be reasonable, and the best that can be hoped is that, by this and similar devices, the liberal rationalist may finally rest content with a prejudice that is not of his own devising.

5

MARXISMS AND POST-MARXISMS

Terrell Carver

INTRODUCTION

The Marxism–Liberalism confrontation is possibly the most important in modern politics and in political theory. The clash has been most dramatically reflected in drastic institutional change and outright warfare, 'cold' and 'hot', on a global scale. On a more theoretical level, debates have often merely tracked the politically expedient lines of attack, rather than making visible the longer-term and more interesting approaches to what is at stake. Now that global politics has become less polarized along the Marxism–Liberalism binary, and the discipline of political theory somewhat more sophisticated philosophically, dormant issues have come to the surface. Current controversies between Marxists and post-Marxists have made some of these concerns more apparent – a process that will continue as political alignments shift along new lines of difference.

In this chapter, I take a long and critical view in order to analyse the Marxist–post-Marxist debate, albeit in ways that the participants may not accept or recognize. My hope is that this will lead to an appreciation of the complex and productive relationship between Liberalism and Marxism that is available theoretically, if not in practice historically, or at least not as yet. This is intended to bear out one of the tasks of theoretical reflection, which is to articulate views and possibilities beyond those already current. To do this, I will be introducing the relationship between Karl Marx and liberalism, and Marx and Marxism. Following that, I will organize a discussion of the current controversy between Marxists and post-Marxists in a way that links to the readings included in this volume from works by Alex Callinicos, and by Ernesto Laclau and Chantal Mouffe. The issues will be considered under three headings: history, class and agency. I will then summarize the way that these ideas impact on current political developments, or might have an impact on future ones. My overall conclusion is that, insofar as Liberalism aims to bury Marxism, it runs considerable risks; that insofar as Marxists aim to expunge post-Marxism, they isolate themselves from post-liberal politics; and that Marx's own post-liberal project remains a pertinent diagnosis of the relevant issues, though a very problematic guide to their resolution.

MARX AND LIBERALISM

One way to make the relationship between Marxism and Liberalism unproductively simple is to map Marxism itself back onto Marx, and then to pose Marxism and Liberalism as exclusive and oppositional. On the contrary, I propose to de-link Marx from Marxism, to a certain extent, and to identify Marxism with the liberal project, again, to a certain extent. This runs counter to the vast majority of commentary on both these binaries (Marx/Marxism and Marxism/liberalism), but it is my contention that in current circumstances my moves are helpful if unusual ones to make. On my view, then, Marx himself was a post-liberal thinker of sorts, in that his earliest journalism about social conditions, and his earliest critique of current political concepts, were both directed to the shortcomings of liberal reform, as it was understood at the time – 1842–3 in the Prussian Rhineland (Levin, 1989: 15–18, 34–66).

Marx's earliest journalism was written for the liberal press during a brief respite from the censorship enforced by authoritarian monarchism. In it, he addressed himself to economic issues, in particular the hardships of the local peasantry and wine-growers, victims of a process of economic liberalization that abolished feudal rights of use and subjected smallholders to the rigour of market forces. Marx's critique was twofold: the peasants and smallholders were not enfranchised nor allowed other political freedoms, and, concomitantly, the liberalizing establishment was concerned to keep economic issues off the political map entirely. Economic liberals were thus not automatically on-side for mass political participation, and indeed one reason for opposing this was precisely the supposition that the labouring classes would 'interfere' with the presumed efficiency and naturalized necessity of private property and market relationships (Carver, 1982: 5–12; Marx, 1977: 20–1 'The Law on Thefts of Wood', 24–5 'Defence of the Moselle Correspondent').

Liberalism itself, in Marx's analysis, was shown to have an uneasy relationship with the economy. On the one hand, most liberals argued for a separation of the political from the economic, on grounds that the latter was a realm of self-generating and self-regulating activity that would work to best advantage when left to run in mechanical fashion. While the property system and market forces required a framework of legality initiated and enforced by the state, that marked the limit of what was needed, and any further political 'regulation' smacked of 'interference' and suboptimality for all. On the other hand, economic liberals had gained political power by arguing that participation in government and in politics generally should be broadened out beyond the monarchist cliques that claimed to rule by divine right rather than rationality and social science. Drawing a line between the state, which they sought to manage, and political participation, which they sought to control, was easy to do if private property and market forces were accepted as natural and progressive to the human species and if further enfranchisement of the labouring classes could be represented as a danger to science and industry. Thus the liberal strategy was to enfranchise their own participation in politics and in government at the expense of both the authoritarian monarchists and the mass democracy of the labouring classes (Marx, 1977: 124–7 'Critical Remarks on the Article: "The King of Prussia and Social Reform"').

Marx was solidly aligned with the liberals in their opposition to monarchical reaction, and he had no time for nostalgia for a pre-industrial age. However, against the liberals he aligned himself with the labouring classes both in their campaigns for enfranchisement and participation, and in their evident refusal to accept that a reformed state could have no purchase on the economic disadvantages that they were suffering. In Marx's analysis, this suffering was not something mechanistic or natural, but rather a result of an economic transition that was in fact politically sanctioned. For the peasantry, this was a transition from feudal rights of use to modern commercial private property, and for the wine-growers it was a transition from smallholdings to larger-scale production as markets in products and capital enforced labour-saving efficiencies. In Marx's view, there were no inherent barriers to political sanctions in economic life that worked the other way, namely the harnessing of modern productive resources to benefit and liberate the labouring classes, rather than to disadvantage and disempower them (Marx, 1977: 63–74 *Towards a Critique of Hegel's Philosophy of Right: Introduction*).

The value of examining Marx's early journalism is that it critically exposes the liberal project of widening political participation (to a point) but drawing a line between politics and economic realities (at a point). In his more theoretically orientated works, Marx developed this idea as an opposition between the 'political' citizen envisaged by liberals as a participant in a (falsely) universalized democratic politics, and the 'economic' producer envisaged by liberals as an economic actor in commodified bargaining relationships of 'freedom' and 'equality' (Marx, 1977: 39–62 'On the Jewish Question'). What is recognized today as Marx's critique of Liberalism was itself a development not only from, but also within, his project in practical politics. As the censors cracked down, so his publications took a more coded turn, and his politics appeared more philosophical than empirical. In more favourable circumstances, during the revolutionary days of 1848–9 and in the immediate aftermath, his overt engagement with class struggle reappeared in radical journalism and speeches (Marx, 1977: 159–91 '*The German Ideology*'; 221–47 *The Communist Manifesto*).

Marx's critique of Liberalism envisaged an exposure of the problem – the self-serving politics and policies of the property-owning classes – and an outline of the solution – the entry of the broad masses of labouring men into political participation and a concomitant engagement of the state with the economy. Marx presumed the gendered view of mass labour as male, as did much, though not all, of the feminism then current (Lopes and Roth 2000). *The Communist Manifesto* of 1848 and the broadsheet summary issued at the time listed the initial demands that would bring the financial institutions of each nation under the control of the producers, through majoritarian means (Marx, 1977: 237–8). The result would be a redistribution of wealth and power that the property-possessing classes would obviously resist. The means for this political revolution, and for major economic restructuring, would thus have to be violent. Marx's vision was one of absorbing liberal gains as against monarchical reaction, both in the form of political advancement in widened democratic participation and extended political institutions, and in the form of vastly increased powers of production through the use of modern industrial processes and organizations (Marx, 1977: 539–58 *The Civil War in France*).

Marx's project was post-liberal in its expansion of the franchise to the male working classes, and in its explicit assignment of economic responsibilities to the state. For Marx, post-Liberalism was ultimately an economy in which market forces were abandoned, and money abolished, in favour of a planned and democratically controlled system of production and distribution of goods and services. Rather than following the principle of assigning power and possessions to those with money and property, the new 'communist' regime would ensure that the conditions of production were such that labour would become 'life's prime want', and goods and services would flow to all the citizenry on the basis of need (Marx, 1977: 231–8, 544–5, 564–70 'Critique of the Gotha Programme'). At what point, and in what way, the democratic politics and industrial technologies that Liberalism had unleashed would effectively transform themselves into something quite different, and even more widely and individually liberating, was rather unclear in Marx's account. But then he expected this human emancipation to be a practical political process through which the liberal 'citizen' and the liberal 'producer' would merge. Thus his abstract critique of Liberalism would be available as a guiding light for this process, but the process itself would proceed in a way consistent with liberal values of majoritarian decision-making in politics and with liberal ambitions for economic advancement through increased productivity.

MARXISTS AND POST-MARXISTS

In 1859, Engels announced the outlines of Marxism as an intellectual system. The extent to which this gloss on Marx's life and works accurately mirrored his activities and ideas, or the extent to which he agreed with this account as an acceptable approximation, remains a matter of debate (Carver, 1981: 31–44). What is clear is that Marxism was post-liberal in a somewhat different way from that of Marx himself, engaging with liberalism's lack of self-conscious historical grounding, and with its denial of class politics. An exploration of this line of critique will build on my account of Marx's own post-liberalism, and will help to set the terms for understanding current post-Marxist debates.

Marxism as it developed from 1859 onwards was founded on a theory of history and a dialectical method (Carver, 1981: 45–61). This represented a critique of liberal thought, in that liberal principles were generally assigned to humanity in a nearly timeless way, or at least to 'civilized' (as opposed to colonized) humanity without much historical investigation. The human individual was represented as almost biologically rational and calculating, and an animal to which monetary trade came naturally. A proclivity for deferring gratification and economizing on labour completed the picture. History was not itself important, nor particularly developmental, in that societies were either within the 'civilized' zone of trade and industry, or candidates for inclusion, on more or less paternalistic and violent terms.

According to Marxists, liberals were wrong to make 'human nature' timeless, and wrong to simplify the past so drastically. Moreover, they were wrong in lacking a mechanism to account for human development in the long term through a more accurate scheme of stages, wrong in lacking a method by which to do this, and wrong in lacking a philosophy of science to establish the facts of the matter. Because of these deficiencies relating to history, method and science, liberals were said to lack a future any different from the present (Carver, 1981: 62–78).

Marxists, of course, were crucially interested in a socialist or communist future that would reform and revolutionize the liberal order. From the Marxist perspective, liberals were becoming conservative in relation to historical development, and defensive in relation to the advancement of their own democratizing political principles and their own promises of prosperity based on individual labour and 'private' wealth. From the liberal perspective, Marxists were dangerous revolutionaries who would destroy the individuals and organizations that produced wealth through market forces and technological innovation, and so bring down the legality of the state and the values of society through which 'private' property was protected and individual liberties secured.

In their response to Marxists, liberals were thus engaged with Marx's original critique, which had questioned the linkage between doctrines of individual liberty to own property and engage in political participation and the realities of political exclusion and economic deprivation. Given their lack of interest in history and method as such, this is unsurprising, as neither was essential in a self-conscious way to the liberal project (Hayek, 1960). Marxists have rather pursued their 'theory of history' and 'scientific method' in a self-conscious way that has mystified liberals, precisely because they do not see the point (Cohen, 1978). Thus liberals and Marxists have had a distinct tendency to talk past each other.

Callinicos emphasizes the centrality of a theory of history to Marxism when he says: 'Marxist historiography is, of course, the most obvious instance of such self-consciously theoretically guided historical research' (see p. 222). He then explains that, in his view, a theory of history requires theories of structure, transformation and directionality, and summarizes how Marxist 'historical materialism' fills this out with substantive claims. Directionality is a problem for Callinicos, as he wants to resist the merger of this theory of history with a philosophy of history that is 'teleological'. Marxists, he suggests, have in the past come too close to Hegel in this respect, and have thus given grounds for the criticism that they are claiming to know in advance what the end or 'telos' of any historical sequence of events must inevitably be. In defending his version of the Marxist theory of history, Callinicos appeals to 'the Marxist political project, with its stress on working-class self-emancipation and revolutionary subjectivity', in contrast with more determinist, and less defensible, versions of Marxism. In that way, Callinicos is updating Marxism, and maintaining the centrality of a theory of history, in line with late twentieth-century critiques of determinism in human affairs and metaphysical or quasi-religious philosophies of progress.

Marxists had underpinned their view of history with claims that it resulted from the application of a unique method in social science, one that was consistent with philosophical determinism (of a sort presupposed by the physical sciences). This determinism was, in turn, linked to the master concept of the dialectic outlining the principles according to which change and development of any kind – in nature, history and logic – takes place. Those principles were adapted by Engels from Hegel, thus reconciling (so Engels thought) philosophical **idealism** with materialism, science with philosophy, and Marx's critique of political economy with an explanatory 'system' of the largest and most ambitious kind. By contrast, Marx's critique of political economy, as he envisaged its overall scope, could be read as a detailed theoretical and empirical deconstruction of liberal doctrines, social structures and political forms. Engels had more grandiose intellectual ambitions for Marx's arguably much more limited, post-liberal project (Carver, 1983).

Engels's focus on a theory of history, a Hegelian methodology and a unifying philosophy of science made Marx's post-liberal working-class politics problematic as a matter of 'theory'. Arguably, it had been problematic in Marx's revolutionary years as a matter of political possibilities, tactics and negotiations. Within Engels's determinism, dialectics and science, class politics became a matter of intellectualized analysis. Theoreticians were needed to determine the relationship between any current political conjuncture and a schema of historical stages and transitions, such that actions could be judged progressive (or not) in terms of an expected, and in some sense ultimately determined, 'communist' outcome. In Engels's schema, class politics, and in particular the modern, industrial working class, had a place of metaphysical privilege within an overall theory of reality, rather than a political privileging that had to be forged and maintained contingently in practice. Moreover, the social phenomena through which Engels's determinism manifested itself seemed to shift uneasily between the sphere of human will and choice in politics, and the sphere of 'material forces' in economic production and technological development.

Marx's own concept of class, and promotion of working-class politics, were both highly problematic to liberals. Liberals characteristically deny the existence of class, arguing that individuals and their choices comprise the entire realm of sociological, moral and political validity, or they construe class distinctions and inequalities as an inherent feature of any social system that generates production over and above a bare subsistence. In the case of the modern industrial system, some liberals were prepared to argue that increases in productivity, expansion of markets and innovations in products could only be had at the cost of an increasingly inegalitarian class system, and that the price was well worth paying. Class, for Marx, seems to have been a rough-and-ready collective concept loosely linked to economic interest and status within the property system. Class, for Marxists, was also a figure in a complex theoretical system of historical stages, decisive struggles and political transformations, underpinned in principle by determinism, method and science.

Post-Marxists have rebelled from this overarching explanatory system, and queried its basic constituents. They have criticised its theories of history, class and agency. Does this make them liberals?

POST-MARXISTS AND LIBERALS

Post-Marxists have objected to the determinism that Marxists defend; to theorizing history as a unity that can be known in terms of a singular truth; to the Marxist privileging of class, in particular the working class, within a teleological and eschatological system; and to the way that Marxists devalue individuals as effective agents in politics in very diverse ways. From the post-Marxist perspective, traditional Marxism is philosophically untenable, and certainly not guaranteed in its validity by any supposed linkage with the natural sciences. Its master concept of dialectic is tautologous and mystical. And its assignment of a special role in politics to intellectual theoreticians is deeply suspect.

Laclau and Mouffe have stated forthrightly that 'It is no longer possible to maintain the conception of subjectivity and classes elaborated by Marxism, nor its vision of the historical course of capitalist development, nor, of course, the conception of communism as a transparent society from which antagonisms have disappeared'. To support this radical critique, they treat the categories of Marxism deconstructively, that is, as discourse through which politics is contingently done. This method does not promise a 'universal history' or knowledge of the 'real'. Rather, it provides an 'anchorage' from which contemporary social struggles are 'thinkable' in their specificity (see p. 212).

Laclau and Mouffe are further concerned to confront the Marxist understanding of 'the subject', that is, the human individual, with the critiques of rationalism and empiricism mounted by **Nietzsche**, **Freud**, **Heidegger** and

Foucault. For Laclau and Mouffe, the human subject becomes a way of occupying 'subject positions' within a discursive structure. This understanding is then used to demolish Marxist mythologies of unity, especially within the working class, and of objectivity, particularly with respect to the way that a 'vanguard party' was said to represent class interests.

Working from the new linguistic philosophies of **deconstruction**, and breaking from traditional Marxist forms of materialism and **positivism**, Laclau and Mouffe dispense not only with the 'theory of history' but also with the priority given to economically defined interests over which classes (as collectives of similar individuals) are supposed necessarily to struggle: 'Let us accept instead that neither the political identity nor the economic identity of the agents crystallizes as differential moment of a unified discourse, and that the relation between them is the precarious unity of a tension' (see p. 218). For Laclau and Mouffe, politics should be the 'struggle for a radical, libertarian and plural democracy', acknowledging the force of 'new social movements' and no longer attempting to privilege, in theory or in practice, a universal 'working class' (see pp. 212–13).

Post-Marxists have thus turned history as an important issue back onto Marxists, by arguing that there has been enough time for the expected historical transition to a post-capitalist future to occur, and that it hasn't. The contingent excuses, post-Marxists argue, have run out. If the working class occupied a privileged place in history, and if history were moving forward in line with their interests towards a new system of production and new principles of distribution, then these developments would be well advanced, or at least the prospects clearly visible. While some Marxists might argue that the working class had been betrayed by power-hungry elites, post-Marxists took the point a stage further and indicated that class politics itself has become less important. In making this point, they referred to the plethora of post-1960s '**identity politics**' movements and groups, typically motivated by demands for recognition and participation that could not be reduced to economic interests. Indeed the politics of these groups, and their visions of success and liberation, often did not turn crucially on economic goals and schemes. Marxists typically did not notice these groups, or dismissed them as divisive and confusing with respect to the all-important class binary into which, they assumed, modern society had to be divided. These 'identity' groups were typically listed as 'black power' and other racial/ethnic movements for recognition and participation, the women's movement and gay and lesbian movements, and movements encompassing, or on behalf of, other disadvantaged minority groups.

Post-Marxists have broken decisively with Engels's determinism, dialectical method, science and system-building in favour of more pragmatic outlooks embracing contingency and **deconstruction**. The pragmatic side derives from Antonio **Gramsci**'s focus on the role of ideas, in particular traditions and ideologies, within working-class politics (Martin, 1998). The deconstructive side derives from Foucauldian sociologies that take the 'linguistic turn' in philosophy very seriously, focusing on the way that knowledge-production assigns power in society and produces micro-changes in individuals (Barker, 1998). In this way, they have challenged the 'materialism' (always confused between 'matter-in-motion' and economic activities and structures) that Marxists have continually affirmed as fundamental. In focusing on the open-ended and constructive character of language, post-Marxists have come perilously close to the philosophical '**idealism**' that Marxists have accommodated, only by assimilating it to their materialism as a determinist dialectic of motion and development. By renouncing the politically and historically privileged concept of class, post-Marxists have effectively abandoned Marxism altogether, at least as Marxists see it.

In summary, post-Marxists have broken with Marxists over any kind of 'grand narrative' of history at all; any *a priori* privileging of groups, such as the working class, in political action; and any notion that effective agents in change and development have to be groups rather than individuals. This leaves us with two questions. How far have post-Marxists departed from Marx, and is this important? What, if anything, separates post-Marxists from liberals, and why should we care?

Marx can be read, and reinterpreted, as much more in line with post-Marxist critiques of Marxism, and much more in line, therefore, with post-Marxist political theory, than Marxists would like to admit. This rereading of Marx predates the current school of post-Marxism by decades, having its origins in reworkings of Marx in the 1920s by **Gramsci** and **Lukács**. Both thinkers were concerned to produce a less deterministic and less scientific Marx than Marxists would allow, and both were concerned to emphasize the contingent and open-ended character of political engagement, without metaphysical guarantees of inevitable success. In turn, these revisionist currents of the 1920s reflected the earlier revisionism of the early 1900s and late 1890s, in which Eduard **Bernstein** and Antonio **Labriola** questioned the systemization of Marx's thought into a materialist dialectic and queried the effects that this would have on political agitation and action. The problems posed by Marxism concerning history, class and agency have been there from an early stage, and the controversy between orthodoxy and revisionism has a long history (Carver, 2003).

What is important at the present moment, however, is not so much the deconstructive philosophies that post-Marxists have brought to bear on these questions as their openness to concepts of political progress independent of class politics and independent of the economy. Earlier revisionists kept to a view that the effective politics of the modern age revolved around class struggle and its resolution, with or without violence and revolution (Steger, 1997). Post-Marxists are likely to support this view, and indeed often identify themselves as social democrats, concerned with issues of production and distribution in the economy. However, they have also been concerned to broaden the political space through which coalition issues, as well as practical coalitions themselves, can be articulated and pursued, and to remove the privileged position that economic redistribution has occupied in theoretical and political terms, as opposed to the demands for participation and recognition that the 'new social movements' have identified and secured. The prior distinction in theory between fundamental and fringe issues has thus been dissolved in post-Marxism, and the role of theory in making that kind of distinction *a priori*, or at least in advance, has been abandoned. In the post-Marxist view, politics arises unpredictably from the people, and the task of theory is to promote the principles and practices that allow this to occur – not to legislate the historical, moral or any other form of political validity from a position of intellectualized authority and privilege.

This raises the issue of the boundary line, if any, between post-Marxists and liberals, especially since post-Marxists identify with Marx's own post-liberal project of building on the participatory principles and processes of democratization (Grugel, 2002). Indeed, few liberals today would identify themselves directly with the kind of Liberalism that Marx was criticizing in his own time. 'Classical' Liberalism of that time demarcated the economy as a sphere best treated as pre-political and outside politics, a mechanism that must be supported in its essentials but left to operate without 'interference'. Liberals who pursue that line of thought and practice today are sometimes identified as 'libertarians', whereas more mainstream liberals have tended to accept the social democratic contention that economies need considerable state intervention, precisely because the mechanisms need constant adjustment, improvement and support. Moreover, electorates have come to expect the economy to feature in political debates and voter evaluation, and their overall judgements, and personal gains and losses, rightly feature in the democratic process of making political choices. Contemporary liberals have strongly supported many of the interest groups and coalitions that have pursued goals of recognition and participation through the democratic process, and have indeed used these successes (or at least substantial gains) of these 'new social movements' to validate the open and pluralistic character of the processes themselves. These processes admit plurality both in terms of their openness to an array of unpredictable goals and in terms of their openness to individual and group participation on a self-validating basis.

It would seem that Marx's post-liberal project is no longer relevant, as liberals have taken the message that the economy is far from off-limits in the political process, but is instead quite central, precisely because voters want it to be. It would seem that contemporary Liberalism and current post-Marxism have come from different directions towards the same thing: an individualism of human rights covering participation and recognition as well as economic well-being; a pluralism of self-starting groups in a public space through which political change and development is effected contingently rather than predictably. It would seem that Marxists have been sidelined, defending a 'system' that is outdated by both philosophical developments (away from determinism and grand narrative) and political developments (away from cohesive class politics organized around structural issues in the economy). It would seem from the Marxist perspective that post-Marxists have simply capitulated to 'the market' and to 'liberal individualism', and that any invocation of Marx in their work is not merely revisionist but spurious.

CONCLUSION

Post-Marxists have not been shy about attacking Marxists; indeed, that is why they are post-Marxists. Nor have they been shy about borrowing from liberals; indeed, that is where their theoretical and political pluralism comes from. What they have been shy about is explaining in what way, if any, they are different from liberals, and why we should care about this. This is not too surprising, as liberals and post-Marxists have come not only from different philosophical traditions but also from different perspectives on themselves. Shortly after the liberal revolutions of the 1830s and 1840s, liberals no longer saw themselves as revolutionary and certainly not violent. This erases a good deal of the story of how representative and responsible government came to succeed authoritarian, monarchical regimes, but it also reflects a common tendency of groups that have come to power: the tendency to write their own histories selectively, making their own rise to power look inevitable and only minimally violent, thus disarming any further revolutionary critique. Marxists were not immune to this by any means; but, insofar as they persisted in using working-class politics as a reason for resisting democracy (rather than aiding it, as in Marx's day), they have fallen victim to spectacular, large-scale collapse, as in Eastern Europe, or to a visible process of piecemeal backtracking, as in the People's Republic of China (at least on the economic if not the political front). This is to say that post-Marxists could do themselves a political favour by breaking even more sharply with Marxism than they do, especially in political terms, and learning the liberal language in order to pursue something like Marx's own post-liberal project – focusing on the alienations of class-ridden capitalism in order to produce a political system that is even more egalitarian and empowering than the one that democracy currently provides. Marx's message that the roots of political inequality lie in unequal and exploitative economic structures of ownership and control is still very timely.

However, it seems that the desire to form an effective coalition between liberals and post-Marxists is not intense, probably because of old suspicions and a desire to maintain familiar identities. Liberals have little incentive to welcome recanting Marxists, who look to them like social democrats with added but unnecessary philosophy; post-Marxists have little desire to lose themselves in what has become a liberal mainstream with few incentives to question inequality, at least in any radical way. The value of post-Marxists today, as was the case with Marx more than 150 years ago, is the value of critique from an 'outside' position, and the push towards the limits of radicalism, at least in theory.

'THE PROLIFERATION OF STRUGGLES AND THE CATEGORY OF THE SUBJECT' BY
ERNESTO LACLAU AND CHANTAL MOUFFE

Ernesto Laclau is a Professor of Political Theory in the Department of Government at the University of Essex in the UK. Greatly influenced by the Althusserian approach to Marxism, he has written a number of notable essays on Marxist theory and analyses of Latin American politics. These can be found in *Politics and Ideology in Marxist Theory* (Verso, 1979). After that, he began to make a series of moves away from orthodox Marxism. This culminated in *Hegemony and Socialist Strategy: Towards a Radical Democratic Politics* (Verso, 1985), co-written with Chantal Mouffe. It established an influential form of post-Marxist theorising based on the attempted fusion of Marxism with poststructuralist linguistic-orientated philosophy. Subsequent works by Laclau have developed and clarified his position and have attempted to specify the 'logic of the political' in ways that do not reduce it to a rationalist or empiricist basis. His books include *New Reflections on the Revolution of our Time* (Verso, 1990) and *Emancipations* (Verso, 1996). He continues to research political theory, focusing on the discursive construction of social antagonism and the links between deconstruction and politics.

Chantal Mouffe is Professor of Political Theory at the Centre for the Study of Democracy, University of Westminster, London. She is well known for her collaboration with Ernesto Laclau on *Hegemony and Socialist Strategy* and for that book's contribution to theories of politics in the period of 'new social movements'. Since then, she has continued to develop such themes as part of a broader project of developing a political theory of radical democracy drawing on Marxism but incorporating the insights of theoretical schools such as deconstruction, psychoanalysis and (in a critical fashion) some parts of Liberalism. Her aim is to develop a non-rationalist political theory explicating an agonistic form of democracy based on continuing argument and 'antagonism' (the term is given a specific inflection in her and Laclau's work). Her books include *The Return of the Political* (Verso, 1993) and *The Democratic Paradox* (Verso, 2000). There is an interesting overlap between the work of Laclau and Mouffe, Wolin, Connolly, Butler and Foucault (all of whose work is presented elsewhere in this volume).

In this extract from *Hegemony and Socialist Strategy*, the authors outline their project of taking account of the proliferation, beyond class antagonism, of points of struggle within the Western democracies, and in so doing to 'work through' Marxism theoretically. Crucial here is the recognition of the importance of the theoretical category of the 'subject' and of comprehending how subjects are the expression not of a fixed and ahistorical essence but of a complex process of political and discursive construction that cannot be reduced to the structures of class conflict.

'THE PROLIFERATION OF STRUGGLES AND THE CATEGORY OF THE SUBJECT' (1985)*

Ernesto Laclau and Chantal Mouffe

INTRODUCTION

Left-wing thought today stands at a crossroads. The 'evident truths' of the past – the classical forms of analysis and political calculation, the nature of the forces in conflict, the very meaning of the Left's struggles and objectives – have been seriously challenged by an avalanche of historical mutations which have riven the ground on which those truths were constituted. Some of these mutations doubtless correspond to failures and disappointments: from Budapest to Prague and the Polish coup d'état, from Kabul to the sequels of Communist victory in Vietnam and Cambodia, a question mark has fallen more and more heavily over a whole way of conceiving both socialism and the roads that should lead to it. This has recharged critical thinking, at once corrosive and necessary, on the theoretical and political bases on which the intellectual horizon of the Left was traditionally constituted. But there is more to it than this. A whole series of positive new phenomena underlie those mutations which have made so urgent the task of theoretical reconsideration: the rise of the new feminism, the protest movements of ethnic, national and sexual minorities, the anti-institutional ecology struggles waged by marginalized layers of the population, the anti-nuclear movement, the atypical forms of social struggle in countries on the capitalist periphery – all these imply an extension of social conflictuality to a wide range of areas, which creates the potential, but no more than the potential, for an advance towards more free, democratic and egalitarian societies.

This proliferation of struggles presents itself, first of all, as a 'surplus' of the social vis-à-vis the rational and organized structures of society – that is, of the social 'order'. Numerous voices, deriving especially from the liberal-conservative camp, have insistently argued that Western societies face a crisis of governability and a threat of dissolution at the hands of the egalitarian danger. However, the new forms of social conflict have also thrown into crisis theoretical and political frameworks closer to the ones that we shall seek to engage in

* From Ernesto Laclau and Chantal Mouffe, *Hegemony and Socialist Strategy* (London: Verso, 1985), pp. 1–5, 115–22.

dialogue in the major part of this book. These correspond to the classical discourses of the Left, and the characteristic modes in which it has conceived the agents of social change, the structuring of political spaces, and the privileged points for the unleashing of historical transformations. What is now in crisis is a whole conception of socialism which rests upon the ontological centrality of the working class, upon the role of Revolution, with a capital 'r', as the founding moment in the transition from one type of society to another, and upon the illusory prospect of a perfectly unitary and homogeneous collective will that will render pointless the moment of politics. The plural and multifarious character of contemporary social struggles has finally dissolved the last foundation for that political imaginary. Peopled with 'universal' subjects and conceptually built around History in the singular, it has postulated 'society' as an intelligible structure that could be intellectually mastered on the basis of certain class positions and reconstituted, as a rational, transparent order, through a founding act of a political character. Today, the Left is witnessing the final act of the dissolution of that Jacobin imaginary.

Thus, the very wealth and plurality of contemporary social struggles has given rise to a theoretical crisis. It is at the middle point of this two-way movement between the theoretical and the political that our own discourse will be located. At every moment, we have tried to prevent an impressionist and sociologistic descriptivism, which lives on ignorance of the conditions of its own discursivity, from filling the theoretical voids generated by the crisis. Our aim has been the exact opposite: to focus on certain discursive categories which, at first sight, appeared to be privileged condensation-points for many aspects of the crisis; and to unravel the possible meaning of a history in the various facets of this multiple refraction. All discursive eclecticism or wavering was excluded from the very start. As is said in an inaugural 'manifesto' of the classical period, when one enters new territory, one must follow the example of 'travellers who, finding themselves lost in a forest, know that they ought not to wander first to one side and then to the other, nor, still less, to stop in one place, but understand that they should continue to walk as straight as they can in one direction, not diverging for any slight reason, even though it was possibly chance alone that first determined them in their choice. By this means if they do not go exactly where they wish, they will at least arrive somewhere at the end, where probably they will be better off than in the middle of a forest.'[1]

The guiding thread of our analysis has been the transformations in the concept of hegemony, considered as a discursive surface and fundamental nodal point of Marxist political theorization. Our principal conclusion is that behind the concept of 'hegemony' lies hidden something more than a type of political relation *complementary* to the basic categories of Marxist theory. In fact, it introduces a *logic of the social* which is incompatible with those categories. Faced with the rationalism of classical Marxism, which presented history and society as intelligible totalities constituted around conceptually explicable laws, the logic of hegemony presented itself from the outset as a *complementary* and *contingent* operation, required for conjunctural imbalances within an evolutionary paradigm whose essential or 'morphological' validity was not for a moment placed in question. (One of the central tasks of this book will be to determine this specific logic of contingency.) As the areas of the concept's application grew broader, from Lenin to Gramsci, the field of contingent articulations also expanded, and the category of 'historical necessity' – which had been the cornerstone of classical Marxism – withdrew to the horizon of theory. As we shall argue, the expansion and determination of the social logic implicit in the concept of 'hegemony' – in a direction that goes far beyond Gramsci – will provide us with an *anchorage* from which contemporary social struggles are *thinkable* in their specificity, as well as permitting us to outline a new politics for the Left based upon the project of a radical democracy.

One question remains to be answered: why should we broach this task through a critique and a deconstruction of the various discursive surfaces of classical Marxism? Let us first say that there is no *one* discourse and *one* system of categories through which the 'real' might speak without mediations. In operating deconstructively within Marxist categories, we do not claim to be writing 'universal history' to be inscribing our discourse as a moment of a single, linear process of knowledge. Just as the era of normative epistemologies has come to an end, so too has the era of universal discourses. Political conclusions similar to those set forth in this book could have been approximated from very different discursive formations – for example, from certain forms of Christianity, or from libertarian discourses alien to the socialist tradition – none of which could aspire to be *the* truth of society (or 'the insurpassable philosophy of our time', as Sartre put it). For this reason, however, Marxism is *one* of the traditions through which it becomes possible to formulate this new conception of politics. For us, the validity of this point of departure is simply based on the fact that it constitutes our own past.

Is it not the case that, in scaling down the pretensions and the area of validity of Marxist theory, we are breaking with something deeply inherent in that theory: namely, its monist aspiration to capture with its categories the essence or underlying meaning of History? The answer can only be in the affirmative. Only if we renounce any epistemological prerogative based upon the ontologically privileged position of a 'universal class' will it be possible seriously to discuss the present degree of validity of the Marxist categories. At this point, we should state quite plainly that we are now situated in a post-Marxist terrain. It is no longer possible to maintain the conception of subjectivity and classes elaborated by Marxism, nor its vision of the historical course of capitalist development, nor, of course, the conception of communism as a transparent society from which antagonisms have disappeared. But if our intellectual project in this book is *post*-Marxist, it is evidently also post-*Marxist*. It has been through the development of certain intuitions and discursive forms constituted within Marxism, and the inhibition or elimination of certain others, that we have constructed a concept of hegemony which, in our view, may be a useful instrument in the struggle for a radical, libertarian and plural democracy. Here, the reference to Gramsci, though partially critical, is of capital importance. In the text, we have tried to recover some of the variety and richness of Marxist discursivity in the era of the Second International, which tended to be obliterated by that impoverished monolithic image of 'Marxism-Leninism' current in the Stalin and post-Stalin eras and now reproduced, almost intact though with opposite sign, by certain forms of contemporary 'anti-Marxism'. Neither the defenders of a glorious, homogeneous and invulnerable 'historical materialism', nor the professionals of an anti-Marxism à la nouveaux philosophes, realize the extent to which their apologias or diatribes are equally rooted in an ingenuous and primitive conception of a doctrine's role and degree of unity which, in all its essential determinations, is still tributary to the Stalinist imaginary. Our own approach to the Marxist texts has, on the contrary, sought to recover their plurality, to grasp the numerous discursive sequences – to a considerable extent heterogeneous and contradictory – which constitute their inner structure and wealth, and guarantee their survival as a reference point for political analysis. The surpassing of a great intellectual tradition never takes place in the sudden form of a collapse, but in the way that river waters, having originated at a common source, spread in various directions and mingle with currents flowing down from other sources. This is how the discourses that constituted the field of classical Marxism may help to form the thinking of a new left: by bequeathing some of their concepts, transforming or abandoning others, and diluting themselves in that infinite intertextuality of emancipatory discourses in which the plurality of the social takes shape.

[. . .]

THE CATEGORY OF 'SUBJECT'

Discussion of this category requires us to distinguish two very different problems, which have frequently been confused in recent debates: the problem of the discursive or pre-discursive character of the category of subject, and the problem of the relationship among different subject positions.

The first problem has received more consistent attention, and has led to a growing questioning of the 'constitutive' role that both rationalism and empiricism attribute to 'human individuals'. This critique has essentially borne upon three conceptual targets: the view of the subject as an agent both rational and transparent to itself; the supposed unity and homogeneity of the ensemble of its positions; and the conception of the subject as origin and basis of social relations (the problem of constitutivity in the strict sense). We do not need to refer in detail to the main dimensions of this critique, as its classical moments – Nietzsche, Freud, Heidegger – are well enough known. More recently, Foucault has shown how the tensions of the 'analytic of finitude', characteristic of what he has called the 'Age of Man', are resolved into a set of oppositions – the empirical/the transdendent, the Cogito/the unthought, withdrawal/

return of the origin – which are insurmountable insofar as the category of 'Man' is maintained as a unified subject.[2] Other analyses have pointed out the difficulties in breaking with the category of 'originative subject', which continues to creep into the very conceptions that seek to implement the rupture with it.[3]

With regard to this alternative, and to its diverse constitutive elements, our position is clear. Whenever we use the category of 'subject' in this text, we will do so in the sense of 'subject positions' within a discursive structure. Subjects cannot, therefore, be the origin of social relations – not even in the limited sense of being endowed with powers that render an experience possible – as all 'experience' depends on precise discursive conditions of possibility.[4] This, however, is only an answer to our first problem, which in no way anticipates the solution that will be given to the second. From the discursive character of all subject positions, nothing follows concerning the type of relation that could exist among them. As every subject position is a discursive position, it partakes of the open character of every discourse; consequently, the various positions cannot be totally fixed in a closed system of differences. We can see why these very different problems were confused. Since the affirmation of the discursive character of every subject position was linked to the rejection of the notion of subject as an originative and founding totality, the analytic moment that had to prevail was that of dispersion, detotalization or decentring of certain positions with regard to others. Every moment of articulation or relation among them broke the cognitive effects of the dispersion metaphor, and led to the suspicion of a retotalization which would surreptitiously reintroduce the category of subject as a unified and unifying essence. From here, it was but one step to transform that *dispersion* of subject positions into an effective *separation* among them. However, the transformation of dispersion into separation obviously creates all the analytical problems we signalled earlier – especially those inherent in the replacement of the essentialism of the totality with an essentialism of the elements. If every subject position is a discursive position, the analysis cannot dispense with the forms of overdetermination of some positions by others – of the contingent character of all necessity which, as we have seen, is inherent in any discursive difference.

Let us consider two cases which have recently given rise to important discussions: that relating to the status of apparently abstract categories (above all, 'Man'); and that relating to the 'subject' of feminism. The first is at the centre of the entire recent debate on humanism. If the status of 'Man'[5] were that of an *essence*, its location with regard to other characteristics of 'human beings' would be inscribed on a logical scale proceeding from the abstract to the concrete. This would open the way for all the familiar tricks of an analysis of concrete situations in terms of 'alienation' and 'misrecognition'. But if, on the contrary, 'Man' is a discursively constructed subject position, its presumed abstract character in no way anticipates the form of its articulation with other subject positions. (The range is here infinite, and it challenges the imagination of any 'humanist'. For example, it is known how, in the colonial countries, the equivalence between 'rights of Man' and 'European values' was a frequent and effective form of discursively constructing the acceptability of imperialist domination.) The confusion created by E. P. Thompson in his attack on Althusser[6], rests precisely on this point. When referring to 'humanism', Thompson believes that if humanist values are denied the status of an essence, then they are deprived of all historical validity. In reality, however, what is important is to try to show how 'Man' has been produced in modern times, how the 'human' subject – that is, the bearer of a human identity without distinctions – appears in certain religious discourses, is embodied in juridical practices and is diversely constructed in other spheres. An understanding of this dispersion can help us to grasp the fragility of 'humanist' values themselves, the possibility of their perversion through equivalential articulation with other values, and their restriction to certain categories of the population – the property-owning class, for example, or the male population. Far from considering that 'Man' has the status of an essence – presumably a gift from heaven – such an analysis can show us the historical conditions of its emergence and the reasons for its current vulnerability, thus enabling us to struggle more efficiently, and without illusions, in defence of humanist values. But it is equally evident that the analysis cannot simply remain at the moment of *dispersion*, given that 'human identity' involves not merely an ensemble of dispersed positions but also the forms of overdetermination existing among them. 'Man' is a fundamental nodal point from which it has been possible to proceed, since the eighteenth century, to the 'humanization' of a number of social practices. To insist on the dispersion of the positions from which 'Man' has been produced constitutes only a first moment; in a second stage, it is necessary to show the relations of overdetermination and totalization that are established among these. The non-fixation or openness of the system of discursive differences is what makes possible these effects of analogy and interpenetration.

Something similar may be said about the 'subject' of feminism. The critique of feminist essentialism has been carried out in particular by the English journal *m/f*: a number of important studies have rejected the notion of a preconstituted category 'women's oppression' – whether its cause is located in the family, the mode of production or elsewhere – and have attempted to study 'the particular historical moment, the institutions and practices through which the category of woman is produced'.[7] Once it is denied that there is a single mechanism of women's oppression, an immense field of action opens up for feminist politics. One can then perceive the importance of punctual struggles against any oppressive form of constructing sexual differences, be it at the level of law, of the family, of social policy, or of the multiple cultural forms through which the category of 'the feminine' is constantly produced. We are, therefore, in the field of a dispersion of subject positions. The difficulty with this approach, however, arises from the one-sided emphasis given to the moment of dispersion – so one-sided that we are left with only a heterogeneous set of sexual differences constructed through practices which have no relation to one another. Now, while it is absolutely correct to question the idea of an original sexual division represented *a posteriori* in social practices, it is also necessary to recognize that overdetermination among the diverse sexual differences produces a systematic effect of sexual *division*.[8] Every construction of sexual differences, whatever their multiplicity and heterogeneity, invariably constructs the feminine as a pole subordinated to the masculine. It is for this reason that it is possible to speak of a sex/gender system.[9] The ensemble of social practices, of institutions and discourses which produce woman as a category, are not completely isolated but mutually reinforce and act upon one another. This does not mean that there is a single cause of feminine subordination. It is our view that once female sex has come to connote a feminine gender with specific characteristics, this 'imaginary signification' produces concrete effects in the diverse social practices. Thus, there is a close correlation between 'subordination', as a general category informing the ensemble of significations constituting 'feminity', and the auton- omy and uneven development of the diverse practices which construct the concrete forms of subordination. These latter are not the *expression* of an immutable feminine essence; in their construction, however, the symbolism which is linked to the feminine condition in a given society plays a primordial role. The diverse forms of concrete subordination react, in turn, by contribut- ing to the maintenance and reproduction of this symbolism.[10] It is therefore possible to criticize the idea of an original antagonism between men and women, constitutive of the sexual division, without denying that in the various forms of construction of 'femininity' there is a common element which has strong overdetermining effects in terms of the sexual division.

Let us now move on to consider the different forms which the determination of social and political subjects has adopted within the Marxist tradition. The starting point and constant *leitmotif* is clear: the subjects are social classes, whose unity is constituted around interests determined by their position in the relations of production. More important than insisting on this common theme, however, is to study the precise ways in which Marxism has politically and theoretically responded to the diversification and dispersion of subject positions with regard to the paradigmatic forms of their unity. A first type of response – the most elementary – consists of an illegitimate passage through the referent. It involves, for example, the assertion that the workers' political struggle and economic struggle are unified by the concrete social agent – the working class – which conducts them both. This type of reasoning – common not only in Marxism but also in the social sciences as a whole – is based on a fallacy: the expression 'working class' is used in two different ways, to define a specific subject position in the relations of production, and to *name* the agents who occupy that subject position. The resulting ambiguity allows the logically ille- gitimate conclusion to slip through that the other positions occupied by these agents are also 'working-class positions'. (They are obviously 'working-class' in the second sense, but not necessarily in the first.) The implicit assumption of the unity and transparency of the consciousness of every social agent serves to consolidate the ambiguity – and hence the confusion.

This subterfuge, however, can only operate when one tries to affirm the unity among *empirically given* positions, not when one tries to explain – as has been most frequently the case in the Marxist tradition – the essential heterogeneity of some positions with regard to the others (that is, the characteristic splits of 'fake consciousness'). In this case, as we have seen, the unity of the class is conceived as a future unity; the way in which that unity manifests itself is through the category of representation, the split between real workers and their objective interests requiring that the latter be represented by the vanguard party. Now, every relation of representation is founded on a fiction: that of the presence at a certain level of something which, strictly speaking, is absent from it. But because it is *at the same time* a fiction and a principle organizing actual social relations, representation is the terrain of a game whose result is not predetermined from the beginning. At one end of the spectrum of possibilities, we would have a dissolution of the fictitious character of representation, so that the means and the field of representation would be totally transparent vis-à-vis what is represented; at the other end, we would have total opaqueness between representative and represented: the fiction would become a fiction in a strictly literal sense. It is important to note that neither of these extremes constitutes an impossible situation, as both have well-defined conditions of possibility: a representative can be subjected to such conditions of control that what becomes a fiction is the very fictitiousness of the representation; and, on the contrary, a total absence of control can make the representation literally fictitious. The Marxist conception of the vanguard party shows this peculiarity: that the party represents not a concrete agent but its historical interests, and that there is no fiction since representative and represented are constituted by the same discourse and on the same plane. This tautological relation, however, exists in its extreme form only in tiny sects which proclaim themselves to be the vanguard of the proletariat, without the proletariat ever realizing, of course, that it has a vanguard. In every political struggle of a certain significance, there is on the contrary a very clear effort to win the allegiance of concrete social agents to their supposed 'historical interests'. If the tautology of a single discourse constituting both represented and representative is abandoned, it is necessary to conclude that represented and representative are constituted at different levels. A first temptation would then be to make total that separation of planes, and to derive the impossibility of the relation of representation from its fictitious character. Thus, it has been stated: 'To deny economism is to reject the classical conception of the economic-political-ideological unity of classes. It is to maintain that political and ideological struggles cannot be conceived as the struggles of economic classes. There is no middle way . . . Class "interests" are not given to politics and ideology by the economy. They arise within the political practice, and they are determined as an effect of definite modes of political practice. Political practice does not recognize class interests and then represent them: it constitutes the interests which it represents.'[11]

This assertion could, however, only be upheld if political practice was a perfectly delimited field, whose frontiers with the economy could be drawn *more geometrico* – that is, if we excluded as a matter of principle any overdetermination of the political by the economic or vice versa. But we know that this separation can only be established *a priori* in an essentialist conception, which derives a real separation among elements from a conceptual separation, transforming the conceptual specification of an identity into a fully and absolutely differentiated discursive position. Yet, if we accept the overdetermined character of every identity, the situation changes. *There is* a different way which – although we do not know whether it is middle – is in any case a third way. The 'winning over of agents to their historical interests' is, quite simply, an articulatory practice which constructs a discourse wherein the concrete demands of a group – the industrial workers – are conceived as steps towards a total liberation involving the overcoming of capitalism. Undoubtedly, there is no essential necessity for these demands to be articulated in this way. But nor is there an essential necessity for them to be articulated in any other way, given that, as we have seen, the relation of articulation is not a relation of necessity. What the discourse of 'historical interests' does is to *hegemonize* certain demands. On this point, Cutler et al. are absolutely right: political practice constructs the interests it represents. But if we observe closely, we will note that, far from being consolidated, the separation between the economic and the political is hereby *eliminated*. For, a reading in socialist terms of immediate economic struggles discursively articulates the political and the economic, and thus does away with the exteriority existing between the two. The alternative is clear: either the separation between the political and the economic takes place on an extra-discursive plane which secures it *a priori*; or else that separation is the result of discursive practices, and it is not possible to immunize it *a priori* from every discourse constructing their unity. If the dispersion of positions is a condition of any articulatory practice, there is no reason why that dispersion should *necessarily* take the form of a separation between the political and the economic identity of social agents. Were economic identity and political identity to be sutured, the conditions of any relation of representation would evidently disappear: we would have returned to the tautological situation in which representative and represented are moments of a single relational identity. Let us accept instead that neither the political identity nor the economic identity of the agents crystallizes as differential moment of a unified discourse, and that the relation between them is the precarious unity of a tension. We already know what this means: the subversion of each of the terms by a polysemy which prevents their stable articulation. In this case, the economic *is* and *is not* present in the political and vice versa; the relation is not one of literal differentiations but of unstable analogies between the two terms. Now, this form of presence through metaphorical transposition is the one that the *fictio iuris* of representation attempts to think. Representation is therefore constituted not as a definite type of relation, but as the field of an unstable oscillation whose vanishing point is, as we saw, either the literalization of the fiction through the breaking of every link between representative and represented, or the disappearance of the separate identity of both through their absorption as moments of a single identity.

All this shows us that the specificity of the category of subject cannot be established either through the absolutization of a dispersion of 'subject positions', or through the equally absolutist unification of these around a 'transcendental subject'. The category of subject is penetrated by the same ambiguous, incomplete and polysemical character which overdetermination assigns to every discursive identity. For this reason, the moment of closure of a discursive totality, which is not given at the 'objective' level of that totality, cannot be established at the level of a 'meaning-giving subject', since the subjectivity of the agent is penetrated by the same precariousness and absence of suture apparent at any other point of the discursive totality of which it is part. 'Objectivism' and 'subjectivisim'; 'holism' and 'individualism' are symmetrical expressions of the *wish* for a fullness that is permanently deferred. Owing to this very absence of a final suture, the dispersion of subject positions cannot constitute a solution: given that none of them manages ultimately to consolidate itself as a *separate position*, there is a game of overdetermination among them that reintroduces the horizon of an impossible totality. It is this game which makes hegemonic articulation possible.

NOTES

1. Descartes, 'Discourse on Method', in *Philosophical Works*, vol. 1, (Cambridge, 1968), p. 96.
2. Cf. M. Foucault, *The Order of Things*, London 1970.
3. Cf. with regard to this B. Brewster, 'Fetishism in *Capital* and *Reading Capital*', *Economy and Society*, 1976, vol. 5, no. 3; and P. Hirst, 'Althusser and the Theory of Ideology', *Economy and Society*, 1976, vol. 5, no. 4.
4. Cf. ibid.
5. The ambiguity arising from the use of 'Man' to refer at the same time to 'human being' and 'male member of the species' is symptomatic of the discursive ambiguities which we are attempting to show.
6. E. P. Thompson, *The Poverty of Theory*, London 1978. We should not, however, jump to the conclusion that Thompson has simply misread Althusser. The problem is considerably more complex, for if Thompson proposed a false alternative by opposing a 'humanism' based on the postulate of a human essence and an anti-humanism founded on the negation of the latter, it is equally true that Althusser's approach to humanism leaves little room for anything other than its relegation to the field of ideology. For, if history has an intelligible structure given by the succession of modes of production, and if it is this structure which is accessible to a 'scientific' practice, this can only be accompanied by a notion of 'humanism' as something constituted on the plane of ideology – a plane which, though not conceived as false consciousness, is ontologically different and subordinate to a mechanism of social reproduction established by the logic of the mode of production. The way out of the blind alley to which these two essentialisms – constituted around 'Man' and 'mode of production' – lead is the dissolution of the differentiation of planes wherein the appearance/reality distinction is founded. In that case, humanist

discourses have a status which is neither privileged *a priori* nor subordinated to other discourses.

7. *m/f*, 1978, no. 1, editorial note.
8. Cf. C. Mouffe, 'The Sex/Gender System and the Discursive Construction of Women's Subordination', in S. Häninen and L. Paldan, eds, *Rethinking Ideology: A Marxist Debate*, Berlin 1983. A historical introduction to feminist politics from this viewpoint can be found in Sally Alexander, 'Women, Class and Sexual Difference', *History Workshop* 17, Spring 1984. On the more general question of sexual politics, see Jeffrey Weeks, *Sex, Politics and Society*, London 1981.
9. This concept has been developed by Gayle Rubin, 'The Traffic in Women: Notes on the "Political Economy" of Sex', in R. R. Reiter, ed., *Toward an Anthropology of Women*, New York/London 1975, pp. 157–210.
10. This aspect is not totally ignored by the editors of *m/f*. Thus, P. Adams and J. Minson state: 'there are certain forms of "all-purpose" responsibility which cover a multitude of social relations – that persons are held "responsible" in general, in a multiplicity of evaluations (being held "irresponsible" in the negative pole). But however diffuse this all-purpose responsibility appears to be it is nonetheless still subject to the satisfaction of definite social conditions and "all-purpose" responsibility must be construed as a heterogeneous bundle of statuses' ('The "Subject" of Feminism', *m/f*, 1978, no. 2, p. 53).
11. A. Cutler et al., vol. 1, pp. 236–7.

'HISTORY AS THEORY' BY ALEX CALLINICOS

At the time of writing, Alex Callinicos is Professor in the Department of Politics at York University in the UK. Well known for his active involvement in anti-capitalist politics (in September 2000, for example, he participated in the Counter-Summit to the IMF/World Bank Meeting in Prague) he is also a well-regarded Marxist political and social theorist. He is the author of numerous books including *Althusser's Marxism* (Pluto, 1976), *Marxism and Philosophy* (Clarendon, 1983), *Against Postmodernism* (Polity, 1989), *Trotskyism* (Open University Press, 1990), *Theories and Narratives* (Polity, 1995) and, most recently, a critique of some trends in the political thought and strategy of social democracy, *Against the Third Way* (Polity, 2001). In the extract reproduced below, Callinicos reviews various theories of history and addresses the question of what a theory of history is (as opposed to a philosophy of it). Part of his point here is to defend the Marxist approach of historical materialism and show it to be a viable theory of history, immune from the sorts of criticisms (such as that it is rigidly determinist) implied by, for example, post-Marxists. Readers might like to consider Callinicos' approach to the philosophies of history and theories of historiographical method found elsewhere in this book, such as those advanced by Collingwood and Dunn, as well as to the poststructuralism of Foucault.

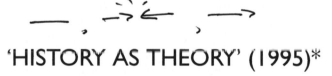

'HISTORY AS THEORY' (1995)*

Alex Callinicos

> The inner meaning of history . . . involves speculation and an attempt to get at the truth, subtle explanation of the causes and origins of existing things, and deep knowledge of the how and why of events. [History,] therefore, is firmly rooted in philosophy. (Ibn Khaldûn)

Historians, in seeking to reconstruct the past, draw (albeit in most cases tacitly) on theories about the nature and transformation of human society. There is, however, an important distinction between this kind of unacknowledged reliance on theory – where the historian may quite sincerely deny that she is doing more than recount what happened – and the self-conscious pursuit of a research

---

* From Alex Callinicos, *Theories and Narratives: Reflections on the Philosophy of History* (Cambridge: Polity Press, 1995), pp. 95–109.

programme in history. In the latter case, the historian is likely explicitly to articulate the theoretical basis of her research and may indeed be seeking to corroborate some hypotheses formulated within the programme. Marxist historiography is, of course, the most obvious instance of such self-consciously theoretically guided historical research. There are, however, other examples. One of the distinguishing features of the 'New History' developed by the *Annales* school was its resort to what in France tend to be called the 'human sciences' – anthopology, economics, sociology, psychoanalysis and so on. The New Economic History – heavily reliant on sophisticated statistical techniques and on the concepts and propositions of neo-classical economics – is perhaps the closest counterpart of this approach to be found in the English-speaking world, but a variety of other historians have made much more individual uses of sociology and anthropology – for example, Keith Hopkins in his studies of the Roman state, and Keith Thomas in his path-breaking exploration of popular beliefs and practices in early modern England, *Religion and the Decline of Magic.*

In many of the cases mentioned above, the historian resorts, often quite eclectically, to ideas derived from some social theory or other, to clarify issues that have arisen in her research, or even to define its objective. Though self-conscious enough, this kind of theoretically guided historiography does not involve a particularly tight relationship between a set of hypotheses which bear on, *inter alia*, the nature of the historical process itself, and the research being pursued by the historian. A much more sustained dialogue between theory and evidence is, however, attempted in other cases, for example, that of the historical sociologies developed by various neo-Weberian theorists, which are discussed at length below. Recent years, too, have seen an efflorescence of historical research pursued by scholars influenced by poststructuralism, and particularly by Foucault's writings – for example, the work of cultural historians, notably on the English Renaissance, that achieved notoriety in the 1980s under the label of 'New Historicism'.[1]

These examples suggest a heterogeneous collection of different types of research. Indeed, one might argue that a consistent Foucauldian should eschew historiography *tout court*: after all, Foucault himself said that his books 'aren't treatises in philosophy or studies of history: at most, they are philosophical fragments put to work in a historical field of problems'.[2] Many historians would in any case deny that historical sociology is 'proper' history, since it lacks the research on primary sources – archival documents and the like – which is the defining characteristic of what Sir Geoffrey Elton calls 'a reliable historiography'.[3] Matters are not quite so simple, however. It is not clear, for example, how in principle one could differentiate the kind of wide-ranging interpretive essay of which Hugh Trevor-Roper is the master – I have in mind especially his two great essays on the gentry and the crisis of the seventeenth century – from the outstanding work of Weberian historical sociology, the first volume of Michael Mann's *The Sources of Social Power*. It is true that Mann covers a vastly greater sweep of history, as he traces the course of Western state-building from Sargon to the Elder Pitt. But does not Trevor-Roper cut himself loose from any firm anchorage in the sources when he seeks to offer an account of the crisis which gripped European society in its entirety in the seventeenth century? Nor is historical sociology (as the caricatured versions of it offered by some historians suggest) speculation uncontrolled by the discipline of empirical evidence: the culmination of Mann's narrative, where he recounts the rise of the modern European state system, makes systematic use of a careful analysis of English state finances from the twelfth century onwards.[4]

The difference is, the sceptical historian might respond, that Trevor-Roper's large-scale interpretations are informed by an understanding of early modern European societies gained by a lengthy training in and practice of historical scholarship based on close study of the sources, while the historical sociologist is likely to treat particular historical cases as mere exemplifications of some general proposition derived from social theory, and therefore to efface the singularity of the phenomena under examination. Elton, for example, argues that the practice of the trained historian provides the only available guarantee of reliable knowledge of the past:

> The two uncertainties of the historian – lack of knowledge, and the need to select – have their cure in the proper practice of scholarship and research. The methods of the trained professional historian are designed to protect him against his human difficulties, and they very often do achieve their purpose.[5]

There is something to this. Their lengthy engagement with the sources seems to give some historians the ability to go beyond them in intuitive flashes. Consider, for example, this anecdote, told by A. J. P. Taylor to illustrate the difference between Lewis Namier and himself as historians:

> I often relied on intuition; Lewis believed in laborious research . . . reviewing Weizsäcker's memoirs, I remarked that of course his criticisms of Hitler's policy were merely put in a drawer and not shown to anyone. Lewis said to me: 'How did you know that Weizsäcker's memoranda had no registration number on them? I worked in the archives for a fortnight to establish this point.' I said I felt it must be so. Lewis groaned: 'Ah, you have green fingers. I have not.'[6]

This is a good story. But, of course, having green fingers isn't enough to make a good historian – Namier managed to be a great one without them. At most, what Norman Stone calls Taylor's 'inspired guesses' allowed him to formulate hypotheses which other scholars were able to corroborate by checking them against the sources.[7] Close acquaintance with the sources may let some historians take short cuts based on intuition, but the critical examination of the accounts they give using these inspired guesses cannot itself rely on intuition but must rather rest on intersubjectively acceptable standards – perhaps those

criteria of scientific progress formulated by Imre Lakatos. The scholarly practice of even the most experienced and inspired historian is thus accountable to
a process of public adjudication of the writing that issues from this practice.
Once this is granted, it is hard to draw a clear line of demarcation between a
broad interpretive essay written by a historian and one produced by a historical sociologist: whatever their origins, whether only one has been sanctified by
the chrism of direct contact with the sources, both are subject to the same
progress of critical appraisal. Unless legitimate historical inquiry is to be
restricted to the research monograph – a step which even the most fuddled
empiricist would hesitate at taking – then it seems hard to exclude from its
domain interpretations generated by the kind of theories of history accepted by
Marxists and Weberians.

But what is such a theory of history? A theory of history must, it seems to
me, meet three conditions.[8]

(1) A theory of history includes a *theory of structure*. That is, it must give some
account of the differences between various kinds of society, differences typically
explained by appeal to the concept of social structure – of the fundamental relationships constitutive of a particular kind of society. These relationships have
a number of important properties: their existence does not depend on the participation in them of particular named persons; they are sets of empty places,
which can be filled by any suitably trained and motivated individuals.
Moreover, structures exist independently of those occupying them being aware
of their existence: the most important social relationships are those which, as
Hegel put it, go on behind the backs of the human beings making up the society
in question.[9]

A theory of structure seems to me a necessary condition of any theory of
history, for two reasons. First, if all human societies shared the same structure
then what Eero Loone calls 'the *presumption of qualitative difference*' that is
'one of the most important socio-theoretical presuppositions of historical
knowledge' would fall away.[10] No theory can be a theory of *history* that does
not include among its premises some account of the singularity of indifferent
human societies. Secondly, the concept of structure implies that the accounts
given by participants in a given society cannot be taken at face value but must
be subjected to critical examination if they are to provide evidence of the nature
of that society. To borrow formulations used by Marx in *Capital*, how a society
presents itself to those participating in it and how its inner structure actually
functions do not correspond; hence the need for a theory of history, which is
not content to register the surface appearances of social life but formulates
explanatory concepts designed to uncover the underlying relationships which
make that society what it is.[11] That the historian's concepts do not correspond
with those she finds in the sources is, I think, a general feature of historical
inquiry: otherwise, Marc Bloch observes, 'history would have little left to do';
he compares the historian who inherits terms such as 'feudal' and gives them

new meanings to 'the physicist who, in disregard of Greek, persists in calling an "atom" something which he spends his time in dividing'.[12] This characteristic of historical inquiry is, however, given a systematic rationale in theories of history.

Historical materialism involves a theory of structure in the sense outlined above. This consists especially in the concept of mode of production. In contemporary usage (which does not correspond exactly to Marx's), this treats each social system as defined by a particular combination of the forces and relations of production – that is, of, on the one hand, the material elements of production (labour power and the means of production), the specific combination of which in the labour process represents a particular level of development of productive technique; and, on the other hand, a specific form of effective control of the productive forces, which, in class societies, gives rise to the appropriation of surplus labour by the controlling minority, and, on the basis of the definite form this exploitation takes, to the division of society into classes with antagonistic interests. Although the mode of production is constituted by the forces and relations of production, it is not exhausted by them: it comprises also law, politics and ideology, the superstructure whose movements are explained (in a manner whose precise character has been the subject of endless controversy among Marxist theorists) by the economic base. Finally, modes of production, basic types of human society such as slavery, feudalism and capitalism, are distinguished from social formations, actually existing societies which may involve a combination of more than one mode of production, though one mode is always dominant over the others.[13]

The Weberian counterpart of this theory of structure is perhaps most perspicuously stated by W. G. Runciman when he argues that social structure is defined by three 'dimensions of power', 'access to or control of the *means of production, means of persuasion* and *means of coercion*'. Consistent with a preoccupation with power that derives ultimately from Nietzsche, Weberian historical sociologists tend to conceptualize societies as different forms of domination: thus Runciman distinguishes between various 'modes of the distribution of power'.[14] The most obvious difference between this style of theory and historical materialism is that the Weberian theory of structure is pluralist in the way it frames explanations. As Perry Anderson puts it, 'there is no primacy of economic causation . . .: military-political and ideological-cultural determinations are of equivalent significance'.[15]

(2) A *theory of transformation* is required to make a theory properly historical. On its own, a theory of structure would merely issue in a typology of social forms, a theoretically informed inventory of the differences between societies. To avoid being merely a principle of societal classification, a theory of history must contain some account of the mechanism or mechanisms responsible both for the changes that take place within a particular society and, more importantly, for the transformation of a society, that is, for the process through which

it ceases to embody one particular structure, and comes instead to embody another.

Theories of history thus differ not simply in the accounts they give of social structure but in the mechanism or mechanisms they claim govern the transformation of societies. In principle, each kind of society could have its own distinctive mechanism, but I know of no theory of history representing this possibility: its explanatory power would in any case be comparatively weak, since a defining characteristic of a theory (as opposed to a description) is that it explains a wide range of phenomena on the basis of a comparatively small number of propositions. The strongest theory of history, therefore, is the one which claims that the same mechanism is responsible for all historical transformations. One example is provided by Arnold Toynbee, for whom the rise and fall of civilizations are consequences of 'the interplay between challenges and responses': this mechanism produces a universal pattern, in which a civilization breaks down when it polarizes between a 'dominant minority' and 'internal and external proletariats' alienated from this ruling group; ultimately the proletariat, invigorated by a process of spiritual renewal, breaks away to found a new civilization.[16] But what *A Study of History* thereby gains in empirical range it loses in theoretical specificity, since the mechanism of challenge-and-response is characterized in such vague and loose terms that it is difficult to see what could constitute a counter-example to the explanatory claims made for it, so that the theory explains nothing and everything at the same time.[17]

The two most interesting theories of history occupy positions intermediate between the two extremes of allocating to each structure its own mechanism of change and explaining all social transformations by the same mechanism. Neo-Weberian theories are as pluralist in the accounts they give of change as in their conceptualizations of social structure. Each of the kinds of domination they identify is capable of effecting transformations in particular historical circumstances. As Anderson puts it, 'different societies and different epochs exhibit different dominants, which have to be established case by case'.[18] Thus, if the same mechanisms are at work throughout history, the role they play varies from situation to situation. The thought is expressed with especial vigour by Mann (who differs from Runciman in treating as basic, not three dimensions, but four sources of power – ideological, economic, military and political):

> there is no obvious, formulaic, general patterning of the interrelations of power sources. It will be evident by now, for example, that this volume cannot support a general 'historical materialism' . . . Economic power relations, modes of production, and social classes come and go in the historical record. In occasional world-historical moments they decisively reorganize social life; usually they are important in conjunction with other power sources; occasionally they are decisively reorganized by them. The same can be said of all the power sources, coming and going, weaving in and out of the historical record.[19]

Historical materialism is, by comparison, strongly monist. Social transformation – the transition from one mode of production to another – is explained in terms of the same mechanism, the development of conflicts within the domain of social production. These conflicts (or contradictions – a term which *restrain* in the Marxist traditions is used to highlight the claim that they are inherent in the social form concerned) are of two kinds: the <u>fettering</u> of the productive forces by the relations of production (itself a consequence of the prior development of the productive forces) and the class struggle between exploiters and exploited. Although distinct, these two social contradictions are interrelated, since, generally speaking, the economic crises produced by fettering intensify class antagonisms. But though Marxism thus specifies a universal mechanism of change, albeit one conceptualized with far greater precision than Toynbee's, the forms taken by the two kinds of conflict vary significantly according to the nature of the prevailing mode of production. Each mode of production has its own 'laws of motion': this implies that the dynamics of economic crisis will differ significantly from one mode to another. Thus, whereas Marx's theory of capitalist crises conceives these as crises of *overproduction*, in which productive forces go to waste because it is unprofitable to use them, Marxist historians tend to treat the crisis of feudal society in the late Middle Ages as one characterized by scarcity, involving an imbalance between population and productive resources. Again, the forms taken by the class struggle differ significantly according to the manner in which the conflicting classes are constituted by the relations of exploitation. In these respects, the Marxist theory of history is a compromise between accounting for all change by the same mechanism and identifying a mechanism for every different social structure.[20]

(3) Every theory of history has, finally, a *theory of directionality*, that is, it offers an account of the overall pattern described by the historical process. If the theory of transformation specifies the mechanism(s) responsible for the transition between one social form and another, the theory of directionality is concerned with the overall shape given to human history by the sum of these transitions. Three principal patterns have been identified. First, *progress*: each successive social form represents an increase in some property common to all kinds of society. Marxism conceives history as progress in this sense since it claims that there is a tendency for the productive forces to develop from one mode of production to another. Secondly, *regress*: the succession of social forms involves a cumulative decrease in the property in terms of which a pattern in the course of history is sought. Claims of this sort are common enough in Christian theologies in as much as, following Augustine, they posit a radical disjunction between two polities, one heavenly and governed by divine providence, the other secular and subject to human wills suffering from the inherent flaw of original sin: thus, as Georges Duby puts it, European intellectuals around the year 1000 'thought human history in the grip of the forces of evil and consequently a history of decline'.[21] Modern theories which conceive

history straightforwardly as a regress are comparatively rare: Rousseau's *Discourse on the Origins of Inequality* might be considered an example. It is more usual to explain what are thought to be periods of decline as the final stage in a historical cycle. For, thirdly, there are modern theories of history which revive the ancient idea that the course of history follows a *cycle* of progress and regression: Spengler and Toynbee represent the most important twentieth-century examples of this way of thinking.

It might be thought that giving an account of the directionality of history is not a necessary condition of a theory of history in the way that the first two are. After all, theories of structure and transformation serve to specify the explanatory objectives of a theory of history. By contrast, arriving at a judgement about the overall pattern described by the course of history might seem to be a super-added and dispensable element, a distinct intellectual operation from those closely linked explanatory activities laid down in the theories of structure and transformation, the ascription of a value to the process analysed by these theories. There are, I think, three reasons for resisting this line of thought. First, conditions (1) and (2) provide the conceptual means of giving an overall account of the historical process. Such an account would, however, surely be incomplete if it did not involve at least the attempt to discern some pattern emerging from the transformations of human societies. Secondly, this attempt need not be intrinsically evaluative in the sense of passing an ethical judgement on the course of history. All that is required for a theory of directionality is that it specify some property whose increase or decrease represents, respectively, progress or regress, and that it advance the claim that the historical process involves a tendency for progress or regression thus defined to occur (or, in the case of a cyclical theory, for progress and regress to alternate in some law-governed fashion). The theory need not involve the further claim that the increase of this property contributes to the good as defined by some ethical theory. Thirdly, and more pragmatically, the two most important theories of history, the Marxist and the Weberian, both involve theories of progress in the sense just specified.

This latter claim has been most effectively defended by Erik Olin Wright, Andrew Levine and Elliott Sober in a critical discussion of Anthony Giddens's theory of history. They give what amount to the necessary conditions of a theory of historical progress (which they call 'directionality', thus giving the latter term a narrower meaning than the sense in which it is used here):

> The probability of staying at the same point is greater than the probability of regressing . . . In a proper theory of history, social forms must be 'sticky downward'.
> There must be some probability of moving from a given level to the next higher level.
> The probability of a 'progressive' change is greater than the probability of 'regression'.[22]

Plainly, historical materialism is a theory of progress in this sense, since it asserts that there is a tendency for the productive forces to develop (though there is, of course, considerable debate among Marxists about the precise character of this tendency and its implications for the nature of social transformation).[23] It is, however, much more controversial to claim that Weberian theories discern a progressive direction in history. Giddens, for example, sets his account of historical development explicitly in opposition to evolutionism (of which he counts Marxism an instance).[24] Nevertheless, as Wright, Levine and Sober point out, he does claim that successive social forms represent an increase in 'time–space distanciation', the processes through which societies gain access to larger expanses of space and time, thereby enhancing agents' control over economic and ideologico-military resources, and in this respect Giddens implicitly contradicts his explicit 'rejection of the idea that historical change has an epochal directionality'.[25]

Other Weberian theories have been much less shy about acknowledging that they see history taking a progressive course. Runciman, who explicitly seeks to develop an evolutionary theory of society, declares: 'As in biological evolution, there has unquestionably been a progression towards more and more complex forms of social organization'.[26] And Mann, at the conclusion of his 'history of power to AD 1760', gives this retrospective judgement:

> Social power has continued to develop, somewhat unsteadily perhaps, but nonetheless cumulatively throughout this volume . . . Seen in the very long run, the infrastructure available to power holders and to societies at large has steadily increased. Many different societies have contributed to this. But, once invented, the major infrastructural techniques seem almost never to have disappeared from human practice. True, often powerful techniques have seemed inappropriate to the problems of a succeeding society and thus have declined. But, unless obsolete, their decline has proved temporary and they have been subsequently recovered.[27]

These remarks of Mann's are especially helpful since they serve to dramatize the logical gap separating the claim that history has a progressive direction from an ethical judgement which finds this movement good. The property which, according to Mann, increases over time is social power. Since this embraces more particularly the destructive capacities of states and their ability to penetrate and control the everyday existence of their subjects, this is a process of development which we may have good ethical and political reasons for condemning. Giddens is the contemporary theorist whose view of history is perhaps closest to Weber's when he described modernity as the confinement of humankind in an 'iron cage', but there is no reason why we should not draw a similar moral conclusion to Weber's from other accounts which conceptualize history as the growth of the resources of domination.[28] There is much more to be said about the question of historical progress. There is, however, a remaining issue to be clarified before I consider the differences between Marxist and Weberian theories of history more closely.

How do theories of history as defined by the three conditions given above differ from philosophies of history? It is time to say more about Maurice Mandelbaum's definition of a philosophy of history as (1) covering the whole of the historical process, (2) offering a general principle of explanation of this process in all its aspects and (3) seeking out the meaning of history. I suggest that theories of history such as Marxism and Weberian historical sociologies meet conditions (1) and (2) but not condition (3). For it is undeniably the case that embedded within what are, on Mandelbaum's definition, philosophies of history are accounts which, on the face of it, meet the three conditions I have argued are necessary features of the theory of history. Hegel's philosophy of history is a case in point: the social forms that make up the subject matter of history have the constitution of a state (structure); their succession is explained as a dialectical movement generated by internal contradictions (transformation); and this movement represents the development of the consciousness of freedom (directionality). Or take Toynbee's *Study*, which offers an account of the nature of complex civilizations (structure), of the mechanism – challenge-and-response – responsible for their rise and fall (transformation) and of the pattern of historical development, in which 'recurrence' is 'concurrent with progress' (directionality).[29] There are, nevertheless, good reasons for regarding Hegel and Toynbee as philosophers rather than theorists of history.

The overlap between philosophies and theories of history arises, of course, from the fact that both seek to offer explanations applicable to the whole of the historical process (Mandelbaum's condition (2)). The differences separating these two forms of theoretical discourse are best seen as consequences of the kinds of explanation they offer. One might say that theories of history are empirical whereas philosophies of history are not. This statement seems to me correct. One way of characterizing theories of history is to say that they are research programmes subject to the criteria of theoretical and empirical progress – respectively, the prediction of novel facts and the corroboration of some of these predictions – developed by Imre Lakatos. They are therefore empirical theories in a way that Hegel's philosophy of history certainly is not. For Hegel, the proposition that history is governed by reason requires no empirical confirmation, since it derives from a 'real proof' which 'comes from knowledge of reason itself' provided by philosophy, and more particularly by a grasp of the self-movement of the categories of Hegel's own speculative logic.

Important though this difference is, it does not, however, seem to me to cut to the core of what separates theories from philosophies of history. This is that philosophies of history are teleological – that is, the account they give of the meaning of the historical process, and more particularly of the state of affairs in which it culminates, explains the succession of social forms making up the content of that process. Once again, Hegel provides a good illustration of this pattern: the 'real proof' of reason's rule over the world reveals a teleological structure in which the conclusion of the dialectical process justifies its starting point, so that 'the science is seen to be a circle which returns upon itself'.[30] Kant's critical philosophy seeks to avoid ontotheological speculation, but is no less teleological in its application to history: '*The history of the human race can be regarded as the realization of a hidden plan of nature to bring about an internally . . . perfect political constitution as the only possible state within which all the natural capacities of mankind can be developed completely*'. The mechanism through which nature's aim of fully developing humankind's 'natural capacities' is to be realized is 'the *unsocial sociability* of man': in rather the same fashion as Hegel's cunning of reason, human beings' 'self-seeking pretensions' lead them to develop these capacities, a process that is likely (but not certain) in the future to draw them into republican government and a federation of peoples.[31]

Theories of history, by contrast, seek to give non-teleological explanations of the historical process. Both Marxist and Weberian theories discern a progressive directionality in the course of history – respectively, the development of the productive forces and the growth of social power. But the existence of such a pattern does not provide the rationale for the explanations each theory gives of specific social transformations. The nature of every social form is to be understood not in terms of the final state of affairs towards which it is a step, but on the basis of the powers and relations constituting it, which give that form its identity but may threaten its survival.

This is not a particularly controversial claim to make of Weberian theories of history, since positing a multiplicity of mechanisms as the causes of historical change – in Runciman's terminology, control over the means of production, coercion and persuasion, or, as the title of Ernest Gellner's main work of historical sociology has it, *Plough, Sword and Book* – would sit ill with projecting a single path of historical development predetermined by its outcome. Anderson ascribes to Weberian theorists the claim that 'the procession of variant institutional hierarchies that makes up the record of human development is contingent – not a chapter, but an encyclopaedia of accidents'.[32] This is perhaps to put it a bit strongly; Mann, for example, does highlight the importance of historical accidents – 'the "might have beens" and "almost weres" [that] could have led into fundamentally different historical tracks' from those which actually unfolded – but his narrative of the growth of social power in the West seems in fact to draw on an interplay of 'pattern' and 'accident' in which 'power struggles are the principal patternings of history, but their outcomes have often been close-run'.[33] What is undoubtedly true is that all Weberian theorists are committed to giving an account of historical development which makes no appeal, overt or tacit, to concepts of predetermination or inevitability. Thus Runciman makes clear that his is a non-teleological theory of social evolution:

> Evolution is more than qualitative change: it is change in a definite direc-
> tion. But it must not be equated with progress in either of the two senses
> to which it was tied by nineteenth-century evolutionary sociologists who,
> for all their other differences, shared an unquestioned presupposition that
> evolution was not only change for the better but change in the direction
> of a predetermined goal.[34]

Runciman's and Mann's historical sociologies are instances of what Wright,
Levine and Sober call a 'theory of *historical trajectories*', a theory, that is, that
'acknowledge[s] an overall directionality to historical change' (directionality in
the sense given above, where it is equivalent to what I prefer to call progress,
and involves a tendency for historical change to increase some property), but
rejects 'the view that directionality implies a unique path and sequence of development'.[35] But Wright, Levine and Sober argue that Marxism also is a theory
of historical trajectories – or, rather, that a non-teleological version of historical materialism would meet the conditions of such a theory. The decisive move
in any attempt to strip Marxism of teleology comes with the rejection of what
G. A. Cohen calls the Primacy Thesis – the proposition defended by Second
International Marxists such as Kautsky and Plekhanov that '[t]he nature of the
production relations of a society is explained by the level of development of its
productive forces'.[36] While Cohen's own defence of the Primacy Thesis does not
depend, strictly speaking, on a resort to teleological explanations (that is, explanations of an event by the future events it brings about), his claim that the production relations are functionally explained by their tendency to promote the
development of productive forces seems impossible to sustain without the
further claim that the replacement of a mode of production that is less progressive (in the sense of developing the productive forces) by one that is more progressive is inevitable. The effect of dropping the Primacy Thesis is to introduce
an element of irreducible contingency into historical materialism: the crisis of
every mode of production may arise from the fettering of the productive forces
by the relations of production, but the outcome of that crisis – whether it leads
to a social revolution inaugurating a new, more progressive mode of production, or whether instead prevailing production relations survive, giving rise to
stagnation or even regression – is not predetermined. A space is thus created for
Mann's 'might have beens' and 'almost weres' that articulates with the Marxist
political project, with its stress on working-class self-emancipation and revolutionary subjectivity, far better than does Cohen's Primary Thesis.[37]

There is much more to be said on the subject of Marxism and historical
progress. The upshot of this has, I hope, been to establish the respects in which
both historical materialism and Weberian historical sociology are similar kinds
of social theory. Both meet the three conditions set out above for a theory of
history; both – or, perhaps better, versions of both – further differ from philosophies of history in refusing to conceptualize the historical process as a
sequence whose course is predetermined by its outcome. One implication of this

latter feature is that it sets the limits any theory of history must respect. One way to deny the doctrine of historical inevitability is to say that the outcome of any major historical crisis, in which the survival of a particular social structure is in question, cannot be predicted on the basis of whatever general propositions a theory of history happens to assert. The interplay of factors which led to the actual outcome can only be reconstructed by careful empirical research. James McPherson justifies his use of a 'narrative format' in writing the history of the American Civil War by appeal to 'the dimension of *contingency* – the recognition that at numerous critical points during the war things might have gone altogether differently'. The contingencies inherent in historical situations do not render social theory otiose: on the contrary – to take the example of the American Civil War – it is indispensable to any understanding of the nature of the 'irrepressible conflict' between North and South, of the forces at work on both sides, and of the society which emerged from it. The point is, once again, that general theories of history and concrete historical inquiries are dependent on, and irreducible to, one another.

NOTES

1. See, for example, H. A. Veeser, ed., *The New Historicism* (London, 1989).
2. M. Foucault, 'Questions of Method', *I & C*, 8 (1981), p. 4. Paul Veyne brings out the philosophical underpinnings of Foucault's 'histories' in 'Foucault révolutionne l'histoire', in *Comment on écrit l'histoire* (2nd edn, Paris, 1978).
3. G. R. Elton, *The Practice of History* (London, 1969), p. 87.
4. H. R. Trevor-Roper, 'The Gentry 1540–1660', *Economic History Review*, supp., 1 (1953), and 'The General Crisis of the Seventeenth Century', in T. Ashton, ed., *Crisis in Europe 1560–1660* (London, 1965); M. Mann, *The Sources of Social Power*, vol. 1 (Cambridge, 1986), chs 14 and 15.
5. Elton, *Practice*, p. 84.
6. A. J. P. Taylor, *A Personal History* (London, 1984), p. 147. Ernst von Weizsäcker was State Secretary at the German Foreign Office under the National Socialist regime.
7. N. Stone, 'Taylorism', in K. Miller, ed., *London Review of Books Anthology One* (London, 1981), pp. 18–19, where other examples of Taylor's green fingers are given.
8. See the admirable discussion in E. Loone, *Soviet Marxism and Analytical Philosophies of History* (London, 1992), esp. part 3, ch. 5.
9. See A. Callinicos, *Making History* (Cambridge, 1987), ch. 2.
10. Loone, *Soviet Marxism*, p. 94. Among the variants of historical theory Loone lists is 'the theory that records differences in systems that belong to its referents', ibid., p. 132.
11. For example: 'All science would be superfluous if the outward appearance and the essence of things coincided', K. Marx, *Capital*, vol. 3 (Moscow, 1971), p. 817.
12. M. Bloch, *The Historian's Craft* (Manchester, 1992), p. 140, and *Feudal Society* (2 vols, London, 1965), vol. 1, p. xviii. See also A. C. Danto, *Analytical Philosophy of History* (Cambridge, 1965), pp. 182–3.
13. For classic treatments of the concept of mode of production, see L. Althusser and E. Balibar, *Reading Capital* (London, 1970), and G. A. Cohen, *Karl Marx's Theory of History* (Oxford, 1978). What Loone, following Soviet usage, calls 'socio-economic formations' are what western Marxists tend to name 'modes of production': see *Soviet Marxism*, part 4, ch. 2. The distinction between mode of production and

social formation was first formally stated by Althusser: see his discussion in 'On Theoretical Work', in *Philosophy and the Spontaneous Philosophy of Scientists and Other Essays* (London, 1990).

14. W. G. Runciman, *A Treatise on Social Theory*, vol. 2 (Cambridge, 1989), pp. 12, 55.

15. P. Anderson, *English Questions* (London, 1992), p. 231.

16. A. J. Toynbee, *A Study of History* (abr. edn, 2 vols, ed. D.C. Somervell, London, 1960), vol. 1, pp. 76–7.

17. For a comparatively sympathetic critical discussion of Toynbee, see W. H. Dray, *Philosophy of History* (Englewood Cliffs, 1964), ch. 7.

18. Anderson, *English Questions*, p. 231.

19. Mann, *Sources*, p. 523; Mann's general theory of power is expounded in chs 1 and 16. See Runciman, *Treatise*, pp. 14–15 for a critical discussion of Mann's attempt to distinguish between political and military power.

20. See Callinicos, *Making History*, ch. 2. On the dynamics of feudal crisis, see G. Bois, *Crisis of Feudalism* (Cambridge, 1984), and Robert Brenner's essays in T. S. Aston and C. E. Philpin, eds, *The Brenner Debate* (Cambridge, 1985).

21. G. Duby, *The Three Orders* (Chicago, 1980), p. 37.

22. E. O. Wright, A. Levine and E. Sober, *Reconstructing Marxism* (London, 1992), p. 79.

23. Cf. Cohen, *Karl Marx's Theory of History*, ch. 6, and Wright et al., *Reconstructing Marxism*, ch. 2 and pp. 80–2.

24. A. Giddens, *A Contemporary Critique of Historical Materialism* (London, 1981), pp. 19–25.

25. Wright et al., *Reconstructing Marxism*, p. 85. On time–space distantiation, see Giddens, *Contemporary Critique*, pp. 90ff.

26. Runciman, *Treatise*, p. 39.

27. Mann, *Sources*, p. 524; see more generally ibid., pp. 524–7. Note that Mann here more or less explicitly gives a version of Wright et al.'s condition (1), that social forms are sticky downward.

28. M. Weber, *The Protestant Ethic and the Spirit of Capitalism* (London, 1976). Cf. A. Giddens, *The Nation State and Violence* (Cambridge, 1985).

29. Toynbee, *Study*, vol. 1, p. 253. The critical discussion of 'Deterministic Solutions' (ibid., pp. 247–54) from which this quotation is taken makes clear that Toynbee does not offer a straightforwardly cyclical theory of directionality.

30. G. W. F. Hegel, *The Science of Logic* (2 vols, London, 1966), vol. 2, p. 484.

31. I. Kant, *Political Writings* (2nd edn, Cambridge, 1991), pp. 50, 44–5.

32. Anderson, *English Questions*, p. 231.

33. Mann, *Sources*, pp. 531–2.

34. Runciman, *Treatise*, p. 296.

35. Wright et al., *Reconstructing Marxism*, p. 79.

36. Cohen, *Karl Marx's Theory of History*, p. 134.

37. See generally ibid., chs 9 and 10, Joshua Cohen, review of *Karl Marx's Theory of History*, *Journal of Philosophy*, 79 (1982), Callinicos, *Making History*, ch. 2, C. Harman, 'Base and Superstructure', *IS*, 2: 32 (1986), and G. A. Cohen and W. Kymlicka, 'Human Nature and Social Change in the Marxist Conception of History', in G. A. Cohen, *History, Labour and Freedom* (Oxford, 1988).

SECTION 2: QUESTIONS FOR DISCUSSION

- To what does 'the Enlightenment Project' typically refer in contemporary political thought?
- How accurately does the concept of an Enlightenment project reflect the nature of the various intellectual currents found in the historical period of the Enlightenment?
- When we debate political matters, is it ever appropriate to offer purely personal (and perhaps self-interested) opinions on what should be done, or should we attempt to offer viewpoints that it might be reasonable to expect our fellow citizens to share (which may be very different from our personal preferences)?
- What are the advantages and disadvantages of continuing the search for a 'foundation' in human nature from which we might 'justify' morality? (What might 'justification' mean here?)
- What might be the purposes or goals of the 'ideal' political order? To what extent should they figure in any account of when and why we ought to obey the state? (On what other grounds might political obligation be based?)
- What is the historical relationship between liberals and mass democracy; between liberals and the capitalist economy; between liberals and post-war social democracy?
- What are the building blocks of the Marxist theoretical 'system'? What has been the relationship between that system and political action?
- What do liberals presume about history and politics? Do post-Marxists differ significantly in their approach?

- Is there a way of reading Marx independent of the Marxist system? What are the consequences for Marxism of raising this question?
- Is the post-Marxist critique merely negative and destructive? Does it offer a basis for political action?
- What is most distinctive about conservatism as a political theory?
- Why do Conservatives see tradition as the greatest source of wisdom? Are they right to do so?
- Is rationalism necessarily an attitude lacking in poetry or passion? What are the differences and similarities between the sort of 'anti-rationalism' found in post-Marxism and that found in Conservatism or in Rorty's 'postmodern' Liberalism?
- What do we get from our 'tradition', and how important is it in orientating us in the world? Can we be sure what we mean when we speak of our customs, habits or traditions?
- Does Conservative theory contradict itself when it seems to argue simultaneously for a strong sense of moral community and laissez-faire capitalism?
- Does less government necessarily lead to more freedom?
- How do liberals and conservatives differ in their views about the dangers of concentrating power in the hands of government?
- What are the key differences between the Marxist, Conservative and Liberal conceptions of the proper role of government?

SECTION 2: FURTHER READING

Those interested in grasping Liberalism more fully should begin with Kant himself. The Cambridge edition, *Political Writings*, edited by Hans Reiss (Cambridge University Press, 1996), has a good introduction and an excellent selection of the most important readings, some of which are surprisingly accessible (especially the famous essay 'What is Enlightenment?'). Other landmark texts of liberal thinking include John Stuart Mill's *On Liberty* (Penguin, 1985) and Leonard Hobhouse's *Liberalism* (Oxford University Press, 1964), whose brand of 'new' social Liberalism has recently been revived in some quarters. More recent key texts could include Ronald **Dworkin**'s *Taking Rights Seriously* (Duckworth, 1977) and the collection edited by Alan Ryan, *The Idea of Freedom* (Oxford University Press, 1979). Of course, the major landmark of recent liberal theory is Rawls's *A Theory of Justice* (various editions). For a useful introduction to this strand of thinking, consult the chapter 'Liberal Equality' in Will Kymlicka's *Contemporary Political Philosophy: An Introduction* (Oxford University Press, 1990). Another useful set of commentaries is Chandran Kukathas and Philip Petit (eds), *A Theory of Justice and its*

Critics (Polity, 1990). Try also Rex Martin's *Rawls and Rights* (University of Kansas Press, 1985). On the more recent Rawls, try Victoria Davion and Clark Wolf (eds) *The Idea of a Political Liberalism* (Rowman and Littlefield, 2000).

To find out more about Berlin, try the readable biography *Isaiah Berlin: A Life* by Michael Ignatieff (Vintage, 2000), and for a more philosophical analysis *Isaiah Berlin* by John Gray (HarperCollins, 1995). But also consult Berlin himself, especially *Four Essays on Liberty* (Oxford University Press, 1969). On our other key liberal thinkers, see Gray's *Two Faces of Liberalism* (Polity, 2000), Gewirth's *Reason and Morality* (University of Chicago Press, 1978) and Rorty's *Contingency, Irony and Solidarity* (Cambridge University Press, 1989). Also well worth consulting is Mark Evans (ed.), *The Edinburgh Companion to Contemporary Liberalism* (Edinburgh University Press, 2001).

The best way to get to grips with the Conservative mindset is to plunge into Burke's highly readable (and actually rather passionate polemic) *Reflections on the Revolution in France* (various editions). Also go straight to Oakeshott by looking at the essays in *Rationalism in Politics* (Methuen, 1967); and (to get a sense of the 'free market' shift) see Hayek's *The Road to Serfdom* (Routledge, 1944) or Milton Friedman, *Capitalism and Freedom* (University of Chicago Press, 1962). For a general selection of conservative writers, Scruton's collection *Conservative Texts: An Anthology* (Macmillan, 1991) is excellent. Noel O'Sullivan presents an alternative to Scruton's version in *Conservatism* (J. M. Dent, 1976).

On specifically American Conservatism, Clinton Rossiter's *Conservatism in America* (Random House, 1962) still has merit, and the collection *American Conservative Thought in the Twentieth Century* edited by William F. Buckley Jr (Bobbs-Merrill, 1970) contains an excellent range of essays. For a range of perspectives on the history and variety of right-wing thought (beyond Conservatism alone), see the essays in Roger Eatwell and Noel O'Sullivan (eds), *The Nature of the Right* (Pinter, 1992). A good comparison of the British and American approaches is presented by Arthur Aughey, Greta Jones and W. T. M. Riches in *The Conservative Political Tradition in Britain and the United States* (Pinter, 1992), while Robert Devigne explains the nature of contemporary conservatism (with specific reference to Oakeshott and Strauss and with pointers to the policies derived from recent conservative thought) in *Recasting Conservatism* (Yale University Press, 1994). For a critique by a left-wing philosopher, try Ted Honderich, *Conservatism* (Penguin, 1991).

If you want to look further into Marxist political thinking and to follow through the debates surrounding 'post-Marxism', then Alex Callinicos's *The Revolutionary Ideas of Karl Marx* (Bookmarks, 1995) spells out his revised but still recognisably 'Marxist' Marx. Stefan Sullivan's *Marx for a Post-Communist Era* (Routledge, 2002) uses an orthodox account of Marx to critique contemporary global capitalism in relation to poverty, corruption and the banality of consumerism.

A collection that explores the ways that post-Marxists explore class as a discursive yet still 'economic' phenomenon in politics is *Re/presenting Class: Essays in Postmodern Marxism* edited by J. K. Gibson-Graham, Stephen Resnick and Richard Wolff (Duke University Press, 2001). *Marxism Beyond Marxism*, edited by Saree Makdisi, Cesare Casarino and Rebecca Karl (Routledge, 1996), presents the ways that Marx and Marxism have been more or less drastically critiqued in order to accommodate poststructuralism and 'new social movements'. In her collection of essays *The Return of the Political* (Verso, 1993), Chantal Mouffe outlines a post-liberal project based on her discursive approach to politics, while Anna Marie Smith's *Laclau and Mouffe: The Radical Democratic Imaginary* (Routledge, 1998) presents the philosophical and political background to the post-Marxist thought of Laclau and Mouffe and develops their ideas in relation to contemporary political and philosophical issues (some of which she touches on in Chapter 12 of the present volume).

SECTION 3
ALTERNATIVE VISIONS AND REVISIONS

INTRODUCTION

Traditions as broad and all-encompassing as Liberalism, Conservatism and Marxism are enduring and powerful because of their breadth. But, for the same reason, they are also weak. In saying so much in general, they may not say enough about particular concerns, including those that are particular to our time. As we saw in the general introduction and in Chapter 1, the social and political challenges with which we are all faced today may well necessitate new ways of thinking and may not be amenable to the sorts of broad and all-encompassing theory put forward at the height of European modernity.

The strands or schools of thought examined in this section all set out with varying sorts of challenge to the dominant conceptions advanced by the mainstream traditions. Yet, in formulating new and alternative perspectives, they often find themselves drawing on the themes of the larger and older traditions. Perhaps, in the attempt to move beyond our traditions, we find ourselves forced to draw on them in search of the resources we need. This is one of the questions to keep in mind when thinking about the alternative visions and revisions discussed here. Are they completely novel attempts to think about politics? Do they really move beyond what has gone before? Is it actually necessary to so move beyond? It may be that we have simply forgotten what it was that our traditions were actually arguing.

Our answer to these questions depends on the seriousness with which we greet the implicit charges made against the mainstream traditions. Communitarian thought sets out, it appears, as a critique, or at least a corrective, to Liberalism, which it finds to be so focused on the rights of the individual that it misses the importance for people of being part of a strong and active community. If this were the only aspect to such a charge, we might regard it as requiring only a minor corrective or perhaps only clarification: that Liberalism has simply overlooked a dimension of social and political life or has overemphasised one aspect to the detriment of others. If this is so, then we need only effect some small repairs. But the charge of communitarianism is greater than this: that Liberalism, in basing itself on the rights of the individual, has fundamentally misunderstood social life and has produced a political philosophy that is itself the cause of the problems with which we are beset. For communitarians, it is only in the context of community that there can be the sort of moral framework that gives us a sense of duty or responsibility to others and so makes us respect others' rights. In treating community as something that can limit people's rights and which they should thus be protected from, Liberalism is undermining the very ground on which its claims to rights can actually grow. This is an altogether greater charge and represents a greater challenge to Liberalism.

But, as Mike Kenny shows in Chapter 6, in advancing this critique communitarianism returns to older and earlier forms of liberalism, to a more holistic approach that pre-dates thinkers such as Rawls. Simultaneously, some communitarians draw heavily on conservative ideas about the importance of tradition in providing a coherent framework of values within which we can live. Furthermore, socialism has generally understood itself as advocating a strong sense of social solidarity as opposed to the individualism of liberal capitalism. So communitarianism is, at least in part, a reworking of older themes in political philosophy.

If the charge feminism makes against Liberalism is that it has overlooked women or been a little biased towards men, then we might be able to repair it simply by making sure that from now on we do think about the rights of women and ensure they are properly protected. Some strands of feminism do indeed emphasise the demand for equality between the sexes and have their roots in arguments about equality advanced by liberal thinkers. But, for many strands of feminism, the charge made against Liberalism is that it is not only incidentally exclusionary of women but constitutively so: that blindness to women and to gender inequality actually structures these theories in their entirety (and society also). Thus Liberal notions of justice, rights and emancipation are not merely inadequate but fundamentally flawed, and considerable effort is required to put things right. The claim here is that the universalism of Liberalism is in fact nothing of the sort and that it is really a disguised particularism that benefits men.

In Chapter 7, Kate Nash concentrates on this charge against universalism and examines a range of claims that women may in fact best be thought of not through their 'sameness' to men but in terms of their difference. She also pays particular attention to arguments that try to show how Liberalism may be intrinsically biased towards men. For example, it is premised on a division between the public and the private where the public can properly be the subject of political dispute but the private is beyond the realms of state and politics. Many feminist writers have argued that this maps onto a gendered division of labour rooted in structural inequality between the sexes whereby women are confined to the private, household realm and men occupy the positions of public life. As such, the liberal principle of the public–private distinction actually serves to prevent scrutiny of men's exploitation of women. A more radical version of this sort of argument, also reviewed by Nash, suggests that it is universalism itself that is at fault, that difference is intrinsic to human existence and that Enlightenment itself may have to be seriously reconsidered. As such, it also challenges the presumptions of Marxism (that often elevated the class to the position of universality and so may have downplayed the importance of gendered exploitation). Feminism then represents a challenge to the traditional ideologies, but at the same time it draws on the emancipatory claims of both Liberalism and Marxism.

The extent to which a liberal approach can deal with varieties of new problems is again questioned by Tim Hayward in Chapter 8 on ecologism. Here, the liberal interest in justice is brought to the fore but reconceived through an awareness of the way our actions are always embedded in the natural environment of which we are a part. Indeed, the distinctiveness of ecologism can be seen as lying in the ways in which it sets limits upon human actions. This is quite a contrast to dominant aspects of Liberalism that tend to lift all limits to human actions and aspirations, or socialism and Marxism that sees itself as abolishing the limits set by Liberalism. In this sense, we may think that environmentalism and ecologism have more in common with conservatism in as much as that ideology also wants us to recognise and put in place limits to human aspirations. But, while ecologism has its 'conservative' aspect, it wants to rethink the reasons for such limitations. It would be better to say that ecologism recognises a limit internal to the thought of mainstream political theory, one that produced contradictions and crises not only within theory but also within the realm of social action. Just as feminism was able to show that much political theory was premised on a blindness to gender-differentiation and even an active involvement in the marginalisation of women, so ecologism has shown the complicity of liberal and other forms of thought in the exploitation of the natural environment. Once we recognise this, we reformulate our political and social thinking not just in part but in its entirety and from the root.

If communitarianism, feminism and ecologism all accuse liberal political thinking of being insufficiently aware of the complexity and difference of human societies, and if all set limits to the capacity of reason to order human affairs (not least because they regard that reason based on a particular and biased conception of the world), then they are perhaps brought together by the powerful strand of contemporary thought known as poststructuralism. There are so many different forms of work carried out under the name of poststructuralism that it is a task in itself even to pinpoint the area, let alone explain it and evaluate it. In Chapter 9, MacKenzie locates poststructuralism within a particular intellectual milieu – that of French Structuralism – and insists on seeing it as formed by its critique of this approach. At the same time, he argues, we should not seek to limit poststructuralism to this context but see it as defined by a particular project: the attempt properly to conceptualise 'the political'. This brings us back to issues already raised by thinkers such as Arendt and Wolin, who likewise concentrated on the experience of the political. But, as MacKenzie presents it, poststructuralism has a more radical perspective and hence a stronger criticism of 'methodism' in politics. For poststructuralists, reason is inseparable from power. The reasoned arguments of political philosophers and political scientists are themselves political acts, and they cannot be extracted from the wider cultural, historical context from which they come. They are always already acts of power. For MacKenzie, the challenge we face is to think politics without pretending to have established a point outside it. Presented in this way, we can perhaps understand poststructuralism as emerging out of the same sorts of problems identified by communitarianism, feminism and ecologism. Political thought that thinks itself to be universal in scope turns out on investigation to be partial and so to perpetuate certain kinds of exclusion. In excluding certain issues, types of people or phenomena, political thought can treat them as not political. But, as society becomes ever more complex and diverse, we begin to see clearly the range of things that need to be addressed by political thinking – and that includes, we might say, considering the politics of politics. All the chapters in this section present bodies of ideas that force us to reconsider our very idea of what is political and to see that beyond the actions of governments we have to address the ways in which we begin to conceive of our world and turn our political attentions even to our own bodies and our very selves.

6

COMMUNITARIANISM

Mike Kenny

Introduction: from liberalism to communitarianism?

In a relatively short space of time, communitarianism has become one of the most salient schools of contemporary political thought, regarded by many as the most serious rival to the dominant strains of liberal political theorising. In the 1980s, a highly polarised 'debate' between liberal and communitarian political theorists unfolded, a recurrent argument that engaged many leading exponents of Anglo-American political philosophy. Simultaneously there has emerged, most notably within the United States, a social movement of sorts united by communitarian values. Two questions are considered in this short guide to this strand of contemporary political theory. Why has this perspective arisen so quickly and become so salient within the spectrum of political thinking? And has communitarianism come to bury Liberalism or revive it?

The reasons for the advance of communitarian ideas, as well as the question of its exact philosophical 'status' and ideological positioning, are all more complex than the popular picture of straightforward rivalry between a historically embedded Liberalism and a disrespectful new challenger suggests (Caney, 1992). In the first place, attention to the genealogy of communitarianism undermines the presumption that it is a newcomer on the intellectual scene. Many of the motifs and arguments associated with this perspective have been an integral element in the repertoire of political theorising since at least the late nineteenth century (Freeden, 1996). Contemporary communitarianism is at heart a revival rather than a brand-new production. What has altered is the positioning of these emphases in relation to liberal thought. Early twentieth-century thinkers such as T. H. **Green** and Leonard **Hobhouse**, in the British context, and John **Dewey**, in the American, were able to incorporate into their thinking the value of 'community' understood in a range of philosophical and sociological ways. Yet their writings were regarded as integral parts of the liberal family of thought. More recently, communitarianism has found advocates from beyond the liberal horizon, and been placed in apparent opposition to some of the core tenets of liberal thought (Mulhall and Swift, 1992).

A number of reasons can be adduced for this shift, but two are of particular significance. The most obvious concerns important transformations in the character of liberal theorising that have taken place since the Second World War. As liberal parties have experienced a downturn in fortunes, liberal political ideas have taken refuge in the academy. In this location, the character of liberal ideas has changed markedly. Where earlier generations of liberal thinkers speculated on the virtues and kinds of character necessary for the realisation of a liberal society, more recent exponents of the tradition have come under the influence of **analytical philosophy** and jurisprudential theory with which they have set out to formulate rationally ordered and non-contradictory moral theories (Bellamy, 1992). These have then provided the underpinnings for proposed liberal arrangements, of both a legal and political kind. This retreat of 'high' liberal theory to the realms of philosophy and law has been a crucial factor in the production of a counter-response. This has come in the form of a communitarian perspective that claims to be the antithesis of Liberalism. In fact, this current has to some degree occupied the ground once staked out by liberal theory, particularly through its insistence upon the centrality of the particular virtues associated with intercommunal existence and attention to the character of the citizens that populate liberal states.

But communitarianism has some distinctly non-liberal antecedents as well. One source of the current concern for community can be found in the republican philosophy that motivated the founders of the American Constitution, and which they imported from seventeenth-century England (Rodgers, 1996). The tradition of civic **republicanism** has undergone something of a revival as well as a radical reinterpretation among historians in recent years (Skinner, 1998). For thinkers like Michael Sandel (1996), the 'social imaginary' of the republic was one in which a strong sense of the common good prevailed, and individuals conceived of themselves as united in a shared moral purpose. A rather different source of current thinking can be located in the development among sociological thinkers of an awareness of the psychological and social benefits of healthy intersubjective identities and the needs that individuals have for stable community relations. These concerns are expressed in the writings of contemporary authors appalled by the narcissism, atomism and egotism that appear to have flourished in Western societies following the shift towards market-orientated economic policies from the early 1980s.

Much communitarian philosophy revolves around a sharp critique of a supposedly hegemonic liberal individualism. This critique typically takes shape in opposition to three features of liberal thought – the tenets of liberal individualism, the universalist claims of Liberalism, and the priority accorded by some leading philosophers of 'the right' over 'the good'. In examining each of these in turn, we will get a clearer idea of what communitarianism is and of what it imagines Liberalism to be.

THE CRITIQUE OF LIBERAL INDIVIDUALISM

Communitarians frequently reject liberal models of the self. Many liberals have drawn upon an image of the subject of liberal society as a 'self' which is defined by its capacity to make meaningful choices and to come to an unforced view of what is important in life. This notion stems in part from the philosophy of Immanuel Kant but equally depends upon the injection by thinkers such as John Stuart **Mill** of the value of '**autonomy**' into liberal thought. The concept of choice plays a foundational role in the principal variants of liberal theory. For utilitarians, it emerges through their commitment to the goods attendant upon the unhindered pursuit of preferences. For other liberals, following **Mill**, it is the capacity for autonomous decision-making that provides a defining feature of the self. For '**deontological**' philosophers like the American John Rawls, the self is imagined as the subject of the social contract it would strike were it in an '**original position**' stripped of its various social and cultural attributes (1971). From behind 'the **veil of ignorance**', the self still retains the capacity to make meaningful choices about the principles which will shape its and others' interests.

Communitarians reject the reification of choice at the heart of such a vision, in particular the implicit elevation of the conscious choosing of ends and goals by citizens above the values and commitments that are learned from others. As Mulgan puts it in the extract below, communitarians claim that: 'By turning choice into a totem, a good that stands above all others, Western societies have not only misread human nature but also misunderstood morals and ethics which, far from being things that can simply be picked off the supermarket shelf, are embedded in the ways we live our lives'.

Communitarian philosophers wonder how the self can be said to exist prior to or outside social settings and communal attachments. Surely, it is the latter that create the possibility of a self which develops preferences and goals. The myth of the unencumbered self has been attacked in the work of the philosopher Michael Sandel, who shows how the very notion of a self which is analytically prior to its ends or choices is logically flawed (1982, 1986). Only a socially and intersubjectively constituted self can plausibly be said to possess goals. Equally, these critics suggest that liberal individualism not only misrepresents the individual self but also cannot render meaningful the communal contexts which citizens inhabit. Liberal individualism generates accounts of political society as arising from the contracts made by sovereign individuals who are accorded a number of basic rights as well as the right of 'exit'. In the minds of many liberal individualists, and libertarians more generally, the state should be considered as a partial association – a body into which we contract for particular advantages and benefits, and which never commands our deepest loyalties (Kukathas, 1996).

Communitarians counter with an account of the self which is both more pluralistic and particularistic: many of the features of persons are shaped by the intersubjective values and traditions of the communities into which they are born. They suggest that the acquisition of a stable sense of self is a much lengthier and more contingent process than liberals glibly assume, one which involves absorbing the socially constituted practices and values of a particular society. Alasdair **MacIntyre** has refined this conception in a particularly influential way, exploring the self as an entity which is constituted through narratives (1985). These are interwoven and refined as the self takes shape around the assemblage of traditions within a particular community. As Ronald Beiner argues, some critics have incorporated liberal societies within their critiques of liberal thought, and thus ask whether the former, which 'basically define and understand themselves within a framework of individualistic categories, can offer the rich experiences of mutual involvement that make for a meaningful human life' (1996: 190–1).

AGAINST LIBERAL UNIVERSALISM

Liberals have frequently claimed to be able to develop foundations for their beliefs by adopting an apparently impartial viewpoint. This is a 'view from nowhere' built on what is believed to be a rational, non-subjective account of the principles that should order political society. Through such arguments, liberals purport to be above subjective and partisan attachments. Liberalism thus retains a propensity for universalistic theorising, and its adherents typically presume that their arguments are intrinsically superior to 'local' forms of reasoning. The correlation of this assumption is that liberal society represents an advance upon other kinds of political community and culture. Communitarians are profoundly unhappy with such presumptions. Reason, it is frequently suggested, can only be grasped as operative within the traditions of belief of particular communities. What liberal universalists regard as rationally justified principles, independent of social and temporal contexts, are seen by communitarian critics as examples of liberal hubris. Liberal universalism, they argue, is in fact the product of some very particular, culturally confident contexts (Bell, 1993).

An interesting exponent of such an argument is the philosopher Michael **Walzer**. Writing in opposition to attempts by liberal philosophers to construct universal theories about the appropriate rules governing **distributive justice**, Walzer has suggested that the search for a single overarching principle of this kind is flawed (1983). This is so partly because he rejects the liberal starting point – the perspective of the autonomous self which holds a set of compossible rights – and hence he refuses to think of the problem of distributive justice as a matter of balancing the conflicting rights claims of independent individuals

(D'Entrèves, 1990: 80–1). Equally, Walzer suggests a particularist approach to the justification of distributive justice. In any complex society, there are different prevailing 'goods' (for instance, solidarity in the domain of welfare, efficiency in the economy, and diversity in the cultural realm) which ought to be articulated within their own appropriate sphere. It is a mistake, he argues, to presume that a single principle can be regarded as applicable to every social good: different goods ought to be distributed for different reasons and according to different criteria. The latter stem from the various conceptions that members of communities have of these goods. Walzer's theory of justice is pluralistic in two senses. Justice varies according to the particular social domain in which a good prevails, and the meaning of a particular good is shaped by the particular intersubjective consensus which pertains in a given community. His argument is indicative of the broad pattern of communitarian thinking in rejecting the derivation of moral principles from universal reason and in placing value upon the existing tissue of common values and meanings that arise from and sustain the social life of a particular community.

Though all communitarians profess to reject the universalist pretensions of liberal thought, there are some important differences in how they take this argument forward. **MacIntyre**, for instance, disagrees fundamentally with Walzer's embrace of pluralism and suggests that the revival of 'strong' communities is in fact dependent upon the abolition of the moral pluralism that Walzer encourages. The proliferation in contemporary society of apparently irreconcilable visions of 'the good', MacIntyre argues, is highly socially divisive and destructive (think of the apparently insoluble conflicts around abortion in the United States, for example) and a consequence of the hegemony of liberalism. The 'universalist' justification of the pursuit of particular goods by individuals, MacIntyre claims, encourages a moral free-for-all in which established traditions and patterns of authority are reduced to the role of one choice among many (the 'supermarket of religions' that Mulgan refers to), and no overarching moral code can be justified (1988). As we will now see, this particular divergence of opinion is rather significant.

THE RIGHT OR THE GOOD

John Rawls's theory of justice has been influential within the communities of anglophone political philosophy in numerous respects, not the least of which is his philosophically rigorous articulation of the view that a just society is one that does not promote a particular vision of what is important in human life and what human flourishing means (1971). In this, he is typical of a broad trend in modern liberal philosophy which has tended to prioritise the rational derivation of a 'neutral' framework of rights and liberties within which individuals can pursue their own values and goals (Larmore, 1987). As Sandel puts it in the excerpt below, for such liberals 'a just society seeks not to promote any particular ends, but enables its citizens to pursue their own ends, consistent with a similar liberty for all; it therefore must govern by principles that do not presuppose any conception of the good'. Communitarians reject the claim that the principles of justice articulated by Rawlsian liberals can be said to exist independently of any particular conception of the good. Recognising the constitutive character of the communal values that we share means that the prioritisation of 'the right' over conceptions of what is valuable, what is 'good', in life is simply illogical. Equally, the pretension to moral impartiality claimed by 'deontological' philosophers is deemed a sham. The influential Canadian thinker Charles **Taylor**, for example, argues that any theory about 'the right' must rely upon a (usually hidden) conception of what is valuable as well as a particular view of the persons to whom the theory applies (1992). Thus he shows how Rawls's theory is indeed 'premised on a prior conception of the human good (the exercise of free moral agency) and of the good of human association (securing the conditions for the full development and exercise of our moral powers)' (D'Entrèves, 1990: 82).

This stance carries a number of implications for communitarian thought. For some thinkers, it has legitimated the reintroduction into the political lexicon of values that have been downplayed and marginalised within liberal thought and culture. Thus we find notions such as reciprocity, solidarity and trust in Sandel's account of the 'virtuous republic' (1996). And, interestingly, some feminist thinkers have allied themselves with this aspect of the communitarian project, highlighting the possibilities of re-legitimating values suppressed by the (masculine) conception of liberal reason (Frazer and Lacey, 1993). For others, the 'dethroning of certain liberal goals enables a recognition of the deeply pluralistic character of moral life, and the incommensurability of many social and moral goods (Walzer, 1983; Taylor, 1992). And finally, some conservative communitarians – MacIntyre being one such example – point to the necessity of reviving strong and coherent traditions of 'virtue' in contemporary life as liberal proceduralism fails to secure the legitimacy of its own moral order (1985).

THE POLITICS OF COMMUNITARIANISM

Though the new philosophers of community broadly agree on these critical points, they differ markedly over their implications for actually existing liberal societies. Thinkers like **Walzer** and **Taylor** are uneasy about some of the new political expressions of communitarianism that have arisen separately from, but in parallel with, these abstract philosophical and metaphysical debates. Writers like Philip Selznick (1994), James Q. Wilson (1993) and Amitai Etzioni (1995, 1997) approach the task of 'reviving' community in a much more direct, programmatic vein than their philosophical counterparts. They approach contemporary problems from the vantage point of a sociological concern for the fracturing of national cultural life, the rise of alienated and anti-social forms of cultural expression, and the decline of some of the institutional features of (particularly) American life that provided meaning and solidarity for individuals. It is not the abstractions of liberal theory that receive their critical attention but the purported historical impact of forms of liberal values.

Figures such as Etzioni and Wilson are the 'organic intellectuals' of the new communitarian movement, thinkers who have played a key role in shaping the demands and outlook of this new political force and have brought these ideas to a wide public. Yet social communitarianism also possesses a broad internal spectrum. At the one end, it incorporates activists from the secular and religious poles of conservatism. They stress the decline of the family and the impact of nihilistic popular cultural practices upon America's youth, and blame the 'permissive' culture established in the 1960s for both. Such exponents of communitarian themes have explicitly adopted an authoritarian or fundamentalist approach to politics, seeing in 'community' the repository of values and goods that liberal decadence has endangered or suppressed (Wilson and Kelling, 1996). At the other end of this spectrum are social entrepreneurs, civic activists and concerned public figures keen to stress the value of what is sometimes called 'the third sector' – networks and associations which might provide more flexible and sensitive solutions to social problems than either state or market (Tam, 1998). A great deal of space lies between these extremes. Somewhere in the middle lie a number of communitarian 'public intellectuals', such as Etzioni, who have brought intellectual rigour to the claims and arguments of these different brands of activist.

Etzioni is a particularly important figure both as a public and articulate voice of communitarian themes and as an intellectual conduit for them. In the extract from his book, *The Spirit of Community* (1995), reprinted below, he outlines the platform of the fledgling communitarian movement. The major points animating these proposals are purported to emerge between the poles of excessive social authoritarianism and the play of the unbridled market. Yet close inspection reveals Etzioni's construction to be an assemblage of two rather distinct political discourses. On the one hand, like other contemporary communitarians, he echoes civic republicans who call for the re-establishment of a common ethos of citizenship and the revival of a pluralistic and diverse civil society. Thus we find Etzioni lamenting the decline of voting as an integral form of political participation in the United States. Yet this emphasis is combined with a more bluntly conservative ethos. In this mode, Etzioni refers to Americans as people 'who have long been concerned with the deterioration of private and public morality, the decline of the family, high crime rates, and the swelling of corruption in government' (1995: 2). The emphasis on federal corruption, inner-city crime and the 'decline' of the family clearly locate part of the communitarian appeal within the conservative tradition and, in terms of American political geography, among predominantly white suburban communities. Etzioni's skill and significance stem from his attempted reconciliation of these diverse discourses as he seeks to retain a broad coalition of support for communitarian goals. Critics suggest that this perspective trades upon nostalgia for the sexual and cultural values associated with a particular community-form – small-town America in the 1950s, in which women play the role of 'home-maker' and men are engaged in stable employment. These views are wrapped in the apparently common-sense notion that rights have to be recombined with a recognition of responsibilities. Yet this piece of wisdom is also given a particular edge: there ought to be 'a tight lid on the manufacturing of new rights' because '[t]he incessant issuance of new rights, like the wholesale printing of currency, causes a massive inflation of rights that devalues their moral claims' (1995: 5). In the American context, the 'code' used by Etzioni is not hard to break: the rights-claims associated with marginal and 'progressive' groups, such as women, gays and African Americans, have been pursued too strongly; measures such as positive discrimination legislation are threatening to unravel the common cultural fabric of the nation as a whole.

Many critics see, in this call for the revival of community, an essentially anti-liberal politics. Here there are some interesting echoes of the philosophical debates between liberal individualists and communitarians. Conservative communitarians in the United States have been particularly active in calling for restrictions on freedom of expression on behalf of the moral fabric of the community (Kristol, 1996). It is also not accidental that communitarians are often found battling against feminists. Etzioni repeatedly criticises the deployment of rights as 'trump cards' against other moral considerations, and he frequently refers to the assertion of gender-equality rights as particularly damaging for the polity.

Yet it would be a mistake to endorse wholeheartedly the judgement of many liberals, leftists and feminists that popular communitarianism is an entirely reactionary and conservative force. In the hands of some of its central intellectuals, a subtle and significant combining of diffuse anxieties and republican political argument takes place. Etzioni is aware that this agenda does not sit entirely easily with the traditions of American conservatism, especially those parts of the right that simultaneously espouse free-market ideology and defend traditional institutions and practices against the encroachment of modernity. Communitarian agendas do not align easily with left–right political models of political affiliation, though they do gain sustenance from existing traditions of political thought. Communitarianism comes in different ideological shades and is best regarded as a spectrum which possesses a number of variants. Hence, calls for the revival of community in political and moral life can be deployed to sustain and justify different kinds of ideological projects. The British writer Henry Tam, for example, uses communitarian themes to re-legitimate values associated with the social democratic tradition (1996). The political positioning of communitarianism is, moreover, complicated by the tendency of the main political parties to appropriate sections of its platform. In part, as Mulgan suggests below, this has occurred because the parties have sensed that the strong concern for social cohesion expressed by communitarians in the wake of the pro-market tilt of public policy overseen by the New Right, British and American governments of the 1980s and early 1990s is widely echoed in both these societies. He observes too how communitarian goals have arisen against the backdrop of the waning of the 'narratives' associated with the left and right of the political spectrum.

THE DILEMMAS OF COMMUNITARIANISM

Communitarianism in its different guises has received numerous criticisms, of both a theoretical and a political nature. Do the philosophical concerns enunciated by communitarian political theorists and the more sociological emphases of popular communitarian writers, like Etzioni, share any common strengths and weaknesses? And is communitarianism an essentially anti-liberal force?

Many critics have observed the lack of a precise focus on policy issues in the speculative offerings of the philosophical communitarians. Underlying this absence is an acute difference among communitarians of all kinds about what kind of community-form is to be recommended, and more generally over the different values that 'community' as an ideal ought to realise. Some of this disagreement arises from the highly indeterminate character of the concept of 'community', a term which is articulated and defined in a range of modern political ideologies: socialists, conservatives, anarchists and religious fundamentalists all claim to subscribe to this value, and it is invoked in an almost infinite number of ways in political and social debate. However, several kinds of usage are especially recurrent in the academic literature. Community is invoked as: a local, geographically bounded place; a particular community-form which is deemed to be especially virtuous (for example, small-town communities); the single most binding identity we share in common; and a normative ideal against which the individualism and anomie of contemporary society is found wanting (Plant, 1991; Kenny, 1991). Most typically, some of these different senses are intermingled when the apparently innocent notion of 'community' is deployed. What is less common in the philosophical literature is any precise reference to actually existing communities: readers are frequently left to infer the kinds of community life and ties that are being referenced.

Moreover, given their adherence to a particularistic epistemology, whereby the values and identities associated with actually existing communities are invoked as the starting point for moral reflection, we ought to wonder whether the normative arguments that communitarians offer for the benefits of community *in general* can really be justified at all. Critics have been quick to observe that this particularistic mode of argument implies a conflation of actual communities with the ideal of community, a position that leaves these thinkers endorsing some highly unpleasant forms of communal attachment and sliding towards a philosophical stance of '**relativism**', whereby no particular community practice or value can be legitimately criticised by any member of a rival community (Bell, 1993).

A related theoretical problem haunts not just these theorists but popular communitarians as well. In nearly all of its incarnations, communitarianism offers an account of identities that are 'stabilised' by a particular narrative, tradition or practice: for **MacIntyre** and other conservative communitarians, identity is regarded as 'given' by the moral traditions of particular communities, while for **Walzer** and **Taylor**, identities stem in part from the values which arise from our membership of nation states. Critics reply that these are constraining and 'essentialist' ways of understanding community. In theoretical terms, we may wonder whether any community can really be defined around a singular 'tradition' or 'loyalty' without doing damage to the plural character of social identities and moral beliefs. Communities might alternatively be regarded as arising out of the complex intertwining of the lives of individuals who are in many ways different to each other, yet come to recognise and learn common interests and values. Fixing a particular tradition or stable moral order may actually be harmful to the subtle tissue of mutual tolerance and interest that characterises communal interrelations. The lack of sociological 'realism' in these philosophers' invocation of community has been widely observed. As John Gray puts it, 'the community invoked by these writers is not one that anyone has ever lived in, an historic human settlement with its distinctive exclusivities, hierarchies and bigotries . . .' (1995a: 7).

Indeed, the singular view of the good life that appears to be at the heart of the ideal community vaunted by these thinkers raises an ethical dilemma for modern citizens. Is this an inherently intolerant philosophy which privileges one perspective about what is valuable in life over the claims of others, and which also legitimates the quashing of alternative perspectives and views? Such is the view of many of its critics. Thinkers like Iris Young, influenced by recent philosophical trends such as poststructuralism and feminism, regard the assertion of community as inherently tyrannical, given that some identities are *necessarily* marginalised and suppressed as communities privilege certain identities over others (1990).

It is for this reason that, while some contemporary political thinkers sympathise with hostility to the liberal model of the self, many steer clear of the normative positions associated with communitarian philosophy, principally because pluralism is only weakly enunciated in this framework. Furthermore, the recurrent critique of 'rights talk' within populist forms of communitarianism concerns liberals as well. How far would communitarians be prepared to go in preserving the dominant values and way of life of a particular community? What will happen to those civil and social rights that have been won following decades, sometimes centuries, of intercommunal struggle by subordinated groups and identities? Would you or I be allowed to be different and to dissent from the 'ideal' community posited by these thinkers? This is a particular concern, given that communitarians deny our right to appeal to transcultural norms such as individual human rights or universal values such as social justice. On what grounds, then, could we assert our own dignity and rights?

Such questions elicit a variety of responses from these thinkers. And a major fault-line does open up within this perspective if we consider its relationship to values that are cherished within liberal society. Two broad stances vis-à-vis Liberalism can be discerned, positions which cut across the differences between the arguments of the philosophical and political communitarians. First, we can see that, for some communitarians, liberal thought and culture are the sources of numerous contemporary problems; and the solution is deemed to consist of the abolition, marginalisation or transcendence of liberalism. It is clear that some of the political energy of this perspective has been generated by recoil at the impact of increasingly unfettered patterns of commodification within market-dominated societies that are associated (rightly or wrongly) with the political economy of classical liberalism. Others locate the malign impact of Liberalism in the political culture of, for instance, the United States, where the prevalence of a juridico-constitutionalist political discourse has infected the body politic at large. Writers like Mary Ann Glendon (see the extract below) have therefore polemicised against the pernicious effects of liberal notions of rights which are wielded in a 'zero-sum fashion' with the effect of rendering notions of citizenship, obligation to others and reciprocity damagingly thin. 'Rights talk', it is suggested, produces a highly atomised, mutually suspicious and antagonistic polity which prefers to seek solutions to social problems in the courtroom rather than encouraging citizens to perceive their common interests and bonds, or to appreciate that their conflicts are outweighed by the loftier goals of the community. Nor is such thinking confined to the United States, where the judicial and legal domains have always played a central role within social and political life. Plenty of doom-mongers in Britain bemoan the increasing recourse to the law to solve conflicts and advance interests.

Yet not all communitarians are so ready to blame Liberalism for the ills of contemporary culture, and some advance more measured criticisms of features of liberal society. According to William Galston, for example, communitarianism serves as a useful reminder that liberals were for a long time unashamed about developing arguments about the character of virtuous individuals and the characteristics necessary for the construction of robust liberal democracies (1991). In this vein, we might well ask whether some communitarian philosophers are really liberals in disguise. Both **Taylor** and **Walzer**, for instance, subscribe to many core liberal values – pluralism, justice and **autonomy** most notably (Friedman, 1994). Certainly they offer 'particularistic' defences of such values, claiming that they arise within the available intersubjective meanings of liberal cultures, yet they hold to them as tenaciously as many liberal individualists. Equally, when pressed to defend their conception of the self, in opposition to that posited by Rawls, it is clear that they stray onto liberal terrain. If the self is regarded as shaped by the various traditions or practices of the community it inhabits, in what sense can agency be ascribed to individual selves at all? Some philosophical communitarians reply by weakening the putative relationship between community and the individual's moral ends. Thus Sandel and **Taylor** posit a self which possesses the capacity to reflect, semi-autonomously, upon the character and commitments given by their community (Sandel, 1996;

Taylor, 1985). It remains unclear, however, quite what makes this a non-liberal metaphysic (Mason, 2000). In a number of senses, therefore, it would appear that, for all their radical rhetoric, some communitarian philosophers are engaged in the project of justifying broadly liberal political values, but by a different route to that taken by rival liberal philosophers.

The recognition of these apparent similarities and overlaps between some philosophical kinds of communitarianism and liberal thought points to the danger of presuming that these bodies of theory are entirely antithetical. It is significant that, in many of its philosophical incarnations, communitarianism is advanced in the kind of abstract vein typical of contemporary liberal philosophy. Though this perspective has tended to prosecute Liberalism for failing to incorporate sociological insight in its theories, philosophical communitarianism is equally characterised by its abstract, metaphysical quality. This state of affairs is highly revealing about the turn in contemporary political theory away from questions that were once deemed of central concern to political philosophers, in particular the relationship between regime types and the moral character of citizens, and that between institutions and moral purposes. Communitarianism may ultimately be significant within the history of modern political thought because it reveals the deleterious impact of disengagement from such questions by political philosophers.

CONCLUSION: THE FUTURE FOR COMMUNITARIANISM

The interpretation that Mulgan gives of the rise of communitarianism in the 1990s is compelling. He points to the centrality of a kind of moral revivalism to this perspective at a time when a host of moral traditions, institutions and common forms of living do appear to be under considerable strain. The dilemma for communitarianism is whether it sets out to connect its advocacy of community with a defence of *certain* traditions and institutions which are deemed to be under threat. This is the stance adopted by some conservative communitarians in Britain, who plead, rather angrily, for a return to the cultural and moral certainties embodied in institutions such as the royal family or selective schools (for instance Hitchens, 1999). Or should such thinkers seek to locate new sources of cultural and moral authority around which communal attachments and identities might be ordered in today's shifting social and cultural contexts? In considering this question, communitarians may have to pay more attention to the task of theorising the role and character of the state, clarifying in particular what role it may legitimately play in assisting the revival of community and the creation of new forms of citizenship. Equally, while liberal communitarians have talked convincingly of the need for an enhanced and diverse 'public domain' in which the public interest can be determined, it is now apparent that such a domain may have to be imagined and actualised on different scales from simply the national. Are there spaces within the realm of international society where a sense of global community could be rendered meaningful? How can the voices of local communities, that are frequently under tremendous threat from the cold winds of global economic forces, be projected onto a wider stage?

It is equally important for this perspective to grapple with the sociological realities of actually existing communities. Within existing nation states, many communities based on ethnicity, religion and place are mutually antagonistic. What forms of political regulation are required to prevent multi-cultural communalism from issuing into a brutal fight for resources and political influence between communities of various sizes and strengths? These are exactly the issues and questions that are emerging within the strands of contemporary communitarian writing which strive to articulate the possibility of more cosmopolitan and heterogeneous communities. While the metaphysical debates that sustained the liberal–communitarian debate of the 1980s and early 1990s appear to have waned, it is notable that communitarianism has been recently deployed in relation to questions about the impact of multiculturalism and communal differences in particular states as well as about the nature of a putative global community. While some communitarians will continue to engage with these challenges within a broadly liberal framework and will seek to amend and improve the character of liberal democracy, others will hold more resolutely than ever to selected models and traditions from the past. Perhaps the major challenge facing both strands is to render 'community' meaningful in societies in which different kinds of moral, cultural and social pluralism are now irredeemably ingrained.

'THE PROCEDURAL REPUBLIC AND THE UNENCUMBERED SELF' BY
MICHAEL SANDEL

At the time of writing, Michael Sandel is Professor of Government at the University of Harvard. He is known as a communitarian philosopher and in particular as a critic of Rawls's notions of justice and of the self. In a common variation on the communitarian theme, Sandel argues that the self cannot be understood in isolation from the social and cultural context that gives selfhood meaning. He also joins in criticism of Rawls's elevation of justice to the primary position in moral and political theory, advocating instead the primacy of the good over the right. Sandel has gone on to diagnose the ills of the American polity, principally the lack of interest in democratic participation caused by the predominance of legalistic individualism. See his *Liberalism and the Limits of Justice* (Cambridge University Press, 1982) and the more populist *Democracy's Discontent: America in Search of a Public Philosophy* (Belknap Press of Harvard University Press, 1996). The communitarian philosophy well represented by Sandel here can usefully be compared to the approach of John Gray (found in Chapter 3 of this volume) and, since there is a kind of republicanism to Sandel, with the rather different arguments of Arendt, Connolly or Wolin. It should also be compared to the views of conservatives such as Scruton and Oakeshott which will produce some interesting questions.

The extract should serve as a good introduction to Sandel's criticisms of the 'procedural' liberalism he believes to predominate in the USA. He takes on the way Liberalism officially denies any overall purpose to political society as embodied in the prioritisation of the 'right' over the 'good'. This has generated mistaken notions of the self as unencumbered and caused us to feel disconnected from our political institutions.

'THE PROCEDURAL REPUBLIC AND THE UNENCUMBERED SELF' (1984)*

Michael Sandel

Political philosophy seems often to reside at a distance from the world. Principles are one thing, politics another, and even our best efforts to 'live up' to our ideals typically founder on the gap between theory and practice.[1]

* Michael Sandel, 'The Procedural Republic and the Unencumbered Self', *Political Theory*, 12 (1984), 81–96.

But if political philosophy is unrealizable in one sense, it is unavoidable in another. This is the sense in which philosophy inhabits the world from the start; our practices and institutions are embodiments of theory. To engage in a political practice is already to stand in relation to theory.[2] For all our uncertainties about ultimate questions of political philosophy – of justice and value and the nature of the good life – the one thing we know is that we live *some* answer all the time.

In this essay, I will try to explore the answer we live now, in contemporary America. What is the political philosophy implicit in our practices and institutions? How does it stand, as philosophy? And how do tensions in the philosophy find expression in our present political condition?

It may be objected that it is a mistake to look for a single philosophy, that we live no 'answer', only answers. But a plurality of answers is itself a kind of answer. And the political theory that affirms this plurality is the theory I propose to explore.

THE RIGHT AND THE GOOD

We might begin by considering a certain moral and political vision. It is a liberal vision, and like most liberal visions gives pride of place to justice, fairness, and individual rights. Its core thesis is this: a just society seeks not to promote any particular ends, but enables its citizens to pursue their own ends, consistent with a similar liberty for all; it therefore must govern by principles that do not presuppose any particular conception of the good. What justifies these regulative principles above all is not that they maximize the general welfare, or cultivate virtue, or otherwise promote the good, but rather that they conform to the concept of *right*, a moral category given prior to the good, and independent of it.

This liberalism says, in other words, that what makes the just society just is not the *telos* or purpose or end at which it aims, but precisely its refusal to choose in advance among competing purposes and ends. In its constitution and its laws, the just society seeks to provide a framework within which its citizens can pursue their own values and ends, consistent with a similar liberty for others.

The ideal I've described might be summed up in the claim that the right is prior to the good, and in two senses: the priority of the right means, first, that individual rights cannot be sacrificed for the sake of the general good (in this it opposes utilitarianism), and, second, that the principles of justice that specify these rights cannot be premissed on any particular vision of the good life. (In this it opposes teleological conceptions in general.)

This is the liberalism of much contemporary moral and political philosophy, most fully elaborated by Rawls, and indebted to Kant for its philosophical foundations.[3] But I am concerned here less with the lineage of this vision than with what seem to me three striking facts about it.

First, it has a deep and powerful philosophical appeal. Second, despite its philosophical force, the claim for the priority of the right over the good ultimately fails. And, third, despite its philosophical failure, this liberal vision is the one by which we live. For us in late twentieth-century America, it is our vision, the theory most thoroughly embodied in the practices and institutions most central to our public life. And seeing how it goes wrong as philosophy may help us to diagnose our present political condition. So, first, its philosophical power; second, its philosophical failure; and, third, however briefly, its uneasy embodiment in the world.

But before taking up these three claims, it is worth pointing out a central theme that connects them. And that is a certain conception of the person, of what it is to be a moral agent. Like all political theories, the liberal theory I have described is something more than a set of regulative principles. It is also a view about the way the world is, and the way we move within it. At the heart of this ethic lies a vision of the person that both inspires and undoes it. As I will try to argue now, what makes this ethic so compelling, but also, finally, vulnerable, are the promise and the failure of the unencumbered self.

KANTIAN FOUNDATIONS

The liberal ethic asserts the priority of right, and seeks principles of justice that do not presuppose any particular conception of the good.[4] This is what Kant means by the supremacy of the moral law, and what Rawls means when he writes that 'justice is the first virtue of social institutions'.[5] Justice is more than just another value. It provides the framework that *regulates* the play of competing values and ends; it must therefore have a sanction independent of those ends. But it is not obvious where such a sanction could be found.

Theories of justice, and, for that matter, ethics, have typically founded their claims on one or another conception of human purposes and ends. Thus Aristotle said the measure of a *polis* is the good at which it aims, and even J. S. Mill, who in the nineteenth century called 'justice the chief part, and incomparably the most binding part of all morality', made justice an instrument of utilitarian ends.[6]

This is the solution Kant's ethic rejects. Different persons typically have different desires and ends, and so any principle derived from them can only be contingent. But the moral law needs a *categorical* foundation, not a contingent one. Even so universal a desire as happiness will not do. People still differ in what happiness consists of, and to install any particular conception as regulative would impose on some the conceptions of others, and so deny at least to some the freedom to choose their *own* conceptions. In any case, to govern ourselves in conformity with desires and inclinations, given as they are by nature or circumstance, is not really to be *self*-governing at all. It is rather a refusal of freedom, a capitulation to determinations given outside us.

According to Kant, the right is 'derived entirely from the concept of freedom in the external relationships of human beings, and has nothing to do with the end which all men have by nature [i.e. the aim of achieving happiness] or with the recognized means of attaining this end'.[7] As such, it must have a basis prior to all empirical ends. Only when I am governed by principles that do not presuppose any particular ends am I free to pursue my own ends consistent with a similar freedom for all.

But this still leaves the question of what the basis of the right could possibly be. If it must be a basis prior to all purposes and ends, unconditioned even by what Kant calls 'the special circumstances of human nature',[8] where could such a basis conceivably be found? Given the stringent demands of the Kantian ethic, the moral law would seem almost to require a foundation in nothing, for any empirical precondition would undermine its priority. 'Duty!' asks Kant at his most lyrical, 'What origin is there worthy of thee, and where is to be found the root of thy noble descent which proudly rejects all kinship with the inclinations?'[9]

His answer is that the basis of the moral law is to be found in the *subject*, not the object of practical reason, a subject capable of an autonomous will. No empirical end, but rather 'a subject of ends, namely a rational being himself, must be made the ground for all maxims of action'.[10] Nothing other than what Kant calls 'the subject of all possible ends himself' can give rise to the right, for only this subject is also the subject of an autonomous will. Only this subject could be that 'something which elevates man above himself as part of the world of sense' and enables him to participate in an ideal, unconditioned realm wholly independent of our social and psychological inclinations. And only this thoroughgoing independence can afford us the detachment we need if we are ever freely to choose for ourselves, unconditioned by the vagaries of circumstance.[11]

Who or what exactly *is* this subject? It is, in a certain sense, *us*. The moral law, after all, is a law we give *ourselves*; we don't *find* it, we *will* it. That is how it (and we) escape the reign of nature and circumstance and merely empirical ends. But what is important to see is that the 'we' who do the willing are not 'we' *qua* particular persons, you and me, each for ourselves – the moral law is not up to us as individuals – but 'we' *qua* participants in what Kant calls 'pure practical reason', 'we' *qua* participants in a transcendental subject.

Now what is to guarantee that I *am* a subject of this kind, capable of exercising pure practical reason? Well, strictly speaking, there *is* no guarantee; the transcendental subject is only a possibility. But it is a possibility I must *presuppose* if I am to think of myself as a free moral agent. Were I wholly an empirical being, I would not be capable of freedom, for every exercise of will would be conditioned by the desire for some object. All choice would be heteronomous choice, governed by the pursuit of some end. My will could never be a first cause, only the effect of some prior cause, the instrument of one or another impulse or inclination. 'When we think of ourselves as free,' writes Kant, 'we transfer ourselves into the intelligible world as members and recognize the autonomy of the will.'[12] And so the notion of a subject prior to and independent of experience, such as the Kantian ethic requires, appears not only possible but indispensable, a necessary presupposition of the possibility of freedom.

How does all of this come back to politics? As the subject is prior to its ends, so the right is prior to the good. Society is best arranged when it is governed by principles that do not presuppose any particular conception of the good, for any other arrangement would fail to respect persons as being capable of choice; it would treat them as objects rather than subjects, as means rather than ends in themselves.

We can see in this way how Kant's notion of the subject is bound up with the claim for the priority of right. But for those in the Anglo-American tradition, the transcendental subject will seem a strange foundation for a familiar ethic. Surely, one may think, we can take rights seriously and affirm the primacy of justice without embracing the *Critique of Pure Reason*. This, in any case, is the project of Rawls.

He wants to save the priority of right from the obscurity of the transcendental subject. Kant's idealist metaphysic, for all its moral and political advantage, cedes too much to the transcendent, and wins for justice its primacy only by denying it its human situation. 'To develop a viable Kantian conception of justice,' Rawls writes, 'the force and content of Kant's doctrine must be detached from its background in transcendental idealism' and recast within the 'canons of a reasonable empiricism.'[13] And so Rawls's project is to preserve Kant's moral and political teaching by replacing Germanic obscurities with a domesticated metaphysic more congenial to the Anglo-American temper. This is the role of the original position.

FROM TRANSCENDENTAL SUBJECT TO UNENCUMBERED SELF

The original position tries to provide what Kant's transcendental argument cannot – a foundation for the right that is prior to the good, but still situated in the world. Sparing all but essentials, the original position works like this: it invites us to imagine the principles we would choose to govern our society if we were to choose them in advance, before we knew the particular persons we would be – whether rich or poor, strong or weak, lucky or unlucky – before we knew even our interests or aims or conceptions of the good. These principles – the ones we would choose in that imaginary situation – are the principles of justice. What is more, if it works, they are principles that do not presuppose any particular ends.

What they *do* presuppose is a certain picture of the person, of the way we must be if we are beings for whom justice is the first virtue. This is the picture of the unencumbered self, a self understood as prior to and independent of purposes and ends.

Now the unencumbered self describes first of all the way we stand towards the things we have, or want, or seek. It means there is always a distinction between the values I *have* and the person I *am*. To identify any characteristics as *my* aims, ambitions, desires, and so on, is always to imply some subject 'me' standing behind them, at a certain distance, and the shape of this 'me' must be given prior to any of the aims or attributes I bear. One consequence of this distance is to put the self *itself* beyond the reach of its experience, to secure its identity once and for all. Or to put the point another way, it rules out the possibility of what we might call *constitutive* ends. No role or commitment could define me so completely that I could not understand myself without it. No project could be so essential that turning away from it would call into question the person I am.

For the unencumbered self, what matters above all, what is most essential to our personhood, are not the ends we choose but our capacity to choose them. The original position sums up this central claim about us. 'It is not our aims that primarily reveal our nature,' writes Rawls, 'but rather the principles that we would acknowledge to govern the background conditions under which these aims are to be formed . . . We should therefore reverse the relation between the right and the good proposed by teleological doctrines and view the right as prior.'[14]

Only if the self is prior to its ends can the right be prior to the good. Only if my identity is never tied to the aims and interests I may have at any moment can I think of myself as a free and independent agent, capable of choice.

This notion of independence carries consequences for the kind of community of which we are capable. Understood as unencumbered selves, we are of course free to join in voluntary association with others, and so are capable of community in the co-operative sense. What is denied to the unencumbered self is the possibility of membership in any community bound by moral ties antecedent to choice; he cannot belong to any community where the self *itself* could be at stake. Such a community – call it constitutive as against merely co-operative – would engage the identity as well as the interests of the participants, and so implicate its members in a citizenship more thoroughgoing than the unencumbered self can know.

For justice to be primary, then, we must be creatures of a certain kind, related to human circumstance in a certain way. We must stand to our circumstance always at a certain distance, whether as transcendental subject in the case of Kant, or as unencumbered selves in the case of Rawls. Only in this way can we view ourselves as subjects as well as objects of experience, as agents and not just instruments of the purposes we pursue.

The unencumbered self and the ethic it inspires, taken together, hold out a liberating vision. Freed from the dictates of nature and the sanction of social roles, the human subject is installed as sovereign, cast as the author of the only moral meanings there are. As participants in pure practical reason, or as parties to the original position, we are free to construct principles of justice unconstrained by an order of value antecedently given. And as actual, individual selves, we are free to choose our purposes and ends unbound by such an order, or by custom or tradition or inherited status. So long as they are not unjust, our conceptions of the good carry weight, whatever they are, simply in virtue of our having chosen them. We are, in Rawl's words, 'self-originating sources of valid claims'.[15]

This is an exhilarating promise, and the liberalism it animates is perhaps the fullest expression of the Enlightenment's quest for the self-defining subject. But is it true? Can we make sense of our moral and political life by the light of the self-image it requires? I do not think we can, and I will try to show why not by arguing first within the liberal project, then beyond it.

JUSTICE AND COMMUNITY

We have focused so far on the foundations of the liberal vision, on the way it derives the principles it defends. Let us turn briefly now to the substance of those principles, using Rawls as our example. Sparing all but essentials once again, Rawl's two principles of justice are these: first, equal basic liberties for all, and, second, only those social and economic inequalities that benefit the least-advantaged members of society (the difference principle).

In arguing for these principles, Rawls argues against two familiar alternatives – utilitarianism and libertarianism. He argues against utilitarianism that it fails to take seriously the distinction between persons. In seeking to maximize the general welfare, the utilitarian treats society as a whole as if it were a single person; it conflates our many, diverse desires into a single system of desires, and tries to maximize. It is indifferent to the distribution of satisfactions among persons, except insofar as this may affect the overall sum. But this fails to respect our plurality and distinctness. It uses some as means to the happiness of all, and so fails to respect each as an end in himself. While utilitarians may sometimes defend individual rights, their defence must rest on the calculation that respecting those rights will serve utility in the long run. But this calculation is contingent and uncertain. So long as utility is what Mill said it is, 'the ultimate appeal on all ethical questions',[16] individual rights can never be secure. To avoid the danger that their life prospects might one day be sacrificed for the greater good of others, the parties to the original position therefore insist on certain basic liberties for all, and make those liberties prior.

It utilitarians fail to take seriously the distinctness of persons, libertarians go wrong by failing to acknowledge the arbitrariness of fortune. They define as just whatever distribution results from an efficient market economy, and oppose all redistribution on the grounds that people are entitled to whatever they get, so long as they do not cheat or steal or otherwise violate someone's rights in getting it. Rawls opposes this principle on the ground that the distribution of talents and assets and even efforts by which some get more and others get less is arbitrary from a moral point of view, a matter of good luck. To distribute the good things in life on the basis of these differences is not to do justice, but simply to carry over into human arrangements the arbitrariness of social and natural contingency. We deserve, as individuals, neither the talents our good fortune may have brought, nor the benefits that flow from them. We should therefore regard these talents as common assets, and regard one another as common beneficiaries of the rewards they bring. 'Those who have been favored by nature, whoever they are, may gain from their good fortune only on terms that improve the situation of those who have lost out . . . In justice as fairness, men agree to share one another's fate.'[17]

This is the reasoning that leads to the difference principle. Notice how it reveals, in yet another guise, the logic of the unencumbered self. I cannot be said to deserve the benefits that flow from, say, my fine physique and good looks, because they are only accidental, not essential facts about me. They describe attributes I *have*, not the person I *am*, and so cannot give rise to a claim of desert. Being an unencumbered self, this is true of *everything* about me. And so I cannot, as an individual, deserve anything at all.

However jarring to our ordinary understandings this argument may be, the picture so far remains intact; the priority of right, the denial of desert, and the unencumbered self all hang impressively together.

But the difference principle requires more, and it is here that the argument comes undone. The difference principle begins with the thought, congenial to the unencumbered self, that the assets I have are only accidentally mine. But it ends by assuming that these assets are therefore *common* assets and that society has a prior claim on the fruits of their exercise. But this assumption is without warrant. Simply because I, as an individual, do not have a privileged claim on the assets accidentally residing 'here', it does not follow that everyone in the world collectively does. For there is no reason to think that their location in society's province, or, for that matter, within the province of humankind, is any *less* arbitrary from a moral point of view. And if their arbitrariness within *me* makes them ineligible to serve *my* ends, there seems no obvious reason why their arbitrariness within any particular society should not make them ineligible to serve that society's ends as well.

To put the point another way, the difference principle, like utilitarianism, is a principle of sharing. As such, it must presuppose some prior moral tie among these whose assets it would deploy and whose efforts it would enlist in a common endeavour. Otherwise, it is simply a formula for using some as means to others' ends, a formula this liberalism is committed to reject.

But on the co-operative vision of community alone, it is unclear what the moral basis for this sharing could be. Short of the constitutive conception, deploying an individual's assets for the sake of the common good would seem an offence against the 'plurality and distinctness' of individuals this liberalism seeks above all to secure.

If those whose fate I am required to share really are, morally speaking, *others*, rather than fellow participants in a way of life with which my identity is bound, the difference principle falls prey to the same objections as utilitarianism. Its claim on me is not the claim of a constitutive community whose attachments I acknowledge, but rather the claim of a concatenated collectivity whose entanglements I confront.

What the difference principle requires, but cannot provide, is some way of identifying those *among* whom the assets I bear are properly regarded as common, some way of seeing ourselves as mutually indebted and morally engaged to begin with. But as we have seen, the constitutive aims and attachments that would save and situate the difference principle are precisely the ones denied to the liberal self; the moral encumbrances and antecedent obligations they imply would undercut the priority of right.

What, then, of those encumbrances? The point so far is that we cannot be persons for whom justice is primary, and also be persons for whom the difference principle is a principle of justice. But which must give way? Can we view ourselves as independent selves, independent in the sense that our identity is never tied to our aims and attachments?[18]

I do not think we can, at least not without cost to those loyalties and convictions whose moral force consists partly in the fact that living by them is inseparable from understanding ourselves as the particular persons we are – as members of this family or community or nation or people, as bearers of that history, as citizens of this republic. Allegiances such as these are more than values I happen to have, and to hold, at a certain distance. They go beyond the obligations I voluntarily incur and the 'natural duties' I owe to human beings as such. They allow that to some I owe more than justice requires or even permits, not by reason of agreements I have made but instead in virtue of those more or less enduring attachments and commitments that, taken together, partly define the person I am.

To imagine a person incapable of constitutive attachments such as these is not to conceive an ideally free and rational agent, but to imagine a person wholly without character, without moral depth. For to have character is to know that I move in a history I neither summon nor command, which carries consequences nonetheless for my choices and conduct. It draws me closer to some and more distant from others; it makes some aims more appropriate, others less so. As a self-interpreting being, I am able to reflect on my history and in this sense to distance myself from it, but the distance is always precarious and provisional, the point of reflection never finally secured outside the history itself. But the liberal ethic puts the self beyond the reach of its experience, beyond deliberation and reflection. Denied the expansive self-understandings that could shape a common life, the liberal self is left to lurch between detachment on the one hand and entanglement on the other. Such is the fate of the unencumbered self, and its liberating promise.

THE PROCEDURAL REPUBLIC

But before my case can be complete, I need to consider one powerful reply. While it comes from a liberal direction, its spirit is more practical than philosophical. It says, in short, that I am asking too much. It is one thing to seek constitutive attachments in our private lives; among families and friends, and certain tightly knit groups, there may be found a common good that makes justice and rights less pressing. But with public life – at least today, and probably always – it is different. So long as the nation state is the primary form of political association, talk of constitutive community too easily suggests a darker politics rather than a brighter one; amid echoes of the moral majority, the priority of right, for all its philosophical faults, still seems the safer hope.

This is a challenging rejoinder, and no account of political community in the twentieth century can fail to take it seriously. It is challenging not least because it calls into question the status of political philosophy and its relation to the world. For if my argument is correct, if the liberal vision we have considered is not morally self-sufficient but parasitic on a notion of community it officially rejects, then we should expect to find that the political practice that embodies this vision is not *practically* self-sufficient either – that it must draw on a sense of community it cannot supply and may even undermine. But is that so far from the circumstance we face today? Could it be that, through the original position darkly, on the far side of the veil of ignorance, we may glimpse an intimation of our predicament, a refracted vision of ourselves?

How does the liberal vision – and its failure – help us make sense of our public life and its predicament? Consider, to begin, the following paradox in the citizen's relation to the modern welfare state. In many ways, we in the 1980s stand near the completion of a liberal project that has run its course from the New Deal through the Great Society and into the present. But notwithstanding the extension of the franchise and the expansion on individual rights and enti-tlements in recent decades, there is a widespread sense that, individually and collectively, our control over the forces that govern our lives is receding rather than increasing. This sense is deepened by what appear simultaneously as the power and the powerlessness of the nation state. On the one hand, increasing numbers of citizens view the state as an overly intrusive presence, more likely to frustrate their purposes than advance them. And yet, despite its unprece-dented role in the economy and society, the modern state seems itself disem-powered, unable effectively to control the domestic economy, to respond to persisting social ills, or to work America's will in the world.

This is a paradox that has fed the appeals of recent politicians (including Carter and Reagan), even as it has frustrated their attempts to govern. To sort it out, we need to identify the public philosophy implicit in our political practice, and to reconstruct its arrival. We need to trace the advent of the pro-cedural republic, by which I mean a public life animated by the liberal vision and self-image we've considered.

The story of the procedural republic goes back in some ways to the founding of the republic, but its central drama begins to unfold around the turn of the century. As national markets and large-scale enterprise displaced a decentral-ized economy, the decentralized political forms of the early republic became out-moded as well. If democracy was to survive, the concentration of economic power would have to be met by a similar concentration of political power. But the Progressives understood, or some of them did, that the success of democracy required more than the centralization of government; it also required the nation-alization of politics. The primary form of political community had to be a recast on a national scale. For Herbert Croly, writing in 1909, the 'nationalizing of

American political, economic, and social life' was 'an essentially formative and enlightening political transformation'. We would become more of a democracy only as we became 'more of a nation . . . in ideas, in institutions and in spirit'.[19]

This nationalizing project would be consummated in the New Deal, but, for the democratic tradition in America, the embrace of the nation was a decisive departure. From Jefferson to the populists, the party of democracy in American political debate had been, roughly speaking, the party of the provinces, of decentralized power, of small-town and small-scale America. And against them had stood the party of the nation – first Federalists, then Whigs, then the Republicans of Lincoln – a party that spoke for the consolidation of the union. It was thus the historic achievement of the New Deal to unite, in a single party and political programme, what Samuel Beer has called 'liberalism and the national idea'.[20]

What matters for our purpose is that, in the twentieth century, liberalism made its peace with concentrated power. But it was understood at the start that the terms of this peace required a strong sense of national community, morally and politically to underwrite the extended involvements of a modern industrial order. If a virtuous republic of small-scale, democratic communities was no longer a possibility, a national republic seemed democracy's next best hope. This was still, in principle at least, a politics of the common good. It looked to the nation, not as a neutral framework for the play of competing interests, but rather as a formative community, concerned to shape a common life suited to the scale of modern social and economic forms.

But this project failed. By the mid- or late twentieth century, the national republic had run its course. Except for extraordinary moments, such as war, the nation proved too vast a scale across which to cultivate the shared self-understandings necessary to community in the formative or constitutive sense. And so the gradual shift, in our practices and institutions, from a public philosophy of common purposes to one of fair procedures, from a politics of good to a politics of right, from the national republic to the procedural republic.

OUR PRESENT PREDICAMENT

A full account of this transition would take a detailed look at the changing shape of political institutions, constitutional interpretation, and the terms of political discourse in the broadest sense. But I suspect we would find in the *practice* of the procedural republic two broad tendencies foreshadowed by its philosophy: first, a tendency to crowd out democratic possibilities; second, a tendency to undercut the kind of community on which it nonetheless depends.

Where liberty in the early republic was understood as a function of democratic institutions and dispersed power,[21] liberty in the procedural republic is defined, in opposition to democracy, as an individual's guarantee against what the majority might will. I am free insofar as I am the bearer of rights, where rights are trumps.[22] Unlike the liberty of the early republic, the modern version permits – in fact even requires – concentrated power. This has to do with the universalizing logic of rights. Insofar as I have a right, whether to free speech or a minimum income, its provision cannot be left to the vagaries of local preferences but must be assured at the most comprehensive level of political association. It cannot be one thing in New York and another in Alabama. As rights and entitlements expand, politics is therefore displaced from smaller forms of association and relocated at the most universal form – in our case, the nation. And even as politics flows to the nation, power shifts away from democratic institutions (such as legislatures and political parties) and towards institutions designed to be insulated from democratic pressures, and hence better equipped to dispense and defend individual rights (notably the judiciary and bureaucracy).

These institutional developments may begin to account for the sense of powerlessness that the welfare state fails to address and in some ways doubtless deepens. But it seems to me a further clue to our condition recalls even more directly the predicament of the unencumbered self – lurching, as we left it, between detachment on the one hand and entanglement on the other. For it is a striking feature of the welfare state that it offers a powerful promise of individual rights, and also demands of its citizens a high measure of mutual engagement. But the self-image that attends the rights cannot sustain the engagement.

As bearers of rights, where rights are trumps, we think of ourselves as freely choosing, individual selves, unbound by obligations antecedent to rights, or to the agreements we make. And yet, as citizens of the procedural republic that secures these rights, we find ourselves implicated willy-nilly in a formidable array of dependencies and expectations we did not choose and increasingly reject.

In our public life, we are more entangled, but less attached, than ever before. It is as though the unencumbered self presupposed by the liberal ethic had begun to come true – less liberated than disempowered, entangled in a network of obligations and involvements unassociated with any act of will, and yet unmediated by those common identifications or expansive self-definitions that would make them tolerable. As the scale of social and political organization has become more comprehensive, the terms of our collective identity have become more fragmented, and the forms of political life have outrun the common purpose needed to sustain them.

Something like this, it seems to me, has been unfolding in America for the past half-century or so. I hope I have said at least enough to suggest the shape a fuller story might take. And I hope in any case to have conveyed a certain view about politics and philosophy and the relation between them – that our practices and institutions are themselves embodiments of theory, and to unravel their predicament is, at least in part, to seek after the self-image of the age.

NOTES

1. An excellent example of this view can be found in S. Huntington, *American Politics: The Promise of Disharmony* (Cambridge, Mass., 1981). See especially his discussion of the 'ideals versus institutions' gap, pp. 10–12, 39–41, 61–84, 221–62.

2. See, e.g., the conceptions of a 'practice' advanced by A. MacIntyre and C. Taylor. MacIntyre, *After Virtue* (Notre Dame, Ind., 1973), 175–209. Taylor, 'Interpretation and the Sciences of Man', *Review of Metaphysics*, 25 (1971), 3–51.

3. J. Rawls, *A Theory of Justice* (Oxford, 1971). I. Kant, *Groundwork of the Metaphysics of Morals*, trans. H. J. Paton (1785; New York, 1956). Kant, *Critique of Pure Reason*, trans. N. Kemp Smith (1781, 1787; London, 1929). Kant, *Critique of Practical Reason*, trans. L. W. Beck (1788; Indianapolis, 1956). Kant, 'On the Common Saying: "This may be true in theory, but it does not apply in practice"', in H. Reiss (ed.), *Kant's Political Writings* (1793; Cambridge, 1970). Other recent versions of the claim for the priority of the right over good can be found in R. Nozick, *Anarchy, State and Utopia* (New York, 1974); R. Dworkin, *Taking Rights Seriously* (London, 1977); B. Ackerman, *Social Justice in the Liberal State* (New Haven, Conn., 1980).

4. This section, and the two that follow, summarize arguments developed more fully in M. Sandel, *Liberalism and the Limits of Justice* (Cambridge, 1982).

5. Rawls, *A Theory of Justice*, p. 3.

6. J. S. Mill, *Utilitarianism*, in *The Utilitarians* (1893; New York, 1973), p. 465. Mill, *On Liberty*, in *The Utilitarians*, p. 485 (originally published 1849).

7. Kant, 'On the Common Saying', p. 73.

8. Kant, *Groundwork*, p. 92.

9. Kant, *Critique of Practical Reason*, p. 89.

10. Kant, *Groundwork*, p. 92.

11. Kant, *Critique of Practical Reason*, p. 89.

12. Kant, *Groundwork*, p. 92.

13. Rawls, 'The Basic Structure as Subject', *American Philosophical Quarterly* (1977), 165.

14. Rawls, *A Theory of Justice*, p. 560.

15. Rawls, 'Kantian Constructivism in Moral Theory: The Dewey Lectures 1980', *Journal of Philosophy*, 77 (1980), 543.

16. Mill, *On Liberty*, p. 485.

17. Rawls, *A Theory of Justice*, pp. 101–2.

18. The account that follows is a tentative formulation of themes requiring more detailed elaboration and support.

19. H. Croly, *The Promise of American Life* (Indianapolis, 1965), pp. 270–3.

20. S. Beer, 'Liberalism and the National Idea', *The Public Interest*, Fall (1966), 70–82.

21. See, e.g., L. Tribe, *American Constitutional Law* (Mineola, NY, 1978), pp. 2–3.

22. See R. Dworkin, 'Liberalism', in S. Hampshire (ed.), *Public and Private Morality* (Cambridge, 1978), 136.

'THE MISSING DIMENSION OF SOCIALITY' BY MARY ANN GLENDON

At the time of writing, Mary Ann Glendon is Learned Hand Professor of Law at Harvard Law School and a well-known writer on constitutional law and international human rights. She has written numerous books including *A World Made New: Eleanor Roosevelt and the Universal Declaration of Human Rights* (Random House, 2001), *Comparative Legal Traditions* (West, 1999) and *A Nation under Lawyers* (Farrar, Straus & Giroux, 1994). The extract is from *Rights Talk: The Impoverishment of Political Discourse* (Free Press, 1991). In an argument that complements the general communitarian concern with the way individual rights, understood predominantly in legal terms, have undermined civic ties, she looks at the spread of rights talk and links it to the downgrading of attention given to civic duties and responsibilities – the missing dimension of sociality in our public discourse.

'THE MISSING DIMENSION OF SOCIALITY' (1991)*

Mary Ann Glendon

In *The Republic* and *The Laws*, Plato offered a vision of a unified society, where the needs of children are met not by parents but by the Government, and where no intermediate forms of association stand between the individual and the State. The vision is a brilliant one, but it is not our own. (Justice William J. Brennan)[1]

The American dialect of rights talk disserves public deliberation not only through affirmatively promoting an image of the rights-bearer as a radically autonomous individual, but through its corresponding neglect of the social dimensions of human personhood. In his studies of language and thought in simple societies, Claude Lévi-Strauss demonstrated how discourse and syntax can operate in countless ways to color and supplement a group's vocabulary.[2] Though the American rights dialect has little in common with the unwritten languages to which the great anthropologist devoted much of his attention, it is a case in point. Just as our stark rights vocabulary receives subtle amplification from its encoded image of the lone rights-bearer, our weak vocabulary of

---

* From Mary Ann Glendon, *Rights Talk* (New York: The Free Press, 1991), pp. 109–20.

responsibility is rendered fainter still by our underdeveloped notion of human sociality. Neglect of the social dimension of personhood has made it extremely difficult for us to develop an adequate conceptual apparatus for taking into account the sorts of groups within which human character, competence, and capacity for citizenship are formed. In a society where the seedbeds of civic virtue – families, neighborhoods, religious associations, and other communities – can no longer be taken for granted, this is no trifling matter. For individual freedom and the general welfare alike depend on the condition of the fine texture of civil society – on a fragile ecology for which we have no name.

These deficiencies in the deep structure are not readily detectable when we listen to rights talk. It is always harder to discern what is absent than to hear what is present. One becomes aware, however, that something is missing from the underlying assumptions of public discourse, as well as from its basic vocabulary, in many situations where people have difficulty translating an important concern into political or legal language. The flag-burning dispute, to recur to a familiar example, elicited passionate defenses of freedom of expression on the one hand, and equally fervent protests against desecration of the national symbol on the other. The arguments for the former position were easy to make, fitting into familiar First Amendment grooves. They carried the day. The rebuttals tended to have a sputtering quality; they sounded more in emotion than in reason. The problem for the flag-defenders, in part, was that the flag-burning controversy pitted individual rights against community standards. Accustomed as we are to the notion that a person's liberty should not be curtailed in the absence of direct and immediate harm to specified others, we can barely find the words to speak of indirect harms, cumulative injury, or damages that appear only long after the acts that precipitated them. The flag dispute was, in fact, a skirmish in what some have called a 'culture struggle' – a contest over the fundamental understandings of what kind of society we are, and the role of common moral intuitions in contributing to those understandings.[3]

What was never fully brought to expression in the controversy was the underlying disagreement between those who equate all widely held standards with majoritarian oppression, and those who regard the extension of constitutional protection to, say, flag-burning, child pornography, or sadomasochistic art, as an assault on all the practices and procedures through which a society constantly defines and redefines itself. The maintenance of a vital democratic society, a society with a creative tension between individual freedom and the general welfare, requires that a continuing debate take place about just such matters. If political discourse all but closes out the voices on one side of the debate, liberalism itself is at risk. Yet that is precisely what our simple rights dialect regularly does.

Even more difficult than common moral standards to explain and defend in current political language are the interests of communities and their members in staving off threats to their very existence. Communities are often caught in a pincer between individual rights on the one hand, and reasons of state on the other. Thus, when Detroit's Poletown residents mounted their campaign to prevent the taking and destruction of their neighborhood, they found that the most readily available vocabulary – that of individual property rights – enabled them to speak about only part of the problem. They could not find a way to communicate effectively with legislators, judges, or the press about other kinds of losses: a rich neighborhood life; shared memories and hopes; roots; a sense of place. When, as a last resort, they brought a lawsuit, they were, in effect, laughed out of court when they resorted to the only legal terms that even came close to enabling them to voice their deepest concerns – the analogy to environmental protection. Nor was Poletown an isolated tragedy. Urban 'renewal' programs in the 1950s and 1960s carelessly wiped out many other neighborhoods and destroyed irreplaceable social networks in the name of a cramped (and frequently mistaken) vision of progress.

It has been difficult, similarly, for persons in areas affected by plant-closings to air the full range of their concerns within the standard framework of legal and political discourse. When a Youngstown, Ohio, coalition of unions, religious groups, and community organizations went to court to try to delay, and explore alternatives to, the departure of the steel mills that had been the lifeblood of that city since the turn of the century, their arguments were as halting and awkward as the Poletown 'environmental' claim. One theory advanced by the Youngstown plaintiffs was that a kind of 'community property right' had arisen somehow from the lengthy relationship between the steel companies and the city, a right that gave rise to an obligation on the part of the companies not to leave the city in a state of devastation. The federal appellate judge who denied relief was sympathetic, agreeing that the mill closing was an 'economic tragedy of major proportions' for Youngstown.[4] The judge pointed out, however, that American law recognizes no property rights in the 'community'. Dubbing their lawsuit a 'cry for help', he advised the plaintiffs that their plea should be addressed to those bodies where public policy regarding plant-closings is formulated – the federal and state legislatures.

But the Youngstown plaintiffs, like the Poletown residents, had already failed to make their case in the ordinary political arena. In Ohio, as in nearly all American states, efforts to draw legislative attention to problems related to plant-closings had been unsuccessful. Legislative discussions of the matter have been framed chiefly in terms of a clash between the need and right of businesses to adapt to new circumstances, on the one hand, and the merely economic interests of individual workers, or organized labor, on the other. It is impossible, of course, to know whether legislative outcomes would have been different if the terms of the discussion had been more capacious. But it is noteworthy that the United States is practically alone among the industrialized nations in lacking broad-gauged legislative programs addressed to the non-economic as well as economic effects of factory-closings on families, communities, and workers.[5]

Once again, from a comparative perspective, we are in the presence of a kind of puzzle. The dislocations caused by plant-closings, partial shutdowns, relocations, and mass economic layoffs have given rise everywhere to broadly similar problems. Ripples go out through entire communities when work disappears and workers remain. In the nations of Western Europe, a wide variety of statutory schemes have long been in place to ease the transitions made necessary by obsolescence and competition. These statutes, at a minimum, require that substantial advance notice of proposed closings be given to affected workers and local governments; and that owners and managers consult with worker representatives and local government officials concerning the effects of the closing. Most of those countries, in addition, have established programs for the retraining and, if necessary, relocation of affected workers. Such legislation is not seen as specially 'pro-labor', but rather as addressed to the long-term general interest in maintaining the conditions that promote family life, community life, and a productive work force.[6] In the United States, by contrast, a modest federal plant-closing bill that merely requires large companies to give sixty days' notice of a proposed major layoff was adopted only in 1988, and even then only over then-President Reagan's veto.

A kind of blind spot seems to float across our political vision where the communal and social, as distinct from individual or strictly economic, dimensions of a problem are concerned. In a leading environmental-law decision, the Supreme Court held that the Sierra Club had no standing to argue for preservation of federal parkland as a *shared* natural resource. The only way the association could remain in court was to establish that particular *individuals* would be harmed by the recreational development proposal it was challenging. Justice Blackmun, in dissent, rhetorically posed the key question: 'Must our law be so rigid and our procedural concepts so inflexible that we render ourselves helpless when the existing methods and the traditional concepts do not quite fit and do not prove to be entirely adequate for new issues?'[7] While this question awaits a negative answer, long-term interests are often held hostage to the short-run, and communities are often at a disadvantage when pitted against the state and a large corporation, as in Poletown, or against the market and corporate actors, as in Youngstown. The same is often true when individual rights are in conflict with the general interests of the community of which they are members – as witness a recent Supreme Court decision involving Indian lands. In the late nineteenth century, Congress (in an effort to promote the assimilation of Native Americans into the larger society) had divided some communal reservations of Indian tribes into modest individual land allotments. Over time, as successive generations of owners died, the original parcels were split up through inheritance into ever-smaller fractions. Eventually, some parcels had hundreds, and many had dozens, of co-owners. In such cases, the only way for the 'owners' to profit from their holdings is to lease out the land and divide the rental income in proportion to their shares. Even then, an individual's share of the rent is often so small that it is less than the administrative cost of transferring it to him or her. By the 1980s, there was a wide recognition that the allotment policy had been 'disastrous for the Indians'.[8]

To remedy the situation, Congress passed a statute in 1983 that would have begun gradually to reconsolidate the smallest and most unprofitable of these individually owned interests under tribal ownership. The statute provided that any share which constituted less than 2 per cent of the tract to which it belonged, and which had earned less than $100 in the year preceding the death of the owner, would return to the tribe when its owner died, rather than passing by will or intestate succession. This consolidation scheme was challenged by certain heirs and devisees of three deceased members of the Oglala Sioux Tribe. The trial court in South Dakota, close to the situation, ruled against the plaintiffs. As a threshold matter, the trial court found that the plaintiffs had no standing to attack the statute. The deceased property-owners may have been deprived of something (the right to pass the property in question on to their heirs), but this deprivation occurred at a time when the plaintiffs had no rights whatsoever in the property. For an heir or devisee has no rights in the property of his ancestor or testator until that person's death. In any event, the court went on, the statute was constitutional under a long line of cases recognizing that Congress has extensive power to alter the law of intestate succession and testamentary disposition.[9] The statute did not interfere with anyone's ownership rights so long as he or she lived; it merely removed one stick from the owner's bundle of rights – the power to transmit ownership upon death.

The United States Supreme Court agreed that the Congressional aim of encouraging consolidation in the hope 'that future generations of Indians would be able to make more productive use of the Indians' ancestral lands' was 'a public purpose of high order'. The Court noted also that the current state of the law under the 'takings' clauses of the Constitution gives legislators 'considerable latitude in regulating property in ways that may adversely affect the owners'. Furthermore, the Court agreed that the heirs or devisees of the deceased owners had no standing to complain in their own names, for no rights had ever vested in them. Nevertheless, the Court unanimously held that the statute could not stand.

Writing for the Court, Justice O'Connor found that Congress had crossed the line into unconstitutionality by removing one of the components of the ownership rights belonging to the *deceased* Indians. Congress's broad powers to restrict or even eliminate intestate or testamentary succession, she wrote, did not extend to completely extinguishing both kinds of succession, even where a small individual interest and a high public purpose were involved. As for standing, the heirs and devisees could be permitted to assert the rights of the deceased Indians in the same way that an administrator of a decedent's estate can prosecute the dead person's claims and collect his debts. Weighing but 'weakly' on the other side, said Justice O'Connor, was the fact that the deceased individuals had belonged to the tribe, and that consolidation of Indian lands in the tribe would benefit the group of which they had been members. That consideration could not prevail against the right of an individual to pass on even a small, unprofitable, fractional share of property. The Indian lands case, together with the *Poletown* case, is revealing of the extreme vulnerability of communities to individual rights on the one hand, and to imperatives of the state on the other.

The catalog is lengthy of instances where the Supreme Court has had difficulty bringing into focus the social dimension of human personhood, and also the kinds of communities that nourish this aspect of an individual's personality. Except for corporations (which the Court has recognized as 'persons' and endowed with rights), groups or associations that stand between the individual and the state all too often meet with the judicial incomprehension. Even in labor law, though Congress firmly committed the nation in the 1930s to a policy of protecting employee organizational activity and promoting collective bargaining, the Court's decisions in recent years have increasingly permitted individual rights to erode that policy. One searches these opinions in vain for any significant affirmation of the basic idea of labor law: that the best and surest way to protect individual workers is through protecting their associational activity. The justices often seem to be at odds with the underlying assumption of our labor legislation, that an individual might willingly agree to subordinate her own interests to some extent by casting her lot together with fellow workers in pursuit of common ends which are frequently, but not exclusively, economic. Judicial adroitness at applying the constitutional principles of liberty and equality is rarely matched by a corresponding skill in implementing the congressionally endorsed principle of solidarity.[10]

The linguistic and conceptual deficiency in question here is not confined to the judiciary, as the Poletown and Youngstown situations demonstrate. American political discourse generally seems poorly equipped to take into account social 'environments' – the criss-crossing networks of associations and relationships that constitute the fine grain of society. When associations do claim public attention, it is chiefly as 'interest groups', that is, as collections of self-seeking individuals pursuing limited, parallel aims. The connection between the health of the sorts of groups where character, competence, and values are formed, and the problem of maintaining our republican form of government, is generally kept out of sight, and therefore out of mind. An implicit anthropology – an encoded image of the human person as radically alone and as 'naturally' at odds with his fellows – certainly contributes to this scotoma in our political and legal vision. Another factor, however, seems to be simply that favourable American circumstances have long fostered a sense of complacency about social environments.

In the beginning, that is, at the Founding, there was no particular reason for American statesmen to pay special attention to families, neighborhoods, or other small associations. These social systems were just there, seemingly 'natural', like gravity on whose continued existence we rely to keep us grounded, steady, and attached to our surroundings. In all likelihood, the Founders just took for granted the dense texture of eighteenth-century American society, with its economically interdependent families and its tight-knit communities. With most of the population clustered in self-governing towns and cities, the architects of our Constitution would have been hard put to conceive of the degree to which local and state government now has been displaced by federal authority. As for religion, whatever views men like Jefferson and Madison may have entertained personally, they probably supposed that churches deeply embedded in community life would always be around, too. How could they have foreseen that even families would lose much of their importance as determinants of individual social standing and economic security? Living in a country dotted with small farms and businesses, how could they have anticipated the rise and decay of great cities (so despised by Jefferson)? Of the eventual economic dependence of a large proportion of Americans on large, bureaucratic, public and private organizations? Or how much power these organizations would wield? Nor could they have imagined the rise and decline of broadly representative political parties; or the flourishing of public education, followed by its alarming deterioration.

This is not to say that the Founders underestimated the importance of the institutions whose durability they assumed. On the contrary, there is much evidence that they counted on families, custom, religion, and convention to preserve and promote the virtues required by our experiment in ordered liberty. Jefferson, Adams, and especially Madison, knew that the Constitution and laws, the institutionalized checks on power, the army, and the militia could not supply all the conditions required for the success of the new regime. They often explicitly acknowledged the dependence of the entire enterprise on the qualities of mind and character with which they believed the American population had been blessed. Madison, in *Federalist* No. 55, put it most plainly: 'As there is a degree of depravity in mankind which requires a certain degree of circumspection and distrust, so there are other qualities in human nature which justify a certain portion of esteem and confidence. Republican government presupposes the existence of these qualities in a higher degree than any other form.' Admitting that he could not foresee whether these qualities would endure as the country grew, Madison expressed great confidence that 'the present genius' and 'political character' of the American people were equal to the challenge.[11] With a variety of social institutions in place to nourish the 'germ' (as Burke called it) of 'public affections',[12] the statesmen of our formative period concentrated their energies on the laws, and produced a remarkable design for government. The notion of civil society did not enter into the mainstream of American political and legal thought. The social environment, like the natural environment, was simply there. In both respects, we seemed endowed with inexhaustible riches.

On the European continent, by contrast, the French Revolutionaries inadvertently guaranteed that 'society', as something quite distinct from the state, would become and remain a major subject of political and legal discourse. In imitation of the program of the Reformation to eliminate institutional intermediaries between man and God, the men of '89 set out to abolish the intermediate groups (*corps intermédiaires*) of the old regime that stood between citizen and state. Feudal statuses, the Church, guilds, and many aspects of family organization were targeted both as oppressive to individuals and as competitors with the state for the loyalty of citizens. In the Napoleonic era, the focus shifted. The revolutionary attack on family, religion, and craft associations lost much of its vigor, but communal and regional centers of power had to bow before the centralization of government. Part of the legacy of the period was an important political discussion that continued throughout the nineteenth century in continental Europe. Tocqueville, Durkheim, Hegel, Marx, Gierke, and others wrote at length about what the relations were or should be among individuals, the institutions of 'Civil society', and the state.

In France, where state and society first had been placed sharply in confrontation with one another, their theoretical speculation took the form of concern about what might ensue if social institutions became weaker as government became stronger. Examining the same historical developments that many of his contemporaries interpreted, with satisfaction, as effecting a continuous liberation of the free, self-determining individual from family and group ties, Tocqueville expressed some reservations. He pointed out that, with the growth of powerful centralized states, the very same groups that had once seemed to stifle individual development and to obstruct the consolidation of national power could help to protect personal freedom and to provide useful checks on government. With his astonishing ability to see deeply into the long-term implications of developments that were just gathering momentum in his lifetime, Tocqueville anticipated that the loosening of group ties would present hazards, as well as opportunities, for the cause of human liberty. Like Burke, he insisted on the connection between rootedness and civic virtue:

> For in a community in which the ties of family, of caste, of class, and craft fraternities no longer exist, people are far too much disposed to think exclusively of their own interests, to become self-seekers practising a narrow individualism and caring nothing for the public good.[13]

He was especially concerned that individualism ('a word unknown to our ancestors'), and excessive preoccupation with material comfort, would render people susceptible to new and insidious forms of tyranny. America, he thought, stood a good chance of forestalling such a fate through its many little associations that served as schools for citizenship. In the settings of townships, families, and other groups, citizens would accumulate 'clear, practical ideas about the nature of their duties and the extent of their rights'.[14] Each generation would learn anew to appreciate the benefits of, and sacrifices necessary for, a constitutional order. Tocqueville especially admired local governments like those he saw operating in New England, for he feared that destruction of regional and communal centers of power in France would take a heavy toll on democracy there.

> Local institutions are to liberty what primary schools are to science; they put it within the people's reach; they teach people to appreciate its

peaceful enjoyment and accustom them to make use of it. Without local institutions a nation may give itself a free government, but it has not got the spirit of liberty.[15]

Another French social theorist, writing several decades later, warned of a different kind of loss. Emile Durkheim's concern was less for the political than for the social and personal consequences of the decline of what he called 'secondary groups'.

> [C]ollective activity is always too complex to be able to be expressed through . . . the State. Moreover, the State is too remote from individuals; its relations with them too external and intermittent to penetrate deeply into individual consciences and socialize them within. Where the State is the only environment in which men can live communal lives, they inevitably lose contact, become detached, and thus society disintegrates. A nation can be maintained only if, between the State and the individual, there is intercalated a whole series of secondary groups near enough to the individuals to attract them strongly in their sphere of action and drag them, in this way, into the general torrent of social life.[16]

It was only much later – with the rise of the powerful states and business corporations of the twentieth century – that Tocqueville's and Durkheim's insights could be fully appreciated. Just as certain works of great nineteenth-century mathematicians seemed useless until chaos science and the computer caught up with them,[17] so theories of civil society have only begun to come into their own as social conditions that were imagined a century ago become reality. To a great extent, urbanization, industrialization, bureaucracy, geographic mobility, mass culture, and centralization of political power have accomplished the project of the French revolutionaires, bringing citizens everywhere into ever more unmediated relationships with government. All over the industrialized world, 'society' with its particularistic communities of memory and mutual aid, its relationships that cannot be captured in purely economic terms, appears to be in considerable disarray.

Many Eastern European thinkers have blamed the expansion of the state for the 'withering away' of society. Thus Czeslaw Milosz has said: 'Quite contrary to the predictions of Marx, . . . instead of the withering away of the state, the state, like [a cancer], has eaten up all the substance of society. Destroying society, as a matter of fact.[18] But observers in the West have pointed out that the market economy, too, can take a toll on society, including the family, by orienting human beings to means – especially money and power – rather than to ends.[19] Men and women in capitalist and socialist regimes alike may now glimpse their own reflections in Tocqueville's haunting passage on the loss of civic virtue:

> There are countries in Europe where the inhabitants feel like some sort of farm laborer indifferent to the fate of the place where he dwells. The

greatest changes may take place in his country without his concurrence; he does not even know precisely what has happened; . . . Worse still, the condition of his village, the policing of his road, and the repair of his church and parsonage do not concern him; he thinks that all those things have nothing to do with him at all, but belong to a powerful stranger called the government . . . Furthermore, this man who has so completely sacrificed his freedom of will does not like obedience more than the next man. He submits, it is true, to the caprice of a clerk, but as soon as force is withdrawn, he will vaunt his triumph over the law as soon as over a conquered foe. Thus he oscillates the whole time between servility and licence.[20]

When nations reach this point, Tocqueville surmised, 'either they must modify both laws and mores or they will perish, for the fount of public virtues has run dry; there are subjects still, but not citizens'.[21]

Now that so much less 'society' flourishes between the individual and the state, certain questions – long unasked in the United States – press for recognition: where does a republic, depending on a citizenry capable of participating in democratic political processes, find men and women with a grasp of the skills of governing and the willingness to use them in the public service? Where does a welfare state find citizens with enough fellow feeling to reach out to others in need, yet with enough sense of personal responsibility to assume substantial control over their own lives? What, if anything, needs to be done to protect social environments – families, neighborhoods, workplace associations, and religious and other communities of obligation – that traditionally have provided us with our principal opportunities to observe, learn, and practice self-government as well as government of the self?

Though these questions are increasingly urgent, our current public discourse makes it difficult to talk about them. Our legal and political vocabularies deal handily with rights-bearing individuals, market actors, and the state, but they do not afford us a ready way of bringing into focus smaller groups and systems where the values and practices that sustain our republic are shaped, practiced, transformed, and transmitted from one generation to the next.[22]

NOTES

1. *Bowen v. Gilliard*, 483 U.S. 587, 632 (1987) (Brennan, J., dissenting).
2. Glaude Lévi-Strauss, *The Savage Mind* (Chicago: University of Chicago Press, 1966), 1.
3. On the idea of a contemporary *Kulturkampf*, see George Weigel, *Catholicism and the Renewal of American Democracy* (New York: Paulist Press, 1989), 4–6.
4. *Local 1330, United Steelworkers of America v. United States Steel Corp.*, 631 F. 2d 1264 (6th Cir. 1980).
5. Benjamin Aaron, 'Plant Closings: American and Comparative Perspectives', 59 *Chicago-Kent Law Review* 941 (1983).
6. A recent study of the restructuring of the steel industry in Western Europe finds that, while strong laws regulating layoff practices may have slowed restructuring of that industry, they also generated important social benefits, including community

stability and a broader distribution of the risks and costs of economic change than would otherwise have occurred. See Susan N. Houseman, *Industrial Restructuring in the European Community: The Case of European Steel* (Cambridge: Harvard University Press, 1991).

7. *Sierra Club v. Morton*, 405 U.S. 727, 755–6 (1972) (Blackmun, J., dissenting).
8. *Hodel v. Irving*, 107 S. Ct 2076 (1987).
9. Ibid.
10. See, generally, Julius Getman, 'The Courts and Collective Bargaining', 59 *Chicago-Kent Law Review* 969, 977 (1983); Thomas C. Kohler, 'Setting the Conditions for Self-Rule: Unions, Associations, Our First Amendment Discourse, and the Problem of *De Bartolo*', 1990 *Wisconsin Law Review* 149.
11. *Federalist* No. 55.
12. Edmund Burke, *Reflections on the Revolution in France* (New York: Doubleday Anchor, 1973):

> To be attached to the subdivision, to love the little platoon we belong to in society, is the first principle (the germ as it were) of public affections. It is the first link in the series by which we proceed towards a love to our country and to mankind. (59)

13. Alexis de Tocqueville, *The Old Regime and the French Revolution*, trans. Stuart Gilbert (New York: Doubleday Anchor, 1955), xiii.
14. Alexis de Tocqueville, *Democracy in America*, trans. George Lawrence, ed. J. P. Mayer (Garden City, New York: Doubleday Anchor, 1969), I, 70.
15. Ibid., 63.
16. Emile Durkheim, *The Division of Labor in Society*, trans. George Simpson (New York: Free Press, 1964), 28.
17. James Gleick, *Chaos: Making a New Science* (New York: Viking, 1987), 46 (Henri Poincaré 'was the first to understand the possibility of chaos [science]').
18. 'An Interview with Czeslaw Milosz', *New York Review of Books*, 27 February 1986, 34.
19. Robert Bellah, 'The Invasion of the Money World', in *Rebuilding the Nest*, ed. David Blankenhorn, Steven Bayme and Jean Bethke Elshtain (Milwaukee: Family Service America, 1990) 227, 228; Christopher Lasch, *Haven in a Heartless World* (New York: Basic Books, 1977).
20. Tocqueville, *Democracy in America*, I, 93–4.
21. *Ibid.*
22. Scholars in many fields, especially those with a sociological orientation, are beginning to make this point. See, especially, Alan Wolfe, *Whose Keeper? Social Science and Moral Obligation* (Berkeley: University of California Press, 1989). Wolfe has insisted that the 'recovery of sociology and its moral tradition' is essential for the health of liberal politics:

> Markets and states have gotten people fairly far along the road to a better life, offering greater freedom on the one hand and a recognition of obligations to others on the other. But they have done so by taking real people living in specific social situations and removing them from the process by which morality is understood. (188)

See also Robert Bellah et al., *Habits of the Heart: Individualism and Commitment in American Life* (Berkeley: University of California Press, 1985); Amitai Etzioni, *An Immodest Agenda* (New York: McGraw-Hill, 1983); Nathan Glazer, *The Limits of Social Policy* (Cambridge: Harvard University Press, 1988).

'THE FALL AND RISE OF AMERICA' BY AMITAI ETZIONI

At the time of writing, Amitai Etzioni is the first University Professor of The George Washington University, where he is also involved in the Communitarian Network which describes itself as a 'coalition of individuals and organisations who have come together to shore up the moral, social and political environment'. A sociologist, starting his career as a specialist in organisational sociology, he has frequently been referred to as the guru of communitarianism, successfully bridging the gap between academic studies and public political engagement. He is the author of numerous books and related articles including *The Monochrome Society* (Princeton University Press, 2001), *Next: The Road to the Good Society* (Basic Books, 2001), *The Limits of Privacy* (Basic Books, 1999), *The New Golden Rule: Community and Morality in a Democratic Society* (Profile Books, 1997), *The Spirit of Community: Rights, Responsibilities and the Communitarian Agenda* (Fontana, 1995) and *The Moral Dimension: Toward a New Economics* (Free Press, 1988). The extract here is from *The New Golden Rule*. It is more a work of sociology than of political theory, but its political claims are quite clear. Using survey data, Etzioni examines an apparent change in American society between the 1950s and the 1980s leading to an increase in autonomy but a decrease in shared values and hence in social order. But he also argues that in the 1990s the pendulum has swung back in the direction of communitarians, who, it would seem, have history on their side. Etzioni's arguments could usefully be read in conjunction with the critique of communitarianism made by feminists and discussed in Chapter 7. It is also worth thinking about the different approach taken by this sort of work to that found in the more philosophical communitarians such as Sandel.

'THE FALL AND RISE OF AMERICA' (1996)*

Amitai Etzioni

BASELINE FIFTIES: THE OLD REGIME – ORDERLY, BUT HOW MORAL?

Any historical analysis requires a starting point which affects the insights and conclusions that follow. Thus, if one chooses American society in the 1950s as the baseline, that society may seem highly ordered from a vantage point in the

---

* From Amitai Etzioni, *The New Golden Rule: Community and Morality in a Democratic Society* (London: Profile Books, 1996), pp. 60–77, 80–4.

1990s, but it may not seem as orderly if examined from the viewpoint of earlier generations. (The same holds from the comparative sociological perspective: if one compares American society to some Asian societies it may be perceived as less orderly, but if one compares it to Russia of the mid-1990s, it is seen as rather orderly.) Those who argue that the 1950s were atypical[1] may have a case, but a similar case could be made for any period, and the analysis requires some kind of baseline.

The year 1960 is used as a baseline here because the society of the 1950s is often cited as the model of the orderly society we lost, one in which virtues were well in place. 'Three decades later, the fifties appear to be an orderly era, one with a minimum of social dissent. . . . In that era of general good will and expanding affluence, few Americans doubted the essential goodness of their society', comments David Halberstam.[2]

> It was a time when America still reigned as the strongest nation in the world. . . . It was a time when the Cold War was still seen as an unambiguous battle between good and evil. It was a time when people were proud to be Americans, trusted their leaders, and shared a consensus on basic beliefs and values.[3]

One can argue that the social order of the 1950s was atypical; sustained the 'wrong' values; that it was based on social conventions that papered over underlying tensions; and even that the order was based on a considerable measure of coercion (all issues explored below). However, one cannot deny that the occurrence of anti-social behavior in the American society of the 1950s (and that of other Western societies) was much lower than it was by the end of the 1980s.

Core values in the 1950s were relatively widely shared and strongly endorsed;[4] and to these a newly established anti-Communist ideology was added. Most Americans were united in the idea that America was the leader of the free world, and most strongly endorsed fighting a cold war against an 'evil empire'.[5] Patriotism was high – America had won World War II, saving the free world, and it had the strongest economy in the world. Indeed, the 1950s were thought of as the beginning of the American century.[6]

Members of society had a strong sense of duty to their families, communities, and society. In 1961, when President John F. Kennedy challenged Americans to ask not what their country could do for them, but what they could do for their country, his call was very warmly received. The establishment of the Peace Corps that followed was much more widely supported than AmeriCorps, President Clinton's attempt to introduce national service some thirty years later.

The dominant religion was Christianity, and it was more established than in 1990. For instance, prayers in schools were common and rarely questioned.[7] Laws made divorce difficult and costly; abortion was illegal in all states.[8] Families were much more intact. Illegitimacy was relatively low.[9] The cultural pollution proffered by television had barely begun.

In the 1950s, the roles of men and women were relatively clearly delineated, although not all abided by the normative expectations built into these roles. Those who did not were often chastised by their community. Women who did not marry were stigmatized as spinsters; married women who did not produce children were frequently pressured to account for their decision. As one historian of the decade puts it, '[I]t was a supreme sign of personal health and well-being to be engaged in the social act of marriage and family-raising'.[10] Promiscuous women were labeled 'sluts'. By and large, women were supposed to do housekeeping, mothering, and community service, and to be submissive and loving. Men were supposed to be providers (if they were not, they were made to feel guilty) and strong. Douglas T. Miller and Marion Nowak write: 'Only by accepting her place as wife, mother, [and] homemaker . . . could woman be content. Man, similarly, must exercise his active and competitive role. The human halves linked together in that basic human wholeness, the natural marital state.'[11]

Respect for authority figures (which embodies and helps sustain a society's values), from presidents to priests, from generals to doctors to labor leaders, was high.[12] Few in the 1950s would have dared to ask for a second opinion when ordered by a physician to undergo surgery. At work, alliances between industrial captains and labor bosses were common. The government was rather firmly trusted. The proportion of people who voted was relatively high and alienation was low.

The *extent* to which this order was *based on moral suasion* (versus various forms of coercion) is of particular importance for a communitarian evaluation, but unfortunately this is a subject very rarely studied, and hence very difficult to gauge. It is particularly difficult to establish the depth to which people internalized the core values of the 1950s versus the extent to which many conformed because of social pressure, economic considerations, or fear (for instance, African Americans in the South).[13] On the one hand, most Americans were quite satisfied with their lot and protests were few and far between. Feminist Betty Friedan, who formed the ideology for one of the protest movements that followed, argues that in the 1950s women often appeared satisfied in their traditional roles, which she explains by noting that women '[grew] up no longer knowing that they have . . . desires and capacities' other than those defined by the prevailing social norms of the time.[14] On the other hand, the fact that in the decade that followed, African Americans, youth, women, and liberal men attacked the old regime and stripped it of much legitimacy strongly suggests that these Americans at least did not fully commit themselves to the existing social order, even in the 1950s.

In the 1950s, divisiveness was low and a sense of *shared bonds, of community, was relatively high*. American society was even at that time a more heterogeneous one (objectively speaking) and had a stronger sense of being diverse (subjectively speaking) than most European societies. But it did not perceive itself to be deeply divided. Group consciousness along racial or gender lines was relatively low compared to what followed. Ethnic groups stressed that their first loyalty was to American society and not to their country of origin. Groups that were suspected of placing their prime loyalty elsewhere were viewed with disdain, and their leaders were kept out of many public offices, especially the presidency. Communists were suspect because, among other reasons, they were said to toe the line of the Communist capital, Moscow. When John F. Kennedy ran for office, he felt he had to convince Americans that his first loyalty was not to the Pope. Similarly, there were very few activists seeking to speak for a fundamentally different lifestyle – Zen, gay, or any other – although at the margins of society there were small assortments of so-called bohemians, deviants, and rabble-rousers.

Indicators of anti-social behavior, such as violent crime, drug abuse, alcoholism, and other sources of social disorder were relatively low (or relatively concealed, such as gambling, frequenting prostitutes, and the consumption of pornography).

Most Americans felt that they lived in safe and orderly places. In many parts of the country, people could use public spaces without fear; they left their front doors unlocked, their ignition keys in place, and their children playing outside unsupervised. More generally, the majority had the sense that theirs was an orderly and relatively tranquil society.

Relatively low autonomy. American society of the 1950s restricted individual and subgroup choice, although not nearly as much as authoritarian societies (not to mention totalitarian ones). For instance, college students were typically expected to take a fair number of prescribed courses that were considered 'good for them' by the faculty, while 'electives' were rather limited. The core curricula reflected unabashedly (and often with little self-awareness) the dominant set of values.

The 1950s were called the age of the 'silent generation', one in which people were expected to be uncritical and not to challenge authority. Godfrey Hodgson notes that 'to dissent from the broad axiom of consensus was to proclaim oneself irresponsible or ignorant'.[15] A witch-hunt was raging across the land in which Senator Joseph McCarthy and his investigators pursued perceived Communists and Communist sympathizers, driving people out of work or into exile and even to suicide.[16] Street justice, in which the policeman's nightstick settled many issues on the spot without any hearing or appeal, was common. Law enforcement showed a strong and clear bias along class, racial, and ethnic lines.[17]

In Congress, a small group of Southern senators dominated. They retained their elected offices for many terms, chaired the key committees, and ran roughshod over everyone else in Congress. When Speaker Tom Foley left the House in 1994 after thirty years, he reminisced about the days when he arrived in Congress. He and other new representatives were told by the then speaker, in public and quite openly, that there was one thing that was expected from them: silence.

The autonomy of several social groups was constricted. Women and minorities were treated as second-class citizens. Widespread racial segregation of public schools, transportation, hotels, and restaurants was enforced by law and custom. Various bureaucratic devices were used, especially in the South, to prevents blacks from voting. Powerful stereotypes, traditions, and interpersonal networks effectively kept most women out of political office, high positions in most companies and associations, and influential professions. Sexual partners were expected to be heterosexual, married, and even then limit their sexual conduct to culturally defined behaviors. In short, society was rather orderly (by present-day American standards, not those of, say, Singapore), but life choices, opportunities for self-expression and creativity, and cultural choices, opportunities for self-expression and creativity, and cultural alternatives were limited for many members of the American society (certainly when compared to what was about to come).

The Pendulum swings: 1960 to 1990, moral order deteriorates, autonomy expands, but so does anarchy

The strong consensus on *core values* of the 1950s was increasingly undermined in the years that followed as some values were contested and others waned but were not replaced by new ones. Americans increasingly doubted the merit of a grand role for their country in the world (especially in the wake of the war in Vietnam). Anti-Communist fervor slowly subsided but was not replaced with any new shared doctrine. The rise of the counter-culture in the 1960s further weakened the country's values of hard work and thrift, as well as compliance with most rules of conduct, from dress codes to table manners, from established tastes in music to cuisine.[18]

While the number of those who fully embraced the counter-culture was relatively small (although still in the millions) and many who joined it did so only for a transitional period, many other millions of 'orderly' Americans embraced, in varying degrees, some of the tenets of the counter-culture. The rise of the counter-culture in the 1960s was followed in the 1970s, and especially in the 1980s, by a strong endorsement of a different, instrumental brand of individualism.[19] It provided a normative seal of approval to a focus on the self rather than on responsibilities to the community, and saw in self-interest the best base for social order and virtue. Books such as *Looking Out for Number One* and *How to Be Your Own Best Friend*, which assert that 'we are accountable only to ourselves for what happens to us in our lives',[20] became popular. Milton Friedman and Peter Drucker argued that the business of business was business and it therefore had no social obligations.[21]

If the hallmark of the 1950s was a strong sense of obligation, from 1960 to 1990 there was a rising sense of entitlement and a growing tendency to shirk social responsibilities. Americans felt that government should be curtailed and that they should pay less taxes, but at the same time they demanded more government services on numerous fronts.[22]

The role and influence of religion declined. Divorce and abortion were legalized. Prayer was removed from most public schools.

A significant exception to the trend toward individualism was that environmental protection became a shared value. Early in the 1970s, a general consensus emerged in favor of a national environmental policy.[23] By 1990, about three-quarters of Americans consistently considered themselves environmentalists.[24]

In a widely cited article entitled 'Defining Deviancy Down', Senator (and sociologist) Daniel Patrick Moynihan pointed out that when there is too much deviance, societies relax their notions of deviance, and allow previously deviant behavior to become 'acceptable' or even 'normal'.[25] For example, Moynihan points out that our most significant response to the decline of the traditional family has been the redefinition of the term 'family' such that it came to include a wider variety of households. Similarly, the soaring rate of crime has led to a redefinition of what constitutes an 'acceptable level' of criminal activity.[26]

By the 1980s, many Americans paid only lip service to some core values and showed significantly lower commitment to others – marriage, for instance. Contentiousness rose considerably on other issues. Either way, the moral order was either hollowed out or weakened.

Respect for authority declined sharply. The index of people's overall confidence in the leadership of a long list of American institutions has fallen on average from a 1966 baseline (earliest data available) of 100 to 46 in 1990.[27] The list includes the military, Congress, the president, educational institutions, the media, and corporations.

In the process, Americans have become a tribe that savages and consumes its leaders. The average terms of police chiefs, school superintendents, and heads of universities were shortened. Heads of hospitals, the Post Office, the Department of Defense, the CIA, and the FBI were subject to intense criticism.

Above all, Americans came to treat presidents as if they were raw meat. For most of his years in office, Ronald Reagan could do no wrong; but then he retired under a cloud because of the Iran-Contra affair. Lyndon Johnson was consumed by controversy over the Vietnam War. Richard Nixon had to resign in mid-term. Gerald Ford was openly disrespected. And Jimmy Carter was treated as if he were grossly incompetent. The last president to survive two terms without having his legitimacy challenged was Dwight Eisenhower.

Voter turnout decline: 63 per cent of eligible voters voted in the 1960 presidential election, but in 1988 only 50 per cent of Americans voted. Polls found a growing number of Americans (by 1990, the overwhelming majority) were highly dissatisfied with politics, especially at the national level.[28] Running against Washington became a widely used political device, even by those who spent much of their adult life as 'insiders' in the nation's capital. Party loyalty declined while the proportion of Americans who see themselves as independent rose from 23 per cent in 1960 to 37 per cent in 1990.[29]

Alienation rose. Americans have been often asked whether they agree with such pointed statements as 'Do you feel that the rich get richer, and the poor get poorer?' and, 'Do you feel that the people running the country don't really care what happens to you?' The average response to a battery of such questions stood at 29 per cent in 1966, the first year of the poll. It more than doubled by 1990 to 61 per cent.[30]

A study that covered ten years of that period found that the percentage of persons in 'stable' job conditions (defined as either no job change or only a single change) fell from 67 per cent in the 1970s to 52 per cent in the 1980s. Meanwhile, the percentage of persons in 'unstable' job conditions (three or more job changes) doubled from 12 per cent to 24 per cent.[31] And this was before large-scale downsizing started.

Socioeconomic conditions and autonomy, 1960s to 1990s

The focus of my analysis is on what some call 'cultural' factors, on values and the ways they are embodied in society (the moral infrastructure), rather than on economic factors. For this reason, I do not examine changes in poverty levels, differential wages, and so on. These factors deserve a major study of their own. I discuss here only briefly the effect of these factors on one cardinal element of the good society, the scope of autonomy.

In the period under study, changes in socioeconomic conditions contributed both to enhancing autonomy – and dependency, and hence the loss of autonomy. The first development occurred as the socioeconomic conditions of the disadvantaged improved, even if their relative condition often did not. The second development was reflected in an increase in the number of those who have become dependent on government support. From 1960 to 1990, the number of persons on welfare increased by a factor of more than five, to 4.2 million by 1990.[32] How many of those who received benefits became more autonomous as their basic needs were met and how many grew psychologically dependent, and thus lost autonomy, or both, is a subject of much ideological debate, but little reliable social-scientific evidence.

In broader terms, there are strong data to show that although household income increased in the period at hand, this was due much more to more people people working per household than to an increase in real income per worker, especially after 1973. This development had strong autonomy-reducing effects as more and more members of the family felt they were forced to work outside the household and had severely limited time for other purposes, including family, community, and volunteer action.[33] Rising job insecurity added to the sense of constricted autonomy.

Family. The family declined, although it neither 'vanished' nor became an 'endangered species' as some argued. The proportion of all households that were families (married couples with at least one child) declined from 42 per cent in 1960 to 26 per cent in 1990.[34] However, more than 60 per cent of all children lived with both their biological parents,[35] and more than 70 per cent of all children still lived with two parents in 1990.[36]

The rate of divorce doubled between 1960 and 1990, with nearly half of all marriages ending in divorce by 1990.[37] While many of those who remarried divorced a second and third time, still half of all couples stayed married.[38] Both the rate of illegitimacy and its significance are particularly difficult to determine, but it should be noted that it rose sharply, nearly doubling from 21.6 per 1,000 births in 1960 to 41.8 in 1989.[39] The percentage of all births to single mothers rose by a factor of five from 1960 to 1990.[40]

Diversity. The percentage of non-white and Hispanic Americans more than doubled from 1960 to 1990.[41] The percentage of the population that is foreign-born increased from 5.4 per cent in 1960 to 7.9 per cent in 1990.[42] Men and women, hardly considered distinct social groups in the 1950s, have grown apart. Tension has resulted as the traditional definitions of gender roles were largely cast aside, while no new consensus arose as to what the expected, approved roles were.

Among racial and ethnic groups, an early indication of the rising division and tension came in race-based urban riots that occurred between 1965 and 1967, followed by the US Riot Commission's report, which declared the United states to be two nations, separate and unequal along racial lines.[43] Tensions between Jews and African Americans, once a liberal coalition for social change, rose.[44] African Americans felt threatened by immigrants and resented the special status accorded to them, leading to conflict with Hispanics and Asian Americans.

Tensions among many other ethnic and racial groups seem to have increased in the thirty years under scrutiny. While there is no reliable trend data, according to recent evidence from the early 1990s 'one out of every four or five adult Americans is harassed, intimidated, insulted, or assaulted for reasons of prejudice during the course of [each] year'.[45]

Indications of a thinning social fabric were not limited to gender, ethnic, and racial relations. The proportion of people who feel that 'most people can be trusted' declined from 58 per cent in 1960 to 37 per cent in 1993.[46] (The importance of trust to a community is expansively investigated by Francis Fukuyama.[47]) Loyalty of corporations to employees declined and so did the loyalty of employees to their corporations,[48] making corporations even less of a community.

Moral suasion versus other means of order. The mix of means used to sustain order changed in complex ways between 1960 and 1990. The picture is complicated because there were several changes in direction during this period, as well as cross-currents. The following serves only as a preliminary sketch.

The 1960s were marked by a fairly broad-based *reduction in the reliance on coercive means to maintain order without a parallel increase – indeed, with a decrease – in reliance on moral suasion.* Note that this is a relative statement: the reliance on coercive means was never as high in American society as in authoritarian societies, and it was not reduced sharply. Still 'street justice' was cut back following strong advocacy of individual rights and the rise of the civil-rights movement. The Civil Rights Voting Act was passed in 1964, numerous

African American mayors and police chiefs were elected, and police abuse of blacks declined (although it far from disappeared). Revulsion at the beating of dissenters during the Democratic Convention in Chicago in 1968 and the shooting of anti-war protesters at Ohio's Kent State University in 1970 made the National Guard and police departments show more restraint. The US Supreme Court, in a 1966 ruling (*Miranda vs Arizona*), imposed new limits on the police. Sodomy laws were repealed in eighteen states by 1975, and as of 1993, sodomy was legal in twenty-seven states.[49] Abortion, under most circumstances, was removed from the list of acts punishable by the state. Divorce was made easier in the late 1960s and early 1970s by 'no-fault' laws. Public support for corporal punishment in schools diminished.[50]

In the 1970s and especially in the 1980s, however, this trend of relying less on coercion reversed direction. Penalties for violating laws were increased, raised some more, and toughened again. The number of incarcerated Americans increased significantly, surpassing those of any industrial nation.[51] The incarceration rate rose per 100,000 from 120 in 1960 to 300 by 1990.[52] Though the Supreme Court overturned all existing death-penalty laws in 1972, within ten years thirty-seven states had reinstituted capital punishment.[53] Several states introduced new limitations on abortion and on homosexual activities. The federal Sentencing Reform Act, which took effect in 1987 (it was passed in 1984), ended the federal parole system and sharply increased sentencing generally.[54] Many states also enacted mandatory sentencing laws, beginning in the 1980s.

Moral suasion as a foundation of social order also declined in the 1960s as coercion declined, and as first welfare-liberal then laissez-faire conservative ideas gained in following. Traditional virtues lost much of their power, and no strong new shared values arose. The notion that one should not be judgmental gained currency;[55] various social and psychological theories that blamed the system for the misconduct of its 'victims' caught on, a trend that continued to evolve in the two decades that followed. Permissiveness was much extended, especially in areas such as sexual conduct and lack of achievement in schools. Even etiquette, Miss Manners reports, declined.[56]

As coercion increased again to some extent, moral suasion also changed direction. By the 1970s and especially the 1980s, the so-called cultural issues gained attention. They were put on the national agenda first by groups such as the Moral Majority, followed by the Christian Coalition, conservative elected officials such as Ronald Reagan and Dan Quayle, and then other public figures, ranging from Pat Buchanan to William J. Bennett. However, at least initially, these voices led to intensified divisiveness and intergroup conflict rather than a recommitment to old values or a new core of shared values. Intensive conflicts in school boards over issues such as the teaching of creationism, sex education, book-banning, and school prayers all illustrate the contentiousness of the era, leading some to refer to the rise in 'culture wars' in America.[57]

Taken *in toto*, the changes in the forces that maintained social order from

1960 to 1990 were paralleled by a sharp increase in *social disorder*. The data about the rise of anti-social behavior are well known: the crime rate rose from 1,126 incidents reported per 100,000 people in 1960 to 5,820 in 1990. Violent crime rose by four and a half times in that period, and the rate of murder doubled.[58]

In 1990, the percentage of the labor force in the United States that was in federal or state prison was 0.584, almost twice what it had been in 1960 (0.295 percent). If one includes persons on parole, probation, and otherwise under the jurisdiction of the criminal justice system, the number is much higher; over 6 per cent of the labor force was entangled in the criminal justice system.[59] Drug abuse, rather confined in 1960, spread considerably in the following decades.[60] (Less is known about changes in the incidence of alcoholism.[61])

While signs of antisocial behavior were on the rise, so was autonomy. The rise in *autonomy* can be seen in minorities gaining most legal rights and quite a few social and political ones. For example, the number of elected African American officials increased dramatically. Between 1970 and 1990, the number of African Americans elected to education posts had quadrupled; in local political office, the number increased by a factor of six; and the number of law enforcement offices more than tripled.[62]

The rise of autonomy for women is widely noted. By 1990, women were legally entitled to the same choices as men, with a few exceptions, such as certain combat duties and entering the Catholic priesthood. Furthermore, gender discrimination and sexual harassment in the workplace became illegal. However, several de facto barriers to women's equality persisted – for instance, the 'glass ceiling'.

Americans between the ages of eighteen and twenty-one gained the right to vote in 1971. The young were anything but a silent generation during the 1960s, leading the counter-culture (including the sexual revolution and the movement into drugs). They played a key role in the civil-rights movement and in the movement against the war in Vietnam.

THE LINE BETWEEN AUTONOMY AND ANARCHY

To what extent did the increase in autonomy in American society, and in other Western societies between 1960 and 1990, cross over the line that separates bounded autonomy from social anarchy? Before answering this question, the conceptual issues involved in drawing such a distinction must be further explored.

Conceptually, the line between bounded autonomy for individuals and sub-groups (a range of legitimate options within an affirmed normative framework) and social anarchy (the absence of order, regulation, and normative guidance) is relatively clear. So is the difference between less strict norms and anomie, between a reformed law and lawlessness. For an example of the difference, one may examine the life of tenured faculty members in university towns in less conservative parts of the country (such as Berkeley, California; Cambridge,

Massachusetts; and Palo Alto, California). They lead a rather autonomous life: they are strongly protected from economic and political pressures, but they are subject to the extensive norms of their college communities and even subject to some possible disciplinary acts (for instance, when they mismanage research funds or make hateful speeches) above and beyond those imposed by the law. They lead autonomous but hardly anarchic lives.

In contrast, outsiders who must traverse parts of the inner cities, in which open drug markets, rampant violence, and economic insecurity prevail, face anarchic conditions in which few mores protect the autonomy of outsiders. Anarchy also prevails in many public spaces, such as parks, plazas, and sidewalks, which people fear to use (especially after dark).

The sexual 'liberation' of the 1960s provides another example of the issue involved when autonomy and anarchy are not carefully separated. The movement started as a rebellion against tight mores that limited sexual relations to those between married, heterosexual couples, and then further regulated that relationship (e.g. religious prohibitions on the use of contraceptives even by married couples). Launched from this traditional basis, the sexual liberation movement did expand people's autonomy. However, it eventually led quite a few Americans to a state of normless anarchy which, for example, the Antioch guidelines try to overcome. At the extreme, this lack of moral guidelines led to movies that romanticize incest, such as *Spanking the Monkey*; the campaign by NAMBLA (the North American Man/Boy Love Association) to repeal the age of consent for sex, arguing that sex at age eight is 'too late'; and to less extreme developments, such as the spread of hard-core pornography and highly offensive sexually violent material on television and in rap songs.[63]

One indicator that helps to determine whether or not the line between autonomy and social anarchy has been crossed is if the mores are truly endorsed by those involved, or they are foisted on members of the community. There are several reports that show that many female teenagers feel they are under great pressure to engage in sexual intercourse from both young males and from males significantly older than themselves,[64] and that college women are often subject to date rape. These are indicators of social anarchy, not of autonomy.

Another area in which bounded autonomy has slipped toward anarchy is deregulation. To the extent that deregulation entailed removing meddlesome, costly, redundant, and unnecessary government interventions, the autonomy of private economic actors has been increased. To the extent that new modes of regulation (e.g. indirect regulation), less frequent inspections for those found to be compliant, or professional self-regulation have replaced earlier, tighter government controls, autonomy has advanced. However, to the extent that economic behavior has been left without effective public oversight, anti-social behavior in the private sector followed. This can be seen in the marketing of drugs that are known to be harmful, stonewalling by tobacco companies and large-scale manipulation of the books by defense contractors, among other examples.

The slippage of bounded autonomy toward anarchy is also evident in the deterioration of the content of television programs for children, in the re-emergence of sweatshops, and in the explosion of private funds contributed to politicians in exchange for legislative favors.

By these standards, if one focuses on the elements of society that are relatively intact, one finds that the changes from 1960 to 1990 enhanced the autonomy of many millions of Americans, especially women, minorities, and the young. At the same time, anarchy rose in terms of the waning of sexual mores. The net effect of deregulation and privatization and that of changes in many other sectors is not settled enough at this time to draw a firm conclusion, although it is evident that the absence of laws, or their slack enforcement, has caused pockets of anarchy. When all is said and done, it is difficult to assess clearly how much of the change between 1960 and 1990 enhances autonomy or increases anarchy. A good deal of both is a safe conclusion.

In general, the fact that erosion has been gradual, uneven, and far from complete is rather significant. Regeneration is much more attainable when the foundations are cracked but the building remains standing than after the foundations crumble and the building collapses. And although a regeneration of the moral order, to reiterate, does not require a return to the specific arrangements or values of an earlier era, American society requires a functional alternative to traditional virtue: a blend of voluntary order with well-protected yet bounded autonomy.

A NEW SWING: THE 1990S CURL BACK

Beginning with the 1990s, a regeneration has begun to set in, centripetal forces have increased, and they have begun to push the pendulum back to stave off anarchy and to restore social order. I refer to these new developments as a *curl back*, to stress that after a long movement in one direction, society began to turn the corner and face in the other direction (without, however, retracing its steps), but has not yet moved far enough in the new direction. Moreover, some of the first regenerative measures have been misdirected, and American society remains engaged in a profound moral dialogue regarding the nature of the renewed order. This includes debates about the proper combination of moral suasion and coercive means, and the limits of what is proper versus what is excessive in bringing autonomy back within bounds.

The specific direction of the curl back is still far from clear. Will it lead to the restoration of a traditional, 1950s-style social order? A fundamentalist religious order? A moderate social conservative one? Or regenerative communitarian? Behind these alternative scenarios lies the basic question of *whether curtailing individualism and re-establishing virtues will also cause a significant diminution of autonomy*. This is the core issue for the near-term future of American society, as it is for other societies in similar circumstances.

There were a fair number of signs even before the end of the 1980s that some social groups were seeking to restore a higher level of order but at the time, society at large did not follow their lead. Among the first to react to the decline in social order was a group of blue-collar workers (known as 'hard hats') who objected to the counter-culture as early as the late 1960s. The Christian right made its first significant organized public-political forays in the 1970s.

The main increase in power of the groups seeking restoration of an earlier order came in the early 1990s. The Christian right rose in membership and influence, as did secular social-conservative groups (such as the Council for National Policy, the John Randolph Club, and the Progress and Freedom Foundation). Together these groups dominated the 1992 GOP platform committee and its national convention. In 1994, the religious right controlled the GOP organization in twenty states and had substantial influence in thirteen more states, and on many schools boards.[65] In 1994, the religious right played a major role in the landslide election that resulted in Republican control of the House and Senate, for the first time since 1954, as well as numerous governorships and state assemblies.[66] Democratic political candidates increasingly courted these religious groups and responded to conservative cultural demands. (President Clinton often sought them out, speaking on family values and the importance of faith, and issuing a memo clarifying the right to pray in public schools.) William J. Bennett became a cultural hero. His *Book of Virtues*, which his publisher feared would not sell, became a run-away best-seller.[67]

The communitarian movement rose in this context and contributed to the newly intensified concern with the moral order. It called for a regeneration of virtue, drawing on some traditional values but deeply recasting others and formulating still other new ones, rather than attempting to reconstruct the past. Its platform and leaders argued that strong individual rights (autonomy) presumed strong personal and social responsibilities (moral order) rather than a return to an order based on imposed duties. Communitarians called for a shoring-up of the moral, social, and political foundations. Objecting to a liberal notion that the family was dysfunctional, defunct, or unnecessary, but not advocating a return to the traditional family, communitarians have favored a peer marriage in which father and mother have the same rights and responsibilities and both are more dedicated to their children.[68] Communitarians favored relying on moral dialogues, education, and suasion to win people to their ideals, rather than imposing their values by force of law. They showed faith in faith.

As of 1990, communitarian ideas and ideals, as a positive statement rather than mainly as a critical (and largely academic) stance, gained growing public attention. A new publication was launched and a platform was issued, along with several position papers on specific issues.[69] The platform was endorsed by more than 100 public leaders, not merely academics, including Betty Friedan; Richard John Neuhaus; the first head of the Environmental Protection Agency. William Ruckelshaus; the president of the American Federation of Teachers, Albert Shanker; former Congresswoman Claudine Schneider; and Daniel

Kemmis, the mayor of Missoula, Montana. Leaders from a variety of social and political positions embraced several of the communitarian ideas.[70] Soon leaders in other Western societies followed suit.[71]

The movement has had a considerable effect on public dialogue. Discussions of communitarian thinking appeared in all the major papers, magazines, and political journals. The number of articles written on the subject increased seven times between 1990 and 1995.[72] Senator Bill Bradley stated that communitarianism 'promises to shape a new political era in much the way progressivism reshaped our nation a century ago'.[73] It is the only significant group that provides a 'cultural' alternative to the religious right; but the extent of its effect on the direction of the curl back cannot yet be determined.

On numerous social issues, the intensified moral dialogue of the early to mid-1990s moved away from individualist notions toward social conservative or communitarian conceptions. There was a growing agreement among Americans about the importance of families, character education in schools, community bonds, and reciprocity among members of society – and their active participation in providing services to one another, including safety (note, for instance, the increase in community policing and neighborhood-watch patrols). It has been more and more widely recognized that the individualism of earlier decades (referred to as 'me-ism' in this curl-back period) had swung too far, and that one must reaffirm John F. Kennedy's often-cited credo: 'Ask not what your country can do for you, ask what you can do for your country'. Personal responsibility for self and social responsibilities toward others and the community became oft-invoked virtues.

Sexual permissiveness, driven in the 1960s by the mass introduction of the birth-control pill and a permissive individualistic ideology, was beginning to be reined in by the rise of sexually transmitted diseases, particularly AIDS, and a new normative thinking that struggled between a return to Victorianism and a linkage of sex to responsible conduct.

While the regeneration of values and institutions had begun, the debate between social conservatives and communitarians about the best direction for regeneration to follow was far from settled. The axis of debate has been along the question of whether moral regeneration must rely on traditional, especially religious, values, or whether it could draw on an inclusive moral dialogue that could include those who are committed to values on secular, humanistic grounds. This debate was paralleled by a discussion of whether the regenerated morality should rely mainly on suasion, or whether it could be rebuilt through legislation concerning social/moral matters, even if millions – even the majority – of members of society do not endorse these values. Typical were the debates on how to deal with homosexuals, abortion, school prayer, criminals, drug abuse, welfare mothers, violence on television, and teen sex.

As the debates raged, punitive measures reached a new high after 1990. Congress passed a bill mandating life sentences for repeat violent offenders ('three strikes and you're out') in 1994.[74] The numbers of prisoners and police were further increased.[75] Death sentences were more common, and appeals were curbed.

Indicators of anti-social behavior 'stabilized' after 1990 or began to recede. The overall rate of crime per 100,000 people fell from 5,820 in 1990 to 5,374 in 1994.[76] Violent crime, including murder, rape, and aggravated assault, has been on a downward trend, as are burglary and car theft.[77] In several major cities, including New York and most cities with populations of over 1 million, murder rates fell back in the early to mid-1990s.[78]

While alienation did not decline, voter turnout has bounced back from its low in 1988, when 50.2 per cent of eligible voters went to the polls, to 55.9 percent in 1992. Though participation in off-year congressional elections remains at little over one third, the participation in 1994 was slightly higher than in 1990.

Families may have stabilized, and, according to at least one study, more traditional families may be making a comeback: since 1990, the number of two-parent families with children has increased (between 1990 and 1995, there were 700,000 more two-parent families, reversing a twenty-year decrease);[79] the divorce rate has begun to fall back from its highs in the 1980s (20.5 in 1994 from 23.0 in 1980);[80] and the rate of teen pregnancy has decreased.[81]

As of the mid-1990s, it seems that the pendulum has begun to swing back toward more social order and some diminution of anti-social behaviour and anarchy, while the extent that the new order will be based on moral factors or on state powers, and its effect on autonomy, are still particularly unclear.[82] And there was no indication that in the future American society will resemble, come close to, or even significantly move in the direction of the kind of society individualists envision.

[. . .]

IMPLICATIONS FOR PRACTICE AND POLICY

To advance the regeneration of American society requires that the members of the society come together to commit themselves to a core of shared values, and find ways to embody these in the members' daily conduct and in social formations such as the family and the schools. There is, though, an overarching contextual matter that is of great importance for the foreseeable future. It concerns the relationship among the centrifugal effects of global economic forces, the responsive policies that have been developed to cope with them, and the social order, especially its moral foundation. Communitarian progress may be severely hobbled unless this issue is addressed.

In this area, too, the United States is leading a parade of Western nations that have committed their public and corporate policies to compete economically on a global level. This is reflected in the reduction of trade barriers; the development of free trade zones (e.g. by the European Community and the North American Free Trade Agreement); international agreements (e.g. GATT);

downward pressures on labor costs (to be able to compete with low-wage countries, which provide few benefits to their workers and have low social costs, especially environmental ones); the lowering of public benefits (the welfare state, in the European sense, which provides benefits not merely for the poor but for all members of society – for instance, low-cost college loans); and deregulation and cutting of inspections in matters ranging from the quality of meats to the safety of drugs. Corporations also have reduced their contributions to healthcare plans, pensions, and other benefits.

Benefits, wages, and job security have also been significantly curtailed by means of a sharply increased reliance on part-time employees. American dependence on 'contingent labor' has risen consistently, nearly doubling between 1990 and 1995 (from 1.2 million workers in 1990 to 2.0 million in 1994).[83] All of these measures together, which I shall refer to as the 'downsizing society', have resulted in a deep-seated and widespread sense of deprivation, insecurity, anxiety, pessimism, and anger.[84] These resentments have been further exacerbated by technological changes that seem to differ from previous ones in that they cause lasting high levels of unemployment, especially in Europe.

The social effects of these developments have been softened to some extent as second members of the same household (typically women and often mothers) turned to gainful employment, thus enabling the household income to rise since 1973 while that of each worker rose only marginally. But this adaptation had social costs of its own, and it cannot be drawn upon in the future as new socioeconomic pressures arise, unless child labor is to be further increased. (A large number of teenagers already work more than twenty hours a week while still in school).

Hence, the crowning contextual question for regeneration for the foreseeable future is *how far can a society tolerate public and corporate policies that give free rein to economic interests* and that seek to enhance global competitiveness, *without undermining the moral legitimacy of the social order?*[85]

Champions of individualism argue that, after a transition period, the increased ability to compete will generate many new jobs and a higher standard of living for most (if not all) members of society. If this is the case, the tension between the centrifugal forces of competitiveness and the needs of an orderly, good society will resolve itself. Communitarians, though, need to inquire which policies need to be followed if these individualists' predictions turn out to be excessively optimistic and the indicators of anger and social unrest continue to rise and to find additional expression in rising extremist movements, fundamentalism, xenophobia, and other forms of public resentment and rebellion, all of which threaten the social order.

This is a subject for which there are no ready answers, especially as the moral dialogue about these questions has just begun. Among the options that can be considered and which are communitarian in nature are:

1: *Slowing down the adjustments globalization entails.* This approach entails allowing employees and citizens in general more time to adjust to new policies and socioeconomic conditions. Western Europe, Australia, and New Zealand clearly choose to follow a slower path in these matters than the United States.[86] Removing tariffs, quotas, and other trade barriers and national subsidies gradually rather than rapidly is one such policy.

2: *Community jobs*.[87] American public policies tend to assume that there are jobs for people, and hence training is the way to deal with the unemployed and welfare recipients. However, if jobs are scarce, neither training nor disincentives for those who have grown to depend on welfare will work; at best they will lead some people (at high public cost) to find jobs, replacing others who would have held those jobs otherwise.

Politicians have talked about accelerating economic growth while keeping inflation down, thus creating millions of new jobs, but suitable macroeconomic policies have been elusive. Providing a massive number of public jobs, as was done during the Depression, is costly, while the resulting production is often of limited social merit.[88] Public funds might be allocated (under a workfare program to replace part of welfare, for example) to schools, hospitals, public libraries, environmental protection agencies, and other community institutions, to hire people to carry out work which these institutions would otherwise not have been able to afford. The institutions, in turn, would be required to provide monitoring, transportation, and child care. Boards need to be set up to include community and labor representatives to ensure that the new community jobs will not replace existing jobs.

3: *Work-sharing and enhancing job security*. Corporations and workers might agree to reduce overtime, and maybe even to introduce a shorter work week, if this will allow the employment of more people. One must note, though, that work-sharing on a significant scale would be possible only if wages were proportional to the time worked (rather than keeping full pay for shorter periods), a position even a few labor unions have come to endorse in Europe.

Agreements that 'trade' various desiderata (from the employees' viewpoint – e.g. higher health benefits) with enhanced job security also help soften the transition.

4: *Social basics*. While in Western Europe most political parties agree that the welfare state needs to be scaled back, few seek to dismantle it. In the United States, individualists (including laissez-faire conservatives and libertarians) have sought to roll up the social safety nets altogether, or indirectly destroy them by means-testing or partial privatization. One can reduce social costs, public expenditures, and dependency by lowering the safety nets without removing them. Psychological security does not rely so much on the specific level of support available if a person is out of work, disabled, or sick, as on the firm conviction that they and their children will receive some basic help; that they will not be cast into the street, without medical assistance or basic provisions.

A bi- or multi-partisan agreement to keep a basic social safety net out of politics, as part of the core of shared values, and to limit the partisan debate to the specifics of what is to be included would significantly curb the rising anxiety in the populace. This would provide an important prerequisite for a good society. Without secure social basics, autonomy is not available to millions of members of the society, a deficiency that, in turn, also undermines the social order.

5: *Voluntary simplicity*. In the longer run, a profound question must be faced: the pursuit of the affluent way of life by 6 billion people (as the underlying goal of global competitiveness) assumes that the earth can sustain a world that is like an American suburb (a direction in which China and India, for instance, have been moving), and that this is a world in which people will generally be content. Both assumptions seem ill-founded. After a worldwide sharing of social basics and the enhancement of autonomy that this entails, more consideration will need to be given to sources of satisfaction that are not resource-intensive (a search the affluent societies may best lead).

I cannot stress enough that this does not entail that the poor remain in their misery in order to leave enough resources for the affluent societies (and the elites in their societies) to maintain their standard of living. On the contrary, the more the affluent find other satisfactions, the more practical and political it will become to ensure that all members of the world's communities will be able to meet their basic needs.

Of interest in this context are values reflected in the notions of *combining* voluntary simplicity (willingly limiting one's consumption to materials that meet true needs and avoiding 'status goods', such as whatever is currently fashionable and the most recent technological devices) with *pursuit of other sources of satisfaction* that are not resource-intensive, such as those found in culture, family life, bonding with others, community-building, participation, voluntarism, and transcendental projects.

The counter-culture of the 1960s championed the rejection of consumerism, often in an extreme form, arguing that if people would consume little, they could drop out of work and find satisfaction in sunsets, cheap wine, and being high on marijuana. These ideas are incompatible with a modern economy (in which work generates not merely consumer goods but also health services, education, science, and art). But a considerable number of suburbanites, city-based young professionals, and campus-based academicians have adopted a much more moderate version of the same basic idea. They have recognized that the acquisition of marginal consumer goods (especially status goods) is a lower source of satisfaction than several other pursuits, which are low in cost: exercise and sports, for instance. And increased involvement in these reduces the need to work overtime, to become career-obsessed, and to suffer the attendant psychic and social consequences. Such a change in attitude toward status goods is also associated with an enhanced sense of security (social basics are easier to secure than a consumerist way of life) and a way to break out of the curse of the time squeeze.

People who embrace voluntary simplicity may also be those most willing to share goods with those in need, because such sharing will not threaten their satisfactions. This is the place where voluntary simplicity and communitarian thinking most clearly converge.

How can the ideals of voluntary simplicity be shared more widely? What practices can best embody them and which public policies can help promote them? The answer lies in moral dialogue that opinion-makers and public leaders can help initiate and nourish, but which they neither control nor command.

NOTES

1. Stephanie Coontz, *The Way We Never Were: American Families and the Nostalgia Trap* (New York: BasicBooks, 1992); Michael Elliott, *The Day Before Yesterday: Reconsidering America's Past, Rediscovering the Present* (New York: Simon & Schuster, 1996).
2. David Halberstam, *The Fifties* (New York: Villard Books, 1993), x. See also Alan Ehrenhalt, *The Lost City: Discovering the Forgotten Virtues of Community in the Chicago of the 1950s* (New York: BasicBooks, 1995).
3. J. Ronald Oakley, *God's Country: America in the Fifties* (New York: Dembner Books, 1986), 434–35.
4. Robin M. Williams Jr., *American Society: A Sociological Interpretation* (New York: Alfred A. Knopf, 1951). Williams outlines American values in fourteen 'value systems' to which Americans generally adhere. See also Ralph H. Gabriel, *American Values: Continuity and Change* (Westport, Conn.: Greenwood Press, 1974), 148–211.
5. The term itself was popularized much later by President Reagan.
6. Halberstam, *Fifties*, 116–20. The term 'American Century' was first used by Henry Luce, who, to quote Halberstam, envisioned 'an all-powerful America spreading democracy and riches across the globe' (ibid., 207). See also Ronald Steel, *Walter Lippmann and the American Century* (New York: Vintage Books, 1981).
7. Seventy-nine per cent of Americans approved of religious observances in public schools in a 1962 poll. *The Gallup Poll: Public Opinion 1935–1971, vol. III* (New York: Random House, 1972), 1779. See also Oakley, *God's Country*, 320–21.
8. Mary Ann Glendon, *Abortion and Divorce in Western Law* (Cambridge, Mass.: Harvard University Press, 1987), 10–11, 63–64.
9. Illegitimate births were approximately 5.3 percent of all births in 1960, calculated from data in George Thomas Kurian, *Datapedia of the United States 1790–2000* (Lanham, Md.: Bernan Press, 1994), 37, 40. The rate of illegitimacy is a complex statistic because many of the births are to couples in common-law marriages.
10. Douglas T. Miller and Marion Nowak, *The Fifties: The Way We Really Were* (Garden City, N.Y.: Doubleday, 1977), 147.
11. Ibid., 153–54.
12. Ehrenhalt, *Lost City*, 8–32.
13. For some comments on these points, see David Riesman, *The Lonely Crowd: A Study of the Changing American Character* (New Haven, Conn.: Yale University Press, 1950) and William Hollingsworth Whyte, *The Organization Man* (New York: Simon & Schuster, 1956).
14. Betty Friedan, *The Feminine Mystique* (New York: W. W. Norton, 1963), 68. See also pp. 15–32.
15. Godfrey Hodgson, *America in Our Time* (Garden City, N.Y.: Doubleday, 1976), 72.
16. Richard M. Fried, *Nightmare in Red: The McCarthy Era in Perspective* (New York: Oxford University Press, 1990).
17. Homer Hawkins and Richard Thomas, 'White Policing Black Populations: A History of Race and Social Control in America,' in *Out of Order?*, eds. Ellis Cashmore and Eugene McLaughlin (New York: Routledge, 1991), 65–86; Pamela

Irving Jackson, *Minority Group Threat, Crime, and Policing: Social Context and Social Control* (New York: Praeger, 1989).

18. Daniel Yankelovich Inc., *The Changing Values on Campus: Political and Personal Attitudes of Today's College Students* (New York: Washington Square Press, 1972); Morris Dickstein, *Gates of Eden: American Culture in the Sixties* (New York: BasicBooks, 1977).

19. For a discussion of the two kinds of individualism, expressive and instrumental, see Robert N. Bellah, Richard Madsen, William M. Sullivan, Ann Swidler, and Steven M. Tipton, *Habits of the Heart: Individualism and Commitment in American Life* (Berkeley, Cal.: University of California Press, 1985). Regarding the level of individualism, on page viii, the authors state: 'We are concerned that this individualism may have grown cancerous – that it may be destroying those social integuments that Tocqueville saw as moderating its more destructive potentialities, that it may be threatening the survival of freedom itself.'

20. Mildred Newman and Bernard Berkowitz, *How to Be Your Own Best Friend: A Conversation with Two Psychoanalysts* (New York: Random House, 1971), 7; Robert J. Ringer, *Looking Out for Number One* (Beverley Hills, Cal.: Los Angeles Book Corp., 1977).

21. Milton Friedman with the assistance of Rose D. Friedman, *Capitalism and Freedom* (Chicago: University of Chicago Press, 1962, 1982), 133–36; and Peter F. Drucker, *Management: Tasks, Responsibilities, Practices* (New York: Harper & Row, 1985), 343–45.

22. Lloyd A. Free and Hadley Cantril, *The Political Beliefs of Americans: A Study of Public Opinion* (New Brunswick, N.J.: Rutgers University Press, 1967). See especially table III-2 on p. 32.

23. Richard G. Niemi, John Mueller, and Tom W. Smith, *Trends in Public Opinion: A Compendium of Survey Data* (New York: Greenwood Press: 1989), 79. Since 1973, those thinking we spend too little on the environment have heavily outnumbered those thinking we spend too much.

24. *The Gallup Poll Monthly* (April 1991): 6.

25. Daniel Patrick Moynihan, 'Defining Deviancy Down,' *American Scholar* 62 (Winter 1993): 17.

26. Moynihan, 'Defining Deviancy,' 23–24, 27–29.

27. *Harris Poll* 11 (1 March, 1993). See also the *Gallup Poll Monthly* (April 1993): 24.

28. For example, R. W. Apple Jr., 'Polls Shows Disenchantment with Politicians and Politics,' *New York Times*, 12 August 1995.

29. Bruce E. Keith, David B. Magleby, Candice J. Nelson, Elizabeth Orr, Mark C. Westlye, and Raymond E. Wolfinger, *The Myth of the Independent Voter* (Berkeley, Cal.: University of California Press, 1992), 18.

30. Humphrey Taylor, *Harris Poll* 1 (4 January 1993): 3.

31. G. Pascal Zachary, 'Sharp Decline in Job Stability Is Found in a New Study, Contradicting Prior Data,' *Wall Street Journal*, 6 June 1995.

32. Kurian, *Datapedia*, 132. As a percentage of the total population, this represents a fourfold increase.

33. Juliet B. Schor, *The Overworked American: The Unexpected Decline of Leisure* (New York: BasicBooks, 1991).

34. U.S. Department of Commerce, *Household and Family Characteristics: March 1993* (Washington, D.C.: GPO, 1994), fig. 1; U.S. Department of Commerce, *Statistical Abstract of the United States* (Washington, D.C.: GPO, 1975), table 51, 56.

35. Calculated from statistics in Wade F. Horn, *Father Facts* (Lancaster, Pa.: National Fatherhood Initiative, 1995), 2, 10.

36. Ibid., 2.

37. Kurian, *Datapedia*; and U.S. National Center for Health Statistics, *Vital Statistics of the United States* (Washington, D.C.: GPO, 1993).

38. David Popenoe, 'American Family Decline, 1960–1990: A Review and Appraisal,' *Journal of Marriage and the Family* 55, no. 3 (August 1993): 532.
39. Kurian, *Datapedia*, 40.
40. U.S. National Center for Health Statistics, 'The Advance Report: Final Natality Statistics,' *Monthly Vital Statistics Report* 44, no. 3, supplement (September 21, 1995).
41. Kurian, *Datapedia*, 16–17.
42. 'The Immigration Story,' *Public Perspective* 6, no. 5 (August/September 1995): 13.
43. *Report of the National Advisory Commission on Civil Disorders* (New York: Bantam, 1968), v.
44. Jonathan Kaufman, *Broken Alliance: The Turbulent Times Between Blacks and Jews in America* (New York: Scribner, 1988); Michael Lerner and Cornel West, *Jews and Blacks: Let the Healing Begin* (New York: Putnam, 1995); Paul Berman, ed., *Blacks and Jews: Alliances and Arguments* (New York: Delacorte, 1994).
45. U.S. Commission on Civil Rights, *Racial and Ethnic Tension in American Communities: Poverty, Inequality, and Discrimination – A National Perspective* (Washington, D.C.: GPO, 1992, 71). From the testimony of Howard Ehrlich, director of research at the National Institute Against Prejudice and Violence.
46. Seymour M. Lipset, 'Malaise and Resiliency in America,' *Journal of Democracy* 6, no. 3 (July 1995): 7.
47. Francis Fukuyama, *Trust: The Social Virtues and the Creation of Prosperity* (New York: Free Press, 1995).
48. N. R. Kleinfield, 'The Company as Family, No More,' *New York Times*, 4 March 1996.
49. Hayden Curry, Denis Clifford, and Robin Leonard, *A Legal Guide for Lesbian and Gay Couples* (Berkeley, Cal.: Nolo Press, 1994).
50. 'Solutions? One Response to Lack of Discipline – Spanking – Has Lost Favor,' *Public Perspective* (October/November 1995): 32. Approval fell from 62 per cent in 1958 to 38 per cent in 1994.
51. Michael Wolff, Peter Rutten, and Albert F. Bayers III, *Where We Stand* (New York: Bantam, 1992), 296.
52. Alfred Blumstein, 'Prisons,' in *Crime*, ed. James Q. Wilson and Joan Petersilia (San Francisco: Institute for Contemporary Studies Press, 1995), 388, fig. 17.1.
53. Lee Epstein and Joseph F. Kobylka, *The Supreme Court and Legal Change: Abortion and the Death Penalty* (Chapel Hill, N.C.: University of North Carolina Press, 1992), 6–7.
54. Brian Forst, 'Prosecution and Sentencing,' in *Crime*, ed. Wilson and Petersilia, 377.
55. For discussion and references, see Amitai Etzioni, *The New Golden Rule* (London: Profile Books, 1997), chapter 5.
56. Judith Martin, 'Who Killed Modern Manners?,' *Responsive Community* 6, no. 2 (Spring 1996): 50–57.
57. James Davison Hunter, *Culture Wars: The Struggle to Define America* (New York: BasicBooks, 1991). See also Todd Gitlin, *The Twilight of Common Dream: Why America is Wracked by Culture Wars* (New York: Metropolitan Books, 1995).
58. U.S. Department of Justice, *Uniform Crime Reports for the United States: 1993* (Washington, D.C.: GPO, 1993), table 1; and U.S. Department of Commerce, *Historical Statistics of the United States: Colonial Times to 1970, Part 1* (Washington, D.C.: GPO, 1975), H952–61. The violent crime rate was 160 in 1960, and 732 in 1990; the rate of murder was 4.7 in 1960 and 9.4 in 1990.
59. Calculated from Kurian, *Datapedia*, 74, 164; and Richard B. Freeman, 'The Labor Market,' in *Crime*, ed. Wilson and Petersilia, 172.
60. Deborah M. Barnes, 'Drugs: Running the Numbers,' *Science* 240, no. 4860 (24 June 1988): 1729–31.
61. In 1960, the per capita consumption was 2.04 gallons. In 1990 it was 2.76 gallons, an increase of about 35 per cent. Kenneth J. Meier, *The Politics of Sin: Drugs, Alcohol, and Public Policy* (Armonk, N.Y.: M.E. Sharpe, 1994), 166.

62. Alfred N. Garwood, ed., *Black Americans: A Statistical Sourcebook* (Boulder, Colo.: Numbers & Concepts, 1991), 162.

63. For example, 'Pop That Pussy' and 'A F**k is a F**k' by 2 Live Crew, and 'Ain't No Fun (If the Hornies Can't Have None)' by Snoop Doggy Dogg.

64. Studies find that two-thirds of pregnant teens are impregnated by men over the age of twenty. (State of California, Department of Health Service, Vital Statistics Section, 1993.)

65. Steven V. Roberts, 'Onward Christian Soldiers,' *U.S. News & World Report*, 6 June 1994, 43.

66. People for the American Way, '60 Percent of Religious Right-Aligned Candidates Victorious,' press release issued 11 November 1994.

67. William J. Bennett, ed., *The Book of Virtues: A Treasury of Great Moral Stories* (New York: Simon & Schuster, 1993); see also Ben J. Wattenberg, *Values Matter Most: How Republicans or Democrats or a Third Party Can Win and Renew the American Way of Life* (New York: Free Press, 1995).

68. The Communitarian Network, *The Responsive Communitarian Platform: Rights and Responsibilities* (Washington D.C.: Communitarian Network, 1991), 5–7; Jean Bethke Elshtain, Enola Aird, Amitai Etzioni, William Galston, Mary Ann Glendon, Martha Minow, and Alice Rossi, *A Communitarian Position Paper on the Family* (Washington, D.C.: Communitarian Network, 1993). Also, William Galston, 'A Liberal-Democratic Case for the Two-Parent Family,' *Responsive Community* 1, no. 1 (Winter 1990/1991): 14; Pepper Schwartz, *Peer Marriage: How Love Between Equals Really Works* (New York: Free Press, 1994).

69. Communitarian position papers have been issued on gun control, character education, the family, health-care reform, organ donation, and diversity.

70. Among those whom the press has cited as supporting communitarian ideas are President Bill Clinton (Michael Kranish, 'Communitarianism: Is Clinton a Convert?,' *Boston Globe*, 22 May 1993; Charles Trueheart, 'At Death's Door – and Back Again,' *Washington Post*, 11 February 1992); Housing and Urban Development Secretary Henry Cisneros (Michael D'Antonio, 'I or We,' *Mother Jones*, May/June 1994); Jack Kemp (*Guardian*, 13 March 1995); Senator Bill Bradley (Jacob Weisberg, 'All Together Now,' *New York*, 24 July 1995); Vice President Albert Gore ('Communitarian Conceits,' *Economist*, 18 March 1995); and William J. Bennett (*Guardian*, 13 March 1995). See also 'The False Politics of Values,' *Time*, 9 September 1996.

71. Among them were German Chancellor Helmut Kohl; British Prime Minister John Major and his opposition leader, Tony Blair; and former European Union president Jacques Delors.

72. Data available from the Communitarian Network.

73. Michael D'Antonio and Michael Krasney, 'I or We?,' *Mother Jones*, May/June 1994, 23.

74. Forst, 'Sentencing,' 377–78.

75. Lawrence W. Sherman, 'The Police,' in *Crime*, ed. Wilson and Petersilia, 328; and Forst, 'Sentencing,' 377.

76. U.S. Department of Justice, Federal Bureau of Investigation, *Crime in the United States, 1994: Uniform Crime Reports* (Washington, D.C.: GPO, 1995), 5.

77. Ibid., 10, 38, 49.

78. Ibid., 14.

79. Carol J. De Vita, 'The U.S. at Mid-Decade' *Population Bulletin* 50, no. 4 (March 1996): 34.

80. Ibid., 34.

81. 'Rate of Births for Teen-agers Drops Again,' *New York Times*, 22 September 1995.

82. *A disclaimer*: societies are complex beings, that as a rule change direction gradually; and on some fronts before others. One can always find indicators that point in different directions, and hence both reasonable people and social scientists can

reach different conclusions as to their meanings. However, just as economists can draw a picture when seven (or even six) out of eleven leading indicators point one way, and so can the Federal Reserve when it receives conflicting reports from different parts of the country, so can a sociologist.

83. Barnaby J. Feder, 'Bigger Roles for Suppliers of Temporary Workers,' *New York Times*, 1 April 1995.
84. The New York Times, *The Downsizing of America* (New York: Times Books, 1996); Susan J. Tolchin, *The Angry American: How Voter Rage is Changing the Nation* (Boulder, Colo.: Westview Press, 1996).
85. Ralf Dahrendorf, 'A Precarious Balance: Economic Opportunity, Civil Society, and Political Liberty,' *Responsive Community* 5, no. 3 (Summer 1995): 13–39.
86. Joan Warner, 'Clinging to the Safety Net,' *Business Week* (Industrial/Technology Edition), 11 March 1996, 62. 'Australia, and John Howard, Opt for Change,' *Economist*, 9 March 1996, 31–32.
87. Amity Shlaes, 'Germany's Chained Economy,' *Foreign Affairs* 73, no. 5 (September/October 1994): 109–24. See also Amitai Etzioni, *A Compassionate Approach: Community Jobs and Prevention* (Washington, D.C.: Communitarian Network, 1995); and Jeremy Rifkin, *The End of Work: The Decline of the Global Labor Force and the Dawn of the Post-Market Era* (New York: Putnam, 1995).
88. James P. Pinkerton, *What Comes Next: The End of Big Government – And the New Paradigm Ahead* (New York: Hyperion, 1995), 313–17.

'Beyond the Lure of Off-the-Shelf Ethics' by Geoff Mulgan

Geoff Mulgan was the co-founder and first director of the London-based think-tank Demos, which forged close links in the 1990s to the British Labour Party, especially its leader Tony Blair, who became Prime Minister in 1997. Mulgan was then taken on as an advisor and, at the time of writing, works for the Prime Minister's Policy Unit. He has written many pamphlets and short articles on numerous areas of public policy. His books include *Connexity* (Chatto and Windus, 1997) and *Politics in an Antipolitical Age* (Polity Press, 1995). The extract is from a newspaper article published at a time when the communitarian agenda was most prevalent in British political debate and formed a part of the way in which the Labour Party responded to conservative anxiety about morality.

'BEYOND THE LURE OF OFF-THE-SHELF ETHICS' (1995)*

Geoff Mulgan

Five years ago, it was not unreasonable to expect that the 1990s would be a decade of peace and prosperity, when, as John Major put it, nations would be at ease with themselves. Instead the dominant mood of the mid-1990s has turned out to be insecurity, not only about jobs, but about everything from crime to the state of public values.

In some parts of the world, anxieties of this kind tend to push people into reaction: to cling to nationalism or racism, and to search for scapegoats. In the Western world insecurity seems to be having a rather more benign effect, promoting an intensive search for a sense of community or cohesion, for ties that can bind people together.

The smarter politicians have all been sensitive to this shift. In Britain, the language of community and neighbourhood has rapidly moved from the margins of Liberal pavement politics to become a defining part both of Tony Blair's new Labour and John Major's softer civic Conservatism. In America, the shift has found expression in the communitarian movement, which has won support on both left and right for its programme of self-help and moral education, and for

---

* Geoff Mulgan, 'Beyond the Lure of Off-the-shelf Ethics', *The Independent* (30 January 1995).

its call for new responsibilities to match the growth of new rights. In Germany, Chancellor Helmut Kohl has explicitly drawn on communitarian ideas, and in France, Sir James Goldsmith's manifesto, *The Trap*, crystallised a widespread desire to return to a more localised, more traditional way of life against the depredations of rationalism, high science and free trade.

Some have tried to interpret this swing away from the high individualism of the 1980s, from the promise that freedom could be expanded without limit or side-effects, as a classic pendulum swing from right to left. But this misreads the significance of what may turn out to be a rather deeper climatic shift, which is just as threatening for the libertarian new left and the technocratic social democrats as it is for the free-market right. For what seems to be happening is a return to clearly articulated principles of right and wrong, and a rejection of the common alibis of recent decades that made it possible for crime to be blamed on society, or for a deceitful and intrusive newspaper to justify its actions on the grounds of market demand.

This shift, towards what can loosely be termed communitarianism, has drawn on several diverse currents. One is philosophy. Since the late 1970s, many of the ablest political philosophers have been leading a powerful re-evaluation of the dominant liberal assumption that individuals are free-standing entities, able to choose whatever values, identities or roles they wish. According to thinkers such as Alasdair MacIntyre, Michael Sandel, Charles Taylor and Michael Walzer, this view is not only philosophically flawed, but also likely to foster societies without any soul or any capacity to cohere or generate mutual trust. By turning choice into a totem, a good that stands above all others, Western societies have not only misread human nature but also misunderstood morals and ethics which, far from being things that can simply be picked off the supermarket shelf, are embedded in the ways we live our lives.

Such ideas have had little direct political influence. But they have given intellectual backbone to the second source of communitarian ideas, a political swing of the pendulum away from the more extreme radical free-market individualism of Britain and the USA in the 1980s, and the claim that there is no such thing as society and no virtue in intermediate institutions. A decade later, it is striking that these societies that went farthest towards deregulation now have the most anxious, insecure populations. They also have the most vocal commentators arguing that rising crime, bad behaviour and the decline of traditional forms of authority are symptoms of societies that are out of balance and have lost some important, if invisible, glue that held them together.

In some respects this is nothing new; a century ago there was no shortage of thinkers and politicians warning that new industries and cities were destroying old communities and corroding people's sense of moral values. But the sheer pace of change in recent years, driven forward by rapid globalisation and declining deference, has lent new force to such fears.

The third source of the turn to communitarianism is a shift in attitudes about how change is achieved. According to the communitarians, a culture that emphasises only rights and freedoms inevitably tends to engender irresponsible behaviour: promiscuous HIV-carriers, selfish drivers, parents who do not consider their children's interests, citizens who demand the right to be tried by jury but are unwilling to serve on one. The answer, they argue, is a change of heart, a cultural shift towards an acceptance of greater personal responsibility. Like Green politicians, they argue that people should act for themselves rather than wait for governments to solve problems.

The fourth source is a change in perceptions about government. Throughout most of this century, politics has been shaped by the idea that government can act on society through professionals working in ordered, top-down bureaucracies. Social workers, social citizenship, social security and socialism were all manifestations of belief in a (usually national) society. In the last quarter of a century, however, this cluster of ideas has fallen apart. Governments now seek to act on the choices of individuals and families, to develop services through a multiplicity of agents, to relate to specific communities rather than a single society, and to pass moral responsibility down from the whole to the parts. In this sense, Margaret Thatcher was not so far off the mark in saying there is no such thing as society. Society may still exist but it is less tangible, less meaningful and less useful as a guide to policy.

Together these factors are transforming the political climate. Evangelistic faith in the transformative powers of the market seems as absurd as the faith in government of an earlier generation of social democrats. But the swing is not understandable solely as one from individualism to communitarianism. It is also a swing away from ideologies (both of the free market and of the left) and back to ethics, away from large solutions to small ones, and away from universal analyses and prescriptions towards a concern for the particular and the incommensurable.

Needless to say, none of these ideas is uncontested. The clearest expression of communitarian ideas, set out in *The Spirit of Community* by Amitai Etzioni, the founder of the American movement, has called forth an extraordinary range of attacks from all sorts of guardians of orthodoxy, whether liberals or feminists, traditional socialists or free-market conservatives.

Two criticisms stand out. The first is that communitarian ideas are essentially nostalgic, harking back to a lost world of happy families and tight-knit neighbourhoods. Although, as the Henley Centre has shown, two-thirds of British people still live within five miles of where they were born and brought up, today's societies are far more mobile. It is easy to drive miles to work, shop, or enjoy ourselves. Telecommunications and television widen horizons and detach people from those who happen to live around them. And life (as in the film *Four Weddings and a Funeral*) revolves more around networks of friends than settled families. If there are communities, they are as likely to define themselves around work, fun, religion or interests as place. Rather than bringing people together, they are just as likely to be defined by the ways in which they differ from dominant values.

The second criticism is that communitarian arguments inevitably become illiberal. If they can't succeed in persuading people to change their behaviour, they will find it hard to resist the temptation to use the law as a tool of social engineering – by making it harder to divorce, by introducing compulsory community service for teenagers, or by penalising mothers who knowingly have children without the means to support them.

The problem with this line of argument, however, is that it is hard to conceive of any government which doesn't make some judgements about right and wrong, better and worse, and which doesn't make some attempt at social engineering. This is as true of taxes as it is of penal policy, and it was as true of the new right (as Margaret Thatcher put it, 'economics is the means, the aim is to change the soul') as it was of social democrats.

But for now, few of the communitarians have quite such ambitious objectives. Most favour a soft communitarianism of persuasion and pluralism, rather than a more strident and legally enforced assertion of how people should behave. In this guise, they win wide support for their call for stronger intermediate-level institutions, neighbourhood schools, family centres or voluntary organisations to give expression to community in ways that the top-down models of local government can no longer achieve.

Communitarian arguments have also won over many to the virtues of self-help and self-reliance that were strong on both left and right in the nineteenth century, before the huge expansion of the state. And the idea of balancing responsibilities and rights in practical ways, by policies which end 'something for nothing' benefits systems, or require state-subsidied university students to give something back, not only by repaying their loans but also by taking part in community service, fit rather well with public common sense.

In these softer forms, communitarianism is likely to be an important fixture in politics of the late 1990s. Its themes can be found in the ideas of politicians as diverse as Paddy Ashdown, Gordon Brown, David Willetts, Alan Howarth and Frank Field. It appears to offer a partial solution to the upward pressure on public spending and to fears that our society is fragmenting into mutual indifference. So long as it does not go too far in seeking to impose consensus on contested issues such as family life, and so long as it does not appear to roll back hard-won rights, particularly of women, it has a powerful appeal.

But behind these arguments there is a deeper problem. In the era of MTV and supermarket religions, where is the authority that will make people behave in more communitarian, more responsible ways? Many on the right still argue that the old institutions of church and family, monarchy and traditional authority can call forth better behaviour with a language of duty. But this may be a vain hope.

Instead, ours is an age where, as Gilles Lipovetsky argued in his fascinating, if extreme, book *Le Crépuscule de Devoir* ('The Twilight of Duty'), inherited duties and commandments have lost their pull. Today, for better or worse, everyone is brought up to question and to contest, and to think about ethics in much more personal terms. This may be why a more personal language of responsibility, rooted not in duty but in individual choices and the values each of us learns and experiences through school and life, fits much better with the times. But if this is true, it may become hard to find any institution with the authority to call on people to make significant sacrifices for others, for their children, and still less for future generations.

This distinction between responsibility and duty suggests both the power and the limit of the communitarians' argument. In its socially conservative guise, where community is used as a codeword for shoring up older institutions that can no longer either win legitimacy or delivery, it may divide far more than it unites. It may even remind people why their ancestors strove so hard to reject the oppressive demands of ancient institutions that claimed authority and demanded allegiance.

But as a way of bringing ethics back into the mainstream, and overturning the dominant economic view that individuals are only selfish, materially moti- vated and separate, it has huge potential. It can bring new insights to bear on the ties between individuals and larger groups, on the deficiencies of welfare and problems of social order. It can illuminate the vital role of self-help in the future delivery of everything from the environment and health to education. Perhaps it can even restore to politics and leadership some of the meaning it has lost during a grey period of underachievement.

7

FEMINISM

Kate Nash

INTRODUCTION

INTRODUCTION

As a movement, feminism has long been dealing with the difficulties of fitting women *as* women into political discourses couched in universal terms but actually developed with men in mind (Bacchi, 1990). In recent years, however, in conjunction with the rising influence of postmodernism and poststructuralism, feminists have undertaken a systematic critique of the universalism through which 'justice' has been conceived in Western political philosophy. This questioning links the most topical themes of contemporary feminist political theory – public/private distinctions, equality and difference, group rights, **essentialism** and the subject of feminism – and marks a break with previous classifications of feminism into liberal, Marxist/socialist and radical feminism. The emphasis on sexual difference within poststructuralist feminism does give it a certain affinity with 'radical feminism'. But, as we shall see, the anti-essentialist thrust of much contemporary feminist political theory also problematises the terms on which radical feminism was based, calling into question the very subject of feminism itself, 'women'. Debates over whether sexual difference is fundamental and how differences within the category 'women' are to be conceived make recourse to the radical feminist concepts of 'patriarchy' and 'women's oppression' unattractive to many contemporary feminist theorists.

THE FEMINIST CRITIQUE OF ENLIGHTENMENT UNIVERSALISM

Contemporary feminists have an ambivalent relationship to the ideal of universal equality around which the women's movement has actually mobilised since the nineteenth century. As Anne Phillips notes in an article called 'Universal Pretensions in Political Thought', the Enlightenment ideal of universalism has given feminists a critical distance from contingencies of time and place, providing standards of equality and justice against which to measure the legitimacy of actual differences in the world. The view of human beings as essentially equal and therefore deserving of universal rights or capable of living according to abstract rules of justice has proved a powerful tool in the struggle against women's inferiority (Phillips, 1992: 10).[1] However, in recent years, suspicions that Enlightenment universalism is not inherently progressive have been growing.

In some cases, this suspicion hardens into the certainty that women have nothing to gain from 'malestream' theory and practice. Carole Pateman, for example, has analysed texts in the history of political philosophy to show how the way in which Enlightenment universalism was modelled on men means that its very concepts and categories exclude women's specificity *as* women. Political philosophers have tended to politely ignore how women are described by writers from previous centuries, supposing that their ideas are simply out of date in this respect and irrelevant to their political philosophy as such. Locke's statement in the *Second Treatise*, for example, that a wife's subordination to her husband has a 'Foundation in Nature' and that his will must prevail in the household since he is naturally 'the abler and the stronger' (quoted in Pateman, 1989: 121) has been passed over without comment. Similarly, feminists themselves, while not ignoring how women have been described, have tended not to see the basic terms of political theory itself as shot through with sexism. The assumption has been that universalism should be extended to incorporate women; that it is the anomalous descriptions of women that are wrong and not the universalism itself. Pateman's position has, however, been very influential, so that the current tendency in feminist political theory is to see political philosophy as constructed with male characteristics and specifically masculine social positions in mind such that its normative principles can never be genuinely universal.[2] There are two strands to this argument.

First, it is argued that the sexes are different in the ways in which they reason. While men are detached, preferring to judge according to rights and universal principles – an 'ethic of justice' – women experience a closer relationship to others and prefer to make judgements based on feelings of responsibility in particular situations – an 'ethic of care' (**Gilligan**, 1982). Interestingly, this critique takes traditional ideas of differences in women's and men's capacities to reason, and reverses them: women's resistance to Kantian moral reasoning is taken as valid, and indeed, superior to 'empty' masculine judgements. It is based on Nancy **Chodorow**'s work on women's psychology as it has developed in capitalist society. She argues that, given that women mother, the masculinity with which boys must identify in order to become men is that of the distant father, uninvolved in the concrete relationship of care for the child (Chodorow, 1978). One of the chief topics for 'maternalist' political theorists is the way in which masculine subjectivity has influenced the formulations of political philosophy itself: the very categories of rights, universal principles, the rational individual itself, are seen as aspects of a masculine defence of the self against the dangers of love and the fear of losing oneself in the (m)other (DiStefano, 1991). However, although this strand of feminist political thought has obvious appeal in its promise to displace 'malestream' theory altogether, the project of creating a new form of political philosophy based on love and care has proved problematic (see e.g. Noddings, 1984). So far, no attempt has met with great acclaim from feminists. In part, this is no doubt due to the **anti-essentialist** impetus of feminist thought. It is also related, however, to the difficulty of thinking justice without universals (Phillips, 1992) and to unease with the dangers of reproducing ancient stereotypes about differences between the sexes, even if their value has been reversed.

The second strand of this feminist critique argues that the universalism of modern political theory is premised on individuals who have roles and activities that have been limited to men. This is not just of historical interest, since it precludes individuals engaged in the types of activities in which women continue to be primarily involved. The differences in this case are those of biology and social position rather than of psychology. They include differences in reproductive capacities as well as roles in the traditional sexual division of labour in which men are breadwinners and women are responsible for work in the home and the care of children, the sick and elderly. Feminists have long recognised that political philosophy has been constructed with male heads of households in mind so that the 'universal rights of man' were just that and did not include women. However, whereas it tended to be argued that women *should* have the rights that men enjoyed – that rights should be genuinely universal – it is now being asked whether justice can be achieved in this way. If women and men are different and rights have been granted to men *as* men, then perhaps gaining those rights cannot be expected to advance the cause of justice between the sexes. However, without a model of gender-neutral, universal rights, how can we conceive of justice at all? It is at this point that the question of universalism links to the themes of the public/private distinction and contemporary debates over equality and difference.

PUBLIC/PRIVATE DISTINCTIONS

The question of universalism raises the issue of the public/private distinction because, both in political philosophy and also in practice, women have been positioned in the private, domestic sphere, while universalism applies only to the public sphere. It is this distinction which has allowed political philosophers to build models of the polity supposedly premised on the attributes of universal humanity and yet to see women as naturally subordinate. Where women have been mentioned at all, it is usually in relation to their duties and 'natural subordination' in the private domestic sphere. In fact, for most philosophers, if women 'fail' to occupy their proper position as women, social disorder will be the inevitable result. This is strongly stated in many cases. For Rousseau, for example, women must submit to their husbands; even in cases of overt injustice, a wife must 'suffer the wrongs inflicted on her . . . without complaint', because social stability depends on the 'natural' order of the family (Rousseau, 1974: 333; Pateman, 1989: ch. 1). Feminists have also, however, uncovered less overt statements of women's inferiority as a result of their position in the private domestic sphere. John Stuart **Mill** – chief philosopher of first-wave feminism – argued that women confined to the home were likely to be narrow-minded and lacking a sense of justice. This was one reason why Mill thought they should have access to education and the possibility of professional occupation. However, he assumed that most women would 'choose' to be wives and mothers, even if they had the right to work outside the home, thereby implying that they would continue to suffer from inferior political judgement in comparison with their husbands, actively involved in the public sphere. From this point of view, they would continue to be a block on modern progress (Mill, 1989: 202–5; Pateman, 1989: 26–7).

For contemporary feminist political theorists, these examples open up two important, but quite different, lines of argument. The first concerns the fact that the universal rights exercised by individuals have no place in the private domestic sphere, seen as the domain of 'natural' family relations. Feminists have long been concerned with this problem, campaigning against domestic violence and sexual abuse, and, in the nineteenth century, for married women's right to their own property and wages, equal rights to divorce and so on (Shanley, 1989). In principle, these battles have been won. These days, it is rarely publicly argued that, for example, wife-beating is a private matter. It should be noted, though, that marital rape was only made illegal in Britain in 1991, and sexual violence is far from being a thing of the past (Lovenduski and Randall, 1993: 330).

However, in recent years, the public/private distinction itself has become a matter of debate in feminist theory. Feminist political theorists have given their attention to reconceptualising the relationship between public and private rather than dismissing it as an ideological construction perpetuating the subordination of women. *Some* kind of distinction between public and private, if not quite that prescribed by Liberalism, is seen as necessary to provide appropriate limits on state action. This has become especially pertinent with the demise of Soviet communism, given the way in which totalitarianism in these societies was linked to the lack of any distinction between public and private. The reconceptualisation of the public/private distinction by feminists is also marked by concerns that women lack privacy in the domestic sphere and that this is a right that needs to be articulated and defended (Okin, 1991).

Feminists are also concerned with the complexities of the distinction between public and private in contemporary society. It is, in fact, quite common now to refer in the plural to public/private distinctions. This is due, in part, to the complexity of advanced capitalist society itself in comparison with the models of political philosophy developed with simpler societies in mind. In fact, as

Pateman has pointed out, there has always been ambiguity about precisely where the public/private distinction is drawn. The distinction between political society and the domestic sphere that is clear in Enlightenment political philosophy is often forgotten in more recent political theory, displaced by the distinction between state and civil society which then implicitly includes it (Pateman, 1989: 119–24). Furthermore, gendered public/private distinctions have multiplied, in part as a result of feminist politics. In an article on the contested confirmation of **Clarence Thomas** as a member of the Supreme Court in 1991, Nancy Fraser analyses the meanings given to publicity and privacy by those engaged in the debate over whether Thomas, accused of sexual harassment by **Anita Hill**, was a suitable appointee. This example brings out the way 'public' and 'private' may be thought of less as separate spheres and more as categories that are always coded with gendered meanings. It also brings out the way 'public' and 'private' are deployed in relation to racial and ethnic meanings, since Thomas demanded that privacy be accorded to him as a black man, a member of a group whose sexual activities have long been subjected to unjust scrutiny by whites. Fraser invites feminists to see public/private distinctions as specifically constructed in particular contexts, as multiple in meaning, and as political: it is the power to define what should count as public or private that is crucial (Fraser, 1998).

This understanding of public/private distinctions is in sharp contrast to the topography of liberal political theory in which it is implied, if not explicitly stated, that the public sphere is synonymous with politics, while the private sphere is that of personal freedom.[3] The reading selected here, 'Public–Private Distinctions', extracted from *The Politics of Community* by Elizabeth Frazer and Nicola Lacey, deals in more detail with this issue. Frazer and Lacey argue that justice for women requires legal rights but also transformation of practices of work, access to political power and so on, that are not readily achieved simply through the exercise of the law. We must take seriously the feminist slogan 'the personal is political' if such changes are to be possible.

This brings us to the second line of argument opened up by women's position in the private domestic sphere: the way this circumscribes participation in the public sphere. The difficulties of participation are easily understood at the most basic and practical of levels: in many cases, women's domestic responsibilities work against full participation in paid work on the same terms as men and also inhibit their involvement in civic associations and political parties. Furthermore, participation in the public sphere is gendered in meaning. Women's capacities and domestic responsibilities continue to be categorised as natural rather than political, or to be ignored altogether in the public sphere. We will look at this question in the following two sections: in relation to the inadequacies of universalist legislation aimed at achieving equality, and at the solution offered by group rights to participation in political decision-making in the public sphere.

EQUALITY AND DIFFERENCE

Legal reforms aimed at achieving equality, like the **British Sex Discrimination Act,** the **Equal Treatment Directive** issued by the **European Union** and the modern interpretation of the **equal protection clause** of the US Constitution are universal in form. They are designed to realise equality by decategorising, proscribing the use of sex or marital status as a basis for action in particular social spheres (Frazer and Lacey, 1993: 79). Legally, they operate to ensure that women have the same formal rights as men, outlawing discrimination on the basis of sex.

As feminists have pointed out, however, decategorisation does not thereby ensure women's equal access to social, economic and political benefits enjoyed by men. If women have the right to be treated the same as men, this is of only limited value where physical and social differences remain significant. Feminists argue that, insofar as rights have been modelled on the masculine individual, wherever women do not conform to the male norm, specifically female differences are impossible to accommodate. This is most graphically illustrated in the case of the 'male comparator test' that has been used in US law to decide on cases of discrimination in the case of pregnancy. The principle is that if a man in a similar situation would have been treated differently, then the woman claiming discrimination has a case. Of course, this is literally impossible in the case of pregnancy. Nevertheless, rulings have been made on this basis. In 1975, judges in the Court of Appeals ruled that a pregnant woman dismissed from her job was not treated less favourably than a similarly situated man, while, on other occasions, judges more sympathetic to women's rights have ruled that pregnancy may be compared to disability or illness for the purposes of carrying out the comparison with a similarly situated man (Bacchi, 1990: 115; Frazer and Lacey, 1993: 81–2). Similarly, the way in which universalist law works according to the male norm makes it very difficult to contest inequalities in the public sphere arising from women's different position in the domestic sphere. Universalism makes policies of affirmative action that would enable women to 'catch up' with men in male-dominated spheres impossible to consider, let alone defend; and 'family-friendly' working practices are difficult to institute in the name of equality between the sexes.

A further challenge to the universalist model of equality has come from black feminists, who ask the pertinent question 'equality with whom'? The feminist preoccupation with equality tends to neglect the fact that all men are far from equal, that black men are systematically disadvantaged in relation to white men and that, with respect to inequalities of 'race' and ethnicity, black women share more with black men than with white women. For example, high rates of unemployment and low wages for black men contribute to the fact that black mothers are more likely to work full-time than white mothers, either as the main breadwinners of a household or sharing that role with a man. Black women's experiences of combining work and care for their homes and children have been quite different from those of white women (hooks, 1984: 133–4). The challenge of black feminists is, then, a challenge to the white feminist pre-occupation with differences between the sexes at the expense of other structures of inequality, structures in which white feminists are themselves directly implicated insofar as they ignore racism. Again, insofar as this issue has been taken on in feminist political theory, the emphasis has shifted from difference to differences. Not only differences of race and ethnicity, but also those of sexuality, class and disability are put forward as inequalities with which feminism must be concerned if we are to bring about changes that will benefit all women.

The feminist critique of the principle of legal equality is highly developed, then. It has, however, been much less easy to come up with alternatives. In part, this is because feminist political theorists are often concerned with practicalities, so that utopian models of sexual equality have little appeal insofar as they have no purchase on existing reality. It is true that, in the USA, 'special rights' feminists have argued that the law should be sexually differentiated so that women's specificity *as* women will be valued rather than ignored or an obstacle to equality. This position is allied to that of the 'maternalists' outlined above; their ultimate aim is the revaluation of caring in society (Bacchi, 1990: 115–17). For the most part, however, feminist political theorists have been unsympathetic to this position, especially since it has led to feminists facing each other on opposite sides in the US courts (for example, in the notorious '**Sears case**': see Bacchi, 1990: 10; Scott, 1990). Furthermore, this 'maximalist' model of sexual difference makes it difficult to appreciate differences between women. Even if it were possible to gain special rights for women, the danger is that stereotypes of women would be confirmed, leading to discrimination against those women who do not conform to either the female or the male norm.

As Anne Phillips argues, a convergence between the sexes so that gendered differences are minimised would seem to be a better alternative if equality is the aim. This convergence need not be orientated towards the male norm, leading to the disappearance of the activities and values previously associated with women, as maternalists fear. It is possible that men might take on a greater share of unpaid care, changing social values in the process. This leaves the question of physical differences, much more difficult to deal with on this 'minimisation' model. If convergence were combined, however, with greater attention to human welfare needs, including those of reproduction, then sex-specific activities, like pregnancy, would no longer be so problematic. Carol Bacchi argues that historically it is only where there is a lack of welfare provision that feminists have been forced into the unhelpful dichotomy of 'sameness–difference' (Bacchi, 1990: xvi–xviii).

GROUP RIGHTS AND POLITICAL PARTICIPATION

The principal alternative to legal equality through universalism with which contemporary feminist political theorists have been concerned is democratic political equality through difference. It is at the level of political participation that contemporary feminist theorists have been most inclined to argue for 'special rights'. One of the best examples of such a model of democracy is that of Iris Marion Young.

In the extract reproduced here from 'Polity and Group Difference', Young sets out an argument against universalism, arguing that the generality of the common view ideally achieved through democratic politics according to the civic republican tradition actually produces inequalities. While Young situates her own work in this tradition, insofar as it opposes the virtues of public participation to the private interests of Liberalism and capitalism, she sees its universalism as supporting already existing exclusions rather than including all citizenship on an equal basis. Following the line of the feminist critique of universalism with which we are now familiar, Young argues that modernity involves a split between public and private, reason and emotion, men and women, such that women's concerns are not seen as appropriate to the public sphere. Furthermore, she claims that other groups suffer similar exclusion on the basis of their differences from the white, male norm; notably ethnic minorities, sexual minorities, poor, disabled and old people. The genuine inclusion of all citizens in political participation requires group-differentiated rights to collective organisation, to input into policy-making and to veto policies that directly affect the groups to which they belong. This kind of heterogeneous but equal participation, will, according to Young, be likely to produce further demands for group-specific rights, to affirmative action, for example. In this respect, her model of political participation is also a theory of special legal rights to counteract the inequalities produced by the universalist form of the law where some people do not conform to the privileged norm.

There is, however, an important difference between Young's position on special rights and that of 'maternalists'. According to Young, rights are specifically political. Insofar as they depend on the ideal of inclusiveness in political participation, group rights are themselves a political matter. Young argues that a group should not be seen as 'an essence or nature with a specific set of common attributes' but rather as fluid and salient only in particular circumstances, when it is defined as such. Furthermore, groups are multiple and cut across each other, so that any specific individual may belong to many groups. Which groups are relevant at any one time and which individuals belong to those groups is, then, a matter of political contestation and decision. It cannot be established on the basis of the privileged knowledge of women's specificity *as* women, which is claimed by maternalists as true regardless of whether women themselves are willing to group themselves in this way.

However, it is precisely Young's anti-essentialist theory of the political definition of groups that makes her theory of group *representation* in politics problematic. Anne Phillips, who herself argues that quotas for marginalised groups are necessary to ensure equal political participation (Phillips, 1995), has clearly argued the difficulties of Young's theory in this respect. The problem is that if an individual is a member of multiple, fluid groups, how is s/he to be represented as the member of a single group? If a woman votes in a group of women, is she voting *as* a woman, or as a complex of different identities, or even as something different altogether, a Christian, say, or a member of the green movement (Phillips, 1991: 77)? Phillips proposes that quotas should be set, not to represent women or ethnic minorities, but rather to give them a voice in policymaking that they would not otherwise have simply because there are so few involved in the political process who are not white men. However, Phillips's own argument, in suggesting that women share common needs, begs the question: are the differences between women less significant than the differences between women and men? This is particularly important from the point of view of feminist political strategy, because, as we have already noted, special rights risk 'freezing' group identities and producing new exclusions and inequalities.

Finally on this topic, it is worth noting a limitation of the feminist debate concerning political equality through difference. As Phillips has argued persuasively in *Which Equalities Matter?* (an extract of which appears below), the issue of political equality has been severed from that of economic equality. With the demise of communism and the demonisation of socialism by the New Right, in contemporary Western societies the argument that greater economic equality is an important condition of political equality has been neglected. Phillips argues that status is important, and that where there are extremes of poverty and wealth it is very difficult for fellow citizens to treat each other as genuinely of equal worth. This argument is important because it puts economic inequalities back into the frame of feminist political theory.

ANTI-ESSENTIALISM AND THE SUBJECT OF FEMINISM

The idea that differences between men and women and between women are political poses a question that goes to the heart of the feminist project: how are we to understand the subject of feminism, 'women'? This question has been raised in a particularly strong form by the poststructuralist critique of **essentialism**.

Diana Fuss has made a useful distinction between two different types of essentialism with which feminists are concerned. 'Metaphysical' essentialism presupposes that women have something fundamental, prior to their description in language, in common. 'Nominalist' essentialism, on the other hand, assumes that they have something in common, however minimal, as a result of socially significant descriptions of themselves as such (Fuss, 1989: 4–5). For those feminists who criticise 'women' as an exclusionary category – including black feminists and those for whom maternalist theories are unconvincing – the problem is that certain women who do not fit a particular, metaphysical definition involving biological sexual difference become invisible in feminist theory and unrepresented in feminist political strategies. For poststructuralists, however, all representations of women are necessarily contingent and partial. The term 'women' does not designate in advance a group of actual embodied persons who share a set of characteristics; rather, it may construct its referent, a group who are identified with or identify themselves with the term as it is used in a particular context. From the poststructuralist point of view, there is no aggregate of individuals who consistently identify with all uses of the term 'women', nor, indeed, is this possible, since it is used in such a multiplicity of contradictory and highly specified ways.

To attempt to establish a subject of feminism in advance of politics is, then, as Judith Butler argues in the article extracted here, 'to foreclose the domain of the political'. She sees this as an authoritarian move which silences those who do not identify with the particular version of 'women' invoked in a particular feminist theory or project. This is particularly pertinent, she argues, given the politics of **postcolonialism**. Butler takes issue with characterisations of postmodernism and poststructuralism that group theorists like **Irigaray**, Foucault and **Derrida** together, seeing this as a way of dismissing argument rather than engaging with it. However, her position is linked to the **anti-foundationalism** usually seen as thematic of theories that are 'post-', although it is important to be clear about precisely what anti-foundationalism involves. For Butler, the argument is not that there are, or should be, no foundations, but rather that politics involves the continual contestation of foundations.

The continual contestation of foundations is also, somewhat paradoxically, necessary for universalism according to Butler. From a poststructuralist perspective, universalism is necessarily exclusionary. There is no possibility of naming any substantive notion of universalism, of filling it with any content (human rights, rules, participation) that would not be exclusive. By definition, to name something (and naming is necessary to thinking) is to essentialise it, at least nominally, to create a bounded set of attributes which it is supposed to possess. We have seen how this has worked historically in the case of universal human rights: the attributes supposed to be possessed by humans have actually referred only to white men under certain conditions. The importance of anti-foundationalism, however, is that it does not confuse nominal and metaphysical **essentialism**. As Butler argues, it is impossible for thought to do without foundations, and it is impossible for an inclusive, democratic politics to do without universalism. It is the horizon that makes democratic politics possible. Nevertheless, it is possible to keep both 'women' and 'universalism' open by not assuming that such terms can ever exhaustively describe the multiple significations and differences they designate. 'Women' does not name a metaphysical essence that is somehow beyond the deployment of the term itself. For Butler, politics opens the terms of feminism itself to resignification, 'to expand the possibilities of what it means to be a woman and in this sense to condition and enable an enhanced sense of agency'.

Insofar as feminists are concerned to rethink the political, poststructuralism provides an inspiring model. For poststructuralists, nothing is ruled out as non-political, and the insistence that none of the **foundationalist** claims on which feminism has relied is off the political agenda has been exhilarating for many contemporary feminist political theorists. What poststructuralist feminism does not inspire, however, are bold normative claims like those formalised in Young's model of political participation and Phillips's plea for consideration of the importance of economic inequality. As Butler's arguments show, however, there is no necessary opposition between these two different directions of contemporary feminist political theory. Universalism is as necessary to feminism as feminism is to universalism; and, while normative claims continually offer the danger of the repression of politics, politics offers the possibility of the continual contestation of repression.

NOTES

1. It is possibly for this reason that feminist political theorists have rarely taken up a position in the liberal-communitarian debate. Feminists tend to be unimpressed by Liberalism as a political philosophy; but, despite commonalities between some strands of feminist political theory and aspects of communitarian thinking, it has exercised little appeal because of the difficulties it presents of making a critical assessment of the status quo (Frazer and Lacey, 1993).
2. This deconstructive orientation towards political philosophy may have been stimulated initially by the failure of Marxist-feminism (although Marxism itself has an ambivalent relationship to the Enlightenment). Marxist-feminists grappled with the difficulties of explaining women's oppression using sex-blind categories such as 'worker', 'mode of production' and 'ideology' (Barrett, 1980). The way in which Marxism's supposedly gender-neutral abstractions came to be seen as irredeemably male no doubt influenced the 'turn' in feminist theory away from using traditional theories for analysis and towards their deconstruction.
3. Anne Phillips argues for defining the private sphere as non-political from a feminist point of view. She thinks feminists should privilege the public sphere of politics as the space within which we 'stand back from ourselves' to consider the general interest (Phillips, 1991: 115–19, 161). For a criticism of this rather unconventional feminist view, see Nash (1998).

'EQUALITY AND DIFFERENCE' BY ANNE PHILLIPS

At the time of writing, Anne Phillips is Professor of Gender Theory and Director of the Gender Institute at the London School of Economics. Hers is an important voice, in British feminism particularly but internationally also. She is notable for developing feminist theory within the context of democratic organisation and citizenship, and can justly be called a leading theorist of gender within democratic theory. In *Engendering Democracy* (Polity, 1991), she showed how various types of democratic theory conceive of citizenship in a gender-neutral way that surreptitiously encodes a male bias. In *Democracy and Difference* (Polity, 1993), she sought to conceive of democracy without the presupposition of neutrality so that it could respond to facts of difference and diversity. In this extract, she examines the argument that gender-neutrality is in fact part of the problem to which feminists must address themselves because it is blind to the 'differences' of the sexes. She suggests that it is one thing to be difference-blind with regard to economic inequality (all should be treated fairly regardless of who they are), but that new problems arise when one is considering group-based inequality – but Phillips is also clear that material inequality cannot be ignored. This can usefully be read in conjunction with the arguments about radical democracy put forward by Anna Marie Smith in Chapter 12.

'EQUALITY AND DIFFERENCE' (1999)*

Anne Phillips

Feminist analyses of the liberal democratic tradition have drawn attention to the way seemingly innocent notions of freedom, equality or consent were founded on an equation between the citizen and the male. This was most apparent in the formative literature of the sixteenth and seventeenth centuries, where exciting new ideas about government being based on consent were welded on to less thrilling ideas about men as the 'natural' heads of their households, and the emerging discourse of free self-government came to be premised on sexual subordination. Similar deformations have continued right through the twentieth century. The rights of citizenship have been variously associated with the responsibility to fight for the defence of one's country, or the dignities and

---

* From Anne Phillips, *Which Equalities Matter?* (Cambridge: Polity Press, 1999), pp. 23–7, 129–33. (Copyright held by Anne Phillips.)

responsibilities of labour (both defined very much out of a masculine experience); and as late as the 1970s, one still finds political theorists writing as if the individual is a male head of household, whose rights can be discussed in abstraction from gender relations.[1]

Left to itself, such evidence of male preferentialism might point towards a more genuine gender-neutrality that no longer discriminates between the two sexes. In much of the feminist literature, however, the critique of male bias has been combined with a more challenging argument that treats gender-neutrality itself as the culprit. All democracies now present themselves as indifferent to sexual difference, proclaiming their citizenship as equally available to both women and men. This very indifference is part of the problem. 'To become a citizen is to trade one's particular identity for an abstract, public self',[2] and this trade-in can be said to be peculiarly advantageous to men. Consider the different balances men and women have had to strike between their public and private lives, and the far greater ease with which men detach themselves (both practically and emotionally) from their private or domestic concerns. In the 'male' norm of democratic politics, the boundaries between public and private worlds are relatively well policed, and those who stray across these boundaries (taking their babies to political meetings, letting their emotions 'intrude' on rational debate) will be regarded as disruptive or peculiar, as failing to abide by the standards of democratic life. These standards are of course presented as neutral – the same criticisms would apply equally to a woman or a man – but, since social characteristics *are* gendered, what passes for neutrality turns out to be preferential treatment for men.

Under the banner of gender-neutrality, sex would have to be treated as an irrelevant consideration. One consequence is that it would be difficult to argue for affirmative action policies designed to raise the proportion of women elected as political representatives: if sex is meant to be irrelevant, why should it matter whether our representatives are women or men? In a world that is patently not neutral between the sexes, proclamations of gender-neutrality then have the effect of affirming the status quo. We carry on with business as usual, which means carrying on with politics monopolized by men. Under the banner of gender-neutrality, it also becomes difficult to tackle deep-rooted assumptions about the nature of justice and rights. One argument developed by feminists is that the ethic of impartial justice needs to be supplemented by an ethic of responsibility or care, and that the impersonal implementation of abstract rules of justice can make us less attentive than we should be to the concrete circumstances of different people's lives and the responsibilities we owe to others.[3] It is probably a mistake to equate the 'ethics of justice' with men and the 'ethics of care' with women, but there is an important gender component here, and easy proclamations of gender-neutrality make it harder to get at the issues.

Feminists have taken issue with supposedly sex-blind versions of equality that require women to simulate the activities of the men who constructed these norms. Black activists have developed similar arguments against the race-blindness that makes equality depend on simulating the language and conventions of those who are white.[4] When people have been denied jobs, education or housing because they are black, it does of course seem right that employers or landlords should be required to ignore the skin colour of applicants and block out the 'accidents' of ethnicity or race. But that kind of race-blindness can also be deeply insulting. It gives the impression that racial identity is incidental to an individual's sense of self; worse still, it can send a message about 'blackness' being a problem, something others will live with only when they are able to pretend it away. The suggestion that white is normal and black an unhappy deviation is part of what has been challenged in recent decades.

Despite overtly good intentions, the notion that we make people equal by ignoring or suppressing their difference easily turns into a statement of inequality: a bit like saying 'I regard you as my equal *despite* your peculiarities, despite those surface characteristics that mark you as my inferior'. The idea that equality depends on everyone being treated the same can also be regarded as an inequitable assimilationism that imposes the values and norms of one group on those who were historically subordinate. Consider the much-discussed example from Canadian politics, which arose when the prime minister, Pierre Trudeau, decided to tackle the unequal status of indigenous peoples by dismantling the reservation system that had protected the First Nations from assimilation.[5] The reservation system enabled native Indians to retain control over reservation lands, setting limits to the mobility, residence and voting rights of non-Indians in Indian territory. But when the majority of Indians still lived in (impoverished) separate reserves, this also limited their participation in mainstream Canadian life. The government concluded that 'separate but equal' was no guarantee of equality and – in an impeccably liberal move – decided to abandon all differential legislation and treatment. What looked like neutrality was, however, perceived as imposition, and the policy was withdrawn six months later in the face of almost unanimous Indian opposition.

Representatives of indigenous peoples have criticized the assimilationism that requires all peoples to conform to the constitutional preferences of the victorious settlers, and have argued for forms of self-government that will respect traditional practices and customs rather than imposing another group's norms. In similar fashion, migrant communities have sometimes looked askance at the legal equalities that promise identical treatment regardless of one's culture or religion, arguing that exceptions should be made in respect of particular practices that are embedded in the traditions of their group. The resulting emphasis on equality *through* difference is probably the most distinctive feature of contemporary thinking on democracy. The idea that equality requires us all to be the same has long been considered a breach of individuality, and the depressing conformism associated with this was challenged more than a century ago by John Stuart Mill. The idea that equality means treating everyone the same has survived for much longer, as has the related idea that equality is to be promoted by eliminating at least some of the differences.

When class was the paradigmatic example of inequality, the notion that equality meant bracketing out or else getting rid of difference seemed more plausible than it does today. One can treat workers and capitalists as equals by discounting the difference between them (what Marx described and criticized as the political annulment of difference). This is what is supposed to happen in the law courts or in the allocation of the same number of votes to each. Or one can go beyond the traditionally liberal understanding of equality to attack differences themselves: abolish private property, abolish the distinction between capitalist and worker, abolish those differences that just can't be discounted, and then let us talk of equality. Difference, in either case, is treated as a problem. In the first scenario, differences in status have to be ignored in order to guarantee people their equal civil and political rights. In the second, they have to be eliminated in order to make people genuine equals. The disagreement is about how much has to be changed in order to prevent difference having its deleterious effect.

Once attention shifts to other forms of group difference that are not so amenable to erasure, it becomes less appropriate to treat difference as always and inevitably a problem. It is clearly inappropriate to make sexual equality depend on sex-change operations that convert all the men to women or all the women to men, or to make racial equality depend on mass programmes of racial intermarriage that produce a uniform world population. And if those differences must remain – must be made in some way compatible with equality – why should it be so difficult to articulate a vision of equal citizenship that is premised on continuing differences in culture and practices and beliefs? As many now argue, treating people as equals does not have to mean treating them the same; indeed, when treating people the same means subjecting everyone to the norms and institutions that were developed by only one of many groups, this is the opposite of equal treatment. These considerations draw us back (rightly, in my view) into unfinished business around the nature of equal citizenship. It is not just that political equality is being subverted by economic inequality. We need a more adequate understanding of political and civil equality that recognizes and respects our differences.

[. . .]

Hannah Arendt once described political equality as 'an equality of unequals who stand in need of being "equalized" in certain respects and for certain purposes'.[6] It then arises only when people are not equal and would hardly be coherent if everyone were already the same. At one level, Arendt's observation must be correct. If 'political equality' is to mean anything distinct from unqualified 'equality' – if there is to be any point in talking of a specifically *political* equality – it must refer in some way to inequality. Why do people insist that they are politically equal? Because in some other respect, they are not regarded as equal: maybe in respect to something you take more seriously than I do, like my lack of connections in high places; maybe in respect to something we both recognize as significant, like the discrepancy in our incomes; maybe in respect to something that bothers me more than you, like my ignorance of nuclear physics? Claims to political equality always carry a background echo of something that makes this equality surprising. We are equals despite various significant inequalities; we are political, even if not total, equals.

If we accept that this is part of what is implied by political equality, we can hardly see it as contradicted by *any* evidence of inequality in other aspects of our lives. The question, rather, is whether democracies can 'equalize unequals' through a pure act of proclamation (what might be described as the town-crier theory of equality), or have to establish certain conditions. There are indeed conditions, and it is never enough just to proclaim that citizens must have 'free and equal access' to political life. So long as large sections of the citizenry are constrained in the exercise of their political rights by lack of money, education, contacts, or time, declarations of basic equality will always ring rather hollow. Formal rights to participate in politics always raise questions about what makes these rights effective. The answers to these questions will include strong measures to equalize educational and employment opportunities and to sustain social mobility throughout people's lives; they will also include remedial measures (such as gender quotas) to counteract what would otherwise be the 'natural' effects of an existing distribution of occupation or income.[7]

Inequalities in political access disturb the complacent surface of democratic life, but even more telling, in my view, is the difficulty of ensuring equality of status when people are so markedly unequal in their material conditions. When the case for greater economic equality is made to turn exclusively on whether individuals have the effective right to participate in politics, it turns on a patronizing – and in its starker formulations, unconvincing – thesis about the rich being politically energetic and the poor politically inert. This does not fit too well with the history of political activism, but it also loads political life with more importance than it can bear. If the only reason for redistributing income and wealth is that this will allow me to participate more fully in politics, I might well decline the favour: I might feel my life is busy enough already without having to take up politics as well. Understood in the narrower sense of equality in political participation and influence, political equality is not a strong enough basis on which to build arguments for economic reform. It is when we take it as a deeper claim about holding all citizens in equal regard that the connections become more compelling.

Political equality, in this deeper sense, has become one of the defining beliefs of the current age – in a way that makes a nonsense of unqualified assertions about people giving up on egalitarian ideals. In my perception, people now care more rather than less about equality. They are more insistent on their standing as equals (what makes him think he is better than I? what makes her think she can tell me what to do?), less prepared to accept a subordinate position or believe everything the authorities say. Faced with evidence that political influence is distributed according to wealth or family connections, many budding egalitarians may still shrug their shoulders: who, in the end, cares? But faced with evidence that one kind of person is regarded as of less account than some other – that office workers are considered of less account than executives, plumbers of less account than doctors, or women of less account than men – the most accommodating of individuals is likely to register a complaint. Taken in this broader sense, this is a time of great egalitarianism, not less.

Because there *is* a relationship between social standing and material conditions, certain things then follow about the way democracies have to organize their economic affairs. A society that condones excesses of poverty in the midst of wealth, or arbitrarily rewards one skill with 100 times the wages of another, is not recognizing its citizens as of equal human worth. On the contrary, it is making it harder than ever for the members of that society to keep up their pretence that they consider their fellow citizens their equals. There are always some individuals capable of that act of imagination that discards social and economic stereotypes and looks through differences in income, experience, or wealth to the essential humanity beyond: the best of novelists do this in their writing, though only rarely in their personal lives. The majority of us succumb to more surface impressions. It is hard to sustain a strong sense of equal worth between people whose life experiences are fundamentally different, and all too easy to fall back on self-serving justifications that present the poor as less sensitive to hardship than the wealthy, or women as more able to cope with the repetitive tedium of semi-skilled work. Strict equality may not be necessary to sustain equality of worth (given the unlikelihood of achieving such an equality, one can only hope this isn't a necessary condition), but ideals of equal citizenship cannot survive unscathed by great differentials in income and wealth. When the gap between rich and poor opens up too widely, it becomes meaningless to pretend we have recognized all adults as equals.

[. . .]

Against this background, it might seem that the real question is not which equalities matter but what (if anything) can be done to make market societies more equal, and that, failing serious investigation of alternatives, the arguments I pursue here will have minimal effect. In many ways, I agree with this. However compelling the theoretical connections between political, cultural and economic equality, these have to be combined with evidence about what is viable; and the crucial outstanding questions are about what kind of change is possible within the broad framework of a market economy and what kind of redistribution has worked elsewhere. My main concern is that too little is currently said even about the injustice of economic inequality. If economic equality matters, it is clearly incumbent on social critics to work out the best means of approximating this condition. Against the contemporary wall of indifference, the first task is to establish that.

NOTES

1. For an example of this last point, see Susan Moller Okin's critique of John Rawls in *Justice, Gender and the Family* (New York, Basic Books, 1989).
2. Kathleen B. Jones, 'Citizenship in a Woman-Friendly Polity', *Signs* 15/4, 1990, p. 784.
3. Carol Gilligan, *In a Different Voice* (Cambridge, Mass., Harvard University Press, 1982).
4. See Patricia J. Williams, *Seeing a Color-Blind Future: The Paradox of Race (Reith Lectures)* (New York, Noonday Press, 1998).
5. See the discussion in Will Kymlicka, *Liberalism, Community and Culture* (Oxford, Clarendon Press, 1989), pp. 142–57.
6. Hannah Arendt, *The Human Condition* (Chicago, University of Chicago Press, 1958).
7. Though I do not address this here, they would also include free access to public media of communication so as to ensure under-resourced campaign groups an effective voice.

At the time of writing, Elizabeth Frazer is a Fellow and Tutor in Politics at New College, Oxford, and a University Lecturer in the Department of Politics and International Relations. She is the author of numerous papers and articles on feminism, political theory and questions of education. At the time of writing, Nicola Lacey is Professor of Criminal Law at the London School of Economics. She is a respected writer on criminal law, criminal justice, legal and social theory, with a particular interest in feminist theory. Her publications include *State Punishment: Political Principles and Community Values* (Routledge, 1988) and *Unspeakable Subjects: Feminist Essays in Legal and Social Theory* (Hart Publishing, 1998). The extract is from their jointly written book *The Politics of Community* (Harvester Wheatsheaf/University of Toronto Press, 1993), concerned with a feminist interpretation of the debate between liberals and communitarians. In this section, they examine the public/private distinction, endorsing the feminist critique of its gendered nature yet sounding a note of caution about advocating state intervention into the private realm.

'PUBLIC–PRIVATE DISTINCTIONS' (1993)*

Elizabeth Frazer and Nicola Lacey

Perhaps the best-known and most deeply contested feature of feminist critique of the liberal tradition is its attack on the dichotomy between public and private, in both its analytic and its prescriptive aspects. The liberal conception of the limited, neutral state carries with it an implicit conception of a private, non-political sphere in which state intervention is inappropriate and where individual autonomy is to be exercised.[1] Feminism is critical of this argument for several reasons, yet itself takes up a somewhat ambivalent position.[2]

In the first place, feminists have argued that the public–private distinction is analytically flawed. At a material level, it turns out to be extremely difficult to identify where the line between public and private is to be drawn. There have been many shifts over time: in the nineteenth century, *laissez-faire* liberalism constructed the economic market as private; in the late twentieth century, mixed-economy liberalism has shifted this boundary, and the quintessentially

---

* From Elizabeth Frazer and Nicola Lacey, *The Politics of Community* (Brighton: Harvester Wheatsheaf, 1993), pp. 72–6.

private sphere is seen as being constituted by the family and sexual relations. In recent years, the state/civil society distinction has been resurrected, in the context both of 'Western' and of East European ex-communist systems. The revival of free-market ideology has begun to push economic relations back into the 'private' sphere. And in actuality in most modern states, family life itself is hedged around with regulation and intervention, with legal definitions of marriage and divorce, conditions under which the custody of children will be granted or maintained, conditions under which state support will be given, and so on. So in a sense there simply is no 'private sphere' in twentieth-century liberal states.[3]

Furthermore, even to the extent that there is a difference in the level of intervention and regulation between different spheres, feminism contests the assumption that the distinction between intervention and non-intervention is of absolute significance. Non-intervention is just as political as intervention, and calls for its own justification. Furthermore, what from one point of view is seen as non-intervention, from another appears to be intervention. Consider the issue of marital rape. From the point of view of some feminist campaigners, the call has been for the state to step in and regulate relations within marriage. But that marital rape has not been and in many states still is not a crime is, of course, the upshot of state regulation of the marriage relation and legal definitions of a wife's status. Arguments like these tend to engender a straightforwardly sceptical analysis of public–private distinctions, which aims to reinterpret their significance for political theory.

However, liberals counter this kind of scepticism about the public–private distinction by reference to its normative credentials: the ideal of the limited state and the worth of individual human freedom. Feminists, as we have seen, reply with the argument that negative freedom is worth little if it is not accompanied by the positive conditions for self-determination. Indeed, it is women's lack of these with which the public–private distinction is associated. More than this, feminists focus on the discursive power of the distinction, a power which somehow survives its analytic incoherence.[4]

The idea of public and private spheres is often hived off from the freedom-based argument for the limited state, and is applied in an apparently descriptive, yet ultimately question-begging, way to particular activities and institutions. Once a sphere is labelled 'private', normative conclusions that no intervention is appropriate are drawn, usually without the full argument for non-intervention being spelled out. The attribution of privacy, which should be the conclusion of argument, is taken for the argument itself. And the discourse of privacy in areas such as sexuality and family life has, in political fact, become a mechanism whereby women's oppression is not only constituted and maintained, but also and most damagingly, rendered apolitical. Similarly, the ascription 'public' has been unproblematically associated with the state, leaving out of account the interpenetration of state and non-state institutions. In modern societies, there are a number of non-state forums for public, political debate, such as social movements, trades unions, pressure groups and so on. Hence it is no longer possible (if ever it was) to elide the terms 'state' and 'public', any more than it is appropriate to see political theory as concerned only with state power. It is against this political marginalisation of women's subordination, and against the narrow conception of 'the political', that feminists have taken up the slogan 'the personal is political'.

While we accept both the importance and the essential validity of the critique of the public–private distinction, we would argue that there is a need to draw a sharper distinction than have many recent feminist analyses between the argument about state intervention on the one hand, and the depoliticisation of 'private' issues on the other. For, although liberalism itself is disingenuous in its assertion of the illegitimacy of state intervention in the private sphere, given such massive intervention in all social-democratic liberal states (intervention which is unquestioned as such by social democratic liberal theory), the feminist critique of this tension without liberalism has often led to a simplistic conclusion in favour of the appropriateness and legitimacy of state intervention in the private sphere. The answer, it is suggested, is simply to extend state regulation of women's oppression into the private sphere.

Leaving aside evident difficulties about both the potential efficacy of state regulation in many areas of life, and the identification of 'state' institutions (especially in a time when such functions as policing and social work have been to some extent and might be further 'privatised'), it is clear that this solution is not only too simple but also too risky. For it appears to commit feminism to the view that there are no moral limits on proper state action. The proper goal for feminism should rather be the reinterpretation of some form of public–private distinction along less gender-exploitative lines.[5] For women even more than disadvantaged men in our culture have suffered from the lack of a real 'private' space in which to pursue our own concerns, given the double burden inherent in current gender arrangements which means that most women have, in effect, both more than one job and relatively few resources. A total critique of the public–private distinction in terms of a rejection of the idea of some limits on proper state intervention and control would be a grave mistake for feminist politics.

Furthermore, the inference from the critique to a solution in terms of legal change partakes of what we argue to be a naive and distinctively liberal attitude to how social change comes about. For it assumes that deliberate state intervention, via legal regulation of, for example, the family or the labour market, would be the best way to tackle the problems engendered by the traditional public–private divide. As we shall argue, however, an adequate theory would rather see potential for political change in terms of gradual changes in culture and practices brought about in important part by the operation of critical discourses such as feminism and, indeed, liberalism. On this view, the really important feminist claim here remains intact. This claim is not so much about state intervention or lack of it, as about the recognition of the political significance of aspects of life lived in what have been culturally constructed as private spheres. The recognition of the political relevance of women's family responsibilities for their effective access to political power, their position in civil society, the 'public' labour market and so on, are a fundamentally important aspect of feminist political theory. Indeed, this insight engenders a critique which has relevance beyond the way liberal political theory has continued to construct its notion of 'the political'. It also, by the same token, reveals the inadequacy of a construction of 'political institutions' as the traditional organs of government. This conception is utterly inadequate for theorising the conditions of the modern social-democratic state, in which a wide range of institutions ranging from the legislature through quangos, pressure groups, businesses, banks, unions, the family, the Church and so on must all be acknowledged to wield what are properly seen as forms of political power. And political theory must attend not only to relatively concrete institutions but also to institutions in the broader sense of cultural practices and discourses, if it is to give a satisfactory account of, let alone an attractive vision of the potential for, political society.

The historically contingent but politically significant fact, then, that women have lived their lives to a disproportionate extent in what has been known as 'the private sphere', marks out the ideological power of the public–private distinction as an important focus of feminist deconstruction and critique. But the crucial part of the argument is the reconstruction of 'private' matters as political, as of central importance to political theory, rather than any general prescription about remedies in terms of state regulation of the private sphere. The feminist argument is that the private sphere is not beyond political critique: this does not imply any general prescriptive position on the aptness of state intervention in response to the critique.

NOTES

1. See Wolfenden 1957; J. S. Mill 1974; Hart 1963.
2. There is a vast feminist literature on this topic. See for example Elshtain 1981; Pateman 1989, ch. 6; MacKinnon 1989, ch. 10; Jaggar 1983; Olsen 1983; O'Donovan 1985; Okin 1989.
3. Lacey 1993, p. 91.
4. Young 1989; MacKinnon 1989; Smart 1989.
5. Young 1989, pp. 116–21; Dietz 1991; Lacey 1993.

REFERENCES

Dietz, Mary G. (1991) 'Hannah Arendt and feminist politics', in Shanley and Pateman (eds).
Elshtain, Jean Bethke (1981) *Public Man, Private Woman: woman in social and political thought*, Princeton, NJ: Princeton University Press.
Hart, H. L. A. (1963), *Law, Liberty and Morality*, Oxford: Oxford University Press.
Jaggar, Alison M. (1983) *Feminist Politics and Human Nature*, Brighton: Harvester.
Lacey, Nicola (1993) 'Theory into practice? Pornography and the public/private dichotomy', *Journal of Law and Society*, 20.
MacKinnon, Catharine A. (1989) *Towards a Feminist Theory of the State*, Cambridge, Mass: Harvard University Press.

Mill, John Stuart (1974) *On Liberty* [1859], Harmondsworth: Penguin.

O'Donovan, Katherine (1985) *Sexual Divisions in Law*, London: Weidenfeld & Nicholson.

Okin, Susan Moller (1989) *Justice, Gender and the Family*, New York: Basic Books.

Olsen, Frances (1983) 'The family and the market', *Harvard Law Review*, 96: 1,497.

Pateman, Carole (1989) *The Disorder of Women*, Oxford: Polity Press.

Shanley, Mary Lyndon and Carole Pateman (eds) (1991) *Feminist Interpretations and Political Theory*, Oxford: Polity Press.

Smart, Carol (1989) *Feminism and the Power of Law*, London: Routledge.

Wolfenden Committee (1957) *Report of the Committee on Homosexual Offences and Prostitution*, Cmnd 247, London, HMSO.

Young, Iris Marion (1989) 'Politics and group difference: A critique of the ideal of universal citizenship', *Ethics*, 99.

'POLITY AND GROUP DIFFERENCE' BY IRIS MARION YOUNG

At the time of writing, Iris Young is Professor of Political Science at the University of Chicago. She is renowned primarily for her attempts to bring together the insights of postmodernism and identity politics with normative liberal theorising; to think through how it may be possible to maintain liberal ideals of universal rights while respecting diversity and difference. In *Justice and the Politics of Difference* (Princeton University Press, 1990), she argued for the extension of the notion of justice from issues of resource-redistribution to those of recognition. The former, she argued, downplayed or ignored other aspects or forms of oppression such as those that exclude or dominate culturally. It is therefore essential for democratic theory to take account of inclusiveness in its fullest sense covering issues of representation, cultural presence, decision-making and so forth. Part of her critique of mainstream liberal theorising is thus focused on the assumption that society is homogeneous or culturally unified. Normative theorising (and the policies flowing from it) needs to take account of group differences and affirm rather than deny or try to eradicate them. Subsequent work such as *Throwing Like a Girl and Other Essays in Feminist Philosophy and Social Theory* (Indiana University Press, 1990), *Intersecting Voices: Dilemmas of Gender, Political Philosophy, and Policy* (Princeton University Press, 1997) and *Inclusion and Democracy* (Oxford University Press, 2000) have developed and refined her position, extending it into more and more areas of public policy. The politics of recognition are now a wide part of North American political theory, partly due to Young's work. However, this has come in for criticism from those who argue that, while recognition matters, there are still even more fundamental issues of redistribution that should be given priority. In the extract reproduced here, Young examines some of the exclusions generated by dominant conceptions of citizenship, suggesting that these conflict with other universalist aspirations such as that for equal treatment. Young argues that a polity should recognise the presence of a variety of groups within it and make provision for listening to those groups and recognising them politically as well as, on some occasions, treating them differently. Only with this particularistic approach can true universality be achieved.

'POLITY AND GROUP DIFFERENCE' (1989)*

Iris Marion Young

An ideal of universal citizenship has driven the emancipatory momentum of modern political life.

[. . .]

Citizenship for everyone, and everyone the same *qua* citizen. Modern political thought generally assumed that the universality of citizenship in the sense of citizenship for all implies a universality of citizenship in the sense that citizenship status transcends particularity and difference. Whatever the social or group differences among citizens, whatever their inequalities of wealth, status, and power in the everyday activities of civil society, citizenship gives everyone the same status as peers in the political public. With equality conceived as sameness, the ideal of universal citizenship carries at least two meanings in addition to the extension of citizenship to everyone: (1) universality defined as general in opposition to particular; what citizens have in common as opposed to how they differ, and (2) universality in the sense of laws and rules that say the same for all and apply to all in the same way; laws and rules that are blind to individual and group differences.

[. . .]

In this article, I argue that, far from implying one another, the universality of citizenship, in the sense of the inclusion and participation of everyone, stands in tension with the other two meanings of universality embedded in modern political ideas: universality as generality, and universality as equal treatment. First, the ideal that the activities of citizenship express or create a general will that transcends the particular differences of group affiliation, situation, and interest has in practice excluded groups judged not capable of adopting that general point of view; the idea of citizenship as expressing a general will has tended to enforce a homogeneity of citizens. To the degree that contemporary proponents of revitalized citizenship retain the idea of a general will and common life, they implicitly support the same exclusions and homogeneity. Thus I argue that the inclusion and participation of everyone in public

* From Iris Marion Young, 'Polity and Group Difference', *Ethics*, 99:2 January 1989), pp. 250–74.

discussion and decision-making requires mechanisms for group representation. Second, where differences in capacities, culture, values, and behavioral styles exist among groups but some of these groups are privileged, strict adherence to a principle of equal treatment tends to perpetuate oppression or disadvantage. The inclusion and participation of everyone in social and political institutions, therefore, sometimes requires the articulation of special rights that attend to group differences in order to undermine oppression and disadvantage.

CITIZENSHIP AS GENERALITY

Many contemporary political theorists regard capitalist welfare society as depoliticized. Its interest-group pluralism privatizes policy-making, consigning it to back-room deals and autonomous regulatory agencies and groups. Interest-group pluralism fragments both policy and the interests of the individual, making it difficult to assess issues in relation to one another and set priorities. The fragmented and privatized nature of the political process, moreover, facilitates the dominance of the more powerful interests.[1]

In response to this privatization of the political process, many writers call for a renewed public life and a renewed commitment to the virtues of citizenship. Democracy requires that citizens of welfare corporate society awake from their privatized consumerist slumbers, challenge the experts who claim the sole right to rule, and collectively take control of their lives and institutions through processes of active discussion that aim at reaching collective decisions.[2]

[. . .]

I agree that interest-group pluralism, because it is privatized and fragmented, facilitates the domination of corporate, military, and other powerful interests. I think that democratic processes require the institutionalization of genuinely public discussion. There are serious problems, however, with uncritically assuming as a model the ideals of the civic public that come to us from the tradition of modern political thought.

[. . .]

Several commentators have argued that, in extolling the virtues of citizenship as participation in a universal public realm, modern men expressed a flight from sexual difference, from having to recognize another kind of existence that they could not entirely understand, and from the embodiment, dependency on nature, and morality that women represent.[3] Thus the opposition between the universality of the public realm of citizenship and the particularity of private interest became conflated with oppositions between reason and passion, masculine and feminine.

The bourgeois world instituted a moral division of labor between reason and sentiment, identifying masculinity with reason and feminity with sentiment, desire, and the needs of the body. Extolling a public realm of manly virtue and citizenship as independence, generality, and dispassionate reason entailed creating the private sphere of the family as the place to which emotion, sentiment, and bodily needs must be confined.[4] The generality of the public thus depends on excluding women, who are responsible for tending to that private realm and who lack the dispassionate rationality and independence required of good citizens.

[. . .]

It is important to recall that universality of citizenship conceived as generality operated to exclude not only women, but other groups as well. European and American republicans found little contradiction in promoting a universality of citizenship that excluded some groups, because the idea that citizenship is the same for all translated in practice to the requirement that all citizens be the same. The white male bourgeoisie conceived republican virtue as rational, restrained, and chaste, not yielding to passion or desire for luxury, and thus able to rise above desire and need to a concern for the common good. This implied excluding poor people and wage workers from citizenship on the grounds that they were too motivated by need to adopt a general perspective. The designers of the American Constitution were no more egalitarian than their European brethren in this respect; they specifically intended to restrict the access of the laboring class to the public, because they feared disruption of commitment to the general interests.

These early American republicans were also quite explicit about the need for the homogeneity of citizens, fearing that group differences would tend to undermine commitment to the general interest. This meant that the presence of Blacks and American Indians, and later Mexicans and Chinese, in the territories of the republic posed a threat that only assimilation, extermination, or dehumanization could thwart. Various combinations of these three were used, of course, but recognition of these groups as peers in the public was never an option. Even such republican fathers as Jefferson identified the Red and Black people in their territories with wild nature and passion, just as they feared that women outside the domestic realm were wanton and avaricious. They defined moral, civilized republican life in opposition to this backward-looking, uncultivated desire that they identified with women and non-whites.[5] A similar logic of exclusion operated in Europe, where Jews were particular targets.[6]

These republican exclusions were not accidental, nor were they inconsistent with the ideal of universal citizenship as understood by these theorists. They were a direct consequence of a dichotomy between public and private that defined the public as a realm of generality in which all particularities are left behind, and defined the private as the particular, the realm of affectivity, affiliation, need, and the body. As long as that dichotomy is in place, the inclusion of the formerly excluded in the definition of citizenship – women, workers, Jews, Blacks, Asians, Indians, Mexicans – imposes a homogeneity that suppresses group differences in the public and in practice forces the formerly excluded groups to be measured according to norms derived from and defined by privileged groups.

[. . .]

A repoliticization of public life should not require the creation of a unified public realm in which citizens leave behind their particular group affiliations, histories, and needs to discuss a general interest or common good. Such a desire for unity suppresses but does not eliminate differences and tends to exclude some perspectives from the public.[7] Instead of a universal citizenship in the sense of this generality, we need a group-differentiated citizenship and a heterogeneous public. In a heterogeneous public, differences are publicly recognized and acknowledged as irreducible, by which I mean that people from one perspective or history can never completely understand and adopt the point of view of those with other group-based perspectives and histories. Yet commitment to the need and desire to decide together the society's policies fosters communication across those differences.

DIFFERENTIATED CITIZENSHIP AS GROUP REPRESENTATION

[. . .]

The concept of a social group has become politically important because recent emancipatory and leftist social movements have mobilized around group identity rather than exclusively class or economic interests. In many cases, such mobilization has consisted of embracing and positively defining a despised or devalued ethnic or racial identity. In the women's movement, gay-rights movement, or elders' movements, differential social status based on age, sexuality, physical capacity, or the division of labor has been taken up as a positive group identity for political mobilization.

[. . .]

A social group involves first of all an affinity with other persons by which they identify with one another and by which other people identify them. A person's particular sense of history, understanding of social relations and personal possibilities, her or his mode of reasoning, values, and expressive styles are constituted at least partly by her or his group identity. Many group definitions come from the outside, from other groups that label and stereotype certain people. In such circumstances, the despised-group members often find their affinity in their oppression. The concept of social group must be distinguished from two concepts with which it might be confused: aggregate and association.

[. . .]

A social group should not be understood as an essence or nature with a specific set of common attributes. Instead, group identity should be understood in relational terms. Social processes generate groups by creating relational differentiations, situations of clustering and affective bonding in which people feel affinity for other people. Sometimes groups define themselves by despising or excluding others whom they define as other and whom they dominate and oppress. Although social processes of affinity and separation define groups, they do not give groups a substantive identity. There is no common nature that members of a group have.

As products of social relations, groups are fluid; they come into being and may fade away. Homosexual practices have existed in many societies and historical periods, for example, but gay-male group identification exists only in the West in the twentieth century. Group identity may become salient only under specific circumstances, when in interaction with other groups. Most people in modern societies have multiple group identifications, moreover, and therefore groups themselves are not discrete unities. Every group has group differences cutting across it.

I think that group differentiation is an inevitable and desirable process in modern societies. We need not settle that question, however. I merely assume that ours is now a group-differentiated society and that it will continue to be so for some time to come. Our political problem is that some of our groups are privileged and others are oppressed.

But what is oppression? In another place, I give a fuller account of the concept of oppression.[8] Briefly, a group is oppressed when one or more of the following conditions occurs to all or a large portion of its members: (1) the benefits of their work or energy go to others without those others reciprocally benefiting them (exploitation); (2) they are excluded from participation in major social activities, which in our society means primarily a workplace (marginalization); (3) they live and work under the authority of others and have little work autonomy and authority over others themselves (powerlessness); (4) as a group they are stereotyped at the same time that their experience and situation is invisible in the society in general, and they have little opportunity and little audience for the expression of their experience and perspective on social events (cultural imperialism); (5) group members suffer random violence and harassment motivated by group hatred or fear. In the United States today, at least the following groups are oppressed in one or more of these ways: women, Blacks, American Indians, Chicanos, Puerto Ricans and other Spanish-speaking Americans, Asian Americans, gay men, lesbians, working-class people, poor people, old people, and mentally and physically disabled people.

[. . .]

I assert, then, the following principle: a democratic public, however that is constituted, should provide mechanisms for the effective representation and recognition of the distinct voices and perspectives of those of its constituent groups that are oppressed or disadvantaged within it. Such group representation implies institutional mechanisms and public resources supporting three activities: (1) self-organization of group members so that they gain a sense of collective empowerment and a reflective understanding of their collective experience and interests in the context of the society; (3) voicing a group's analysis of how social-policy proposals affect them and generating policy proposals themselves, in institutionalized contexts where decision-makers are obliged to show that they have taken these perspectives into consideration; (3) having veto power regarding specific policies that affect a group directly – for example, reproductive rights for women or use of reservation lands for American Indians.

[. . .]

Group representation is the best means to promote just outcomes to democratic decision-making processes. The argument for this claim relies on Habermas's conception of communicative ethics. In the absence of a philosopher-king who reads transcendent normative verities, the only ground for a claim that a policy or decision is just is that it has been arrived at by a public that has truly promoted free expression of all needs and points of view. In his formulation of a communicative ethic, Habermas retains inappropriately an appeal to a universal or impartial point of view from which claims in a public should be addressed. A communicative ethic that not merely articulates a hypothetical public that would justify decisions, but also proposes actual conditions tending to promote just outcomes of decision-making processes, should promote conditions for the expression of the concrete needs of all individuals in their particularity.[9] The concreteness of individual lives, their needs and interests, and their perception of the needs and interests of others, I have argued, are structured partly through group-based experience and identity. Thus full and free expression of concrete needs and interests under social circumstances where some groups are silenced or marginalized requires that they have a specific voice in deliberation and decision-making.

[. . .]

UNIVERSAL RIGHTS AND SPECIAL RIGHTS

A second aspect of the universality of citizenship is today in tension with the goal of full inclusion and participation of all groups in political and social institutions: universality in the formulation of law and policies. Modern and contemporary liberalism hold as basic the principle that the rules and policies of the state, and in contemporary liberalism also the rules of private institutions, ought to be blind to race, gender, and other group differences. The public realm of the state and law properly should express its rules in general terms that abstract from the particularities of individual and group histories, needs, and situations to recognize all persons equally and treat all citizens in the same way.

[. . .]

Where group differences in capacities, values, and behavioral or cognitive styles exist, equal treatment in the allocation of reward according to rules of merit composition will reinforce and perpetuate disadvantage. Equal treatment requires everyone to be measured according to the same norms, but in fact there are no 'neutral' norms of behavior and performance. Where some groups are privileged and others oppressed, the formulation of law, policy, and the rules of private institutions tend to be biased in favor of the privileged groups, because their particular experience implicitly sets the norm. Thus where there are group differences in capacities, socialization, values, and cognitive and cultural styles, only attending to such differences can ensure the inclusion and participation of all groups in political and economic institutions. This implies that instead of always formulating rights and rules in universal terms that are blind to difference, some groups sometimes deserve special rights.[10]

[. . .]

The issue of a right to pregnancy and maternity leave and the right to special treatment for nursing mothers is highly controversial among feminists today. I do not intend here to wind through the intricacies of what has become a conceptually challenging and interesting debate in legal theory. As Linda Krieger argues, the issue of rights for pregnant and birthing mothers in relation to the workplace has created a paradigm crisis for our understanding of sexual equality, because the application of a principle of equal treatment on this issue has yielded results whose effects on women are at best ambiguous and at worst detrimental.[11]

In my view, an equal-treatment approach on this issue is inadequate because it either implies that women do not receive any right to a leave with job security when having babies, or it assimilates such guarantees under a supposedly gender-neutral category of 'disability'. Such assimilation is unacceptable because pregnancy and childbirth are normal conditions of normal women; they themselves count as socially necessary work, and they have unique and variable characteristics and needs.[12] Assimilating pregnancy into disability gives a negative meaning to these processes as 'unhealthy'. It suggests, moreover, that the primary or only reasons that a woman has a right to a leave with job security are that she is physically unable to work at her job or that doing so would be more difficult than when she is not pregnant and recovering from childbirth. While these are important reasons, depending on the individual woman, another reason is that she ought to have the time to establish breastfeeding and to develop a relationship and routine with her child, if she chooses.

[. . .]

Issues of difference arise for law and policy not only regarding bodily being, but also, and just as important, for cultural integrity and invisibility. By culture I mean group-specific phenomena of behavior, temperament, or meaning. Cultural differences include phenomena of language, speaking style or dialect, body comportment, gesture, social practices, values, group-specific socialization, and so on. To the degree that groups are culturally different, however, equal treatment in many issues of social policy is unjust because it denies these cultural differences or makes them a liability.

[. . .]

Whether they involve quotas or not, affirmative-action programs violate a principle of equal treatment because they are race- or gender-conscious in setting criteria for school admissions, jobs, or promotions. These policies are usually defended in one of two ways. Giving preference to race or gender is understood either as just compensation for groups that have suffered discrimination in the past or as compensation for the present disadvantage these groups suffer because of that history of discrimination and exclusion.[13] I do not wish to quarrel with either of these justifications for the differential treatment based on race or gender implied by affirmative-action policies. I want to suggest that, in addition, we can understand affirmative-action policies as compensating for the cultural biases of standards and evaluators used by the schools or employers. These standards and evaluators reflect at least to some degree the specific life and cultural experience of dominant groups – whites, Anglos, or men. In a group-differentiated society, moreover, the development of truly neutral standards and evaluations is difficult or impossible, because female, Black, or Latino cultural experience and the dominant cultures are in many respects not reducible to a common measure. Thus affirmative-action policies compensate for the dominance of one set of cultural attributes. Such an interpretation of affirmative action locates the 'problem' that affirmative action solves partly in the understandable biases of evaluators and their standards, rather than only in specific differences of the disadvantaged group.

[. . .]

Many opponents of oppression and privilege are wary of claims for special rights because they fear a restoration of special classifications that can justify exclusion and stigmatization of the specially marked groups. Such fear has been particularly pronounced among feminists who oppose affirming sexual and gender difference in law and policy. It would be foolish for me to deny that this fear has some significant basis.

Such fear is founded, however, on accession to traditional identification of group difference with deviance, stigma, and inequality. Contemporary movements of oppressed groups, however, assert a positive meaning to group difference, by which a group claims its identity as a group and rejects the stereotypes and labeling by which others mark it as inferior or inhuman. These social movements engage the meaning of difference itself as a terrain of political struggle, rather than leaving difference to be used to justify exclusion and subordination. Supporting policies and rules that attend to group difference in order to undermine oppression and disadvantage is, in my opinion, a part of that struggle.

[. . .]

NOTES

1. Theodore Lowi's classic analysis of the privatized operations of interest-group liberalism remains descriptive of American politics; see *The End of Liberalism* (New York: W. W. Norton, 1969). For more recent analyses, see Jürgen Habermas, *Legitimation Crisis* (Boston: Beacon Press, 1973); Claus Offe, *Contradictions of the Welfare State* (Cambridge, Mass.: MIT Press, 1984); John Keane, *Public Life in Late Capitalism* (Cambridge, Mass.: MIT Press, 1984); and Benjamin Barber, *Strong Democracy* (Berkeley: University of California Press, 1984).

2. For an outstanding recent account of the virtues of and conditions for such democracy, see Philip Green, *Retrieving Democracy* (Totowa, N.J.: Rowman and Allenheld, 1985).

3. Hannah Pitkin performs a most detailed and sophisticated analysis of the virtues of the civic public as a flight from sexual difference through a reading of the texts of Machiavelli; see *Fortune Is a Woman* (Berkeley: University of California Press, 1984). Carol Pateman has an important analysis of contract theory in this respect, in *The Sexual Contract* (Stanford, Conn.: Stanford University Press, 1988). See also Nancy Hartsock, *Money, Sex and Power* (New York: Longman, 1983), chapters 7 and 8.

4. See Susan Okin, 'Women and the Making of the Sentimental Family', *Philosophy and Public Affairs*, vol. 11, no. 1 (Winter 1982), 65–88; see also Linda Nicholson, *Gender and History: The Limits of Social Theory in the Age of the Family* (New York: Columbia University Press, 1986).

5. See Ronald Takaki, *Iron Cages: Race and Culture in 19th-Century America* (New York: Knopf, 1979). Don Herzog discusses the exclusionary prejudices of some other early American republicans; see 'Some Questions for Republicans', *Political Theory*, vol. 14, no. 3 (August 1985), 473–93.

6. George Mosse, *Nationalism and Sexuality* (New York: Howard Fertig, 1985).

7. See Carole Pateman, 'Feminism and Participatory Democracy,' *Participation and Democratic Theory* (Cambridge, Mass.: Cambridge University Press, 1970).

8. I have developed a fuller account of oppression in 'Five Faces of Oppression', *The Philosophical Forum*, vol. XIX, no. 4 (Summer 1988), 270–90.

9. Jürgen Habermas, *Reason and the Rationalization of Society* (Boston: Beacon New York: Columbia University Press, 1986); and my 'Impartiality and the Civic Public: Some Implications of Feminist Critiques of Moral and Political Theory', *Praxis International*, vol. 5, no. 4 (January 1986), 381–401.

10. I use the term 'special rights' in much the same way as Elizabeth Wolgast does in *Equality and the Rights of Women* (Ithaca, N.Y.: Cornell University Press, 1980). Like Wolgast, I wish to distinguish a class of rights that all people should have, general rights, and a class of rights that categories of people should have by virtue of particular circumstances. That is, the distinction should refer only to different levels of generality, where 'special' means only 'specific'. Unfortunately, 'special rights' tends to carry a connotation of *exceptional*, that is, specially marked and deviating from the norm. As I assert below, however, the goal is not to compensate for deficiencies in order to help people be 'normal', but to denormalize, so that in certain contexts and at certain levels of abstraction everyone has 'special' rights.

11. Linda J. Krieger, 'Through a Glass Darkly: Paradigms of Equality and the Search for a Women's Jurisprudence', *Hypatia: A Journal of Feminist Philosophy*, vol. 2, no. 1 (Winter 1987), 45–62. Deborah Rhode provides an excellent synopsis of the dilemmas involved in this pregnancy debate in feminist legal theory in *Justice and Gender* (Cambridge, Mass.: Harvard University Press, 1989), chapter 9.

12. See Ann Scales, 'Towards a Feminist Jurisprudence', *Indiana Law Journal*, vol. 56 (1983). Christine Littleton provides a very good analysis of the feminist debate about equal vs different treatment regarding pregnancy and childbirth, among other legal issues for women, in 'Reconstructing Sexual Equality', *California Law*

Review, vol. 75, no. 4 (July 1987), 1,279–337. Littleton suggests, as I have stated above, that only the dominant male conception of work keeps pregnancy and birthing from being conceived of as work.

13. For one among many discussions of such 'backward-looking' and 'forward-looking' arguments, see Bernard Boxill, *Blacks and Social Justice* (Totowa, N.J.: Rowman and Allenheld, 1984), chapter 7.

'CONTINGENT FOUNDATIONS: FEMINISM AND THE QUESTION OF
"POSTMODERNISM"' BY JUDITH BUTLER

At the time of writing, Judith Butler is Maxine Elliot Professor in the
Departments of Rhetoric and Comparative Literature at the University of
California, Berkeley, and one of the leading figures in Anglo-American poststructuralist theory. She focuses particularly on the ways in which bodies
'acquire' a sex and a sexuality that affirms both the division of sexes into just
two and maintains heterosexuality as the norm. According to Butler, sex is not
a natural category, and the apparent viability of a binary sex/gender division
depends on its continual reaffirmation. Butler's repeated appearance in this
book is testament to her influence. However, she has been heavily criticised by
others, including other feminists, because her work is considered difficult and
insufficiently focused on the 'mainstream' areas of political argument. In this
extract, Butler defends the idea that there can be a political or feminist theory
that does not start from a given foundation and which does not understand 'the
subject' of politics in closed or unitary terms. It is precisely the attempt to establish a basis to political claims that is presumed to be outside of politics that
Butler wants to unmask as a disguised act of power. It follows that feminism
cannot theorise the political properly unless it is first accepted that we cannot
define the content of the category 'woman' in advance. Such an argument is
considered further in Chapter 9 on poststructuralism and deepened in Chapter
12.

'CONTINGENT FOUNDATIONS: FEMINISM AND THE QUESTION OF "POSTMODERNISM"' (1992)*

Judith Butler

The question of postmodernism is surely a question – for is there, after all,
something called postmodernism? Is it an historical characterization, a certain
kind of theoretical position, and what does it mean for a term that has described
a certain aesthetic practice now to apply to social theory and to feminist social

---

* Judith Butler, 'Contingent Foundations: Feminism and the Question of "Postmodernism"',
Judith Butler and Joan Scott (eds), *Feminists Theorize the Political* (London: Routledge, 1992).

and political theory in particular? Who are these postmodernists? Is this a name that one takes on for oneself, or is it more often a name that one is called if and when one offers a critique of the subject, a discursive analysis, or questions the integrity or coherence of totalizing social descriptions?

I know the term from the way it is used, and it usually appears on my horizon embedded in the following critical formulations: 'if a discourse is all there . . .,' or 'if everything is a text . . .,' of 'if the subject is dead . . .,' 'if real bodies do not exist . . . .'

"Zf it is real at all"

[. . .]

Against this postmodernism, there is an effort to shore up the primary premises, to establish in advance that any theory of politics requires a subject, needs from the start to presume its subject, the referentiality of language, the integrity of the institutional descriptions it provides. For politics is unthinkable without a foundation, without these premises.   *F Arg. Aciant PMoD.*

To begin the Arg. submissing to ones "rules"
 # is to reinforce their rule?   [. . .]

To claim that politics requires a stable subject is to claim that there can be no *political* opposition to that claim. Indeed, that claim implies that a critique of the subject cannot be a politically informed critique but, rather, an act which puts into jeopardy politics as such. To require the subject means to foreclose the domain of the political, and that foreclosure, installed analytically as an essential feature of the political, enforces the boundaries of the domain of the political in such a way that that enforcement is protected from political scrutiny. The act which unilaterally establishes the domain of the political functions, then, as an authoritarian ruse by which political contest over the status of the subject is summarily silenced.   *By declaring it doesnot follow rules,*
declares it invalid 3a neutral threat

[. . .]

I don't know about the term 'postmodern', but if there is a point, and a fine point, to what I perhaps better understand as poststructuralism, it is that <u>power pervades</u> the very <u>conceptual apparatus</u> that <u>seeks to negotiate its terms</u>, including the subject position of the critic; and further, that this implication of the terms of criticism in the field of power is *not* the advent of a nihilistic relativism incapable of furnishing norms, but, rather, the very precondition of a politically engaged critique. To establish a set of norms that are beyond power or force is itself a powerful and forceful conceptual practice that sublimates, disguises and extends its own power play through recourse to tropes of normative universality. And the point is not to do away with foundations, or even to champion a position that goes under the name of anti-foundationalism. Both of those positions belong together as different versions of foundationalism and the skeptical problematic it engenders. Rather, the task is to interrogate what the theoretical move that establishes foundations *authorizes*, and what precisely it excludes or forecloses.

the regiananh metachallenging is impossible to meet

345

It seems that theory posits foundations incessantly, and forms implicit metaphysical commitments as a matter of course, even when it seeks to guard against it; foundations function as the unquestioned and the unquestionable within any theory. And yet, as these 'foundations', that is, those premises that function as authorizing grounds, are they themselves not constituted through exclusions which, taken into account, expose the foundational premise as a contingent and contestable presumption? Even when we claim that there is some implied universal basis for a given foundation, that implication and that universality simply constitute a new dimension of unquestionability.

How is it that we might ground a theory or politics in a speech situation or subject position which is 'universal', when the very category of the universal has only begun to be exposed for its own highly ethnocentric biases? How many 'universalities' are there, and to what extent is cultural conflict understandable as the clashing of a set of presumed and intransigent 'universalities', a conflict which cannot be negotiated through recourse to a culturally imperialist notion of the 'universal' or, rather, which will only be solved through resource at the cost of violence?

[. . .]

A social theory committed to democratic contestation within a postcolonial horizon needs to find a way to bring into question the foundations it is compelled to lay down. It is this movement of interrogating that ruse of authority that seeks to close itself off from contest that is, in my view, at the heart of any radical political project. Inasmuch as poststructuralism offers a mode of critique that effects this contestation of the foundationalist move, it can be used as a part of such a radical agenda. Note that I have said, 'it can be used': I think there are no necessary political consequences for such a theory, but only a possible political deployment.

If one of the points associated with postmodernism is that the epistemological point of departure in philosophy is inadequate, then it ought not to be a question of subjects who claim to know and theorize under the sign of the postmodern pitted against other subjects who claim to know and theorize under the sign of the modern. Indeed, it is that very way of framing debate that is being contested by the suggestion that the position articulated by the subject is always in some way constituted by what must be displaced for that position to take hold, and that the subject who theorizes is constituted as a 'theorizing subject' by a set of exclusionary and selective procedures. For, indeed, who is it that gets constituted as the feminist theorist whose framing of the debate will get publicity? Is it not always the case that power operates in advance, in the very procedures that establish who will be the subject who speaks in the name of feminism, and to whom?

[. . .]

The critique of the subject is not a negation or repudiation of the subject, but, rather, a way of interrogating its construction as a pre-given or foundationalist premise.

[. . .]

We may be tempted to think that to assume the subject in advance is necessary in order to safeguard the *agency* of the subject. But to claim that the subject is constituted is not to claim that it is determined; on the contrary, the constituted character of the subject is the very precondition of its agency. For what is it that enables a purposive and significant reconfiguration of cultural and political relations, if not a relative that can be turned against itself, reworked, resisted? Do we need to assume theoretically from the start a subject with agency *before* we can articulate the terms of a significant social and political task of transformation, resistance, radical democratization? If we do not offer in advance the theoretical guarantee of that agent, are we doomed to give up transformation and meaningful political practice? My suggestion is that agency belongs to a way of thinking about persons as instrumental actors who confront an external political field. But if we agree that politics and power exist already at the level at which the subject and its agency are articulated and made possible, then agency can be *presumed* only at the cost of refusing to inquire into its construction. Consider that 'agency' has no formal existence or, if it does, it has no bearing on the question at hand. In a sense, the epistemological model that offers us a pre-given subject or agent is one that refuses to acknowledge that *agency is always and only a political prerogative*. As such, it seems crucial to question the conditions of its possibility, not to take it for granted as an *a priori* guarantee. We need instead to ask, what possibilities of mobilization are produced on the basis of existing configurations of discourse and power? Where are the possibilities of reworking that very matrix of power by which we are constituted, or reconstituting the legacy of that constitution, and of working against each other those processes of regulation that can destabilize existing power regimes? For if the subject is constituted by power, that power does not cease at the moment the subject is constituted, for that subject is never fully constituted, but is subjected and produced time and again. That subject is neither a ground nor a product, but the permanent possibility of a certain resignifying process, one which gets detoured and stalled through other mechanisms of power, but which is power's own possibility of being reworked. It is not enough to say that the subject is invariably engaged in a political field; that phenomenological phrasing misses the point that the subject is an accomplishment regulated and produced in advance. And it is as such fully political; indeed, perhaps *most* political at the point in which it is claimed to be prior to politics itself. To perform this kind of Foucaultian critique of the subject is not to do away with the subject or pronounce its death, but merely to claim that certain versions of the subject are politically insidious.

For the subject to be a pre-given point of departure for politics is to defer the question of the political construction and regulation of the subject itself; for it is important to remember that subjects are constituted through exclusion, that is, through the creation of a domain of deauthorized subjects, presubjects, figures of abjection, populations erased from view. This becomes clear, for instance, within the law when certain qualifications must first be met in order to be, quite literally, a claimant in sex-discrimination or rape cases. Here it becomes quite urgent to ask who qualifies as a 'who', what systematic structures of disempowerment make it impossible for certain injured parties to invoke the 'I' effectively within a court of law? Or less overtly, in a social theory like Albert Memmi's *The Colonizer and the Colonized*, an otherwise compelling call for radical enfranchisement, the category of women falls into neither category, the oppressor or the oppressed.[1] How do we theorize the exclusion of women from the category of the oppressed? Here the construction of subject positions works to exclude women from the description of oppression, and this constitutes a different kind of oppression, one that is effected by the very *erasure* that grounds the articulation of the emancipatory subject. As Joan Scott makes clear in *Gender and the Politics of History*, once it is understood that subjects are formed through exclusionary operations, it becomes politically necessary to trace the operations of that construction and erasure.[2]

[. . .]

There is the refrain that, just now, when women are beginning to assume the place of subjects, postmodern positions come along to announce that the subject is dead (there is a difference between positions of poststructuralism which claim that the subject *never* existed, and postmodern positions which claim that the subject *once* had integrity, but no longer does). Some see this as a conspiracy against women and other disenfranchised groups who are now only beginning to speak on their own behalf. But what precisely is meant by this, and how do we account for the very strong criticisms of the subject as an instrument of Western imperialist hegemony theorized by Gloria Anzaldúa,[3] Gayatri Spivak[4] and various theorists of postcoloniality? Surely there is a caution offered here, that in the very struggle toward enfranchisement and democratization, we might adopt the very models of domination by which we were oppressed, not realizing that one way that domination works is through the regulation and production of subjects. Through what exclusions has the feminist subject been constructed, and how do those excluded domains return to haunt the 'integrity' and 'unity' of the feminist 'we'? And how is it that the very category, the subject, the 'we' that is supposed to be presumed for the purpose of solidarity, produces the very factionalization it is supposed to quell? Do women want to become subjects on the model which requires and produces an anterior region of abjection, or must feminism become a process which is self-critical about the processes that produce and destabilize identity categories? To take the construction of the subject as a political problematic is not the same as doing away with the subject; to deconstruct the subject is not to negate or throw away the concept; on the contrary, deconstruction implies only that we suspend all commitments to that to which the term 'the subject' refers, and that we consider the linguistic functions it serves in the consolidation and concealment of authority. To deconstruct is not to negate or to dismiss, but to call into question and, perhaps most importantly, to open up a term, like the subject, to a reusage or redeployment that previously has not been authorized.

Within feminism, it seems as if there is some political necessity to speak as and for *women*, and I would not contest that necessity. Surely, that is the way in which representational politics operates, and in this country, lobbying efforts are virtually impossible without recourse to identity politics. So we agree that demonstrations and legislative efforts and radical movements need to make claims in the name of women.

But this necessity needs to be reconciled with another. The minute that the category of women is invoked as *describing* the constituency for which feminism speaks, an internal debate invariably begins over what the descriptive content of that term will be. There are those who claim that there it is an ontological specificity to women as childbearers that forms the basis of a specific legal and political interest in representation, and then there are others who understand maternity to be a social relation that is, under current social circumstances, the specific and cross-cultural situation of women. And there are those who seek recourse to Gilligan and others to establish a feminine specificity that makes itself clear in women's communities or ways of knowing. But every time that specificity is articulated, there is resistance and factionalization within the very constituency that is supposed to be *unified* by the articulation of its common element. In the early 1980s, the feminist 'we' rightly came under attack by women of color who claimed that the 'we' was invariably white, and that that 'we' that was meant to solidify the movement was the very source of a painful factionalization. The effort to characterize a feminine specificity through recourse to maternity, whether biological or social, produced a similar factionalization and even a disavowal of feminism altogether. For surely all women are not mothers; some cannot be, some are too young or too old to be, some choose not to be, and for some who are mothers, that is necessarily the rallying point of their politicization in feminism.

I would argue that any effort to give universal or specific content to the category of women, presuming that that guarantee of solidarity is required *in advance*, will necessarily produce factionalization, and that 'identity' as a point of departure can never hold as the solidifying ground of a feminist political movement. Identity categories are never merely descriptive, but always normative, and as such, exclusionary. This is not to say that the term 'women' ought not to be used, or that we ought to announce the death of the category. On the contrary, if feminism presupposes that 'women' designates an undesignatable field of differences, one that cannot be totalized or summarized by a descriptive identity category, then the very term becomes a site of permanent openness and resignifiability. I would argue that the rifts among women over the content of the term ought to be safeguarded and prized, indeed, that this constant rifting ought to be affirmed as the ungrounded ground of feminist theory. To deconstruct the subject of feminism is not, then, to censure its usage, but, on the contrary, to release the term into a future of multiple significations, to emancipate it from the maternal or racialist ontologies to which it has been restricted, and to give it play as a site where unanticipated meanings might come to bear.

[. . .]

One might well ask: but doesn't there have to be a set of norms that discriminate between those descriptions that ought to adhere to the category of women and those that do not? The only answer to that question is a counter-question: who would set those norms, and what contestations would they produce? To establish a normative foundation for settling the question of what ought properly to be included in the description of women would be only and always to produce a new site of political contest. That foundation would settle nothing, but would of its own necessity founder on its own authoritarian ruse. This is not to say that there is no foundation, but rather, that wherever there is one, there will also be a foundering, a contestation. That such foundations exist only to be put into question is, as it were, the permanent risk of the process of democratization. To refuse that contest is to sacrifice the radical democratic impetus of feminist politics. That the category is unconstrained, even that it comes to serve anti-feminist purposes, will be part of the risk of this procedure. But this is a risk that is produced by the very foundationalism that seeks to safeguard feminism against it. In a sense, this risk is the foundation, and hence is not, of any feminist practice.

[. . .]

NOTES

1. Albert Memmi, *The Colonizer and the Colonized* (Boston: Beacon Press, 1965), p. 129.
2. Joan W. Scott, *Gender and the Politics of History* (New York: Columbia University Press, 1988), introduction.
3. Gloria Anzaldúa, *La Frontera/Borderlands* (San Francisco: Spinsters Ink, 1988).
4. Gayatri Spivak, 'Can the Subaltern Speak?', in *Marxism and the Interpretation of Culture*, ed. Nelson and Grossberg (Chicago: University of Illinois Press, 1988).

8

ECOLOGISM AND ENVIRONMENTALISM

Tim Hayward

INTRODUCTION: FROM ENVIRONMENTALISM TO ECOLOGISM

The term 'environmentalism' can be taken to refer, quite generally, to the belief that environmental protection is a significant ethical, social and political value. Until relatively recently, it was considered by many to be a marginal and combative creed. But environmental campaigners have been successful over the last few decades in bringing to public awareness the force of their case, and the situation has changed markedly. The importance of environmental issues is now so widely acknowledged that social and political activists are almost as likely to claim a commitment to principles of environmentalism as they are to those of democracy.

But while environmentalists have been successful in raising general awareness of the extent and gravity of environmental problems, this has not always been matched by effective action to deal with them. Even when action is taken in good faith, the remedies often fall short of what is required. One reason for the inadequacy of responses to environmental problems is that they tend to be viewed as discrete issues for policy-makers to deal with. Consequently, their interconnections and underlying causes are not fully addressed. Another reason is that to deal with environmental problems can require measures that conflict with other important policy aims that compete for resources. And it is these that are often accorded priority, particularly when they favour economic growth and development. An underlying problem, therefore, is that environmental objectives are often perceived as representing unacceptable costs against socioeconomic objectives. Correspondingly, politicians and the public are not always strongly motivated to take a longer-term view of what is environmentally desirable when this looks unfavourable from the perspective of a short-term cost/benefit analysis. As long as the environment is seen as just one policy area among many, and with no particular priority, then the aims of environmentalism are always liable to remain unfulfilled. Hence many green thinkers and activists believe that a more radical approach is called for than that of environmentalism.

Such radicals criticise attempts to manage or regulate discrete environmental problems within existing institutional structures and without considering their ecological and social interrelations. They consider environmentalism too restricted in failing to question radically the very way of life that gives rise to these problems. They believe it is not enough to aim for policies that deal with problems as they arise. Rather, it is necessary to rethink the basic organisation of the societies that generate such problems in the first place. Those who believe that 'managerial' approaches to environmental problems fail to tackle the root causes of the problems in humans' interaction with the non-human, natural world see environmentalism as not only inadequate but also shallow and insufficiently holistic in its understanding of the nature of the problem. Hence green parties, environmental activists and green political theorists have often appealed to principles and values that they believe go deeper than those of environmentalism. In both theory and ideology, these more radical ideas have begun to coalesce around the idea of 'ecologism'.

ECOLOGISM

Within green political theory, Andrew Dobson has been an influential promoter of the idea that ecologism is a distinct political ideology. He presents it in terms of a set of contrasts with environmentalism. As he writes in the extract reproduced below, '*environmentalism* argues for a managerial approach to environmental problems, secure in the belief that they can be solved without fundamental changes in present values or patterns of production and consumption', but '*ecologism* holds that a sustainable and fulfilling existence presupposes radical changes in our relationship with the non-human natural world, and in our mode of social and political life' (Dobson, 2000: 2). For instance, where environmentalism would have us use unleaded petrol in our cars, ecologism would question not only our reliance on road transport but also our petroleum-based economy, our energy usage generally, and our entire relationship with the non-human world.

Ecologism, moreover, can lay better claim to being a political ideology than environmentalism. Indeed, it is difficult to conceive of environmentalism as a political ideology at all, for, on the one hand, its aims are confined within just part of the spectrum of general political concerns, and any party adopting it as an ideology would likely be marginalised as a 'single-issue party'. On the other hand, proponents of most other ideologies can, as they increasingly do, incorporate elements of environmental concern alongside their more traditional preoccupations, adopting these in a selective and piecemeal fashion while still prioritising their own core concerns. Ecologism, by contrast, is claimed by Dobson to be an ideology on a par with the established ideologies of Liberalism, socialism and conservatism. Like them, he believes, ecologism has not only a distinctive take on what a good society ought (and ought not) to look like, but also core values that are irreducible to the core values of other ideologies. Thus, as liberty is the core value of Liberalism and equality of socialism, the core value of ecologism, he believes, is 'ecocentrism'. This, as Dobson notes, is a contested notion; but so too are liberty and equality. If ecologism admits of a variety of interpretations, so too do the other ideologies.

Nevertheless, contest over the meaning and validity of ecologism's core value may be more thoroughgoing than that relating to liberty and equality. The latter are values which, however they are interpreted, mean something about how humans live together in political society. The idea of 'ecocentrism' is rather less clear in its range of meanings, and does not seem so directly to focus guidance on human relations.

Still, we might interpret the idea in a quite general way, as referring to political beliefs and values that in some way are 'centred in ecology'. There is a family of nascent ideological groupings at whose core is some reference to ecology: these include deep ecology and social ecology, as well as hybrids such as **eco-feminism, eco-anarchism** and eco-socialism. If we focus on the **ontological** sense of 'centred in ecology', then the general distinctiveness of ecologism as an ideology may be indicated in the following way: Liberalism presupposes the human individual as its basic unit; socialism presupposes human collectivities; but ecologism presupposes that humans are part of nature. This is its basic **ontological** assumption.

HUMANS AS PART OF NATURE: THE PHILOSOPHICAL BASIS OF ECOLOGISM

The term 'ecology' was originally coined to refer to the totality of relationships between organisms and their environments, including both their **biotic** and **abiotic** constituents. It refers both to the reality of these interrelationships and to the scientific study of them as a biological discipline.

One question, then, is how a biological science can yield knowledge, let alone values, of relevance to political thought. In the early days of political ecological writings, one found suggestions such as 'one can and should follow nature' in one's human behaviour. Notwithstanding the kernel of wisdom that may underlie such a general proposition, it is all but impossible to operationalise in a determinate fashion. It is not obvious how one can follow nature when nature teaches contradictory lessons. After all, nature can exemplify benign harmony but can also appear 'red in tooth and claw'. Even where certain values – such as resilience, diversity and so on – might be thought to have some purchase on human affairs, as in ecosystems, one must still be cautious about their translatability into, and applicability for, social and political organisation. One should also take due heed of philosophical warnings about committing the naturalistic fallacy or the fallacy of ecologism. Writing before 'ecologism' designated a political ideology, Arne Naess, a founding theorist of its values, referred to the fallacy of 'excessive generalisation or generalisation of ecological concepts and theories' (Naess, 1989: 39).

Another sort of question arises from the claim that ecologism is both 'deeper' ecologically and more socially aware than environmentalism. As we have noted, ecologism proposes radical changes in our relationship *both* with the non-human natural world and in our mode of social and political life. But is there a coherent basis for this proposition? Disputes, for instance, between proponents of deep ecology and social ecology (see Dobson, 2000: chapter 2) highlight considerable tensions concerning whether the two sorts of change are mutually compatible or even flow from a single source. For, while the emphasis on changing our relation with non-human nature is at the heart of deep ecology, the need to change our mode of social and political life is emphasised by social ecology; yet the latter's positive evaluation of **humanism** seems to go against the anti-anthropocentric impulse of deep ecology.

The key to seeking a firm basis and coherent conceptual framework for ecologism perhaps lies in starting from that part of nature that we humans, so to speak, are. Nature should not be seen as something 'out there', apart from us, whether we want to exploit it, dominate it or learn lessons from it. To take an ecological view is to see humans as a part of nature, not as a kind of being that exists apart from it. Humans are not 'part nature' and 'part something else' (part rational or part social). They are natural beings who have certain capacities which some, or perhaps all, other natural beings do not have. These capacities may set humans apart from other natural beings – as any characteristic of a species might set it off from others – but they do not set them apart from nature. Humans, like all other organisms, stand within a web of ecological relations. To take an ecological perspective is to take a fuller and more complex view of humans in relation to the rest of nature than is taken by an environmentalism that considers the environment only in terms of humans' 'life-support system'.

In seeing humans as a part of nature, and in taking this to have constitutive implications for political theory and practice, ecologism is clearly contrasted with other ideologies that are premised on humans' radical apartness from the rest of nature. This does not mean denying, though, that humans can appropriately be conceived as rational individuals (as in liberalism) or as social beings (as in socialism), but it is to say that neither of these characterisations is exhaustive of what is relevant about humans for political thought. They need to be supplemented, and perhaps underpinned, by an account of how humans are also natural beings.

There are three distinct implications for political theory of the assumption of humans' naturalness. The first is that humans have *natural capacities*, as individuals and as members of the species. These condition possible forms of individual development and social co-operation. They also constitute limits to possible adaptation to changed environments. Although natural capacities are always socially and culturally inflected, they do establish parameters within which concepts of the good life may be characterised.

Second, there are *natural limits* of both 'internal' and 'external' sorts to human development: there are limits to what the human organism can achieve or tolerate; there are limits to the demands humans can place on natural resources. These limits not only have to do with defining the good life, but also bear on questions of justice. As natural and finite beings in a natural and finite world, therefore, humans must heed this finitude, and not assume that distributive principles can be developed in abstraction from it.

Third, like other beings, humans exist in webs of *natural relations*. These are of numerous kinds: natural relations of biological kinship between humans, on which familial and social relations are supervenient; between humans who are not blood relatives, relations are naturally *mediated*, for instance in the sense that reproductive and productive activities occur in a natural medium; and all humans, individually and collectively, have relations to their environment. Moreover, humans not only *have* an environment, they themselves *are* the environment of other beings – this is the case for humans individually (as hosts for various micro-organisms), socially (as beings whose practices and institutions provide an anthropogenic environment) and as (populations of) a species, to the extent that they participate in ecosystemic relations as organic beings. Finally, there are among other natural beings many, especially animals, with which humans have work and leisure relations, forms of co-operation and communication, that are more like relations with other humans than with their environment.

The assumption that humans' natural being is of political significance thus has three important implications for normative political theory. It places constraints on, and provides some determinations for, accounts of the good; of justice or right; and on our dealings with non-human nature. Full recognition of each of these is necessary for an adequate political theory under contemporary conditions, and is perhaps sufficient to distinguish a political theory, informed by what we might call the philosophy of ecologism, from other political philosophies. Certainly, other political philosophies may, in some versions, take on board one or both of the first two of these implications. These can be seen as extensions of, rather than radical departures from, more traditional concerns with the right and the good. This helps explain the plausibility of claims to green credentials by certain liberals, socialists and conservatives. However, in such cases we still find only a green tinge, so to speak. Only when all three are fully adopted can a political ideology be considered fully 'ecological'.

ECOLOGISM AND ETHICS

In establishing the normative implications that follow from the premises of ecologism, two general lines of inquiry can be distinguished. First, does ecologism offer new insights regarding the ways human behaviour affects non-human organisms and ecological systems? Second, does it offer a novel take on how humans should act in their relations with other humans? Let us focus on the first of these questions.

From an ecologistic perspective, questions about the ethically appropriate treatment of non-human beings assume an importance they do not have for other political philosophies. The latter take it for granted that political organisation and ethical norms relate exclusively to humans. Even environmentalism, understood as concern for the human environment, does not necessarily confront such questions if its concern is essentially with the maintenance of the human life-support system. Such an approach advocates care for the environment because, and to the extent that, we need it for our survival and well-being. This is an instrumental and human-centred view of environmental values which ecologism seeks to challenge and transcend. Ecologistic theorists identify reasons to care about non-human beings 'for their own sake' and not only because their survival and flourishing may have benefits for humans. Central to such an argument are the rejection of 'anthropocentrism' and advocacy of respect for 'nature's intrinsic value'.

Anthropocentrism literally means 'human-centredness' and has increasingly come to be applied to attitudes, values or practices which give exclusive or preferential concern to human interests at the expense of the interests or well-being of other species or the environment. Ethical criticism of anthropocentrism in part draws out the consequences of the belief that humans are a part of nature. If humans can no longer be thought to occupy a special and privileged position in the world, this calls into question their prerogative to use natural creatures and the environment however they see fit. Many human practices can be criticised on these grounds, including those which involve cruelty to animals, destruction of habitats, endangering species, upsetting the balance of ecosystems and so on. There are also practical problems involved in avoiding anthropocentrism. A concern with human interests is in some ways inescapable and legitimate while applied ethics has to deal with 'hard cases' where vital human interests oppose those of non-humans. Furthermore, there are limits as to how much humans can actually know about what is good for non-humans. Such difficulties can perhaps be overcome, however, by recognising that there are different types of anthropocentrism: for instance, between 'strong' forms which are rejected because they involve unjustifiable human preferentiality, and 'weak' forms which are accepted because they allow only the unobjectionable features.

A normative commitment to the *intrinsic value of non-human nature* is supposed, on many accounts of ecological values, to be one thing which is distinctive about them. This idea is invoked to oppose the assumption that humans need have no regard to the effects on non-human nature of their activities. Of course, humans seldom, if ever, completely disregard the effects of their actions on non-human nature; but, according to ecologism, their concern should be for nature for its 'own sake'. But there are problems here. In particular, what is the locus of the intrinsic value of nature? Which kind of entity is to be deemed to have it: individual organisms, populations, species or entire ecosystems? Much debate within environmental ethics concerns precisely this question. After all, what is good for one constituency might be bad for another. Hence, in practice, a general commitment to nature's intrinsic value does not always yield unequivocal guidance for action.

A basic problem in trying to transcend a human-centred ethical viewpoint is that, as humans, we are stuck with a human perspective: our perceptual, cognitive and evaluative capacities are species-specific; we cannot be certain that the judgements we make about the good of other species or their members are absolutely reliable. Moreover, given that there is competition between other species, we have to recognise that any human ethic must be selective in what it attaches importance to. Such considerations problematise the very idea that we can ever really value or act towards other beings 'for their own sake' as opposed to, at best, imputing to them certain interests on the basis of human assumptions about value. Moreover, general criticisms of human-centredness can overlook how harm to and exploitation of non-human nature may be caused and benefited from by particular groups of humans at the expense of other humans.

But perhaps these problems are not completely insurmountable or utterly damaging to ecological ethics. Some views of the goods of non-humans seem to be pretty reliable, at least to the extent necessary for understanding the conditions of their flourishing. Some ecological criteria seem pretty reliable. We certainly need some caution, humility and provisionality in our views of the goods of non-humans, but the key point for ecological ethics is that we try, in good faith, to arrive at a reasonable view of them. We are already interfering with ecosystems and non-humans. To the extent that we are acting in this way, we need to inform our actions with the best possible reasons and values.

What follows for specifically political values? What specific recommendations might ecologism offer to those interested in the values that should guide the conduct of affairs between humans? Does it have a specific conception of the good life or offer a distinctive take on the question of justice?

Certain value commitments can be derived from the basic idea of living within our ecological means. These can be understood as imperatives that are both constraining and enabling: constraining in that humans must put less strain on ecological resources (by reducing consumption, waste and the general exploitation of non-human nature, allowing ecological systems to work within their 'carrying capacity' and biological diversity to be preserved, and ensuring resources are not used at rates faster than they naturally reproduce themselves); enabling in that it is about fostering a way of life that incorporates patterns of consumption and production which contribute better to human flourishing. Under conventional economic imperatives, much production and consumption is geared to engendering new needs, which in turn give rise to demand for production of further 'goods'. The ecological view involves a step back from this process to ask what humans *really* need for a good life. In this, inspiration is sometimes drawn from earlier, utopian writers such as Charles **Fourier** or William **Morris**. Of course, there are varying, and sometimes conflicting, accounts of the details of a green utopia, just as there are about the roots of contemporary malaise; and there is even greater uncertainty about how to realise utopian visions in practice. Nevertheless, the ideals of cultivating a focus on needs rather than wants, on *being* rather than *having*, and developing a conception of 'wealth' through an orientation to human flourishing rather than acquisition of things or money, are arguably more truly realistic. Indeed, the ecological view underpinning the critique of conventional economics is much closer to the real facts of life in recognising the economy's tremendous debt to nature and that the true source of all wealth lies in life's processes, driven by the energy of the sun, rather than in humans' 'productive' activity, much less in the abstract dealings of an exchange economy (see for example Hayward, 1995, chapter 3).

Hence certain central tenets of the good life from an ecological perspective can be summed up in popular green slogans such as 'simple in means, rich in ends' or 'to be rather than to have'. For many greens, moreover, a spiritual dimension is important; and some look to Eastern traditions, particularly those grounded in **Taoist** or **Buddhist** beliefs, for models of a more spiritual relation to non-human nature and to one's fellow humans.

Because of these emphases, some commentators have considered it appropriate to characterise green values as *postmaterialist*. This describes values appealed to by sections of a population that are secure in the meeting of their material needs and now look for some meaning to life beyond what can be represented in material terms. However, while this view may have some truth as a sociological thesis about the composition and motivations of green movements in affluent countries, it is rather restrictive, and perhaps even misleading. Criticism of consumerism and economic growth for its own sake point to a commitment to values that do not depend on a 'materialist' attitude in the everyday sense of the term. It is also true that, in developed countries, green movements have tended more to attract disaffected members of the affluent middle classes than the less materially secure. Yet political ecology also has highly 'material' concerns 'about food, work, health, the quality of life, and most materially of all, the very issue of survival' (Wall, 1990: 66), especially in poorer parts of the world, where ecological politics is about securing the most fundamental processes of material production and reproduction of the conditions of existence.

So ecological politics is not only about questions of the good life, or about aggregative limits; it also has to do with the distribution of benefits and burdens. And here its concerns converge on those of recognisable positions on the issue of social justice.

JUSTICE AND RIGHTS

Arguably, early green thinking underemphasised the importance of justice. A key feature of green thinking has always been a distinctive concern with natural limits on human consumption, production and population growth. However, as others have emphasised, natural limits are always and necessarily *socially mediated* (see for example Benton, 1993). Natural limits do not make themselves felt at the same time, in the same way, in all places. Quite generally, it is those whose situation is socially and economically most precarious who are liable to bear the brunt of their effects, whereas the wealthier can pay to avoid or export many of the most serious problems, or to ensure they are dealt with. It is notable that often, perhaps even typically, those whose activities are the root cause of greatest ecological disruption, and who reap its economic benefits, are not the same people who bear the brunt of its environmental consequences. This is especially the case when interests are compared and contrasted on a global scale. So it is not necessarily, or even typically, humans in general whose interests are served by ecological disruption. How natural limits actually make themselves felt is a result of social, economic and political choices.

Given that there are ecological constraints to the possible extent of sustainable economic development, there are limits to how much the worst-off can expect to benefit from it. Hence pro-active redistribution seems more appropriate, with limits on growth for the richer. For this reason, a concern with social justice is integral to green thinking, and is normally a central plank of Green Party platforms and manifestos. So too are human rights.

Greens' support for human rights follows not just from concerns of social justice, but also from ecological concerns. For one thing, serious environmental harms are frequently accompanied by civil and political oppression, and there is reason to see common cause between struggles against both. Social and economic rights can also be mobilised to contribute to environmental protection through providing substantive standards of human well-being. Rights to health, decent living conditions and decent working conditions may all bear directly upon environmental conditions. If certain social and economic rights may be considered material preconditions for the effective enjoyment of civil and political rights, it seems equally arguable that the effective enjoyment of an adequate environment is a precondition for the enjoyment of any of those rights.

An advantage of pursuing environmental ends by means of human rights is that, in doing so, one can draw normative and practical support from an established discourse of fundamental human rights. The human-rights discourse, which does enjoy considerable consensus in international law, embodies just the sort of non-negotiable values which seem to be required for environmental legislation (see for example Aiken, 1992). Indeed, the view has been advanced, not least influentially by the Brundtland Report (World Commission on Environment and Development, 1987), that the goals of environmentalism can be presented as essentially an extension of the existing human-rights discourse. There is evidence that governments, as well as social scientists and environmental campaigners, consider this a natural extension of human rights.

Certainly, one would not expect environmental rights themselves to be a panacea for all ecological and social challenges. Some critics even see rights as counterproductive: if natural ecosystems have a limited carrying capacity which simply cannot support all the demands of a growing human population, then they cannot necessarily support all the rights that might be claimed. So the pursuit of a full range of rights for an unlimited number of people would be unsustainable and ultimately self-defeating. Moreover, it would perpetuate the anthropocentric view that the world is merely a resource or background for humans arrogating rights to themselves, heedless of the good of non-human nature. Still, paying due heed to limits and, crucially, to responsibilities, it seems likely that human rights do have an important and constructive role to play in ecological politics and in opening up debate about the foundations and institutional design of an ecologically sustainable polity.

ECOLOGY AND POLITICAL ORGANISATION

The question remains, though, whether ecologistic thought has anything distinctive to offer with regard to political organisation and institutions. In the early green literature, which was above all concerned to highlight the seriousness and urgency of ecological problems, dramatic political solutions were advanced. Markedly contrasting solutions were proposed, however, with some being highly authoritarian while others were radically democratic and even anarchistic.

Authoritarian solutions appeared necessary to a number of early green writers in the wake of newly perceived limits to growth and concerns about population expansion. Garrett Hardin's (1968) analysis of these in terms of the 'Tragedy of the Commons' was influential in formulating the idea that only by the imposition of strong restrictions from above could disaster be averted. However, not only would authoritarian solutions be objectionable to anyone committed to principles of democracy, there is also reason to think that they would be unsuccessful in dealing with ecological problems. For one thing, there is no very good reason to suppose that an authoritarian government would be seriously committed to the implementation of ecological principles, given that these are often likely to conflict with the imperatives associated with securing an authoritarian regime in power. This is not to say that an authoritarian regime would necessarily ignore the need to maintain an ecological infrastructure; and it could of course espouse certain 'green' values: indeed, as Anna Bramwell has noted in an attempt to cast green thought in an essentially authoritarian mould, the Nazi Party's ideology, for instance, appealed to the anti-modernist values of the 'soil', and Hitler was a vegetarian (Bramwell, 1989). But even allowing for such contingent 'greenness' of authoritarians, there would remain the practical problem that an authoritarian form of government is peculiarly unresponsive, in virtue of its hierarchical organisation, to feedback about appropriate responses to diffuse and complex problems such as those of ecology (see for example Dryzek, 1987).

Far more typical of actual green parties and movements has been a commitment to radical democracy, some influential examples of which historically emerged out of anarchistic and left-libertarian traditions. Green politics has aspired to new political forms based in grass-roots social movements committed to extra-parliamentary, non-conventional and decentralised forms of political action. Green parliamentary parties have sought to preserve this impetus, as mediators of grass-roots politics, through radically democratic internal organisation.

However, in practice, they have had difficulty devising robust solutions to standard problems with the operationalising of radical democracy, and green parties generally have tended to be taken over by moderate reformists within them. These take a view which is consonant to that articulated by Goodin, namely that what is important is the achievement of green policy aims; how this is brought about is a secondary question. Goodin's crucial observation is that there is in fact no necessary connection at all between democracy and green values. 'To advocate democracy is to advocate procedures, to advocate environmentalism is to advocate substantive outcomes: what guarantee can we have that the former procedures will yield the latter sorts of outcomes?' On his view, there is no guarantee.

Nevertheless, many ecological thinkers would dispute the view that green ends can so clearly be set apart from ungreen procedures. The aims of ecological politics include the manner in which people relate to and act with one another, while policy aims, and the values informing them, are the product of democratic deliberation. Hence there is a marked preference in the theory and practice of ecological politics for some form of deliberative or discursive democracy, whereby all questions relating both to ends and to means are open to debate among participants. To be sure, even proponents of deliberative democracy recognise that it is not necessarily a panacea for the sorts of problem Goodin highlights; and, as John Dryzek, for instance, acknowledges, individuals engaged in discursive practices might still 'reflectively and competently choose to downgrade environmental concerns in comparison with (say) economic prosperity or social integration' (Dryzek, 1992: 38). Nevertheless, it may be suggested that when reasons for decisions have to be publicly defended, as they do in discursive fora, more transparent decisions may be reached; and if the ecological case has a stronger basis with regard to the rationality of the situation, this truth might out.

THE AGENTS OF ECOLOGICAL POLITICS AND THEIR RATIONALITY

But does ecologism have rationality on its side? Some critics argue that only the more restricted aims of environmentalism can claim to be supported by rationality. For instance, a group of eminent scientists who launched an appeal to those assembled at the Rio Summit in 1992 mounted a defence of treating environmental concerns *within* the prevailing modes of thought and action challenged by ecologism. They affirmed a commitment to 'the preservation of our common heritage, the Earth', but expressed their concern at 'the emergence of an irrational ideology which is opposed to scientific and industrial progress, and impedes economic and social development' (quoted in Holland, 1992: 189). They claim that 'many essential human activities are carried out either by manipulating hazardous substances and that progress and development have always involved control over hostile forces, to the benefit of mankind'. For them, the 'greatest evils which stalk our Earth are ignorance and oppression'; and, in the struggle against these, science, technology and industry are our indispensable weapons.

This is in marked contrast to ecologism, which takes a view more consonant with that of Vandana Shiva, who claims that the unbridled pursuit of progress, guided by science and development, has tended 'to destroy life without any assessment of how fast and how much of the diversity of life on this planet is disappearing' (Shiva, 1989: xiv). Thus Shiva, in common with other radical ecologists, challenges the scientists' unreconstructed view of what is rational on the grounds that it is precisely the application of apparent advances in human reason which lies at the root of an increasing irrationality of the human relation with nature:

> 'Rational' man of the modern West is exposed today as a bundle of irrationalities, threatening the very survival of humankind. When we find that those who claimed to carry the light have led us into darkness and those who were declared to be inhabiting the dark recesses of ignorance were actually enlightened, it is but rational to redefine categories and meanings. (ibid.: 233)

Hence ecologism entails *questioning* the rationality that should be taken as a guide to social and political action.

In questioning competing conceptions of rationality, a central issue is how these relate to human interests. There has, in fact, been a marked tendency shared by greens and their critics to portray green politics as transcending human interests altogether. This makes it appear as a political form of generalised altruism, involving the making of personal sacrifices – of interests and preferences – for the greater ecological good, including the good of non-humans too. Yet, for this reason, green politics has often been unattractive and unpersuasive to many people. A major obstacle to an ecological reorientation of political values or an ecological reconstruction of social institutions is that people often do not consider that such changes would be in their interest (for a fuller discussion, see Hayward, 1998). Thus significant questions for ecological politics concern who is motivated to pursue ecological ends, for what reasons, and by what means. The question of who might be the agents of ecological change is a particularly thorny one, since, unlike other political ideologies, the core values of ecologism do not clearly respond, at least in a direct way, to any identifiable interest-bearers in society. Thus, while a potential strength of ecological politics is the mobilisation of a variety of social forces outside mainstream political channels, this is accompanied by the corresponding problem not only that different grass-roots movements aim at discrete objectives, but that these objectives can also conflict. Furthermore, they exercise limited political *power*.

One of the archetypal ways of characterising ecological problems is in terms of the problem of how to secure collective or public goods when the means of securing them conflict with more particular or private interests. This view of the problem, as a problem of choice for rationally self-interested individuals, has been captured by Garrett Hardin as an instance of the sort of **'free rider problem'** familiar from **rational choice theory**. When resources are commonly owned, or not owned at all, individuals have an interest in exploiting them for maximum private benefit, and have little regard to the costs of doing so since these are distributed more widely and thinly. Yet what is individually rational is collectively irrational. It is thus arguable that environmental goods have the character of public goods and so are not appropriately considered as questions of individual preference at all; decisions about the provision of public goods are appropriately a collective and political matter – a matter of properly informed public debate, involving political deliberation in public fora rather than calculations of private interests; it would involve collective deliberation about social goals, and not the mere aggregation of individual preferences.

In this sense, ecologism can be seen as recalling politics to its own most central and constitutive commitments rather than remaining in thrall to the narrow and short-sighted values associated with individualistic economic incentives. This may leave questions about its motivational force, especially in the shorter term, but not about its longer-term rationality.

CONCLUSION

It is not possible to predict what will become of ecological politics in the future, or to what extent a new ideology will be consolidated around principles of ecologism. Not all ecologically sympathetic writers believe the development of an ecological ideology to be desirable, and some favour instead a more pragmatic approach to incorporating environmental values into democratic politics: even among those who share the radical aspirations of ecologism, as distinct from environmentalism, one may encounter scepticism about how far the radical philosophical claims may actually serve to guide the development of ecological politics (see for example De-Shalit, 2000; Light and Katz, 1996).

Nevertheless, all ideologies arise as a response to specific historical conjunctures of issues, and give expression to new or hitherto unsatisfied interests in ways that may initially be difficult fully to articulate. What is certain is that ecologism focuses on issues of major significance. Whether or not it will formulate a distinctive solution, there seems good reason to believe that its agenda will command increasing attention. At the very least, it will serve to counter hubristic assumptions that Liberalism or socialism represent the end of ideology. As polities guided by both ideologies have demonstrated, the solutions to the problems focused on by them are by no means also solutions to ecological problems. Rather, they are, in some ways, the causes of them.

'ENVIRONMENTALISM AND ECOLOGISM' BY ANDREW DOBSON

At the time of writing, Andrew Dobson is a Professor in the Department of Politics and Government at the Open University in the UK. He is well known as a scholar of environmental political theory and of the links between ecologism and other political ideologies. He has also developed ideas of how to integrate the environment and sustainability into the traditional concern of political theory with justice. He has written a number of books on this, including *Green Political Thought* (Routledge, 2000) and *Justice and the Environment: Conceptions of Environmental Sustainability and Dimensions of Social Justice* (Oxford University Press, 1998). In this extract, Dobson considers the nature of political ideologies as a way into distinguishing between environmentalism and ecologism, arguing that only the latter is an ideology. He goes on to examine some aspects of that ideology in order to show the radical nature of its claims and of its challenge to other forms of political thought.

'ENVIRONMENTALISM AND ECOLOGISM' (2000)*

Andrew Dobson

[From the Introduction]

[. . .]

[It is] important to distinguish *ecologism* from its more visible cousin *environmentalism.* . . . [They] are so different as to make their confusion a serious intellectual mistake – partly in the context of thinking about ecologism as a political ideology and partly in the context of an accurate representation of the radical green challenge to the political, economic and social consensus that dominates contemporary life. In respect of what is to come, the following can be taken as a rough and ready distinction between environmentalism and ecologism:

> *environmentalism* argues for a managerial approach to environmental problems, secure in the belief that they can be solved without fundamental changes in present values or patterns of production and consumption.

---

* From Andrew Dobson, *Green Political Thought*, 3rd edn (London: Routledge, 2000), pp. 2–35.

and

> *ecologism* holds that a sustainable and fulfilling existence presupposes radical changes in our relationship with the non-human natural world, and in our mode of social and political life.

So the Queen of England does not suddenly become a political ecologist by having her fleet of limousines converted to lead-free petrol.

I want to argue that environmentalism and ecologism need to be kept apart because they differ not only in degree but also in kind. In other words, they need to be kept apart for the same reasons that liberalism and socialism, or conservatism and nationalism, need to be kept apart. This may seem controversial because the standard view is that environmentalism and ecologism belong to the same family, with the former simply being a less radical manifestation of concern for the environment than the latter. It is less radical, of course, and this is not without importance, and I wish to establish that the nature of the difference takes us beyond the question of radicalism into territory of a more fundamental kind – the kind of territory, indeed, that obliges us to distinguish liberalism and socialism as families and not simply, or only, as offspring of the same parents.

In the first place, environmentalism is not an ideology at all. Most commentators ascribe the same three basic features to ideologies in the sense in which I am talking about them: they must provide an analytical description of society – a 'map' composed of reference points enabling its users to find their way around the political world. Second, they must prescribe a particular form of society employing beliefs about the human condition that sustain and reproduce views about the nature of the prescribed society. Finally, they must provide a programme for political action, or show how to get from the society we presently inhabit to the one prescribed by the ideology in question.

As far as the first characteristic is concerned, and in the context of keeping ecologism and environmentalism apart, it is important to stress that whatever problem is being confronted by any given ideology, it will be analysed in terms of some fundamental and (as it were) necessary feature of the human condition, and not in terms of contingent features of particular social practices. In our context, ecologism will suggest that acid rain is not simply a result of not fixing enough carbon-dioxide scrubbers to coal-fired power-station chimneys, but rather that it is symptomatic of a misreading of the possibilities (or more properly here, constraints) inherent in membership of an interrelated biotic and abiotic community. My point is that while ideologies will disagree over analysis and prescriptions, they will always couch them in terms of fundamental 'truths' about the human condition. On this score, ecologism counts as political ideology while environmentalism most certainly does not.

A similar remark can be made in respect of the second point raised above: that of political prescription. The prescriptions made by political ideologies will not only be issue-based, but will be founded on some notion of the human condition and its associated limitations and possibilities. Moreover, this will translate into some principled vision of the Good Life and will contrast strongly with prescriptions that amount to no more than a set of technical adjustments which derive their legitimacy from the exercise of instrumental rationality. In other words, the legitimacy of ideological prescriptions will be rooted in the kinds of observations to be found in works of political theory; they will not be thought through with the same rigour, but they will be there. Again, ecologism qualifies as a political ideology in these terms, but environmentalism does not.

The importance of these remarks about the source of legitimacy of ideologies' descriptions and prescriptions should not be underestimated, for they help both to distinguish between 'first-order' sets of description and prescription (like ecologism and liberalism) and 'second-order' sets (like environmentalism and democracy), as well as constituting the markers that separate ideologies from one another. In their *Politics and Ideology*, James Donald and Stuart Hall state that 'In this collection, the term ideology is used to indicate the frameworks of thought which are used in society to explain, figure out, make sense of or give meaning to the social and political world' (1986: xi). In my assessment, the markers that serve to separate these frameworks are those different views of the nature of the human condition in which the legitimacy of ideologies' descriptions and prescriptions are rooted.

[. . .]

However plural the meanings we can construct from the historical experience of any given ideology, and however close some of these meanings in the margins of ideologies might appear to bring them, we still want to keep them apart, and we find ways of doing so. How?

We begin, in Roger Eatwell's words, by describing and assessing the 'intrinsic structure' of ideologies – their 'key tenets, myths, contradictions, tensions, even [their] morality and truth' (Eatwell and Wright, 1993: 1). This implies that each ideology has key tenets, myths and so on that distinguish it from other ideologies, and part of my task will be to outline what these are for ecologism – tenets that distinguish it from other ideologies and (I argue) from environmentalism, too. I am unashamedly involved, then, in producing an 'ideal type', and I say this early on so as to head off criticism that the ideology I describe is not that outlined in the latest manifesto of the Swedish Green Party (for example). Ecologism as presented here should 'not be confused with specific movements, parties or regimes which may bear [its] name' (Eatwell and Wright, 1993: 10).

[. . .]

My position on definitional tenets seems to fly in the face of warnings in all contemporary political ideologies textbooks against the

> misguided belief that ideologies have a definitive essential core of principles and values . . . Each ideology may possess a characteristic set of ideas

and beliefs, but these ideas are constantly being revised and defined. In reality all political concepts are 'elastic'; they have no self-evident or unchallengeable meaning. (Heywood, 1992: 8)

Robert Eccleshall makes a similar point: 'political concepts do not travel through history with a fixed, inherent meaning. They are, rather, essentially contested concepts which embody various, often incompatible meanings' (Eccleshall et al., 1994: 30). Fortunately for me, there is no contradiction between believing that ideologies 'have a definitive essential core of principles and values' and recognizing that these principles and values are 'constantly being revised and defined'. I can believe that liberalism has liberty as a core value and that its meaning is contested; I can believe that equality is a core value of socialism and that its meaning is contested; and I can believe that ecocentrism is a core value of ecologism and that its meaning is contested.

Our distinguishing of ideologies one from another rests not only on identifying distinctive tenets, but also on saying something about the relationship between them. Most understandings of ideology refer to the way in which ideologies systematize their key beliefs. This is often loosely put: 'An ideology is a fairly coherent . . . set of ideas' (Ball and Dagger, 1991: 8). 'Here, the concept of ideology will be taken to mean any more or less coherent system of beliefs or views on politics and society' (Leach, 1991: 10) and 'A political ideology is a relatively coherent set of empirical and normative beliefs and thought' (Eatwell and Wright, 1993: 9). These are cagey remarks, and it is striking how rarely the 'fairlys', 'relativelys' and 'more or lesses' are spelled out, even in spaces given over to discussing the nature of ideology *per se*. Malcolm Hamilton, for instance, in his survey of eighty-five sources for defining the notion of ideology, comes up with twenty-seven possible definitional components, six of which he retains together with a combination of a further two. His own amalgam goes like this:

> An ideology is a system of collectively held normative and reputedly factual ideas and beliefs and attitudes advocating a particular pattern of social relationships and arrangements, and/or aimed at justifying a particular pattern of conduct, which its proponents seek to promote, realise, pursue or maintain. (Hamilton, 1987: 37).

Focusing on what he means by a 'system' of ideas, Hamilton writes: 'The ideas may be loosely structured, ambiguous and even contradictory as long as they are in some way, and to some minimal degree, interrelated' (ibid.: 22). Up to a point this is acceptable, but the limits of looseness, ambiguity and contradiction are reached when they threaten the distinctiveness of ideology, built up by describing its central tenets and contrasting them with those of other ideologies. The relationship between an ideology's ideas should not be so loose that the comfortable and non-contradictory importation of ideas from other, distinct ideologies is possible. Indeed, if the importation *is* comfortable and non-contradictory, then we are not talking about a distinct ideology at all. The central tenets should hang together in such a way as to contribute to distinctiveness, and I hope to show that ecologism's tenets can be shown to do this.

All this points up the need to keep ideologies apart as well as respecting the differences to be found within them. [W]e typically signal differences within ideologies by placing adjectives in front of the ideology in question: *social* liberalism, *democratic* socialism, *communist* anarchism and so on. Some adjectives work better than others (in the sense that the resulting hybrid is viable), while some seem not to work at all: we'd be hard pressed, for example, to imagine or describe a liberal fascist. The thing worthy of note here is that the hybrids we are happiest with are those that do not mix ideologies. Put differently, the adjective used to distinguish positions within ideologies is unlikely, itself, to derive from an ideology. Again, as Ball and Dagger observe, 'almost all political ideologies claim to be democratic, a claim they could hardly make if democracy were an ideology itself' (1991: 11). Even when the adjective does appear to derive from an ideology (as in communist anarchism, above), on closer inspection it usually turns out that the adjective refers to a common, rather than a political-ideological, usage of the word. In fact, *communal* anarchism is less likely to sow confusion than *communist* anarchism, and this is a result of the latter term sending off uncomfortable hybrid signals.

These remarks comprise more circumstantial evidence of the stubbornly resistant need to keep ideologies apart. More important in the present context, they allow us further purchase on the nature of, and relationship between, ecologism and environmentalism. For *environmentalism* is a word that could quite happily be pressed into adjectival service by virtually any ideology we care to name without producing any of the contradictions observable in hybrids such as liberal fascist. This fact alone should make us wary of thinking of environmentalism as a political ideology in its own right.

But my second and more controversial claim is that the ideology least susceptible to being hybridized by environmentalism is, curiously, ecologism itself. Environmentalism is so easily accommodated by other ideologies, and ecologism is so different from those ideologies, that we need to be very careful before allowing environmentalism to be a strand within ecologism. A belief in ecocentrism (for example) serves to distinguish ecologism from the other political ideologies, and, as environmentalism does not subscribe to it either, it can only hybridize ecologism at the cost of radically altering it.

[. . .]

Green politics self-consciously confronts dominant paradigms, and my task here is to ensure that it is not swallowed up by them and the interests they often seem to serve. In this sense, it is in a similar position to notions like 'post-industrialism'. Michael Marien is right to suggest that, contrary to general opinion, there is not one but 'two visions of post-industrial society' and, importantly, that one of these is dominant and the other is subordinate. If we allow the subordinate one to disappear, we risk intellectual sloppiness and are likely to mistake consensus for disagreement, and the same goes for light-green and dark-green politics – or what I have called environmentalism and ecologism.

Marien writes that there are 'two completely different modes of usage: 'Post-industrial society' as a technological, affluent, service society, and 'post-industrial society' as a decentralized agrarian economy following in the wake of a failed industrialism' (1977: 416), and suggests that the former is dominant with respect to the latter. Clearly the second usage constitutes a challenge to the first usage in that it calls itself by the same name while reconstituting its meaning. Using his typology, Marien sensitizes us to the variety of possible interpretations of post-industrial society. This variety would be invisible if we were to pay attention to the dominant interpretation: that of an affluent, service economy.

Analogously, I have suggested that dominant and subordinate understandings of green politics have emerged from discussion of the topic as well as its political practice. The point is to remain open to the existence of these understandings rather than to let the bright light of the dominant one obscure the subordinate one behind.

But, of course, it is not simply a question of analogy. It just happens that Marien's dominant version of post-industrialism – a technological, affluent, service society – is a fair description of the twenty-first-century political aspiration to which most people would probably subscribe, if asked. We are certainly encouraged at every turn to aspire to it, at any rate. Now the content of post-industrialism in this dominant sense can work powerful magic on all with which it comes into contact – it moulds challenges to it in its own image and so draws their sting. This is, I think, precisely what has happened to environmental politics as it has emerged from the wings on to the main stage. There is now a perfectly respectable claim to be made that green politics can be a part of a technological, affluent, service society – a part, in other words, of Marien's dominant version of what post-industrial society both is and might be like. This is the green politics of carbon-dioxide scrubbers on industrial chimneys, CFC-free aerosols and car exhausts fitted with catalytic converters.

In this guise, green politics presents no sort of a challenge at all to the twenty-first-century consensus over the desirability of affluent, technological, service societies. But my understanding of the historical significance of radical green politics is that it constitutes precisely such a challenge, and that we shall lose sight of that significance if we conceive of it only in its reformist mode: a mode that reinforces affluence and technology rather than calling them into question. Radical green politics is far more a friend of the subordinate interpretation of post-industrialism – a decentralized economy following in the wake of a failed industrialism – than of its dominant counterpart. Jonathon Porritt and Nicholas Winner assert that

> the most radical [green aim] seeks nothing less than a nonviolent revolu-
> tion to overthrow our whole polluting, plundering and materialistic

industrial society and, in its place, to create a new economic and social order which will allow human beings to live in harmony with the planet. In those terms, the Green Movement lays claim to being the most radical and important political and cultural force since the birth of socialism. (Porritt and Winner, 1988: 9)

It is these terms that I see green politics first, so as to keep a fuller picture of the movement in mind than is presently the case; second, to understand better the challenge that it presents to the dominant consensus; and third, to establish ecologism as a political ideology in its own right.

[. . .]

In a sense, Porritt and Winner do the movement a disfavour by likening the profundity of its challenge to that of early socialism. Much of socialism's intellectual work, at least, had already been done by the time it came on the scene. Liberal theorists had long since laid the ground for calls of liberty and equality, and socialism's job was to pick up and reconstitute the pieces created by liberalism's apparent failure to turn theory into practice. In this sense, the radical wing of the green movement is in a position more akin to that of the early liberals than that of the early socialists – it is self-consciously seeking to call into question an entire world-view rather than tinker with one that already exists. For the sake of convenience, but at the risk of blind blundering on territory where specialists themselves quite properly fear to tread, the world-view that modern political ecologists challenge is the one that grew out of the (early) Enlightenment. Norman Hampson has suggested a number of characteristics salient to the Enlightenment world-view: 'a period when the culture of the educated man was thought to take in the whole of educated knowledge' (1979: 11); 'that man was to a great extent the master of his own destiny' (ibid.: 35); that 'God was a mathematician whose calculations, although infinite in their subtle complexity, were accessible to man's intelligence' (ibid.: 37–8); and that 'universal reason' was held to be preferable to 'local habit', principally because it helps to drive out superstition (ibid.: 152).

[. . .]

Hampson quotes Pluche as writing that 'It is for him [Man] that the sun rises; it is for him that the stars shine', and goes on to observe that 'Almost everything could be pressed into service, from the density of water, which Fenelon considered exactly calculated to facilitate navigation, to the shape of the watermelon, which makes it easy to slice' (Hampson, 1979: 81). In these respects, the Enlightenment attitude was that the world had been made for human beings and that, in principle, nothing in it could be kept secret from them.

In a tortuous way, this attitude has remained dominant ever since in the cultures and societies that have most obviously incubated the modern green movement. They inform, too, Marien's dominant interpretation of what post-industrial society both is and ought to be: Baconian science has helped produce its technology and its material affluence, and the Promethean project to which the Enlightenment gave birth in its modern form is substantially intact. Now the historical significance of radical green politics as I see it is that it constitutes a challenge to this project and to the norms and practices that sustain it. This ecocentric politics explicitly seeks to decentre the human being, to question mechanistic science and its technological consequences, to refuse to believe that the world was made for human beings – and it does this because it has been led to wonder whether dominant post-industrialism's project of material affluence is either desirable or sustainable. All this will be missed if we choose to restrict our understanding of green politics to its dominant guise: an environmentalism that seeks a cleaner service economy sustained by cleaner technology and producing cleaner affluence.

These thoughts on the Enlightenment help to identify ecologism's present historical significance, but there is danger here, too. The analytic temptation is to see the ideology as a recreation of the Romantic reaction that the Enlightenment and then early forms of industrialization themselves brought about. So we cast ecologism in terms of passion opposing reason, of the joys of a bucolic life and of mystery as against transparency. And of course it is true that many manifestations of the green movement argue for a repopulation of the countryside and for the reawakening of a sense of awe in the face of natural phenomena.

At the same time, however, modern green politics turns out to be based on a self-consciously hard-headed assessment of the unsustainability of present political and economic practices – it is remarkable, indeed, to see the extent to which the success of modern political ecology has been mediated and sustained by scientific research. This could hardly be said of the Romantic reaction to the Enlightenment. Similarly, ecologism's political Utopia is (by and large) informed by interpretations of the principle of equality – a principle that was minted and put into circulation during the Enlightenment, and certainly not popular with the Romantics. Again, as far as Romanticism is concerned, green politics has little time for individualism or for geniuses, and one suspects (although this will be disputed by members of the movement) that the nonconformity so beloved of Romantics would be a pretty scarce commodity in green communities. Finally, if we hold the green movement to believe that one can only recognize the value of the natural world through intuition (as we are likely to do if we see it merely as a resurgence of Romanticism), then we are blind to the enormous range and influence of rationalist attempts to account for such value, and which are of great importance to the movement's intellectual archaeology.

So while (in terms of its present historical significance) radical green politics ought to be characterized as a challenge to the contemporary consensus over norms and practices that has its most immediate sources in the early Enlightenment, it would be a mistake to think it pays no mind whatever to those norms and practices. And this would be an especially big mistake if we were to jump to the conclusion that modern green politics is only a form of re-incarnated Romanticism. To guard against this, we should say that its challenge most generally takes the form of an attempt to shift the terms of the burden of persuasion from those who would question the dominant post-industrial embodiment (an affluent, technological, service society) of politics and society, on to those who would defend it. In doing so, greens may sometimes speak, even if often *sotto voce*, in the Enlightenment idiom. Indeed, in the context of an extended inquiry into the relationship between ecology and enlightenment, Tim Hayward writes that 'the ecological challenge, precisely to the extent that it is a critical challenge, can be seen as a renewal of the enlightenment project itself' (1995: 39).

Finally, a remark needs to be made about the use of the word 'ideology' here. The study of ideology is immensely more complex than the standard 'functional' definition of the word would have us believe. At a more profound level than this, ideology 'asks about the bases and validity of our most fundamental ideas' (McLellan, 1986: 1) and as such involves us in critical thought about the most hidden presuppositions of present social and political life – even more hidden than those that political ecologists claim to have uncovered. Drawing on Marx, this conception of ideology urges us to take nothing for granted and suggests that words used in any given description of the world are opaque rather than translucent, and demand deciphering.

However, it seems that there is still something useful to be said about social-ism, liberalism and conservatism from within the functional idiom, if only in the sense that we can indeed sensibly view political ideologies as providing 'the concepts, categories, images and ideas by means of which people make sense of their social and political world, form projects, come to a certain consciousness of their place in that world and act in it' (Donald and Hall, 1986: x).

[. . .]

[From Chapter 1, 'Thinking about Ecologism']

[. . .]

In the Introduction, I began to establish three points: first, that ecologism is not the same as environmentalism; second, that environmentalism is not a political ideology; and third, that while environmentalism is sufficiently non-specific for it to be hybridized with most ideologies, it is at its most uncomfortable with ecologism.

I should say at the outset that these points set my views at odds with most of those who have written recently on political ecology as ideology. The more common position is that both environmentalism and ecologism need to be con-sidered when green ideology is at issue, with writers typically offering a 'spec-trum' of green ideology with all the necessary attendant features such as 'wings' and 'centres'. Elsewhere, I have referred to these two approaches to green ideology as 'maximalist' and 'minimalist' (Dobson, 1993a). Maximalist commentators define ecologism tightly: 'people and ideas will have to pass stringent tests before they can be properly called political-ecological', while minimalists 'cast their net wider so that the definition of ecologism is subject to fewer and/or less stringent conditions' (ibid.: 220). It will be clear that I take a maximalist position, partly because of the ground rules that I consider any description of any ideology must follow, which are betrayed by including environmentalism as a wing within a description of green ideology, partly because the submerging of ecologism in environmentalism is in danger of skewing the intellectual and political landscape, and partly because of how little the minimalist position actually ends up saying.

[. . .]

Andrew Vincent has written the most articulate and robust accounts from the minimalist position that I have come across (Vincent, 1992 and 1993), but even he concludes with some rather limp-looking 'broad themes' in (what he calls) green ideology:

> most [political ecologists] assert the systematic interdependence of species and the environment . . . [and] there is a tendency to be minimally sceptical about the supreme position of human beings on the planet. Furthermore there is a general anxiety about what industrial civilisation is actually doing to the planet. (Vincent, 1993: 270).

Vincent's fourth theme – that there is 'a much less damaging and more positive attitude to nature' than in other ideologies – is only uncontestably true of (what I call) ecologism rather than of environmentalism, so it should not really be in his 'broad theme' list at all. The second and third points are rather watered down by the words 'tendency', 'minimally' and 'general', and the first three points (with the possible exception of the second) are so general as to be acceptable to a large number of people in modern industrial societies today – certainly a larger number than would style themselves political ecologists.

But it is only right to outline two advantages of the minimalist position, both of which are passed up in the present approach. The first is that it reflects clearly the rather eclectic nature of the green movement itself. Many of the people and organizations whom we would want to include in the green movement are environmentalist rather than political-ecologist, and defining ecologism as strictly as I want to can obscure this very important truth about green politics.

[. . .]

The second advantage is that the minimalist approach allows us to see that the movement has a history – a fact which is less obvious from the maximalist point of view because it tends to date the existence of ecologism from the 1960s or even the 1970s. Minimalists will typically look to the nineteenth century for the beginnings of ecologism, and my opposition to this view is based on the observation that while some of the ideas we now associate with ecologism were flagged over 100 years ago, this is a far cry from saying that ecologism itself existed over 100 years ago. . . . These, then, are the general issues at stake in thinking about ecologism, and they will resurface as detail in what remains of this chapter.

The need for the rethink of values proposed in the radical green agenda is derived from the belief that there are natural limits to economic and population growth. It is important to stress the word 'natural', because green ideologues argue that economic growth is prevented not for social reasons – such as restrictive relations of production – but because the Earth itself has a limited carrying capacity (for population), productive capacity (for resources of all types) and absorbent capacity (pollution). 'The earth is finite,' write the authors of *Beyond the Limits*, sequel to the seminal *The Limits to Growth* report, and '[G]rowth of anything physical, including the human population and its cars and buildings and smoke-stacks, cannot continue forever' (Meadows et al., 1992: 7). This ought to make it clear that from a green perspective continuous growth cannot be achieved by overcoming what might appear to be temporary limits – such as those imposed by a lack of technological sophistication: continuous and unlimited growth is *prima facie* impossible.

At this point, ecologism throws into relief a factor – the Earth itself – that has been present in all modern political ideologies but has remained invisible, either because of its very ubiquity or because these ideologies' scheme for description and prescription have kept it hidden. Ecologism makes the Earth as physical object the very foundation-stone of its intellectual edifice, arguing that its finitude is the basic reason why infinite population and economic growth are impossible and why, consequently, profound changes in our social and political behaviour need to take place. The enduring image of this finitude is a familiar picture taken by the cameras of Apollo 8 in 1968 showing a blue-white Earth suspended in space above the moon's horizon. Twenty years earlier, the astronomer Fred Hoyle had written that 'Once a photograph of the Earth, taken from the outside, is available . . . a new idea as powerful as any other in history will be let loose' (in Myers, 1985: 21). He may have been right. The green movement has adopted this image and the sense of beauty and fragility that it represents to generate concern for the Earth, arguing that everyday life in industrial society has separated us from it: 'Those who live amid concrete, plastic, and computers can easily forget how fundamentally our well-being is linked to the land' (ibid.: 22). We are urged to recognize what is and has always been the case: that all wealth (of all types) ultimately derives from the planet.

SUSTAINABLE SOCIETIES

The centrality of the limits-to-growth thesis and the conclusions drawn from it lead political ecologists to suggest that radical changes in our social habits and practices are required. The kind of society that would incorporate these changes is often referred to by greens as the 'sustainable society', and the fact that we are able to identify aspects of a green society distinguishable from the preferred pictures of other ideologies is one of the reasons why ecologism can be seen as a political ideology in its own right.

Political ecologists will stress two points with regard to the sustainable society: one, that consumption of material goods by individuals in 'advanced industrial countries' should be reduced; and two (linked to the first), that human needs are not best satisfied by continual economic growth as we understand it today. Greens argue that, if there are limits to growth, then there are limits to consumption as well. The green movement is therefore faced with the difficulty of simultaneously calling into question a major aspiration of most people – maximizing consumption of material objects – and making its position attractive.

There are two aspects to its strategy. On the one hand, it argues that continued consumption at increasing levels is impossible because of the finite productive limits imposed by the Earth. So it is argued that our aspiration to consume will be curtailed whether we like it or not: 'In common parlance that's known as having your cake and eating it, and it can't be done', announced Porritt (1984a: 118). It is very important to see that greens argue that recycling or the use of renewable energy sources will not, alone, solve the problems posed by a finite Earth – we shall still not be able to produce or consume at an ever-increasing rate. Such techniques might be a part of the strategy for a sustainable society, but they do not materially affect the absolute limits to production and consumption in a finite system:

> The fiction of combining present levels of consumption with 'limitless recycling' is more characteristic of the technocratic vision than of an ecological one. Recycling itself uses resources, expands energy, creates thermal pollution; on the bottom line, it's just an industrial activity like all the others. Recycling is both useful and necessary – but it is an illusion to imagine that it provides any basic answers. (ibid.: 183).

This observation is the analogue of the distinction made earlier between environmentalism and ecologism. To paraphrase Porritt, the recycling of waste is an essential part of being green but it is not the same thing as being radically green. Being radically green involves subscribing to different sets of values. As indicated by Porritt above, greens are generally suspicious of purely technological solutions to environmental problems – the 'technological fix' – and the relatively cautious endorsement of recycling is just one instance of this.

[. . .]

The second strategy employed by green ideologues to make palatable their recommendation for reduced consumption is to argue for the benefits of a less materialistic society. In the first place, they make an (unoriginal) distinction between needs and wants, suggesting that many of the items we consume and that we consider to be needs are in fact wants that have been 'converted' into needs at the behest of powerful persuasive forces. In this sense, they will suggest that little would be lost by possessing fewer objects.

Second, some deep-greens argue that the sustainable society that would replace the present consumer society would provide for wider and more profound forms of fulfilment than that provided by the consumption of material objects. This can profitably be seen as part of the green contention that the sustainable society would be a spiritually fulfilling place in which to live. Indeed, aspects of the radical green programme can hardly be understood without reference to the spiritual dimension on which (and in which) it likes to dwell. Greens invest the natural world with spiritual content and are ambivalent about what they see as mechanistic science's robbery of such content. They demand reverence for the Earth and a rediscovery of our links with it: 'It seems to me so obvious that without some huge groundswell of spiritual concern the transition to a more sustainable way of life remains utterly improbable' (Porritt, 1984a: 210). In this way, the advertisement for frugal living and the exhortation to connect with the Earth combine to produce the spiritual asceticism that is a part of political ecology.

A controversial theme in green politics which is associated with the issue of reducing consumption is that of the need to bring down population levels. As Fritjof Capra explains: 'To slow down the rapid depletion of our natural resources, we need not only to abandon the idea of continuing economic growth, but to control the worldwide increase in population' (1983: 227). Despite heavy criticism, particularly from the left – Mike Simons has described Paul Ehrlich's proposals as 'an invitation to genocide' (Simons, 1988: 13) – greens have stuck to their belief that long-term global sustainability will involve reductions in population, principally on the grounds that fewer people will consume fewer objects.

[. . .]

REASONS TO CARE FOR THE ENVIRONMENT

In an obvious way, care for the environment is one of ecologism's informing (although not exhaustive) principles. Many different reasons can be given for why we should be more careful with the environment, and I want to suggest that ecologism advances a specific mix of them. In this sense, the nature of the arguments advanced for care for the environment comes to be a part of ecologism's definition.

In our context, such arguments can be summarized under two headings: those that suggest that human beings ought to care for the environment because it is in our interest to do so, and those that suggest that the environment has an intrinsic value in the sense that its value is not exhausted by its being a means to human ends – and, even if it cannot be made a means to human ends, it still has value.

Most of the time, we encounter arguments of the first sort: for example, that tropical rainforests should be preserved because they provide oxygen, or raw materials for medicines, or because they prevent landslides. These, though, are not radical green reasons. The ecological perspective is neatly captured in *The Green Alternative* in response to the question, 'Isn't concern for nature and the environment actually concern for ourselves?':

> Many people see themselves as enlightened when they argue that the non-human world ought to be preserved: (i) as a stockpile of genetic diversity for agricultural, medical and other purposes; (ii) as material for scientific study, for instance of our evolutionary origins; (iii) for recreation and (iv) for the opportunities it provides for aesthetic pleasure and spiritual inspiration. However, although enlightened, these reasons are all related to the instrumental value of the non-human world to humans. What is missing is any sense of a more impartial, biocentric – or biosphere-centred – view in which the non-human world is considered to be of intrinsic value. (Bunyard and Morgan-Grenville, 1987: 284).

[. . .]

So the political ideology of ecologism clearly wants to subscribe to a particular set of reasons for care for the environment but is confronted by a culture that appears to engender a crisis of confidence, and that forces it to produce another set – which it would like to see as subordinate – in public. This, then, is another characteristic of ecologism: that its public face is in danger of hiding what it 'really' is; and yet what it 'really' is is its public face.

Something similar might be said of the spirituality that sometimes surfaces in the writings of ecologists. Its advocates argue that radical green politics is itself a spiritual experience in that it is founded on a recognition of the 'oneness' of creation and a subsequent 'reverence for one's own life, the life of others and the Earth itself' (Porritt, 1984a: 111). Moreover, it is suggested that political change will involve such a recognition and that only green politics has the possibility of re-creating the spiritual dimension of life that the grubby materialism of the industrial age has torn asunder. This kind of talk, though, is hardly a vote-winner, and so although 'spirituality' might be conspicuous in the ecologist's private conversation it does not get the public airing this would seem to warrant.

CRISIS AND ITS POLITICAL-STRATEGIC CONSEQUENCES

No presentation of ecologism would be complete without the appropriate (usually heavy) dosage of warnings of doom and gloom. Political ecologists invariably claim that dire consequences will result if their warnings are not heeded and their prescriptions not followed. *Beyond the Limits* provides a typical example:

> Human use of many essential resources and generation of many kinds of pollutants have already surpassed rates that are physically sustainable.

> Without significant reductions in material and energy flows, there will be
> in the coming decades an uncontrolled decline in per capita food output,
> energy use, and industrial production. (Meadows et al., 1992): xv–xvi)

The radical green's consistent use of an apocalyptic tone is unique in the
context of modern political ideologies, and it might be argued that the movement has relied too heavily on these sorts of projections as a means of galva-
nizing people to action. The consequences of this have been twofold. First, there
is the unfounded accusation by the movement's critics that it is informed by an
overwhelming sense of pessimism as to the prospects of the planet and the
human race along with it. The accusation is unfounded because the movement's
pessimism relates only to the likely life expectancy of current social and political practice. Greens are generally unerringly optimistic with respect to our
chances of dealing with the crisis they believe they have uncovered – they merely
argue that a major change of direction is required. As *Beyond the Limits* concludes:

> [T]his decline is not inevitable. To avoid it two changes are necessary. The
> first is a comprehensive revision of policies and practices that perpetuate
> growth in material consumption and in population. The second is a rapid,
> drastic increase in the efficiency with which materials and energy are used.
> (Meadows et al., 1992: xvi)

The second and perhaps more serious consequence of the movement's reliance on gloomy prognostications is that its ideologues appear to have felt themselves absolved from serious thinking about realizing the change they propose.
This, indeed, is another feature of the ideology that ought to be noted: the
tension between the radical nature of the social and political change that it
seeks, and the reliance on traditional liberal-democratic means of bringing it
about. It is as though the movement's advocates have felt that the message was
so obvious that it only needed to be given for it to be acted upon. The obstacles to radical green change have not been properly identified, and the result is
an ideology that lacks an adequate programme for social and political transformation.

UNIVERSALITY AND SOCIAL CHANGE

A related feature that ought to be mentioned, however, is the potentially universal appeal of the ideology. Up to now, it has not been aimed at any particular section of society but is addressed to every single individual on the planet
regardless of colour, gender, class, nationality, religious belief and so on. This
is a function of the green movement's argument that environmental degradation and the social dislocation that goes with it are everybody's problem and
therefore ought to be everybody's concern: 'we are *all* harmed by the ecological crisis and therefore we *all* have a common interest in uniting together with
people of *all* classes and *all* political allegiances to counter this mutually shared
threat' (Tatchell in Dodds, 1988: 45; emphasis in the original). Ecologism thus

has the potential to argue more easily than most modern political ideologies that it is, literally, in everyone's interest to follow its prescriptions.

This is not so obviously true of other modern political ideologies. None of them is able to argue that the penalty for not following its advice is the threat of major environmental and social dislocation for everyone. The potentially universal appeal generated by this observation has undoubtedly been seen by the green movement as a positive characteristic, to be exploited for all its worth.

LESSONS FROM NATURE

The importance of nature to ecologism, already identified, is not exhausted by reasons why we should care for it. Ecologism's thoroughgoing *naturalism* rests on the belief that human beings are natural creatures. On the one hand, this may involve the recognition (already canvassed) that there are natural limits to human aspirations; on the other – and even more controversially – there is often a strong sense in which the natural world is taken as a model for the human world, and many of ecologism's prescriptions for political and social arrangements are derived from a particular view of how nature 'is'. This view – not surprisingly – is an ecological view. 'Professional ecologists', writes Jonathon Porritt, 'study plant and animal systems in relation to their environment, with particular emphasis on the inter-relations and interdependence between different life forms' (1984a: 3). This characterization conveys the benign sense of nature that has been adopted by political ecologists. This is a natural world in which interdependence is given priority over competition and in which equality comes before hierarchy. Nature for ecologism is not 'red in tooth and claw' but pacific, tranquil, lush – and green.

[. . .]

It is an ecological axiom that stability in an ecosystem is a function of diversity in that ecosystem. Thus, the more diverse the flora and fauna (within limits imposed by the ecosystem), the more stable the system will be. Further, stability is seen as a positive feature of an ecosystem because it proves the system to be sustainable; an ecosystem that is subject to fluctuation has not reached the 'climax' stage and is therefore characterized as immature. Socially, this translates into the liberal aspiration of the toleration of peculiarity and generosity with respect to diverse opinions, and these are most certainly characteristics of liberalism that have been adopted by greens. There is a strong sense in ecologism that the 'healthy society' (organic metaphor intended) is one in which a range of opinions is not only tolerated but celebrated, in that this provides for a repository of ideas and forms of behaviour from which to drawn when confronted with political or social problems.

[. . .]

Some will no doubt object that this is too rosy a view of the green movement's political prescriptions, and that its history is full of suggestions described more accurately as authoritarian than democratic. Anna Bramwell's history of ecology in the twentieth century (1989) certainly provokes such an impression, and it is true that even in the modern movement there was a time when avoiding environmental catastrophe was seen as the chief end, and the means used to achieve it were largely irrelevant: 'It [social design leading to a sustainable society] is a process that can be carried out within present authority structures whether they be democratic or dictatorial. It is not necessary, although it might be preferable, that authority relationships be changed' (Pirages, 1977b: 10).

[. . .]

Ecologism's next political 'lesson from nature' is that the view of the natural world as an interlocking system of interdependent objects (both sentient and non-sentient) generates a sense of equality, in that each item is held to be necessary for the viability of every other item. In this view, no part of the natural world is independent and therefore no part can lay claim to 'superiority'. Without the humble bacteria that clean our gut wall, for example, human beings would be permanently ill. Likewise, those particular bacteria need our gut in which to live.

The social ecologist Murray Bookchin presents the scientific picture of ecology in the following way:

> If we recognize that every ecosystem can also be viewed as a food web, we can think of it as a circular, interlacing nexus of plant–animal relationships (rather than as a stratified pyramid with man at the apex) that includes such widely varying creatures as microorganisms and large mammals. What ordinarily puzzles anyone who sees food-web diagrams for the first time is the impossibility of discerning a point of entry into the nexus. The web can be entered at any point and leads back to its point of departure without any apparent exit. Aside from the energy provided by sunlight (and dissipated by radiation), the system to all appearances is closed. Each species, be it a form of bacteria or deer, is knitted together in a network of interdependence, however indirect the links may be. A predator in the web is also prey, even if the 'lowliest' of the organisms merely makes it ill or helps to consume it after death. (Bookchin, 1982: 26)

Bookchin continues with a comment on the social implications of this:

> What renders social ecology so important is that it offers no case whatsoever for hierarchy in nature and society; it decisively challenges the very function of hierarchy as a stabilizing or ordering principle in *both* realms. The association of order as such with hierarchy is ruptured. (ibid.: 36)

In this way, the science of ecology works in favour of egalitarianism through its observations of the interdependence of species.

The kind of assertion made by Bookchin, however, is fraught with difficulties, and I am saying nothing new – although the point bears repetition – if I suggest that extrapolations from 'nature' to 'society' are dangerous to make. It may be the case that the science of ecology has neutered hierarchy as an organizing principle in the 'natural' world (and this is, in any case, disputable), but that is not to say that we can say the same of the social world.

The radical political ecologist would respond to this criticism [by agreeing] that the general point is to encourage different ways of thinking about the 'natural' world. If we accept that a degree of inter-species equality of value is generated by the fact of our interdependence, then the onus will be upon those who want to destroy species to justify their case, rather than upon those who want to preserve them.

[. . .]

Ecologists argue that we should live with, rather than against, the natural world, and this has significant repercussions in the context of the kind of community in which they would have us live. At the same time, the natural world's longevity can help generate a sense of awe and humility and thus contribute to the move away from anthropocentrism that the green movement considers necessary: 'The ecological approach . . . [introduces] an important note of humility and compression into our understanding of our place on earth' (Eckersley, 1987: 10).

Not only, however, is nature held to be our best teacher, but 'she' is also female. This has important consequences for the feminism to which ecologism subscribes, because there is a tendency to map nature's beneficial characteristics on to the 'female personality'. Thus, nature and women come to be tender, nurturing, caring, sensitive to place, and partly defined by the (high) office of giving birth to life. To the extent that much feminist momentum has been geared towards ridding the woman of stereotypical behaviour and character patterns, this ecological vision might seem retrograde. More pertinently, the features of this vision (if we assume women actually possess them to the general exclusion of other characteristics) are precisely those that have consigned women to an inferior status because they are held to be subordinate qualities. It will probably be of little comfort to some feminists that ecologism seeks to turn the tables in this context, arguing that the predominance of 'male' values is part of the reason for the crisis that they have identified, and that nature's 'female' lead is the one to follow. Brian Tokar puts it like this: 'The values of nurturance, cooperation and sharing which are traditionally identified more closely with women than with men need to become the deepest underlying principles of our society' (Tokar, 1994: 91). These are important matters for ecologism and for feminism, both because ecologism claims feminism as a guiding star (not least in terms of how to 'do' politics) and because some feminists have balked at the kind of feminism shunted into ecological service.

LEFT AND RIGHT: COMMUNISM AND CAPITALISM

In standard political terms and in order to help distinguish ecologism from other political ideologies, it is useful to examine the widespread green claim to 'go beyond' the left–right political spectrum: 'In calling for an ecological, non-violent, nonexploitative society, the Greens (*die Grünen*) transcend the linear span of left-to-right' (Spretnak and Capra, 1985: 3). Jonathon Porritt translates this into a transcendence of capitalism and communism, and remarks that 'the debate between the protagonists of capitalism and communism is about as uplifting as the dialogue between Tweedledum and Tweedledee' (Porritt, 1984a: 44). The basis for this claim is that from an ecocentric green perspective the similarities between communism and capitalism can be made to seem greater than their differences:

> Both are dedicated to industrial growth, to the expansion of the means of production, to a materialist ethic as the best means of meeting people's needs, and to unimpeded technological development. Both rely on increasing centralisation and large-scale bureaucratic control and co-ordination. From a viewpoint of narrow scientific rationalism, both insist that the planet is there to be conquered, that big is self-evidently beautiful, and that what cannot be measured is of no importance. (Porritt, 1984a: 44)

The name generally given to this way of life is 'industrialism', which Porritt goes so far as to call a 'super-ideology' within which communism and capitalism are inscribed, and which he describes elsewhere as 'adherence to the belief that human needs can only be met through the *permanent* expansion of the process of production and consumption' (in Goldsmith and Hildyard, 1986: 343–4). This observation is central to green ideology, pointing up both the focus of attack on contemporary politics and society – industrialism – and the claim that ecologism calls into question assumptions with which we have lived for at least two centuries. Ecologists argue that discussion about the respective merits of communism and capitalism is rather like rearranging the deckchairs on the *Titanic*: they point out that industrialism suffers from the contradiction of undermining the very context by which it is possible, by unsustainably consuming a finite stock of resources in a world that does not have a limitless capacity to absorb the waste produced by the industrial process.

Although the green movement appears to view 'left and right' and 'capitalism and communism' as synonymous pairs, I want to look at them separately, if only because the terms used to examine them will be different. It ought nevertheless to be said that the green claim in both cases has come in for criticism, especially regarding the second pair, and especially from the left.

In some respects, we can talk of the green movement quite happily in terms of left and right because the terms we use to discuss the difference between the two can easily be applied to it. If, for example, we take equality and hierarchy as characteristics held to be praiseworthy within left-wing and right-wing thought respectively, then ecologism is clearly left-wing, arguing as it does for forms of equality among human beings and between human beings and other species. However, to argue that ecologism is unequivocally left-wing is not so easy. For instance, green politics is in principle averse to anything but the most timid engineering of the social and natural world by human beings. Since the French Revolution, it has been a theme of left-wing thought that the existence of a concrete natural order of things with which human beings should conform and not tamper is a form of medieval mumbo-jumbo used by the right to secure and ossify privilege. The left has consistently argued that the world is there to be remade in the image of 'man' (usually) in accordance with plans drawn up by 'men' (usually), and in which the only reference to a natural order is to an abstract one outside of time and place.

The radical green aspiration to insert the human being in its 'proper place' in the natural order and to generate a sense of humility in the face of it is clearly 'right-wing' in this context:

> The belief that we are 'apart from' the rest of creation is an intrinsic feature of the dominant world-order, a man-centred or anthropocentric philosophy. Ecologists argue that this ultimately destructive belief must be rooted out and replaced with a life-centred or biocentric philosophy. (Porritt, 1984a: 206)

Ecologists can only perversely be accused of using this idea to preserve wealth and privilege, but the understanding of the place of the human being in a pre-ordained and immensely complex world with which we meddle at our peril is nevertheless a right-wing thought. Joe Weston, writing from a socialist perspective, puts it like this:

> Clearly the green analysis of environmental and social issues is within the broad framework of right-wing ideology and philosophy. The belief in 'natural' limits to human achievement, the denial of class divisions and the Romantic view of 'nature' all have their roots in the conservative and liberal political divisions. (Weston, 1986: 24)

John Gray has picked up some of this and turned it into a virtue, from a conservative point of view. He suggests that there are three 'deep affinities' between green and conservative thinking. The first is that 'both conservatism and Green theory see the life of humans in a multi-generational perspective'; second, '[B]oth conservative and Green thinkers repudiate the shibboleth of liberal individualism, the sovereign subject, the autonomous agent whose choices are the origin of all that has value'; and third, 'both Greens and conservatives consider risk-aversion the path of prudence when new technologies, or new social practices, have consequences that are large and unpredictable' (Gray, 1993b: 136–7). Although Gray does not count a common opposition to 'hubristic humanism' in his list, he might have done (ibid.: 139). The similarities Gray outlines are well chosen, but there is plenty in the detail that may yet provide for lengthy arguments between political ecologists and conservatives (just what is to replace the shibboleth of the liberal individual? What are the rules for distribution across generations to be?) – and of course there is no mention of eco-centrism (as a fundamental distinguishing characteristic) at all.

[. . .]

Second, the green claim to transcend capitalism and communism, in the sense that ecologism calls into question an overriding feature common to them both (industrialism), has drawn heavy criticism from the left. There are two reasons for this. In the first place, it brings back grim memories of the 'end of ideology' thesis of the 1960s. This thesis has been interpreted by the left as itself ideological in the sense of observing a putative veneer of agreement about the basic goals of society, and so obscuring and delegitimizing alternative strategies. The 'end of ideology' position was buttressed by the convergence thesis, which argued that communist and capitalist nations were beginning to converge on a similar course of social and political action. The left pointed out that such analyses served to cement existing power relationships – particularly in the capitalist nations – and therefore performed a conservative social function.

For socialists, there is no more important political battle to be fought than that between capital and labour; and any politics that claims to transcend this battle is regarded with suspicion. The idea that the interests of capital and labour have somehow converged amounts to a betrayal, from the socialist point of view, of the project to liberate labour from capital. The interests of capital and labour are not the same, yet the green belief that both are inscribed in the super-ideology of industrialism makes it seem as though they are.

At root, proposes Joe Weston, the green movement's mistake is to refuse a class analysis of society – it 'argues that traditional class divisions are at an end' (Weston, 1986: 22), and uses the concept 'industrial society . . . to distinguish contemporary society from orthodox capitalism; it is not a neutral term' (ibid.). It is not neutral in the sense that it removes capitalism from the glare of criticism and thus contributes to its survival and reproduction. Similarly, the original 'end of ideology' thesis was accompanied by an analysis of how policies are formulated and social conflicts resolved, collected under the term 'pluralism'. Socialists have always considered this to be a dubious description, principally because the apparently democratic diversity and openness it implies serve to obscure capitalism's hierarchy of wealth and power, based on the domination of labour by capital.

From Weston's point of view, it is no accident, therefore, that the green movement's 'industrialism' thesis, kept company by the abandonment of a class analysis of society, also results in a political practice based around the pressure groups of pluralism. In this sense, there is no difference between Daniel Bell and Jonathon Porritt. In the first place, Porritt's attack on industrialism prevents him from seeing that the real problem is capitalism; second, his failure to subscribe to a class analysis of society leads him to the dead-end of pressure-group politics; and third – and probably most serious from a socialist point of view – not only is he not attacking capitalism as he should, but he is contributing to its survival by deflecting criticism from it.

So the left's belief that it is not possible to transcend capitalism while capitalism still exists makes it suspicious of claims to the contrary. David Pepper, for instance, has suggested that we should not see 'environmentalist concerns or arguments' as 'above or unrelated to traditional political concerns, but stemming from, and used very much as agents to advance, the interests of one traditional political side or the other' (1984: 187). The general conclusion the left draws is that ecologism serves the interests of the *status quo* by diverting attention from the real battleground for social change: the relationship between capital and labour. It is undoubtedly a central feature of ecologism that it identifies the 'super-ideology' of industrialism as the thesis to be undermined, and it has been relatively easy for green ideologues to point to high levels of environmental degradation in Eastern Europe to make their point that there is little to choose – from this perspective – between capitalism and communism. It makes no appreciable difference who owns the means of production, they say, if the production process itself it based on doing away with the presuppositions of its very existence.

CONCLUSION

It needs to be stressed that most people will understand environmentalism – a managerial approach to the environment within the context of present political and economic practices – to be what green politics is about. I do not think it is – at least in its political-ideological guise. Ecologists and environmentalists are inspired to act by the environmental degradation they observe, but their strategies for remedying it differ wildly. Environmentalists do not necessary subscribe to the limits-to-growth thesis, nor do they typically seek to dismantle 'industrialism'. They are unlikely to argue for the intrinsic value of the non-human environment and would balk at any suggestion that we (as a species) require 'metaphysical reconstruction' (Porritt, 1984a: 198–200). Environmentalists will typically believe that technology can solve the problems it creates, and will probably regard any suggestions that only a reduction in material throughout in the production process will provide for sustainability as wilful nonsense. In short, what passes for green politics in the pages of today's newspapers is not the ideology of political ecology, properly understood. This is why the student of green politics needs to do more than scratch the surface of its public image in order to appreciate the full range of the debate that it has opened up.

'PRINCIPLES OF GREEN POLITICS' BY ROBERT GOODIN

At the time of writing, the North American political philosopher Robert Goodin is Professor of Social and Political Theory and Philosophy in the Research School of Social Sciences at the Australian National University. His work has covered a range of areas, but he particularly writes about issues of welfare and public policy in connection with political philosophical issues of morality. Among his numerous books are *Political Theory and Public Policy* (University of Chicago Press, 1982), *Utilitarianism as a Public Philosophy* (Cambridge University Press, 1995), *Reasons for Welfare* (Princeton University Press, 1988), *Social Welfare and Individual Responsibility* (Cambridge University Press, 1998) and *Reflective Democracy* (Oxford University Press, 2002). In the extracts here, from *Green Political Theory* (Polity, 1992), Goodin considers whether or not green thinking offers distinct theories of human value and agency that feed into the way greens conceive of political action and political structures.

'PRINCIPLES OF GREEN POLITICS' (1992)*

Robert Goodin

THE THESIS

That the greens do indeed pose a fundamental challenge to the existing socio-political order is, in one sense, plain for all to see. Politically, the greens are obviously making some awfully radical demands. They call, predictably enough, for drastic measures to curtail pollution of the air, waterways and oceans, to control disposal of hazardous wastes, to protect the ozone layer, and to conserve forests, landscapes, natural resources and ancient monuments. Beyond all that, though, they would also have us: take steps to protect animals, both individually and especially as species; wind down modern technology generally, and nuclear electricity generating plants particularly; disarm militarily, disposing straightaway of our entire nuclear and chemical/biological weapons arsenals; and change our lifestyles quite generally, especially as regards attitudes toward women, children, elders and 'marginalized groups' in society, such as homosexuals, immigrants and gipsies.[1] Accepting all those demands would clearly

---

* From Robert Goodin, *Green Political Theory* (Cambridge: Polity Press, 1992), pp. 13–16, 113–68.

commit us, both domestically and internationally, to a very basic reorientation of crucial components of the present political, economic and social orders.[2]

What is less obvious and requires rather more argument is the further proposition that the greens' demands really do – as greens themselves say they do – have to be taken on something like an all-or-nothing basis. Once established, that proposition logically militates against picking and choosing items off the green political agenda – breaking apart the package, buying some parts of it without buying all the rest as well. Showing the fallacies that are involved in such magpie-like borrowing from the greens is the political punchline of this book as a whole.[3]

What, at root, makes the green political agenda form a peculiarly tight package is the fact that all the elements without it are informed by a single moral vision.[4] Specifically, all are arguably manifestations of one and the same 'green theory of value'. What makes the green agenda form something very much akin to an all-or-nothing political package is the simple incoherence of accepting the validity of that particular theory of value for some purposes but not for others. A theory of the Good holds good regardless of context: goodness does not flicker on and off like some faulty light switch.

That is not to say that we must always accept green conclusions everywhere if we ever accept them anywhere. Of course we do not. Purely as a matter of logic, it is illegitimate for us utterly to disregard for some purposes considerations which we take to be utterly compelling in others. As I shall argue in my conclusions, that logic might come to have real political consequences for any mainstream political parties that try to defy it.

It is my larger thesis that green political theory is actually composed of two quite separate principal components. Typically conjoined with these two elements is yet a third – personal lifestyle recommendations, of an essentially non-political sort – which is actually separate, yet again, from either of the two more specifically political strands in green thought.

These strands in green thought are separate, in the sense that the arguments used to support any one of them do not necessarily commit us to any of the others. All the strands might – or might not – ultimately prove justifiable. My point is just that, by and large, each of them will have to be justified separately, rather than any one piggybacking on the justification given for any one of the others.

At the core of green political theory's public-policy stance is a 'green theory of value'. It is that theory of value that provides the unified moral vision running through all the central substantive planks in the green political programme; it is by virtue of that unified moral vision that the green agenda can legitimately be thought to form something akin to an all-or-nothing package; it is the inconsistency of endorsing that theory of value for some purposes but not for others to which it is equally applicable that allows greens properly to complain, in a way that would not be appropriate for an ordinary single-issue group, when mainstream parties borrow piecemeal from the green agenda. All of that follows from the green theory of value, and from that alone.

The second strand of green political theory is a 'green theory of agency'.[5] Whereas the first strand tells us what things are of value and why, the second strand advises on how to go about pursuing those values. Such a theory is action-guiding in both a negative and a positive direction: it tells us what not to do in pursuit of the Good, as well as what we must (or may) do in pursuit of it. Such a theory is also agent-creating as well as being agent-instructing: as well as telling natural individuals what they should and should not do, directly, it also tells them what sort of collective organizations they should create and what they should and should not do indirectly through the agency of such artificial entities.

Such a theory of agency is pitched at the level of principle rather than of mere pragmatics, to be sure. Of course, greens have to take due account of pragmatics and tactics, too. But that is not all that is at work in their theory of agency. They also have certain principled views as to which sorts of political agency are to be preferred to which others. They are decidedly of the view that decentralized, egalitarian political mechanisms are to be preferred to centralized, hierarchical ones. For them it is a matter of principle and not mere pragmatics that we should 'think globally, act locally'. For them, nonviolence is a matter of principle, not merely a useful tactic.

What the relationship is that is supposed to exist between the green theory of value and this green theory of agency is unclear. Green writers rarely address the problem explicitly. Furthermore, through their silence, they are implicitly suggesting that there is no problem there to be addressed at all. The implication seems to be that all the strands of green political theory hang together, both at root deriving somehow from the one and the same normative premise.

I think that implicit claim is untrue – or anyway, unproven.[6] Basically, greens could derive their theory of agency from their theory of value only by asserting that one mode of human organization was uniquely natural. But that would amount to privileging as uniquely 'natural' one particular phase of human history, such as hunter-gatherer society, for example. Such judgements seem arbitrary and insupportable.

In the end, I think we have to say that the green theory of agency is a separate component of green political theory. It exists in addition to, and substantially independently of, the green theory of value. Furthermore, it ought to be seen as subsidiary to the green theory of value.[7] The green theory of agency is a theory about how best to pursue the Good and the valuable, according to a distinctively green analysis of what is good and valuable. Some theories of agency might elevate right action, regardless of consequences, to an art form in and of itself. Green theory is not among them. It aims first and foremost at producing good green consequences.

[. . .]

[From Chapter 4, 'The Green Theory of Agency']

1   THEORIES OF VALUE AND THEORIES OF AGENCY.

[. . .]

Like all theories of value in general, the green theory of value is not self-implementing. Instead it is a theory that is addressed to moral agents, in hopes that they might themselves use it in guiding their conduct. It is through the deliberate actions and choices of those agents that the recommendations of our theory of value will be implemented, if they are to be implemented at all. Hence any theory of value or any theory of the Good needs to be conjoined with a theory of agency, analysing the nature of the mechanisms by which its recommendations are to be given practical meaning.[8]

The need for a theory of agency is, if anything, greater when the recommendations of the theory of value in view are not purely personal but also interpersonal and, indeed, largely political in nature. Then we will need not only a theory of agency of the ordinary sort – a theory about the nature of (individual) human action. We will also need a theory of agency that embraces interactions between individuals – a theory for analysing coordination of actions among various individuals. And we will also need a theory of agency that embraces notions of genuinely collective agency – a theory for analysing an entirely new sort of collective moral agent (clubs, cadres, firms, parties), which is created by the intentional actions of individuals but which then goes on to acquire something of an independent moral life all its own.[9]

Philosophical analyses of agency often tend to confine themselves to questions of the nature of individual agency. In a way, that emphasis is perfectly proper. Before we can properly address questions of the nature of coordinated or collective action among individuals, we must first get clear on the logically prior question of the nature of individual human agency itself. But we cannot stop there. Many (perhaps most) theories of value have important interpersonal and, indeed, distinctly political implications. In so far as they do, what is crucially required in framing a strategy for implementing them will be some analysis of the coordination and collectivization of individual agency.[10]

Such an account of agency might, in the first instance, be a purely positive theory. It might analyse what human agents are really like, what actually makes them tick, without passing any normative judgement on the matter either way. To a certain extent, any decent theory of agency is going to have to be like this. In so far as there are any hard and fast empirical truths about the nature of different sorts of agents, then a theory of agency must of course report those facts fully and faithfully; and it must respect them as best it can, consistently with respecting other facts of similar standing, in its theorization of the phenomenon.[11]

A theory of agency need not and usually does not stop with that, though. It is partly an empirical theory, to be sure. But it is an empirical theory with normative overtones. In part, those derive from the normative concerns – the desire to get someone to act on our theory of value – that set us looking for a theory of agency in the first place.

Quite apart from that, however, a theory of agency is also often normatively charged in so far as it commends certain forms of agency as being morally especially worthy and condemns others as being morally reprehensible. Furthermore, it commends or condemns those forms of agency at least in part independently of their characteristic consequences, and hence independently of the values or disvalues that would be assigned to them on that account by a theory of value alone.

Some might say, at this juncture, that what is really happening here is that we are finding that we need to conjoin a theory of the Right with our theory of the Good. It is all too tempting to try to cash out the present point in terms of that familiar contrast. A theory of the Good is standardly said to be a theory of value, to be used in assessing outcomes and consequences; a theory of the Right, in contrast, is standardly said to be a largely independent theory of right action, to be used in assessing people's actions and choices regardless of their consequences. Each has an important role in overall moral assessment, most commentators would have to agree.

Notice, however, that what a theory of the Right delivers is not quite what a theory of agency requires. A theory of the Right specifies right actions, whereas what a theory of agency requires is an analysis of the nature of the actors who are supposed to be performing those actions. In that sense, then, a theory of the Right itself needs a theory of agency every bit as much as does a theory of value or a theory of the Good. The prescriptions of a theory of the Right are addressed to agents, every bit as much as are the prescriptions of those other sorts of theories. And it therefore needs an analysis of the nature of the agents it is addressing, every bit as much as do those other theories.

All that is simply to say that theories of value and theories of agency are really rather different sorts of theories. They take as their focus different subjects – outcomes and their values in the former case, actions and choices and the mechanisms producing them in the latter. In that sense, at the very least, they are philosophically separate issues, at least in the sense that they have to be considered separately.

A separate issue?

To say that theories of value and of agency are *logically* separate issues, however, is not necessarily to deny that arguments that bear on the one issue might also bear on the other as well. And if they do, then our answers to those two genuinely separate questions might, in such ways, be indirectly connected. Both might derive from some deeper common theories of humanity and society, for example. The same thing that makes us think that certain outcomes are valuable and to be desired might lead us to prefer certain sorts of human agent and certain sorts of social structure, as well. The fact that the two are logically separate issues, philosophically, ought not automatically to preclude us from giving one and the same style of answer to both sorts of questions.

Green theorists seem to think – or hope or imagine or pretend or presume – that this is the case. They themselves draw no sharp distinction between the arguments that they offer for their theory of agency and those that they offer for their theory of value. That is in part because they rarely appreciate the difference between the two sorts of theory, supposing both are part and parcel of one and the same larger theory. Or if they do see that there is a separate theory of agency at work within their larger theory at all, they do not see the need to offer any separate defence of it. They seem just to presume that whatever they say in defence of their theory of value will apply, *mutatis mutandis*, as a defence of their theory of agency.

I can see only one plausible way to justify this traditionally unargued-for conflation of green theories of agency and green theories of value. That would involve a further unstated premise, postulating the uniquely natural status of small-scale primitive (prototypically, hunter-gatherer) human societies. Suppose it were true that those, and those alone, were the uniquely natural forms of human organization. Then the green theory of value would accord value to those, and only those, forms of human agency which are characteristically embodied in such societies. We would thereby be led to praise, among other things: simple living and plain dealing; societies that are small in scale, modest in material possessions and broadly egalitarian in character; loose authority structures internally, and even looser links between communities.

Greens are of course sensitive to the charge that they are essentially involved in romanticizing a primitive past. They are quick to deny that they are doing any such thing. But there is much to suggest that, for many greens, some such Rousseauian vision is indeed what bridges the gap between their theories of value and their theories of agency. It is not only that green recommendations hauntingly echo Rousseau's discourses.[12] Among the more distinguished green writers, commentaries on ideal green social forms followed from – and one can only presume were at least partly inspired by – studies of primitive societies.[13]

If that is the argument, there is a good reason for its having long remained unstated, for it is obviously a highly suspect one. It amounts to privileging, seemingly arbitrarily, one particular stage in human social development over all others. For the argument to go through, we would need some reason for believing what this argument merely asserts – namely, that hunter-gatherer society (or some such) is a uniquely natural social form.

On the face of it, that claim seems highly implausible. The shifts in social evolution that led from hunter-gatherer society to the social forms which followed it are seemingly of a cloth with the shifts in social evolution which led up to hunter-gatherer society from the social forms that preceded it. If the one sort of shift is 'natural', the other must be likewise. The only way we can deem one natural and the other not is by arbitrarily stipulating what is and is not to be included in the category of the 'natural' for these purposes.

Presumably even greens themselves, trying to argue that hunter-gatherer society and the social forms associated with it are recommended on the same basis as the green theory of value, would not want to argue that hunter-gatherer society is, literally, *uniquely* natural. They may well want to argue that at some point social evolution was artificially pushed off its natural course.[14] Everything that happened after that false turning might be non-natural, or less natural than everything that went before. But greens wanting to argue in this way would not, presumably, be so bold as to claim that hunter-gatherer society is more natural, somehow, than all the even more primitive social forms that *preceded* it. They may want to say that later stages in that process of social evolution count as 'higher' forms of social organization. But up to the crucial wrong turning, they are all equally 'natural' forms of social organization, surely.

On what basis, though, could hunter-gatherer society even be said to be a 'higher' – if not necessarily any more natural – form of social organization? Surely it cannot just be that it is a 'later' stage in social evolution. Then whatever followed hunter-gatherer society must be a yet 'higher' stage.[15] And that, of course, is precisely the result that greens want to avoid.

Similarly, though, they run the very real risk that any other basis on which they end up commending hunter-gatherer society as superior to earlier forms of social organization will lead to the conclusion that other, subsequent forms are superior to hunter-gatherer society, in turn. Suppose we fix on some particular consequence of the evolutionary step in view – greater efficiency in procuring food, for example – as the basis for saying it has led to a 'higher' form of social life. Well, certainly hunter-gatherer society is superior to what preceded it by those standards. But settled agriculture is yet better still, by those standards, than is chasing after herds of itinerant animals or seasonal berries. And so it is likely to go with any criterion we might consider: complexity of cultural artefacts, increasing human knowledge, or what have you.[16]

Ultimately, it seems, the ostensible unity of the green theory of value and the green theory of agency really does have to rest on a claim that there is something uniquely natural about the processes that led to hunter-gatherer society and something peculiarly artificial about the processes that led beyond it. Then and only then will greens have good grounds for stopping with hunter-gatherer society – for praising it as uniquely natural and the form of social organization that it embodies as being uniquely commended by a green theory of value.

I cannot, for my part, see how such a claim can be sustained. The processes of banding together for the hunt, of shaping tools and of the division of labour within the hunter-gatherer society seem of a cloth – no more and no less artificial human contrivances – than the processes of banding together for agricultural cultivation, and shaping tools and dividing labour in that connection. Both are human artifices of a peculiarly low level, agreed. Both might even be considered 'natural' artifices, in the sense of being artifices that come somehow 'naturally' to agents equipped with the ordinary sort of mental machinery standardly possessed by humans. My point is merely that neither of those stages in social evolution – nor any others adjacent to them – involve human artifices that are obviously different in kind from others that immediately precede or follow them.

[. . .]

In short, I agree that there are some forms of society which are to be preferred, on the green theory of value. Those are societies that are living 'in harmony with nature'. But such societies are characterized merely by a certain attitude towards nature. And that has no necessary implications for any particular forms of social agency. Certainly it does not imply the forms of agency ordinarily recommended by green theorists. The green theory of value and those theories of agency really do have to be regarded as separate, not only in the weaker sense that they are logically separable but also in the stronger sense that genuinely different arguments must be given in support of each.

2   PRINCIPLES OF GREEN POLITICAL ACTION

Theories of agency, as I have said, operate first and foremost at the level of individual human agents. Those are not the only sorts of agents that exist, of course. There are also properly constituted groups of people (clubs, movements, parties, states) that have all the properties that would be required for them to count as fully fledged moral agents. Some sufficiently complex automata – super-smart robots and the like – might do likewise. The point about all those artificially created agents, though, is that they are artificial human creations. Logically as well as causally, individual human agency comes first. It is that which any theory of agency must address, first and foremost.

In most respects, there is nothing special – or anyway nothing peculiar – about the green theory of individual human agency. By and large, at the level of individual human actors, it just takes over pretty standard assumptions about the nature of human action and intention, powers and purposes.[17] In taking over those standard analyses rather unreflectively, as a job lot, it runs the risk of embracing contradictory positions and failing to confront tricky issues. But the contradictions that it incorporates are just those that are 'in the air' anyway. In failing to resolve them, the green theory of agency is no worse off than any other which piggybacks on the received wisdom in this way.

It is in the more value-laden aspects of its analysis of individual agency that the green theory shows its distinctive colours, and it is on those that I shall therefore primarily focus in the present discussion. I shall discuss, specifically, the importance which the green theory of agency accords to democratic participation in the life of one's society (which is arguably the central plank in the whole green theory of agency) and the importance that that theory accords to nonviolent action (which, even according to many greens themselves, arguably does not belong there at all).

Democratic participation

Above all else, the green theory treats individual human beings as agents who naturally are, and morally ought to be, autonomous and self-governing entities. Politically, that pretty directly implies the central theme of the green political theory of agency: the importance of the full, free, active participation by everyone in democratically shaping their personal and social circumstances.

Thus, the canonical 1983 manifesto of the German Greens conspicuously and repeatedly claims that the present 'ecological, economic and social crisis can be countered only by the self-determination of those affected . . . [W]e stand for self-determination and the free development of each human being. . . . [W]e want people to shape their lives creatively together in solidarity, in harmony with their natural environment, their own wishes and needs, and free from external threat.' In consequence, the German Greens 'take a radical stand for human rights and far-reaching democratic rights both at home and abroad.'[18] Their manifesto calls for the increased 'use of referenda and plebiscites to strengthen direct democracy'.[19] It urges that large industrial combines 'be broken down into surveyable units which can be run democratically by those working in them'.[20] And so on.

The same phrases recur in several contexts, thus giving the impression of consistency. The images of 'democracy' and 'self-determination' at work in these various propositions are themselves many and varied, though.[21] Perhaps certain background conditions are presupposed by all of them – conditions like freedom from external compulsion, whether physical or economic, for example. Still, green theories on the broader subjects of democracy and self-determination more generally seem to share the same problems as most theories of participatory democracy, self-management or self-determination.

All such theories seem systematically ambivalent as between the following:

1. *Choice of oneself*. On this reading, aspirations of self-determination refer to character formation, to choosing one's personality, preferences and deepest character traits for oneself.[22] This might (indeed, it almost inevitably will) have implications for one's relations with the larger community. But basically self-determination, on this understanding, is restricted to very personal concerns.

2. *Choice for oneself*. The most standard reading of 'self-determination', familiar from Kant and Rousseau, understands it as being 'self-legislating', obeying only those commands which one has given to oneself.[23] On this understanding, the scope of self-determination extends well beyond the purely personal to embrace matters of collective concern. Yet it is unclear how individuals who are self-legislating in this strong sense could yield to any collective determination of these common concerns.[24] This brings us to our third reading of self-determination:

3. *Choice by oneself*. A final way of construing 'self-determination' puts the emphasis on determining whatever it is to be determined all by

oneself. On this interpretation, what is to be determined is left largely open: certainly it is not confined to purely personal matters of 'self-formation' as on the first interpretation; and in principle it is allowed to range as widely as you please. What is crucial to self-determination, on this reading, is simply that one should do the determining all by oneself.

These distinctions make a very real difference. Many of the best philosophical arguments for moral autonomy imply self-determination largely, if not exclusively, in the first ('choice of oneself') sense alone. As such, they have next to no political implications.[25] Certainly they would not, on their face, necessarily dictate active participation in the political institutions of direct democracy as being the best – still less the only – way of achieving self-determination.[26]

That conclusion emerges only if we construe self-determination in the second sense ('choice for oneself'). Seeing self-determination as a matter of obeying only such commands as one has given to oneself might lead us to suppose that only those who have directly and actively participated in the making of laws can obey those laws and at the same time be self-determining, in the sense of being purely self-legislating.

But then self-determination in the second sense shades dangerously over into the third. For how can we pretend that one is obeying a law that one has given to oneself if one were on the losing side of the contest? Only in the rare case of unanimity can we plausibly pretend that we are obeying 'only ourselves' when obeying laws that have been collectively enacted.

In the context of collective decision-making, self-determination in the second sense ('choice for oneself') would therefore seem to require self-determination in the third ('choice by oneself') sense. Each person must be decisive – in effect, each must have a veto – over the ultimate collective outcome.

Notice, however, that the institutions implied by giving everyone a veto are very different from those characteristically associated with participatory democracy. There is not much democracy (certainly not in its majoritarian form, at least) in any of this. Nor is there even much of a case for active participation. (The rule could be phrased, 'We propose that this law should be enacted: if you agree, you need do nothing; only if you disagree do you need to take action to register your veto.') In short, what is implied by self-determination in the 'choice by-and-for oneself' mode is more what Macpherson dubs 'protective democracy' rather than genuinely 'participatory democracy'.

I happen to think that such arguments are both true and important. But all of that, it might fairly be said, amounts to little more than philosophical points-scoring. Arguments conducted on such a plane of conceptual purity and intellectual abstraction are always in danger of missing – sometimes, one suspects, of stubbornly refusing to see – the point which real-world actors are trying, however imprecisely, to make. So let us stand back from such logic-chopping to see what might really lie behind demands for participatory democracy, from a green perspective in particular.

The goal of participatory democracy, as greens (among others) espouse it, is for example to give workers more say in what happens on the shopfloor, rather than having all production decisions being dictated from on high by a handful of managers.[27] Or, for another example, the goal is to give local communities more say in what happens in their own neighbourhoods, rather than having all decisions handed down from on high by a handful of politicians or corporate executives. Or, for yet another example, the goal is to give the local branches of green parties a genuine voice in the affairs of the party, rather than having all policy dictated from some central office.

Clearly, there is a common theme running through all those propositions. What greens are objecting to is, essentially, the concentration of power in the hands of the few. The root idea running through all their demands for 'participatory democracy' is not, as is often claimed, that everyone should be self-determining completely and in all respects. Rather, it is that more people should have more say over more of what happens to them.

That aim, however, is consistent with various different sorts of decision rules. Interminable discussions designed to evoke unanimous agreement is one, but far from the only one, which is consistent with that larger goal. Furthermore, that aim is consistent with a rationale for promoting widespread political participation which is purely pragmatic – and which may well be all the stronger for being so. The idea behind encouraging widespread, active political participation might be no more than this: mass mobilization simply makes it harder for the powers-that-be to resist popular demands. The green theory of democracy might, in those crucial respects, be better characterized as 'populist' – if the term can still be used in its original non-technical, non-pejorative sense – rather than as 'participatory', strictly speaking.

Participation, thus rationalized, would not be an end in itself but instead merely a means designed to promote substantively better decisions. They would be 'substantively better' simply in the sense that they would have to take more seriously into account a larger proportion of the community's self-conceived interests. Of course, people still might conceive their interests incorrectly, and morally there might be more to good public policy than mere interest satisfaction. So widespread, active public participation might not guarantee morally perfect outcomes. But at least in that restricted sense, it is quite likely to promote morally better ones.

What exactly is required to promote widespread public participation in politics is an empirical question, though. Happily, it is one on which political scientists have by now built up considerable expertise. First and foremost, what is required is the elimination of all manner of formal barriers to participation, ranging from the literal disenfranchisement of certain groups (women, blacks, guest workers) to mere deterrents to participating (literacy tests, poll taxes). Merely legally granting everyone the right to vote is not enough in itself, of course; arrangements must also be made for that legal right to be effectively secured (so there are no lynch parties gathering to greet any blacks who appear at the polling station, for example). But once all of that has been done, various requisites of a more sociological sort come to the fore.

Once the right legal structure is in place, it is less a question of whether people are able to vote and participate more generally than of whether they are willing to do so.[28] At this point, political sociologists point to the importance of a wide range of sociological factors (like socioeconomic status, education, group ties) in addition to more transparently political ones (like the activities of political parties) in mobilizing people to participate.

All those things are undeniably important, but they are probably important for reasons other than the social-psychological ones which political sociologists usually tend to suggest.[29] They are right to suppose that all those sociological factors work to increase people's propensity to participate in politics by increasing their 'sense of efficacy'. It stands to reason that people will only bother participating if they think that they can, through their participation, make some real difference to the outcome.

True to their social-psychological groundings, though, political sociologists standardly treat that 'sense of efficacy' as essentially an illusion. People with a good education, high social standing and links to the local elite score highly on 'ego strength'. They feel good about themselves. And that, on this essentially psychological account, is why they are inclined to have a greater 'sense of efficacy' and hence to participate more vigorously.

The model that I, and I suspect most greens (and indeed most radical-left commentators more generally), would want to counterpose to that one interprets the same facts differently. True, people with better education, higher social standing and links to the local elite tend to participate in politics more vigorously. And true, that is because they have a stronger sense of their own efficacy. But their greater efficacy is, on the radical-green account, real rather than illusory. Far from being 'all in their head' – a psychological residue of happy early childhood socialization experiences, or some such – the rich and powerful participate more often because through their participation they can win more often. They have more weight to throw around.[30]

That finding has important implications for political and social structures more generally. Suppose we think that it is important for people to participate actively in the making of decisions that affect them, if only to ensure that their interests are protected. Then we should strive to ensure not only that formal legal institutions allow participation but also that actual social circumstances facilitate it.

That means various things. Minimally, it means ensuring that questions are put to people in terms that they can understand. More demandingly, it requires a generous provision of public education. Those are the easy corollaries of any belief in even a moderately strong democracy. And, if those demands are not necessarily always easy to satisfy, they are at least easy enough to recognize and acknowledge as corollaries of a genuine belief in democratic government.

There are other corollaries to a genuine belief in democratic rule that are perhaps harder to recognize and harder yet again to realize. Creating social circumstances that facilitate democratic rule also means, for example, that the decision units should be small enough for people to comprehend the issues facing the polity, preferably from first-hand experience. (That gives rise to green proposals for decentralization, workplace democracy, and suchlike.) It also means, more importantly still, that there must be at least rough socioeconomic equality within the decision units.[31] For then and only then will people have the sort of rationally well-grounded sense of political efficacy that is required for them to bother participating at all. (That provides yet another reason for the regime of greater social equality which greens would prefer on other, quite separate grounds as well.)

Both of those latter two prescriptions might seem wildly idealistic. Neither decentralization nor radical equalization of social resources is likely to happen any time soon. Greens might of course reply that they have room to compromise on these points. Although they would ideally like both decentralization and equalization worldwide, they can make do with either one or the other. Specifically, if rough equality of socioeconomic resources worldwide is too much to hope for, then it might be enough (so far as promoting participation is concerned, anyway) to decentralize decision-making powers to small communities of a relatively homogeneous character. Rough equality within communities will be enough to ensure high levels of participation within those communities themselves, even if substantial inequalities across communities remain.

Of course, no green theorist would say that gross inequalities across communities would be in any way ideal. Furthermore, green theorists would still need some way of deciding issues that straddle communities – and the smaller the communities, the more that will fall between the cracks in those ways. (I shall have more to say on those matters in section 4 of this chapter.) The thing to notice here is merely that green theory is only half as unrealistic as it sounds, at least in the sociopolitical structural reforms it would advocate as a spur to democratic participation.

[. . .]

4   PRINCIPLES OF GREEN POLITICAL STRUCTURES

[. . .]

Decentralization

If there is anything truly distinctive about green politics, most commentators would concur, it must surely be its emphasis on decentralization. As Theodore Roszak puts it in his influential book, *Person/Planet*, both person and planet are threatened by the same enemy. *The bigness of things.* The bigness of industrial structures, world markets, financial networks, mass political organizations, public institutions, military establishments, cities, bureaucracies. It is the insensitive colossalism of these systems that endangers the rights of the person and the rights of the planet. The inordinate scale of industrial enterprise that must grind people into statistical grist for the market place and the work force simultaneously shatters the biosphere in a thousand unforeseen ways.[32]

The greens seek to substitute for all that 'a decentralized, democratic society with . . . political, economic, and social institutions locating power on the smallest scale (closest to home) that is efficient and practical'.[33] Their 'guiding principle . . . is that no authority be held at a higher level than is absolutely necessary'.[34] They want to see 'politics on a human scale'.[35] They call for decision-making power to be devolved to units that are 'surveyable' – capable of being scanned and understood by ordinary mortals.[36]

In the words of the canonical 1983 manifesto of the German Greens, the basic principle of green politics is that 'decentralized basic units (local community, district) should be given extensive autonomy and rights of self-government'.[37] They propose, more specifically, things like:

- The establishment of democratically controllable self-administration close to the citizens, in place of the increasing monopolisation of economic power and the steadily increasing central administrative apparatus.
- Thoroughgoing decentralization and simplification of units of administration.
- The rights of administration and self-determination for states, regions, districts, local authorities and urban districts are to be increased, as well as their share of financial resources. . . .
- Citizens' initiatives and associations must have the right to be heard by the relevant [federal and state] parliaments and authorities, and to obtain information. They must be given plaintiff rights against administrative measures, even across state borders.
- The vast flood of consultation, far removed from the citizens and without clearly defined responsibilities, is to be replaced by combined consultation and decision-making boards (economic and social councils) at all levels. These boards must be given a hearing everywhere (local authority, county, district, state and federal) that economically important planning and decision-making takes place. They are to make decisions about public investment policy, and be responsible in conjunction with the relevant political authority for the economic sphere of the budget.[38]

While all those specific demands are drawn from the 1983 German Green manifesto, they are nowise peculiar to that document. Decentralism of roughly that

they involve free and equal parties meeting to agree mutually desirable arrangements among themselves, without the intervention of any superior authority.[53]

All of that is just to say that greens are basically libertarians-cum-anarchists, at least as regards relations between communities if not necessarily within them. They think that decentralized communities can and should negotiate voluntary agreements coordinating their activities in various respects. But they think that there need not be – and that there should not be – any central coordinating agency overseeing that process.[54]

They say that not because greens think coordination between decentralized communities does not really matter. On the contrary, greens are the first to recognize the importance of this process. Signatories to *The Ecologist*'s 1972 'Blueprint for survival' wax lyrical on the subject:

> Although we believe that the small community should be the basic unit of society and that each community should be as self-sufficient and self-regulating as possible, we would like to stress that we are not proposing that they be inward-looking, self-obsessed or in any way closed to the rest of the world. Basic precepts of ecology, such as the interrelatedness of all things and the far-reaching effects of ecological processes and their disruption, should influence community decision-making . . .[55]

The question is simply how, exactly, that aim is to be achieved absent the agency of a state.

Some greens see the 'basic precepts of ecology' to which the 'blueprint' refers as providing the solution as well as posing the problem.[56] There is, after all, no central organization imposing order on nature. Rather, the plants and animals of each area simply adapt to their own locality, while at the same time incidentally feeding into the larger scheme of things. Ecologically, the global order emerges out of these local adaptations and interactions between them. And it does so 'naturally', without any self-conscious, intentional interventions on the part of any central coordinating agency or even on the part of any of the local constituents of nature.[57]

Sometimes green writers offer that ecological analogy as a model of coordination among the decentralized political units that they are proposing. They seem to suppose that a 'natural order' will similarly emerge there, too. But the analogy is just an analogy – no more – until they specify the precise mechanism by which order will be imposed, politically. In nature, the mechanism serving that purpose is the familiar one of natural selection. The automatic workings of that mechanism are what obviates the need for any intentional coordination in the ecological setting. Greens appealing to that ecological analogy as a model of political coordination neglect to specify what would on their theory serve as the functional equivalent, in politics, of natural selection in nature.[58]

There is a possible answer here, perhaps, but greens are not likely to be tempted by it. Many writers foresee just such a 'naturally occurring order' in the social world and have a very clear idea as to how that order will come about. The mechanism that they nominate is, of course, the market. Without any intentional interventions on the part of any superior forces, the 'hidden hand' of the market coordinates the activities of all the individual agents involved. For the likes of Hayek and Nozick, this 'spontaneous order' that emerges from the uncoerced market interactions among free individuals is something morally to be cherished.[59]

Greens would usually think otherwise. It is part of their programme that they must be highly sensitive to distributive injustices and exploitative social relations. Both, all too often, come in the wake of markets. So I think we can safely presume that that is not a mechanism that greens can rely on for coordinating decentralized decision-making. Neither, though, is it clear what other mechanism greens could nominate in its place. Until some such mechanism has been specified and its workings adequately explained, we must dismiss the idea of a 'natural order' emerging among decentralized political units that is in any important respect analogous to the 'natural order' that natural selection causes to emerge among decentralized ecological units.

Having emphasized that their decentralized communities must not 'be inward-looking, self-obsessed or in any way closed to the rest of the world', the authors of 'A blueprint for survival' proceed to a relatively limp conclusion. 'Therefore,' they write, 'there must be an efficient and sensitive communications network between all communities. There must be procedures whereby community actions that affect regions can be discussed at global level.'[60]

Clearly, communication between the decentralized communities is a necessary condition for effective coordination among them.[61] But to suggest that that will be sufficient to ensure adequate coordination seems little more than a pious hope. Recall that we are supposed to be dealing here with completely independent communities subject to no common power. So what is being proposed is communications without sanctions – a pure 'talking shop'.

The best single green text on the subject of green decentralization, Kirkpatrick Sale's *Human Scale*, offers an example of how this all might work. He points to the practices of the New England Clamshell Alliance, which is 'based on small 'affinity groups' of ten or twenty people, who meet with some regularity and make all decisions by consensus; these are then conveyed to a central committee by non-voting delegates – 'spokes' – and this committee then coordinates the results into a fixed policy, sending word back and forth to various affinity groups until general agreement is reached'. From this experience, Sale concludes that 'federation of consensus-taking groups is certainly a workable organizational form'.[62]

But the Clamshell Alliance was being rent asunder even as Sale was busy singing its praises, as Sale himself freely admits. That that happened should have come as no surprise to anyone. Even with the best will in the world, a consensus cannot hold forever. In effect, a consensus rule gives each member the power of veto over all group decisions. That veto will naturally be used as a bargaining lever. What it is one is bargaining for, with it, is variable. In politics-as-usual, the lever is characteristically employed by those with most to win or least to lose to feather their own nests.[63] In more highminded politics, it will be used by those wanting to press their particular vision of the public good on others in the group with a different vision. The motives are different, but the resulting deadlock is the same. And such deadlocks will be the inevitable results of adopting consensus rules among groups of people with divergent goals or even just divergent opinions about how best to pursue goals that they all share.

Perhaps in appreciation of those plain truths, the German Greens seem to place their faith instead in institutions of direct democracy. Their 1983 manifesto declares, 'In all political spheres we support the idea of strengthening the participation of the people affected by introducing elements of direct democracy for deciding on major schemes with regional, state and federal referenda'.[64] That is how they propose to secure the 'comprehensive organisation and coordination' that they acknowledge will be required 'if an ecological policy is to be carried through . . . against strong opposition'.[65]

Notice, though, that conducting a referendum at the national, state or even regional level is in stark contrast to green proposals for radical decentralization of decision-making powers to very small, local-level political units.[66] Direct democracy within these larger political units may well be an alternative – another way to achieve the same goals that decentralization was supposed to serve, goals of increasing people's control over what happens to them or whatever. Or, again, direct democracy at the national, state or regional levels may be just an interim measure – a second-best stopgap useful only until such time as the sort of genuine decentralization greens most desire can actually be arranged. Still, it must be said that conducting a referendum at the national, state or even regional level is dramatically different from deciding everything at the sort of small-scale neighbourhood or town meetings which greens seemed originally to be proposing.

'Think globally, act locally'

The catchphrase that at one and the same time best encapsulates both green objectives and preferred green strategies for obtaining them is 'Think globally, act locally'.[67] Greens are strong on the need to overcome traditional constraints of national sovereignty in solving pressing concerns of the global environment. *Only One Earth* was the title of the book that served as an unofficial manifesto for the 1972 Stockholm Conference on the Human Environment that led to the founding of the United Nations Environmental Programme.[68] Similar themes run throughout virtually all contemporary green manifestos.[69]

Certainly it is true that greens are concerned with life on earth as such, quite independently of artificial national boundaries. Certainly they are anti-statist, in that sense. But being anti-statist in that sense is not necessarily equivalent to being 'internationalist', in the Stockholm Conference sense of being in favour of strong international organizations (of which the UNEP is, at most, a feeble precursor) capable of securing protection for the global environment.

On the contrary, greens are more typically concerned with how to 'reshape world order without creating just another enormous nation-state'.[70] Green anti-statism characteristically emanates in proposals not for strong suprastate political institutions but rather in proposals for breaking states up and devolving their powers to smaller units, organized around bioregions or some such. That is the message that is so effectively signalled in the latter half of the slogan, 'Think globally, act locally'.[71]

But of course what gives impetus to the contemporary green movement in its present form is the supposition that we can no longer afford purely local remedies. The problems now before us are genuinely global, in the sense of requiring concerted action worldwide. The paradigmatically contemporary problems of climate change and ozone depletion, unlike the earlier problems of pollution and population control, simply cannot reliably be solved through actions by nations (still less bioregions) one at a time. The systematic, coordinated efforts of all are required.

It is at this international level that the failure of greens to provide any coherent account of coordination among smaller political units is perhaps most serious.[72] What makes the green message especially appealing is that it points to the need for concerted global action. What makes it especially unsatisfying is that it provides no account – apart from the apparently vacuous suggestion to 'think globally' – as to how that concerted global action is to be achieved.

The suggestion to 'think globally' might be less vacuous than it at first appears, though. Perhaps what it is meant to suggest is the proposition that, among communities organized around properly green values, there is a different logic at work – and that there is less need for heavy-handed coordination among those communities, in consequence.

Here I shall summarize four different models of the basic dynamics underlying efforts to coordinate environmental protection worldwide.[73] The first two models are more descriptions of current reality. They serve to explain why it is so standardly supposed that some sort of relatively centralized coordination (binding agreements, if not world governments) will be required to secure the desired goals. The latter two models are, perhaps, more apt characterizations of the sort of dynamics that greens suppose will be operating among decentralized green communities. Greens would presumably hope that they would show how, given these new dynamics, coordination might emerge more automatically without the intervention of any centralized authority. In the end, though, I think I can show that there is still a substantial role for centralized agencies to facilitate that coordination. They will be undoubtedly handy, even if they are not strictly essential.

The basic logic underlying environmental disputes, whether between separate communities or between separate individuals, is ordinarily represented as a Polluter's Dilemma, modelled on the infamous Prisoner's Dilemma. That is the first model I shall be discussing.

In a Polluter's-cum-Prisoner's Dilemma, polluting and environmental degradation more generally is represented as a cheap solution to the otherwise expensive problem of waste disposal. Each side, desiring to minimize costs to itself, is therefore presumed to prefer polluting to not polluting whatever the other side does. As in all Prisoner's Dilemmas, though, each is worse off if all pollute than if none pollutes. Hence each would be willing to be bound to some anti-pollution regulations, if that is the only way that it can ensure that others stop dumping their wastes on it.[74] But since it would be in the narrow interests of each to defect from this regime if it could – polluting others without being polluted by them – these regulations require enforcement.[75] This enforcement might in principle come in any of a variety of forms; most commonly, though, it must come in the form of sanctions imposed by some superior legal authority.[76]

The second model is essentially just a variation on that basic Polluter's-cum-Prisoner's Dilemma logic. The story as just told is a story about a two-person game. But in the real world, environmental protection games involve more than just two players: it is, in the language of game theory, an *n*-person game rather than just a two-person game. Now, let us suppose that the goal in view – protection of a fishery from being overfished, protection of the air or oceans from being overpolluted, or whatever – requires the cooperation of most but not quite all of those *n* players in the game. Suppose that if eighty out of 100 nations did it, the goal would be achieved.

Well, the basic structure of the situation may still be that of a Polluter's-cum-Prisoner's Dilemma. Each nation would certainly rather that others bear the sacrifices, to be sure. But now we have a game within a game. Suppose the world's air, oceans or fisheries can afford for twenty nations to continue polluting. There will be a mad scramble in which each nation tries to lock itself inexorably into a policy of polluting, thereby forcing others to pay the costs of environmental protection that they have avoided. And this attempt to force the other to play cooperatively by locking yourself firmly into a policy of noncooperation is, of course, the defining feature of a Chicken Game.[77] So we might say that, on this second model, there is a Chicken Game nesting inside a Polluter's-cum-Prisoner's Dilemma.

This second model might, on its face, seem to bode even worse for international environmental protection than does the basic Polluter's-cum-Prisoner's Dilemma. But, in fact, it bodes marginally better. For whereas in a Polluter's-cum-Prisoner's Dilemma noncooperation (polluting) is a strictly dominant strategy, better for each whatever the others do, in a Chicken Game there is no strictly dominant strategy. What each side does depends on what it thinks the others are going to do. Specifically, if one side thinks that the others really are locked into a pattern of noncooperative behaviour, then it will itself play cooperatively.[78] In the example above, if we think that twenty other nations really are locked into a policy of polluting and if we think that the world really can afford only twenty polluting nations, then we will sign on to a policy of not polluting ourselves. And we will do so as a matter of pure prudence, without any external sanctioning agency to force us to abide by that agreement.[79]

Of course, mistakes will happen. We will occasionally find ourselves 'calling the bluff' of others who were not bluffing at all – they really were locked into a noncooperative strategy, and they cannot now get out of it even if we try to force them to do so by playing noncooperatively ourselves. Sometimes, in the mad rush to lock themselves into noncooperative policies and thereby secure their place as one of the twenty polluting countries that the world can afford, more than twenty nations might get locked into pollution-intensive policies.[80] And sometimes there might be disagreement – genuine, or more often strategically motivated – about how many polluters the world can really afford. In all these ways, there might still be some substantial scope for a centralized authority to coordinate environmental protection policies even on the nested Chicken Game.

Both of those first two models – the Polluter's-cum-Prisoner's Dilemma and the nested Chicken Game – are essentially attempts to represent the world as it presently is. Both are essentially models of problems facing us in our attempt to coordinate environmental policies of presently existing nations and their presently existing political leaders. And both point to the need for centralized coordination backed by sanctions; enforceable international agreements, if not a world government.

All that is true, however, only in so far as people have the peculiar sorts of preferences characterizing those particular sorts of games. In particular, it is absolutely essential to have a superior legal authority to enforce agreements only if each side thinks it is better off polluting others than not, just so long it can succeed in doing so without being polluted by them in turn.[81] Not everyone manifests such peculiarly beggar-my-neighbour attitudes, though. And in so far as they do not, other models of the situation might be more appropriate.

A third model builds on the observation that – at least sometimes and at least on some issues – most people would actually prefer to behave cooperatively, just so long as others do likewise. Certainly that seems to describe the behaviour of people working on Chinese communal farms, for example. They seem happy enough to work hard without any special rewards or punishments, just so long as others are working hard too. All that they seem to ask is that they not be 'played for suckers', working hard themselves while others loll about. Amartya Sen has coined the term 'Assurance Game' to represent this phenomenon.[82]

In formal terms, this Assurance Game differs from that of the Prisoner's Dilemma in basically just one essential respect. The first choice of everyone with Prisoner's Dilemma preferences is to idle while others work. The first choice of everyone with Assurance Game preferences, in contrast, is to work while others work.

That one small change has important consequences for the need for enforcement, in turn. In a Prisoner's Dilemma there will always be a need for sanctions, usually imposed via some superior legal authority, to induce people to abide by agreements that are best for all concerned. The reason is simply that each would prefer to defect from such agreements whatever others did. In an Assurance Game there may be no need for sanctions. The reason is simply that each would prefer to abide by agreements – in the Chinese commune case, to work hard – if others did likewise.

That Assurance Game model is easily enough adapted to serve as a story about environmental protection. On the Assurance Game model of environmental protection, we are asked to imagine that everyone wants – genuinely wants, as their most preferred outcome – for everyone, themselves included, to do their bit to protect the environment. Everyone is prepared to bear their fair share of those costs, so long as others are likewise. The only reason that it might seem otherwise is that no one wants to be played for a sucker. It is only because of the (mis)perception that others will take advantage of our cooperative behaviour that any of us ever fail to cooperate in these realms.

Now, that may or may not seem like a particularly plausible model of international environmental politics among currently existing nation-states and their present political leaders. Indeed, as a model of that, most would probably dismiss it as really awfully implausible. But remember, the greens are offering this model not as an account of present political preferences but rather as a model of how coordination ought to work among a set of decentralized communities guided by genuinely green principles and values. So the fact that the present rulers of Brazil or Britain or wherever might clearly manifest the beggar-my-neighbour environmental preferences characteristic of a Polluter's-cum-Prisoner's Dilemma ought not be taken as criticism of the green model of how to coordinate transboundary environmental policy among green communities characterized by much more environmentally friendly preferences.

Even setting that obvious but erroneous objection aside, however, there nonetheless remain very real problems with the Assurance Game account of coordination among genuinely green communities. One of them, internal to the logic of the Assurance Game itself, is just that within an Assurance Game such cooperation as naturally emerges is really rather fragile. And in overcoming that fragility, here is a substantial role for a superior legal authority to play.

The source of the fragility of voluntary cooperation in an Assurance Game is that, in such games, people do not want to be 'played for a sucker'. If for any reason they get the idea that not enough others are going to cooperate, then they themselves will not cooperate. Hence, in an Assurance Game there has to be some mechanism for assuring people that enough others are going to cooperate to induce them to cooperate themselves.

Among small groups, perhaps each can assure the other adequately through verbal signals or previous plays in the game. But those mechanisms are unlikely to work among large groups – and if greens decentralize decision-making powers as thoroughly as they say they will, the group of communities to be thus coordinated will be very large indeed.[83]

The most plausible source of the needed assurances among such a large group would, once again, probably be some some superior authority with the power to impose sanctions on those who do not cooperate. So long as that superior authority can threaten sufficiently severe sanctions against noncooperative behaviour, everyone will be thereby assured of others' cooperative behaviour. And having Assurance Game preferences, each will want to play cooperatively so long as there is sufficient confidence that everyone else is going to play cooperatively likewise. That certainly is one way – among a large group of players, probably the best way – of providing the assurance, crucial for evoking cooperation in an Assurance Game, that others are not going to play you for a sucker.

Of course it is perfectly true that, if everything works according to that plan, the upshot would be that sanctions will never actually need to be imposed on anyone. Their mere existence will have been enough to induce cooperative play from everyone in a genuinely Assurance Game. That does not mean that the sanctions have been superfluous, however. Quite the contrary, the threat of sanctions will have played a crucial role in inducing cooperative behaviour from each by providing the crucial assurance that all others will do likewise.

That is just to say that, even in an Assurance Game, there may well be a substantial role for some central legal authority, superior to and with sanctioning power over all the players in that game. Nationally, that constitutes a case for the state. Internationally, that constitutes a case for, if not a world government, at least treaties with teeth. On neither level does the Assurance Game model provide any support for green suppositions that the needed coordination between decentralized jurisdictions will emerge naturally, if only the people within them 'think globally', in an Assurance Game sense.

Thus, even if relations between decentralized green communities are properly characterized as an Assurance Game, that does not necessarily mean that we can count on the needed coordination among all the various players emerging automatically without any central coordinating mechanism. Superior authorities with sanctioning power would still be useful, and may even prove essential.

There is a further, fatal problem with the Assurance Game model as an account of the green theory of policy coordination among decentralized communities. The problem, simply stated, is that people who genuinely embrace green theories of value or agency have no business harbouring Assurance Game preferences at all. Certainly the desire to cooperate in protecting the environment so long as others do likewise is consistent with those fundamentally green values. But the willingness to do so *only* as long as others do likewise is not. The desire not to be 'played for a sucker' simply cannot, on the face of it, be squared with green values. Surely if you really care about environmental protection, the fact that no one else is not going to do it is *prima facie* more of a reason – not less of one – for you to do it.

Of course, there might be special facts about the situation such that it makes sense for you to refuse to try single-handedly to protect the environment, even if you care about the environment deeply. (Perhaps it simply will not do any good for just one person or for just a few people to do it, for example; or perhaps you reckon, strategically, that by refusing to do their job for them this time you will get more people to make more of a contribution on lots of future occasions.) The green theory of intercommunal coordination here in view, though, predicates Assurance Game preferences of green players in general – not merely in those peculiar situations where they make that special kind of sense. And I, for one, cannot see any rationale within green theory that would justify people with genuinely green values in refusing to save the environment when they can, just because others who could and should help refuse to do so.[84]

That observation leads to our fourth and final model of policy coordination among decentralized green communities. Suppose that those communities are all thoroughly green. Suppose that they are so infused with green values that everyone within them 'thinks globally' about what is good for the earth, quite regardless of self-interest of any sort. Suppose that none of them would mind in the least being 'played for a sucker', or at least that brown actions from others would not lead them to deviate from their own truly green course of action. Indeed, suppose that, on the contrary, the less that others are prepared to do to save the planet, the more they are themselves prepared to do.

That is, in my view, the most credible account of what the greens have in mind with the first half of their injunction to 'think globally, act locally'.[85] Certainly it would represent the strongest possible sense of 'thinking globally' – shaping your preferences in accordance with global environmental demands, and those alone. Greens hope that this strongest sort of 'thinking globally' would underwrite the conditions under which 'acting purely locally' would prove feasible. They want to devolve decision-making powers to really very small political units, and they want those powers to remain there rather than being taken back by some centralized coordination mechanisms with strong powers all their own. Greens hope that 'thinking globally' in this strong sense can avoid the need for any such agency. Among such totally self-effacing communities, they trust, coordination will prove easy enough.

It is standardly said that pure altruists would have as much trouble with co-ordination as egoists. Some go so far as to concoct an Altruist's Dilemma, perfectly parallel to the Prisoner's Dilemma.[86] And certainly it is formally true that if you fully internalize my pay-offs and I yours, then the structure of the game remains the same: you just take my place and I yours in the game-theoretic matrix used to represent the game. Then we see the scenario, familiar from vaudeville, of two overly polite people insisting on holding the door for the other: one says, 'After you', the other, 'No, after you'; neither ever gets through the door in consequence.

That problem arises, though, only when – and only because – each party internalizes the other's pay-offs completely, to the exclusion of their own. That is not the situation here in view. What greens propose is that each should 'think globally'. That amounts to saying that each should internalize not the pay-offs of any particular other, but of everyone taken altogether. And in a Prisoner's Dilemma, when each internalizes sum-total pay-offs (one's own plus the other's), you do not get an Altruist's Dilemma. On the contrary, you will characteristically get each regarding cooperative – in the case at hand, pro-environmental – action strategies as being strictly dominant, the best for them regardless of what the other does.[87]

There do however remain other, more serious problems with the green proposal to avoid the need for organized coordination among decentralized units merely by 'thinking globally'. In environmental protection applications just as in so many others, exactly what you should do (as well as how much you should do) depends on how many others are going to cooperate and in what ways.[88]

Adjusting at the margins – doing a little, seeing how it goes, then doing a little more or a little less as needs be – is fine if it is a matter of just increasing or decreasing some homogeneous commodity. It works just fine, for example, in the standard economic settings, where the 'marginal adjustments' in view amount to no more than slight increases or decreases in price or output.

But sometimes the change in view is not just a marginal quantitative adjustment to quantity. The change in view is, rather, an alteration to the kind or quality of the inputs you make.[89] Then it is far from clear that the desired sort of coordination can come from a large number of decentralized actors adjusting to each other at the margins. If it comes at all, certainly it will not come smoothly but rather in fits and starts as each retools radically in response to each act (and again in response each subsequent response) from every other.

Here again, there might be a very useful role to be served by a centralized coordinating mechanism. There might be little need for sanctions to enforce agreements, perhaps; everyone who really does 'think globally' in this totally self-effacing way may well be prepared to bear whatever sacrifices are required quite willingly, without threat of sanction. But there would still be a need for a central coordinating mechanism to collate everyone's action plans.

Each community needs to know how much of what sort of action every other community plans to undertake, in order to choose the right kind and quantity of action itself. And while in principle they could find this out by trial and error, lots of resources would be wasted (and irreversible decisions might have been taken) in the process. Surely it would be better for there to be some centralized agency collecting and disseminating information about everyone's plans and provisional intentions.

Furthermore, since those plans will – in ways just described – naturally change in response to the plans of others, there will be a useful role for a collective forum in which representatives of all the communities can meet and negotiate these responses-to-responses-to-responses. Of course, here again, if everyone is 'thinking globally' in this completely self-effacing way, these 'negotiations' may be far friendlier than those characterizing present international forums. In a way, that might mean that there is less need for negotiations. In another, though, it means that there is more point to them.

In ordinary negotiations, even where a negotiated settlement would be better for all concerned, negotiations often break down because nobody knows how much to discount for bluff and bluster. The only way you can find out if others really mean what they say is to call their bluff and force them to act on it. In negotiations among the totally self-effacing agents of green theory, however, there will be no bluff or bluster. Everyone can be trusted to report fully and honestly on what they would actually do in response to whatever the others propose doing. Everyone can be taken at their word. And precisely because there is no need to test anyone's word, the potentially costly business of mutual adjustment can all be played out virtually costlessly, on paper or in conversations.

In short, even among representatives of totally self-effacing green communities, there may well be a substantial role for a central coordinating mechanism. It may need to amount to little more than a 'talking shop', perhaps. But it is essential that it should be a centralized talking shop, where all parties are represented.

Of course, many would suppose that such totally self-effacing actors are pure figments of green fantasy. No real individuals – certainly no actual communities – can ever be realistically expected to internalize quite so thoroughly as that the green injunction to 'think globally' so totally to the exclusion of local interests and concerns. If those suspicions are right, then there will always be elements of the other three models at work in coordination among decentralized green communities.

The point to notice is just this. On any plausible model of policy coordination among decentralized green communities, there will be a role for centralized coordinating mechanisms. The role will be greater, the need for sanctioning powers more urgent, the more the situation resembles the Polluter's-cum-Prisoner's Dilemma. But even if it is only a relatively tame Assurance Game, sanctions in support of green policies worldwide will prove useful. And even if green communities manage to be as self-effacing as greens imagine only in their fondest dreams, organized information-pooling through a central agency will still prove essential.[90]

This is just to say that greens simply cannot have it both ways. It cannot be true, at one and the same time, that (1) green issues ought to be of pressing concern because only concerted global action is capable of solving them, but that (2) the best way of responding to those issues is to devolve all decision-making powers down to very small political units who lack any way of acting in concert with one another. If green issues are important for the reasons and in the ways that they say they are, then it is essential that greens provide a coherent account of policy coordination among those decentralized communities. And all such accounts, I would argue, must necessarily involve revesting at least some of those powers in centralized coordinating agencies at the global level.

5   CONCLUSION

All of this, in a way, just amounts to variations on this one central theme. If the green theory of agency cannot be *derived from* the green theory of value – as I argue it cannot[91] – then how can we be sure that the agency thereby created would actually serve the values the other half of the green theory specifies?

This conundrum is most apparent, perhaps, in connection with green support for grassroots democracy. To advocate democracy is to advocate procedures, to advocate environmentalism is to advocate substantive outcomes: what guarantee can we have that the former procedures will yield the latter sorts of outcomes?[92] More generally, how can we guarantee that localized, or nonviolent, action will always protect the global environment?

Intuitively, greens feel that both dimensions – both process and substance – must surely matter. But much more remains to be done to show that those two dimensions reinforce rather than cut across one another. For now, pending demonstration of some such necessary linkage, we must conclude that the green theory of agency is a separate issue from the green theory of value that truly lies at the core of the green political agenda.

NOTES

1. This list is based on Die Grünen (1983).
2. Although their full implementation can come only through collectively enforced political decisions, there is much that individuals can do in the meanwhile – in their roles both as consumers and producers – to further these policy goals. When proprietors of major mining corporations or large agricultural holdings adopt environmentally responsible practices in their own operations, that seems more a case of the incomplete implementation of a public policy than of a green personal lifestyle on the part of private green consumers.
3. I see this principally as a moral problem facing mainstream parties trying to capture the green position, rather than as an objection to greens compromising their own programme by joining in coalitions with other parties.
4. In this, their programme really is radically different from those of other more established parties.
5. Discussed in chapter 4 below.
6. For reasons given at the outset of chapter 4 below.
7. As I shall argue in discussing priorities in chapter 4, section 1 below.
8. For a sample of recent philosophical work on agency and action theory in general, see e.g. Goldman 1970; Hornsby 1980; Taylor 1985, esp. ch. 1; and White 1968. For an excellent adaptation of such theories to allied problems, see O'Neill (1986, esp. ch. 3).
9. On coordination, cooperation and the nature of collective agency in general, see Lewis 1969; Goodin 1976, esp. pt 2; Regan 1980; French 1984; Snidal 1985.
10. O'Neill's (1986, ch. 3) discussion of problems of agency as applied to problems of famine relief differs strikingly from standard philosophical accounts in just this way, for example.
11. Likewise, brute empirical (if only institutional) facts constrain the sorts of collective agency that green parties can manifest, as when Die Grünen proposed that the constituency party's mandate should bind MPs whose independence from just such influences is enshrined in the Federal Republic's very constitution (Poguntke 1987).
12. Luke (1988, p. 74) effectively evokes the deep-ecology myth of man's fall: 'Once upon a time, or elsewhere in more primitive regions of the world, humanity lived

in a state of innocence. But now, due to technological domination, humanity lives in a state of corruption or alienation. For deep ecology, however, redemption is possible, in accord with examples set by primal societies, by attaining correct moral consciousness.' Although this is obviously an unsympathetic characterization, it is far from an inaccurate one, is apparent from a comparison of e.g. Bookchin (1990) and Roszak (1978) with Rousseau (1750; 1755); see similarly Bahro's (1986, pp. 87–8) description of small-scale communes as 'anthropologically favourable', in the sense that they correspond better to crucial aspects of 'human nature'.

13. At the risk of an *ad hominem* argument, reflect upon the fact that Kirkpatrick Sale's *Human Scale* (1980) – which is without doubt the best argument in the existing literature for green decentralization – carries opposite its title page a list of the author's previous books, headed by *The Land and People of Ghana*. Lest that be thought a quirk of personal history, notice that Sale (1980, p. 488) actually leans heavily upon anthropological literature about stateless societies – the Dinka, especially, but also the Mandavi, the Amba, the Lugbara, the Konkomba, the Tupi and so on – in his crucial discussion of the optimal size of local communities. See similarly the appeals to the examples of American Indian tribal society in Devall and Sessions (1985) and Tokar (1987, ch. 1).

14. In Rousseau's (1755) tale, with the introduction of notions of private property, for example.

15. Perhaps we should add: 'just so long as it followed equally natural processes of social evolution'.

16. The one candidate that might conceivably be credible – both as an account of what hunter-gatherer groups manifest among themselves and as an account of what greens value societies of broadly that sort – is 'diversity'. That, too, may be a romanticized account of hunter-gatherer societies. (Pressures towards standardization undoubtedly increase in all stages of social development from settled agriculture onwards; but it is, I take it, an open and essentially empirical question just how diverse hunter-gatherer bands themselves actually were.) And, in any case, we need to know what it was about hunter-gatherer societies that made them diverse: in the absence of any strong theoretical understanding of that, we have no good grounds for supposing that replicating some (but, inevitably, not all) attributes of such societies will actually yield the desired levels of diversity.

17. Represented by Goldman (1970), Davidson (1980) and Taylor (1985), to name just three of the most distinguished exemplars.

18. Die Grünen 1983, sec. 1, p. 8. Among the *Ten Key Values* enunciated by the Green Committees of Correspondence in the US (1986, item 2) we find similar concerns: 'How can we develop systems that allow and encourage us to control the decisions that affect our lives? . . . How can we develop planning mechanisms that would allow citizens to develop and implement their own preferences for policies and spending priorities?'

19. Die Grünen 1983, sec. 5, p. 37.

20. Ibid., sec. II.3, p. 11. See similarly the Green Committees of Correspondence in the US (1986, item 6).

21. The best single attempt at unravelling them is, in my view, Berg (1978).

22. Issues of 'choice of self' have recently been discussed, in very different contexts, by Charles Taylor (1976) and John Rawls (1982).

23. Rousseau 1762; Kant 1785. Even today, the standard analysis of 'autonomy' is still couched very much in such terms (Benn 1988; Dworkin 1988).

24. It is a notoriously tricky problem in political theory how a person can, at one and the same time, connive to obey only oneself and yield to the collective will. The problem has driven at least one reluctant theorist to philosophical anarchism (Wolff 1970). And it seems that the problem really is just about insoluble, absent fortuitous unanimity or some peculiar theory of a 'real will' (in Rousseau, uncorrupted by self-interest) or a 'split will' ('I vote for X, and in that way will for it to be

implemented; but above all, I will to be implemented whatever policy the majority votes for').

25. 'Next to no', rather than literally 'none', in deference to familiar arguments for democratic participation as a means of self-development (Pateman 1970, ch. 2; Macpherson 1977b, ch. 3).

26. And, indeed, models emphasizing participation as a means of self-development tend to concentrate primarily on shopfloor democracy in the workplace (Pateman 1970, chs 3–5; Vanek 1975; Greenberg 1986).

27. Still less do greens – or democrats of any other tint, come to that – want the democratically determined decisions of the community at large negated by the actions of powerful private corporations. That is another reason for market-socialist institutions of workers' ownership and control of the firms in which they work. To the minds of many, it is a far more important reason than the considerations of 'self-development' and 'self-expression' to which theorists of participatory democracy typically point. See e.g. Dahl (1970, ch. 3; 1985). Lindblom (1977) and Walzer (1980, ch. 17).

28. And to participate more generally. Voting, though only one mode of political participation (and in many respects a peculiar one), will here be used as a proxy for all others. Everything I say here applies, *mutatis mutandis*, to all other modes as well.

29. Verba, Nie and Kim (1978) represent the culmination of a research tradition. For critiques, see Goodin and Dryzek (1980) and references therein.

30. Pateman (1971; 1974) suggests this model. Goodin and Dryzek (1980) put it to the empirical test, and find it at least as good on all accounts and better on some than the more standard social-psychological analysis.

31. As Rousseau (1762, bk 2, ch. 11) puts it, 'no citizen shall ever be wealthy enough to buy another, and none poor enough to be forced to sell himself'. This theme is picked up by Pateman (1970, ch. 2), in particular.

32. Roszak 1978, p. 33.

33. This is the fifth of the *Ten Key Values* enunciated by the Green Committees of Correspondence in the US (1986).

34. European Greens 1989, preamble.

35. Sale 1980, esp. pp. 419–518.

36. Die Grünen 1983, sec. 1, p. 8. Similarly, in their policy on the economy, the German Greens call for 'decentralized and surveyable production units and a new and democratically controllable application of technology. Large combines are to be broken down into surveyable units which can be run democratically by those working in them' (Die Grünen 1983, sec. 2.3, p. 11).

37. Ibid., sec. 1, p. 8.

38. Ibid., sec. 5, p. 37.

39. The consensus statement among European Greens (1989, preface) describes decentralization as their 'guiding principle'. The Green Committees of Correspondence in the US (1986, item 5) demand, more particularly, that we 'redesign our institutions so that fewer decisions and less regulation over money are granted as one moves from the community toward the national level'. The exception to this rule is the British Green Party's 1987 manifesto (quoted in Dobson 1990, p. 127), proposing merely to shift responsibility for many services (taxation and benefits, social services, housing, education, health care, land reform, policing, transportation and pollution control) to decentralized district level, while leaving central government in place to tend to others (foreign affairs, defence, customs and excise, international trade and transboundary aspects of justice, transportation and pollution). It is unclear whether those more modest goals are embraced by British Greens on grounds of principle or merely on grounds of political pragmatism, however.

40. Goldsmith et al. 1972, pp. 14–15.

41. Kirkpatrick Sale (1980, p. 504; 1985, p. 64), for example, similarly commends neighbourhoods of 500 to 1,000, aggregated into cities of 8,000 to 10,000, set in

turn in 'bioregions' (Sale 1984; 1985) of more variable size. 'A bioregion', Sale writes, 'is a part of the earth's surface whose rough boundaries are determined by natural rather than human dictates, distinguishable from other areas by attributes of flora, fauna, water, climate, soils and land-forms, and the human settlements and cultures those attributes have given rise to' (1984, p. 168). That rather woolly suggestion is sometimes made more precise by saying that boundaries should be drawn so as to encapsulate certain self-contained physical and biological processes of nature, such as airsheds and watersheds (to which Sale himself at one point refers in describing a bioregion (1985, p. 107). See further Ostrom, Tiebout and Warren (1961) and, especially, Haefele (1973, ch. 4).

42. There is actually a considerable literature – in part philosophical, in part empirical – upon the importance of face-to-face meetings in making participatory democracy work. (See e.g. Laslett 1956; Mansbridge 1980, chs 19–20; and Barber 1984, ch. 19.) That is why democracy in the workplace, where interactions are more standardly face to face, is such an important model for advocates of participatory democracy (Pateman 1970; Greenberg 1986).

43. Here is the justification given by Sale (1985, pp. 94–5) for why 'the primary location of decision-making, and of political and economic control, should be the . . . more-or-less intimate grouping' of between 1,000 and 5,000–10,000: 'Here, where people know one another and the essentials of the environment they share, where at least the most basic information or problem-solving is known or readily available, . . . decisions . . . stand at least a fair chance of being correct and a reasonable likelihood of being carried out competently; and even if the choice is misguided or the implementation faulty, the damage to either the society or the ecosphere is likely to be insignificant'.

44. Thus, Dahl (1970, p. 86) says that a 'nation [that] . . . dissolves itself into tiny states in order to create a multiplicity of primary democracies . . . would be very much worse off than before with respect to a vast range of problems', naming 'pollution' as primary among them. See further Dahl and Tufte 1973.

45. Of course, on balance it might still make more sense for people for participate in smaller-scale decisions, if people gain proportionately more power over community decisions than the community loses over ultimate outcomes. My point here is just that matters are less clear-cut than 'power to the people' advocates of decentralization pretend.

46. Frankel (1987, p. 270) similarly bases his critique of 'postindustrial utopians' – greens among them – on the proposition that 'stateless, decentralized, moneyless, small-scale communes or other informal alternatives are not viable without the complex administrative and social structures necessary to guarantee democratic participation, civil rights and egalitarian co-ordination of economic resources'.

47. Greens themselves would hope to minimize the need for such coordination by making the communities self-sufficient and environmentally friendly. The first attribute obviates the necessity to negotiate with other communities to secure needed positive inputs, the latter the necessity to negotiate an end to negative externalities. Try as greens might to minimize such cross-boundary flows, there are always bound to be some of them and hence some need for coordination across different communities. Furthermore, the smaller those communities are, the larger those cross-boundary flows will ordinarily, of necessity, be.

48. French 1984.

49. Sale 1984, p. 170. A better description might be 'self-reliant' rather than 'self-sufficient' (Dobson 1990, pp. 104–7).

50. Tokar 1987, p. 98.

51. Ibid. They should also, greens say, be 'subject to popular control' (ibid.) – thus making them more ephemeral still.

52. In their practical political writings, they take a similarly lackadaisical attitude towards coordination among the various constituent parts of the larger green

movement. Sara Parkin (1988, p. 176), co-spokesperson for the British Green Party, claims in an otherwise astute essay on 'Green strategy' that 'there is no need for rigid or formal battle plans. . . . The most successful sort of co-ordination in these cases takes place in bars and restaurants.' That is fine for modest movements whose effective leadership can all fit around the same table. But it is an obviously unpromising model for any movement of a scale sufficient to capture national government.

53. Sale 1980, p. 513.
54. Bookchin (1990, pp. 182, 193), for example, advocates what he cells 'libertarian municipalism', with each 'humanly scaled, self-governing municipality freely and confederally associat[ing] with other humanly scaled, self-governing municipalities' – 'a confederal Commune of communes', as it were. Other anarchist strands in green thought are effectively evoked by O'Riordan (1976, chs 1 and 9), Dobson (1990, pp. 83–4), Sale (1980, pp. 466–81), Tokar (1987, chs 1, 2 and 7) and Woodcock (1974), as well as by Bookchin's (1971; 1982) own earlier writings.
55. Goldsmith et al. 1972, p. 15. Similarly, the 1983 German Green manifesto emphasizes that 'Grassroots democracy . . . requires comprehensive organisation and co-ordination if an ecological policy is to be carried through at the level of public decision-making against strong opposition' (Die Grünen 1983, sec. 1, p. 8). And the Green Committees of Correspondence in the US (1986, item 5) speak of the need to 'reconcile the need for community and regional self-determination with the need for appropriate centralized regulation in certain [unspecified] matters'.
56. The authors of 'A blueprint for survival' are not among them, I hasten to add. But something rather like the following argument is vaguely suggested by Bookchin's (1971, p. 80) remarks on the theme that 'an anarchist community would approximate an ecosystem'.
57. Or at least so the standard models would have it. But this proposition is itself the subject of some controversy among natural scientists themselves. See e.g. the debate between Engelberg and Boyarsky (1979) and Patten and Odum (1981).
58. The importance of specifying mechanisms to validate non-intentional, non-causal explanations is powerfully brought home by Elster (1983, chs 1 and 2).
59. Hayek 1960; 1973–9; Nozick 1974.
60. Goldsmith et al. 1972, p. 15.
61. Goodin 1976, ch. 5.
62. Sale 1980, pp. 503–4. Elsewhere, Sale (1984) has written that 'bioregions' – a substantially larger unit than the decentralized local communities – should also develop in 'relative autonomy' from each other.
63. Barry 1965, pp. 243–50.
64. Die Grünen 1983, sec. 1, p. 8; see similarly sec. 5.1.2, p. 37.
65. Ibid., sec. 1, p. 8.
66. Direct democracy on the local level is, of course, quite another matter. That is not only consistent with green proposals for decentralization but also at least arguably presupposes them. There is much reason to believe that direct democracy works only among groups small enough for everyone to meet face to face (Sale 1980, pp. 492–507).
67. The phrase is commonly attributed to René Dubois (Tokar 1987, p. 138). The idea obviously predates green parties themselves. In the section of the 1972 'Blueprint for survival' dedicated to decentralization, for example, the signatories are at pains to 'emphasize that our goal should be to create *community* feeling and *global* awareness . . .' (Goldsmith et al. 1972, p. 15).
68. Ward and Dubois 1972.
69. The 1983 German Green manifesto, for example, reads, 'The future of life on our planet Earth can only be safeguarded if a survival community of all peoples and nations is formed. For this reason, cooperation in partnership with all nations of the world is the uppermost principle of our foreign policy' (Die Grünen 1983, sec. 3.1, p. 24).

70. That counts as one of the *Ten Key Values* enunciated by the Green Committees of Correspondence in the US (1986, item 9).
71. The German Greens (Die Grünen 1983, sec. 3.1, pp. 24–5) are systematically ambivalent on this score. On the one hand, they write, 'Though we all undoubtedly live in one world, it would be quite contrary to the principles of an ecological policy if we were to try and solve all problems uniformly and centralistically. Our aim is to maintain the viability of particular regions of the Earth even if they have to depend upon themselves [alone]. This corresponds to our principle of decentralization within the state.' On the other hand, they write, 'As many of the important tasks of the future can only be achieved by a worldwide organisation, we Greens support the strengthening of the United Nations'.
72. Some comfort might be drawn from considerable evidence of norms of 'comity' at work in international law (Paul 1991). But it is an open question how far that will generalize: it is one thing to be willing to apply standards set elsewhere in the relatively rare case of a foreign national standing in the dock in your own jurisdiction; it is quite another to alienate power to set standards for yourselves, at all. The absence of traditions of comity in private international law – where commerce and contracts are concerned – suggests that the model is not likely to generalize very far.
73. For a fuller discussion of coordination problems in general and of the social mechanisms appropriate to solving them, see Goodin (1976, chs 4 and 5 respectively).
74. The Polluter's Dilemma is thus represented in Goodin 1976, ch. 15 and extended to the international environment in ch. 17. On such models of collective action in general, see Olson (1965), Hardin (1982). For an extended application to international environmental regimes, see Ostrom (1991).
75. This is what Garrett Hardin (1968) refers to as 'mutual coercion mutually agreen upon' in his classic paper on 'The tragedy of the commons'; the point, indeed the phrase, is echoed in Schelling (1971).
76. I say 'most commonly' in deference to the possibility that self-enforcement might be possible, on a 'tit-for-tat' basis, among a small group of agents locked into an indefinitely long series of such games with each other (Luce and Raiffa 1957, pp. 97–102; M. Taylor 1976; 1987; Axelrod 1984).
77. Taylor and Ward 1982; Taylor 1987, ch. 2; Ward 1987.
78. For a theoretically elaborated empirical example, see Ward and Edwards 1990.
79. Ward 1987.
80. Taylor and Ward 1982; Taylor 1987, ch. 2; Ward 1987.
81. Indeed, in the peculiar structure of a Polluter's-cum-Prisoner's Dilemma Game, each is better off polluting whatever others do. One would rather pollute if they do not: that way one enjoys the comparative advantage over them of disposing of one's wastes cheaply, whereas they must pay to dispose of them properly. But one would also rather pollute even if they do: certainly one would not want to put oneself at the comparative disadvantage of being the only one to pay to dispose of one's own wastes properly. The peculiarity of the Prisoner's Dilemma is that each following this 'strictly dominant strategy' and doing what is best for each, whatever others do, leads to everyone doing something – polluting – which is worse for everyone than everyone not polluting. But since it is best for each to pollute whatever others do, there is no way to get to that socially preferred world of no pollution, absent some mechanism of enforcing the no-pollution agreement. Individual interests, narrowly calculated, will not naturally yield that result.
82. Sen 1966; 1967.
83. The same is broadly true of the self-enforcement of cooperative agreements in Polluter's-cum-Prisoner's Dilemmas via strategies of tit-for-tat reciprocity. While that is still possible even among a large number of players, the conditions required for that strategy to work are less likely to be satisfied with many players (Taylor 1987, pp. 104–5; see further Taylor and Ward 1982 and Hardin 1982, ch. 3).

84. At most, the refusal to be 'played for a sucker' might be excused rather than justified on green principles. As in the standard analysis of 'saints and heroes' (Urmson 1958), perhaps it is just more than standard human psychology can bear to let others continually take advantage of you. But then the fact that greens have Assurance Game attitudes towards environmental protection is a sad fact, permissible and excusable perhaps but certainly not in any way justifiable.

85. In other respects, it must be said, this model is wildly at odds with green theory – especially the emphasis it places upon 'diversity'. Sale (1985, p. 107) is particularly forthright in acknowledging that, while a 'certain homogeneity would exist' within a bioregion, 'a certain divergence would be bound to exist there also . . . it would be the purpose of a bioregional polity . . . to find agreement between quarrelsome communities'. He goes on to say that 'of course . . . agreement at the cost of squelching variety or imposing uniformity comes at too high a price', and he adds that the stable bioregion, like the stable econiche, 'permits – even, in a sense, encourages – a certain amount of disharmony and conflict . . .'. Whether or not this ecological model offers a viable model for containing political conflict, it is clear that on Sale's model conflict between communities is not expected to disappear in the ways here being contemplated.

86. Buchanan 1975.

87. 'Characteristically', because of course in this formulation things depend on the precise numbers in each cell. The 'sum total' phrasing of this point presupposes interpersonal comparability and additivity, which many would suppose cannot be done; but I put it that way just for expository convenience, and those who find the phrase objectionable should just think in terms of a 'collective rank ordering of outcomes' which each individual player then internalizes.

88. This is formalized by economists as the 'general theory of second best' (Lipsey and Lancaster 1956).

89. For an example that might prove less fanciful than one would like, our community might be happy to reduce our emissions of greenhouse gases if everyone else is going to do likewise, but be inclined to dump lots of carbon-dioxide-eating algae in the world's oceans if not enough others are going to cooperate in controlling emissions at source.

90. These conclusions parallel the insights of Herring (1990, p. 65) concerning the second-order 'role of supra-local authority in providing or denying space for local solutions, mediating between local institutions on overlapping commons dilemmas, and responding to dilemmas which are beyond the reach of any local response'. I am grateful to Claus Offe for drawing this valuable source to my attention.

91. Section 1 above.

92. Saward 1991.

'DEVELOPMENT, ECOLOGY AND WOMEN' BY VANDANA SHIVA

Vandana Shiva is an activist, campaigner, writer and intellectual. Her work and activity are testament to the way in which the environmental movement has come to focus on broad issues of development, trade and the empowerment of the poor. At present, she is Director of the Research Foundation for Science, Technology and Natural Resource Policy (based in India), which she founded to examine issues of sustainable agricultural development. She has worked on a range of linked issues including biodiversity and, more recently, genetic modification and patent rights (which she terms 'biopiracy'). She is also a founder of the social movement Navdanya which campaigns for the conservation of indigenous seeds. Among her numerous works, those perhaps most related to the context of this book are *The Violence of the Green Revolution: Third World Agriculture, Ecology and Politics* (Zed Books, 1991), *Monocultures of the Mind: Perspectives on Biodiversity and Biotechnology* (Zed Books, 1993), *Ecofeminism* (with Maria Mies) (Zed Books, 1993), *Biopiracy: The Plunder of Nature and Knowledge* (South End Press, 1997) and *Biodiversity: Social and Ecological Perspectives* (Zed Books, 1992).

The extract is taken from *Staying Alive* (Zed Books, 1989) and should serve as a good introductory presentation of Shiva's criticism of Western scientism, its imposition on the Third World and the links between ecological disaster and the suppression of women. She challenges the conception of growth that animates most economic analysis, advocating a distinctively feminist approach to ecology and, as with other extracts in this section, showing how Green politics is concerned with the overall organisation of social and political life.

'DEVELOPMENT, ECOLOGY AND WOMEN' (1989)*

Vandana Shiva

[From the Introduction]

> Let them come and see men and women and children who know how to live, whose joy of life has not yet been killed by those who claimed to teach other nations how to live. (Chinua Achebe)[1]

---

* From Vandana Shiva, *Staying Alive* (London: Zed Books, 1989), pp. xiv–xviii, 1–37.

The Age of Enlightenment, and the theory of progress to which it gave rise, was centred on the sacredness of two categories: modern scientific knowledge and economic development. Somewhere along the way, the unbridled pursuit of progress, guided by science and development, began to destroy life without any assessment of how fast and how much of the diversity of life on this planet is disappearing. The act of living and of celebrating and conserving life in all its diversity – in people and in nature – seems to have been sacrificed to progress, and the sanctity of life been substituted by the sanctity of science and development.

Throughout the world, a new questioning is growing, rooted in the experience of those for whom the spread of what was called 'enlightenment' has been the spread of darkness, of the extinction of life and life-enhancing processes. A new awareness is growing that is questioning the sanctity of science and development and revealing that these are not universal categories of progress, but the special projects of modern western patriarchy. This book has grown out of my involvement with women's struggles for survival in India over the last decade. It is informed both by the suffering and insights of those who struggle to sustain and conserve life, and whose struggles question the meaning of a progress, a science, a development which destroys life and threatens survival.

The death of nature is central to this threat to survival. The earth is rapidly dying: her forests are dying, her soils are dying, her waters are dying, her air is dying. Tropical forests, the creators of the world's climate, the cradle of the world's vegetational wealth, are being bull-dozed, burnt, ruined or submerged. In 1950, just over 100 million hectares of forests had been cleared – by 1975, this figure had more than doubled. During 1950–75, at least 120 million hectares of tropical forests were destroyed in South and Southeast Asia alone; by the end of the century, another 270 million could be eliminated. In Central America and Amazonia, cattle ranching for beef production is claiming at least 2.5 million hectares of forests each year; in India 1.3 million hectares of forests are lost every year to commercial plantation crops, river valley projects, mining projects and so on. Each year, 12 million hectares of forests are being eliminated from the face of the earth. At current rates of destruction, by the year 2050 all tropical forests will have disappeared, and with tropical forests will disappear the diversity of life they support.

Up to 50 per cent of all living things – at least five million species – are estimated to live in tropical forests. A typical four-square-mile patch of rainforest contains up to 1,500 species of flowering plants, 750 species of trees, 125 of mammals, 400 of birds, 100 of reptiles, 60 of amphibians and 150 of butterflies. The unparalleled diversity of species within tropical forests means relatively few individuals of each; any forest clearance thus disrupts their life cycles and threatens them with rapid extinction. Current estimates suggest that we are losing one species of life a day from the 5–10 million species believed to exist. If present trends continue, we can expect an annual rate of loss as high as 50,000 species by the year 2000. In India alone, there exist 7,000 species of plant life not found anywhere else in the world; the destruction of her natural forests implies the disappearance of this rich diversity of animal and plant life.

Forests are the matrix of rivers and water sources, and their destruction in tropical regions amounts to the desiccation and desertification of land. Every year, 12 million hectares of land deteriorate into deserts and are unable to support vegetation or produce food. Sometimes land is laid waste through desertification, at other times through ill-conceived land use which destroys the fertility of fragile tropical soils. Desertification in the Sahel in Africa has already killed millions of people and animals. Globally, some 456 million people today are starving or malnourished because of the desertification of croplands. Most agricultural lands cropped intensively with green revolution techniques are either waterlogged or desiccated deserts. Nearly 7 million hectares of land in India brought under irrigation have already gone out of production due to severe salinity, and an additional 6 million hectares have been seriously affected by waterlogging. Green revolution agriculture has decreased genetic diversity and increased the vulnerability of crops to failure through lowering resistance to drought and pests.

With the destruction of forests, water and land, we are losing our life-support systems. This destruction is taking place in the name of 'development' and progress, but there must be something seriously wrong with a concept of progress that threatens survival itself. The violence to nature, which seems intrinsic to the dominant development model, is also associated with violence to women, who depend on nature for drawing sustenance for themselves, their families, their societies. This violence against nature and women is built into the very mode of perceiving both, and forms the basis of the current development paradigm. This book is an attempt to articulate how rural Indian women, who are still embedded in nature, experience and perceive ecological destruction and its causes, and how they have conceived and initiated processes to arrest the destruction of nature and begin its regeneration. From the diverse and specific grounds of the experience of ecological destruction arises a common identification of its causes in the developmental process and the view of nature with which it is legitimised. This book focuses on science and development as patriarchal projects not as a denial of other sources of patriarchy, such as religion, but because they are thought to be class, culture and gender neutral.

Seen from the experiences of Third World women, the modes of thinking and action that pass for science and development, respectively, are not universal and humanly inclusive, as they are made out to be; modern science and development are projects of male, western origin, both historically and ideologically. They are the latest and most brutal expression of a patriarchal ideology which is threatening to annihilate nature and the entire human species. The rise of a patriarchal science of nature took place in Europe during the fifteenth and seventeenth centuries as the scientific revolution. During the same period, the closely related industrial revolution laid the foundations of a patriarchal mode of economic development in industrial capitalism. Contemporary science and development conserve the ideological roots and biases of the scientific and industrial revolutions even as they unfold into new areas of activity and new domains of subjugation.

The scientific revolution in Europe transformed nature from *terra mater* into a machine and a source of raw material; with this transformation it removed all ethical and cognitive constraints against its violation and exploitation. The industrial revolution converted economics from the prudent management of resources for sustenance and basic needs satisfaction into a process of commodity production for profit maximisation. Industrialism created a limitless appetite for resource exploitation, and modern science provided the ethical and cognitive licence to make such exploitation possible, acceptable – and desirable. The new relationship of man's domination and mastery over nature was thus also associated with new patterns of domination and mastery over women, and their exclusion from participation *as partners* in both science and development.

Contemporary development activity in the Third World superimposes the scientific and economic paradigms created by western, gender-based ideology on communities in other cultures. Ecological destruction and the marginalisation of women, we know now, have been the inevitable results of most development programmes and projects based on such paradigms; they violate the integrity of one and destroy the productivity of the other. Women, as victims of the violence of patriarchal forms of development, have risen against it to protect nature and preserve their survival and sustenance. Indian women have been in the forefront of ecological struggles to conserve forests, land and water. They have challenged the western concept of nature as an object of exploitation and have protected her as Prakriti, the living force that supports life. They have challenged the western concept of economics as production of profits and capital accumulation with their own concept of economics as production of sustenance and needs satisfaction. A science that does not respect nature's needs and a development that does not respect people's needs inevitably threaten survival. In their fight to survive the onslaughts of both, women have begun a struggle that challenges the most fundamental categories of western patriarchy – its concepts of nature and women, and of science and development. Their ecological struggle in India is aimed simultaneously at liberating nature from ceaseless exploitation and themselves from limitless marginalisation. They are creating a feminist ideology that transcends gender, and a political practice that is humanly inclusive; they are challenging patriarchy's ideological claim to universalism not with another universalising tendency, but with diversity; and they are challenging the dominant concept of power as violence with the alternative concept of non-violence as power.

The everyday struggles of women for the protection of nature take place in the cognitive and ethical context of the categories of the ancient Indian worldview in which nature is Prakriti, a living and creative process, the feminine principle from which all life arises. Women's ecology movements, as the preservation and recovery of the feminine principle, arise from a non-gender-based ideology of liberation, different both from the gender-based ideology of patriarchy which underlies the process of ecological destruction and women's subjugation, and the gender-based responses which have, until recently, been characteristic of the west.

[. . .]

[From Chapter 1, 'Development, Ecology and Women']

DEVELOPMENT AS A NEW PROJECT OF WESTERN PATRIARCHY

[. . .]

The displacement of women from productive activity by the expansion of development was rooted largely in the manner in which development projects appropriated or destroyed the natural resource base for the production of sustenance and survival. It destroyed women's productivity both by removing land, water and forests from their management and control, as well as through the ecological destruction of soil, water and vegetation systems so that nature's productivity and renewability were impaired. While gender subordination and patriarchy are the oldest of oppressions, they have taken on new and more violent forms through the project of development. Patriarchal categories which understand destruction as 'production' and regeneration of life as 'passivity' have generated a crisis of survival. Passivity, as an assumed category of the 'nature' of nature and of women, denies the activity of nature and life. Fragmentation and uniformity as assumed categories of progress and development destroy the living forces which arise from relationships within the 'web of life' and the diversity in the elements and patterns of these relationships.

The economic biases and values against nature, women and indigenous peoples are captured in this typical analysis of the 'unproductiveness' of traditional natural societies:

> Production is achieved through human and animal, rather than mechanical, power. Most agriculture is unproductive; human or animal manure may be used but chemical fertilisers and pesticides are unknown . . . For the masses, these conditions mean poverty.[2]

The assumptions are evident: nature is unproductive; organic agriculture based on nature's cycles of renewability spells poverty; women and tribal and peasant societies embedded in nature are similarly unproductive, not because it has been demonstrated that in cooperation they produce *less* goods and services for needs, but because it is assumed that 'production' takes place only when mediated by technologies for commodity production, even when such technologies destroy life. A stable and clean river is not a productive resource in this view: it needs to be 'developed' with dams in order to become so. Women, sharing the river as a commons to satisfy the water needs of their families and society, are not involved in productive labour: when substituted by the engineering man, water management and water use become productive activities. Natural forests remain unproductive till they are developed into monoculture plantations of commercial species. Development thus, is equivalent to maldevelopment, a development bereft of the feminine, the conservation, the ecological principle. The neglect of nature's work in renewing herself, and women's work in producing sustenance in the form of basic, vital needs is an essential part of the paradigm of maldevelopment, which sees all work that does not produce profits and capital as non-work or unproductive work. As Maria Mies[3] has pointed out, this concept of surplus has a patriarchal bias because, from the point of view of nature and women, it is not based on material surplus produced *over and above* the requirements of the community: it is stolen and appropriated through violent modes from nature (which needs a share of her produce to reproduce herself) and from women (who need a share of nature's produce to produce sustenance and ensure survival).

From the perspective of Third World women, productivity is a measure of producing life and sustenance; that this kind of productivity has been rendered invisible does not reduce its centrality to survival – it merely reflects the domination of modern patriarchal economic categories which see only profits, not life.

MALDEVELOPMENT AS THE DEATH OF THE FEMININE PRINCIPLE

In this analysis, maldevelopment becomes a new source of male–female inequality. 'Modernisation' has been associated with the introduction of new forms of dominance. Alice Schlegel[4] has shown that under conditions of subsistence, the interdependence and complementarity of the separate male and female domains of work is the characteristic mode, based on diversity, not inequality. Maldevelopment militates against this equality in diversity, and superimposes the ideologically constructed category of western technological man as a uniform measure of the worth of classes, cultures and genders. Dominant modes of perception based on reductionism, duality and linearity are unable to cope with equality in diversity, with forms and activities that are significant and valid, even though different. The reductionist mind superimposes the roles and forms of power of western male-orientated concepts on women, all non-western peoples and even on nature, rendering all three 'deficient', and in need of 'development'. Diversity, and unity and harmony in diversity, become epistemologically unattainable in the context of maldevelopment, which then becomes synonymous with women's underdevelopment (increasing sexist domination) and nature's depletion (deepening ecological crises). Commodities have grown, but nature has shrunk. The poverty crisis of the South arises from the growing scarcity of water, food, fodder and fuel, associated with increasing maldevelopment and ecological destruction. This poverty crisis touches women most severely, first because they are the poorest among the poor, and then because, with nature, they are the primary sustainers of society.

Maldevelopment is the violation of the integrity of organic, interconnected and interdependent systems, that sets in motion a process of exploitation, inequality, injustice and violence. It is blind to the fact that a recognition of nature's harmony and action to maintain it are preconditions for distributive justice. This is why Mahatma Gandhi said, 'There is enough in the world for everyone's need, but not for some people's greed'.

Maldevelopment is maldevelopment in thought and action. In practice, this fragmented, reductionist, dualist perspective violates the integrity and harmony of man in nature, and the harmony between men and women. It ruptures the co-operative unity of masculine and feminine, and places man, shorn of the feminine principle, above nature and women, and separated from both. The violence to nature as symptomatised by the ecological crisis, and the violence to women, as symptomatised by their subjugation and exploitation, arise from this subjugation of the feminine principle. I want to argue that what is currently called development is essentially maldevelopment, based on the introduction or accentuation of the domination of man over nature and women. In it, both are viewed as the 'other', the passive non-self. Activity, productivity and creativity which were associated with the feminine principle are expropriated as qualities of nature and women, and transformed into the exclusive qualities of man. Nature and women are turned into passive objects, to be used and exploited for the uncontrolled and uncontrollable desires of alienated man. From being the creators and sustainers of life, nature and women are reduced to being 'resources' in the fragmented, anti-life model of maldevelopment.

TWO KINDS OF GROWTH, TWO KINDS OF PRODUCTIVITY

Maldevelopment is usually called 'economic growth', measured by the Gross National Product. Porritt, a leading ecologist, has this to say of GNP:

> *Gross* National Product – for once a word is being used correctly. Even conventional economists admit that the hey-day of GNP is over, for the simple reason that as a measure of progress, it's more or less useless. GNP measures the lot, all the goods and services produced in the money economy. Many of these goods and services are not beneficial to people, but rather a measure of just how much is going wrong; increased spending on crime, on pollution, on the many human casualties of our society, increased spending because of waste or planned obsolescence, increased spending because of growing bureaucracies: it's all counted.[5]

The problem with GNP is that it measures some costs as benefits (e.g. pollution control) and fails to measure other costs completely. Among these hidden costs are the new burdens created by ecological devastation, costs that are invariably heavier for women, both in the North and South. It is hardly surprising, therefore, that as GNP rises, it does not necessarily mean that either wealth or welfare increase proportionately. I would argue that GNP is becoming, increasingly, a measure of how real wealth – the wealth of nature and that produced by women for sustaining life – is rapidly decreasing. When commodity production as the prime economic activity is introduced as development, it destroys the potential of nature and women to produce life and goods and services for basic needs. More commodities and more cash mean less life – in nature (through ecological destruction) and in society (through denial of basic needs). Women are devalued first, because their work cooperates with nature's processes, and second, because work which satisfies needs and ensures sustenance is devalued in general. Precisely because more growth in maldevelopment has meant less sustenance of life and life-support systems, it is now imperative to recover the feminine principle as the basis for development which conserves and is ecological. Feminism as ecology, and ecology as the revival of Prakriti, the source of all life, become the decentred powers of political and economic transformation and restructuring.

This involves, first, a recognition that categories of 'productivity' and growth which have been taken to be positive, progressive and universal are, in reality, restricted patriarchal categories. When viewed from the point of view of nature's productivity and growth, and women's production of sustenance, they are found to be ecologically destructive and a source of gender inequality. It is no accident that the modern, efficient and productive technologies created within the context of growth in market economic terms are associated with heavy ecological costs, borne largely by women. The resource- and energy-intensive production processes they give rise to demand ever-increasing resource withdrawals from the ecosystem. These withdrawals disrupt essential ecological processes and convert renewable resources into non-renewable ones. A forest, for example, provides inexhaustible supplies of diverse biomass over time if its capital stock is maintained and it is harvested on a sustained-yield basis. The heavy and uncontrolled demand for industrial and commercial wood, however, requires the continuous overfelling of trees which exceeds the regenerative capacity of the forest ecosystem, and eventually converts the forests into non-renewable resources. Women's work in the collection of water, fodder and fuel is thus rendered more energy- and time-consuming. (In Garhwal, for example, I have seen women who originally collected fodder and fuel in a few hours now travelling long distances by truck to collect grass and leaves in a task that might take up to two days.) Sometimes the damage to nature's intrinsic regenerative capacity is impaired not by over-exploitation of a particular resource but, indirectly, by damage caused to other related natural resources through ecological processes. Thus the excessive overfelling of trees in the catchment areas of streams and rivers destroys not only forest resources, but also renewable supplies of water, through hydrological destabilisation. Resource-intensive industries disrupt essential ecological processes not only by their excessive demands for raw material, but by their pollution of air and water and soil. Often such destruction is caused by the resource demands of non-vital industrial products. In spite of severe ecological crises, this paradigm continues to operate because for the North and for the elites of the South, resources continue to be available, even now. The lack of recognition of nature's processes for survival *as factors in the process of economic development* shrouds the political issues arising from resource transfer and resource destruction, and creates an ideological weapon for increased control over natural resources in the conventionally employed notion of productivity. All other costs of the economic process consequently become invisible. The forces which contribute to the increased 'productivity' of a modern farmer or factory worker, for instance, come from the increased use of natural resources. Lovins has described this as the amount of 'slave' labour presently at work in the world.[6] According to him, each person on earth, on an average, possesses the equivalent of about 50 slaves, each working a 40-hour week. Man's global energy conversion from all sources (wood, fossil fuel, hydroelectric power, nuclear) is currently approximately 8×10^{12} watts. This is more than 20 times the energy content of the food necessary to feed the present world population at the FAO standard diet of 3,600 cal/day. The 'productivity' of the western male compared to women or Third World peasants is not intrinsically superior; it is based on inequalities in the distribution of this 'slave' labour. The average inhabitant of the USA for example has 250 times more 'slaves' than the average Nigerian. 'If Americans were short of 249 of those 250 'slaves', one wonders how efficient they would prove themselves to be?'

It is these resource- and energy-intensive processes of production which divert resources away from survival, and hence from women. What patriarchy sees as productive work is, in ecological terms, highly destructive production. The second law of thermodynamics predicts that resource-intensive and resource-wasteful economic development must become a threat to the survival of the human species in the long run. Political struggles based on ecology in industrially advanced countries are rooted in this conflict between *long-term survival options* and *short-term over-production and over-consumption*. Political struggles of women, peasants and tribals based on ecology in countries like India are far more acute and urgent since they are rooted in the *immediate threat to the options for survival* for the vast majority of the people, *posed by resource-intensive and resource-wasteful economic growth* for the benefit of a minority.

In the market economy, the organising principle for natural resource use is the maximisation of profits and capital accumulation. Nature and human needs are managed through market mechanisms. Demands for natural resources are restricted to those demands registering on the market; the ideology of development is in large part based on a vision of bringing all natural resources into the market economy for commodity production. When these resources are already being used by nature to maintain her production of renewable resources and by women for sustenance and livelihood, their diversion to the market economy generates a scarcity condition for ecological stability and creates new forms of poverty for women.

TWO KINDS OF POVERTY

In a book entitled *Poverty: the Wealth of the People*[7] an African writer draws a distinction between poverty as subsistence, and misery as deprivation. It is useful to separate a cultural conception of subsistence living as poverty from the material experience of poverty that is a result of dispossession and deprivation. Culturally perceived poverty need not be real material poverty: subsistence economies which satisfy basic needs through self-provisioning are not poor in the sense of being deprived. Yet the ideology of development declares them so because they do not participate overwhelmingly in the market economy, and do not consume commodities produced for and distributed through the market *even though they might be satisfying those needs through self-provisioning mechanism*s. People are perceived as poor if they eat millets (grown by women) rather than commercially produced and distributed processed foods sold by global agri-business. They are seen as poor if they live in self-built housing made from natural material like bamboo and mud rather than in cement houses. They are seen as poor if they wear handmade garments of natural fibre rather than synthetics. Subsistence, as culturally perceived poverty, does not necessarily imply a low physical quality of life. On the contrary, millets are nutritionally far superior to processed foods, houses built with local materials are far superior, being better adapted to the local climate and ecology, natural fibres are preferable to man-made fibres in most cases, and certainly more affordable. This cultural perception of prudent subsistence living as poverty has provided the legitimisation for the development process as a poverty-removal project. As a culturally biased project, it destroys wholesome and sustainable lifestyles and creates real material poverty, or misery, by the denial of survival needs themselves, through the diversion of resources to resource-intensive commodity production. Cash-crop production and food-processing take land and water resources away from sustenance needs, and exclude increasingly large numbers of people from their entitlements to food.

> The inexorable processes of agriculture-industrialisation and internationalisation are probably responsible for more hungry people than either cruel or unusual whims of nature. There are several reasons why the high-technology-export crop model increases hunger. Scarce land, credit, water and technology are pre-empted for the export market. Most hungry people are not affected by the market at all . . . The profits flow to corporations that have no interest in feeding hungry people without money.[8]

The Ethiopian famine is in part an example of the creation of real poverty by development aimed at removing culturally perceived poverty. The displacement of nomadic Afars from their traditional pastureland in Awash Valley by commercial agriculture (financed by foreign companies) led to their struggle for survival in the fragile uplands which degraded the ecosystem and led to the starvation of cattle and the nomads.[9] The market economy conflicted with the survival economy in the Valley, thus creating a conflict between the survival economy and nature's economy in the uplands. At no point has the global marketing of agricultural commodities been assessed against the background of the new conditions of scarcity and poverty that it has induced. This new poverty, moreover, is no longer cultural and relative: it is absolute, threatening the very survival of millions on this planet.

The economic system based on the patriarchal concept of productivity was created for the very specific historical and political phenomenon of colonialism. In it, the input for which efficiency of use had to be maximised in the production centres of Europe was industrial labour. For colonial interest, therefore, it was rational to improve the labour resource *even at the cost of wasteful use of nature's wealth*. This rationalisation has, however, been illegitimately universalised to all contexts and interest groups; and, on the plea of increasing productivity, labour-reducing technologies have been introduced in situations where labour is abundant and cheap, and resource-demanding technologies have been introduced where resources are scarce and already fully utilised for the production of sustenance. Traditional economies with a stable ecology have shared with industrially advanced affluent economies the ability to use natural resources to satisfy basic vital needs. The former differ from the latter in two essential ways: first, the same needs are satisfied in industrial societies through longer technological chains requiring higher energy and resource inputs and excluding large numbers without purchasing power; and second, affluence generates new and artificial needs requiring the increased production of industrial goods and services. Traditional economies are not advanced in the matter of non-vital needs satisfaction, but as far as the satisfaction of basic and vital needs is concerned, they are often what Marshall Sahlins has called 'the original affluent society'. The needs of the Amazonian tribes are more than satisfied by the rich rainforest; their poverty begins with its destruction. The story is the same for the Gonds of Bastar in India or the Penans of Sarawak in Malaysia.

Thus are economies based on indigenous technologies viewed as 'backward' and 'unproductive'. Poverty, as the denial of basic needs, is not necessarily associated with the existence of traditional technologies, and its removal is not necessarily an outcome of the growth of modern ones. On the contrary, the destruction of ecologically sound traditional technologies, often created and used by women, along with the destruction of their material base is generally believed to be responsible for the 'feminisation' of poverty in societies which have had to bear the costs of resource destruction.

The contemporary poverty of the Afar nomad is rooted not in the inadequacies of traditional nomadic life but in the *diversion of the productive pastureland of the Awash Valley*. The erosion of the resource base for survival is increasingly being caused by the demand for resources by the market economy, dominated by global forces. The creation of inequality through economic activity which is ecologically disruptive arises in two ways: first, inequalities in the distribution of privileges make for unequal access to natural resources – these include privileges of both a political and economic nature. Second, resource-intensive production processes have access to subsidised raw material on which a substantial number of people, especially from the less privileged economic groups, depend for their survival. The consumption of such industrial raw material is determined purely by market forces, and not by considerations of the social or ecological requirements placed on them. The costs of resource destruction are externalised and unequally divided among various economic groups in society, but are borne largely by women and those who satisfy their basic material needs directly from nature, simply because they have no purchasing power to register their demands on the goods and services provided by the modern production system. Gustavo Esteva has called development a permanent war waged by its promoters and suffered by its victims.[10]

The paradox and crisis of development arises from the mistaken identification of culturally perceived poverty with real material poverty, and the mistaken identification of the growth of commodity production as better satisfaction of basic needs. In actual fact, there is less water, less fertile soil, less genetic wealth as a result of the development process. Since these natural resources are the basis of nature's economy and women's survival economy, their scarcity is impoverishing women and marginalised peoples in an unprecedented manner. Their new impoverishment lies in the fact that resources which supported their survival were absorbed into the market economy while they themselves were excluded and displaced by it.

The old assumption that with the development process the availability of goods and services will automatically be increased, and poverty will be removed, is now under serious challenge from women's ecology movements in the Third World, even while it continues to guide development thinking in centres of patriarchal power. Survival is based on the assumption of the sanctity of life; maldevelopment is based on the assumption of the sacredness of 'development'. Gustavo Esteva asserts that the sacredness of development has to be refuted because it threatens survival itself. 'My people are tired of development,' he says, 'they just want to live.'[11]

The recovery of the feminine principle allows a transcendence and transformation of these patriarchal foundations of maldevelopment. It allows a redefinition of growth and productivity as categories linked to the production, not the destruction, of life. It is thus simultaneously an ecological and a feminist political project which legitimises the way of knowing and being that create wealth by enhancing life and diversity, and which delegitimises the knowledge and practice of a culture of death as the basis for capital accumulation.

[From Chapter 2, 'Science, Nature and Gender']

The recovery of the feminine principle is an intellectual and political challenge to maldevelopment as a patriarchal project of domination and destruction, of violence and subjugation, of dispossession and the dispensability of both women and nature. The politics of life centred on the feminine principle challenges fundamental assumptions not just in political economy, but also in the science of life-threatening processes.

Maldevelopment is intellectually based on, and justified through, reductionist categories of scientific thought and action. Politically and economically, each project which has fragmented nature and displaced women from productive work has been legitimised as 'scientific' by operationalising reductionist concepts to realise uniformity, centralisation and control. Development is thus the introduction of 'scientific agriculture', 'scientific animal husbandry', 'scientific water management' and so on. The reductionist and universalising tendencies of such 'science' become inherently violent and destructive in a world which is inherently interrelated and diverse. The feminine principle becomes an oppositional category of non-violent ways of conceiving the world, and of acting in it to sustain all life by maintaining the interconnectedness and diversity of nature. It allows an ecological transition from violence to non-violence, from destruction to creativity, from anti-life to life-giving processes, from uniformity to diversity and from fragmentation and reductionism to holism and complexity.

It is thus not just 'development' which is a source of violence to women and nature. At a deeper level, scientific knowledge, on which the development process is based, is itself a source of violence. Modern reductionist science, like development, turns out to be a patriarchal project, which has excluded women as experts, and has simultaneously excluded ecological and holistic ways of knowing which understand and respect nature's processes and interconnectedness *as science*.

MODERN SCIENCE AS PATRIARCHY'S PROJECT

Modern science is projected as a universal, value-free system of knowledge, which has displaced all other belief and knowledge systems by its universality and value neutrality, and by the logic of its method to arrive at objective claims about nature. Yet the dominant stream of modern science, the reductionist or mechanical paradigm, is a particular response of a particular group of people. It is a specific project of western man which came into being during the fifteenth and seventeenth centuries as the much-acclaimed Scientific Revolution. During the last few years, feminist scholarship has begun to recognise that the dominant science system emerged as a liberating force not for humanity as a whole (though it legitimised itself in terms of universal betterment of the species), but as a masculine and patriarchal project which necessarily entailed the subjugation of both nature and women. Harding has called it a 'western, bourgeois, masculine project',[12] and according to Keller

> Science has been produced by a particular sub-set of the human race, that is, almost entirely by white, middle-class males. For the founding fathers of modern science, the reliance on the language of gender was explicit; they sought a philosophy that deserved to be called 'masculine', that could

be distinguished from its ineffective predecessors by its 'virile' powers, its capacity to bind Nature to man's service and make her his slave.[13]

Bacon (1561–1626) was the father of modern science, the originator of the concept of the modern research institute and industrial science, and the inspiration behind the Royal Society. His contribution to modern science and its organisation is critical. From the point of view of nature, women and marginal groups, however, Bacon's programme was not humanly inclusive. It was a special programme benefiting the middle-class, European, male entrepreneur through the conjunction of human knowledge and power in science.

[. . .]

In *New Atlantis*, Bacon's Bensalem was administered from Solomon's House, a scientific research institute, from which male scientists ruled over and made decisions for society, and decided which secrets should be revealed and which remain the private property of the institute.

Science-dominated society has evolved very much in the pattern of Bacon's Bensalem, with nature being transformed and mutilated in modern Solomon's Houses – corporate labs and the university programmes they sponsor. With the new biotechnologies, Bacon's vision of controlling reproduction for the sake of production is being realised, while the green revolution and the bio-revolution have realised what in *New Atlantis* was only a utopia.

'We make by act trees and flowers to come earlier or later than their seasons, and to come up and bear more speedily than by their natural course they do. We make them by act greater, much more than their nature, and their fruit greater and sweeter and of differing taste, smell, colour and figure from their nature.'[14] For Bacon, nature was no longer Mother Nature, but a female nature, conquered by an aggressive masculine mind. As Carolyn Merchant points out, this transformation of nature from a living, nurturing mother to inert, dead and manipulable matter was eminently suited to the exploitation imperative of growing capitalism. The nurturing earth image acted as a cultural constraint on exploitation of nature. 'One does not readily slay a mother, dig her entrails or mutilate her body.' But the mastery and domination images created by the Baconian programme and the scientific revolution removed all restraint and functioned as cultural sanctions for the denudation of nature.

[. . .]

PROFITS, REDUCTIONISM AND VIOLENCE

The close nexus between reductionist science, patriarchy, violence and profits is explicit in 80 per cent of scientific research that is devoted to the war industry, and is frankly aimed directly at lethal violence – violence, in modern times, not only against the enemy fighting force but also against the much larger civilian population. In this book, I argue that modern science is related to violence and profits even in peaceful domains such as, for example, forestry and agriculture, where the professed objective of scientific research is human welfare. The relationship between reductionism, violence and profits is built into the genesis of masculinist science, for its reductionist nature is an epistemic response to an economic organisation based on uncontrolled exploitation of nature for maximization of profits and capital accumulation.

Reductionism, far from being an epistemological accident, is a response to the needs of a particular form of economic and political organisation.[15] The reductionist world-view, the industrial revolution and the capitalist economy were the philosophical, technological and economic components of the same process. Individual firms and the fragmented sector of the economy, whether privately owned or state-owned, have only their own efficiency and profits in mind; and every firm and sector measures its efficiency by the extent to which it maximizes its gains, regardless of the maximization of social and ecological costs. The logic of this internal efficiency has been provided by reductionism. Only those properties of a resource system are taken into account which generate profits through exploitation and extraction; properties which stabilise ecological processes but are commercially non-exploitative are ignored and eventually destroyed.

Commercial capitalism is based on specialised commodity production. Uniformity in production, and the uni-functional use of natural resources, is therefore required. Reductionism thus reduces complex ecosystems to a single component, and a single component to a single function. It further allows the manipulation of the ecosystem in a manner that maximizes the single-function, single-component exploitation. In the reductionist paradigm, a forest is reduced to commercial wood, and wood is reduced to cellulose fibre for the pulp and paper industry. Forests, land and genetic resources are then manipulated to increase the production of pulpwood, and this distortion is legitimised scientifically as overall productivity increase, even though it might decrease the output of water from the forest, or reduce the diversity of life forms that constitute a forest community. The living and diverse ecosystem is thus violated and destroyed by 'scientific' forestry and forestry 'development'. In this way, reductionist science is at the root of the growing ecological crisis, because it entails a transformation of nature such that its organic processes and regularities and regenerative capacities are destroyed.

Women in sustenance economies, producing and reproducing wealth in partnership with nature, have been experts in their own right of a holistic and ecological knowledge of nature's processes. But these alternative modes of knowing, which are orientated to social benefits and sustenance needs, are not recognised by the reductionist paradigm, because it fails to perceive the interconnectedness of nature, or the connection of women's lives, work and knowledge with the creation of wealth.

The rationality and efficacy of reductionist and non-reductionist knowledge systems are never *evaluated* cognitively. The rationality of reductionist science is, *a priori*, declared superior. If reductionist science has displaced non-reductionist modes of knowing, it has done so not through cognitive competition, but through political support from the state: development policies and programmes provide the financial and material subsidies *as well as* the ideological support for the appropriation of nature for profits. Since the myths of progress (material prosperity) and superior rationality lost their sheen in the working-out of development patterns and paradigms, and were visibly exploded by widespread ecological crises, the state stepped in to transform the myths into an ideology. When an individual firm or sector directly confronts the larger society in its appropriation of nature on grounds of progress and rationality, people can assess social costs and private benefits for themselves; they can differentiate between progress and regression, rationality and irrationality. But with the mediation of the state, subjects and citizens become objects of change rather than its determinants, and consequently lose both the capability and the right to assess progress. If they have to bear the costs instead of reaping the benefits of 'development', this is justified as a minor sacrifice for the 'national interest'.

The nexus between the state, the dominant elite and the creation of surplus value provides the power with which reductionism establishes its supremacy. Institutions of learning in agriculture, medicine and forestry selectively train people in the reductionist paradigms, in the name of 'scientific' agriculture, medicine and forestry to establish the superiority of reductionist science. Stripped of the power the state invests it with, reductionism can be seen to be cognitively weak and ineffective in responding to problems posed by nature. Reductionist forestry has destroyed tropical forests, and reductionist agriculture is destroying tropical farming. As a system of knowledge about nature or life, reductionist science is weak and inadequate; as a system of knowledge for the market, it is powerful and profitable. Modern science, as we have noted earlier, has a world-view that both supports and is supported by the socio-political-economic system of western capitalist patriarchy which dominates and exploits nature, women and the poor.

The ultimate reductionism is achieved when nature is linked with a view of economic activity in which money is the only gauge of value and wealth. Life disappears as an organising principle of economic affairs. But the problem with money is that it has an asymmetric relationship to life and living processes. Exploitation, manipulation and destruction of the life in nature can be a source of money and profits, but neither can ever become a source of nature's life and its life-supporting capacity. It is this asymmetry that accounts for a deepening of the ecological crises as a decrease in nature's life-producing potential, along with an increase of capital accumulation and the expansion of 'development' as a process of replacing the currency of life and sustenance with the currency of cash and profits. The 'development' of Africa by western experts is the primary cause for the destruction of Africa; the 'development' of Brazil by transnational banks and corporations is the primary cause for the destruction of the richness of Amazonian rainforests, the highest expression of life. Natives of Africa and Amazonia had survived over centuries with their ecologically evolved, indigenous knowledge systems. What local people had conserved through history, western experts and knowledge destroyed in a few decades, a few years even.

It is this destruction of ecologies and knowledge systems that I characterise as the violence of reductionism which results in (1) *violence against women*: women, tribals and peasants as the knowing subject are violated socially through the expert/non-expert divide which converts them into non-knowers even in those areas of living in which, through daily participation, they are the real experts – and in which responsibility of practice and action rests with them, such as in forestry, food and water systems. (2) *Violence against nature*: nature as the object of knowledge is violated when modern science destroys its integrity of nature, both in the process of perception as well as manipulation. (3) *Violence against the beneficiaries of knowledge*: contrary to the claim of modern science that people in general are ultimately the beneficiaries of scientific knowledge, they – particularly the poor and women – are its worst victims, deprived of their productive potential, livelihoods and life-support systems. Violence against nature recoils on man, the supposed beneficiary. (4) *Violence against knowledge*: in order to assume the status of being the only legitimate mode of knowledge, rationally superior to alternative modes of knowing, reductionist science resorts *to the suppression and falsification of facts* and thus commits violence against science itself. It declares organic systems of knowledge irrational, and rejects the belief systems of others without full rational evaluation. At the same time, it protects itself from the exposure and investigation of the myths it has created by assigning itself a new sacredness that forbids any questioning of the claims of science.

[. . .]

The emerging feminist and ecological critiques of reductionist science extend the domain of the testing of scientific beliefs into the wider physical world. Socially, the world of scientific experiments and beliefs has to be extended beyond the so-called experts and specialists into the world of all those who have systematically been excluded from it – women, peasants and tribals. The verification and validation of a scientific system would then be validation in practice where practice and experimentation is real-life activity in society and nature. Harding says:

> Neither God nor tradition is privileged with the same credibility as scientific rationality in modern cultures . . . The project that science's sacredness makes taboo is the examination of science in just the ways any other institution or set of social practices can be examined. If we are not willing to try and see the favoured intellectual structures and practices of science as cultural artifacts rather than as sacred commandments handed down to humanity at the birth of modern science, then it will be hard to understand how gender symbolism, the gendered social structure of

science, and the masculine identities and behaviours of individual scientists have left their marks on the problematics, concepts, theories, methods, interpretation, ethics, meanings and goals of science.[16]

The intellectual recovery of the feminine principle creates new conditions for women and non-western cultures to become principal actors in establishing a democracy of all life, as countervailing forces to the intellectual culture of death and dispensability that reductionism creates.

Ecology movements are political movements for a non-violent world order in which nature is conserved for conserving the options for survival. These movements are small, but they are growing. They are local, but their success lies in non-local impact. They demand only the right to survival, yet with that minimal demand is associated the right to live in a peaceful and just world. With the success of these grassroots movements is linked the global issue of survival. Unless the world is restructured ecologically at the level of world-views and life-styles, peace and justice will continue to be violated, and ultimately the very survival of humanity will be threatened.

NOTES

1. Chinua Achebe, *No Longer at Ease*, London: Heinemann, 1960, p. 45.
2. M. George Foster, *Traditional Societies and Technological Change*, Delhi: Allied Publishers, 1973.
3. Maria Mies, *Patriarchy and Accumulation on a World Scale*, London: Zed Books, 1986.
4. Alice Schlegel (ed.), *Sexual Stratification: A Cross-Cultural Study*, New York: Columbia University Press, 1977.
5. Jonathan Porritt, *Seeing Green*, Oxford: Blackwell, 1984.
6. A. Lovins, cited in S. R. Eyre, *The Real Wealth of Nations*, London: Edward Arnold, 1978.
7. R. Bahro, *From Red to Green*, London: Verso, 1984, p. 211.
8. R. J. Barnet, *The Lean Years*, London: Abacus, 1981, p. 171.
9. U. P. Koehn, 'African Approaches to Environmental Stress; A Focus on Ethiopia and Nigeria', in R. N. Barrett (ed.), *International Dimensions of the Environmental Crisis*, Colorado: Westview, 1982, pp. 253–89.
10. Gustavo Esteva, 'Regenerating People's Space', in S. N. Mendlowitz and R. B. J. Walker, *Towards a Just World Peace: Perspectives from Social Movements*, London: Butterworths and Committee for a Just World Peace, 1987.
11. G. Esteva, Remarks made at a Conference of the Society for International Development, Rome, 1985.
12. Susan Harding, *The Science Question in Feminism*, Ithaca: Cornell University Press, Press, 1985, p. 7, 1986, p. 8.
13. Evelyn F. Keller, *Reflections on Gender and Science*, New Haven: Yale University Press, 1985, p. 7.
14. Carolyn Merchant, *The Death of Nature: Women, Ecology and the Scientific Revolution*, New York: Harper & Row, 1980, p. 182.
15. J. Bandyopadhyay and V. Shiva, 'Ecological Sciences: A Response to Ecological Crises', in J. Bandyopadhyay et al., *India's Environment*, Dehradun: Natraj, 1985, p. 196; and J. Bandyopadhyay and V. Shiva, 'Environmental Conflicts and Public Interest Science', *Economic and Political Weekly*, Vol. XXI, No. 2, Jan. 11, 1986, 84–90.
16. Harding, *op. cit.*, p. 30.

9

POSTSTRUCTURALISM AND POSTMODERNISM

Iain MacKenzie

Introduction

Poststructuralist political theory is one of the most vibrant and exciting areas of contemporary political studies. And yet, it is still a relatively unknown and poorly understood form of political inquiry. This apparent conundrum can be explained, at least in part, by the way poststructuralists often define their approach to politics. Those who identify themselves as poststructuralists typically do so as a way of distancing themselves from the dominant paradigms of political theory. A poststructuralist political theorist, therefore, is a critic of liberalism, Marxism, **Critical Theory**, **rational choice theory**, various feminisms and communitarianism (to name a few). From this generalised oppositional stance, poststructuralist political theorists go on to interrogate the very foundations of our attempts to make sense of the social and political world by questioning the need for foundations in political theory, and by questioning what we mean by 'the social' and 'the political'. The vibrancy that surrounds poststructuralist political theory is derived from this desire to subject the discipline of politics to a thoroughgoing and fundamental critique.

Yet, this concern with fundamental problems in political theory is also the source of the confusion that so often surrounds poststructuralism. It is one thing to pursue mainstream political theory with a view to exposing the shaky foundations upon which it rests. It is quite another to present a cogent and convincing alternative to such dominant paradigms. In one form or another, the question that has dogged poststructuralist political theory since its emergence has been this: 'what can poststructuralism *contribute* to the study of political

438

life?' It is not that poststructuralists have been unable to answer this question, rather that there are so many different and possibly conflicting answers that confusion ensues. There are certainly many possible distinctive poststructuralist contributions to political theory: an unrelenting emphasis on difference; a realisation of the all-pervasive nature of power; a persistent reflection on the nature of political inquiry; a focus on identity and the body as sites of political contest; a shift from a politics of accommodation to one of antagonism; and, to give one last example, a transformation of the political itself such that it becomes less a site of competing agencies and more a site of repressed desires or forces. The problem is that none of these in itself marks out a truly distinctive poststructuralist political theory. They are all aspects of the contribution of poststructuralism to political theory; but, if we are to find out what binds these elements together into a cogent and convincing alternative to the dominant paradigms of political theory, we must dig deeper into the nature of poststructuralism.

The aim of this chapter is to offer an account of poststructuralist political theory that will bring to light its nature and the challenge it poses to mainstream political theory.

WHAT IS POSTSTRUCTURALISM?

There are a number of different ways of understanding the term 'poststructuralism'. While I cannot hope to give a full survey of the ways it is deployed throughout the literature, I shall outline two of the definitions that dominate work in this area. After a brief discussion of their relative merits, I shall propose a definition which aims to retain both a precise meaning to the term and a sense of the potential poststructuralism has to grow and develop within political studies.

Poststructuralism is most closely associated with a number of intellectuals based in France who responded critically to the wave of structuralist analyses that dominated a section of French intellectual life during the late 1950s and through the 1960s. So, when one thinks of poststructuralism, one typically thinks of writers such as **Cixous, Deleuze, Derrida,** Foucault, **Guattari, Irigaray, Kristeva** and **Lyotard** among others. In approaching a definition of poststructuralism, therefore, one is tempted to say that it is a form of inquiry specific to a certain intellectual context (reactions to structuralism), geographical location (France), political situation (the student uprisings of **May 1968** are often associated with poststructuralism, though one must be careful of oversimplifying the relationship between the rise of new social movements and the rise of new theoretical paradigms) and historical moment (typically the relatively short space of time between all the seminal publications of the writers just mentioned, the late 1960s and the 1970s). This 'history of ideas' approach to defining poststructuralism certainly helps to explain the emergence of these ideas within a particularly complex but nonetheless analysable milieu (Schrift, 1995).

The problem with defining poststructuralism in this way is that we fail to account for the fact that it quickly outgrew this context. Although it began as an intellectual response to structuralism, poststructuralism quickly became a way of interrogating a wide range of other dominant paradigms: **hermeneutics, Critical Theory**, liberalism, feminisms of various types, **psychoanalysis**, Marxism and so on. Of course, this is partly due to the wide influence of structuralism in many of these areas; but it also coincided with poststructuralism's move beyond France. Particularly important in this regard was the influence of **Derrida** on 'the Yale School' of the 1970s, one so profound that it marked a sea-change in the American academy, the effects of which are still being felt almost thirty years later. Similarly, the translation and transportation of Foucault's work to America did much to take poststructuralism out of its particular milieu and into the purview of a whole generation of academics who had not necessarily been through the structuralist revolution in social theory. This put poststructuralist ideas into a very different political context, one which gave them a new shape by setting them head-to-head with American social and political concerns. In the UK, the spread of poststructuralism across the English Channel generated a specifically 'leftist' orientation to poststructuralism as those dissatisfied with Marxist and socialist paradigms began to look for ways of grasping the changing nature of what had been rather settled ideological disputes within the academy and in the political world at large. One could mention other places where poststructuralist ideas received a new and distinctive twist – in Italy, for example, poststructuralist figures were associated with the **Autonomia** group of radical activists – but the general point is that what was at one time a specific reaction to certain intellectual and political conditions in 1960s France was quickly transported across the globe. Any attempt, therefore, to limit one's definition of poststructuralism to that very particular context will fail to appreciate the wider significance of a movement that has reached far beyond its original milieu.

But if we should be cautious of defining poststructuralism simply in terms of the place and time of its birth, we must also be wary of forgetting those initial conditions. There is a tendency to define poststructuralism as any theoretical work that uses the lexicon of Foucault, **Derrida**, et al. in any way at all. If the 'history of ideas' approach is too exclusive, then this way of defining poststructuralist work 'by association' is too inclusive to be useful. While it has the benefit of allowing one to focus on how poststructuralism has mutated in a variety of different contexts, it opens the floodgates on what counts as poststructuralist theory. The problem is that, as poststructuralism is increasingly wrenched from its original context, it makes less and less sense to retain the term for work that shows no appreciation of the structuralism that preceded and still pervades poststructuralism. The tendency is to focus on difference, for example, without recognising that the poststructuralist emphasis on difference is a specific response to structuralist concerns. In political theory, this kind of 'non-structuralist poststructuralism' often descends into a variety of liberal political theory. While there is a certain merit in pursuing the claim that liberals are not sensitive enough to difference, if these are the *only* terms of engagement then one is not really a poststructuralist critic of Liberalism but a kind of liberal critic of liberalism. After all, the liberal framework of rights is promoted precisely to enshrine difference in our political institutions; that it may not do this effectively is hardly a fundamental critique of liberalism's core assumptions. Rather than querying liberal politics *per se*, poststructuralism challenges the claims liberals make about 'the political' – by invoking a broadly structuralist account of 'the political' as opposed to a liberal humanist one. So-called 'poststructuralist' critiques of Liberalism that do not interrogate liberal claims about 'the political' do not have a foothold within the context in which poststructuralism was born.

Since definitions which stress the very particular conditions that gave rise to poststructuralism are too exclusive, and those emphasising the impact of poststructuralist writers on a whole range of thinkers and disciplines are too inclusive, how are we to define poststructuralism? The short answer is that we must stress the *project* of poststructuralism. If we begin with an analysis of the major theoretical claims associated with poststructuralism, then we can see the extent to which subsequent writers, whether they use Foucault, **Derrida** et al. or not, can be said to be poststructuralist. This approach has the benefit of adherence to the classic texts of poststructuralism (though one must be wary of treating these texts as canonical) while allowing for a sense of how poststructuralist ideas continue to flourish in areas well beyond the milieu in which they were formed. In other words, an emphasis on the project of poststructuralism can provide an exclusive but not deadening definition of this most nebulous label.

The project that motivated poststructuralism can be summed up quite simply: how can we retain the basic outlines of the structuralist critique of **humanism** without the pitfalls that beset structuralist analyses? Beginning, therefore, with the structuralist critique of humanism, we can discern the nature of poststructuralism. For the structuralists, humanist analyses focused on the actions and intentions of agents without interrogating the deep structures that enabled those agents to act and think in the first place. Humanist work, it was argued, ignored the background frames of reference that were not immediately apparent if one simply sought to observe people and what they do. According to **Lévi-Strauss**, structuralism 'reveals, behind phenomena, a unity and coherence that could not be brought out by a simple description of the facts' (1981: 68). Crucially, though, the structuralist concept of structure was greatly influenced by the insights of **Saussure** (1960). For Saussure, the meaning of a word does not emerge from the relation it has to the thing it describes. Rather, meaning emerges as a result of the other words to which any given word is related (such that 'cat' has meaning by being related to the words 'dog', 'mouse' and so on, rather than by being related to the furry animals it represents). In this sense, everyday speech (*parole*) is dependent upon a set of differential relations which constitute the structure of language (*langue*). The structuralist generalisation of this insight was a way of avoiding the tendency to 'humanise' the structures they unearthed – that is, to treat them as if they are agents that act in the social and political world. More importantly, it led to an emphasis on the important place that *relations*, rather than things in themselves, play in shaping our view of the world around us. Hawkes has summed this up neatly: 'this new concept, that the world is made up of relations rather than things, constitutes the first principle of the way of thinking that can properly be called 'structuralist' (1977: 17–18). So, the aim of structuralism is to move social and political analyses away from a focus on subjects by invoking the deep structures which shape the way subjects act and by treating these structures as a complex series of relationships rather than as things in themselves.

In essence, poststructuralism is the attempt to fulfil the structuralist project. Both envisage a thoroughgoing critique of **humanism**, but the former claims that the latter never managed to live up to this aim. Despite being aware of the danger of treating structures in much the same way as humanists treat agents, the structuralists did not always avoid the trap. This general reproach can be separated into three interrelated criticisms. First, it was thought that the structuralist concept of structure tended to overstress the **synchronic** (spatial) dimension such that the deep structures uncovered by its analyses were unwittingly accorded a timeless role in shaping human activity. Poststructuralists argued for a greater **diachronic** (temporal) sensitivity when analysing the structural features of social and political life. This has led to a new vocabulary that replaces the emphasis on 'structure' with talk of 'discourses', 'assemblages', 'regimes' and so on in order to signal a more temporally astute account of the structures that shape our social and political lives. Foucault's (1977, 1978) genealogies of punishment and sexuality are exemplary in this regard. Second, where the structuralists had stressed relationality, the poststructuralists questioned whether the concept of relation itself was sufficiently developed within structuralism. In essence, the poststructuralist preoccupation with difference comes from this interrogation of the structuralist notion of relation, the argument being that the structuralist concept of relation ultimately tended to nullify difference by treating it in simple oppositional terms. Here we might think of **Derrida**'s (1982) interrogation of *difference/différance* and **Deleuze**'s (1994) concept of non-dialectical difference. Third, taken together, these criticisms pointed to a political problem with structuralism. In trying to outline the structures that shape our activity, structuralism tended to lapse into an uncritical engagement with the dominant forces of the social and political world. To the extent that structures were timeless, universal features of existence, there seemed no room for a critical engagement with them. Furthermore, to the extent that relationality was viewed in simply oppositional terms, it seemed to legitimate dominant conceptual binaries rather than challenge them. Poststructuralists aim to fulfil the critical agenda set by structuralism by making the development of novel strategies of criticism a central plank of their activity. The critical approach adopted by poststructuralists is to expose the contingency and historicity of structures in order to show that the way we conceptualise the social and political world could be radically different to the ways which seem most 'natural' to us. Poststructuralist feminists have been particularly important in this respect, to the extent that they have challenged those most 'natural' and 'fixed' parts of our identity: our bodies, sex, sexuality and gender (Butler, 1990, 1993; Grosz, 1994).

So, poststructuralism is an attempt to fulfil the structuralist project of a thoroughgoing critique of **humanism** by placing the structuralist notions of structure, **difference** and criticism under scrutiny in a way that avoids the surreptitious 'humanising' of the structures that shape our everyday lives. With this definition in mind, we can go on to assess the nature of the challenge poststructuralism poses to the dominant paradigms of political theory.

POSTSTRUCTURALISM AND POLITICAL THEORY

There are a number of different ways of thinking about the poststructuralist challenge to political theory. Many poststructuralists emphasise the discursively constituted nature of subjectivity with a view to drawing out the links back to the critique of **humanism** (Rajchman, 1995). This is a particularly appropriate way of looking at the poststructuralist analysis of the various accounts of human nature that underpin the dominant paradigms of political theory. Similarly, poststructuralists often challenge the grand narratives of political theory, particularly the Hegelian/Marxist narrative of the necessary progress of humanity (Lyotard, 1984). Another approach adopted by poststructuralists is to subject some of the great normative categories of political theory – democracy, justice, freedom and the like – to thoroughgoing **deconstruction** with a view to exposing the inevitable paradoxes that inhabit these concepts (Derrida, 1994; Laclau 1996). Lastly, the great categories of the oppressed that political theory so often seeks to represent – 'woman', 'working class', the excluded and the dominated of all sorts – are scrutinised by poststructuralists who aim to expose how such categories often work to mask the deep plurality of social and political life (Kristeva, 1986; Laclau and Mouffe, 1985). All of these approaches offer fruitful ways into detailing and assessing the challenge that poststructuralism poses to traditional political theory. In what follows, I shall focus on that which underlies all of these approaches: a radically different understanding of the very nature of the political.

As this volume makes abundantly clear, there is wide disagreement over what constitutes politics and the political world. For poststructuralists, though, this wide disagreement tends to obscure an underlying commonality among the dominant paradigms of political thought when it comes to understanding the political world. In one form or another, much political thought views our political lives as distinct from other aspects of our lives, such as family life, commercial life and so on. Crucially, this distinction is turned into a hierarchy such that much contemporary political theory works by positing a non-political realm as a necessary prerequisite for understanding the political world. The most obvious expression of this is the debate within Liberalism regarding the relationship between the public political world and the private world of individual belief and interaction. Moreover, those other dominant paradigms of political thought that criticise liberals for relying upon this distinction between the public and the private are not immune from the poststructuralist challenge. The most obvious example is Marxism. For many Marxists, every aspect of our lives can be linked to the all-pervasive and distorting power of capitalism such that even our most intimate relationships are tainted by an ideology that fosters individualism, competition and greed. From a poststructuralist perspective, though, Marxist analyses usually depend upon the promise of a depoliticised world to the extent that they rely on problematic assumptions about human nature and the progression of history. Furthermore, normative political theory of all persuasions comes under fire from poststructuralists as an attempt to limit the political by reference to depoliticised modes of moral justification. Rather than ask 'what is the right way to organise our political affairs?', poststructuralists typically interrogate the concept of 'right' and assess the consequences of different courses of action without assuming the priority of normative judgement. In general, therefore, the aim of poststructuralist political theory is to analyse the social and political world *immanently*, that is, on its own terms by not subordinating the political to a depoliticised realm of human life. It is worth further clarifying this challenge to mainstream political theory by looking at the way poststructuralists reconceptualise the relationship between reason, power and criticism.

Mainstream political theory is dominated by the Enlightenment understanding of the relationship between these three core concepts. For Enlightenment thinkers, reason was the only legitimate source of critical intervention against the stultifying powers of mysticism and superstition. The irrationality of a dogmatic belief in the authority of the sovereign and the naturally subservient position of the populace was exposed by subjecting all aspects of political life to the demands of reason. Political theory had a new and exciting function in the political world – to act as the standard-bearer for criticism of the dominating powers by providing the reasons for intervening in political life. As Kant (1996a) puts it, 'what on rational grounds holds for theory also holds for practice' (309). In a variety of different guises, most contemporary political theory still clings to this maxim.

For the poststructuralist, the relationship between reason, power and criticism is rather different and so, therefore, is the task of political theory. We can see this in two related ways. First, for poststructuralists, reason is not in itself beyond criticism. In pursuing this line, we can see that poststructuralism follows in the footsteps of **Nietzsche** and early **Frankfurt School Critical Theory**, particularly **Horkheimer** and **Adorno**'s (1973) *Dialectic of Enlightenment*. Where thinkers of the Enlightenment saw reason as the source of critical activity, Horkheimer and Adorno argued that the deployment of Enlightenment reason had led to new forms of enslavement as well as emancipation. One response to this dilemma can be seen in **Habermas**'s (1984, 1987) version of **Critical Theory**. Taking the basic outlines of **Horkheimer** and **Adorno**'s analysis as his point of departure, **Habermas** argues for a differentiated critique of reason such that it is the deployment of instrumental reason in the spheres of value and meaning that has led to the pathologies of modernity while the reconstruction of the communicative basis to reason holds the key to emancipation. Poststructuralists, on the other hand, tend towards a total, though not unsubtle, attack on the primacy of reason by uncoupling it from the base of social and political criticism. **Deleuze**'s Nietzschean-inspired response to Kant sums this up well: 'Kant concludes that critique must be a critique of reason by reason itself. Is this not the Kantian contradiction, making reason both the tribunal and the accused; constituting it as judge and plaintiff, judging and judged?' (1983: 91). Of course, this raises a whole host of challenging questions about the philosophical, political and critical status of reason. From the perspective of political theory, it is especially important that poststructuralism tackles the political consequences of knocking reason off its pedestal. If reason can no longer claim to be the ultimate arbiter of political disputes, then it is right to worry about whether or not poststructuralism is equipped to deal with the business of politics at all. But the force of this criticism is dulled if the critic assumes that poststructuralism ends up in irrationalism. In fact, poststructuralist political theory is an attempt to offer an immanent account of political rationality, and it is misleading to characterise it as an approach to political life that dismisses the power of reason *tout court*. For example, poststructuralists do not deny the relevance of deploying reason when it comes to choosing one course of action over another, but they do deny that reason has, or should have, a special priority as regards decision-making in politics, and they also deny that reason is capable of acting as an extra-political source of legitimation for democratic or other regimes.

Second, the relationship between reason, power and criticism has been reformulated by rethinking power itself. Famously, Foucault's genealogical turn marked a transition in the way we think about power. Traditional conceptions of power viewed it as a substance that could be held and wielded against those without power, as, for example, when the state holds power over and against the people. Foucault challenged us to think of power as productive as well as debilitating, as constitutive as well as constraining and, generally, as positive as well as negative. In reorientating discussions of power in this way, Foucault viewed power as a series of relationships rather than as a thing in itself, as all-pervasive rather than as centralised in any particular part of the social and political world, and as multi-directional rather than 'top-down'. One consequence of this analytic of power is that it mutates the role traditionally accorded to reason as the only valid source of criticism against illegitimate powers. After Foucault, the deployment of reason itself came to be viewed as a technique of power such that social and political criticism can no longer be justified by an appeal to timeless standards of rationality. Critical intervention in the social and political world, for the poststructuralist, must be viewed in terms of strategies and local struggles.

All of this amounts to saying that the challenge poststructuralism poses to political theory is that of understanding and critically engaging with the political world without the need to posit a non-political perspective from which to judge it. Or, to give a different formulation, the aim of poststructuralist political theory is to understand political conflicts from within rather than to bring them before the court of an authority that stands outside the conflict itself.

CONCLUSION

I have argued (1) that poststructuralism is the attempt to continue and complete the structuralist critique of **humanism** and (2) that it challenges the dominant paradigms of political theory on the grounds that our attempts to understand political life will remain problematic unless we have an immanent understanding of the political, that is, one that does not posit or presuppose a non-political benchmark against which to judge the political. It is important to spell out the link between these two ideas. At its most basic, most political theory has always sought to understand political affairs by beginning with an account of human nature. A structuralist understanding of politics is one which eschews this theoretical gesture by conceiving of the political as a series of interlocking structures that condition human action. The problem, from a poststructuralist point of view, is that structuralism tends to become another variant of the human-nature argument; humans will act in such a way as conditioned by whatever structures – class, psychological, mythological or whatever – shape our lives. By highlighting the contingency and historicity of structures and by reconfiguring the notion of structural difference, poststructuralists aim to remove once and for all the drive to understand politics on the basis of transcendental claims about human nature. Only in this way, it is hoped, will an immanent understanding of the political actually emerge.

Undoubtedly, thinking of the political without reference to human nature is not an easy task, largely because it demands a whole new vocabulary of politics. For many critics, this need to explore new ways of talking about political life is enough to condemn poststructuralism as irrelevant, intellectually obtuse and difficult. However, the proliferation of new terms that poststructuralism has brought into our political lexicon – regimes of **power/knowledge, nomadology, libidinal economies,** to name a few – should not be so easily dismissed. After all, the 'great' political philosophers have always been conceptual innovators who have struggled to communicate the relevance and importance of their conceptual inventions. Poststructuralism is simply one of the most recent innovations in political theory, one which is still in the process of struggling for its acceptance. When one recognises the project of poststructuralism as the attempt to understand the structural features of our political life without reifying the structures themselves, one can see why conceptual innovation is required.

One final obstacle stands in the way of reading poststructuralist political theory: the terms of its reception. Having clarified the project of poststructuralism and the challenge it poses to contemporary political theory, it is important to untangle poststructuralism from a set of terms that have been used against it by critics and even adopted by some of its defenders. It is sometimes claimed that poststructuralism is anti-foundational, relativist, normatively confused and critically quietist. I would suggest, instead, that poststructuralism is foundational, perspectivist, ethically astute and critically radical. I shall give a very brief account of each of these differences.

It used to be said by critics and supporters alike that what defined poststructuralist theory was its **anti-foundationalism**. As a critique of all the great foundational gestures in philosophy and politics, poststructuralism was seen as a way of doing critical analysis without reference to overarching and typically transcendental foundations. This view of poststructuralism is, however, rather misleading. Although it was not always clearly expressed, the classic texts of poststructuralism were not concerned with a total rejection of all foundations. Rather, they were looking to expose the problematic nature of certain kinds of foundational strategy, especially the phenomenological and existential attempt to ground criticism in the experiential subject and the Hegelian and Marxist attempt to reveal the logic of history as a basis for political intervention. But it is a mistake to see these critiques as part of a total rejection of foundations. Hardt has put the point well: 'Poststructuralism does critique a certain notion of foundations, but only to affirm another notion that is more adequate to its ends. Against a transcendental foundation we find an immanent one; against a given, teleological foundation we find a material, open one' (1993: xv). A similar distinction must be made when one considers the charge, and it is nearly always a charge against poststructuralism, that it is relativist. While poststructuralists problematise the notion of truth, this does not mean that they necessarily relativise it. Truth may be inextricably linked to operations of power and desire, but this does not amount to affirming the famously contradictory claim that 'there is no such thing as truth'. Rather, truth is viewed by poststructuralists as something that is conditioned by perspective, where perspective is described in terms of relations of power, desire, force and so forth. In this sense, truth is not rejected though it is demystified, interrogated and brought squarely into the realm of politics. These philosophical clarifications can begin to pay dividends when one considers the claims that poststructuralism is normatively confused and critically quietist. The polemics against poststructuralism that dominated its early reception typically argued that it claimed to be non-normative while surreptitiously smuggling norms into every line of its critical endeavour, thus causing confusion as to the nature of its project. For the poststructuralist, there is no confusion if one views the project of criticism as the task of 'thinking differently'. The point is this: criticism is not for the poststructuralist a necessarily normative pursuit, rather it is first and foremost the activity of creatively reconfiguring our understanding of the social and political world. Whatever normative judgements one makes about the act of criticism are second-order and not essential to the critical gesture in the first place. For the poststructuralist, it is the normative political philosophers who elide a key analytical distinction between criticism and judgement. The confusion, for poststructuralists, is with those who assume that all criticism is *essentially* normatively constituted. The astute nature of poststructuralist ethics is the result of this non-normative account of social and political criticism. Nonetheless, this clarification does raise the spectre of quietism. On what grounds can poststructuralists intervene in social and political life if criticism is deemed to be non-normative? For the poststructuralist, though, the very demand for criticism is a structural feature of the political world, as in Foucault's (1978) claim that all power relations create the possibility of resistance. This leads to a radical, rather than a quietist, response to political life because poststructuralism reveals the possibility of critical intervention in areas that are often thought to be beyond criticism.

While these clarifications must remain at the level of assertion in this context, and they will do little to convince the sceptic, it is hoped that they raise the possibility that poststructuralist political theory will not be read through its critics (or even through some of its supporters) without a keen eye for the straw man that is so often set up to represent it.

It is in light of these clarifications that one should read poststructuralist political theory. If one avoids the tendency to assume in advance that poststructuralism is somehow confused, one will find novel analyses of the relationship between the state and capitalism; deconstructive work on the nature of law and justice; genealogical work on the very idea of government; critical analyses of the relationship between sex, gender and sexuality; reconceptualisations of political ideology; novel accounts of the operation of power in social and political life; reconsideration of the idea of political utopias; perceptive analyses of the history of political thought; critiques of Rawls and post-Rawlsian liberalism; interrogations of the idea of community; and much more besides. All this, and yet the riches within poststructuralist political theory have barely begun to be revealed.

Poststructuralism is a relative newcomer on the scene of political theory. Much of the work in this area is still trying to come to grips with the classic texts of poststructuralism in order to reveal their insights for political theory. Increasingly, though, political theorists influenced by poststructuralism are creating new sites for political investigation and, in the process, reconceptualising the nature of the poststructuralist project. It is this reflexive attitude to its own beginnings that makes poststructuralist political theory one of the most vibrant of all contemporary political theories. Although it is still treated with disdain in some quarters of the academy, poststructuralism has long since revealed itself as more than a passing fad. Its future rests on its claim to offer the most thoroughly political approach to politics of all political theories.

We have already encountered Mouffe in Chapter 5, where we saw an example of her work co-written with Ernesto Laclau. Biographical details can be found there. The extract reproduced here is from her collection of essays *The Return of the Political* (Verso, 1993). In Chapter 5, we saw the connections between contemporary currents of post-Marxism and liberal political thinking. In this extract, Mouffe examines what she sees as the limits of Liberalism. Like Butler on the category of the subject (in Chapter 7), Mouffe points out that liberal rationalism presupposes the 'rules of the game' and thus limits contenders. But she does not advocate a complete or extreme pluralism, arguing only that we must recognise what it is that Liberalism does when it excludes other political positions. Her form of pluralism is based not on the claims of moral philosophy but on a recognition that the political realm is one of continual contest. Given her arguments about a non-rationalist pluralism and on the need for citizens' identification with such a politics, it may be interesting to read Mouffe alongside the communitarian critique of Liberalism and the anti-foundationalism of Rorty (both of whom she critically assesses elsewhere in the volume from which this short extract is taken).

'POLITICS AND THE LIMITS OF LIBERALISM' (1993)*

Chantal Mouffe

[. . .]

PLURALISM AND UNDECIDABILITY

In order to create the conditions for successful argumentation, political liberals refuse to open rational dialogue to those who do not accept their 'rules of the game'. In a sense there is nothing objectionable about that, provided one is aware of the implications – but of course in this case the implications would defeat the very purpose of supposedly rational argumentation.

It is now generally acknowledged that argumentation is only possible when there is a shared framework. As Wittgenstein pointed out, to have agreement in opinions, there must first be agreement on the language used. But he also

---

* From Chantal Mouffe, *The Return of the Political* (London: Verso, 1993), pp. 144–54.

alerted us to the fact that those represented 'not agreement in opinions but in forms of life'.[1] In his view, to agree on the definition of a term is not enough and we need agreement in the way we use it. As he puts it: 'If language is to be a means of communication there must be agreement not only in definitions but also (queer as this may sound) in judgements'.[2]

As John Gray indicates, Wittgenstein's analysis of rules and rule-following undermines the kind of liberal reasoning that envisages the common framework for argumentation on the model of a 'neutral' or 'rational' dialogue. According to a Wittgensteinian perspective:

> Whatever there is of definite content in contractarian deliberation and its deliverance, derives from particular judgments we are inclined to make as practitioners of specific forms of life. The forms of life in which we find ourselves are themselves held together by a network of precontractual agreements, without which there would be no possibility of mutual understanding or therefore, of disagreement.[3]

Such an approach offers a fruitful alternative to rationalist liberalism because it can be developed in a way that highlights the historical and contingent character of the discourses that construct our identities. This is exemplified by Richard Flathman when he notes that, notwithstanding the fact that a good deal of agreement has been achieved on many features of liberal democratic politics, certainty is not to be seen as necessary in any of the philosophical senses. In his view, 'Our agreement in these judgments constitutes the language of our politics. It is a language arrived at and continuously modified through no less than a history of discourse, a history in which we have thought about, as we became able to think in, that language.'[4]

This is, I believe, a very promising direction for political philosophy. Contrary to the current brand of liberalism, a reflection on liberal democracy on those lines would not present it as the rational, universal solution to the problem of political order. Neither would it attempt to deny its ultimately ungrounded status by making it appear as the outcome of a rational choice or a dialogical process of undistorted communication. Because of the central role it gives to practices, such a perspective could help us understand how our shared language of politics is entangled with power and needs to be apprehended in terms of hegemonic relations. It might also leave room for 'undecidability' and be better suited to account for conflict and antagonism.

Many rationalists will certainly accuse such a political philosophy of opening the way to 'relativism' and 'nihilism' and thus jeopardizing democracy. But the opposite is true because, instead of putting our liberal institutions at risk, the recognition that they do not have an ultimate foundation creates a more favourable terrain for their defence. When we realize that, far from being the necessary result of a moral evolution of mankind, liberal democracy is an ensemble of contingent practices, we can understand that it is a conquest that needs to be protected as well as deepened.

A political philosophy that makes room for contingency and undecidability is clearly at odds with liberal rationalism, whose typical move is to erase its very conditions of enunciation and deny its historical space of inscription. This was already constitutive of the 'hypocrisy' of the Enlightenment, as Reinhart Koselleck has shown.[5] Many liberals follow suit by refusing to assume their political stand and pretending to be speaking from an impartial location. In that way, they manage to present their views as the embodiment of 'rationality' and this enables them to exclude their opponents from 'rational dialogue'. However, the excluded do not disappear and, once their position has been declared 'unreasonable', the problem of neutrality remains unsolved. From their point of view, the 'neutral' principles of rational dialogue are certainly not so. For them, what is proclaimed as 'rationality' by the liberals is experienced as coercion.

It is not my intention to advocate a total pluralism, and I do not believe it is possible to avoid excluding some points of view. No state or political order, even a liberal one, can exist without some forms of exclusion. My point is different. I want to argue that it is very important to recognize those forms of exclusion for what they are and the violence that they signify, instead of concealing them under the veil of rationality. To disguise the real nature of the necessary 'frontiers' and modes of exclusion required by a liberal democratic order by grounding them in the supposedly neutral character of 'rationality' creates effects of occultation which hinder the proper workings of democratic politics. William Connolly is right when he indicates that 'the pretence to neutrality functions to maintain established settlements below the threshold of public discourse'.[6]

The specificity of pluralist democracy does not reside in the absence of domination and violence but in the establishment of a set of institutions through which they can be limited and contested. It is for that reason that democracy 'maintains a split between law and justice: it accepts the fact that justice is 'impossible', that it is an act which can never be wholly grounded in 'sufficient (legal) reasons''.[7] But this mechanism of 'self-binding' ceases to be effective if violence goes unrecognized and hidden behind appeals to rationality. Hence the importance of abandoning the mystifying illusion of a dialogue free from coercion. It might undermine democracy by closing the gap between justice and law which is a constitutive space of modern democracy.

In order to avoid the danger of such a closure, what must be relinquished is the very idea that there could be such a thing as a 'rational' political consensus, if that means a consensus that would not be based on any form of exclusion. To present the institutions of liberal democracy as the outcome of a pure deliberative rationality is to reify them and make them impossible to transform. The fact that, like any other regime, modern pluralist democracy constitutes a system of relations of power is denied, and the democratic challenging of those forms of power becomes illegitimate.

The political liberalism of Rawls and Larmore, far from being conducive to a pluralistic society, manifests a strong tendency toward homogeneity and leaves little space for dissent and contestation in the sphere of politics. By postulating that it is possible to reach a free moral consensus on political fundamentals through rational procedures and that such a consensus is provided by liberal institutions, it ends up endowing a historically specific set of arrangements with the character of universality and rationality. This is contrary to the indetermination that is constitutive of modern democracy. In the end, the rationalist defence of liberalism, by searching for an argument that is beyond argumentation and by wanting to define the meaning of the universal, makes the same mistake for which it criticizes totalitarianism: it rejects democratic indeterminacy and identifies the universal with a given particular.

Modern democratic politics, linked as it is to the declaration of human rights, does indeed imply a reference to universality. But this universality is conceived as a horizon that can never be reached. Every pretension to occupy the place of the universal, to fix its final meaning through rationality, must be rejected. The content of the universal must remain indeterminate since it is this indeterminacy that is the condition of existence of democratic politics.

The specificity of modern democratic pluralism is lost when it is envisaged merely as the empirical fact of a multiplicity of moral conceptions of the good. It needs to be understood as the expression of a symbolic mutation in the ordering of social relations: the democratic revolution envisaged in Claude Lefort's terms as 'the dissolution of the markers of certainty'. In a modern democratic society, there can be no longer a substantive unity, and division must be recognized as constitutive. It is 'a society in which Power, Law and Knowledge are exposed to a radical indeterminacy, a society that has become the theatre of an uncontrollable adventure'.[8]

MORALITY, UNANIMITY AND IMPARTIALITY

What has been celebrated as a revival of political philosophy in the last decades is in fact a mere extension of moral philosophy; it is moral reasoning applied to the treatment of political institutions. This is manifest in the absence in current liberal theorizing of a proper distinction between moral discourse and political discourse. To recover the normative aspect of politics, moral concerns about impartiality and unanimity are introduced into political argumentation. The result is a public morality for liberal societies, a morality which is deemed to be 'political' because it is 'minimal' and avoids engaging with controversial conceptions of the good and because it provides the cement for social cohesion.

There might well be a place for such an endeavour, but it cannot replace political philosophy and it does not provide us with the adequate understanding of the political that we urgently need. Moreover, its insistence on universalism and individualism can be harmful because it masks the real challenge that a reflection on pluralism faces today with the explosion of nationalisms and the multiplication of particularisms. Those phenomena need to be grasped in political terms, as forms of construction of a 'we/them' opposition, and consequently appeals to universality, impartiality and individual rights miss the mark.

The problems arising from the conflation of morality and politics are evident in the work of another liberal: Thomas Nagel. According to him, the difficulty for political theory is that 'political institutions and their theoretical justification try to externalize the demands of the impersonal standpoint. But they have to be staffed and supported and brought to life by individuals for whom the impersonal standpoint coexists with the personal, and this has to be reflected in their design.'[9] Nagel believes that, in order to be able to defend the acceptability of a political order, we need to reconcile an impartial concern for everyone with a view of how each individual can reasonably be expected to live. Nagel proposes that we should start with the conflict that each individual encounters in himself between the impersonal standpoint that produces a powerful demand for universal impartiality and equality and the personal standpoint that gives rise to individualistic motives which impede the realization of those ideals.

Central to political theory, in his view, is the question of political legitimacy, which requires the achievement of unanimity over the basic institutions of society. Like Rawls and Larmore, he rejects a Hobbesian solution because it does not integrate the impersonal standpoint and only considers personal motives and values, and he insists that some form of impartiality must be central to the pursuit of legitimacy. However, he considers that a legitimate system will have to reconcile the principle of impartiality with one of reasonable partiality so that no one could object that the demands made on them are excessive.

With their insistence on 'partiality', Nagel's views represent, no doubt, progress with respect to the position of those liberals who equate the moral point of view with that of impartiality, and privilege it at the expense of all kinds of personal commitments. The problem is the emphasis he puts on unanimity and on his search for principles that no one could reasonably reject and that all could agree that everyone should follow. He sees the strength of such principles in the fact that they will have a moral character. As a consequence, he argues that when a system is legitimate, 'those living under it have no grounds for complaint against the way its basic structure accommodates their point of view, and no one is morally justified in withholding his cooperation from the functioning of the system, trying to subvert its results, or trying to overturn it if he has the power to do so'.[10]

We find again, stated openly in this case, the same attempt to foreclose the possibility of dissent in the public realm that we have already observed in Rawls and Larmore. For those liberals, a fully realized liberal democratic order is one in which there is perfect unanimity concerning political arrangements and total coincidence between the individuals and their institutions. Their aim is to reach a type of consensus which, by its very nature, will disqualify every move to destabilize it. The pluralism they defend only resides in the private sphere and is restricted to philosophical, moral and religious issues. They do not seem to understand that there can also be unresolvable conflicts in the field of political values.

It must be said that Nagel is not very sanguine about the possibility of realizing the type of consensus he promotes, but he entertains no doubt about its desirability. He declares:

> It would be morally preferable, and a condition of true political legitimacy, if the general principles governing agent-relative reasons limited the reach of those reasons in such a way that they left standing some solutions or distributions of advantages and disadvantages that no one could reasonably refuse, even if he were in a position to do so. Instead of morality being like politics in its sensitivity to the balance of power, we should want politics to be more like morality in its aim of unanimous acceptability.[11]

This is, in my view, a dangerously misguided perspective, and people committed to democracy should be wary of all projects that aspire to create unanimity. Speaking about moral philosophy, Stuart Hampshire warns us that

> Whether it is Aristotelian, Kantian, Humean, or utilitarian, moral philosophy can do harm when it implies that there ought to be, and that there can be, fundamental agreement on, or even a convergence in, moral ideals – the harm is that the reality of conflict, both within individuals and within societies, is disguised by the myth of humanity as a consistent moral unit across time and space. There is a false blandness in the myth, an aversion from reality.[12]

I think the same reasoning applies even more to political philosophy and that a democratic pluralist position cannot aim at establishing once and for all the definite principles and arrangements that the members of a well-ordered society should accept. Divisive issues cannot be confined to the sphere of the private, and it is an illusion to believe that it is possible to create a non-exclusive public sphere of rational argument where a non-coercive consensus could be attained. Instead of trying to erase the traces of power and exclusion, democratic politics requires that they be brought to the fore, making them visible so that they can enter the terrain of contestation.

Tackled from such a perspective, the question of pluralism is much more complex. It cannot be envisaged only in terms of already existing subjects and restricted to their conceptions of the good. What must be addressed is the very process of constitution of the subjects of pluralism. This is indeed where the more crucial issues lie today. And this is where the limitations of the current liberal approach – informed by essentialism and individualism – can have really damaging political consequences for democratic politics.[13]

WHAT KIND OF CONSENSUS?

I agree with political liberals on the need to distinguish between liberalism as a comprehensive doctrine, a philosophy of man, and liberalism as a doctrine that is concerned with the institutions and values of the liberal society. And I am also

committed – although in a way that differs from them – to elucidating the political dimension of liberalism. I want to scrutinize its contribution to the emergence of modern democracy as a new regime. But this requires recognition that
the liberal democratic regime is not exhausted by its liberal component. For it
consists in the articulation of two elements, the liberal one constituted by the
institutions of the liberal state (rule of law, separation of powers, defence of individual rights) and the democratic one of popular sovereignty and majority rule.
Moreover, liberty and equality, which constitute the political principles of the
liberal democratic regime, can be interpreted in many different ways and ranked
according to different priorities. This accounts for the multiple possible forms
of liberal democracy. The 'liberals' privilege the values of liberty and individual
rights, while the 'democrats' insist on equality and participation. But as long as
neither side attempts to suppress the other, we are witnessing a struggle *inside*
liberal democracy, over its priorities, and not one between alternative regimes.

To state, as Larmore does, that 'Liberalism and democracy are separate
values whose relation . . . consists largely in democratic self-government being
the best means for protecting the principles of a liberal political order'[14] is typically a liberal interpretation and is open to challenge. To be sure, the relation
between liberalism and democracy has long been a controversial issue and will
probably never be settled. A pluralist democracy is constantly pulled in opposite directions: towards exacerbation of differences and disintegration on one
side; towards homogenization and strong forms of unity on the other. I consider that the specificity of modern democracy as a new political form of society,
as a new 'regime', lies precisely in the *tension* between the democratic logic of
equality and the liberal logic of liberty. It is a tension that we should value and
protect, rather than try to resolve, because it is constitutive of pluralist democracy. This does not mean that it does not create some specific problems; since
the articulation between liberalism and democracy has been established, a
recurrent concern of liberals has been how to put individual rights outside the
reach of majoritarianism. To that effect, they have wanted to put constraints
on the democratic process of decision-making. Without being openly acknowledged, this is, I believe, one of the subtexts of the present discussion. Presenting
liberal institutions as the outcome of a purely deliberative rationality might be
seen as an attempt to provide them with a ground that forecloses the possibility of reasonable disagreement. This could be seen as a way to protect them
against potential threats from democratic majorities.

There is, no doubt, a need to secure pluralism, individual rights and minorities against a possible majority tyranny. But the opposite danger also exists, of
thereby naturalizing a given set of 'liberties' and existing rights, and at the same
time buttressing many relations of inequality. The search for 'guarantees' can
lead to the very destruction of pluralist democracy. Hence the importance of
understanding that for democracy to exist no social agent should be able to
claim any mastery of the *foundation* of society. The relation between social
agents can only be termed 'democratic' in so far as they accept the particularity

'THE PURITY OF POLITICS' BY WILLIAM CONNOLLY

At the time of writing, William Connolly is Professor of Political Theory in the Department of Political Science, Johns Hopkins University. He is a leading figure in North American political theory, particularly that part of it concerned to develop, broadly speaking, poststructuralist approaches to politics, and has described himself as a 'rhizomatic pluralist'. In his prize-winning *The Terms of Political Discourse* (Heath, 1974), Connolly showed how language is not a neutral mechanism of political communication and that it functions as an institutionalised structure directing political thought and action. There are crossovers (but also differences) here with the perspective of the Cambridge School discussed in Chapter 2. He has developed his ideas in engagement with various thinkers of political modernity (see *Political Theory and Modernity*, Blackwell, 1988), especially Nietzsche, but also with the classics. In *The Ethos of Pluralization* (University of Minnesota Press, 1995), he sought to distinguish between the nature of pluralism in society and the ongoing, dissenting process of pluralisation, developing a particular ethical approach to politics and a conception of democracy in the process. He showed how politics always invokes fundamental presumptions about the nature of existence even as these are downplayed or hidden by contemporary political conceit. This book is helpfully debated by other leading thinkers in a special section of the journal *Philosophy and Social Criticism* (vol. 24, 1998). In *Why I Am Not a Secularist* (University of Minnesota Press, 1999), he continues this vein, criticising the way in which secularism downplays the significance of fundamental questions, flattening out public life and public discourse and limiting rather than encouraging pluralism.

The extract below is from a short article by Connolly in which he uses the experience of disgust as a way into asking some troubling questions about the way politics occurs and is conceived. He uses Kant and Arendt as a way into these themes, but the extract includes only his comments on Arendt. Here we see how his criticism leads him to consider the ways in which bodily matters (including the cultural organisation of disgust) can be politicised. Underlying this is an interest (common to many forms of poststructuralism) in the ways in which political and ethical 'techniques of the self' work on our bodies and can rewrite those things we thought were automatic biological responses. The links to Foucault's concept of biopower (introduced in Chapter 1) should be clear. It is recommended that readers consider thinking about Connolly's arguments in relation to those of authors with a related approach and also found in this volume. In addition to Foucault, Butler is of particular relevance.

'THE PURITY OF POLITICS' (1997)*

William Connolly

We have identified an irreducible element of wildness in the Kantian will. It must be there for radical evil to be defined as a propensity of the will rather than prior to it. But Kant wants desperately to nullify this unruliness that he cannot eliminate. That is why this devotee of moral purity calls the element of wildness perversity and pretty much identifies it with evil. Everything else in his characterization of the supersensible and sensible realms moves in the direction of nullification too. For the sensible is the realm of appearance as lawful *regularity* and the supersensible properly the source of morality as lawful *obedience*. The Kantian world thus becomes doubled over in regularity. This double regularity is then further reinforced by giving pure practical reason unilateral authority whenever it 'intervenes' in the sensible world.

Hannah Arendt responds to the element of wildness in an un-Kantian way. She could easily include Kant when she says that 'professional thinkers, whether philosophers or scientists, have not been "pleased with freedom" and its ineluctable randomness; they have been unwilling to pay the price of contingency for the questionable gift of spontaneity, of being able to do what could also be left undone'.[1] Arendt resists the Kantian morality of law; she prizes the element of opacity, division and wildness in the will; and she resists any metaphysic that gives singular priority to foundational authority, law, regularity, routine, or the unworldly. Arendt, indeed, is impressed by the extent to which the morality of law was impotent under the onslaught of totalitarianism; she is even, perhaps, wary of the degree to which the vaunted simplicity of morality carries with it a disposition to obedience and thoughtlessness that might spawn widespread acquiescence in the face of a fascist takeover of the state. Arendt worries about the underside of moral purity.

Arendt, by contrast to Kant, is a philosopher of *births and beginnings* as the introduction of new and surprising events into the world; of *action* as a mode of politics in which people enact something new exceeding the intentions of the participants prior to their mutual engagement; of *gratitude for being and the appreciation of cultural plurality* as crucial conditions of ethical thoughtfulness in political action;[2] and of *publicity, promising, forgiving and augmentation* as

---

* From William Connolly, 'A Critique of Pure Politics', *Philosophy and Social Criticism*, 23:5 (September 1997), 14–20, 24–6.

ways to build islands of stability, trust and responsibility in a world ungoverned by a set of preordained moral laws.[3]

But, while Arendt dissolves the purity of morality into a solution of politics, she is sorely tempted to reinstate a corollary model of purity inside the political 'realm' itself. To consider Arendt in relation to Kant is to probe again sources of the temptation to purity, the extent to which the temptation is avoidable, and alternative ways in which it might be negotiated. We will focus on three closely interwoven issues: the Arendtian bracketing of 'the social question' and opposition to the nation; her depreciation of 'the body' in ethics and politics; and the restrictive spaces of political action she recognizes.

Arendt is opposed to all modes of politics organized around a general will, sovereignty, or a nation. These ideals, she insists, engender a politics that suffocates diversity and drowns out the capacity for political action in concert. They reduce politics either to administration or to the thoughtless pressure of social movements. Therefore, among other things, these ideals jeopardize the only sort of legitimacy political governance can attain in the modern age. For today to appeal to one universal moral source to justify governance over a plurality of people is to ensure that a whole series of constituencies will be assaulted, suppressed, or excluded; the 'we' of governance itself emerges, then, out of a series of promises across lines of difference that enable action in concert to occur.

Arendt's avoidance of the nation is admirable, and I endorse a version of it. Nonetheless, it is in the context of this avoidance that her attempt to avoid the social question is generally posed. The social question speaks above all to the drive to escape poverty. But it might also involve questions about the organization of work, the governance of the household, the organization of gender and sensual relations. Such questions of economy and identity, when urgently felt, draw the multitude into politics, as they did for the first time in the French Revolution. 'And this multitude, appearing for the first time in broad daylight, was actually the multitude of the poor and the downtrodden, who every century before had hidden in darkness and shame.' It becomes a paradigm of the multitude as such.

> What from then on has been irrevocable, and what the agents and spectators of the revolution immediately recognized as such, was that the public realm – reserved as far as memory could reach, to those who *were free*, namely carefree of all the worries that are connected with life's necessity, with bodily needs – should offer its space and its light to this immense majority who are not free because they are driven by bodily needs.[4]

Several Arendtian themes and anxieties are discernible in this formulation. First, she knows that the emergence of the masses into politics is irrevocable; this knowledge informs the melancholy that permeates her writing about modern democratic politics. Second, the eruption of the social question into 'broad daylight' introduces a compulsory mood into politics that threatens to overwhelm its deliberative and creative possibilities. Third, this 'immense majority who are not free' is translated by the last line into the present tense, signalling again Arendt's recognition that a force has been unleashed that cannot be pushed back into the private realm, combined with her sense that nothing very good can come from it. And fourth, the social question – poverty – is closely connected by Arendt to 'bodily needs', to that domain of the automatic and the moody structurally resistant to political elaboration and refinement.

Arendt is alert to how corruptions of the rich and the high so easily incite corollary violences and brutalities by the lowly. 'Wherever society was permitted to overgrow, and eventually to absorb the political realm, it imposed its own mores and "moral" standards, the intrigues and perfidies of high society, to which the lower strata responded by violence and brutality.'[5] And she makes powerful points when she compares the left's tendency to idealize the motives and nobility of the poor with her judgment that 'abundance and endless consumption are the ideals of the poor' and that the experience of poverty is more likely to lead to a politics of demand and condemnation of difference rather than deliberation and free action in concert. But Arendt is also caught in a dilemma that may not be articulated explicitly in her work. Some of the forces and constituencies she would insulate from the political realm become ripe, through the very politics of insulation, for mobilization by disaffected elites to *renationalize* the democratic state. If, for example, many Americans chafing under job insecurity and authoritarianism at work are also white, Christian males, failure to engage the social question helps to set this constituency up for mobilization by elites who promise to restore a nation of ethnic purity, masculine superiority and religious unity. Arendtian exclusion of the social question thus fosters political effects she resists. Arendt herself acknowledges how Indians and slaves were excluded from the founding of the American Republic. But now the dynamics of early American exclusions and entitlements intersect with contemporary effects of the social question upon working-class males of European descent to produce the very effect Arendt wants to avoid (almost) the most: implacable pressures to renationalize the state to restore a putative unity it never really had. Arendtians, then, must reconfigure the parameters of 'the political' to resist compensatory drives to (re)nationalize the state.

Arendt, however, does not read the danger in this way. 'Nothing, we might say today, could be more obsolete than to attempt to liberate mankind from poverty by political means; nothing could be more futile and more dangerous.'[6] Arendt binds 'liberation' to the social question by restricting her attention to a 'Marxist' engagement with that question. But there are other approaches that proceed against poverty without binding that pursuit to liberation. The two are bound together by Arendt, perhaps, to use the impossibility of the latter to discredit the credibility of the former. Against Arendt's formulation, it must be said that nothing could be more dangerous and futile from the standpoint of a politics seeking to move beyond the nation and the general will than to try to bracket the social question from politics. This also means that the Arendtian ideal of politics in small islands of action, such as the Soviet councils, the localities of early America, and syndicalist organizations, must be diversified further too. The state itself must be embraced as *one* indispensable site of politics, a site containing its share of dangers but also the one most capable of supporting general conditions for the cultural plurality she admires. Indeed, to the extent the social question and the body are purged together from Arendtian plurality, that plurality itself becomes bleached and aristocratic, expunging dimensions of diversity that might otherwise enrich and fortify it.

The masses, Arendt says, are governed by interests or moods whenever they exist in need and remain outside the small precincts of political discussion. Moods and interests are thereby resistant to the type of public discussion that might elevate and refine them. Opinions alone can be discussed and elevated because they are 'carefree'. There are other things Arendt says that implicitly qualify this odd disjunction between mood and opinion. But the consideration that presses Arendt to join interests and moods so ponderously to imperative need while linking opinions so lightly to carefree engagement is above all her rendering of the body in relation to thinking, judgment, action, freedom and politics. Here is a dramatic formulation that binds those elements together:

> The most powerful necessity of which we are aware in self-introspection is the life process which permeates our bodies and keeps them in a constant state of a change whose movements are automatic, independent of our activities and irresistible – i.e., of an overwhelming urgency. The less we are doing ourselves, the less active we are, the more forcefully will this biological process assert itself, impose its inherent necessity upon us, and overawe us with the fateful automatism of sheer happening that underlies all human history.[7]

Here Arendt gives priority to thought-imbued action over the inherent necessity of fateful automatism in a way designed to protect the former from the fateful effects of the latter. She takes one step in the right direction ('the less we are doing ourselves, the less active we are, the more forcefully will this biological process assert itself'), but then almost cancels its positive effect with another step in the opposite direction. To invoke terms introduced earlier, she implicitly treats the amygdala as being sunk in 'fateful automatism'; she then declines to come to terms sharply enough with its regular effects in the *active world of intersubjective thought and action*; and she thereby fails to engage the micropolitics by which those thought-imbued feelings of anxiety, disgust, resentment, responsiveness and generosity, that enter so profoundly into private and public ethics, are shaped. As a result of this combination Arendt devalues the profound importance of arts of the self and micro-politics to the quality of ethical life.

Arendt does not seem to me always to follow her own most programmatic statements in this complex domain. But such a perspective, *if* relentlessly pressed, removes several important dimensions of life from the politics of enactment such as diet, gender identity, the organization of sensuality, health, the cultural organization of dying, and the cultivation of critical responsiveness; it does so by treating a profoundly important dimension of ethical life as if it were first automatic and then automatically beyond the reach of practical action. In general, the Arendtian compound of active thinking and corporeal automatism obscures the extent to which numerous dimensions of corporeality are always already *objects* of extensive political action as well as protean *sources* from which new possibilities of being might be cast into the world of public debate.

If Arendt rejects the Kantian 'supersensible' – and her repudiation of Kant's conception of morality does not suffice to make that certain to me – and if she then intensifies his dull presentation of sensibility, there remains little space in the Arendtian world for selves to work upon each other to render themselves more responsive to the fundamental contingency of things and less resentful about the human condition as she understands it. These activities occur, of course, but they operate below the threshold of Arendtian attentiveness, and they often assume directions Arendt would resist. Arendt's automatization of the corporeal renders her tone-deaf to complex cultural/corporeal strategies by which some of the very 'urgencies' she fears the most are both installed and rendered implacable. The body is more profound and multiplicitous than the soul. But it all sounds like humming to her.

In her book on Kant, Arendt works upon the Kantian idea of 'common sense', to render it suitable for a philosophy of judgment she can endorse. It never becomes entirely clear (to me) where Arendt stands on the Kantian relation between common sense and the supersensible. For him, the judgment of beauty, refracted through the common sense of 'taste', both manifests a free accord of the faculties and symbolizes something fundamental about the form of nature beyond the mechanistic appearance it necessarily presents to our understanding. Arendt focuses upon the way common sense mediates the experiences of taste and smell.

> Hence we may be tempted to conclude that the faculty of judgment is wrongly derived from this sense. Kant being aware of all of the implications of this derivation, remains convinced that it is a correct one. And the most plausible thing in his favor is his observation, entirely correct, that the true opposite of the Beautiful is not the Ugly, but 'that which excites disgust'.[8]

Disgust, on my reading, is reducible neither to the manifestation of a spontaneous accord of the faculties nor to a brute datum of the body. It is a complex corporeo-cultural code of feeling scripted into the cortical organization of the stomach and the brain. Moreover, since disgust, when it becomes strong enough to turn the stomach, can easily foster thoughtlessness, the cultural organization of disgust has profound implications for political and ethical life. Sometimes a feeling of disgust becomes ripe material to work on by experimental methods, say, when a heterodox practice of sexuality disgusts you and threatens the claim to natural superiority of your own sensual disposition. Or when 'the Jew' offends your natural pursuit of ethnic purity even as you endorse equal respect for 'persons'. The predicament for Arendt is this: either acknowledge that disgust is a (sometimes) movable feeling of appraisal and thus affirm the ethico-political importance of arts of the self, or deny both of these claims and leave little space for selves to cultivate the sort of sensibility her politics admires. Of course Arendt believes the sensibility she admires emerges within politics itself, when the conditions are right. And there is a lot to her point. But a preliminary condition for the salutary effect of publicity in politics is lacking if most of the parties involved are already predisposed to thoughtlessness on the most important corporeo-cultural issues of the day.

Tactics to modify thought-imbued feelings already there must be experimental because, since you seldom know exactly how the initial feeling became installed and since you lack direct access to triggering scripts in the amygdala, stomach and elsewhere, you do not quite know in advance how the tactics you adopt might act on the existing shape and intensity of your appraisals. So you act cautiously and experimentally on those feelings that curtail the capacity for responsiveness or thoughtfulness in specific domains. Surely some dimensions in Arendt's thought press in the direction of such tactics. For she herself emphasizes the significant relation between thoughtlessness and the 'banality of evil'. And yet her banal portrayal of corporeality then drives a wedge between its manifold complexity and those tactics that might modify the sensibility within which thoughtfulness and thoughtlessness are set.

Arendt is admirable in her resistance to the Kantian purification of morality. But her intercoded orientations to the social question, the body, and spaces of political action relocate purity in the domain of politics itself. Her rendering of the body is the pivot upon which the other two dispositions turn. And yet the body does not simply exist outside or below the field of culture, action, innovation, freedom and beginnings; 'it' is a relatively mobile, unfinished set of sources *from* which new energies and surprising experiments emerge and *upon* which multiple scripts of culture are unevenly and imperfectly written. The Arendtian politics of action will be enriched immeasurably when the body becomes admitted among its sources, sites and effects. Cultural scripts written upon it might then periodically become issues of political engagement. And the difficulties Arendt faces – though she is not alone here – in delineating a defensible mode of political legitimacy, in a world in which the old banisters of morality have fallen away, might be informed by admission of the social question and bodies together into the admixtures of politics.[9]

NOTES

1. Arendt, *The Life of the Mind*, Vol. II, *Willing* (New York: Harcourt Brace Jovanich, 1994), p. 198.
2. In a book which remains (after all the new studies) the wisest study of Arendt available in English, George Kateb explores the critical role that wonder and gratitude play in the Arendtian sensibility: 'Altogether, wonder at and gratitude for Being may help to diminish resentment of the human condition, just as inflamed resentment may close off susceptibility to wonder and gratitude. Where resentment proceeds . . .

alienation ensues and works to block widespread commitment to the world (as culture) and to the life of political action.' *Hannah Arendt: Politics, Conscience, Evil* (Totowa, NJ: Rowman & Allanheld, 1984), p. 268. To push my thesis further than is accomplished in this essay would be to join my (forthcoming) discussion of embodiment and disgust to the cultivation of gratitude for the contingency of being. It would be to continue the discussion between Nietzsche and Arendt on gratitude that Kateb has already started.

3. Bonnie Honig, in *Political Theory and the Displacement of Politics* (Ithaca, NY: Cornell University Press, 1993), brings out superbly these dimensions in Arendt's work. She also poses some of the reservations I will pursue, 'augmenting Arendt until she has elevated Arendtian politics above them. Here is a summary of how Arendtian bracketing of the social question becomes overdetermined: 'Indeed, any reading of Arendt that takes seriously the agonistic, virtuosic, and performative impulses of her politics must, for the state of that politics, resist the *a priori* determination of a public–private distinction that is beyond contestation. . . . Arendt secures her public–private distinction with a multi-tiered edifice . . . "We hold" versus "self-evident truth", self versus body, male versus female, resistible versus irresistible, courageous versus risk-aversive, multiple versus univocal, speech versus silence, active versus passive, open versus closed, power versus violence, necessity versus freedom, action versus behavior, extraordinary versus repetition, light versus dark, – in short, public versus private' (p. 119).

4. Hannah Arendt, *On Revolution* (New York: Penguin Books, 1965), p. 48.

5. Ibid., p. 105.

6. Ibid., p. 114.

7. Ibid., p. 58.

8. Arendt, *Lectures on Kant's Political Philosophy*, ed. and with an Introduction by Ronald Beiner (Chicago, IL: University of Chicago Press, 1982), p. 68; Arendt's emphasis. Ronald Beiner, in his interpretive essay, suggests that Kant's analysis of common sense sets a model from which Arendt proceeds. But that seems to commit her to Kant's metaphysic of the supersensible. And Beiner also says, 'Arendt does not really face up to this question of the ultimate cognitive status of shared judgements' (p. 115). I suspect that Arendt wants to retain the authority of Kantian judgment while remaining wary of the philosophy that endows it with such authority. But if she repudiates the Kantian philosophy of the supersensible while sticking with a deaf and dumb model of the corporeal, there is not much space left in which to work on the ethical sensibility of the self. Others may doubt that Arendt uses the Kantian theory of judgment as a model at all, reading her engagement primarily as an attempt to understand Kant in preparation for future work never accomplished. Here is a quotation from *On Revolution* that speaks to that issue: 'The same is true with respect to judgment, where we would have to turn to Kant's philosophy, rather than to the men of the revolution, if we wished to learn something about its essential character and amazing range in the realm of human affairs' (p. 229).

9. It does not seem to me that Arendt has succeeded in delineating the elements needed in an ethos that both respects the ambiguities and contingencies of political action and enables authority and legitimacy to emerge as stabilizing factors within them. She is right to conclude that you cannot simply invoke a theory of morality as command and issue a few governing criteria. Proceduralism, too, while pertinent, is radically insufficient to the issue. A cultural ethos is necessary. The practices of promising and forgiveness that Arendt explores will provide crucial elements in it. For a fine exploration of their possibilities and limits, see Alan Keenan, 'Promises, Promises: The Abyss of Freedom and the Loss of the Political in the Work of Hannah Arendt', *Political Theory* (May 1994): 297–322. I attempt, in *The Ethos of Pluralization*, to show how the cultivation of 'agonistic respect' and 'critical responsiveness' can contribute to such an ethos while respecting those pluralities, uncertainties and innovations that form constitutive ingredients of politics.

'FROM PARODY TO POLITICS' BY JUDITH BUTLER

We have already encountered Judith Butler, writing in the context of feminist theory and conceptions of the category of 'woman' (biographical details can be found in Chapter 7). The extract reproduced here is also concerned with gender and shows some aspects of her general approach to politics and the idea of the subject. It comes from an influential book, *Gender Trouble*, that raised many questions about the nature of gender identity and in which Butler tried to push beyond a simple notion of the 'social construction' of gender to question the very categories of sex and sexuality as such. Theories arguing that identity is constituted through 'discourse' are often taken to entail the idea that such subjectivity is determined in a restrictive and closed fashion. But Butler argues that we should regard identity as a kind of ongoing (if constrained) practice of signification. The injunction to conform to a dominant identity is subject to failure, and at these moments there arises the opportunity for a subversion of identity. This moment, that of the articulation of identity, is one of the most important for politics and its theorisation a major challenge.

'FROM PARODY TO POLITICS' (1990)*

Judith Butler

I began with the speculative question of whether feminist politics could do without a 'subject' in the category of women. At stake is not whether it still makes sense, strategically or transitionally, to refer to women in order to make representational claims in their behalf. The feminist 'we' is always and only a phantasmatic construction, one that has its purposes, but which denies the internal complexity and indeterminacy of the term and constitutes itself only through the exclusion of some part of the constituency that it simultaneously seeks to represent. The tenuous or phantasmatic status of the 'we', however, is not cause for despair or, at least, it is not *only* cause for despair. The radical instability of the category sets into question the *foundational* restrictions on feminist political theorizing and opens up other configurations, not only of genders and bodies, but of politics itself.

The foundationalist reasoning of identity politics tends to assume that an identity must first be in place in order for political interests to be elaborated

---

* From Judith Butler, *Gender Trouble: Feminism and the Subversion of Identity* (London: Routledge, 1990), pp. 142–9.

and, subsequently, political action to be taken. My argument is that there need not be a 'doer behind the deed', but that the 'doer' is variably constructed in and through the deed. This is not a return to an existential theory of the self as constituted through its acts, for the existential theory maintains a prediscursive structure for both the self and its acts. It is precisely the discursively variable construction of each in and through the other that has interested me here.

The question of locating 'agency' is usually associated with the viability of the 'subject', where the 'subject' is understood to have some stable existence prior to the cultural field that it negotiates. Or, if the subject is culturally constructed, it is nevertheless vested with an agency, usually figured as the capacity for reflexive mediation, that remains intact regardless of its cultural embeddedness. On such a model, 'culture' and 'discourse' *mire* the subject, but do not constitute that subject. This move to qualify and enmire the pre-existing subject has appeared necessary to establish a point of agency that is not fully *determined* by that culture and discourse. And yet, this kind of reasoning falsely presumes (1) agency can only be established through recourse to a prediscursive 'I', even if that 'I' is found in the midst of a discursive convergence, and (2) that to be *constituted* by discourse is to be *determined* by discourse, where determination forecloses the possibility of agency.

Even within the theories that maintain a highly qualified or situated subject, the subject still encounters its discursively constituted environment in an oppositional epistemological frame. The culturally enmired subject negotiates its constructions, even when those constructions are the very predicates of its own identity. In Beauvoir, for example, there is an 'I' that does its gender, that becomes its gender, but that 'I', invariably associated with its gender, is nevertheless a point of agency never fully identifiable with its gender. That *cogito* is never fully *of* the cultural world that it negotiates, no matter the narrowness of the ontological distance that separates that subject from its cultural predicates. The theories of feminist identity that elaborate predicates of color, sexuality, ethnicity, class, and able-bodiedness invariably close with an embarrassed 'etc.' at the end of the list. Through this horizontal trajectory of adjectives, these positions strive to encompass a situated subject, but invariably fail to be complete. This failure, however, is instructive: what political impetus is to be derived from the exasperated 'etc.' that so often occurs at the end of such lines? This is a sign of exhaustion as well as of the illimitable process of signification itself. It is the *supplément*, the excess that necessarily accompanies any effort to posit identity once and for all. This illimitable *et cetera*, however, offers itself as a new departure for feminist political theorizing.

If identity is asserted through a process of signification, if identity is always already signified, and yet continues to signify as it circulates within various interlocking discourses, then the question of agency is not to be answered through resource to an 'I' that pre-exists signification. In other words, the enabling conditions for an assertion of 'I' are provided by the structure of signification, the rules that regulate the legitimate and illegitimate invocation of that pronoun, the practices that establish the terms of intelligibility by which that pronoun can circulate. Language is not an *exterior medium or instrument* into which I pour a self and from which I glean a reflection of that self. The Hegelian model of self-recognition that has been appropriated by Marx, Lukács, and a variety of contemporary liberatory discourses presupposes a potential adequation between the 'I' that confronts its world, including its language, as an object, and the 'I' that finds itself as an object in that world. But the subject/object dichotomy, which here belongs to the tradition of Western epistemology, conditions the very problematic of identity that it seeks to solve.

What discursive tradition establishes the 'I' and its 'Other' in an epistemological confrontation that subsequently decides where and how questions of knowability and agency are to be determined? What kinds of agency are foreclosed through the positing of an epistemological subject precisely because the rules and practices that govern the invocation of that subject and regulate its agency in advance are ruled out as sites of analysis and critical intervention? That the epistemological point of departure is in no sense inevitable is naively and pervasively confirmed by the mundane operations of ordinary language – widely documented within anthropology – that regard the subject/object dichotomy as a strange and contingent, if not violent, philosophical imposition. The language of appropriation, instrumentality, and distantiation germane to the epistemological mode also belong to a strategy of domination that pits the 'I' against an 'Other' and, once that separation is effected, creates an artificial set of questions about the knowability and recoverability of that Other.

As part of the epistemological inheritance of contemporary political discourses of identity, this binary opposition is a strategic move within a given set of signifying practices, one that establishes the 'I' in and through this opposition and which reifies that opposition as a necessity, concealing the discursive apparatus by which the binary itself is constituted. The shift from an *epistemological* account of identity to one which locates the problematic within practices of *signification* permits an analysis that takes the epistemological mode itself as one possible and contingent signifying practice. Further, the question of *agency* is reformulated as a question of how signification and resignification work. In other words, what is signified as an identity is not signified at a given point in time after which it is simply there as an inert piece of entitative language. Clearly, identities *can* appear as so many inert substantives; indeed, epistemological models tend to take this appearance as their point of theoretical departure. However, the substantive 'I' only appears as such through a signifying practice that seeks to conceal its own workings and to naturalize its effects. Further, to qualify as a substantive identity is an arduous task, for such appearances are rule-generated identities, ones which rely on the consistent and repeated invocation of rules that condition and restrict culturally intelligible practices of identity. Indeed, to understand identity as a *practice*, and as a signifying practice, is to understand culturally intelligible subjects as the resulting effects of a rule-bound discourse that inserts itself in the pervasive and mundane signifying acts of linguistic life. Abstractly considered, language refers to an open system of signs by which intelligibility is insistently created and contested. As historically specific organizations of language, discourses present themselves in the plural, coexisting within temporal frames, and instituting unpredictable and inadvertent convergences from which specific modalities of discursive possibilities are engendered.

As a process, signification harbors within itself what the epistemological discourse refers to as 'agency'. The rules that govern intelligible identity, i.e., that enable and restrict the intelligible assertion of an 'I', rules that are partially structured along matrices of gender hierarchy and compulsory heterosexuality, operate through *repetition*. Indeed, when the subject is said to be constituted, that means simply that the subject is a consequence of certain rule-governed discourses that govern the intelligible invocation of identity. The subject is not *determined* by the rules through which it is generated because signification is *not a founding act, but rather a regulated process of repetition* that both conceals itself and enforces its rules precisely through the production of substantializing effects. In a sense, all signification takes place within the orbit of the compulsion to repeat; 'agency', then, is to be located within the possibility of a variation on that repetition. If the rules governing signification not only restrict but enable the assertion of alternative domains of cultural intelligibility, i.e., new possibilities for gender that contest the rigid codes of hierarchical binarisms, then it is only *within* the practices of repetitive signifying that a subversion of identity becomes possible. The injunction *to be* a given gender produces necessary failures, a variety of incoherent configurations that in their multiplicity exceed and defy the injunction by which they are generated. Further, the very injunction to be a given gender takes place through discursive routes: to be a good mother, to be a heterosexually desirable object, to be a fit worker, in sum, to signify a multiplicity of guarantees in response to a variety of different demands all at once. The coexistence or convergence of such discursive injunctions produces the possibility of a complex reconfiguration and redeployment; it is not a transcendental subject who enables action in the midst of such a convergence. There is no self that is prior to the convergence or who maintains 'integrity' prior to its entrance into this conflicted cultural field. There is only a taking up of the tools where they lie, where the very 'taking up' is enabled by the tool lying there.

What constitutes a subversive repetition within signifying practices of gender? I have argued ('I' deploy the grammar that governs the genre of the philosophical conclusion, but note that it is the grammar itself that deploys and enables this 'I', even as the 'I' that insists itself here repeats, redeploys, and – as the critics will determine – contests the philosophical grammar by which it is both enabled and restricted) that, for instance, within the sex/gender distinction, sex poses as 'the real' and the 'factic', the material or corporeal ground upon which gender operates as an act of cultural *inscription*. And yet gender is not written on the body as the torturing instrument of writing in Kafka's 'In the

Penal Colony' inscribes itself unintelligibly on the flesh of the accused. The question is not: what meaning does that inscription carry within it, but what cultural apparatus arranges this meeting between instrument and body, what interventions into this ritualistic repetition are possible? The 'real' and the 'sexually factic' are phantasmatic constructions – illusions of substance – that bodies are compelled to approximate, but never can. What, then, enables the exposure of the rift between the phantasmatic and the real whereby the real admits itself as phantasmatic? Does this offer the possibility for a repetition that is not fully constrained by the injunction to reconsolidate naturalized identities? Just as bodily surfaces are enacted *as* the natural, so these surfaces can become the site of a dissonant and denaturalized performance that reveals the performative status of the natural itself.

Practices of parody can serve to re-engage and reconsolidate the very distinction between a privileged and naturalized gender configuration and one that appears as derived, phantasmatic, and mimetic – a failed copy, as it were. And surely parody has been used to further a politics of despair, one which affirms a seemingly inevitable exclusion of marginal genders from the territory of the natural and the real. And yet this failure to become 'real' and to embody 'the natural' is, I would argue, a constitutive failure of all gender enactments for the very reason that these ontological locales are fundamentally uninhabitable. Hence, there is a subversive laughter in the pastiche-effect of parodic practices in which the original, the authentic, and the real are themselves constituted as effects. The loss of gender norms would have the effect of proliferating gender configurations, destabilizing substantive identity, and depriving the naturalizing narratives of compulsory heterosexuality of their central protagonists: 'man' and 'woman'. The parodic repetition of gender exposes as well the illusion of gender identity as an intractable depth and inner substance. As the effects of a subtle and politically enforced performativity, gender is an 'act', as it were, that is open to splittings, self-parody, self-criticism, and those hyperbolic exhibitions of 'the natural' that, in their very exaggeration, reveal its fundamentally phantasmatic status.

I have tried to suggest that the identity categories often presumed to be foundational to feminist politics, that is, deemed necessary in order to mobilize feminism as an identity politics, simultaneously work to limit and constrain in advance the very cultural possibilities that feminism is supposed to open up. The tacit constraints that produce culturally intelligible 'sex' ought to be understood as generative political structures rather than naturalized foundations. Paradoxically, the reconceptualization of identity as an *effect*, that is, as *produced* or *generated*, opens up possibilities of 'agency' that are insidiously foreclosed by positions that take identity categories as foundational and fixed. For an identity to be an effect means that it is neither fatally determined nor fully artificial and arbitrary. That the *constituted* status of identity is misconstrued along these two conflicting lines suggests the ways in which the feminist discourse on cultural construction remains trapped within the unnecessary binarism of free will and determinism. Construction is not opposed to agency; it is the necessary scene of agency, the very terms in which agency is articulated and becomes culturally intelligible. The critical task for feminism is not to establish a point of view outside of constructed identities; that conceit is the construction of an epistemological model that would disavow its own cultural location and, hence, promote itself as a global subject, a position that deploys precisely the imperialist strategies that feminism ought to criticize. The critical task is, rather, to locate strategies of subversive repetition enabled by those constructions, to affirm the local possibilities of intervention through participating in precisely those practices of repetition that constitute identity and, therefore, present the immanent possibility of contesting them.

The theoretical inquiry has attempted to locate the political in the very signifying practices that establish, regulate, and deregulate identity. This effort, however, can only be accomplished through the introduction of a set of questions that extend the very notion of the political. How to disrupt the foundations that cover over alternative cultural configurations of gender? How to destabilize and render in their phantasmatic dimension the 'premises' of identity politics?

This task has required a critical genealogy of the naturalization of sex and of bodies in general. It has also demanded a reconsideration of the figure of the body as mute, prior to culture, awaiting signification, a figure that cross-checks with the figure of the feminine, awaiting the inscription-as-incision of the masculine signifier for entrance into language and culture. From a political analysis of compulsory heterosexuality, it has been necessary to question the construction of sex as binary, as a hierarchical binary. From the point of view of gender as enacted, questions have emerged over the fixity of gender identity as an interior depth that is said to be externalized in various forms of 'expression'. The implicit construction of the primary heterosexual construction of desire is shown to persist even as it appears in the mode of primary bi-sexuality. Strategies of exclusion and hierarchy are also shown to persist in the formulation of the sex/gender distinction and its recourse to 'sex' as the prediscursive as well as the priority of sexuality to culture and, in particular, the cultural construction of sexuality as the prediscursive. Finally, the epistemological paradigm that presumes the priority of the doer to the deed establishes a global and globalizing subject who disavows its own locality as well as the conditions for local intervention.

If taken as the grounds of feminist theory or politics, these 'effects' of gender hierarchy and compulsory heterosexuality are not only misdescribed as foundations, but the signifying practices that enable this metaleptic misdescription remain outside the purview of a feminist critique of gender relations. To enter into the repetitive practices of this terrain of signification is not a choice, for the 'I' that might enter is always already inside: there is no possibility of agency or reality outside of the discursive practices that give those terms the intelligibility that they have. The task is not whether to repeat, but how to repeat or, indeed, to repeat and, through a radical proliferation of gender, *to displace* the very gender norms that enable the repetition itself. There is no ontology of gender on which we might construct a politics, for gender ontologies always operate within established political contexts as normative injunctions, determining what qualifies as intelligible sex, invoking and consolidating the reproductive constraints on sexuality, setting the prescriptive requirements whereby sexed or gendered bodies come into cultural intelligibility. Ontology is, thus, not a foundation, but a normative injunction that operates insidiously by installing itself into political discourse as its necessary ground.

The deconstruction of identity is not the deconstruction of politics; rather, it establishes as political the very terms through which identity is articulated. This kind of critique brings into question the foundationalist frame in which feminism as an identity politics has been articulated. The internal paradox of this foundationalism is that it presumes, fixes, and constrains the very 'subjects' that it hopes to represent and liberate. The task here is not to celebrate each and every new possibility *qua* possibility, but to redescribe those possibilities that *already* exist, but which exist within cultural domains designated as culturally unintelligible and impossible. If identities were no longer fixed as the premises of a political syllogism, and politics no longer understood as a set of practices derived from the alleged interest that belong to a set of ready-made subjects, a new configuration of politics would surely emerge from the ruins of the old. Cultural configurations of sex and gender might then proliferate or, rather, their present proliferation might then become articulable within the discourses that establish intelligible cultural life, confounding the very binarism of sex, and exposing its fundamental unnaturalness. What other local strategies for engaging the 'unnatural' might lead to the denaturalization of gender as such?

SECTION 3: QUESTIONS FOR DISCUSSION

- Liberal theorists (such as Rawls) seem to argue for a state that is neutral on questions of 'values' and about the nature of the 'good life'. What would be the communitarian response to this? Can liberals defend themselves from the charges that might follow?
- Does individualism necessarily corrode the sense of solidarity required to support a meaningful set of shared values?
- Are communitarians right to conceive of the self as 'embedded' in a social role or roles? Do liberals really think that the self is independent of such roles, and do they really ignore our embeddedness in social practices?
- Feminists and communitarians both attack the idea of a neutral liberal state. Does this mean they really agree with each other?
- How important is it for feminist political theorists to make the analysis of the category of 'woman' central to their work? Are feminists right to concentrate on the issue of **'difference'**? Can we think of 'women' as a unified subject of political thought and action?
- Do you think feminists are right to argue that mainstream political theories are committed to a public–private distinction that renders them unable to acknowledge many important gender inequities? What sorts of politics flow from this charge?
- Young argues that the ideal of 'citizenship as generality' actually excludes many groups of people. What do you understand by this? Does this have implications for the arguments of liberals such as Rawls? What would communitarians say about it?

- Do you think that the predominant structure of marriage and the family renders women vulnerable or exploited? Can (or should) politics be concerned with such areas of life? How might feminists and communitarians differ on this issue and why?
- Can poststructuralist, liberal and socialist feminisms usefully be distinguished on the grounds that they have markedly different concepts of power? How do these different conceptions lead to differing political strategies?
- Is green political theory just a generally environmental ethic, or is it a new political theory altogether? If so, what is new about it?
- How do we understand 'nature'? Are our understandings of nature shaped by political ideology?
- Is the Enlightenment idea of reason implicated in the domination of nature? Is science 'bad' for nature?
- Is the critique of anthropocentrism made by some ecological theorists anti-humanist?
- Can liberal notions of the self, freedom, rights and property ever be made compatible with green thinking? What distinguishes liberal and green conceptions of self, society and nature?
- Is the problem of ecological crisis also a feminist issue? What are the core insights of the eco-feminist argument about the relationship between the domination of women and the domination of nature? Does eco-feminism reintroduce an essentialist notion of womanhood that other feminisms have tried to undermine?
- What is novel in the poststructuralist conception of political criticism? How might this affect concepts of the political?
- What connections might there be between the feminist, ecological and poststructuralist criticisms of Enlightenment?
- How do you think communitarians, feminists, liberals and poststructuralists might approach a concrete moral/political issue such as abortion, crime or genetic experimentation? Does one of these perspectives seem more helpful to you than others?

SECTION 3: FURTHER READING

Each of the areas examined in this section is an ever-growing and expanding one, featuring some of the most important and exciting debates in contemporary political theory. There are, for example, several useful collections of essays on communitarian political thought and the challenges it poses for liberalism. The reader is advised to start with the clear and insightful chapters on leading communitarian and liberal thinkers in Stephen Mulhall and Adam Swift's

Liberals and Communitarians (Blackwell, 1992), as well as the essays collected by S. Avineri and A. De-Shalit in *Communitarianism and Individualism* (Oxford University Press, 1992); see also F. D. Miller Jr and J. Paul (eds), *The Communitarian Challenge to Liberalism* (Cambridge University Press, 1996). Two perceptive essays on the dangers of overstating the communitarian–liberal dichotomy are A. Mason's 'Communitarianism and its Legacy', in Noel O'Sullivan (ed.), *Political Theory in Transition* (Routledge, 2000) and Simon Caney's 'Liberalism and Communitarianism: A Misconceived Debate', in *Political Studies* (1992: 273–90). Those interested in recent developments in communitarian thinking should consult the essays collected in Amitai Etzioni, *The Spirit of Community: Rights, Responsibilities and the Communitarian Agenda* (Fontana, 1995).

On feminist debates concerning the tension between the demands of equality and the recognition of difference, see the collection edited by G. Bock and S. James, *Beyond Equality and Difference: Citizenship, Feminist Politics and Female Subjectivity* (Routledge, 1992). b. hooks *Feminist Theory: From Margin to Center* (South End Press, 1984) considers race and gender issues. Also recommended are J. B. Landes (ed.), *Feminism, the Public and the Private* (Oxford University Press, 1998), Linda Nicholson, *Feminist Contentions: A Philosophical Exchange* (Routledge, 1995), Carol Pateman, *The Disorder of Women* Cambridge (Polity Press, 1989) and Anne Phillips's edited volume *Feminism and Politics* (Oxford University Press, 1998). For further investigation into French poststructuralist feminism, see Luce Irigaray's *Speculum of the Other Woman* (Cornell University Press, 1985) and *This Sex Which Is Not One* (Cornell University Press, 1985), as well as Julia Kristeva's *Revolution in Poetic Language* (Columbia University Press, 1984). Judith Butler's *Gender Trouble: Feminism and the Subversion of Identity* (Routledge, 1990) and the follow-up *Bodies that Matter: On the Discursive Limits of Sex* (Routledge, 1993) are both a kind of contemporary classic of poststructuralist feminism.

There is, of course, a very wide range of reading related to Green thinking. In addition to following up on the work of those represented here (Dobson, Goodin and Shiva), readers will probably find the following useful introductions: Robyn Eckersley, *Environmentalism and Political Theory* (State University of New York Press; UCL Press, 1992), Tim Hayward, *Ecological Thought: An Introduction* (Polity Press, 1995) and Luke Martell, *Ecology and Society: An Introduction* (Polity Press, 1994). On the idea of the natural, see Kate Soper, *What is Nature?* (Blackwell, 1995) and Michael E. Soule and Gary Lease (eds), *Reinventing Nature: Responses to Postmodern Deconstruction* (Island Press, 1995). On the issue of ecology and science, try George Robertson et al., *Future Natural: Nature, Science and Culture* (Routledge, 1996).

Those following the argument of Iain MacKenzie may wish to find out more about structuralism. A useful introduction is Terence Hawkes's *Structuralism and Semiotics* (Routledge, 1977), while Roland Barthes's *Image–Music–Text* (Fontana, 1977) is an illuminating and entertaining example of the method of analysis it proposed. For those really serious about sampling the structuralist approach, Claude Lévi-Strauss's *The Naked Man: Introduction to a Science of Mythology* (Jonathan Cape, 1981) may be a starting point, and reference has to be made to the founding text of Ferdinand de Saussure, *Course in General Linguistics* (Peter Owen, 1960 [1916]). The following are a selection of classic texts of poststructuralism: Hélène Cixous with Catherine Clément, *The Newly Born Woman* (University of Minnesota Press, 1986), Gilles Deleuze, *Difference and Repetition* (Columbia University Press, 1994), Gilles Deleuze and Felix Guattari, *Anti-Oedipus* (University of Minnesota Press, 1983) and also their *A Thousand Plateaus* (University of Minnesota Press, 1987). Felix Guattari's own work is also worth investigation. See his *Molecular Revolution* (Penguin, 1984).

Jacques Derrida's major works include *Of Grammatology* (Johns Hopkins University Press, 1976), *Margins – Of Philosophy* (University of Chicago Press, 1982) and *Spectres of Marx: The State of Debt, the Work of Mourning and the New International* (Routledge, 1994). Key works of Michel Foucault are *Discipline and Punish: The Birth of the Prison* (Penguin, 1977), *The History of Sexuality, Vol. 1: An Introduction* (Penguin, 1978) and *Power/Knowledge: Selected Interviews and Other Writings 1972–1977* (Harvester Wheatsheaf, 1980). Another variety of poststructuralism is that developed by Jean-François Lyotard in *Libidinal Economy* (Athlone, 1993) and his famous short book *The Postmodern Condition: A Report on Knowledge* (Manchester University Press, 1984).

For work that builds on poststructuralism and explicitly working within the concerns of political theory, the reader should follow up the thinkers mentioned at numerous points in this volume: William Connolly, *Identity/Difference: Democratic Negotiations of Political Paradox* (Cornell University Press, 1991) and Ernesto Laclau's *Emancipations* (Verso, 1996).

SECTION 4
NEW DIRECTIONS?

INTRODUCTION

Anyone who has read this volume in order from front to back may have noticed that, while a large number of themes have been touched upon, there is one that seems to recur insistently and that manifests itself in many different ways in each section. That theme is 'difference'. Its accompaniment is a challenge to political theories presumed to be universal in scope and application. Just consider the numerous contexts in which something like this has come up in the course of the book so far: Evans discussed Liberalism particularly in terms of the ways it might justify itself in a world marked by plurality and the absence of any single 'comprehensive doctrine' subscribed to by all; Carver considered post-Marxists who reject the totalising claims of Marxism and examine the multiple identities (in addition to social class) that might form political identities; Kenny examined communitarianism and its critique of Liberalism on the grounds that it is insensitive to communal contexts; Nash showed how contemporary debates in feminism are greatly shaped by the question of how the subject 'woman' is to be conceived and specifically of whether or not it can be understood as a universal category or identity; MacKenzie demonstrated that poststructuralism is basically a critique of philosophies that seek a pre-political unifying foundation rather than accept an irreducible plurality. This repetition attests to a very important shift in political thinking over the last thirty years and refers us back to something touched upon in the General Introduction. There, I argued that political theory today has to respond to the sorts of issue or problem created by current waves of social change. Among these, I highlighted presumed cultural globalisation and differentiation as well as the growth of **identity politics**. I also discussed, very briefly, the presumed collapse of 'grand narratives'. This was related in part, I argued, to the commingling of cultures and perspectives and to the related suspicion that the claims to universality made on behalf of European Enlightenment were in fact based on obscured or hidden particularisms.

This suspicion formed a starting point for the growth in importance of the idea of difference in political thought – the sense that our political concepts and practices have been far too reliant on presumptions about the universality of humanity and have downplayed the importance of the various things that differentiate us, and that political thought has proceeded on the basis of an assumption about the universal 'nature' of humanity and thus (wittingly or unwittingly) played a part in imposing a way of thinking and being upon others (which in turn may generate new and unacknowledged political problems and conflicts). In a number of ways, this final section is focused entirely upon this difference in a variety of contexts in which it manifests itself as a central theme in political thinking today as well as the challenges that it poses for us.

The first issue raised in this section is that of multiculturalism. In complex and plural societies, the population may come from many different cultural backgrounds; and peoples are increasingly asserting their need for a state that recognises this differentiation, whether it be the French Canadians, who think they should not be ruled in the same way as all the other Canadians, or minority populations within unitary states who, as a result of experiencing discrimination, exclusion or simply the dilution of their culture, demand that the state recognise their allegiance to it without expecting them to be exactly the same as everyone else. This raises difficult practical issues as well as theoretical and ethical ones.

As Modood and Favell demonstrate in Chapter 10, political theory is challenged by its being put to applied use. For here, unavoidably, the universalism of philosophical and academic approaches becomes a definite hindrance. This is especially the case when that to which one wants to apply the generality of political theory is the particular issues raised by cultural specificity. Can theories of multiculturalism and minority relations that have been developed in the contexts of North America be applied without serious revision to European contexts which have such a different history? Modood and Favell lay out a challenge to normative political philosophy and an alternative. Where political theory deals in a 'clean hands' way with actual policy and principle dilemmas, it should have a better understanding of how those in political or legal institutions make decisions and should try to build up a philosophical picture on the basis of an understanding of these contexts and on 'real-world' case studies. If political thought is to confront the facts of difference in our polities, then it too must be able to focus properly upon the differences of those polities. This might entail a specific way of 'doing' political theory in which a study of how institutions make decisions (and the values behind them) shapes normative theoretical assessment, which then feeds back into the original study, creating a virtuous circle in which theory can be both grounded in the actuality of the world and able to contribute ideals to it.

One of the central issues multiculturalism raises is that of religion in the context of cultural identity and diversity. Officially, Liberalism is committed to pluralism, and in the early history of liberal thought this meant religious pluralism and was translated into the demand for a neutral state that would not prescribe a particular form of worship to its citizens. The USA is probably the archetype of such a state founded in order to secure a space of religious freedom. But, more generally, one might say that a central feature of liberal democratic political societies is that no one group or ideology is able to take over the state and force it to reflect its particular world view and then impose it on others. But liberal societies have in practice not been so absolutely neutral. This has become clearer as society has become ever more obviously diverse. We noted in the General Introduction the proliferation of **identity politics**, of demands that particular identities, be they based on ethnicity, gender or sexuality, be properly respected as full members of the polity. Each of these can charge that what appears to be a free and open society is in fact not: that rights are afforded only to certain sorts of subject, to those who are of the dominant culture and to those who agree to fit into its ethic; that the state is not truly neutral because society itself isn't. Thus, for example, the liberal state has been asked to adopt policies that grant 'special' rights to some, usually minority, groups. However, this introduces an apparent contradiction into liberal principles. In order to make the neutral liberal society possible, the state has to be partial. Thus, Liberalism, in finding itself open to the charge that it is partial, can remedy itself only by being partial. This is an even greater problem when the liberal state is faced by those who are opposed to it: those who want not more openness but less. The archetype of this is the religious fundamentalist (of whatever sort), since one of the essential beliefs of such fundamentalism is that society ought to be organised in accordance with the principle of that religion and that an ungodly state is an unhealthy state. Can a liberal state accommodate to the demands of those who do not accept liberal principles? If it refuses to accommodate them, is it still a liberal state neutral with regard to citizens' conceptions of the 'good' life? In Chapter 10, Modood and Favell point out that too often our theories lack contextual sensitivity and so fail to understand what is and is not at stake in the conflicts that sometimes arise between religious cultures and the neutral state. It can be possible to resolve disputes if we properly understand the context of what is happening and appreciate the pragmatism behind some policy decisions.

The need for such sensitivity, now more than ever, extends across the globe. This is one reason why we have included a chapter on non-Western political thinking. It is a small gesture (perhaps tokenistic), but we do have to make a start at understanding across all borders; and, as Leaman points out in Chapter 11, the variety of forms of thought in each of the other regions in the world is as great as, sometimes greater than, the variety found within the tradition of the West. He then introduces us to work emerging from the Chinese, Japanese and Islamic traditions. Here too, we see the importance of the relationship between religion and the state. Buddhist themes permeate Japanese political thinking just as Islamic thought is central to the politics of the Middle East. We have seen in previous chapters that the question of communality, and the linked issue of religion, has never really left political thought of the West. It persists in forms of conservatism and has been resuscitated by the communitarian movement. It is interesting therefore to compare the ways in which Suzuki and Khomeini address the issue of religion with the themes that have run throughout this book. In some respects, the concerns of non-Western political thought are not very far removed from those of the West. Khomeini, for example, emphasises communality, shared values and social order in a way that is not at all foreign to Western ways of thinking. However, at the same time, his hard line and sectarian attitude (especially towards Jews) is likely to concern many.

There are also important 'real-world' political reasons for looking at the traditions of, say, China (the most populous nation on Earth, playing an increasingly large part in world politics, economics and culture), or of Islam, which is not only one of the major world religions but also the fastest-growing. The Christian liberal West has to understand these cultures and traditions, and it has to think about its relationship to them. That means appreciating their varied patterns of thought and establishing the points where they complement or conflict with each other. Khomeini and Mao were responding not only to intellectual currents but also to popular political discontents, and we need to understand this context if we are to establish the points of complement or contradiction between traditions. We also have to understand how our own traditions came about, since they too have been formed by leaders seeking to respond to and shape popular feeling. Perhaps the very division of politics and thought into that of the 'West' and 'the rest' is a political and theoretical problem in need of resolution (as if each region were really unified and grown from shared traceable roots, as if all the peoples of one part of the world share and agree on their interests and that these are the opposite of the shared interests of other peoples).

In Chapter 12 on the future of democracy, Smith presents a particular take on the ways in which the democratic experience should be furthered, focusing 'difference' to provide a radical perspective. She argues for a radical democracy understood as an extension of the rights of those communities or identities that have been excluded and seeking their inclusion but not incorporation. Drawing on the ideas of poststructuralist and post-Marxist writers (as discussed in Chapters 5 and 9), she outlines a different sort of approach to democratic theory rooted in a particular understanding of identity. The liberal tradition certainly sees itself as founded on a notion of the individual subject, but this is taken to be external to the theorisation and practice of liberal politics. MacKenzie argued that poststructuralism rejects this starting point in favour of a political theory of political theory. Here, Smith provides something like that. Building on Foucault and Butler, she focuses attention on how the practices of governmental institutions and other authorities serve to regulate and define us, in our bodies and in our selves 'constructing, authorising and policing' identities. This is more, then, than an extension of **identity politics**, for it raises the crucial and deeply problematic question of what identity is. She argues that we need to look not at identity so much as at identification, at how we attain a sense of identity by identifying with certain things which in turn are subject to policing and control. This means that the question ceases to be that of how we can balance the demands of rival identities in the context of some form of pluralism and becomes that of how we come to conceive of ourselves the way we do (and of how we might think ourselves anew). From this perspective, Smith advances a very radical form of egalitarianism linking into concerns about wealth and inequality as well as with 'recognition'. Her argument and approach has something of importance to say to those concerned with the application of political theory and with 'real-world' processes. She draws attention to the ways in which the discourses, the frames of thought and speech, within which legislators and officials consider policy-formation and change, can have encoded into them unjustifiable and highly prejudicial assumptions. As such, she shows how the work of political theory now always extends across the range of social relations and cannot be confined to a narrow sphere of governmental politics or law. Ultimately, this last section suggests that, despite arguments that politics has come to an end and there are no large-scale political conflicts to be addressed, we are in fact witnessing an extension of politics – upwards at the global level where different civilisations encounter each other, and downwards into the microscopic relations between ourselves. More than ever, it seems, thinking about politics is essential for life.

10

MULTICULTURALISM AND THE THEORY AND PRACTICE OF NORMATIVE POLITICAL THEORY

Adrian Favell and Tariq Modood

INTRODUCTION

Subjects can become 'hot' topics in seminar-room philosophy discussions for a variety of reasons. The salience of a particular subject politically, out in the 'real world' so to speak, is one important factor. Philosophy students are not impervious to political rioting in the streets or to a furious controversy raging in the daily press; and universities, despite their ivory-tower characterisation, can sometimes be the epicentre of contentious national and international political debate. Yet theoretical discussion can also turn to specific practical material for reasons internal to the field itself. The dynamics of a particular theoretical debate may itself drive protagonists to look for more applied examples that push theorising forward.

A mix of such reasons lie behind the popularity in normative political theory of applied references to multicultural dilemmas and issues of race, ethnicity and identity. Many such multicultural dilemmas – to do with the claims of group rights versus those of individuals, the fair representation of minority groups or demands made by liberal democratic citizenship on members of non-Western cultures – have indeed risen on the public political agenda in many Western countries in recent years. The experience of postcolonialism, the recognition of claims of oppressed native minorities, and the emergence of an Islamic presence in Western countries have all influenced the intellectual agenda of the philosophical seminar room.

However, this consciousness of the political salience of issues is not the whole story. The internal dynamic of an evolving debate within political philosophy has itself pushed practitioners to engage in applying political theorising outside of pure or abstract concerns of justice, equality, liberty and so on. That is for reasons to do with the advancement of the field of political philosophy itself. There has been an internal change, in other words, in the nature of political philosophy: the recognition that the practice of 'practical reason' actually does involve some engagement with real examples taken from everyday political and social issues. Much less common now are the unreal armchair examples familiar from the utilitarian 'thought experiments' once so beloved of moral and political philosophers. Theorists have come to believe that contributions to an engaged, politically aware form of multicultural theorising might actually cast some light on the murky business of actual political debate or public policy-making. They see that holding up clear principles of liberal-democratic practice (however counterfactual they might prove to be) might bear some relation to the actions and thinking of those who legislate or make decisions on these issues. This is, of course, a very different 'applied' goal for moral and political philosophers more used to seeing their work as a contribution to 'classic' issues in philosophy reflecting on 'timeless' thoughts of writers from the canon.

THE RAWLSIAN LEGACY

This is the first of four cleavages that we will use to make sense of the contemporary political philosophy of multiculturalism. The work of John Rawls, as in other applied debates, is absolutely central, but there is a big difference between those who read his work principally as a contribution to abstract debates about the nature of reason, equality, justice or pluralism – part of an ongoing dialogue with the fundamental issues found in **Aristotle, Hobbes, Locke, Hume, Mill** or (especially) **Kant** – and those inspired to think how his principles might actually enlighten political issues arising in contemporary liberal democratic societies. The canonical importance of his work, of course, lies in its suggestive powers to do *both*; but it is only the latter group of theorists – both followers and critics – that are of relevance and interest here.

The opening for applied multicultural theorists in the Rawlsian moral universe arose from the internal development of the Rawlsian framework as it moved from *A Theory of Justice* (1971) to *Political Liberalism* (1993). In the series of articles that marked this transition, Rawls became increasingly preoccupied with the problem of pluralism: the question of how individuals of different moral beliefs could be persuaded to believe in and affirm the basic principles of justice in a constitutional regime. As in **Locke**'s discussion of toleration, Rawls's focus on the limits of pluralism is imagined principally in terms of the political reconciliation of opposed *religious* views of the world, seeking a publicly recognised 'overlapping' consensus of common principles that would enable a workable framework of political decision-making. Other multicultural dilemmas do not really appear in Rawls's frame itself, but have been read in by successive interpretations seeking to push Rawls in a more applied, political direction.

Rawls's abstract and technical discussions on pluralism and consensus as the essence of liberal-democratic principled thinking became the starting point for all subsequent Anglo-American normative theory on the subject. It set the dominant axes of recent applied philosophical inquiry: centred around the reconciliation of Liberalism with communitarianism, universalism with the value of ethnic and cultural belonging, or equality with membership in a specific national society.

LIBERALS AND COMMUNITARIANS

Early interpreters of the field read the basic stand-off in terms of a second cleavage, as one between 'liberals' and 'communitarians' (for the best overview, see Mulhall and Swift, 1992). That is, between a liberal position that put the choices and **autonomy** of the individual as uppermost in any theory (Dworkin, 1977; Gutmann, 1985) and those who argued that a broader communal socialisation in a historically rooted culture was necessary to enable the preconditions of such individualism identified in the pure theory (Sandel, 1982; Raz, 1986; Taylor, 1994). As such, at a pure philosophical level, the debate was simply between two kinds of liberals, arguing about the source of reason and **autonomy** in a modern liberal democratic society: those of a Kantian disposition and those of a Hegelian one. However, under the influence of imported examples from current politics, the cleavage began to take the form of a tension between liberal Western values and the defence of non-Western traditions, minorities and immigrants.

The evolution of Will Kymlicka's work is a case in point, showing how the liberal and communitarian debate changed. *Liberalism, Community and Culture* (1989) was a predominantly abstract Oxford philosophy text, focusing on **Dworkin** and **Taylor**. *Multicultural Citizenship* (1995), however, was something very different, discussing the applied history of liberal principles on minorities, and wanting to engage with specific, contemporary hard cases. The text represents a high point of applied liberal thinking because, while retaining a core belief in liberal **autonomy**, it takes very seriously the sociological claim that any individualism needs community, culture and history to stand a chance of taking root: hence its strong defence of 'national' cultural contexts as sources of the liberal self. Yet, it also undoubtedly represented a crucial moment in another sense, of a pure discipline crossing the Rubicon into genuinely applied work. Unusually, it showed sensitivity and awareness (in both sociological and legal terms) of the complexity of real issues surrounding principally the native American population in liberal Canada. It is Kymlicka's example as perhaps the leading and most widely read applied theorist that has led to what he now points to as a 'liberal culturalist' consensus in the field (Kymlicka, 1998). The extract from *Multicultural Citizenship* (reproduced below) represents the heart of his liberal multiculturalism.

It is no accident that, in general, 'liberal culturalist' writers such as Kymlicka have offered the richest theorisations in contexts where the dilemmas are most sharply drawn and most pertinent to the issues dominating everyday politics. Canadian (and **Quebecois**) writers, particularly, have proven adept at translating the paradoxical difficulties of reconciling the rights of a minority dominant nation (**Quebec**) with the rights of native minorities and the rights of new immigrants in a multicultural, federal and multinational society (Carens, 2000; Beiner and Norman, 2000). These distinctive North American origins undoubtedly bias the theorisation. Yet there clearly is some weight in Kymlicka's distinction between the strong right of national indigenous minorities to territory, self-government and cultural lenience, and the much weaker rights of immigrant populations, who can only claim group rights provisions in order to ease the process of integration over time. It draws a tough but *prima facie* realistic line between the historical responsibilities of nations to populations they conquered and their ongoing prerogative to engage in the nation-building socialisation of new migrant groups who choose to stay and participate in the new host society. This line is, however, not going to work in all circumstances, and liberal culturalists are likely to find themselves facing rather stronger claims on behalf of newly naturalised ethnic minorities, who feel they have paid their due to the new society and that it should now offer them the chance of personal development in their own cultural terms. The question remains, then, as to what extent the central theoretical concepts of North American philosophy are informed by an experience that is different from that of Europe and where an uncritical application of the former to the latter is highly damaging.

For example, what in Britain is called multiculturalism (for example, the provision of **halal** meat in hospitals or the marking of **Diwali** by a school holiday), Kymlicka calls 'polyethnicity' (Kymlicka, 1995). His distinction between national minorities and voluntary migrants may be helpful for conceiving of immigration-derived polyethnicity in Canada, but it is less helpful for Britain. British 'polyethnicity' is a legacy of empire; most migrants came from states that had been incorporated into the British Empire in ways not dissimilar to the incorporations of 'nations' in Canada and the USA. These states contributed to Britain's economic development and to its superpower status; some migrants were ex-servicemen, with many others having relatives who had risked or given their lives for Britain. For the West Indians, England was the 'mother country'; for the children of the **Raj**, the Queen was the head of the British Commonwealth and the migrants were subjects of the Crown with free rights of entry, settlement and indeed British citizenship (albeit circumscribed by increasingly restrictive legislation). Moreover, most migrants came to meet Britain's demand for cheap labour. Migration from South Asia certainly did not consist of unconnected individuals but was largely structured through kinship networks, to the extent that sometimes streets and localities in England have been residentially constructed as extensions of **Punjabi** villages. Kymlicka's framework cannot capture these kinds of ties and so, inevitably, weakens the kinds of claims the 'new British' make upon Britain.

A further point of difference between Kymlicka's world and Britain is that at the core of British multiculturalism is South Asian religious ethnicity. Kymlicka does make some reference to issues concerning British Muslims, but the demands of religion are primarily conceived in terms of individual conscience, freedom of worship and the exemptions enjoyed by the **Amish** in the USA. This is a public-policy model of religion that might just fit parts of North America but is far too narrow to be helpful in Europe (Modood, 1998, 2001). Amy Gutmann's religious exceptionalism, too, seems to be an unacknowledged country-based argument. She recognises that multicultural equality between groups can take a neutralist or interventionist version and suggests that the former is more suited to religious groups and the latter to non-religious educational policy (Gutmann, 1994). No justification is offered for this differential approach except the implicit one that it reflects US constitutional and political arrangements.

Another controversial application has been debating the limits of minority-rights representation for territorial minorities in Eastern and Central Europe (Kymlicka, 2000). Kymlicka's ideas on nationhood push us dangerously towards ethnocultural secession if taken seriously in this context, but his crisp formulation does show why there is and has to be a stand-off between the drive for improved cultural rights and representation for minorities and the need to build (or rebuild) inclusive federal citizenship regimes that can include all within the nation. The toughness of these dilemmas has often led hard-line liberal individualists to denounce all culture-sensitive arguments as condoning the slippery slope to 'tribal' **identity politics** and the undermining of liberal values. A recent example of an attack on the liberal culturalist consensus – and the work of Kymlicka in particular – is Brian **Barry**'s *Culture and Equality* (2001).

RADICAL CRITIQUES

Besides pure versus applied theorising and the liberal–communitarian debate, a third helpful cleavage to make sense of the field is that between liberals and radicals. While the former are content to work within a clearly mainstream liberal framework that affirms the basic soundness of contemporary liberal democratic arrangements (this spans both liberals and communitarians in the original debate), the latter fundamentally reject it. Carrying forward the Marxist critical tradition in social and political theory, there came into this field writers influenced by the expansion of feminism and minority studies, and the more 'liberational' drive contained in multicultural **identity politics** springing from **postcolonial** critique or radical black politics, attacking the ethnocentrism of Western liberal values and promoting forms of cross-cultural dialogue with a relativist sensibility (Benhabib, 1992; Hall, 2000; Mouffe,1993; Said, 1978; Young, 1990).

Black and gender city politics in the USA has provided one context within which some of this work hits home, though it might be said that even more important have been the fierce American campus debates over multiculturalism in the curriculum. The USA has provided several issues in which multicultural dilemmas become clear: for example, legal dilemmas about positive discrimination; the under-representation of the black populations; or the provision of Spanish language in a predominantly anglophone society. It is Iris Marion Young's work which best captures the thrust of US-centred radical multiculturalism. Much of her thinking was built on an explicit critique of Rawls. It challenged an important blind spot in all mainstream liberal thinking: the inescapable effects of power, domination and historical oppression on the political and personal chances of true participation for minority and ethnic groups. Young's catch-all rainbow coalition of distinct minority interests – spanning women, the old and the disabled, racial and ethnic groups, immigrant minorities and indigenous native populations – in fact adds up to a majority of the population of any country. Indeed, it means anyone not white, male and middle-class. But leaving this absurdity aside – and the fact that religious minorities are comprehensively omitted – the theory did bring back to centre stage a sociological concern with the effects of substantive inequality on people's ability to choose, and a political scientist's awareness of the pervasiveness of power. Notably, she emphasised the distorting effects of so-called neutral institutions which, in fact, reflect and embody sedimented, historically legitimated patterns of power and interest. She is also the philosopher who best expressed and advocated a conception of equality that incorporated a politics of 'difference' – of a refusal to conform to a dominant culture – as brought out in the extract reproduced below.

Some ex-Marxists, especially in social theory and cultural studies, have argued that groups do not have the unitary character that political theorists and others assume, and that culture needs to be analysed as an interactive process rather than a fixed set of properties (Gilroy, 1987; Hall, 1992). The central idea is that ethnic identities are not pure or static but change in new circumstances or by sharing social space with other heritages and influences. Blackness, for example, is necessarily a **syncretic** identity, for it has historically grown alongside, in interaction with, and influenced by dominant and dissenting European or white cultural forms (Gilroy, 1993). This lack of pure identities means that minority groups are not homogeneous and cannot be represented through formal group structures. The mixing of populations and the influences of global media cultures is such that many people are refusing to be defined by their ethnic descent or any one group, but consciously create new identities for themselves and cultural expressions to celebrate their **hybridity**. In his latest work, **Gilroy** identifies the bonds of racial solidarity as one of the biggest obstacles to moving forward towards a new 'planetary humanism' (Gilroy, 2000).

Other inheritors of the Marxist tradition have themselves seen their objections to the contemporary liberal-democratic order melt away as they test their ideals on the hard edge of ethnic or nationalist dilemmas. In these situations, an anti-liberal critique can end up pointing back towards quite illiberal conclusions. It is highly significant that the great German inheritor of the Marxist social-theoretical tradition – Jürgen **Habermas** – has come to converge on a

Rawlsian-style logic in recent years, despite their widely different starting points in classic sociological theory and classic political philosophy respectively. His 'ideal speech' communication situation – in which the iniquities of power and the unevenness of relativist difference are ironed out into a space in which some kind of principled constitutional agreement can be found – resembles very closely Rawlsian ideals of the **overlapping consensus**. Where Habermas differs is in his explicitly cosmopolitan vision of these principles being embodied in a post-national (European) order that has transcended the traditional liberal idea of citizenship in the democratic nation state, in favour of an international order based on rights and international co-operation (Habermas, 1992). This is also echoed in the writings of French theorists (Ferry, 1992; Kastoryano, 1998). Moreover, some radicals go on to hold up a post-Marxist mirror to the iniquities of the current world order, balancing the idealist implications of a 'real' enforced human-rights regime and global redistribution against the sullied limitations of the actual human-rights regime and liberal capitalist system we in fact live in (Held, 1996; Castles and Davidson, 2000).

In part, the emergence of this style of global normative theory owes a lot to the fallout of the post-1989 'end of history' period. It forced a search for a new kind of critical idealism that might at least embrace the liberal principles seen to be embodied in the demise of the Marxist alternative. Hence the emergence of a new left-leaning Kantianism, embracing human rights and idealisations of justice. So, while one set of ex-Marxists emphasised 'difference' and the need for a popular 'cultural revolution' and the capture of civil society on behalf of the excluded, another looked for constitutional human-rights solutions at an international level.

But there is no easy place to stand, and the imperfections of 'actually existing' liberal practice as seen in empirical institutions and policy perhaps reflect better the efforts of Liberalism to deal with these dilemmas than the abstract efforts of theorists. These institutions have, after all, emerged after decades of dealing with policy dilemmas in an adequately complex yet sufficiently pragmatic and principled way. So much 'ideal' theory simply trades in a naively unsullied attitude to the world that it never really has to deal with. The interesting point here is that both hard-line liberals and Marxist cosmopolitans are **postpositivists**. All of the theorists so far discussed reject the mainstream disciplinary view of other social sciences, instead arguing first that value-free social-policy research is undesirable (they believe that what they are doing is inherently normative, politically engaged and so on), but also that the work they do can claim a privileged, moral 'objective' standpoint for ideal 'constitutive' theory (the liberals) or a 'clean hands' critique (the Marxists) that prescribes changing the world in its own image.

THE CONTEXTUALIST CRITIQUE

What this form of **postpositivism** forecloses is any constructive engagement with the kinds of methodologies basic to other social-science disciplines, stressing the need for empirical comparative approaches before any generalisations can be drawn. The lack of awareness often shown by political theorists of all kinds for the logic and substantive findings of empirical researchers working on similar topics is striking. Any responsible and genuinely contextual engagement with the way liberal politics and institutions actually work would surely demand this. A fourth cleavage might be drawn here, then, between pure theorists and those whose theorising fits with and interacts with the methodology of mainstream political and social sciences.

Seen this way, the oft-derided 'communitarianism' of Michael **Walzer**, for example, in this respect reveals itself much more to be a position that follows from his empirically sensitive, methodological approach to 'doing' liberal political philosophy than an artificial opposition with individualist liberals. **Walzer**, in his work, sets out a wholly different way of generating philosophical judgements through interpretation and historical analogy. It is clear when reading *Spheres of Justice* (1983) that this is a work which, unlike that of Rawls, sits easily alongside the givens of other disciplines such as history, anthropology, sociology, social psychology and empirical political science. **Walzer** thus prefers to read off liberal principles interpretively from the liberal-democratic institutions that we in fact inhabit, seeking a complex historical argument about the principles that have emerged, and the inner logic that gives them progressive force. Such theory shows a Wittgensteinian awareness of the futility of searching for essences, understanding family resemblances within Liberalism instead; and of the different trajectories that historical examples of liberal democracy have taken. Meaning and context are made primary in the work of the philosopher.

A good example of how this gets lost in the work of so many theorists is the celebrated case of *l'affaire foulard* in France – when three girls were prevented from attending school for insisting on wearing the Islamic headscarf in class. It has been typically read in seminar-room discussions as a dilemma for an ideal law-maker that decided to uphold a tough, individualist French republican line against the 'communitarian' claim of an ethnic religious community. In fact, this anecdotal way of picturing the story scarcely does any justice at all to the complexity of the case. The case was the first controversial outburst in a pattern of similar cases over a number of years, which did indeed provoke a typically liberal multicultural dilemma, but were in fact decided in an opposite way to the philosophical edict by the French *Conseil d'État*, for largely pragmatic reasons. Their reasoning embodied the institutionalised translation of the issue into a longer public political and legal process, which eventually, by deliberation and contestation, produced a result consistent with Republican principles of respect for religion and pragmatic considerations about the evolution of Islam in France. A comparative understanding of the case would have revealed how it was solved in a way not so different to the British or Dutch pragmatism in this area, despite the dramatic differences in the kind of ideological rhetoric used in republican public discussions in France (Favell, 2001). The case basically demonstrated the reluctance of the state to intervene in an area where space for cultural tolerance had already been allowed by its withdrawal from legislative intervention in this area.

The example crops up in recent work by Bhikhu Parekh, which offers much suggestive thinking on how more contextual sensitivity might be incorporated into political philosophy. He is a leading proponent of the grounding of political philosophy through discussion of real multicultural dilemmas and is unusual in that the majority of the cases he explores are religious. Reproduced below is his elaboration of his philosophy through relating it to the *foulard* case. It is, however, preceded by an extract which states an original aspect of his theory. He points out that liberal arguments about why culture matters to individuals cannot reach the purported conclusion that cultural diversity matters. It can make the majority aware that minority cultures matter to their members – but that's only an indirect argument for diversity. For Parekh, multiculturalism is not about the rights of minority cultures but about the value of cultural diversity. The value of the presence of a variety of cultures in a society cannot be understood as increasing our options, for other cultures are rarely options for us. Rather, their sense of contrast gives us a deeper understanding of our own culture and makes us reflect on and learn about the diversity of humanity.

Other suggestive contextual styles of doing political theory can be found in the work of **Elster** (1992) or Goodin (1995), in which the everyday mechanisms of policy-making or the reasoning of the state are broken down to reveal the mix of principles and pragmatism that drives decision-making on hard cases. As yet, none of the theorists associated with this branch of analytical political theory have sought to apply their insights to the playing-out of multicultural dilemmas in actual institutional contexts. As Favell argues (2001) in his full-length exploration along these lines of multicultural issues in France and Britain, there is a richly promising line of philosophical work here: the comparative normative analysis of how actual existing liberal institutions have dealt with multiculturalism in the post-war period. This would fundamentally reject the ideal 'clean hands' philosophising that has dominated the field. In exploring the false application of North American theories to European examples of multiculturalism, and the development of a new case-study-led theoretical methodology, Modood, Favell and others are now pursuing this line of work. While recognising the vitality and productiveness of reflection inspired by the pluralist turn in Rawls's later works, it does need to be asked whether this paradigm for the translation of multicultural dilemmas into principled liberal policy positions is at all the right one. It is surely alarming that this style of normative 'applied' thinking in fact has little or no connection with the way public-policy scholars themselves might study the question.

WHAT IS WRONG WITH APPLIED POLITICAL PHILOSOPHY?

Theoretically minded researchers and students turned to these various applied political philosophies of multiculturalism because they provided clear, problem-generating analytical frameworks for the kind of discussions that thrive in seminar-room discussion. The *apparent* congruence between how theorists have pictured ethnic and multicultural dilemmas, and the way an ideal legislator or policy-maker might approach the subject, has encouraged them in the thought that such theories might capture the essence of the political problem as faced by practitioners. For sure, there is much enlightenment to be had from clear reflection on the normative principles at work in liberal reasoning. However, as we have suggested, such a way of approaching real-life policy problems is, to the say the least, an odd way of characterising the nature of issues as they in fact appear in real legal or policy-making situations. The idealisation of how judgements are made in liberal democracy in fact works through a dangerous denial of this fact, which creates a gap between the idealised articulation of how liberal democracy *should* work and the empirical understanding of how in fact people in decision-making positions make decisions – usually through a combination of pragmatism, institutional habit and (perhaps) a sense of principle. The real limitations of contemporary political philosophy emerge here. There are at least three key problems with the approach as it is practised in the seminar room, arising from its disconnection from other social-scientific ways of understanding the way policy and legal decisions are actually made by institutions.

One is the unfortunately *anecdotal* nature of the 'hard cases' as they tend to get portrayed in philosophical material. This is endemic to even the very best philosophical work. Studies almost never grow out of comparative empirical methods and inquiry. Instead, theorists tend simply to rely on the unchallenged reproduction of anecdotal facts usually taken from newspapers, everyday discussion, or other theorists. Invariably, these 'examples' fail to do justice to the complex context from which a hard case might be taken. Examples are ripped from complex political and social circumstances that might have a variety of different possible interpretations and which always need to be given a full history in order to capture the nature of the dilemma. The 'clean hands' reasoning of political philosophers also misses the element of practical reasoning that must be aware of possible consequences and perverse effects of any principled line. Without this, it is impossible to capture dilemmas as they are faced by a judge or policy-maker only too aware of all the historical, political or symbolic stakes that might be riding on a particular liberal decision. Moreover, any empirical study builds into its methodology a logic for the selection of representative case studies, leaving the possibility that the researchers' initial hypothesis might be refuted. Philosophers, magpie-like, simply take what best suits their argument, ensuring that their reading of the case will become self-fulfilling interpretations.

Linked to this, it can also be said that the overwhelmingly *specific origins* of some of the most popular theoretical discussions in Canada and the USA actually might do violence to the varieties and complexities of other cases in other geographical locations. When solutions to European dilemmas on Islam or racism are proposed which take their inspiration from norms more appropriate to the North American continent of voluntary immigration or a North American rights-based legal system, we are likely to mischaracterise completely the nature and logic of solutions as they might be found in Europe. In Europe, liberal policy solutions reflect a context where limited immigration, often shaped by colonial histories, confronts ongoing nation-building projects in old nation states, and where more mobilisation-based forms of citizenship, not law, have provided forms of minority representation. Again, any kind of comparative empirical methodology would teach theorists not to generalise for all liberal democracies across inappropriately matched comparisons.

Finally, it needs to be pointed out that political philosophers, because they are thinking constitutionally, are always *thinking for the state*; they are state-centred by definition. This way of thinking, however, may miss many of the true sources of multiculturalism in Western liberal societies, which are multicultural not only because the state legislates for these practices, with positive rights, entitlements and policy frameworks, but also because of what it does *not* do. Many Western liberal states became multicultural by default because of the *laissez-faire* attitude of the state towards cultural or market-led mechanisms that would have been very difficult to legislate for in terms of the state-centred logic of rights or citizenship.

Other ways, then, might be found to do normative work on multiculturalism in liberal democracies that step definitively out of the paradigm laid by Rawls and followers. Better applied political philosophy would link itself more with mainstream empirical approaches in other social sciences. One necessary crossover is the missing interaction between liberal theorists and the empirical comparative-institutional study of immigration, citizenship and ethnic politics which has, in Europe particularly, focused on the ways these issues get translated differently into different national contexts (Koopmans and Statham, 2000). A variety of key normative issues are thrown up by these comparative efforts: the political process of creating rights (or anti-discrimination laws) for migrants/minorities; the recognition of diverse 'ethnic' groups as the way in which different groups are recognised/categorised for policy/legal purposes; or the mobilisation opportunities/channels that are opened up and used by different ethnic groups. There is a need to recognise differences as much as commonalities between and within North American and European cases, and a constant need to build history and the comparison of differences within liberal democracies into any normative reflections on the 'nature' or 'essence' of Liberalism. And beyond this, there is a need for much deeper reflection among normative theorists about the sociological basis of integration or successful multiculturalism: 'the mystery of ties that bind', as Kymlicka calls it.

The challenge here is to bring normative theory back *within* mainstream empirical theories of society and politics, fully integrating historical, political science and sociological insights into the characterisation of normative questions. It remains to be seen if the ongoing development of the field of political philosophy can provide much more here, short of the kind of methodological overhaul we would prescribe in the application of theorising to actual cases and examples. It would seem that the most interesting theorists – such as Will Kymlicka or Bhikhu Parekh – are those most willing to incorporate a genuinely empirical sensibility into the work they do. But this step, of necessity, is likely to push such theorists further into considering more explicitly empirical and comparative methodologies. Political philosophers have at least put a toe in the Rubicon, and one or two have got their feet wet. It remains to be seen if any are prepared to cross it fully.

'FREEDOM AND CULTURE' BY WILL KYMLICKA

At the time of writing, the Canadian political theorist Will Kymlicka is Professor of Philosophy at Queen's University in Ontario, Canada. He is a leading liberal political philosopher emphasising aspects of community and culture that he believes have been underappreciated by liberalism. This has led him to a great interest in questions of multiculturalism and to the attempt to specify clearly the rights of minority cultures throughout the world. He is one of the most widely read and debated political theorists of multiculturalism, though his arguments are not uncontroversial. An important book is his *Liberalism, Community and Culture* (Clarendon, 1989). The extract below is from *Multicultural Citizenship: A Liberal Theory of Minority Rights* (Clarendon, 1995). Here, while staying firmly within the liberal framework, Kymlicka argues for the intrinsic value of membership within a group or shared culture on the grounds that this alone gives meaning to the choices we make regarding the 'good' life. But, unlike communitarians, he does not see this as grounds for restricting freedom, advocating that people should be able (and are able) to stand back a little and assess the merits of their ideas of the good. Consequently, he endorses a broader (or thinner) notion of the community than the hard-line communitarians.

'FREEDOM AND CULTURE' (1995)*

Will Kymlicka

[. . .]

LIBERALISM AND INDIVIDUAL FREEDOM

I believe that societal cultures are important to people's freedom, and that liberals should therefore take an interest in the viability of societal cultures. To show this, however, I need briefly to consider the nature of freedom, as it is conceived within the liberal tradition.[1]

The defining feature of liberalism is that it ascribes certain fundamental freedoms to each individual. In particular, it grants people a very wide freedom of

---

* From Will Kymlicka, *Multicultural Citizenship: A Liberal Theory of Minority Rights* (Oxford: Oxford University Press, 1995), pp. 80–93.

choice in terms of how they lead their lives. It allows people to choose a conception of the good life, and then allows them to reconsider that decision, and adopt a new and hopefully better plan of life.

Why should people be free to choose their own plan of life? After all, we know that some people will make imprudent decisions, wasting their time on hopeless or trivial pursuits. Why then should the government not intervene to protect us from making mistakes, and to compel us to lead the truly good life? There are a variety of reasons why this is not a good idea: governments may not be trustworthy; some individuals have idiosyncratic needs which are difficult for even a well-intentioned government to take into account; supporting controversial conceptions of the good may lead to civil strife. Moreover, paternalistic restrictions on liberty often simply do not work – lives do not go better by being led from the outside, in accordance with values the person does not endorse. Dworkin calls this the 'endorsement constraint', and argues that 'no component contributes to the value of a life without endorsement . . . it is implausible to think that someone can lead a better life against the grain of his profound ethical convictions than at peace with them' (Dworkin 1989: 486).[2]

However, the fact that we can get it wrong is important, because (paradoxically) it provides another argument for liberty. Since we can be wrong about the worth or value of what we are currently doing, and since no one wants to lead a life based on false beliefs about its worth, it is of fundamental importance that we be able rationally to assess our conceptions of the good in the light of new information or experiences, and to revise them if they are not worthy of our continued allegiance.[3]

This assumption that our beliefs about the good life are fallible and revisable is widely endorsed in the liberal tradition – from John Stuart Mill to the most prominent contemporary American liberals, such as John Rawls and Ronald Dworkin. (Because of their prominence, I will rely heavily on the works of Rawls and Dworkin in the rest of this chapter.) As Rawls puts it, individuals 'do not view themselves as inevitably tied to the pursuit of the particular conception of the good and its final ends which they espouse at any given time'. Instead, they are 'capable of revising and changing this conception'. They can 'stand back' from their current ends to 'survey and assess' their worthiness (Rawls 1980: 544; cf. Mill 1982: 122; Dworkin 1983).

So we have two preconditions for leading a good life. The first is that we lead our life from the inside, in accordance with our beliefs about what gives value to life. Individuals must therefore have the resources and liberties needed to lead their lives in accordance with their beliefs about value, without fear of discrimination or punishment. Hence the traditional liberal concern with individual privacy, and opposition to 'the enforcement of morals'. The second precondition is that we be free to question those beliefs, to examine them in light of whatever information, examples, and arguments our culture can provide. Individuals must therefore have the conditions necessary to acquire an awareness of different views about the good life, and an ability to examine these views intelligently. Hence the equally traditional liberal concern for education, and freedom of expression and association. These liberties enable us to judge what is valuable, and to learn about other ways of life.

It is important to stress that a liberal society is concerned with both of these preconditions, the second as much as the first. It is all too easy to reduce individual liberty to the freedom to pursue one's conception of the good. But in fact much of what is distinctive to a liberal state concerns the forming and revising of people's conceptions of the good, rather than the pursuit of those conceptions once chosen.

Consider the case of religion. A liberal society not only allows individuals the freedom to pursue their existing faith, but it also allows them to seek new adherents for their faith (proselytization is allowed), or to question the doctrine of their church (heresy is allowed), or to renounce their faith entirely and convert to another faith or to atheism (apostasy is allowed). It is quite conceivable to have the freedom to pursue one's current faith without having any of these latter freedoms. There are many examples of this within the Islamic world. Islam has a long tradition of tolerating other monotheistic religions, so that Christians and Jews can worship in peace. But proselytization, heresy, and apostasy are generally prohibited. This was true, for example, of the 'millet system' of the Ottoman Empire. Indeed, some Islamic states have said the freedom of conscience guaranteed in the Universal Declaration of Human Rights should not include the freedom to change religion (Lerner 1991: 79–80). Similarly, the clause in the Egyptian constitution guaranteeing freedom of conscience has been interpreted so as to exclude freedom of apostasy (Peters and de Vries 1976: 23). In such a system, freedom of conscience means there is no forced conversion, but nor is there voluntary conversion.

A liberal society, by contrast, not only allows people to pursue their current way of life, but also gives them access to information about other ways of life (through freedom of expression), and indeed requires children to learn about other ways of life (through mandatory education), and makes it possible for people to engage in radical revision of their ends (including apostasy) without legal penalty. These aspects of a liberal society only make sense on the assumption that revising one's ends is possible, and sometimes desirable, because one's current ends are not always worthy of allegiance. A liberal society does not compel such questioning and revision, but it does make it a genuine possibility.

SOCIETAL CULTURES AS CONTEXT OF CHOICE

I have just outlined what I take to be the predominant liberal conception of individual freedom. But how does this relate to membership in societal cultures? Put simply, freedom involves making choices among various options, and our societal culture not only provides these options, but also makes them meaningful to us.

People make choices about the social practices around them, based on their beliefs about the value of these practices (beliefs which, I have noted, may be wrong). And to have a belief about the value of a practice is, in the first instance, a matter of understanding the meanings attached to it by our culture.

Societal cultures involve 'a shared vocabulary of tradition and convention' which underlies a full range of social practices and institutions (Dworkin 1985: 231). To understand the meaning of a social practice, therefore, requires understanding this 'shared vocabulary' – that is, understanding the language and history which constitute that vocabulary. Whether or not a course of action has any significance for us depends on whether, and how, our language renders vivid to us the point of that activity. And the way in which language renders vivid these activities is shaped by our history, our 'traditions and conventions'. Understanding these cultural narratives is a precondition of making intelligent judgements about how to lead our lives. In this sense, our culture not only provides options, it also 'provides the spectacles through which we identify experiences as valuable' (Dworkin 1985: 228).[4]

[. . .]

This argument about the connection between individual choice and culture provides the first step towards a distinctively liberal defence of certain group-differentiated rights. For meaningful individual choice to be possible, individuals need not only access to information, the capacity to reflectively evaluate it, and freedom of expression and association. They also need access to a societal culture. Group-differentiated measures that secure and promote this access may, therefore, have a legitimate role to play in a liberal theory of justice.[5]

This connection between individual choice and societal cultures raises three obvious questions. (1) Is individual choice tied to membership in one's *own* culture, or is it sufficient for people to have access to some or other culture? (2) If (as I will argue) people have a deep bond to their own culture, should immigrant groups be given the rights and resources necessary to recreate their own societal cultures? (3) What if a culture is organized so as to preclude individual choice – for example, if it assigns people a specific role or way of life, and prohibits any questioning or revising of that role?

THE VALUE OF CULTURAL MEMBERSHIP

I have tried to show that people's capacity to make meaningful choices depends on access to a cultural structure. But why do the members of a national minority need access to their *own* culture?[6] Why not let minority cultures disintegrate, so long as we ensure their members have access to the majority culture (e.g. by teaching them the majority language and history)? This latter option would involve a cost to minorities, but governments could subsidize it. For example, governments could pay for the members of national minorities to learn about the majority language and history.

This sort of proposal treats the loss of one's culture as similar to the loss of one's job. Language training for members of a threatened culture would be like worker retraining programmes for employees of a dying industry. We do not feel obliged to keep uncompetitive industries afloat in perpetuity, so long as we help employees to find employment elsewhere, so why feel obliged to protect minority cultures, so long as we help their members to find another culture?

This is an important question. It would be implausible to say that people are never able to switch cultures. After all, many immigrants function well in their new country (although others flounder and many return home). Waldron thinks that these examples of successful 'cosmopolitan' people who move between cultures disprove the claim that people are connected to their own culture in any deep way. Suppose, he says, that

> a freewheeling cosmopolitan life, lived in a kaleidoscope of cultures, is both possible and fulfilling . . . Immediately, one argument for the protection of minority cultures is undercut. It can no longer be said that all people need their rootedness in the particular culture in which they and their ancestors were reared in the way that they need food, clothing, and shelter . . . (Waldron 1992a: 762)

Because people do not need their own culture, minority cultures can ('at best') claim the same negative rights as religious groups – that is, the right to non-interference, but not to state support.

I think Waldron is seriously overstating the case here. For one thing, he vastly overestimates the extent to which people do in fact move between cultures, because (as I discuss below) he assumes that cultures are based on ethnic descent. On his view, an Irish-American who eats Chinese food and reads her child *Grimms' Fairy-Tales* is thereby 'living in a kaleidoscope of cultures' (e.g. Waldron 1992a: 754). But this is not moving between societal cultures. Rather it is enjoying the opportunities provided by the diverse societal culture which characterizes the anglophone society of the United States.

Of course, people do genuinely move between cultures. But this is rarer, and more difficult. In some cases, where the differences in social organization and technological development are vast, successful integration may be almost impossible for some members of the minority. (This seems to be true of the initial period of contact between European cultures and indigenous peoples in some parts of the world.)

But even where successful integration is possible, it is rarely easy. It is a costly process, and there is a legitimate question whether people should be required to pay those costs unless they voluntarily choose to do so. These costs vary, depending on the gradualness of the process, the age of the person, and the extent to which the two cultures are similar in language and history.[7] But even where the obstacles to integration are smallest, the desire of national minorities to retain their cultural membership remains very strong (just as the members of the majority culture typically value their cultural membership).

In this sense, the choice to leave one's culture can be seen as analogous to the choice to take a vow of perpetual poverty and enter a religious order. It is not impossible to live in poverty. But it does not follow that a liberal theory of justice should therefore view the desire for a level of material resources above bare subsistence simply as 'something that particular people like and enjoy' but which 'they no longer can claim is something that they need' (Waldron 1992a: 762). Liberals rightly assume that the desire for non-subsistence resources is so normal – and the costs of forgoing them so high for most people's way of life – that people cannot reasonably be *expected* to go without such resources, even if a few people voluntarily choose to do so.

[. . .]

[As Rawls says,] cultural ties 'are normally too strong to be given up, and this fact is not to be deplored'. Hence, for the purposes of developing a theory of justice, we should assume that 'people are born and are expected to lead a complete life' within the same 'society and culture' (Rawls 1993a: 277).

I agree with Rawls's view about the difficulty of leaving one's culture.[8] Yet his argument has implications beyond those which he himself draws. Rawls presents this as an argument about the difficulty of leaving one's political community. But his argument does not rest on the value of specifically political ties (e.g. the bonds to one's government and fellow citizens). Rather it rests on the value of cultural ties (e.g. bonds to one's language and history). And cultural boundaries may not coincide with political boundaries. For example, someone leaving East Germany for West Germany in 1950 would not be breaking the ties of language and culture which Rawls emphasizes, even though she would be crossing state borders. But a francophone leaving Quebec City for Toronto, or a Puerto Rican leaving San Juan for Chicago, would be breaking those ties, even though she is remaining within the same country.

According to Rawls, then, the ties to one's culture are normally too strong to give up, and this is not to be regretted. We cannot be expected or required to make such a sacrifice, even if some people voluntarily do so. It is an interesting question why the bonds of language and culture are so strong for most people. It seems particularly puzzling that people would have a strong attachment to a liberalized culture. After all, as a culture is liberalized – and so allows members to question and reject traditional ways of life – the resulting cultural identity becomes both 'thinner' and less distinctive. That is, as a culture becomes more liberal, the members are less and less likely to share the same substantive conception of the good life, and more and more likely to share basic values with people in other liberal cultures.

The Québécois provide a nice illustration of this process. Before the Quiet Revolution, the Québécois generally shared a rural, Catholic, conservative, and patriarchal conception of the good. Today, after a rapid period of liberalization, most people have abandoned this traditional way of life, and Québécois society now exhibits all the diversity that any modern society contains – e.g. atheists and Catholics, gays and heterosexuals, urban yuppies and rural farmers, socialists and conservatives, etc. To be a 'Québécois' today, therefore, simply means being a participant in the francophone society of Quebec. And francophones in Quebec no more agree about conceptions of the good than anglophones in the United States. So being a 'Québécois' seems to be a very thin form of identity.

[. . .]

In short, liberalization in Quebec has meant both an increase in differences among the Québécois, in terms of their conceptions of the good, and a reduction in differences between the Québécois and the members of other liberal cultures. This is not unique to Quebec. The same process is at work throughout Europe. The modernization and liberalization of Western Europe has resulted both in fewer commonalities within each of the national cultures, and greater commonalities across these cultures. As Spain has liberalized, it has become both more pluralistic internally, and more like France or Germany in terms of its modern, secular, industrialized, democratic, and consumerist civilization.

This perhaps explains why so many theorists have assumed that liberalization and modernization would displace any strong sense of national identity. As cultures liberalize, people share less and less with their fellow members of the national group, in terms of traditional customs or conceptions of the good life, and become more and more like the members of other nations, in terms of sharing a common civilization. Why then would anyone feel strongly attached to their own nation? Such an attachment seems, to many commentators, like the 'narcissism of minor differences' (Ignatieff 1993: 21; Dion 1991).

Yet the evidence is overwhelming that the members of liberal cultures *do* value their cultural membership. Far from displacing national identity, liberalization has in fact gone hand in hand with an increased sense of nationhood. Many of the liberal reformers in Quebec have been staunch nationalists, and the nationalist movement grew in strength throughout the Quiet Revolution and afterwards. The same combination of liberalization and a strengthened national identity can be found in many other countries. For example, in Belgium, the liberalization of Flemish society has been accompanied by a sharp rise in nationalist sentiment (Peterson 1975: 208). The fact that their culture has become tolerant and pluralistic has in no way diminished the pervasiveness or intensity of people's desire to live and work in their own culture. Indeed, Walker Connor goes so far as to suggest that few if any examples exist of recognized national groups in this century having voluntarily assimilated to another culture, even though many have had significant economic incentives and political pressures to do so (Connor 1972: 350–1; 1973: 20).

Why are the bonds of language and culture so strong for most people? Commentators offer a number of reasons. Margalit and Raz argue that membership in a societal culture (what they call a 'pervasive culture') is crucial to people's well-being for two reasons. The first reason is the one I have discussed above – namely, that cultural membership provides meaningful options, in the sense that 'familiarity with a culture determines the boundaries of the imaginable'. Hence if a culture is decaying or discriminated against, 'the options and opportunities open to its members will shrink, become less attractive, and their pursuit less likely to be successful' (Margalit and Raz 1990: 449).

But why cannot the members of a decaying culture simply integrate into another culture? According to Margalit and Raz, this is difficult, not only because it is 'a very slow process indeed', but also because of the role of cultural membership in people's self-identity. Cultural membership has a 'high social profile', in the sense that it affects how others perceive and respond to us, which in turn shapes our self-identity. Moreover, national identity is particularly suited to serving as the 'primary foci of identification', because it is based on belonging, not accomplishment:

> Identification is more secure, less liable to be threatened, if it does not depend on accomplishment. Although accomplishments play their role in people's sense of their own identity, it would seem that at the most fundamental level our sense of our own identity depends on criteria of belonging rather than on those of accomplishment. Secure identification at that level is particularly important to one's well-being.

Hence cultural identity provides an 'anchor for [people's] self-identification and the safety of effortless secure belonging'. But this in turn means that people's self-respect is bound up with the esteem in which their national group is held. If a culture is not generally respected, then the dignity and self-respect of its members will also be threatened (Margalit and Raz 1990: 447–9). Similar arguments about the role of respect for national membership in supporting dignity and self-identity are given by Charles Taylor (1992a) and Yael Tamir (1993: 41, 71-3).

[. . .]

No doubt all of these factors play a role in explaining people's bond to their own culture. I suspect that the causes of this attachment lie deep in the human condition, tied up with the way humans as cultural creatures need to make sense of their world, and that a full explanation would involve aspects of psychology, sociology, linguistics, the philosophy of mind, and even neurology (Laponce 1987).

But whatever the explanation, this bond does seem to be a fact, and, like Rawls, I see no reason to regret it. I should emphasize, again, that I am only dealing with general trends. Some people seem most at home leading a truly cosmopolitan life, moving freely between different societal cultures. Others have difficulty making sense of the cultural meanings within their own culture. But most people, most of the time, have a deep bond to their own culture.

It may seem paradoxical for liberals like Rawls to claim that the bonds to one's culture are 'normally too strong to be given up'. What has happened to the much-vaunted liberal freedom of choice? But Rawls's view is in fact common within the liberal tradition. The freedom which liberals demand for individuals is not primarily the freedom to go beyond one's language and history, but rather the freedom to move around within one's societal culture, to distance oneself from particular cultural roles, to choose which features of the culture are most worth developing, and which are without value.

This may sound like a rather 'communitarian' view of the self. I do not think this is an accurate label. One prominent theme in recent communitarian writing is the rejection of the liberal view about the importance of being free to revise one's ends. Communitarians deny that we can 'stand apart' from (some of) our ends. According to Michael Sandel, a leading American communitarian, some of our ends are 'constitutive' ends, in the sense that they define our sense of personal identity (Sandel 1982: 150–65; cf. MacIntyre 1981: ch. 15; Bell 1993: 24–54). It makes no sense, on his view, to say that my ends might not be worthy of my allegiance, for they define who I am. Whereas Rawls claims that individuals 'do not regard themselves as inevitably bound to, or identical with, the pursuit of any particular complex of fundamental interests that they may have at any given moment' (1974: 641), Sandel responds that we are in fact 'identical with' at least some of our final ends. Since these ends are constitutive of people's identity, there is no reason why the state should not reinforce people's allegiance to those ends, and limit their ability to question and revise these ends.

I believe that this communitarian conception of the self is mistaken. It is not easy or enjoyable to revise one's deepest ends, but it is possible, and sometimes a regrettable necessity. New experiences or circumstances may reveal that our earlier beliefs about the good are mistaken. No end is immune from such potential revision. As Dworkin puts it, it is true that 'no one can put everything about himself in question all at once', but it 'hardly follows that for each person there is some one connection or association so fundamental that it cannot be detached for inspection while holding others in place' (Dworkin 1989: 489).

Some people may think of themselves as being incapable of questioning or revising their ends, but in fact 'our conceptions of the good may and often do change over time, usually slowly but sometimes rather suddenly', even for those people who think of themselves as having constitutive ends (Rawls 1985: 242). No matter how confident we are about our ends at a particular moment, new circumstances or experiences may arise, often in unpredictable ways, that cause us to re-evaluate them. There is no way to predict in advance when the need for such a reconsideration will arise. As I noted earlier, a liberal society does not compel people to revise their commitments – and many people will go years without having any reason to question their basic commitments – but it does recognize that the freedom of choice is not a one-shot affair, and that earlier choices sometimes need to be revisited.

Since our judgements about the good are fallible in this way, we have an interest, not only in pursuing our existing conception of the good, but also in being able to assess and potentially revise that conception. Our current ends are not always worthy of our continued allegiance, and exposure to other ways of life helps us make informed judgements about what is truly valuable.

The view I am defending is quite different, therefore, from the communitarian one, although both views claim that we have a deep bond to a particular sort of social group. The difference is partly a matter of scope. Communitarians typically talk about our attachment to subnational groups – churches, neighbourhoods, family, unions, etc. – rather than to the larger society which encompasses these subgroups. But this difference in scope reflects an even deeper divergence. Communitarians are looking for groups which are defined by a shared conception of the good. They seek to promote a 'politics of the common good', in which groups can promote a shared conception of the good, even if this limits the ability of individual members to revise their ends. They believe that members have a 'constitutive' bond to the group's values, and so no harm is done by limiting individual rights in order to promote shared values.

As most communitarians admit, this 'politics of the common good' cannot apply at the national level. As Sandel puts it, 'the nation proved too vast a scale across which to cultivate the shared self-understandings necessary to community in the . . . constitutive sense' (Sandel 1984: 93; cf. MacIntyre 1981: 221; Miller 1988–9: 60–7). The members of a nation rarely share moral values or traditional ways of life. They share a language and history, but often disagree fundamentally about the ultimate ends in life. A common national identity, therefore, is not a useful basis for communitarian politics, which can only exist at a more local level.

The liberal view I am defending insists that people can stand back and assess moral values and traditional ways of life, and should be given not only the legal right to do so, but also the social conditions which enhance this capacity (e.g. a liberal education). So I object to communitarian politics at the subnational level. To inhibit people from questioning their inherited social roles can condemn them to unsatisfying, even oppressive lives.[9] And at the national level, the very fact which makes national identity so inappropriate for communitarian politics – namely, that it does not rest on shared values – is precisely what makes it an appropriate basis for liberal politics. The national culture provides a meaningful context of choice for people, without limiting their ability to question and revise particular values or beliefs.

Put another way, the liberal ideal is a society of free and equal individuals. But what is the relevant 'society'? For most people, it seems to be their nation. The sort of freedom and equality they most value, and can make most use of, is freedom and equality within their own societal culture. And they are willing to forgo a wider freedom and equality to ensure the continued existence of their nation.

For example, few people favour a system of open borders, where people could freely cross borders and settle, work, and vote in whatever country they desired. Such a system would dramatically increase the domain within which people would be treated as free and equal citizens. Yet open borders would also make it more likely that people's own national community would be overrun by settlers from other cultures, and that they would be unable to ensure their survival as a distinct national culture. So we have a choice between, on the one hand, increased mobility and an expanded domain within which people are free and equal individuals, and, on the other hand, decreased mobility but a greater assurance that people can continue to be free and equal members of their own national culture. Most people in liberal democracies clearly favour the latter. They would rather be free and equal within their own nation, even if this means they have less freedom to work and vote elsewhere, than be free and equal citizens of the world, if this means they are less likely to be able to live and work in their own language and culture.

[. . .]

NOTES

1. The following argument is presented in much more detail in Kymlicka 1989a: chs 2–4; 1990: ch. 6.
2. Liberals often make an exception where individuals are particularly vulnerable to weakness of will (e.g. paternalistic legislation against addictive drugs). The connection between rational revisability, the endorsement constraint, and the liberal prohibition on state paternalism is quite complicated. For Rawls's discussion of perfectionism, see Rawls 1988: 260, 265. For Dworkin's account, see 1989: 486–7; 1990. For general discussions see Kymlicka 1989b; Waldron 1989; Moore 1993: ch. 6; Caney 1991; Mason 1990; McDonald 1992: 116–21; Hurka 1994.
3. Allen Buchanan calls this the 'rational revisability' model of individual choice (Buchanan 1975). The claim that we have a basic interest in being able rationally to assess and revise our current ends is often phrased in terms of the value of 'autonomy'. This label may be misleading, since there are many other conceptions of autonomy. For example, on one account of autonomy, the exercise of choice is intrinsically valuable, because it reflects our rational nature (this view is ascribed to Kant). Another account of autonomy argues that nonconformist individuality is intrinsically valuable (this view is often ascribed to Mill). I am making the more modest claim that choice enables us to assess and learn what is good in life. It presupposes the we have an essential interest in identifying and revising those of our current beliefs about value which are mistaken. When I use the term autonomy, therefore, it is in this (relatively modest) sense of 'rational revisability'. I discuss these different conceptions of autonomy in Kymlick 1989a: ch. 4; 1990: ch. 6.
4. I discuss this in greater length in Kymlicka 1989a: ch. 8; 1995. Of course, the models we learn about in our culture are often closely related to the models in other cultures. For example, models derived from the Bible will be part of the structure of many cultures with a Christian influence. And there are international bodies, like the Catholic Church, which actively seek to ensure this commonality among models in different cultures. So in saying that we learn about conceptions of the good life through our culture, I do not mean to imply that the goods are therefore culture-specific, although some are.
5. In Rawls's terminology, we can say that access to such a culture is a 'primary good' i.e. a good which people need, regardless of their particular chosen way of life, since it provides the context within which they make those particular choices. I explore how this argument relates to Rawls's account of 'primary goods' in more depth in Kymlicka 1989a: ch. 7. For related arguments about the dependence of freedom on culture, see Taylor 1985; Tamir 1993: chs 1–2; Margalit and Raz 1990.
6. I am trying to respond here to the cogent questions raised by Binder 1993: 253–5; Buchanan 1991: 54–5; Waldron 1992; Tomasi 1995; Nickel 1995; Lenihan 1991; Margalit and Halbertal 1994, among others.

7. For a discussion of these costs, and the extent to which they vary between children and adults, see Nickel 1995.

8. It is worth remembering that, while many immigrants flourish in their new country, there is a selection factor at work. That is, those people who choose to uproot themselves are likely to be the people who have the weakest psychological bond to the old culture, and the strongest desire and determination to succeed elsewhere. We cannot assume *a priori* that they represent the norm in terms of cultural adaptability. As John Edwards notes, the ability to communicate does not only involve pragmatic language skills, but also the 'inexpressible' knowledge of historical and cultural associations tied up with the language, and this may be difficult or impossible for immigrants to acquire fully: 'the symbolic value of language, the historical and cultural associations which it accumulates, and the "natural semantics of remembering" all add to the basic message a rich underpinning of shared connotations . . . the ability to read between the lines, as it were, depends upon a cultural continuity in which the language is embedded, and which is not open to all. Only those who grow up within the community can, perhaps, participate fully in this expanded communicative interaction' (Edwards 1985: 17).

9. The danger of oppression reflects the fact that many traditional roles and practices were defined historically on the basis of sexist, racist, classist, and homophobic assumptions. Some social roles are so compromised by their unjust origins that they should be rejected entirely, not just gradually reformed (Phillips 1993). In some places, Sandel qualifies his idea of constitutive ends in a way that suggests that people can, after all, stand back and assess even their most deeply held ends. But once these qualifications are added in, it is no longer clear how Sandel's conception of the person differs from the liberal one he claims to be criticizing (see Kymlicka 1989a: chs 2–4; 1990: ch. 5). In his more recent work, Rawls has attempted to accommodate the communitarian view and defend liberalism without insisting on the rational revisability of our ends. I do not think his new defence works.

REFERENCES

Binder, Guyora (1993), 'The Case for Self-Determination', *Stanford Journal of International Law*, 29: 223–70.

Buchanan, Allen (1975), 'Revisability and Rational Choice', *Canadian Journal of Philosophy*, 5: 395–408.

Buchman, Allen (1991), *Secession: The Legitimacy of Political Divorce* (Westview Press, Boulder, Col.).

Caney, Simon (1991), 'Consequentialist Defenses of Liberal Neutrality', *Philosophical Quarterly*, 41/165: 457–77.

Dworkin, Ronald (1989), 'Liberal Community', *California Law Review*, 77/3: 479–504.

Edwards, John (1985), *Language, Society and Identity* (Blackwell, Oxford).

Hurka, Thomas (1994), 'Indirect Perfectionism: Kymlicka on Liberal Neutrality', *Journal of Political Philosophy*.

Kymlicka, Will (1989a), *Liberalism, Community, and Culture* (Oxford University Press, Oxford).

——(1989b), 'Liberal Individualism and Liberal Neutrality', *Ethics*, 99/4: 883–905.

——(1990), *Contemporary Political Philosophy: An Introduction* (Oxford University Press, Oxford).

——(1995), 'Dworkin on Freedom and Culture', in Justine Burley (ed.), *Reading Dworkin* (Blackwell, Oxford).

Lenihan, Donald (1991), 'Liberalism and the Problem of Cultural Membership', *Canadian Journal of Law and Jurisprudence*, 4/2: 401–19.

McDonald, Michael (1992), 'Liberalism, Community, and Culture', *University of Toronto Law Journal*, 42: 113–31.

Margalit, Avishai and Moshe Halbertal (1994) 'Liberalism and the Right to Culture', *Social Research*, 61/3: 491–510.

Margalit, Avishai and Joseph Raz (1990), 'National Self-Determination', *Journal of Philosophy*, 87/9: 439–61.

Mason, Andrew (1990), 'Autonomy, Liberalism and State Neutrality', *Philosophical Quarterly*, 40/160: 433–52.

Moore, Margaret (1993), *Foundations of Liberalism* (Oxford University Press, Oxford).

Nickel, James (1995), 'The Value of Cultural Belonging: Expanding Kymlicka's Theory', *Dialogue*, 33/4: 635–42.

Phillips, D. Z. (1993), *Looking Backward: A Critical Appraisal of Communitarian Thought* (Princeton University Press, Princeton, NJ).

Rawls, John (1988), 'The Priority of Right and Ideas of the Good', *Philosophy and Public Affairs*, 17/4: 251–76.

Tamir, Yael (1993), *Liberal Nationalism* (Princeton University Press, Princeton, NJ).

Taylor, Charles (1985), *Philosophy and the Human Sciences: Philosophical Papers 2* (Cambridge University Press, Cambridge).

Tomasi, John (1995), 'Kymlicka, Liberalism, and Respect for Cultural Minorities', *Ethics*, 105/3: 580–603.

Waldron, Jeremy (1989), 'Autonomy and Perfectionism in Raz's *Morality of Freedom*', *Southern California Law Review*, 62/3–4: 1,097–152.

——(1992), 'Minority Cultures and the Cosmopolitan Alternative', *University of Michigan Journal of Law Reform*, 25/3: 751–93.

'OPPRESSION AND GROUP DIFFERENCE' BY IRIS MARION YOUNG

We have already encountered Young (in Chapter 7, where a fuller description of her work can be found). This extract is from *Justice and the Politics of Difference*. Here, Young argues (in a way similar to the previous extract) that being blind to group differences can actually lead to the perpetuation of oppression. She is thus critical of the ideal of assimilation and presents a strong case in favour of fully recognising group difference which, she argues, will promote equality, enhance solidarity and promote self-government. This sort of radical democratic pluralism can usefully be considered in relation to the different approaches to pluralism expressed by Mouffe or Berlin.

'OPPRESSION AND GROUP DIFFERENCE' (1990)*

Iris Marion Young

Though in many respects the law is now blind to group differences, some groups continue to be marked as deviant, as the Other. In everyday interactions, images, and decisions, assumptions about women, Blacks, Hispanics, gay men and lesbians, old people, and other marked groups continue to justify exclusion, avoidance, paternalism, and authoritarian treatment. Continued racist, sexist, homophobic, ageist, and ableist institutions and behavior create particular circumstances for these groups, usually disadvantaging them in their opportunity to develop their capacities. Finally, in part because they have been segregated from one another, and in part because they have particular histories and traditions, there are cultural differences among social groups – differences in language, style of living, body comportment and gestures, values, and perspectives on society.

Today in American society, as in many other societies, there is widespread agreement that no person should be excluded from political and economic activities because of ascribed characteristics. Group differences nevertheless continue to exist, and certain groups continue to be privileged. Under these circumstances, insisting that equality and liberation entail ignoring difference has oppressive consequences in three respects.

---

* From Iris Marion Young, *Justice and the Politics of Difference* (Princeton, NJ: Princeton University Press, 1990), pp. 164–8.

First, blindness to difference disadvantages groups whose experience, culture, and socialized capacities differ from those of privileged groups. The strategy of assimilation aims to bring formerly excluded groups into the mainstream. So assimilation always implies coming into the game after it is already begun, after the rules and standards have already been set, and having to prove oneself according to those rules and standards. In the assimilationist strategy, the privileged groups implicitly define the standards according to which all will be measured. Because their privilege involves not recognizing these standards as culturally and experientially specific, the ideal of a common humanity in which all can participate without regard to race, gender, religion, or sexuality poses as neutral and universal. The real differences between oppressed groups and the dominant norm, however, tend to put them at a disadvantage in measuring up to these standards, and for that reason assimilationist policies perpetuate their disadvantage.

Second, the ideal of a universal humanity without social group differences allows privileged groups to ignore their own group specificity. Blindness to difference perpetuates cultural imperialism by allowing norms expressing the point of view and experience of privileged groups to appear neutral and universal. The assimilationist ideal presumes that there is a humanity in general, an unsituated group-neutral human capacity for self-making that left to itself would make individuality flower, thus guaranteeing that each individual will be different. Because there is no such unsituated group-neutral point of view, the situation and experience of dominant groups tend to define the norms of such a humanity in general. Against such a supposedly neutral humanist ideal, only the oppressed groups come to be marked with particularity; they, and not the privileged groups, are marked, objectified as the Others.

Thus, third, this denigration of groups that deviate from an allegedly neutral standard often produces an internalized devaluation by members of those groups themselves. When there is an ideal of general human standards according to which everyone should be evaluated equally, then Puerto Ricans or Chinese Americans are ashamed of their accents or their parents, Black children despise the female-dominated kith and kin networks of their neighborhoods, and feminists seek to root out their tendency to cry, or to feel compassion for a frustrated stranger. The aspiration to assimilate helps produce the self-loathing and double consciousness characteristic of oppression. The goal of assimilation holds up to people a demand that they 'fit', be like the mainstream, in behavior, values, and goals. At the same time, as long as group differences exist, group members will be marked as different – as Black, Jewish, gay – and thus as unable simply to fit. When participation is taken to imply assimilation, the oppressed person is caught in an irresolvable dilemma: to participate means to accept and adopt an identity one is not, and to try to participate means to be reminded by oneself and others of the identity one is.

A more subtle analysis of the assimilationist ideal might distinguish between a conformist and a transformational ideal of assimilation. In the conformist ideal, status-quo institutions and norms are assumed as given, and disadvantaged groups who differ from those norms are expected to conform to them. A transformational ideal of assimilation, on the other hand, recognizes that institutions as given express the interests and perspective of the dominant groups. Achieving assimilation therefore requires altering many institutions and practices in accordance with neutral rules that truly do not disadvantage or stigmatize any person, so that group membership really is irrelevant to how persons are treated. Wasserstrom's ideal fits a transformational assimilation, as does the group-neutral ideal advocated by some feminists (Taub and Williams, 1987). Unlike the conformist assimilationist, the transformational assimilationist may allow that group-specific policies, such as affirmative action, are necessary and appropriate means for transforming institutions to fit the assimilationist ideal. Whether conformist or transformational, however, the assimilationist ideal still denies that group difference can be positive and desirable; thus any form of the ideal of assimilation constructs group difference as a liability or disadvantage.

Under these circumstances, a politics that asserts the positivity of group difference is liberating and empowering. In the act of reclaiming the identity the dominant culture has taught them to despise (Cliff, 1980), and affirming it as an identity to celebrate, the oppressed remove double consciousness. I am just what they said I am – a Jewboy, a colored girl, a fag, a dyke, or a hag – and proud of it. No longer does one have the impossible project of trying to become something one is not under circumstances where the very trying reminds one of who one is. This politics asserts that oppressed groups have distinct cultures, experiences, and perspectives on social life with humanly positive meaning, some of which may even be superior to the culture and perspectives of mainstream society. The rejection and devaluation of one's culture and perspective should not be a condition of full participation in social life.

Asserting the value and specificity of the culture and attributes of oppressed groups, moreover, results in a relativizing of the dominant culture. When feminists assert the validity of feminine sensitivity and the positive value of nurturing behavior, when gays describe the prejudice of heterosexuals as homophobic and their own sexuality as positive and self-developing, when Blacks affirm a distinct Afro-American tradition, then the dominant culture is forced to discover itself for the first time as specific: as Anglo, European, Christian, masculine, straight. In a political struggle where oppressed groups insist on the positive value of their specific culture and experience, it becomes increasingly difficult for dominant groups to parade their norms as neutral and universal, and to construct the values and behavior of the oppressed as deviant, perverted, or inferior. By puncturing the universalist claim to unity that expels some groups and turns them into the Other, the assertion of positive group specificity introduces the possibility of understanding the relation between groups as merely difference, instead of exclusion, opposition, or dominance.

The politics of difference also promotes a notion of group solidarity against the individualism of liberal humanism. Liberal humanism treats each person as an individual, ignoring differences of race, sex, religion, and ethnicity. Each person should be evaluated only according to her or his individual efforts and achievements. With the institutionalization of formal equality, some members of formerly excluded groups have indeed succeeded, by mainstream standards. Structural patterns of group privilege and oppression nevertheless remain. When political leaders of oppressed groups reject assimilation, they are often affirming group solidarity. Where the dominant culture refuses to see anything but the achievement of autonomous individuals, the oppressed assert that we shall not separate from the people with whom we identify in order to 'make it' in a white Anglo male world. The politics of difference insists on liberation of the whole group of Blacks, women, American Indians, and that this can be accomplished only through basic institutional changes. These changes must include group representation in policy-making and an elimination of the hierarchy of rewards that forces everyone to compete for scarce positions at the top.

Thus the assertion of a positive sense of group difference provides a standpoint from which to criticize prevailing institutions and norms. Black Americans find in their traditional communities, which refer to their members as 'brother' and 'sister', a sense of solidarity absent from the calculating individualism of white professional capitalist society. Feminists find in the traditional female values of nurturing a challenge to a militarist world-view, and lesbians find in their relationships a confrontation with the assumption of complementary gender roles in sexual relationships. From their experience of a culture tied to the land, American Indians formulate a critique of the instrumental rationality of European culture that results in pollution and ecological destruction. Having revealed the specificity of the dominant norms which claim universality and neutrality, social movements of the oppressed are in a position to inquire how the dominant institutions must be changed so that they will no longer reproduce the patterns of privilege and oppression.

From the assertion of positive difference, the self-organization of oppressed groups follows. Both liberal humanist and leftist political organizations and movements have found it difficult to accept this principle of group autonomy. In a humanist emancipatory politics, if a group is subject to injustice, then all those interested in a just society should unite to combat the powers that perpetuate that injustice. If many groups are subject to injustice, moreover, then they should unite to work for a just society. The politics of difference is certainly not against coalition, nor does it hold that, for example, whites should not work against racial injustice or men against sexist injustice. This politics of group assertion, however, takes as a basic principle that members of oppressed groups need separate organizations that exclude others, especially those from more privileged groups. Separate organization is probably necessary in order for these groups to discover and reinforce the positivity of their specific experience, to collapse and eliminate double consciousness. In discussions within autonomous organizations, group members can determine their specific needs and interests. Separation and self-organization risk creating pressures toward homogenization of the groups themselves, creating new privileges and exclusions. But contemporary emancipatory social movements have found group autonomy an important vehicle for empowerment and the development of a group-specific voice and perspective.

Integration into the full life of the society should not have to imply assimilation to dominant norms and abandonment of group affiliation and culture (Edley, 1986; cf. McGary, 1983). If the only alternative to the oppressive exclusion of some groups defined as Other by dominant ideologies is the assertion that they are the same as everybody else, then they will continue to be excluded because they are not the same.

Some might object to the way I have drawn the distinction between an assimilationist ideal of liberation and a radical democratic pluralism. They might claim that I have not painted the ideal of a society that transcends group differences fairly, representing it as homogeneous and conformist. The free society envisaged by liberalism, they might say, is certainly pluralistic. In it, persons can affiliate with whomever they choose; liberty encourages a proliferation of lifestyles, activities, and associations. While I have no quarrel with social diversity in this sense, this vision of liberal pluralism does not touch on the primary issues that give rise to the politics of difference. The vision of liberation as the transcendence of group difference seeks to abolish the public and political significance of group difference, while retaining and promoting both individual and group diversity in private, or non-political, social contexts. This way of distinguishing public and private spheres, where the public represents universal citizenship and the private individual differences, tends to result in group exclusion from the public. Radical democratic pluralism acknowledges and affirms the public and political significance of social group differences as a means of ensuring the participation and inclusion of everyone in social and political institutions.

'CULTURAL DIVERSITY AND EQUALITY' BY BHIKHU PAREKH

At the time of writing, Bhikhu Parekh (Lord Parekh of Kingston-upon-Hull) is Professor of Political Theory at the University of Hull. He is a leading figure in debates about multiculturalism in Britain and abroad, in his capacity as a political theorist and as a member of the House of Lords (one of the two Houses of Parliament, the British legislature). He has written numerous works on aspects of political theory including Liberalism, and also on aspects of Indian political philosophy (see e.g. *Gandhi's Political Philosophy: A Critical Examination*, Macmillan, 1989). His most recent work, *Rethinking Multiculturalism: Cultural Diversity and Political Theory* (Macmillan, 2000), has been an important contribution to a much wider debate. It links in with *The Future of Multi-Ethnic Britain* (Profile Books, 2000), the report of a Commission on the Future of Multi-Ethnic Britain that was chaired by Parekh. In this extract (from *Rethinking Multiculturalism*), Parekh develops a new argument in favour of cultural diversity that stresses the importance of being in contact with radically different cultures from our own because they challenge us (and give us the opportunity) to think through what is good and bad about the way we live and see things. He then goes on to consider a particular case where cultural diversity became a source of conflict – *l'affaire foulard* in France. Parekh shows the need properly to contextualise the case in hand and suggests this has important implications for the way we conceive of equal treatment for communities. Because the arguments presented here touch so much on the nature of politics and governance, they can helpfully be considered in conjunction with other writers also found in this volume, including Young and Butler.

'CULTURAL DIVERSITY' (2000)*

Bhikhu Parekh

CULTURAL DIVERSITY

Cultural diversity or the presence of a variety of cultures and cultural perspectives within a society has much to be said for it. The first systematic case for it was made by J. S. Mill, Humboldt, Herder and others and has been recently

---

* From Bhikhu Parekh, *Rethinking Multiculturalism: Cultural Diversity and Political Theory* (London: Macmillan, 2000), pp. 165–8, 249–54, 256.

restated with important modifications by Berlin, Raz and Kymlicka in particular. Briefly, they advance one or more of the following four arguments in support of it. First, cultural diversity increases the available range of options and expands freedom of choice. Since it values other cultures only as options or potential objects of choice, it gives no good reason to value such cultures as those of indigenous peoples, religious communities, the Amish or the Gypsies which are not realistic options for us. Indeed, the argument implies that the more different other cultures are from our own, the less reason we have to cherish them. As we shall see, the opposite is often the case. It does not make out a convincing case for mainstream cultures either. Since we are deeply shaped by our culture and find it too much of a moral and emotional wrench to give it up or radically revise it or even introduce into it the beliefs and practices of another, other mainstream cultures are rarely options for us. Furthermore, the argument gives no good reason to cherish cultural diversity to those who are perfectly happy with their culture and have no wish to add to the options provided by it.

Second, some writers argue that since human beings are culturally embedded, they have a right to their culture, and that cultural diversity is an inescapable and legitimate outcome of the exercise of that right. This argument shows the inescapability but not the desirability of cultural diversity. It establishes why membership of one's culture is important but not why cultural diversity is; why one should enjoy access to one's own culture, not why one should also have access to others. Furthermore, giving individuals a right to their culture does not by itself ensure cultural diversity. If the wider society has an assimilationist thrust, or if the dominant culture is overpowering and respects and rewards only those who conform to it, members of other cultures would lack the capacity, the confidence and the incentive to retain their cultures, leading over time to the withering-away of cultural diversity. It is therefore not enough to grant them the formal right to their culture. Society should also create conditions conducive to the exercise of that right, such as respect for differences, nurturing minority self-confidence, and provision of additional resources to those in need of them. The wider society would not wish to incur the cost involved, welcome the required changes in its institutions and way of life, and restrain its assimilationist impulse unless it can be persuaded that cultural diversity is in its interest or a value worth cherishing.

Third, Herder, Schiller and other romantic liberals advance an aesthetic case for cultural diversity, arguing that it creates a rich, varied and aesthetically pleasing and stimulating world. They make a valid point, but it is too weak and vague to carry the moral burden placed on it. Aesthetic considerations are a matter of taste, and it is not easy to convince those who prefer a uniform moral and social world. Cultures, furthermore, are not merely objects of aesthetic contemplation. They are moral systems, and we need to show that their diversity is not only aesthetically but also morally justified. If we cannot, as the monist insists, then either the moral case for uniformity overrides the aesthetic one for diversity or we need to find some way of resolving their conflict.

Finally, Mill, Humboldt and others link cultural diversity to individuality and progress, arguing that it encourages a healthy competition between different systems of ideas and ways of life, and both prevents the dominance of any one of them and facilitates the emergence of new truths. Although Mill weakened the force of this argument by tying it too closely to a particular view of human excellence, it contains important insights. However, it suffers from several limitations. It takes a largely instrumental view of cultural diversity and does not appreciate its intrinsic value. Since it stresses progress, it also needs to provide criteria of it; these are not only difficult to agree upon but predetermine the outcome of cultural diversity and delimit its permissible range – hardly the way to encourage the unexpected and the new. Finally, since cultural diversity is linked to competition, it cannot defend the rights of indigenous peoples, the Amish, orthodox religious groups and others who have no wish either to compete or to discover new truths.

Although a convincing case for cultural diversity must include these and other arguments, I suggest that it can best be made by approaching the subject from a different perspective. Since human capacities and values conflict, every culture realizes a limited range of them and neglects, marginalizes and suppresses others. However rich it might be, no culture embodies all that is valuable in human life and develops the full range of human possibilities. Different cultures thus correct and complement each other, expand each other's horizon of thought and alert each other to new forms of human fulfilment. The value of other cultures is independent of whether or not they are options for us. Indeed, they are often valuable precisely because they are not. Although a native people's way of life is not an option for us, it serves important cultural purposes. By cherishing such commendable values and sensibilities as harmony with nature, a sense of ecological balance, contentment, innocence and simplicity, which our way of life has to sacrifice in order to attain its characteristic form of excellence, it both reminds us of our limitations and reassures us that the values are not lost altogether. Its unassimilable otherness challenges us intellectually and morally, stretches our imagination, and compels us to recognize the limits of our categories of thought.

Cultural diversity is also an important constituent and condition of human freedom. Unless human beings are able to step out of their culture, they remain imprisoned within it and tend to absolutize it, imagining it to be the only natural or self-evident way to understand and organize human life. And they cannot step out of their culture unless they have access to others. Although human beings lack an Archimedean standpoint or a 'view from nowhere', they do have mini-Archimedean standpoints in the form of other cultures that enable them to view their own from the outside, tease out its strengths and weaknesses, and deepen their self-consciousness. They are able to see the contingency of their culture and relate to it freely rather than as a fate or a predicament. Since cultural diversity fosters such vital preconditions of human freedom as self-knowledge, self-transcendence and self-criticism, it is an objective good, a good whose value is derived not from individual choices but from its being an essential condition of human freedom and well-being (Weinstock, 1994).

The diversity of cultures also alerts us to that within our own. Used to seeing differences between cultures, we tend to look for them within our own and learn to do them justice. We appreciate that our culture is a product of different influences, contains different strands of thought, and is open to different interpretations. This makes us suspicious of all attempts to homogenize it and impose on it a simplified and singular identity. It also encourages an internal dialogue within the culture, creates a space for critical and independent thought, and nurtures its experimental vitality. Tolerance of external and internal differences [allows them to] complement and reinforce each other. A culture or a religion that considers itself the best and suppresses others or fears and avoids contacts with them tends to take a unified and homogeneous view of itself and suppress its internal differences and ambiguities as well.

Cultural diversity creates a climate in which different cultures can engage in a mutually beneficial dialogue. Different artistic, literary, musical, moral and other traditions interrogate, challenge and probe each other, borrow and experiment with each other's ideas, and often throw up wholly new ideas and sensibilities that none of them could have generated on their own. What creative writers do at a sophisticated level, ordinary men and women do unselfconsciously in their daily encounters. A British Indian taking invasive pictures at a religious ceremony was gently asked by an English friend if that was a common practice in India and did not offend the feelings of the gathering. The Indian and his friends got the message and behaved better on future occasions. When their white colleague died, an Afro-Caribbean asked their common white friend to join him in calling on the widow. His friend reluctantly agreed, was pleasantly surprised by her welcome, and came to appreciate that the largely unquestioned English practice of leaving the bereaved alone could do with a change. In these and other ways, communities educate and even 'civilize' each other provided, of course, that none is too overbearing and self-righteous to welcome criticism. They also represent different talents, skills, forms of imagination, ways of looking at things, forms of social organization, different senses of humour, and psychological and moral energies, all of which constitute a most valuable resource which can be fruitfully harnessed in such different areas of life as scholarship, sports, business, management, creative arts, industry and government.

[. . .]

CONTEXTUALIZING EQUALITY

Sometimes we know what is relevant in a given context, but find it difficult to decide if two individuals are equal in relation to it. Take *l'affaire du foulard*, which first surfaced in France in September 1989 and has haunted it ever since.[1] Three Muslim girls from North Africa, two of them sisters, wore the *hijab* (headscarf) to their ethnically mixed school in Creil, some 60 km, north of Paris. In the previous year twenty Jewish students had refused to attend classes on Saturday mornings and autumn Friday afternoons when the Sabbath arrived before the close of the school, and the headmaster, a black Frenchman from the Caribbean, had to give in after initially resisting them. Worried about the trend of events, he objected to the Muslim girls wearing the *hijab* in the classroom on the grounds that it went against the *laïcité* of French state schools. Since the girls refused to comply, he barred them from attending the school. As a gesture of solidarity, many Muslim girls throughout France began to wear *hijabs* to school, and the matter acquired national importance. To calm the situation, the Education Minister, Lionel Jospin, sought an opinion (*avis*) from the *Conseil d'État*. The *Conseil* ruled in November 1989 that pupils had a right to express and manifest their religious beliefs within state schools and that the *hijab* did not violate the principle of *laïcité*, provided that such religious insignia did not 'by their character, by their circumstances in which they were worn . . . or by their ostentatious or campaigning nature constitute an act of pressure, provocation, proselytism or propaganda', the decision on which was to be made by the local education authority on a case-by-case basis.

The vagueness of the ruling not only failed to give the headmaster clear guidance but publicly revealed the ambiguities of the official policy. Soon there were more incidents of *hijab*-wearing and protests by Muslims, provoking counter-protests by secular Frenchmen. The stand-off was finally resolved when one of the girls voluntarily, and the other two under pressure from King Hassan of Morocco, agreed to drop the scarves to the shoulders in the classroom. The issue flared up again in November 1993 when the principal of a middle school in another city barred two girls from the school for wearing the *hijab*. In response, hundreds of Muslim girls, their number at one stage reaching 2,000, started wearing the *hijab* to the school. On 10 September 1994, the Education Minister, François Bayrou, ruled that while wearing 'discreet' religious symbols was acceptable, 'ostentatious symbols which in themselves constitute elements of proselytism or discrimination' were unacceptable and that the *hijab* fell under that category. Headscarves were now banned as a matter of public policy, and school decisions to the contrary were declared void.[2]

The national debate on the *hijab* went to the heart of the French conceptions of citizenship and national identity and divided the country. Some advocated *laïcité ouverte*, which largely amounted to a search for a negotiated solution with the Muslims. Some others, including Madame Miterrand, saw no reason for banning the *hijab* and advocated the right to difference and the concomitant celebration of plurality. Yet others questioned the rigid application of the principle of *laïcité* and argued for the teaching of religion in schools, both because of its cultural importance and because pupils would not be able to make sense of contemporary global conflicts without some knowledge of it.

These views, however, were confined to a minority. The dominant view was firmly committed to the practice of *laïcité* and hostile to any kind of compromise with the Muslim girls. It was eloquently stated in a letter to *Le Nouvel Observateur* of 2 November 1989, signed by several eminent intellectuals and urging the government not to perpetrate the 'Munich of Republican Education'. As the 'only institution consecrated to the universal', the school must be a 'place of emancipation' and resist 'communal, religious and economic pressures' with 'discipline' and 'courage'. For the signatories to the letter, as for a large body of Frenchmen, France was a single and indivisible nation based on a single culture. The school was the central tool of assimilation into French culture and could not tolerate ethnic self-expression. The *hijab* was particularly objectionable because it symbolized both a wholly alien culture and the subordinate status of women. Wearing it implied a refusal to become French, to integrate, to be like the rest. Since *laïcité* was a hard-won principle of long historical standing, the French state could not compromise with it without damaging its identity. As Serge July, the editor of *Libération*, put it, 'behind the scarf is the question of immigration, behind immigration is the debate over integration, and behind integration the question of *laïcité*'.

The principal argument against allowing Muslim girls to wear the *hijab*, then, was that it violated the principle of *laïcité* and went against the secular and assimilationist function of state schools. If Muslim spokesmen were to argue their case persuasively, they needed to counter this view. While some tried to do so, most realized that it raised many large and complex questions that did not admit of easy and conclusive answers, and that such a debate would take years to settle and did not help them in the short run. As it happened, French state schools did not strictly adhere to the principle of *laïcité*, and allowed Catholic girls to wear the cross and other insignia of religious identity and the Jews to wear the *kipa*. Muslims decided to articulate their demand in the language of equality and argued that, since they were denied the right enjoyed by the other religious groups, they were being treated unequally.

Defenders of the ban, including the Minister of Education, rejected the Muslim charge of discrimination on the ground that the *hijab* was not equivalent to the cross, and that the two groups of girls were *not* equal in relevant respects. First, unlike the 'discreetly' worn cross, the 'ostentatious' *hijab* was intended to put pressure on other Muslim girls and entailed 'proselytization'. Second, unlike the freely worn cross, the *hijab* symbolized and reinforced women's oppression. Third, unlike the unselfconsciously worn cross, the *hijab* was an ideologically motivated assertion of religious identity inspired by a wider fundamentalist movement which the schools had a duty to combat.

Although there is a good deal of humbug, misplaced anxiety and false alarm in these arguments, they are not totally devoid of substance. Both the cross and the *hijab* are religious symbols, and hence bases of equal claims. However, religious symbols cannot be defined and compared in the abstract, both because they rarely have exactly equivalent significance and because they acquire different meanings in different contexts and historical periods and might sometimes even cease to be religious in nature. We need to contextualise them and compare them not abstractly or 'in themselves' but in terms of the character and significance they might have acquired at a particular point in time. The question is not whether the *hijab* is the Islamic equivalent of the Christian cross, but whether in contemporary France wearing the *hijab* has broadly the same religious significance for Muslims as wearing the cross has for Christians. Since we cannot therefore dismiss the ban in the name of an abstract right to equal religious freedom, we need to take seriously the three arguments made in support of it and assess their validity.

As for the first argument, the *hijab* is certainly visible, but there is no obvious reason why religious symbols should be invisible or be of the same type. Besides, there is no evidence to support the view that the *hijab* was intended to proselytize among non-Muslims or to put religious pressure on other Muslim girls beyond the minimum inherent in the wearing of religious symbols. Conversely, the cross is not necessarily discreet, for Catholic girls do sometimes display, flaunt and talk about it, it is clearly visible when they engage in sports, swimming and such other activities, and it is visible even otherwise except that we do not see it because of its familiarity. Once the *hijab* is allowed, it too would become invisible.

The second argument which contrasts the freely worn cross with the coerced *hijab* is no more persuasive. It assumes that parental pressure is necessarily wrong, a strange and untenable view, and that choices by adolescent girls are always to be preferred over parental preferences, which is no more tenable. Furthermore, we have no means of knowing that wearing the cross was a free choice by Catholic girls and that Muslim girls wore the *hijab* only under parental or communal pressure. It is true that the latter had hitherto avoided it. However, nothing follows from this, for it is quite possible that they now defined their identity differently or felt more confident about expressing it. Indeed, the father of the two Creil girls said that the decision to wear the *hijab* was theirs and that he had been trying to convince them out of it. Since he might be saying this under pressure or to avoid embarrassment, we might refer to the remark of a young girl who was inspired by the three Creil girls to start wearing the headscarf in 1994:

> I feel completely liberated by the veil. As soon as I put it on, I felt as if I'd blossomed. The veil allows a woman no longer to be a slave to her body. It is the belief that a woman can go far through means other than using her body.

The third argument for the ban is equally unconvincing, for wearing the *hijab* need not be a form of ideological self-assertion any more than wearing the cross is. As for the fears about the rise of fundamentalism, a term that was never clearly defined, they were speculative and irrelevant to the argument. Only three out of scores of Muslim girls had worn the *hijab*, and the father of two of them had not only no history of religious activism but was positively embarrassed by the publicity. There was not much evidence either that most of the French Muslim community was becoming religiously militant. Some of them did show considerable sympathy for traditional values, but that was not against the law, represented a kind of cultural conservatism shared by many a Frenchman, and hardly amounted to fundamentalist militancy.

Allowing the cross and other Christian symbols but not the *hijab* then clearly amounted to treating Muslim girls unequally. Some French leaders conceded this, but insisted that the inequality was justified in order to liberate the girls from their traditional patriarchal system and to prepare them for an autonomous life. There is something to this argument, as equality is one value among many and needs to be balanced against others. However, it is open to several objections. It assumes without evidence that the girls' decision to wear the *hijab* was not autonomous. Furthermore, autonomy is difficult to define and impossible to measure or demonstrate, and any attempt to violate equality in its name opens the door to all manner of specious reasoning and arbitrary interference with pupils' ways of life. What is more, if the school started aggressively promoting autonomy, it would create a threatening and alienating environment in which girls would not feel relaxed enough to pursue their education. Parents, too, would lose confidence in it and deny it their support and cooperation.

The widely shared belief that the *hijab* symbolizes and reinforces female subordination ignores its complex cultural dialectic. Muslim immigrants in France, Britain and elsewhere are deeply fearful of their girls entering the public world including the school. By wearing the *hijab*, their daughters seek to reassure them that they can be culturally trusted and will not be 'corrupted' by the norms and values of the school. At the same time, they also reshape the semi-public world of the school and protect themselves against its pressures and temptations by subtly getting white and Muslim boys to see them differently to the way they eye white girls. The *hijab* puts the girls 'out of bounds' and enables them to dictate how they wish to be treated. Traditional at one level, the *hijab* is transgressive at another, and enables Muslim girls to transform both their parental and public cultures. To see it merely as a sign of subjection, as most secular Frenchmen and feminists did, was to be trapped into crude cultural stereotypes and fail to appreciate the complex processes of social change and intercultural negotiation it symbolized and triggered. This is not at all to say that all Muslim girls saw the *hijab* in this way, but rather that at least some did. Since the school and local authorities had no reliable means of ascertaining who wore it for what reasons, and since female subordination is too large an issue to be tackled by banning the *hijab*, they should have restrained their republican zeal and left the girls alone subject to the requirement of non-proselytization.

[. . .]

It should be clear that equal treatment of cultural communities is logically different from that of individuals. Unlike the latter, it is deeply embedded in and inseparable from the wider cultural and political relations between the communities involved. Besides, cultural communities often contain a wide variety of views on a subject and cannot be homogenized and reified. The case for intercultural equality should therefore not be made in such abstract and ahistorical terms that it ignores genuine differences between and within the communities involved or fails to address the deepest anxieties of the wider society. We should take a contexualized view of equality, identify what respects are relevant, and demand equal treatment of those shown to be equal in these respects. *If* the *hijab* really is different from the cross (which it is not), then Muslim girls may legitimately be denied the right to wear it without incurring the charge of discriminating against them. And *if* Muslim schools do really run the risk that their critics fear (which they do not), or if the British state does really wish to discontinue religious schools (which it does not), then they may legitimately be denied state funding without offending against the principle of equality.

NOTES

1. For good discussion of the headscarf controversy, see Galeotti (1993) and Moruzzi (1994). For a similar controversy in Germany, see Mandel (1989).
2. For an interesting summary and interpretation, see 'La saga des foulards', *Le Monde*, 13 October 1994.
3. The *Conseil d'Etat*'s decision on 14 April 1995 permits Jewish students to miss Saturday classes to observe the Sabbath. Since this does not violate the principle of *laïcité*, the Conseil's attitude to Muslims is puzzling. See *Le Monde*, 16–17 April 1995, pp. 1 and 9. The French government heavily subsidizes the 'private' Roman Catholic school system, but refuses public funds to Jewish, Muslim and even other Christian schools.

REFERENCES

Galeotti, A. (1993) 'Citizenship and Equality: The Place for Toleration', in *Political Theory* vol. 21, no. 4.

Mandel, R. (1989) 'Turkish Headscarves and the "Foreigners Problem": Constructing Difference Through Emblems of Identity', *New German Critique*, vol. 46.

Moruzzi, N. C. (1994) 'A Problem with Headscarves', in *Political Theory*, vol. 22, no. 2.

11

POLITICAL THOUGHT BEYOND THE WESTERN TRADITION

Oliver Leaman

INTRODUCTION

There is no such singular thing as non-Western political philosophy, of course, given the huge variety of cultures and political systems in what might be called 'the East'. This geographical term is not used that much now due to fears of being accused of Orientalism: of both romanticising and demonising 'the Other'; seeing the East as opposed to the West and as irretrievably mysterious, devious or (in positive terms) more spiritual and less materialistic than the industrialised Western countries. But, when one looks closely at such a comparison, it quickly falls to pieces. Japan, for example, is irretrievably Eastern yet seems to have an economy which is predominantly Western, and it can hardly be called a more spiritual place than the West. There is no common approach to political thought which exists in any one of the major Eastern centres of civilisation. The title 'Eastern political philosophy' is very much a misnomer.

It is also worth saying that there is a great deal more political philosophy in the East than is represented here. The extracts reproduced below include nothing from India, surely the cultural capital of Eastern philosophy and the place from which **Buddhism** originated and spread out to China, Japan and elsewhere. What there is of Indian political thought in the contemporary period is not that distinctive, although much of the thought of Gandhi is quite interesting and unusual. In all books on Eastern philosophy, Indian thought is given a central role. It is interesting that this is not the case for contemporary political philosophy, but the omission of India accurately reflects an omission in much of a contemporary tradition.

When it comes to China, it is difficult to decide what might count as representative of thinking there. The thought of Maozedong (Mao Tze Tung) has undoubtedly been politically important in practical terms, but it does not seem to be very Chinese (readers will see that the notes to the extract reproduced here refer exclusively to European thinkers). Furthermore, with the collapse of communism as an ideology in China (in everything except name), Mao appears to be passé. Some modern Confucian thinkers embody the spirit of China in a way that a new doctrine like **dialectical materialism** could not. But Mao is a very Chinese thinker, and his interpretation of Marxism is heavily marked by a long tradition of Chinese thought of which he was aware (although this is not explicit in the extract found here).

In Japan, there have been quite a few interesting nationalistic pieces of writing in the modern period, and these could easily have been included. The extract reproduced here, 'Zen and the Samurai', brings out the links between these two apparently very different schools of thought and argues persuasively that they are closely linked. Suzuki is an important thinker in contemporary Japan, having like so many in that tradition an excellent grasp of both Japanese and Western schools of thought.

Deciding who might represent Islamic political thought is fraught with problems also. Imam Khomeini was an important contemporary thinker, and best known in the West as an advocate of Islamic government, but his work in other areas of philosophy is more creative than his writings on political thought. Also, he was a Shi'i Muslim, and so a member of a substantial but still minority group within Islam. On the other hand, his writings on politics are clear and well arranged, and they are actually respected far outside the Shi'i world.

Before these writings from Chinese, Japanese and Islamic political thought are considered, it is worth noting that much non-Western political philosophy is very similar to the work which takes place in the West. For example, the doctrine of Liberalism has been widely adopted by many non-Western thinkers. One of the most frequent topics of consideration is that of modernity: of how cultures which initially were very distinct from what is found in the West come to terms with Western forms of thought. Many Eastern thinkers see some variety of Liberalism, with its stress on democracy, individualism and economic independence, as the theoretical path to follow. I have not included any liberal thinkers here, but that should not be taken as suggesting that they do not exist. They do, and they are important, but it would be difficult to argue that they have defined the area as firmly as some of the thinkers we have included here.

THE POLITICAL PHILOSOPHY OF MAO TZE TUNG

Mao's essay, while it bristles with references to **dialectical materialism**, is really in a long tradition of Chinese thought that deals with the relationship between theory and practice. What is more important – what we do or what we know? Many Chinese thinkers, like Mao, argued that action is more significant than what we know or the concepts we have. This is an interesting debate and particularly important in Chinese thought, much of which is ethical in nature. There is certainly work in Chinese philosophy that is concerned with epistemology or metaphysics, and much on logic; but, if one were to characterise Chinese philosophy in any general way, it would be as primarily ethical. So it is hardly surprising that Mao ends up prioritising practice over our ideas. He argues that it is only by developing ideas out of practice, by reflecting on our experience in the right sort of way, that we can use ideas which are accurate and fit the objective world. Even ideas which are abstract in the sense that we do not ourselves have any experience of what they describe are not entirely divorced from experience, since at some stage they were linked with someone's or some culture's experience, and hence part of the system of practice by which ideas become validated as relevant and accurate.

Mao sets himself against the traditional doctrine of the sage who is able to understand reality while at the same remaining distant from it: the philosophy of those thinkers for whom theory precedes practice. This view, the priority of the intellectual, clearly implies a thoroughgoing elitism since only those who possess the knowledge are likely to be regarded as appropriate candidates for political authority. One of the main schools of thought in Chinese philosophy, Confucianism, embodied this sort of doctrine, emphasising the significance of the status quo and the authority of those who have been brought up to exercise it. In the contemporary People's Republic of China at the start of the new millennium, **Confucius** has undergone something of a transformation in reputation. In the past, he was seen as a dreadful conservative. Now he is seen as a thinker who correctly emphasises the significance of rules and the common standards of behaviour that underpin social harmony. This is in contrast to the moral anarchism consequent on the collapse of communism as an ideology and the inability of the capitalism which is taking over in China to provide an acceptable social philosophy. Confucianism has often been called the right philosophy for the twenty-first century: a potent combination stressing respect for rules, the importance of education and the circumscribing of individual freedom within a notion of a community as the source of ideas of social value.

From a Marxist perspective, Mao makes two unusual claims. One is that classical Marxism knew little about imperialism – a very eccentric claim to make about Marx, who lived at the centre of world imperialism in nineteenth-century Britain. The other claim is that Marxism-Leninism itself is only valid temporarily, since everything is part of a process of change, and one cannot tell what theories will emerge in the future to reflect changing material and cultural circumstances. The first of these claims indicates that Mao's version of communism is intended to take into account the specific conditions under which Chinese communists find themselves, thus emphasising the significance of practice. He is distancing himself from Marxist theory insofar as it purports to present an account of reality which is valid and objective at every time and in every place. This thesis is strengthened by Mao's argument that theory is only as good as the conditions under which it operates. That means that one cannot just use a theory perpetually, because to do so is to ignore the fact that the conditions which make it valid have changed. In fact, as we know, Mao during his long period of rule in China adopted some very radical policy shifts in order to reflect better what he thought were changing material events. For example, the **Cultural Revolution** was supposed to reinvigorate a revolution which had begun to grow old and stale, which had been appropriate in the past but which in the new circumstances of the People's Republic was no longer functioning in accordance with the nature of reality. Although the present regime in China has, to a degree, distanced itself from Mao and his approach to communism, this pragmatism seems to have persisted. If theories are to change as circumstances change, then we should not be surprised that the same sort of political regime produces a very different economic policy from the past, since this is obeying the Maoist point that everything changes. The question which is often asked about China is how long a government that pays lip service to a political system which is no longer linked with the economic system can last. Mao's response would be that it will last as long as it can last, and, when the material conditions make it no longer viable, it will collapse.

Mao also argues that what makes a political operator effective is not just his understanding of the facts but his ability to put those facts within a wider perspective. Only in so doing will he be able properly to understand what the situation really is and what he should do with respect to it. Two things are necessary for knowledge: experience and the correct theory. Now, this looks like **dialectical materialism**, and the references which Mao gives are to the right sort of authorities in Marxism. But his description of theory is not at all Marxist in that it does not refer to historical processes and their grounding in material facts and relations. We get here a vestige of the traditional Chinese idea that there is a **Tao**, a Way. If our actions are in accordance with this Way, they are effective. If we are not aligned with it, then our actions are vacuous. The way in which the **Taoists** describe this path can be very mystical. There is no hint of that in Mao. On the other hand, in the past the Taoist notion was taken up enthusiastically by the **Legalists**, who used it to defend autocratic government and the necessity of the ruler to fit his strategies with the general pattern of change. This suggests that the Taoist notion can be adapted to a wide range of different theories. Of course, in Chinese philosophy, the notion of there being a path or Tao is not restricted to Taoism and Legalism. It exists across the philosophical spectrum, and it certainly seems to emerge in Mao's thought. As someone who was trying to mould China into a particular pattern, the idea that only he really knew what that pattern is, what the Tao is, is very attractive, and explains the theoretical basis to the many changes of direction which took place under Mao's extensive rule in China. It also explains the ability of a communist regime to reconstruct itself as an entirely different form of polity while at the same time retaining the old label of communist.

'On Practice' looks superficially like an orthodox example of Marxist analysis, but on closer analysis it is very different from that. In particular, it fails to ground political change in objective material and cultural conditions. The theory looks Marxist because it insists that change can only properly take place when the conditions are right. But who can tell when the conditions are right, what the Tao is in accordance with which one must act? The implication is that only a restricted number of people know the answer to that question, and it is for them to instruct the masses in the solution. Again, this is a very traditional view in Chinese political philosophy, and it is not surprising that it should figure in Mao's thinking. Nor is it surprising that it should figure in the thinking of his successors, who in this general doctrine at least continue to be faithful Maoists, if not orthodox Marxists.

POLITICAL PHILOSOPHY IN JAPAN

The twentieth century was a time of great expansion for Japan, at first militarily and then economically. A country which had been used to seeing itself as very different from others had to come to terms with its increasing contact with the outside world. Much of the political literature was xenophobic in nature, stressing the uniqueness and superiority of Japanese culture over that of its neighbours and imperial competitors. There were also thinkers who saw Japan's future lying in becoming a liberal democracy on a par with Europe and the United States. But one of the most interesting features of Japanese thought is its use of **Buddhism**, and the specifically Japanese school of Buddhism – Zen – to underpin its military spirit.

One might think that **Buddhism** is a particularly poor philosophy for the martial spirit since it emphasises compassion, non-violence and the lack of significance of the self. If the self is of no significance, then how significant could the state be? There is a tradition in Japan of what might be called 'muscular Buddhism', constructed by **Nichiren** as a response to the difficult times in which Buddhists found themselves. His argument was that the passive message of early Buddhism was right for the early period, but not for the deteriorating circumstances in which he lived. As a result, it was not only permissible for Buddhists to take up arms to defend themselves and their communities but incumbent on them.

Zen is the Japanese version of the Chinese chan, and refers to a particular attitude to the attainment of enlightenment. There was a protracted debate in China between those Buddhists who thought that enlightenment could only be reached through long and difficult processes of training and meditation, and the chan Buddhists who argued that sudden enlightenment was possible. The difference between these two groups is not as extreme as might be thought, since the chan Buddhists also believed that one should be trained for enlightenment, and the sudden methods often seem just as difficult as the gradual ones. One of the central aspects of Zen Buddhism, as it developed in Japan, is the use of the koan, the riddle, to tease the intellect of the practitioner and get him to see the truth suddenly, often through a ridiculous action or absurd remark. The point is to demonstrate the limitations of rationality, the restricted nature of language and the significance of pursuing a single goal.

As Suzuki points out (in the extract below), the military mind found the apparent simplicity of Zen attractive. It could be used to help train the minds of soldiers to attain one objective and to direct their entire lives towards it. Another characteristic of Zen is its contempt for life, in the sense that the difference between life and death is regarded as of no significance. It might be thought useful for a soldier to have little or no fear of death.

What is distinct about the Zen attitude to death is that it does not try to ignore it or refuse to regard it as an evil. This very effort of concentration goes against what Zen is trying to do, which is to help us act naturally and in that way discover what it is to align ourselves with where we should be going. That is very much a principle of the martial arts: that the best fighter is not the person who responds to the attacks of his opponent but one who uses the attacks of his opponent as part of his response. For example, in judo, a skilful practitioner will often use the move of his opponent to defeat him, turning the opponent's strength against him. An opposing advance is not directly resisted. On the contrary, it is immediately successful: the other fighter retreats, but while doing so he manipulates the advance in order to transform it from a successful movement into something which will work against its creator.

Suzuki's description of **Tokimune** as a **bodhisattva** is interesting, since a bodhisattva is an enlightened being who participates in the ordinary events of the world in order to bring others to Enlightenment. It is not a description normally applied to a military leader! But the whole meaning of his life was the importance of peace and in particular the peace of Japan and its imperial dynasty. What made him such an impressive general was the fact that his primary interest was not war but peace, in just the same way that what makes a physical opponent impressive is his lack of anger or aggression in his response to attack. This is a difficult attitude to cultivate, and Zen is seen as a means to that cultivation, since it implies that once the artificial accumulation of ordinary ideas has been removed the light of Enlightenment can freely radiate. Everyone is naturally enlightened, and all that is needed is the right technique to achieve this natural state. Normally, when we are attacked we are nervous about our future well-being. We try to preserve our lives by reacting to the attack, but in so doing we perform another action, one designed to counter the action of the aggressor. What we should do is make the aggressor's action part of our action. In that way, we can respond much more effectively to it. If we have perpetually before us a nervous anticipation of the effect of the aggression, then we are fighting less well, since our attention is directed not at what is taking place but at some possible future consequence.

Does this mean that the fighter or samurai should ignore the possibility of death? On the contrary, all the Zen manuals on this topic emphasise the importance of constantly thinking about death. This fascination with death might be thought self-defeating since, surely, it would make the samurai less brave, constantly aware of the immanence of his death. But, according to Zen, the opposite is the case. It is the fact that he is prepared to think of death constantly that enables the samurai to put it in its proper place. Having thought of it every day, the fact of death loses its capacity to shock him. Similarly, if one is prepared to be attacked, then when one is attacked it is not regarded as a surprising and shocking event, and one can react to it rationally and effectively.

There is another aspect of Zen which is relevant here, and that is its stress on feeling and intuition and relative devaluation of rationality. Many varieties of Buddhism place great importance on rationality, and even Zen requires considerable intellectual work at many stages if one is to understand what is going on. Yet the ultimate aim is a state of mind which goes beyond rationality, since rationality and language are irretrievably mired in the world of generation and corruption and do not allow us to transcend it.

The Zen ways of working things out are actually very complex, but they present themselves as cutting through the artificialities of language and culture to attain a grasp of reality as it is in itself, and how one should act as a result becomes obvious. Not only is it obvious, but any attempt at investigating it further, judging its merits and disadvantages, is nugatory. It defeats the whole project of going beyond language and rationality through the appropriate use of one intuition if one then returns to those more limited forms of finding out. The political consequences of such an approach are clear, in that once the mind of the individual is made up in a particular way, Zen ensures that it stays made up, and any arguments for a different view will remain ignored. This perhaps explains not only why, for a period during the twentieth century, the Japanese military was such a formidable force, but also why a particular kind of nationalism has remained so powerful a factor in Japanese life in modern times.

ISLAMIC POLITICAL PHILOSOPHY

For much of the twentieth century, Islam seemed politically to be a dormant force. There were a few states like Pakistan which had been created as specifically Islamic, but there was nothing especially unusual about such states, and as a global ideology Islam was not seen as particularly effective. The growth of secular states such as Turkey and Algeria in countries with predominantly Muslim populations, and the repeated defeats of the Arab armies by the state of Israel, suggested that Islam as an ideology had limited political thrust. However, the **Iranian Revolution** and its encouragement to many other Islamic revolutionary movements has put the notion of Islamic government firmly on the agenda.

In his account of the Islamic state, Imam Khomeini follows the familiar pattern of reflecting on the past and what took place then. He points out that the Prophet instituted a practical way of life as well as transmitting God's message, and also made provision for his successors. (It was over this issue of successors that the big divide in Islam between the Sunni and the Shi'a occurred.

The latter believe that the Prophet's son-in-law 'Ali was his legitimate successor as head of the polity). Islam is not only a religion in the sense of a system of belief about spiritual issues. It also includes specific demands about how people ought to live, and if they are to live in those ways then the legal and material provisions of the state must support that form of life. There are three strong arguments for the continuing relevance of Islamic government. As Khomeini points out, the claim that Islamic government was only appropriate in earlier times might be taken as equivalent to the thesis that Islam itself is only valid at earlier times. Also, if Islam was not supposed to be a comprehensive and constant legislative system, why would it in fact consist of such detailed prescriptions? Finally, had there existed a unified Islamic polity, the Jews, Khomeini claims, would not have been able to do what they have done (a reference not only to the creation of the state of Israel, and its dominance in the Middle East, but also to what Khomeini regards as the general influence of Jews in the world).

From an Islamic perspective, there is no such thing as a neutral state. States are either Islamic or they represent unbelief and corruption. The Muslim cannot live in the latter kind of state without being irretrievably affected by it, unless he actively opposes it. It follows that it is the duty of all Muslims to struggle against the state unless the state is Islamic. Khomeini denounces the division of the global Islamic community (umma) into individual states, which he sees as one of the effects of imperialism, weakening and dividing Islam. Everything in Islam, he argues, is opposed to injustice, and yet we see injustice all around us in what goes under the description of the Islamic world. What is needed is the overturning of corrupt regimes and their replacement by appropriately Islamic governments, in which justice would prevail because it is part and parcel of Islam itself.

The establishment of an Islamic government, in its own terms, in Iran had a tremendous effect on the Islamic world. The **Pahlavi** regime which had been overthrown looked very strong and well supported by the United States, and yet it collapsed when steadfastly opposed by the supporters of Khomeini. It is also worth saying that there have been many secular regimes in the Islamic world which do not appear to have been very successful either economically or politically. The slogan 'Islam is the answer' has a ready audience in such a climate. Finally, it is true that Islam can be interpreted as involving a system of government which is attractive and has the advantage over the secular polity of preparing the individual citizen not only for the material world but for the spiritual world also. One of the difficulties which Western analysts have with the notion of Islamic government is that secularism has come to have such deep roots in the West in modern times that a religious government seems a ridiculous, not to say dangerous, prospect in contemporary society.

There is no one notion of Islamic government, in just the same way that there is no one notion of *shari'a*. The model which Khomeini presents here is merely one among the many candidates for an Islamic polity (although he was unlikely to have seen it in this way!). One might expect that Islamic governments would differ from Iran, given the differences between Sunni and Shi'i Islam. The latter tends to be more hierarchical, since it places so much emphasis on the imam as the intermediary between this world and the higher world, and of course on the family of the Prophet, that the status of the ruler-imam is a very powerful one. Sunni Islam, with its emphasis on *ijma'* or consensus of the community, however that is interpreted, might be expected to lead to more participatory forms of government, although in practice this does not really seem to be the case. Some have argued that the concept of *shura* (consultation) in Islam means that it is basically democratic; but that is not at all plausible. Like any religion, Islam has a range of principles which can be interpreted politically in any way one wishes, and the individual Islamic governments which arise have far more to do with the individuals who are in charge and the particular cultures out of which they emerge. So, what is interesting in the different accounts of Islamic government is the creative use of a scripture to give form to a view of the polity.

There has been extensive discussion towards the end of the twentieth century about whether the main threat to the West is now the Islamic world, and in particular the notion of Islamic government. Samuel Huntington suggested (1996) that there is a basic clash of civilisations between Islam and the West, and that, after the disappearance of the Soviet Union as the chief enemy, Islam has taken its place. This debate has, on the whole, radiated more heat than light, but it is worth pointing to one aspect of it which is important and relevant. The notion of religious government does stand opposed to the leading principles of liberal democracy on which Western political thought is based, and in that sense we are likely to see an extended rivalry between two different ways of assessing the role of religious faith in the organisation of the state.

'Zen and the Samurai' by D. T. Suzuki

The Japanese religious philosopher Daisetz Teitaro Suzuki (1870–1966) moved in 1897 from Japan to the USA, where he worked for a publishing company and began translating into English and publishing a number of Oriental religious and philosophical works. Returning to Japan, he became a professor at Otani University in 1921. Having undertaken Zen training, he formed the Eastern Buddhist Society and wrote many works in English on Buddhism, including *Studies in Zen Buddhism* (1927–1934) in three volumes, *Studies in the Lankâvatâra Sûtra* (1933), and *Zen Buddhism and Its Influence on Japanese Culture* (1938), published as *Zen and Japanese Culture*. *Japanese Spirituality* (1972) is regarded by many as a classic of Japanese religious thought. Suzuki lectured widely but especially in America (he was a visiting professor at Columbia University), and is often credited with making Zen accessible to Americans. The extract below is from *Zen and Japanese Culture* and examines the relationship between the Zen philosophy and the Samurai.

'ZEN AND THE SAMURAI' (1959)*

D. T. Suzuki

It may be considered strange that Zen has in any way been affiliated with the spirit of the military classes of Japan. Whatever form Buddhism takes in the various countries where it flourishes, it is a religion of compassion, and in its varied history it has never been found engaged in warlike activities. How is it, then, that Zen has come to activate the fighting spirit of the Japanese warrior?

In Japan, Zen was intimately related from the beginning of its history to the life of the samurai. Although, it has never actively incited them to carry on their violent profession, it has passively sustained them when they have for whatever reason once entered into it. Zen has sustained them in two ways, morally and philosophically. Morally, because Zen is a religion which teaches us not to look backward once the course is decided upon; philosophically, because it treats life and death indifferently. This not turning backward ultimately comes from the philosophical conviction; but, being a religion of the will, Zen appeals to the samurai spirit morally rather than philosophically. From the philosophical

---

* From D. T. Suzuki, 'Zen and the Samurai', in *Zen and Japanese Culture* (Princeton, NJ: Princeton University Press, 1959), pp. 61–73.

point of view, Zen upholds intuition against intellection, for intuition is the more direct way of reaching the Truth. Therefore, morally and philosophically, there is in Zen a great deal of attraction for the military classes. The military mind, being – and this is one of the essential qualities of the fighter – comparatively simple and not at all addicted to philosophizing, finds a congenial spirit in Zen. This is probably one of the main reasons for the close relationship between Zen and the samurai.

Secondly, Zen discipline is simple, direct, self-reliant, self-denying; its ascetic tendency goes well with the fighting spirit. The fighter is to be always single-minded with one object in view: to fight, looking neither backward nor side-wise. To go straight forward in order to crush the enemy is all that is necessary for him. He is therefore not to be encumbered in any possible way, be it physical, emotional, or intellectual. Intellectual doubts, if they are cherished at all in the mind of the fighter, are great obstructions to his onward movement, while emotionalities and physical possessions are the heaviest of encumbrances if he wants to conduct himself most efficiently in his vocation. A good fighter is generally an ascetic or stoic, which means he has an iron will. This, when needed, Zen can supply.

Thirdly, there is an historical connection between Zen and the military classes of Japan. The Buddhist priest Eisai (1141–1215) is generally regarded as the first to introduce Zen into Japan. But his activities were more or less restricted to Kyoto, which was at the time the headquarters of the older schools of Buddhism. The inauguration of any new faith here was almost impossible owing to the strong opposition they offered. Eisai had to compromise to some extent by assuming a reconciliatory attitude towards the Tendai and the Shingon. Whereas in Kamakura, which was the seat of the Hōjō government, there were no such historical difficulties. Besides, the Hōjō regime was militaristic, as it succeeded the Minamoto family, who had risen against the Taira family and the court nobles. The latter had lost their efficacy as a governing power because of their over-refinement and effeminacy and consequent degeneration. The Hōjō regime is noted for its severe frugality and moral discipline and also for its powerful administrative and militaristic equipments. The directing heads of such a strong governing machine embraced Zen as their spiritual guide, ignoring tradition in the matter of religion; Zen thus could not help but exercise its varied influence in the general cultural life of the Japanese ever since the thirteenth century and throughout the Ashikaga and even in the Tokugawa period.

Zen has no special doctrine or philosophy, no set of concepts or intellectual formulas, except that it tries to release one from the bondage of birth and death, by means of certain intuitive modes of understanding peculiar to itself. It is, therefore, extremely flexible in adapting itself to almost any philosophy and moral doctrine as long as its intuitive teaching is not interfered with. It may be found wedded to anarchism or fascism, communism or democracy, atheism or idealism, or any political or economic dogmatism. It is, however, generally animated with a certain revolutionary spirit, and when things come to a dead-lock – as they do when we are overloaded with conventionalism, formalism, and other cognate isms – Zen asserts itself and proves to be a destructive force. The spirit of the Kamakura era was in this respect in harmony with the virile spirit of Zen.

We have the saying in Japan: 'The Tendai is for the royal family, the Shingon for the nobility, the Zen for the warrior classes, and the Jōdō for the masses'. This saying fitly characterizes each sect of Buddhism in Japan. The Tendai and the Shingon are rich in ritualism, and their ceremonies are conducted in a most elaborate and pompous style appropriate to the taste of the refined classes. The Jōdō appeals naturally more to plebeian requirements because of the simpleness of its faith and teaching. Besides its direct method of reaching final faith, Zen is a religion of will-power, and will-power is what is urgently needed by the warriors, though it ought to be enlightened by intuition.

The first Zen follower of the Hōjō family was Tokiyori (1227–63), who succeeded his father Yasutoki in the Hōjō regency. He invited to Kamakura the Japanese Zen masters in Kyoto and also some Chinese masters directly from the Southern Sung, under whom he earnestly devoted himself to the study of Zen. He finally succeeded in mastering it himself, and this fact must have greatly encouraged all his retainers to imitate the example of their master.

Wu-an (Gottan; 1197–1276), the Chinese Zen master, under whom Tokiyori had his final enlightenment after twenty-one years of constant application, composed the following verse for his illustrious disciple:

> I have no Buddhism about which I can this moment talk to you,
> Nor have you any mind with which you listen to me hoping for an
> attainment:
> Where there is neither preaching nor attainment nor mind,
> There Śākyamuni has a most intimate interview with Buddha
> Dīpankara.

After a very successful regency, Tokiyori died in 1263, when he was only thirty-seven years old. When he realized that the time for departure was approaching, he put on his Buddhist robe and sat on a straw seat of meditation. After writing his farewell song, he passed away quietly. The song reads:

> The karma mirror raised high,
> These thirty-seven years!
> 'Tis broken now with one hammer blow.
> The Great Way remains ever serene!

Hōjō Tokimune (1251–84) was his only son, and when his father's mantle fell on him in 1268 he was only eighteen years old. He proved to be one of the greatest personages whom Japan has produced. Without him, indeed, the history of the country would not be what it actually is. He it was who most effectively crushed the Mongolian invasions, lasting several years – in fact during the whole length of his regency, 1268–84. It seems that Tokimune was almost a heaven-sent agent to stave off the direst calamity that might have befallen the nation, for he passed away with the termination of the greatest event in the history of Japan. His short life was simply and wholly devoted to this affair. He was then the body and soul of the whole nation. His indomitable spirit controlled the whole situation, and his body in the form of a most strongly consolidated army stood like a solid rock against the tumultuously raging waves of the Western Sea.

A still more wonderful thing about this almost superhuman figure, however, is that he had time and energy and aspiration to devote himself to the study of Zen under the masters from China. He erected temples for them, especially one for Bukkō Kokushi (1226–86), the National Teacher, which was meant also to console the departed spirits both Japanese and Chinese at the time of the Mongolian invasions. Tokimune's grave is still in this last-mentioned temple known as Engakuji. Some letters are still preserved which were sent to him by his several spiritual masters, and from these we know how studiously and vigorously he applied himself to Zen. The following story, though not quite authenticated, gives support to our imaginative reconstruction of his attitude towards Zen. Tokimune is said to have asked Bukkō, 'The worst enemy of our life is cowardice, and how can I escape it?'

> Bukkō answered, 'Cut off the source whence cowardice comes'.
> Tokumune: 'Where does it come from?'
> Bukkō: 'It comes from Tokimune himself.'
> Tokimune: 'Above all things, cowardice is what I hate most, and how can it come out of myself?'
> Bukkō: 'See how you feel when you throw overboard your cherished self known as Tokimune. I will see you again when you have done that.'
> Tokimune: 'How can this be done?'
> Bukkō: 'Shut out all your thoughts.'
> Tokimune: 'How can my thoughts be shut out of consciousness?'
> Bukkō: 'Sit crossed-legged in meditation and see into the source of all your thoughts which you imagine as belonging to Tokimune.'
> Tokimune: 'I have so much of worldly affairs to look after and it is difficult to find spare moments for meditation.'
> Bukkō: 'Whatever worldly affairs you are engaged in, take them up as occasions for your inner reflection, and some day you will find out who this beloved Tokimune of yours is.'

Something like the above must have taken place sometime between Tokimune and Bukkō. When he received definite reports about the Mongolian invaders coming over the sea of Tsukushi, he appeared before Bukkō the National Teacher and said, 'The greatest event of my life is at last here'.

Bukkō asked, 'How would you face it?'

Tokimune uttered '*Katsu!*' as if he were frightening away all his enemies actually before him.

Bukkō was pleased and said, 'Truly, a lion's child roars like a lion'.

This was the courage with which Tokimune faced the over-whelming enemies coming over from the continent and successfully drove them back.

Historically speaking, however, it was not courage alone with which Tokimune accomplished the greatest deed in the history of Japan. He planned everything that was needed for this task, and his ideas were carried out by the armies engaged in the different parts of the country to resist the powerful invaders. He never moved out of Kamakura, but his armies far out in the western parts of Japan executed his orders promptly and effectively. This was extraordinary in those remote days, when there was no speedier method of communication than relay horses. Unless he had the perfect confidence of all his subordinates, it was impossible for him to achieve such a feat.

Bukkō's eulogy of Tokimune at his funeral ceremony sums up his personality:

> There were ten wonders in his life, which was the actualization of a Bodhisattva's great *praṇidhāna* (vows): he was a filial son to his mother; he was a loyal subject to his Emperor; he sincerely looked after the welfare of the people; studying Zen he grasped its ultimate truth; wielding an actual power in the Empire for twenty years, he betrayed no signs of joy or anger; sweeping away by virtue of a gale the threatening clouds raised by the barbarians, he showed no feeling of elation; establishing the Engakuji monastery, he planned for the spiritual consolation of the dead [both Japanese and Mongolian]; paying homage to the teachers and fathers [of Buddhism] he sought for enlightenment – all this proves that his coming among us was solely for the sake of the Dharma. And then when he was about to depart, he managed to rise from his bed, put the Buddhist robe I gave him over his enfeebled body, and write his death song in full possession of his spirit. Such a one as he must be said to be really an enlightened being, or a Bodhisattva incarnate . . .

Tokimune was born great, no doubt, but his study of Zen must have helped him a great deal in his dealing with state affairs and also in his private life. His wife was also a devout Zen follower, and after his death she founded a nunnery in the hills just opposite the Engakuji.

When we say that Zen is for the warrior, this statement has a particular significance for the Kamakura period. Tokimune was not merely a fighting general, but a great statesman whose object was peace. His prayer offered to the Buddha at the time of a great religious ceremony performed at the Kenchōji under the leadership of the abbot, when an intimation of the first Mongolian invasion was received, runs as follows:

> The only prayer Tokimune, a Buddhist disciple, cherishes is: that the Imperial House continue in prosperity; that for a long time to come he [the

Emperor] may be the guardian of the Buddha's doctrine; that the four seas remain unruffled without an arrow being shot; that all evil spirits be kept under subjection without a spearhead being unsheathed; that the masses be benefited by means of a benevolent administration so that they could enjoy a long life in happiness more than ever; that the darkness of the human mind be illumined by the torch of transcendental wisdom which should be raised high; that the needy be properly ministered to and those in danger be saved by the heart of compassion being widely open. May all the gods come and protect us, all the sages extending their quiet help, and every hour of the day may there be a great gathering of auspicious signs! . . .

Tokimune was a great Buddhist spirit and a sincere follower of Zen, and it was due to his encouragement that Zen came to be firmly established in Kamakura and then in Kyoto and began to spread its moral and spiritual influence among the warrior classes. The constant stream of intercourse thus started between the Japanese and the Chinese Zen monks went even beyond the boundaries of their common cause. Books, paintings, porcelains, potteries, textiles, and many other objects of art were brought from China; even carpenters, masons, architects, and cooks came along with their masters. Thus the trading with China that later developed in the Ashikaga period had its initiation in the Kamakura.

Led by such strong characters as Tokiyori and Tokimune, Zen was auspiciously introduced into the Japanese life, especially into the life of the samurai. As Zen gained more and more influence in Kamakura, it spread over to Kyoto, where it was strongly supported by Japanese Zen masters. The latter soon found strong followers among members of the Imperial family, headed by the emperors Godaigo, Hanazono, and others. Large monasteries were built in Kyoto, and masters noted for their virtue, wisdom, and learning were asked to be founders and successive abbots of such institutions. Shoguns of the Ashikaga regime were also great advocates of Zen Buddhism, and most generals under them naturally followed suit. In those days, we can say that the Japanese genius went either to priesthood or to soldiery. The spiritual co-operation of the two professions could not help but contribute to the creation of what is now generally known as Bushido, 'the way of the warrior'.

At this juncture, let me touch upon one of the inner relationships that exist between the samurai mode of feeling and Zen. What finally has come to constitute Bushido, as we generally understand it now, is the act of being an unflinching guardian-god of the dignity of the samurai, and this dignity consists in loyalty, filial piety, and benevolence. But, to fulfill these duties successfully, two things are needed: to train oneself in moral asceticism, not only in its practical aspect but in its philosophical preparation; and to be always ready to face death, that is, to sacrifice oneself unhesitatingly when occasion arises. To do this, much mental and spiritual training is needed.

There is a document that was very much talked about in connection with the Japanese military operations in China in the 1930s. It is known as the

Hagakure, which literally means 'Hidden under the Leaves', for it is one of the virtues of the samurai not to display himself, not to blow his horn, but to keep himself away from the public eye and be doing good for his fellow beings. To the compilation of this book, which consists of various notes, anecdotes, moral sayings, etc., a Zen monk had his part to contribute. The work started in the middle part of the seventeenth century under Nabeshima Naoshige, the feudal lord of Saga in the island of Kyūshū. The book emphasizes very much the samurai's readiness to give his life away at any moment, for it states that no great work has ever been accomplished without going mad – that is, when expressed in modern terms, without breaking through the ordinary level of consciousness and letting loose the hidden powers lying further below. These powers may be devilish sometimes, but there is no doubt that they are super-human and work wonders. When the unconscious is tapped, it rises above individual limitations. Death now loses its sting altogether, and this is where the samurai training joins hands with Zen.

To quote one of the stories cited in the *Hagakure*: Yagyū Tajima no kami Munenori was a great swordsman and teacher in the art of the Shogun of the time, Tokugawa Iyemitsu. One of the person guards of the Shogun one day came to Tajima no kami wishing to be trained in swordplay. The master said, 'As I observe, you seem to be a master of the art yourself; pray tell me to what school you belong, before we enter into the relationship of teacher and pupil'.

The guardsman said, 'I am ashamed to confess that I have never learned the art'.

'Are you going to fool me? I am teacher to the honorable Shogun himself, and I know my judging eye never fails.'

'I am sorry to defy your honor, but I really know nothing.'

This resolute denial on the part of the visitor made the swordsmaster think for a while, and he finally said, 'If you say so, that must be so; but still I am sure of your being master of something, though I know not just what'.

'Yes, if you insist, I will tell you this. There is one thing of which I can say I am complete master. When I was still a boy, the thought came upon me that as a samurai I ought in no circumstances to be afraid of death, and ever since I have grappled with the problem of death now for some years, and finally the problem has entirely ceased to worry me. May this be what you hint at?'

'Exactly!' exclaimed Tajima no kami. 'That is what I mean. I am glad I made no mistake in my judgment. For the ultimate secrets of swordsmanship also lie in being released from the thought of death. I have trained ever so many hundreds of my pupils along this line, but so far none of them really deserves the final certificate for swordsmanship. You need no technical training, you are already a master.'

The problem of death is a great problem with every one of us; it is, however, more pressing for the samurai, for the soldier, whose life is exclusively devoted to fighting, and fighting means death to fighters of either side. In feudal days, nobody could predict when this deadly encounter might take place, and the samurai worth his name was always to be on the alert. A warrior-writer of the seventeenth century, Daidōji Yusan, therefore, writes in the beginning of his book called a 'Primer of Bushido' as follows:

> The idea most vital and essential to the samurai is that of death, which he ought to have before his mind day and night, night and day, from the dawn of the first day of the year till the last minute of the last day of it. When this notion takes firm hold of you, you are able to discharge your duties to their fullest extent: you are loyal to your master, filial to your parents, and naturally can avoid all kinds of disasters. No only is your life itself therefore prolonged, but your personal dignity is enhanced. Think what a frail thing life is, especially that of a samurai. This being so, you will come to consider every day of your life your last and dedicate it to the fulfillment of your obligations. Never let the thought of a long life seize upon you, for then you are apt to indulge in all kinds of dissipation, and end your days in dire disgrace. This was the reason why Masashige is said to have told his son Masatsura to keep the ideal of death all the time before his mind.

The writer of this 'Primer' has rightly given expression to what has been unconsciously going on in the mind of the samurai generally. The notion of death, on the one hand, makes one's thought extend beyond the limitations of this finite life, and, on the other hand, screws it up so as to take daily life seriously. It was, therefore, natural for every sober-minded samurai to approach Zen with the idea of mastering death. Zen's claim to handling this problem without appealing either to learning or to moral training or to ritualism must have been a great attraction to the comparatively unsophisticated mind of the samurai. There was a kind of logical relationship between his psychological outlook and the direct practical teaching of Zen.

Further, we read the following in the *Hagakure*:

> Bushido means the determined will to die. When you are at the parting of the ways, do not hesitate to choose the way to death. No special reason for this except that your mind is thus made up and ready to see to the business. Some may say that if you die without attaining the object, it is a useless death, dying like a dog. But when you are at the parting of the ways, you need not plan for attaining the object. We all prefer life to death, and our planning and reasoning will be naturally for life. If then you miss the object and are alive, you are really a coward. This is an important consideration. In case you die without achieving the object, it may be a dog-death – the deed of madness, but there is no reflection here on your honor. In Bushido, honor comes first. Therefore, every morning and every evening, have the idea of death vividly impressed in your mind. When your determination to die at any moment is thoroughly established, you attain to perfect mastery of Bushido, your life will be faultless, and your duties will be fully discharged.

'ON PRACTICE' BY MAO TZE TUNG

Mao Tze Tung (1893–1976) was the founder and long-term leader of the People's Republic of China and for a period a widely read and quite influential theorist of Marxism-Leninism. When the Chinese empire collapsed, Mao became a political organiser in his native province of Hunan and was converted to Marxism in 1918 when working as a librarian in Beijing University. In 1921, he helped found the Chinese Communist Party (partly at the instigation of the Soviet Union). When the communists clashed with Chinese nationalists (led by Chiang Kai-Shek), Mao led a peasant guerrilla war against the government, escaping Chiang's armies in the famous 'Long March'. In 1945, China fell into civil war again, and Mao and followers were able to take power, proclaiming the People's Republic of China on 1 October 1949.

The decisive aspect of Mao's political outlook was his commitment to organising the peasants and raising a revolutionary movement among them (in distinction to communist orthodoxy that focused on the industrial proletariat). Mao thus adapted Leninism and Stalinism to the specific context of China at that time. In his philosophical work, he wanted to move beyond the traditional Chinese culture (especially Confucianism and monarchism and religion) and to replace the authority vested in the state, the clan, religion and the family (including male domination of women) with an egalitarian society. The 'New China' was to be based on a 'New Democracy' of bottom-up democracy rising from the local to the national level.

Mao's long period of rule was marked by fractious relations with the Soviet Union, and courting by the USA, and by disasters such as the 'Great Leap Forward', intended to communalise agricultural labour but which led to starvation and ultimately the repressive Cultural Revolution in the 1970s. Mao's influence in the West stems not only from his presentation of an apparently different form of communism to that found in the Soviet Union but also from the publication in 1964 of *The Little Red Book*, which was widely read by young radicals in the West attracted by its advocacy of an apparently 'open' political philosophy. In this extract, Mao stresses the importance of practice – practical engagement within the world – in forming and reforming our theoretical commitments. This legitimates changes in policy and movements away from orthodoxy since it stresses a kind of pragmatism over a purity of theory; but it also has the effect of politicising philosophical reflection, since it is only possible if formed as part of ongoing practical experience of the world.

'ON PRACTICE' (1954)*

Mao Tze Tung

Pre-Marxist materialism could not understand the dependence of knowledge upon social practice, namely, the dependence of knowledge upon production and class struggle, because it examined the problem of knowledge apart from man's social nature, apart from his historical development.

To begin with, the Marxist regards man's productive activity as the most fundamental practical activity, as the determinant of all other activities. In his cognition man, depending mainly upon activity in material production, gradually understands nature's phenomena, nature's characteristics, nature's laws, and the relations between himself and nature; and through productive activity he also gradually acquires knowledge in varying degrees about certain human interrelations. None of such knowledge can be obtained apart from productive activity. In a classless society every person, as a member of society, joins in effort with the other members, enters into certain relations of production with them, and engages in productive activity to solve the problem of material life. In the various kinds of class society, on the other hand, members of society of all classes also enter, in different ways, into certain relations of production and engage in productive activity to solve the problem of material life. This is the primary source from which human knowledge develops.

Man's social practice is not confined to productive activity; there are many other forms of activity – class struggle, political life, scientific and artistic activity; in short, man in society participates in all spheres of practical social life. Thus in his cognition man, besides knowing things through material life, knows in varying degrees the various kinds of human interrelations through political life and cultural life (both of which are closely connected with material life). Among these the various forms of class struggle exert a particularly profound influence on the development of man's knowledge. In a class society everyone lives within the status of a particular class and every mode of thought is invariably stamped with the brand of a class.

The Marxist holds that productive activity in human society develops step by step from a lower to a higher level, and consequently man's knowledge, whether of nature or of society, also develops step by step from a lower to a higher level, that is, from the superficial to the deep and from the one-sided to the

---

* From Mao Tze Tung, *Selected Works of Mao Tze Tung, Vol. 1* (London: Lawrence and Wishart, 1954), pp. 282–92, 296–7.

many-sided. For a very long period in history man was confined to a merely one-sided understanding of social history because, on the one hand, the biased views of the exploiting classes constantly distorted social history and, on the other, small-scale production limited man's outlook. It was only when the modern proletariat emerged along with the big forces of production (large-scale industry) that man could acquire a comprehensive, historical understanding of the development of social history and turn his knowledge of society into science, the science of Marxism.

The Marxist holds that man's social practice alone is the criterion of the truth of his knowledge of the external world. In reality, man's knowledge becomes verified only when, in the process of social practice (in the process of material production, of class struggle, and of scientific experiment), he achieves the anticipated results. If man wants to achieve success in his work, that is, to achieve the anticipated results, he must make his thoughts correspond to the laws of the objective world surrounding him; if they do not correspond, he will fail in practice. If he fails he will derive lessons from his failure, alter his ideas, so as to make them correspond to the laws of the objective world, and thus turn failure into success; this is what is meant by 'failure is the mother of success', and 'a fall into the pit, a gain in your wit'.

The theory of knowledge of dialectical materialism raises practice to the first place, holds that human knowledge cannot be separated the least bit from practice, and repudiates all incorrect theories which deny the importance of practice or separate knowledge from practice. Thus Lenin said, 'Practice is higher than (theoretical) knowledge because it has not only the virtue of universality, but also the virtue of immediate reality'.[1]

Marxist philosophy, i.e. dialectical materialism, has two most outstanding characteristics: one is its class nature, its open declaration that dialectical materialism is in the service of the proletariat; the other is its practicality, its emphasis on the dependence of theory on practice, emphasis on practice as the foundation of theory which in turn serves practice. In judging the trueness of one's knowledge or theory, one cannot depend upon one's subjective feelings about it, but upon its objective result in social practice. Only social practice can be the criterion of truth. The viewpoint of practice is the first and basic viewpoint in the theory of knowledge of dialectical materialism.[2]

But how after all does human knowledge arise from practice and in turn serve practice? This becomes clear after a glance at the process of development of knowledge.

In fact man, in the process of practice, sees at the beginning only the phenomena of various things, their separate aspects, their external relations. For instance, a number of visitors come to Yenan on a tour of observation: in the first day or two, they see the topography, the streets and the houses of Yenan; meet a number of people; attend banquets, evening parties and mass meetings; hear various kinds of talk; and read various documents – all these being the phenomena of things, the separate aspect of things, the external relations between such things. This is called the perceptual stage of knowledge, namely, the stage of perceptions and impressions. That is, various things in Yenan affect the sense organs of the members of the observation group, give rise to their perceptions, and leave on their minds many impressions, together with an idea of the general external relations between these impressions: this is the first stage of knowledge. At this stage, man cannot as yet form profound concepts or draw conclusions that conform with logic.

As social practice continues, things that give rise to man's perceptions and impressions in the course of his practice are repeated many times; then a sudden change (a leap) takes place in the process of knowledge in man's mind, resulting in concepts. Concepts as such no longer represent the phenomena of things, their separate aspects, or their external relations, but embrace their essence, their totality and their internal relations. Conception and perception are not only quantitatively but also qualitatively different. Proceeding farther and employing the method of judgment and inference, we can then draw conclusions that conform with logic. What is described in the *Tale of the Three Kingdoms* as 'knitting the brows one hits upon a strategem', or in our workaday language as 'let me think it over', refers precisely to the procedure of man's manipulation of concepts in his mind to form judgments and inferences. This is the second stage of knowledge.

When our visitors, the members of the observation group, have collected various kinds of data and, furthermore, 'thought them over', they can come to the following judgment: 'the Communist Party's policy of the Anti-Japanese National United Front is thorough, sincere and honest'. Having made this judgment, they can, if they are honest about unity for national salvation, go a step farther and draw the following conclusion: 'the Anti-Japanese National United Front can succeed'. In the whole process of man's knowledge of a thing, conception, judgment and inference constitute the more important stage, the stage of rational knowledge. The real task of knowledge is to arrive at thought through perception, at a gradual understanding of the internal contradictions of objective things, their laws and the internal relations of various processes, that is, at logical knowledge. To repeat, the reason why logical knowledge is different from perceptual knowledge is that perceptual knowledge concerns the separate aspects, the phenomena, the external relations of things; whereas logical knowledge takes a big stride forward to reach the wholeness, the essence and the internal relations of things, discloses the internal contradictions of the surrounding world, and is therefore capable of grasping the development of the surrounding world in its totality, in the internal relations between all its aspects.

Such a dialectical-materialist theory of the process of development of knowledge, based on practice and proceeding from the superficial to the deep, was not put forward by anybody before the rise of Marxism. Marxist materialism for the first time correctly solved the problem of the process of development of knowledge, pointing out both materialistically and dialectically the deepening process of knowledge, the process of how perceptual knowledge turns into logical knowledge through the complex and regularly recurrent practices of production and class struggle of man in society. Lenin said: 'The abstract concept of matter, of a law of nature, of economic value or any other scientific (i.e. correct and basic, not false or superficial) abstraction reflects nature more deeply, truly and fully'. Marxism-Leninism holds that the characteristics of the two stages of the process of knowledge are that, at the lower stage, knowledge appears in perceptual form, while at the higher stage it appears in logical form; but both stages belong to a single process of knowledge. Perception and reason are different in nature, but not separate from each other; they are united on the basis of practice.

Our practice proves that things perceived cannot be readily understood by us and that only things understood can be more profoundly perceived. Perception only solves the problem of phenomena; reason alone solves the problem of essence. Such problems can never be solved apart from practice. Anyone who wants to know a thing has no way of doing so except by coming into contact with it, i.e. by living (practising) in its surroundings.

In feudal society it was impossible to know beforehand the laws of capitalist society, because, with capitalism not yet on the scene, the corresponding practice did not exist. Marxism could only be the product of capitalist society. In the age of free, competitive capitalism, Marx could not have known specifically beforehand some of the special laws pertaining to the era of imperialism, because imperialism – the last stage of capitalism – had not yet emerged and the corresponding practice did not exist; only Lenin and Stalin could take up this task.

Apart from their genius, the reason why Marx, Engels, Lenin and Stalin could work out their theories is mainly their personal participation in the practice of the contemporary class struggle and scientific experimentation; without this no amount of genius could bring success. The saying 'a scholar does not step outside his gate, yet knows all the happenings under the sun' was mere empty talk in the technologically undeveloped old times; and although this saying can be realised in the present age of technological development, yet the people with real first-hand knowledge are those engaged in practice, and only when they have obtained 'knowledge' though their practice, and when their knowledge, through the medium of writing and technology, reaches the hands of the 'scholar', can the 'scholar' know indirectly 'the happenings under the sun'.

If a man wants to know certain things or certain kinds of things directly, it is only through personal participation in the practical struggle to change reality, to change those things or those kind of things, that he can come into contact with the phenomena of those things or those kinds of things; and it is only during the practical struggle to change reality, in which he personally participates, that he can disclose the essence of those things or those kinds of things and understand them. This is the path to knowledge along which everyone actually travels, only some people, distorting things deliberately, argue to the contrary. The most ridiculous person in the world is the 'wiseacre' who, having gained some half-baked knowledge by hearsay, proclaims himself 'the world's number one'; this merely shows that he has not taken a proper measure of himself. The question of knowledge is one of science, and there must not be the least bit of insincerity or conceit; what is required is decidedly the reverse – a sincere and modest attitude. If you want to gain knowledge you must partici-pate in the practice of changing reality. If you want to know the taste of a pear you must change the pear by eating it yourself. If you want to know the composition and properties of atoms you must make experiments in physics and chemistry to change the state of atoms. If you want to know the theory and methods of revolution, you must participate in revolution. All genuine knowledge originates in direct experience. But man cannot have direct experience in everything; as a matter of fact, most of our knowledge comes from indirect experience, e.g. all knowledge of ancient times and foreign lands. To the ancients and foreigners, such knowledge comes from direct experience; if, as the direct experience of the ancients and foreigners, such knowledge fulfils the condition of 'scientific abstraction' mentioned by Lenin, and scientifically reflects objective things, then it is reliable, otherwise it is not. Hence a man's knowledge consists of two parts and nothing else, of direct experience and in-direct experience. And what is indirect experience to me is nevertheless direct experience to other people. Consequently, taking knowledge in its totality, any kind of knowledge is inseparable from direct experience.

The source of all knowledge lies in the perception through man's physical sense organs of the objective world surrounding him; if a person denies such perception, denies direct experience, and denies personal participation in the practice of changing reality, then he is not a materialist. That is why the 'wiseacres' are ridiculous. The Chinese have an old saying: 'How can one obtain tiger cubs without entering the tiger's lair?' This saying is true of man's practice as well as of the theory of knowledge. There can be no knowledge apart from practice.

To make clear the dialectical-materialist process of knowledge arising from the practice of changing reality – the gradually deepening process of knowledge – a few concrete examples are further given below:

In its knowledge of capitalist society in the first period of its practice – the period of machine-smashing and spontaneous struggle – the proletariat, as yet in the stage of perceptual knowledge, only knew the separate aspects and exter-nal relations of the various phenomena of capitalism. At that time the proletar-iat was what we call a 'class in itself'. But when this class reached the second period of its practice (the period of conscious, organised, economic struggle and political struggle), when through its practice, through its experiences gained in long-term struggles, and through its education in Marxist theory, which is a summing-up of these experiences by Marx and Engels according to scientific method, it came to understand the essence of capitalist society, the relations of exploitation between social classes, and its own historical task, and then became a 'class for itself'.

Changing reality from [strikethrough] unknown to known; this changing the way you interact w/ your reality

Similarly with the Chinese people's knowledge of imperialism. The first stage was one of superficial, perceptual knowledge, as shown in the indiscriminate anti-foreign struggles of the Movement of the T'aip'ing Heavenly Kingdom, the Boxer Movement, etc. It was only in the second stage that the Chinese people arrived at rational knowledge, when they saw the internal and external contradictions of imperialism, as well as the essence of the oppression and exploitation of China's broad masses by imperialism in alliance with China's compradors and feudal class; such knowledge began only about the time of the May 4 Movement of 1919.

Let us also look at war. If those who direct a war lack war experience, then in the initial stage they will not understand the profound laws for directing a particular war (e.g. our Agrarian Revolutionary War of the past ten years). In the initial stage they merely undergo the experience of a good deal of fighting, and what is more, suffer many defeats. But from such experience (of battles won and especially of battles lost), they are able to understand the inner thread of the whole war, namely, the laws governing that particular war, to understand strategy and tactics, and consequently they are able to direct the war with confidence. At such a time, if an inexperienced person takes over the command, he, too, cannot understand the true laws of war until after he has suffered a number of defeats (after he has gained experience).

We often hear the remark made by a comrade when he has not the courage to accept an assignment: 'I have no confidence'. Why has he no confidence? Because he has no systematic understanding of the nature and conditions of the work, or because he has had little or even no contact with this kind of work; hence the laws governing it are beyond him. After a detailed analysis of the nature and conditions of the work, he will feel more confident and become willing to do it. If, after doing the work for some time, this person has gained experience in it, and if moreover he is willing to look at things with an open mind and does not consider problems subjectively, one-sidedly and superficially, he will be able to draw conclusions as to how to proceed with his work and his confidence will be greatly enhanced. Only those are bound to stumble who look at problems subjectively, one-sidedly and superficially and, on arriving at a place, issue orders or directives in a self-complacent manner without considering the circumstances, without viewing things in their totality (their history and their present situation as a whole), and without coming into contact with the essence of things (their qualities and the internal relations between one thing and another).

Thus the first step in the process of knowledge is contact with the things of the external world; this belongs to the stage of perception. The second step is a synthesis of the data of perception by making a rearrangement or a reconstruction; this belongs to the stage of conception, judgment and inference. It is only when the perceptual data are extremely rich (not fragmentary or incomplete) and are in correspondence to reality (not illusory) that we can, on the basis of such data, form valid concepts and carry out correct reasoning.

Here two important points must be emphasised. The first, a point which has been mentioned before, but should be repeated here, is the question of the dependence of rational knowledge upon perceptual knowledge. The person is an idealist who thinks that rational knowledge need not be derived from perceptual knowledge. In the history of philosophy there is the so-called 'rationalist' school which admits only the validity of reason, but not the validity of experience, regarding reason alone as reliable and perceptual experience as unreliable; the mistake of this school consists in turning things upside down. The rational is reliable precisely because it has its source in the perceptual, otherwise it would be like water without a source or a tree without roots, something subjective, spontaneous and unreliable. As to the sequence in the process of knowledge, perceptual experience comes first; we emphasise the significance of social practice in the process of knowledge precisely because social practice alone can give rise to man's knowledge and start him on the acquisition of perceptual experience from the objective world surrounding him. For a person who shuts his eyes, stops his ears and totally cuts himself off from the objective world, there can be no knowledge to speak of. Knowledge starts with experience – this is the materialism of the theory of knowledge. \ \ \.

  The second point is that knowledge has yet to be deepened, the perceptual stage of knowledge has yet to be developed to the rational stage – this is the dialectics of the theory of knowledge. It would be a repetition of the mistake of 'empiricism' in history to hold that knowledge can stop at the lower stage of perception and that perceptual knowledge alone is reliable while rational knowledge is not. This theory errs in failing to recognise that, although the data of perception reflect certain real things of the objective world (I am not speaking here of idealing empiricism which limits experience to so-called introspection), yet they are merely fragmentary and superficial, reflecting things incompletely instead of representing their essence. To reflect a thing fully in its totality, to reflect its essence and its inherent laws, it is necessary, through thinking, to build up a system of concepts and theories by subjecting the abundant perceptual data to a process of remodelling and reconstructing – discarding the crude and selecting the refined, eliminating the false and retaining the true, proceeding from one point to another, and going through the outside into the inside; it is necessary to leap from perceptual knowledge to rational knowledge. Knowledge which is such a reconstruction does not become emptier or less reliable; on the contrary, whatever has been scientifically reconstructed on the basis of practice in the process of knowledge is something which, as Lenin said, reflects objective things more deeply, more truly, more fully. As against this, the vulgar plodders, respecting experience yet despising theory, cannot take a comprehensive view of the entire objective process, lack clear direction and long-range perspective, and are self-complacent with occasional successes and peep-hole views. Were those persons to direct a revolution, they would lead it up a blind alley.

[. . .]

The development of the objective process is one full of contradictions and struggles. The development of the process of man's knowledge is also one full of contradictions and struggles. All the <u>dialectical movements</u> of the objective world can sooner or later be reflected in man's knowledge. As the process of emergence, development and disappearance in social practice is infinite, the process of emergence, development and disappearance in human knowledge is also infinite. As the practice directed towards changing objective reality on the basis of definite ideas, theories, plans or programmes develops farther ahead each time, man's knowledge of objective reality likewise becomes deeper each time. The process of change in the objective world will never end, nor will man's knowledge of truth through practice. Marxism-Leninism has in no way summed up all knowledge of truth, but is ceaselessly opening up, through practice, the road to the knowledge of truth. <u>Our conclusion is for the concrete and historical unity of the subjective and the objective</u>, of theory and practice, and of knowing and doing, and against all incorrect ideologies, whether Right or 'Left', which depart from concrete history. With society developed to its present stage, it is upon the shoulders of the proletariat and its party that, from historical necessity, the responsibility for correctly understanding and changing the world has fallen. This process of the practice of changing the world, determined on the basis of scientific knowledge, has already reached a historic moment in the world and in China, a moment of such importance as human history has never before witnessed, i.e. a moment for completely dispelling the darkness in the world and in China and bringing about such a world of light as never existed before.

Perception (subjective) + essence (objective) = totality [handwritten annotation]

NOTES

1. V. I. Lenin, *Philosophical Notebooks*, Russian edition, Moscow 1947, p. 185.
2. Cf. Karl Marx, *Theses on Feuerbach*, published as an Appendix in Frederick Engels's *Ludwig Feuerbach and the End of Classical German Philosophy*; and V. I. Lenin, *Materialism and Empirio-Criticism*, Chapter III, Section 6.
3. V. I. Lenin, loc. cit., p. 146.
4. Cf. Lenin, loc. cit., p. 146: 'For the sake of knowing, one must start to know, to study, on the basis of experience and rise from experience to general knowledge'.

'THE NECESSITY FOR ISLAMIC GOVERNMENT' BY AYATOLLAH KHOMEINI

Time Magazine's 1979 'Man of the Year', Ayatollah Khomeini (1900–89), was one of the most important religious leaders in the world, during his lifetime and, from his subsequent influence, after his death. An *ayatollah* is a supreme religious leader, and Khomeini came from the Shi'ite branch of Islam (the second-largest, accounting for approximately 15 per cent of all Muslims). The precise differences between Shi'ite thought and the mainstream forms of Sunni Islam cannot be explained in full here, but it is worth noting that the Shi'ite form tends to stress that the character of Islam is not isolated to specific religious practices but is also about the empowerment of the oppressed. This has meant that it has often been part of political movements (but note that the form of Islam adhered to by Osama Bin Laden and those taken to be responsible for the attacks on New York and Washington of 11 September 2001 is Wahhabism, a puritanical sect of Sunni Islam). Khomeini came to world prominence when he took power after the Iranian Revolution of 1979 and declared the country an Islamic republic wedded to a conservative vision and hostile to Western intervention. In the extract here, he argues that, for the Islamic law to be properly implemented, the state itself must be Islamic. He outlines some of the elements of such a state and, in urging its necessity, encourages the removal of 'imperialist' rulers who have divided the Islamic community and brought about oppression, poverty and irreligious behaviour.

'THE NECESSITY FOR ISLAMIC GOVERNMENT' (1981)*

Ayatollah Khomeini

A body of laws alone is not sufficient for a society to be reformed. In order for law to ensure the reform and happiness of man, there must be an executive power and an executor. For this reason, God Almighty, in addition to revealing a body of law (i.e., the ordinances of the *shari'a*), has laid down a particular form of government together with executive and administrative institutions.

The Most Noble Messenger (peace and blessings be upon him) headed the executive and administrative institutions of Muslim society. In addition to

---

* From Khomeini, *Islam and Revolution*, trans. H. Algar (Berkeley, CA: Mizan Press, 1981), pp. 40–51.

conveying the revelation and expounding and interpreting the articles of faith and the ordinances and institutions of Islam, he undertook the implementation of law and the establishment of the ordinances of Islam, thereby bringing into being the Islamic state. He did not content himself with the promulgation of law; rather, he implemented it at the same time, cutting off hands and administering lashings and stonings. After the Most Noble Messenger, his successor had the same duty and function. When the Prophet appointed a successor, it was not for the purpose of expounding articles of faith and law; it was for the implementation of law and the execution of God's ordinances. It was this function – the execution of law and the establishment of Islamic institutions – that made the appointment of a successor such an important matter that the Prophet would have failed to fulfill his mission if he had neglected it. For after the Prophet, the Muslims still needed someone to execute laws and establish the institutions of Islam in society, so that they might attain happiness in this world and the hereafter.

By their very nature, in fact, law and social institutions require the existence of an executor. It has always and everywhere been the case that legislation alone has little benefit: legislation by itself cannot assure the well-being of man. After the establishment of legislation, an executive power must come into being, a power that implements the laws and the verdicts given by the courts, thus allowing people to benefit from the laws and the just sentences the courts deliver. Islam has therefore established an executive power in the same way that it has brought laws into being. The person who holds this executive power is known as the *vali amr*.[1]

The Sunna[2] and path of the Prophet constitute a proof of the necessity for establishing government. First, he himself established a government, as history testifies. He engaged in the implementation of laws, the establishment of the ordinances of Islam, and the administration of society. He sent out governors to different regions; both sat in judgment himself and appointed judges; dispatched emissaries to foreign states, tribal chieftains, and kings; concluded treaties and pacts; and took command in battle. In short, he fulfilled all the functions of government. Second, he designated a ruler to succeed him, in accordance with divine command. If God Almighty, through the Prophet, designated a man who was to rule over Muslim society after him, this is in itself an indication that government remains a necessity after the departure of the Prophet from this world. Again, since the Most Noble Messenger promulgated the divine command through his act of appointing a successor, he also implicitly stated the necessity for establishing a government.

It is self-evident that the necessity for enactment of the law, which necessitated the formation of a government by the Prophet (upon whom be peace), was not confined or restricted to his time, but continues after his departure from this world. According to one of the noble verses of the Qur'an, the ordinances of Islam are not limited with respect to time or place; they are permanent and must be enacted until the end of time. They were not revealed merely for the time of the Prophet, only to be abandoned thereafter, with retribution and the penal code of Islam no longer to be enacted, or the taxes prescribed by Islam no longer collected, and the defense of the lands and people of Islam suspended. The claim that the laws of Islam may remain in abeyance or are restricted to a particular time or place is contrary to the essential credal bases of Islam. Since the enactment of laws, then, is necessary after the departure of the Prophet from this world, and indeed, will remain so until the end of time, the formation of a government and the establishment of executive and administrative organs are also necessary. Without the formation of a government and the establishment of such organs to ensure that through enactment of the law, all activities of the individual take place in the framework of a just system, chaos and anarchy will prevail and social, intellectual, and moral corruption will arise. The only way to prevent the emergence of anarchy and disorder and to protect society from corruption is to form a government and thus impart order to all the affairs of the country.

Both reason and divine law, then, demonstrate the necessity in our time for what was necessary during the lifetime of the Prophet and the age of the Commander of the Faithful. 'Ali ibn Abi Talib (peace be upon them) – namely the formation of a government and the establishment of executive and administrative organs.

In order to clarify the matter further, let us pose the following questions. From the time of the Lesser Occultation[3] down to the present (a period of more than twelve centuries that may continue for hundreds of millennia if it is not appropriate for the Occulted Imam to manifest himself), is it proper that the laws of Islam be cast aside and remain unexecuted, so that everyone acts as he pleases and anarchy prevails? Were the laws that the Prophet of Islam labored so hard for twenty-three years to set forth, promulgate, and execute valid only for a limited period of time? Did God limit the validity of His laws to 200 years? Was everything pertaining to Islam meant to be abandoned after the Lesser Occultation? Anyone who believes so, or voices such a belief, is worse situated than the person who believes and proclaims that Islam has been superseded or abrogated by another supposed revelation.[4]

No one can say it is no longer necessary to defend the frontiers and the territorial integrity of the Islamic homeland; that taxes such as the *jizya, kharaj, khums* and *zakat*[5] should no longer be collected; that the penal code of Islam, with its provisions for the payment of blood money and the exacting of requital, should be suspended. Any person who claims that the formation of an Islamic government is not necessary implicitly denies the necessity for the implementation of Islamic law, the universality and comprehensiveness of that law, and the eternal validity of the faith itself.

After the death of the Most Noble Messenger (peace and blessings be upon him), none of the Muslims doubted the necessity for government. No one said: 'We no longer need a government'. No one was heard to say anything of the kind. There was unanimous agreement concerning the necessity for government. There was disagreement only as to which person should assume responsibility for government and head the state. Government, therefore, was established after the Prophet (upon whom be peace and blessings), both in the time of the caliphs and in that of the Commander of the Faithful (peace be upon him); an apparatus of government came into existence with administrative and executive organs.

The nature and character of Islamic law and the divine ordinances of the *shari'a* furnish additional proof of the necessity for establishing government, for they indicate that the laws were laid down for the purpose of creating a state and administering the political, economic, and cultural affairs of society.

First, the laws of the *shari'a* embrace a diverse body of laws and regulations, which amounts to a complete social system. In this system of laws, all the needs of man have been met: his dealings with his neighbors, fellow citizens, and clan, as well as children and relatives; the concerns of private and marital life; regulations concerning war and peace and intercourse with other nations; penal and commercial law; and regulations pertaining to trade and agriculture. Islamic law contains provisions relating to the preliminaries of marriage and the form in which it should be contracted, and others relating to the development of the embryo in the womb and what food the parents should eat at the time of conception. It further stipulates the duties that are incumbent upon them while the infant is being suckled, and specifies how the child should be reared, and how the husband and the wife should relate to each other and to their children. Islam provides laws and instructions for all of these matters, aiming, as it does, to produce integrated and virtuous human beings who are walking embodiments of the law, or to put it differently the law's voluntary and instinctive executors. It is obvious, then, how much care Islam devotes to government and the political and economic relations of society, with the goal of creating conditions conducive to the production of morally upright and virtuous human beings.

The Glorious Qur'an and the Sunna contain all the laws and ordinances man needs in order to attain happiness and the perfection of his state. The book *al-Kafi*[6] has a chapter entitled, 'All the Needs of Man Are Set Out in the Book and the Sunna', the 'Book' meaning the Qur'an, which is, in its own words, 'an exposition of all things'.[7] According to certain traditions, the Imam[8] also swears that the Book and the Sunna contain without a doubt all that men need.

Second, if we examine closely the nature and character of the provisions of the law, we realize that their execution and implementation depend upon the formation of a government, and that it is impossible to fulfill the duty of executing God's commands without there being established properly comprehensive administrative and executive organs. Let us now mention certain types of provision in order to illustrate this point; the others you can examine yourselves.

The taxes Islam levies and the form of budget it has established are not merely for the sake of providing subsistence to the poor or feeding the indigent among the descendants of the Prophet (peace and blessings be upon him); they are also intended to make possible the establishment of a great government and to assure its essential expenditures.

For example, *khums* is a huge source of income that accrues to the treasury and represents one item in the budget. According to our Shi'i school of thought, *khums* is to be levied in an equitable manner on all agricultural and commercial profits and all natural resources whether above or below the ground – in short, on all forms of wealth and income. It applies equally to the greengrocer with his stall outside this mosque and to the shipping or mining magnate. They must all pay one-fifth of their surplus income, after customary expenses are deducted, to the Islamic ruler so that it enters the treasury. It is obvious that such a huge income serves the purpose of administering the Islamic state and meeting all its financial needs. If we were to calculate one-fifth of the surplus income of all the Muslim countries (or of the whole world, should it enter the fold of Islam), it would become fully apparent that the purpose for the imposition of such a tax is not merely the upkeep of the *sayyids*[9] or the religious scholars, but on the contrary, something far more significant – namely, meeting the financial needs of the great organs and institutions of government. If an Islamic government is achieved, it will have to be administered on the basis of the taxes that Islam has established – *khums*, *zakat* (this, of course, would not represent an appreciable sum),[10] *jizya*, and *kharaj*.

How could the *sayyids* ever need so vast a budget? The *khums* of the bazaar of Baghdad would be enough for the needs of the *sayyids* and the upkeep of the religious teaching institution, as well as all the poor of the Islamic world, quite apart from the *khums* of the bazaars of Tehran, Istanbul, Cairo, and other cities. The provision of such a huge budget must obviously be for the purpose of forming a government and administering the Islamic lands. It was established with the aim of providing for the needs of the people, for public services relating to health, education, defense, and economic development. Further, in accordance with the procedures laid down by Islam for the collection, preservation, and expenditure of this income, all forms of usurpation and embezzlement of public wealth have been forbidden, so that the head of state and all those entrusted with responsibility for conducting public affairs (i.e., members of the government) have no privileges over the ordinary citizen in benefiting from the public income and wealth; all have an equal share.

Now, should we cast this huge treasury into the ocean, or bury it until the Imam returns, or just spent it on fifty *sayyids* a day until they have all eaten their fill? Let us suppose we give all this money to 500,000 *sayyids*; they would not know what to do with it. We all know that the *sayyids* and the poor have a claim on the public treasury only to the extent required for subsistence. The budget of the Islamic state is constructed in such a way that every source of income is allocated to specific types of expenditures. *Zakat*, voluntary contributions and charitable donations, and *khums* are all levied and spent separately. There is a *hadith* to the effect that at the end of the year, *sayyids* must return any surplus from what they have received to the Islamic ruler, just as the ruler must aid them if they are in need.

The *jizya*, which is imposed on the *ahl adh-dhimma*,[11] and the *kharaj*, which is levied on agricultural land, represent two additional sources of considerable income. The establishment of these taxes also proves that the existence of a ruler and a government is necessary. It is the duty of a ruler or governor to assess the poll-tax to be levied on the *ahl adh-dhimma* in accordance with their income and financial capacity, and to fix appropriate taxes on their arable lands and livestock. He must also collect the *kharaj* on those broad lands that are the 'property of God' and in the possession of the Islamic state. This task requires the existence of orderly institutions, rules and regulations, and administrative processes and policies; it cannot be fulfilled in the absence of order. It is the responsibility of those in charge of the Islamic state, first, to assess the taxes in due and appropriate measure and in accordance with the public good; then, to collect them; and finally, to spend them in a manner conducive to the welfare of the Muslims.

Thus, you see that the fiscal provisions of Islam also point to the necessity for establishing a government, for they cannot be fulfilled without the establishment of the appropriate Islamic institutions.

The ordinances pertaining to preservation of the Islamic order and defence of the territorial integrity and the independence of the Islamic *umma*[12] also demanded the formation of a government. An example is the command: 'Prepare against them whatever force you can muster and horses tethered' (Qur'an, 8:60), which enjoins the preparation of as much armed defensive force as possible and orders the Muslims to be always on the alert and at the ready, even in time of peace.

If the Muslims had acted in accordance with this command and, after forming a government, made the necessary extensive preparations to be in a state of full readiness for war, a handful of Jews would never have dared to occupy our lands, and to burn and destroy the Masjid al-Aqsa[13] without the people's being capable of making an immediate response. All this has resulted from the failure of the Muslims to fulfill their duty of executing God's law and setting up a righteous and respectable government. If the rulers of the Muslim countries truly represented the believers and enacted God's ordinances, they would set aside their petty differences, abandon their subversive and divisive activities, and join together like the fingers of one hand. Then a handful of wretched Jews (the agents of America, Britain, and other foreign powers) would never have been able to accomplish what they have, no matter how much support they enjoyed from America and Britain. All this has happened because of the incompetence of those who rule over the Muslims.

The verse: 'Prepare against them whatever force you can muster' commands you to be as strong and well-prepared as possible, so that your enemies will be unable to oppress you and transgress against you. It is because we have been lacking in unity, strength, and preparedness that we suffer oppression and are at the mercy of foreign aggressors.

There are numerous provisions of the law that cannot be implemented without the establishment of a governmental apparatus; for example, blood money, which must be exacted and delivered to those deserving it, or the corporeal penalties imposed by the law, which must be carried out under the supervision of the Islamic ruler. All of these laws refer back to the institutions of government, for it is governmental power alone that is capable of fulfilling this function.

After the death of the Most Noble Messenger (peace and blessings be upon him), the obstinate enemies of the faith, the Umayyads[14] (God's curses be upon them), did not permit the Islamic state to attain stability with the rule of 'Ali ibn Abi Talib (upon whom be peace). They did not allow a form of government to exist that was pleasing to God, Exalted and Almighty, and to his Most Noble Messenger. They transformed the entire basis of government, and their policies were, for the most part, contradictory to Islam. The form of government of the Umayyads and the Abbasids,[15] and the political and administrative policies they pursued, were anti-Islamic. The form of government was thoroughly perverted by being transformed into a monarchy, like those of the kings of Iran, the emperors of Rome, and the pharaohs of Egypt. For the most part, this non-Islamic form of government has persisted to the present day, as we can see.

Both law and reason require that we not permit governments to retain this non-Islamic or anti-Islamic character. The proofs are clear. First, the existence of a non-Islamic political order necessarily results in the non-implementation of the Islamic political order. Then, all non-Islamic systems of government are the systems of *kufr*,[16] since the ruler in each case is an instance of *taghut*,[17] and it is our duty to remove from the life of Muslim society all traces of *kufr* and destroy them. It is also our duty to create a favorable social environment for the education of believing and virtuous individuals, an environment that is in total contradiction with that produced by the rule of *taghut* and illegitimate power. The social environment created by *taghut* and *shirk*[18] invariably brings about corruption such as you can now observe in Iran, the corruption termed 'corruption on earth'.[19] This corruption must be swept away, and its instigators punished for their deeds. It is the same corruption that the Pharaoh generated in Egypt with his policies, so that the Qur'an says of him, 'Truly he was among the corruptors' (28:4). A believing, pious, just individual cannot possibly exist in a socio-political environment of this nature and still maintain his faith and righteous conduct. He is faced with two choices: either he commits acts that amount to *kufr* and contradict righteousness, or in order not to commit such acts and not to submit to the orders and commands of the *taghut*, the just individual opposes him and struggles against him in order to destroy the environment of corruption. We have in reality, then, no choice but to destroy those systems of government that are corrupt in themselves and also entail the corruption of others, and to overthrow all treacherous, corrupt, oppressive, and criminal regimes.

This is a duty that all Muslims must fulfill, in every one of the Muslim countries, in order to achieve the triumphant political revolution of Islam.

We see, too, that together, the imperialists and the tyrannical self-seeking rulers have divided the Islamic homeland. They have separated the various segments of the Islamic *umma* from each other and artificially created separate nations. There once existed the great Ottoman State, and that, too, the imperialists divided. Russia, Britain, Austria, and the other imperialist powers united, and through wars against the Ottomans, each came to occupy or absorb into its sphere of influence part of the Ottoman realm. It is true that most of the Ottoman rulers were incompetent, that some of them were corrupt, and that they followed a monarchical system. Nonetheless, the existence of the Ottoman State represented a threat to the imperialists. It was always possible that righteous individuals might rise up among the people and, with their assistance, seize control of the state, thus putting an end to imperialism by mobilizing the unified resources of the nation. Therefore, after numerous prior wars, the imperialists at the end of World War I divided the Ottoman State, creating in its territories about ten or fifteen petty states.[20] Then each of these was entrusted to one of their servants or a group of their servants, although certain countries were later able to escape the grasp of the agents of imperialism.

In order to assure the unity of the Islamic *umma*, in order to liberate the Islamic homeland from occupation and penetration by the imperialists and their puppet governments, it is imperative that we establish a government. In order to attain the unity and freedom of the Muslim peoples, we must overthrow the oppressive governments installed by the imperialists and bring into existence an Islamic government of justice that will be in the service of the people. The formation of such a government will serve to preserve the disciplined unity of the Muslims; just as Fatimat az-Zahra[21] (upon whom be peace) said in her address: 'The Imamate exists for the sake of preserving order among the Muslims and replacing their disunity with unity'.

Through the political agents they have placed in power over the people, the imperialists have also imposed on us an unjust economic order, and thereby divided our people into two groups: oppressors and oppressed. Hundreds of millions of Muslims are hungry and deprived of all form of healthcare and education, while minorities composed of the wealthy and powerful live a life of indulgence, licentiousness, and corruption. The hungry and deprived have constantly struggled to free themselves from the oppression of their plundering overlords, and their struggle continues to this day. But their way is blocked by the ruling minorities and the oppressive governmental structures they head. It is our duty to save the oppressed and deprived. It is our duty to be a helper to the oppressed and an enemy to the oppressor. This is nothing other than the duty that the Commander of the Faithful (upon whom be peace) entrusted to his two great offspring[22] in his celebrated testament: 'Be an enemy to the oppressor and a helper to the oppressed'.

The scholars of Islam have a duty to struggle against all attempts by the oppressors to establish a monopoly over the sources of wealth or to make illicit use of them. They must not allow the masses to remain hungry and deprived while plundering oppressors usurp the sources of wealth and live in opulence.

The Commander of the Faithful (upon whom be peace) says: 'I have accepted the task of government because God, Exalted and Almighty, has exacted from the scholars of Islam a pledge not to sit silent and idle in the face of the gluttony and plundering of the oppressors, on the one hand, and the hunger and deprivation of the oppressed, on the other'. Here is the full text of the passage we refer to:

> I swear by Him Who causes the seed to open and creates the souls of all living things that were it not for the presence of those who have come to swear allegiance to me, were it not for the obligation of rulership now imposed upon me by the availability of aid and support, and were it not for the pledge that God has taken from the scholars of Islam not to remain silent in the face of the gluttony and plundering of the oppressors, on the one hand, and the harrowing hunger and deprivation of the oppressed, on the other hand – were it not for all of this, then I would abandon the reins of government and in no way seek it. You would see that this world of yours, with all of its position and rank, is less in my eyes than the moisture that comes from the sneeze of a goat.[23]

How can we stay silent and idle today when we see that a band of traitors and usurpers, the agents of foreign powers, have appropriated the wealth and the fruits of labor of hundreds of millions of Muslims – thanks to the support of their masters and through the power of the bayonet – granting the Muslims not the least right to prosperity? It is the duty of Islamic scholars and all Muslims to put an end to this system of oppression and, for the sake of the well-being of hundreds of millions of human beings, to overthrow these oppressive governments and form an Islamic government.

Reason, the law of Islam, the practice of the Prophet (upon whom be peace and blessings) and that of the Commander of the Faithful (upon whom be peace), the purport of various Qur'anic verses and Prophetic traditions – all indicate the necessity of forming a government.

NOTES

1. *Vali amr*: 'the one who holds authority', a term derived from Qur'an, 4:59: 'O you who believe! Obey God, and obey the Messenger and the holders of authority (*uli 'l-amr*) from among you.'
2. Sunna: the practice of the Prophet, accepted by Muslims as the norm and ideal for all human behavior.
3. Lesser Occultation: *ghaybat-i sughra*, the period of about seventy years (260/872–329/939) when, according to Shi'i belief, Muhammad al-Mahdi, the Twelfth Imam, absented himself from the physical plane but remained in communication with his followers through a succession of four appointed deputies. At the death of the fourth deputy no successor was named, and the Greater Occultation (*ghaybat-i kubra*) began, and continues to this day.
4. The allusion is probably to the Baha'is, who claim to have received a succession of post-Qur'anic revelations.
5. *Jizya*: a tax levied on non-Muslim citizens of the Muslim state in exchange for the protection they receive and in lieu of the taxes, such as *zakat*, that only Muslims

pay. *Kharaj*: a tax levied on certain categories of land. *Khums*: a tax consisting of one-fifth of agricultural and commercial profits. *Zakat*: the tax levied on various categories of wealth and spent on the purposes specified in Qur'an, 9:60.

6. *al-Kafi*: one of the most important collections of Shi'i *hadith*, compiled by Shaykh Abu Ja'far al-Kulayni (d. 329/941). Two fascicules of this work have recently been translated into English by Sayyid Muhammad Hasan Rizvi and published in Tehran.

7. Qur'an, 16:89.

8. The reference is probably to Imam Ja'far as-Sadiq, whose sayings on this subject are quoted by 'Allama Tabataba'i in *al-Mizan fi Tafsir al-Qur'an* (Beirut, 1390/1979), XII, 327–8.

9. *Sayyids*: the descendants of the Prophet through his daughter Fatima and son-in-law 'Ali, the first of the Twelve Imams.

10. *Zakat* would not represent an appreciable sum presumably because it is levied on surplus wealth, the accumulation of which is inhibited by the economic system of Islam.

11. *Ahl adh-dhimma*: non-Muslim citizens of the Muslim state, whose rights and obligations are contractually determined.

12. *Umma*: the entire Islamic community, without territorial or ethnic distinction.

13. Masjid al-Aqsa: the site in Jerusalem where the Prophet ascended to heaven in the eleventh year of his mission (Qur'an, 17:1); also the complex of mosques and buildings erected on the site. The chief of these was extensively damaged by arson in 1969, two years after the Zionist usurpation of Jerusalem.

14. Umayyads: members of the dynasty that ruled at Damascus from 41/632 until 132/750 and transformed the caliphate into a hereditary institution. Mu'awiya, frequently mentioned in these pages, was the first of the Umayyad line.

15. Abbasids: the dynasty that replaced the Umayyads and established a new caliphal capital in Baghdad. With the rise of various local rulers, generally of military origin, the power of the Abbasids began to decline from the fourth/tenth century and it was brought to an end by the Mongol conquest in 656/1258.

16. *Kufr*: the rejection of divine guidance; the antithesis of Islam.

17. *Taghut*: one who surpasses all bounds in his despotism and tyranny and claims the prerogatives of divinity for himself, whether explicitly or implicitly.

18. *Shirk*: the assignment of partners to God, either by believing in a multiplicity of gods, or by assigning divine attributes and prerogatives to other-than-God.

19. 'Corruption on earth': a broad term including not only moral corruption, but also subversion of the public good, embezzlement and usurpation of public wealth, conspiring with the enemies of the community against its security, and working in general for the overthrow of the Islamic order. See the commentary on Qur'an, 5:33 in Tabataba'i, *al-Mizan*, V, 330–2.

20. It may be apposite to quote here the following passage from a secret report drawn up in January 1916 by T. E. Lawrence, the British organizer of the so-called Arab revolt led by Sharif Husayn of Mecca: 'Husayn's activity seems beneficial to us, because it marches with our immediate aims, the break-up of the Islamic bloc and the defeat and disruption of the Ottoman Empire . . . The Arabs are even less stable than the Turks. If properly handled they would remain in a state of political mosaic, a tissue of small jealous principalities incapable of political cohesion.' See Philip Knightley and Colin Simpson, *The Secret Lives of Lawrence of Arabia* (New York, 1971), p. 55.

21. Fatimat az-Zahra: Fatima, the daughter of the Prophet and wife of Imam 'Ali.

22. I.e., Hasan and Husayn.

23. See *Nahj al-Balagha*, ed. Subhi as-Salih (Beirut, 1397/1967).

12

DEMOCRATIC THEORY FOR A NEW CENTURY

Anna Marie Smith

Introduction

One of the tasks of democratic theory is to develop an understanding of the concept of democracy that is grounded in the historical traditions of emancipatory struggles. At the same time, however, democratic theory must also ensure that the meaning of democracy is constantly interrogated and that, where necessary, it is carefully revised such that it can address contemporary political conditions. In the United States today, for example, women have had the vote for the better part of a century, blacks and other minorities enjoy formal equality thanks to civil-rights gains, and the economy is expanding at such a rate that even the poorest Americans are seeing some increase in their incomes. At the same time, however, women, blacks and Latinos do not have equal access to the most important roles in the political process. Economic inequality, measured in terms of income, household wealth, career opportunities, the distribution of 'life chances' and so on, stubbornly remains a prominent feature of American society. Environmental issues are given a great deal of attention by politicians on the campaign trail, but the results in terms of actual policies are mixed at best. The trade-union movement is emerging once again as a major player in Presidential, Senate and Congressional races and has successfully recruited hundreds of thousands of new members. **Reagan**-era anti-union regulations are nevertheless still the rule, and the USA lags far behind many other Western nation states in unionisation rates, while the lack of campaign-finance reform guarantees an astonishing degree of political access for private corporations. Lesbians and gays have won some gains, including the repeal of various sodomy laws, the passage of civil-rights ordinances and laws against hate crimes, and the introduction of same-sex partner benefits for some private and public employees. Service in the military still remains impossible for any homosexual who does not maintain a strict regime of self-censorship, and same-sex marriage faces formidable opposition from conservative forces. A whole new information-technology era has unfolded, and more Americans are gaining access to the internet as the 'digital gap' is gradually narrowed. It is not clear, however, that the increased availability of information is fostering the creation of a more informed electorate. While new media products are launched every day, the public education system remains woefully underfunded. 'Content providers' on the internet are seeking brand-name recognition and audience share above all else. Mega-mergers are creating huge media conglomerates that overwhelmingly favour popular products with multimedia marketing tie-ins over alternative viewpoints, high-quality reporting and artistic work.

The entire question of democracy also has to be negotiated today simultaneously on transnational, international, nation-state and local terms. Global capitalism has developed to the extent that it is now commonplace to find that the workers performing the unskilled labour needed to produce a good actually live in an entirely different polity from the one inhabited by the experts who contribute technical knowledge to the manufacturing process. The consumers and the investors who reap the profits may live in other political jurisdictions as well. While trade-liberalisation agreements promote the free flow of investment capital, goods and profits across nation-state borders, immigration controls continue to block access to better labour markets and quality of life for the vast majority of foreign workers. Neo-conservative supporters of capitalist globalisation hail the eclipse of national economic boundaries, but human-rights movements continue to insist upon the importance of democratic struggles at both the international and the nation-state levels.

What does it mean in these conditions to demand equality for women, the elimination of racism, equal access to material resources, environmental justice, and lesbian and gay rights? How does this specific historical conjuncture give rise to new tensions between equality, freedom and solidarity? What tools can democratic theory offer that may help us to diagnose contemporary forms of inequality, to stimulate thought about possibilities for progressive struggle, and to imagine alternative worlds?

Democratic theory cannot meet this challenge if it devotes itself exclusively to abstract arguments. When democratic theory sets up abstract puzzles for itself and resolves them on the basis of universal principles and syllogistic arguments, it does gain conceptual clarity, but that is, in itself, insufficient. Democratic theory must also engage in a critical dialogue with contemporary social movements; it must also aim to grasp these movements' concrete historical wisdom – a type of knowledge that can only be generated in the midst of actual struggles – and to subject their utopian aspirations to critical interrogation. In this chapter, I will outline some of the ways in which feminist, queer and anti-racist struggles are generating new questions and theoretical forms of wisdom that are invigorating democratic theory today.

POWER, IDENTITY AND SUBJECTIVITY

Political discourse commonly assumes that identity is a more or less straight-forward matter. The rational, self-conscious, interest-maximising individual is posited as the fundamental unit of analysis. He or she is then grouped together with other individuals on the basis of their shared 'natural' interests. There is of course some disagreement on the nature of these shared interests – theorists such as **Lukes** (1974) do of course note that power relations tend to distort the situation such that the subject cannot grasp their objective interests – but they are nevertheless taken as a foundational dimension of their identity. A specific set of interests – such as bourgeois interests, or that pertaining to women or blacks – is considered as the core of the subject's being. Further, this core is con-ceptualised like an ideal type: even if it is clear that, in a given historical situa-tion, a specific movement has been shaped simultaneously by many different political factors, that subject is nevertheless understood for analytic purposes as the expression of a single, homogeneous and non-contradictory set of inter-ests. In this discourse, then – a discourse that has roots in the liberal-democra-tic and pluralist traditions, and borrows various elements from the Marxist and Weberian traditions as well – the subject is commonly reduced to its ascribed essence, and that essence is given prior to the subject's encounter with histori-cally specific power relations.

Nietzsche (1969) and Foucault (1977, 1978) suggest an entirely different approach. From their perspective, power relations in modern societies are not external and secondary; they are constitutive of the subject. When the delin-quent, to take Foucault's classic example (1979), engages in recidivist acts of reoffending, he or she is not necessarily expressing some sort of primordial pathology. It is the prison – the institution that holds the offender in its grip – that, in a sense, teaches him or her to follow a life of crime. Modern institu-tions such as the prison do not eliminate social disorder; they take these ele-ments of **alterity** into the heart of society, make them useful, and ensure their reproduction. Social outlaws are either put to work in a direct manner – some prisoners are obliged to perform productive labour, for example – or, more gen-erally, they are used as the objects of intricate and intensive experiments in new forms of population-management. The timetables and spatial segregation tech-niques used in the prison may find their way into the army, the school or the hospital. To follow Foucault's account further, the recidivist may imagine that, in the act of reoffending, he or she is freely choosing to pursue his or her own will. What if, Foucault asks, that which the subject imagines as their free will is actually a seductive illusion that has been incited in the course of the recidi-vist's encounter with the prison? And what if the prison system's chronic failure to eliminate recidivism actually serves some sort of purpose? Once it is assured that it will have a steady supply of manageable recidivists at its disposal, the prison system can mount an effective popular campaign for the endless expansion, intensification and refinement of social discipline. What appears to be an act of free will on the part of the outlaw may therefore be much more complicated. There are times in which the subject imagines that he or she has made a free choice to engage in rebellion, when he or she has actually been positioned by disciplinary relations such that he or she always already had a favourable disposition towards a course of action that actually strengthens the entire apparatus of social control.

Butler has emerged as one of the best contemporary interpreters of this tradition. In the text reproduced below, Butler offers a close reading of Foucault's conception of the deployment of sexuality. Moving from the terrain of the prison to that of sex and sexuality in his subsequent work (1980), Foucault maintains that power is constitutive of the subject rather than a simply negative and deductive force, but introduces several significant shifts in his theory. In *Discipline and Punish* (1977), Foucault argues that all modern disciplinary institutions closely resemble one another insofar as they borrow technologies and structures from each other in an almost seamless pattern of homogeneous social control. In *The History of Sexuality, Vol. 1* (1978), by contrast, he emphasises the complex, context-specific, heterogeneous and even contradictory nature of disciplinary tactics and population-management trends in modern Western societies. Foucault nevertheless consistently returns to the idea that the constitutive nature of power has a fundamentally insidious character. Modern emancipatory discourse encourages the subject to engage in a profound struggle to 'liberate' his or her true self – an imaginary entity that is intimately connected to one's sex – but, in the end, our efforts to set our true sexual selves free may only contribute even further to our entanglements in disciplinary regimes.

This paradoxical, contradictory identity regime – one in which the subject is invited to come into being as an active agent but only insofar as he or she conforms to a pre-authorised identity code – is at the heart of Butler's theory. For Butler, the sex/gender/sexuality system that operates in today's Western societies is one of the most effective fundamental identity regimes. The gendering process, from her perspective, does not simply take the shape of straightforward socialisation. According to feminist socialisation theory, young children are basically trained to conduct themselves according to the gender behaviour norms that correspond to their biological sex. In this model, the child arrives at his or her socialisation lessons with a body that has been sexed as male or female in a perfectly objective and non-controversial manner. The political impact of the misogynist tradition is supposed to begin when the child is taught exactly how he or she should inhabit his or her given male or female body. In a discriminatory environment, from this perspective, girls and women suffer oppressive treatment on the basis of their sex, but the assignment of sex itself has nothing to do with discrimination. Socialisation theory draws on a fairly one-dimensional behaviourist account of power relations. The child learns to

conform successfully to gender norms insofar as he or she responds in an instrumental manner to various rewards and punishments. Gender norms themselves
are typically understood in socialisation theory as a more or less arbitrary set
of associations between biologically sexed bodies and gender types of behaviour. Persons with male sex organs are expected to act aggressively, while more
nurturing behaviour is associated with persons who possess female sex organs.
Socialisation theory concludes that these sex–behaviour associations are taken
for granted as the norm only because the misogynist tradition has remained predominant for ages. It is possible, for example, for women to take on positions
of leadership, and for men to care for children. Men, however, have learned
over time how to obtain and defend a virtual monopoly on leadership positions.
Gender norms that equate nurturing, subservience and passivity with women's
true nature constitute a legitimating ideology that assists in the reproduction of
patriarchal authority.

Butler certainly accepts the claims of feminist socialisation theory about the
enduring character of patriarchal power. She disagrees, however, with its
approach to identity-formation and power relations. First, Butler follows the
lead of the lesbian feminist movement: she places homophobia, as well as
sexism, squarely at the centre of the feminist agenda. What if the gender regime
is constructed not only to perpetuate patriarchal power, but also to maintain
the abjection of homosexuality? And what if the entire process begins at a much
more fundamental level, namely at the very moment in which the bodily matter
is officially interpreted as a sexed being? Butler calls into question the process
by which our culture only confers personhood after it has unequivocally and
officially assigned the individual in question to one of the two sanctioned biological sex categories. Why does recognition turn on sex assignment? Why do
we not, for example, categorise each individual according to the day of the
week in which he or she is born, and then organise legal, medical and sociocul-
tural recognition of each individual's personhood according to the seven-day
system? If we must refer to the biological sex system, why do we have only two
sexes, and not the five sexes proposed by **Fausto-Sterling** (1993)? And why
must one indicate that one belongs to one or the other sex to obtain virtually
any official identification document that is issued by a state institution? The
process of becoming a recognised person is necessarily mediated by this binary
biological sex framework. One cannot become an authorised subject except as
a legally recognised male or as a legally recognised female. If someone insisted
that they belonged to both biological sex categories, or to neither of them, their
claims would be dismissed as incoherent by official institutions. As the transgender movement points out, it is the government agency, backed by the
medical profession, that ultimately assigns one of the two recognised sexes; the
views of the persons in question have very little bearing on the matter.

For Butler, the tyranny of the binary sex model is not an accident; it is the
product of a specific misogynist tradition in which sexism has been combined
with homophobia. When a body is interpreted as female, and thus a person is

invited into being, our culture does not just expect that person to conform to gender norms. Each gendering process entails entry into a world of compulsory heterosexuality. Imagine the moment in which the child is welcomed as a full human being into the world. 'It's a girl!' the doctor proclaims, and, unconsciously, the doctor, her parents and the entire culture also silently proclaim together, 'It's a future wife!' If this sounds far-fetched, consider the fact that the transgender movement is currently taking aim against the medical profession where its response to the birth of intersexed and hermaphrodite children is concerned. Doctors typically urge the parents of these perfectly healthy children to rush their infants into a series of operations that will install a legible set of genitalia. Sex-reassignment programmes for young children and teenagers – complete with further operations, synthetic hormone treatments and behaviour-modification therapy, all conducted before the patient reaches an age at which he or she could give consent for these procedures – are considered successful once the subject exhibits desire for a person of the opposite sex. When our official institutions and our culture invites someone into authorised being as a person, it not only insists on establishing their biological sex according to the binary model, but it does so in expectation that the person will desire individuals belonging to the other sex. The two-sex model secures at a fundamental level the myth of heterosexual necessity. A three-sex model would immediately complicate matters, for example, for it would call into question the natural character of male–female bonding.

This dimension of Butler's approach therefore emphasises the incorporation effects of power. Power does not come later to the body; the logic of a prevailing power regime is necessarily inscribed in the body, and the very coherence of the body as such depends upon this process of inscription. To become a recognised person, one must have a body that has already been officially categorised. In this sense, Butler draws our attention to the material dimension of subjectivation: at its most profound, the invitation to become a legitimate subject is only issued to those who already bear the marks of the power regime's corporeal interpretation.

Although we have referred exclusively to sex, gender and sexuality in this discussion, critical race theorists would note that racial politics may be usefully illuminated from this perspective as well. Racism does not simply entail the subordination of African Americans, Asians, native Americans and Latinos/Latinas to white-Anglo authority. In many instances, the person of colour cannot live their own relationship to their body except through the mediation of an interpretive schema that is not of their choosing. In American slave and segregation history, for example, countless individuals who considered themselves of mixed-race or white-European origins found that the law regarded them as African American and, on that basis, as lacking basic human rights. In other cases, the native American peoples who managed to survive the genocidal policies of the early American governments later had their tribal status misrecognised, eliminated or ignored altogether. Struggles for recognition, especially where the authorisation of identity entails rights to land and resources, continue to lie at the core of native American resistance strategies.

The democratic theme that emerges here is self-determination. If identity in modern societies is never a matter of individual will, but is in part determined by official agencies that are prior to the individual, and if those agencies' practices are shaped by prevailing forces, rather than determined by objective facts, then the processes by which identities are authorised must be opened up to democratic scrutiny. If the interpretive work that is done in marking the body is not a neutral process, then its arbitrariness should be made the subject of egalitarian and libertarian interrogation. Perhaps we will always find it necessary to categorise infant bodies in some fashion; perhaps, in the short run at least, we will need to draw lines between population-sized bodies. We should nevertheless ask in each instance: which forces benefit from this specific bodily regime as opposed to that one? And we should struggle to enhance human rights to the greatest extent possible wherever we bring order to bodies – at both the individual and the population levels. Many movements are already taking up various struggles in the bio-politics terrain. People of colour, for example, are questioning the American government's approach to racial census-data collection; many are demanding that official agencies make a new 'mixed race' category available for census respondents. Transsexuals and feminists are pressing for a more sensitive approach to official sex-determination policies. Indigenous peoples and immigrant groups continue to challenge macro-population-management policies that deprive the native peoples of their rights and close national borders to foreigners.

Because Butler shares much of the same poststructuralist and psychoanalytic influences as Althusser (1971), there are many resemblances between her approach and his **interpellation** theory. A power regime 'hails' a proto-subject, and invites him or her into being, but only insofar as the subjectivity that he or she begins to inhabit conforms to the regime's standards. If an interpellation is relatively effective, the subject finds himself or herself thoroughly caught up in its lure. He or she identifies so thoroughly with the subject position into which he or she has been invited that he or she forgets that he or she could inhabit an alternative world view. Everything about that identification – its outlook on the world, the specific set of actions that it encourages the subject to perform, and so on – seems to be already familiar and obvious. Both Althusser and Butler hold that political authority involves the capacity to define the ways in which everyday lived experience is framed. Democratic action therefore cannot be guided solely by appeals to immediate experience. It may very well be true, for example, that wealthy white male citizens genuinely feel threatened by equal-pay programmes, affirmative action for people of colour, redistributive taxation schemes and human-rights campaigns for immigrants and refugees. Having been incited to inhabit a set of identities that confer substantial privilege, and having had that conferral of privilege concealed by various inegalitarian ideologies operating in a subtle and yet pervasive matter, it will not be surprising if these individuals strive at every turn to resist efforts to deepen the democratic tradition and invoke their own right to fair treatment while doing so. Experiential evidence is always already profoundly mediated by powerful discourses. Privileged individuals may honestly speak their own truths in the context of a democratic deliberation – and yet, for all their candour, they may be contributing to the subordination of others at the same time. As democratic activists already know very well, we must always expose experiential discourse to egalitarian and libertarian critique in the context of democratic deliberations. And, in those cases in which the forces of privilege remain particularly recalcitrant, democratic deliberation and critique will be insufficient. Antagonistic democratic struggles will be needed as well – not only to provide a counterweight against the privileged, but also to produce the alternative world views, oppositional forms of interpellation, and counter-cultural imaginaries that can promote resistance practices.

By bringing the whole problematic of identification into the centre of her political philosophy, Butler thereby joins with the **Gramscian** cultural studies theorists such as **Hall** (1988) in insisting on the centrality of cultural practice. If becoming a subject is not simply a matter of discovering one's objective interests and joining the appropriate interest group, but involves instead a complex birthing process through which one answers specific invitations to come into being in this or that form, and then embarks on a series of identifications, then one's exposure to alternative world views that incite oppositional identifications becomes a crucial matter. Struggles to create and to disseminate counter-cultural imaginaries become absolutely central to democratic politics, rather than secondary concerns.

Butler nevertheless differs from Althusser on the possibility of resistance. Inspired by **Derrida**'s notion of **iteration** (Derrida, 1988), Butler explores the processes by which the sex/gender/sexuality matrix has become predominant. Following one of the basic principles of the contemporary feminist movement, Butler contends that the binary sex system is not grounded in nature. As practitioners and anthropologists of reproductive technology have found, there are an infinite number of ways to organise kinship that are perfectly consistent with the goal of birthing and raising children in a humane manner. She argues that the binary sex system owes its hegemonic status not to its natural status but to the fact that it has been authorised and re-authorised time and time again over centuries in Western cultures. This enduring pattern of repetition gives rise to the creation of a formidable tradition that appears to be absolutely necessary. And yet, Butler suggests, study of this pattern and analogous patterns in linguistics should also remind us that this tradition always remains vulnerable to subversion. With every instance in which a linguistic sign is used in a specific text, it can only become meaningful for us insofar as it parasitically cites the meanings that have been associated with it in the past. Hence some degree of repetition is indispensable for every effective form of communication. At the same time, however, even the most conformist and tradition-respecting text adds something new to the sign, for it places the sign in a slightly different context from the ones that it inhabited in the past, and it makes the sign work in a somewhat unique manner. Butler asks, what if sex operates in analogous fashion? What if the gendering process is like the citation of the sign in a text? If that comparison is valid, then it may very well be the case that even the most apparently conformist gender performance actually introduces some element that is at odds with its misogynist and homophobic tradition. (It should be noted here that, by using the term 'performance', Butler is invoking **Austin**'s theory of the **performative** (1975); the concept of 'gender performance' is much broader than a narrowly defined set of explicitly theatrical practices.)

Althusser leaves almost no room whatsoever for resistance in his all-encompassing model of domination. Butler, by contrast, points to the fact that although the binary sex system remains extremely powerful, it is nevertheless constantly confronted by the resistance practices of its discontents. In this sense, she demonstrates that it is perfectly consistent for feminists to adopt the slogan 'biology is not destiny' even though they also hold that patriarchal forms of power remain authoritative in our society; they are simply affirming the hegemonic and yet incomplete character of the sex/gender/sexuality system. The totalising dimension of Althusser's approach is such that he cannot grasp the moments in which the ideological state apparatuses fail to secure the perfect conditions for the reproduction of capitalist relations. Butler does not subscribe to a careless and anti-feminist form of postmodern optimism; she certainly does not claim that all resistances are equally valid or that anyone can make himself or herself into anything they choose. She nevertheless consistently refers to the fact that even the most hegemonic project remains unfinished, prone to 'backfiring' and vulnerable to subversion. Her movement away from the Althusserian 'dominant ideology' theory allows her to provide much more subtle and effective tools for political analysis.

DEMOCRACY AND WELFARE

The work of Mohanty and Mink (reproduced below) supplements Butler's theory in two important respects. Although Butler certainly recognises the fact that identification always takes place in an **overdetermined** manner – the gendering process, for example, never takes place on its own but is always intertwined with sexual, race and class-orientated **interpellation**s – she does not fully explore the theme of multiple identities. Other theorists have taken up the challenges issued by women-of-colour activists to think in imaginative ways about complex and overlapping forms of oppression and resistance. Essentialists tended to argue that one element, such as class or gender, prevailed over all other elements of identity and in all cases. Theorists of **identity politics** constructed hierarchies of oppression and coalition theories. Socialist feminists experimented with **dual systems theory** (Eisenstein, 1979; Sargent, 1986; Rowbotham et al. 1981). Women-of-colour feminists developed theories of intersectionality (Crenshaw, 1992) and oppositional consciousness (Sandoval,

1990). Laclau and Mouffe (1985) suggest that a social agent with multiple identity elements will become something other than the mere sum of its parts. Each identity element will tend to be redefined insofar as it is brought into dialogue and interaction with the other identity elements; the resulting compound – or 'articulation' – will therefore take the form of a somewhat unique hybrid ensemble (Smith, 1998).

Mohanty's exploration of the experiences of women-of-colour workers advances these discussions further. Her research probes the continuities and discontinuities between the condition of women-of-colour workers in the developing countries and in the developed West. She finds that capitalist employers – ranging from the husband in a family shop or crafts business to large corporations – often draw upon prevailing kinship norms, gender roles and racial codes to support the exploitation of these female workers. In the case examined by Mohanty, each exploitative and oppressive force – capitalism, sexism and racism – tends parasitically to feed off the other forces. Together, the forces become all the more powerful as they combine together to create a complex formation. One of the implications of her research is that a progressive form of feminist, anti-racist and labour activism today has to be simultaneously local and global. It has to be sensitive to the multiple forms of exploitation and oppression that prevail in a given community, and, at the same time, it has to be aware of the importance of international solidarity and the opportunities for innovative alliances and coalitions. Mohanty's approach also suggests that the researcher ought to avoid imposing rigid models about identity-formation based on 'objective interests' and should instead engage in careful fieldwork and discourse analyses that detect the historical specificities of the case in question.

As we have seen, Butler's approach implicitly draws upon institutional theory and analysis. If a given sex/gender/sexuality regime is hegemonic, it owes its predominance not to the fact that it mirrors a given nature, but to the power of tradition. In sociopolitical relations, enduring reactionary forces such as misogyny and homophobia shape existing institutions and give rise to the formation of new ones. It is at the level of institutions that specific types of exploitation and oppression are perpetuated. While it is certainly true that reactionary forces have a history – they do not take the form of trans-historical phenomena, since they undergo significant shifts over time – continuities in hierarchical power relations can nevertheless be secured by institutions in an extremely effective manner. Butler's analysis can therefore usefully be supplemented by historically specific institutional analysis. For example, poor women of colour in the United States have been consistently over-represented among the population that is singled out for sexual regulation. During slavery, African American women were routinely subjected to sexual assault by the slave masters, and, because their owners treated their children like chattels, their parental rights were severely violated. Myths about the dangerous nature of black female sexuality were nevertheless commonplace, such that it was the black woman, rather than the white male slave master, who was regarded as a sexual threat. After emancipation, single African American mothers applying for poverty assistance under early welfare programmes were routinely denied benefits on the grounds that they were incapable of providing an appropriate moral environment for their children. By the 1960s, these myths had become so normalised that a key report on African American poverty (United States, 1965) found that where black males failed to succeed in American society, black women were to blame. The report claimed that their sexual excess and abnormal matriarchal authority threatened the very future of the black family. At the height of the 'welfare reform' debates in the 1990s, when the right to poverty assistance was effectively eliminated in the United States, poor African American mothers were typically depicted as the worst kind of undeserving, lazy and immoral recipients in a fundamentally corrupt system.

This specific form of racist and sexist myth-making could not have been perpetuated unless it had found expression in powerful institutions. Indeed, American governments at the federal and state levels have in fact played an important role in the construction and reproduction of these representations. Mink's research, for example, documents and analyses the official discourse of Congress, state legislators, political lobby groups and activists who have played a role in the passage of welfare legislation. She demonstrates that the 1990s welfare reform debate in the United States was heavily racialised and gendered. A bi-partisan consensus emerged in favour of special policies that required all single mothers to participate in work programmes and to disclose the identities of their children's biological fathers. Alternative principles which suggest that every active mother already performs valuable work as a care-giver for her children, that a mother on welfare should not be forced to enter the paid workforce, and that a mother should be able to choose whether or not she will disclose the identity of the biological father of her children were abandoned in favour of a disciplinary approach. It was widely held that poor single mothers indulge in irresponsible sexual activity and an immoral lifestyle, and that they therefore deserve to be subjected to compulsory 'workfare' and paternal notification rules. Throughout these discussions, the poor African American mother was positioned as a special target for corrective legislation. Mink also cites extensive evidence from the legislative record that suggests that policymakers have for decades regarded poor African American women as a special case and as a serious threat to social order.

CONCLUSION

Although Butler, Mohanty and Mink do not cite each other's work, their approaches are complementary in many respects. Butler's theoretical arguments can be used to demonstrate that politics is not simply about the mobilisation of given interest groups, for the very problem of constructing, authorising and policing identities is often at the core of political struggles. Mohanty takes the idea that gender roles are socially constructed as a starting point for an analysis of capital's attempts to turn established kinship relations to its advantage, and sets the stage for an exploration of the perspectives formed by women of colour themselves in diverse working conditions. Mink focuses on the policy implications of racist and misogynist myths about African American women's sexuality, and traces the role of governmental institutions in their perpetuation. Reading Butler, Mohanty and Mink together allows us to ask new questions. We might inquire, for example, about the enormous difficulties that poverty-rights groups will encounter in their campaign against the attack on the poor in the United States. If that assault on the poor is not simply about class and government 'downsizing' but is also about misogyny, racism and a moral panic about non-traditional forms of sexual expression, then we need to find a way to address each of these dimensions simultaneously. More generally, we need to enrich our understanding of progressive politics by grasping the fact that gender equality, racial equality, the right to work – in either the traditional sector or the domestic sector – the right to a liveable wage and to a decent standard of living, the right to live in a healthy environment, and the right to determine one's intimate life are all integral to the very concept of democracy. And we also need to ensure that we constantly reinvigorate each progressive struggle by borrowing and adapting the forms of wisdom that are generated in our sister struggles, and, where appropriate, by combining different struggles together to form new emancipatory movements.

Further, progressive activists must strive to take part in policy reform in one way or another. How can we work effectively within a system that is so thoroughly marked by gendered and racialised exclusions and capitalist interests? How does a movement, or a well-intentioned individual for that matter, achieve credibility as a legitimate actor within a terrain such as the welfare-policy field while simultaneously refusing to accept the punitive logic and the racist and sexist myths that are widely taken for granted in that arena? Indeed, how does a progressive subject guard against the insidious ways in which it is always invited by powerful institutions – through careerism, assimilation, co-optation and so on – to betray its own principles in order to gain access to power? These articles do not, of course, answer these questions; some of the best strategic responses to these dilemmas will continue to come from activists on the ground. Taken together, these articles nevertheless respond to some of the questions posed by contemporary progressive movements, weave together some of these movements' key practical ideas, and generate new theoretical approaches that will give the democratic theory tradition greater historical specificity and depth.

'SEXUAL INVERSIONS' BY JUDITH BUTLER

This is the third extract in this volume by Judith Butler (details about her can be found in Chapter 7). Here she takes us back to one of the first extracts, from Foucault's *History of Sexuality*. Offering a close reading of parts of that text, Butler extends feminist argument about the ways in which fixed gender identity is maintained and addresses the issue of sexuality, linking the prescription of a heterosexual norm to the techniques and processes of modern government. It would be useful for readers to consider this essay not only in the light of this chapter in general but also in relation to the other extracts from Butler and to the discussion of feminism and the wider question of what it is to claim that an identity is natural or universal.

'SEXUAL INVERSIONS' (1992)*

Judith Butler

Some might say that the scandal of the first volume of Foucault's *The History of Sexuality* consists in the claim that we did not always have a sex. What can such a notion mean? Foucault proposes that there was a decisive historical break between a socio-political regime in which sex existed as an attribute, an activity, a dimension of human life, and a more recent regime in which sex became established as an identity. This particularly modern scandal suggests that for the first time sex is not a contingent or arbitrary feature of identity but, rather, that there can be no identity without sex and that it is precisely through being sexed that we become intelligible as humans. So it is not exactly right to claim we did not always *have* a sex. Perhaps the historical scandal is that we *were* not always our sex, that sex did not always have the power to characterize and constitute identity with such thoroughgoing power (later, there will be occasion to ask after the exclusions that condition and sustain the Foucaultian 'we', but for now we will try on this 'we', if only to see where it does not fit). As Foucault points out, sex has come to characterize and unify not only biological functions and anatomical traits but sexual activities as well as a kind of psychic core that gives clues to an essential, or final meaning to, identity. Not only is one one's sex, but one has sex, and in the having, is supposed to show

---

* From Judith Butler, 'Sexual Inversions', in Domna C. Stanton (ed.), *Discourses of Sexuality: From Aristotle to AIDS* (Ann Arbor, MI: University of Michigan Press, 1992), pp. 344–57.

the sex one 'is' even as the sex one 'is' is psychically deeper and more unfathomable than the 'I' who lives it can ever know. Hence, this 'sex' requires and secures a set of sciences that can meditate endlessly on that pervasive indecipherability.

What conditioned the introduction into history of this notion of sex that totalizes identity? Foucault argues that during the course of the eighteenth century in Europe, famines and epidemics start to disappear and that power, which had previously been governed by the need to ward off death, now becomes occupied with the production, maintenance, and regulation of *life*. It is in the course of this regulatory cultivation of life that the category of sex is established. Naturalized as heterosexual, it is designed to regulate and secure the reproduction of life. Having a true sex with a biological destiny and natural heterosexuality thus becomes essential to the aim of power, now understood as the disciplinary reproduction of life. Foucault characterizes early modern Europe as governed by *juridical* power. As juridical, power operates negatively to impose limits, restrictions, and prohibitions; power reacts defensively, as it were, to preserve life and social harmony over and against the threat of violence or natural death. Once the threat of death is ameliorated, as he claims it is in the eighteenth century, those juridical laws are transformed into instances of *productive* power, in which power effectively *generates* objects to control, in which power elaborates all sorts of objects and identities that guarantee the augmentation of regulatory scientific regimes.[1] The category of 'sex' is constructed as an 'object' of study and control, which assists in the elaboration and justification of productive power regimes. It is as if once the threat of death is overcome, power turns its idle attention to the construction of objects to control. Or, rather, power exerts and articulates its control through the formation and proliferation of objects that concern the continuation of life.

[. . .]

LIFE, DEATH AND POWER

In the final section of the first volume, the 'Right of Death and Power over Life', Foucault describes a cataclysmic 'event' which he attributes to the eighteenth century: 'nothing less than the entry of life into history' (1:141). What he means, it seems, is that the study and regulation of life becomes an object of historical concern, that is, that life becomes the site for the elaboration of power. Before this unprecedented 'entry" of life into history, it seems that history and, more important, power were concerned with combating death. Foucault writes:

> the pressure exerted by the biological on the historical had remained very strong for thousands of years; epidemics and famine were the two great dramatic forms of this relationship that was always dominated by the menace of death. *But through a circular process*, the economic – and

primarily agricultural – development of the 18th century, and an increase in productivity and resources even more rapid than the demographic growth it encouraged, allowed a measure of relief from those profound threats: despite some renewed outbreaks, the period of great ravages from starvation and plague had come to a close before the *French Revolution*; death was ceasing to torment life so directly. But at the same time, the development of the different fields of knowledge concerned with life in general, the improvement of agricultural techniques, and the observations and measures relative to man's life and survival contributed to this relaxation: a relative control over life averted some of the imminent risks of death. (1:142)

There are of course several reasons to be suspicious of this kind of epoch-making narrativizing. It appears that Foucault wants to mark an historical shift from a notion of politics and history that is always threatened by death, and guided by the aim of negotiating that threat, to a politics that can to some extent *presume* the continuation of life and, hence, direct its attention to the regulation, control, and cultivation of life. Foucault notes the Eurocentrism in his account, but it alters nothing. He writes,

it is not that life has been totally integrated into techniques that govern and administer it; it constantly escapes them. Outside the Western world, famine exists, on a greater scale than ever; and the biological risks confronting the species are perhaps greater, and certainly more serious, than before the birth of microbiology. (1:143)

Foucault's historical account can perhaps be read only as a wishful construction: death is effectively expelled from Western modernity, cast *behind* it as an historical possibility, surpassed or cast *outside* it as a non-Western phenomenon. Can these exclusions hold? To what extent does his characterization of later modernity require and institute an exclusion of the threat of death? It seems clear that Foucault must tell a phantasmatic history in order to keep modernity and productive power free of death and full of sex. Insofar as the category of sex is elaborated within the context of productive power, a story is being told in which sex, it seems, surpasses and displaces death.

If we accept the historically problematic character of this narration, can we accept it on logical grounds? Can one even defend against death without also promoting a certain version of life? Does juridical power in this way entail productive power as its logical correlate? 'Death', whether figured as *prior* to modernity as that which is warded off and left behind or as a threat *within* premodern nations *elsewhere*, must always be the death, the end of a specific way of life; and the life to be safeguarded is always already a normatively construed *way* of life, not life and death pure and simple. Does it make sense, then, to reject the notion that life entered into history as death took its exit from history? On the one hand, neither one ever entered or departed, since the one can only appear as the immanent possibility of the other; on the other hand, life and death might be construed as the incessant entering and departing that characterizes any field of power. Perhaps we are referring neither to an historical shift nor to a logical shift in the formation of power. For even when power is in the business of warding off death, that can only be in the name of some specific form of life and through the insistence on the right to produce and reproduce that way of life. At this point, the distinction between juridical and productive power appears to collapse.

And yet this shift must make sense for Foucault to argue convincingly that 'sex' enters history in later modernity and becomes an object that productive power formulates, regulates, and produces. When sex becomes a site of power, it becomes an object of legal and regulatory discourses; it becomes that which power in its various discourses and institutions *cultivates* in the image of its own normative construction. There is no 'sex' to which a supervening law attends; in attending to sex, in monitoring sex, sex itself is constructed, produced as that which calls to be monitored and *is* inherently regulatable. There is a normative development to sex, laws that inhere in sex itself, and the inquiry that attends to that lawlike development postures as if it merely discovers in sex the very laws that it has itself installed at the site of sex. In this sense, the regulation of 'sex' finds no sex there, external to its own regulation; regulation produces the object it comes to regulate; regulation has regulated in advance what it will only disingenuously attend to as the object of regulation. In order to exercise and elaborate its own power, a regulatory regime will generate the very object it seeks to control.

And here is the crucial point: it is not as if a regulatory regime first controls its object and then produces it or first produces it in order then to control it; there is no temporary lag between the production and the regulation of sex; they occur at once, for regulation is always generative, producing the object it claims merely to discover or to find in the social field in which it operates. Concretely, this means that we are not, as it were, (merely) discriminated against on the basis of our sex; power is more *insidious* than that: either discrimination is built into the very formulation of our sex, or enfranchisement is precisely the formative and generative principle of someone else's sex. And this is why, for Foucault, sex can never be liberated *from power*: the formation of sex is an enactment of power. In a sense, power works on sex more deeply than we can know, not only as an external constraint or repression but as the formative principle of its intelligibility.

Here we can locate a shift or inversion at the center of power, in the very structure of power, for what appears at first to be a law that imposes itself upon 'sex' as a ready-made object, a juridical view of power as constraint or *external* control, turns out to be – all along – performing a fully different ruse of power; silently, it is *already productive* power, forming the very object that will be suitable for control and then, in an act that effectively disavows that production, claiming to discover that 'sex' outside of power. Hence, the category of 'sex' will be precisely what power produces in order to have an object of control

What this suggests, of course, is that there is no historical shift from juridical to productive power but that juridical power is a kind of dissimulated or concealed productive power from the start and that the shift, the inversion, is within power, not between two historically or logically distinct forms of power.

The category of 'sex', which Foucault claims is understandable only as the result of an historical shift, is actually, as it were, produced in the midst of this shift, this very shiftiness of power that produces in advance that which it will come to subordinate. This is not a shift from a version of power as constraint or restriction to a version of power as productive but a production that is *at the same time* constraint, a constraining in advance of what will and will not qualify as a properly sexed being. This constraining production works through linking the category of sex with that of identity; there will be two sexes, discrete and uniform, and they will be expressed and evidenced in gender and sexuality, so that any social displays of non-identity, discontinuity, or sexual incoherence will be punished, controlled, ostracized, reformed. Hence, by producing sex as a category of identity, that is, by defining sex as one sex or another, the discursive regulation of sex begins to take place. It is only after this procedure of definition and production has taken place that power comes to posture as that which is external to the object – 'sex' – that it finds. In effect, it has already installed control in the object by defining the object as a self-identical object; its self-identity, presumed to be immanent to sex itself, is precisely the trace of this installation of power, a trace that is simultaneously erased, covered over, by the posturing of power as that which is external to its object.

What propels power? It cannot be human subjects, precisely because they are one of the occasions, enactments, and effects of power. It seems, for Foucault, that power seeks to augment itself within modernity just as life sought to augment itself prior to modernity. Power acts as life's proxy, as it were, taking over its function, reproducing itself always in excess of any need, luxuriating in a kind of self-elaboration that is no longer hindered by the immanent threat of death. Power thus becomes the locus of a certain displaced vitalism in Foucault; power, conceived as productive, is the form life takes when it no longer needs to guard itself against death.

SEX AND SEXUALITY

How does this inversion from early to late modern power affect Foucault's discussion of yet another inversion, that between *sex and sexuality*? Within ordinary language, we sometimes speak, for instance, of being a given sex, and having a certain sexuality, and we even presume for the most part that our sexuality in some way *issues* from that sex, is perhaps an *expression* of that sex, or is even partially or fully *caused* by that sex. Sexuality is understood to come from sex, which is to say that the biological locus of 'sex' in and on the body is somehow conjured as the originating source of a sexuality that, as it were, flows out from that locus, remains inhibited within that locus, or somehow takes its bearings with respect to that locus. In any case, 'sex' is understood logically and temporally to *precede* sexuality and to function, if not as its primary cause, then at least as its necessary precondition.

However, Foucault performs an *inversion* of this relation and claims that this inversion is correlated with the shift from early to late modern power. For Foucault, 'it is apparent that the deployment of sexuality, with its different strategies, was what established this notion of "sex"' (1:154). Sexuality is here viewed as a discursively constructed and highly regulated network of pleasures and bodily exchanges, produced through prohibitions and sanctions that quite literally give form and directionality to pleasure and sensation. As such a network or regime sexuality does not emerge from bodies as their prior causes; sexuality takes bodies as its instrument and its object, the site at which it consolidates, networks, and extends its power. As a regulatory regime, sexuality operates primarily by *investing bodies with the category of sex*, that is, making bodies into the *bearers of a principle of identity*. To claim that bodies are one sex or the other appears at first to be a purely *descriptive* claim. For Foucault, however, this claim is itself a *legislation* and a *production* of bodies, a discursive demand, as it were, that bodies become produced according to principles of heterosexualizing coherence and integrity, unproblematically as either female or male. Where sex is taken as a principle of identity, it is always positioned within a field of two mutually exclusive and fully exhaustive identities; one is either male or female, never both at once, and never neither one of them.

> the notion of sex brought about a fundamental reversal; it made it possible to invert the representation of the relationships of power to sexuality, causing the latter to appear, not in its essential and positive relation to power, but as being rooted in a specific and irreducible urgency which power tries as best it can to dominate; thus the idea of 'sex' makes it possible to evade what gives 'power' its power; it enables one to conceive power solely as law and taboo. (1:155)

For Foucault, sex, whether male or female, operates as a principle of identity that imposes a fiction of coherence and unity on an otherwise random or unrelated set of biological functions, sensations, pleasures. Under the regime of sex, every pleasure becomes symptomatic of 'sex', and 'sex' itself functions not merely as the biological ground or cause of pleasure but as that which determines its directionality, a principle of teleology or destiny, and as that repressed, psychical core which furnishes clues to the interpretation of its ultimate meaning. As a fictional imposition of uniformity, sex is 'an imaginary point' and an 'artificial unity', but as fictional and as artificial, the category wields enormous power.[2] Although Foucault does not quite claim it, the science of reproduction produces intelligible 'sex' by imposing a compulsory heterosexuality on the description of bodies. One might claim that sex is here produced according to a heterosexual morphology.

The category of 'sex' thus establishes a principle of intelligibility for human beings, which is to say that no human being can be taken to be human, can be recognized *as* human unless that human being is fully and coherently marked by sex. And yet it would not capture Foucault's meaning merely to claim that there are humans who are marked by sex and thereby become intelligible; the point is stronger: to qualify as legitimately human, one must he coherently sexed. The incoherence of sex is precisely what marks off the abject and the dehumanized from the recognizably human.

Luce Irigaray would clearly take this point further and turn it against Foucault. She would, I think, argue that the only sex that qualifies as a sex is a masculine one, which is not marked as masculine but parades as the universal and thereby silently extends its dominion. To refer to a sex which is not one is to refer to a sex which cannot be designated univocally as sex but is outside identity from the start. Are we not right to ask, which sex is it that renders the figure of the human intelligible, and within such an economy, is it not the case that the feminine functions as a figure for unintelligibility? When one speaks of the 'one' in language – as I do now – one makes reference to a neuter term, a purely human term. And whereas Foucault and Irigaray would agree that sex is a necessary precondition for human intelligibility, Foucault appears to think that any sanctioned sex will do, but Irigaray would argue that the only sanctioned sex is the masculine one; that is, the masculine that is reworked as a 'one', a neuter, a universal. If the coherent subject is always sexed as masculine, then it is constructed through the abjection and erasure of the feminine. For Irigaray, masculine and feminine sexes are not similarly constructed as sexes or as principles of intelligible identity; in fact, she argues that the masculine sex is constructed as the only 'one', and that it figures the feminine other as a reflection only of itself; within that model, then, both masculine and feminine reduce to the masculine, and the feminine, left outside this male autoerotic economy, is not even designatable within its terms or is, rather, designatable as a radically disfigured masculine projection, which is yet a different kind of erasure.[3]

This hypothetical critique from an Irigarayan perspective suggests something problematic about Foucault's constructivism. Within the terms of productive power, regulation and control work through the discursive articulation of identities. But those discursive articulations effect certain exclusions and erasures; oppression works not merely through the mechanism of regulation and production but by foreclosing the very possibility of articulation. If Foucault claims that regulation and control operate as the formative principles of identity, Irigaray in a somewhat more Derridean vein would argue that oppression works through other means as well, through the *exclusion* and *erasure* effected by any discursive formation, and that here the feminine is precisely what is erased and excluded in order for intelligible identities to be produced.[4]

CONTEMPORARY IDENTITY IN THE AGE OF EPIDEMIC

This is a limitation of Foucault's analysis. And yet he offers a counterwarning, I think, to those who might be tempted to treat femaleness or the feminine as an identity to be liberated. To attempt that would be to repeat the gesture of the regulatory regime, taking some aspect of 'sex' and making it stand synecdochally for the entirety of the body and its psychic manifestations. Similarly, Foucault did not embrace an identity politics that might in the name of homosexuality combat the regulatory effort to produce the symptomatic homosexual or to erase the homosexual from the domain of intelligible subjects. To take identity as a rallying point for liberation would be to subject oneself at the very moment that one calls for a release from subjection. For the point is not to claim, 'yes, I am fully totalized by the category of homosexuality, just as you say, but only that the meaning of that totalization will be different from the one that you attribute to me'. If identity imposes a fictive coherence and consistency on the body or, better, if identity is a regulatory principle that produces bodies in conformity with that principle, then it is no more liberatory to embrace an unproblematized gay identity than it is to embrace the diagnostic category of homosexuality devised by juridico-medical regimes. The political challenge Foucault poses here is whether a resistance to the diagnostic category can be effected that does not reduplicate the very mechanism of that subjection, this time – painfully, paradoxically – under the sign of liberation. The task for Foucault is to refuse the totalizing category under either guise, which is why Foucault will not confess or 'come out' in the *History of Sexuality* as a homosexual or privilege homosexuality as a site of heightened regulation. But perhaps Foucault remains significantly and politically linked to this problematic of homosexuality all the same.

Is Foucault's strategic *inversion* of identity perhaps a redeployment of the medicalized category of the invert? The diagnostic category 'invert' presumes that someone with a given sex somehow acquired a set of sexual dispositions and desires that do not travel in the appropriate directions; sexual desire is 'inverted' when it misses its aim and object and travels wrong-headedly to its opposite or when it takes itself as the object of its desire and then projects and recovers that 'self' in a homosexual object. Clearly, Foucault gives us a way to laugh at this construction of the proper relation between 'sex' and 'sexuality', to appreciate its contingency, and to question the causal and expressive lines that are said to run from sex to sexuality. Ironically, or perhaps, tactically, Foucault engages a certain activity of 'inversion' here but reworks that term from a noun to a verb. His theoretical practice is, in a sense, marked by a series of inversions: in the shift to modern power, an inversion is performed; in the relation of sex and sexuality, another inversion is performed. And with respect to the category of the 'invert', yet another inversion is performed, one that might be understood to stand as a strategy of refiguration according to which the various other inversions of the text can be read.[5]

The traditional invert gets its name because the *aim* of its desire has run off the rails of heterosexuality. According to the construction of homosexuality as narcissism, the aim has turned back against itself or exchanged its position of identification for the position of the object desired, an exchange that constitutes a kind of psychic mistake. But to locate inversion as an exchange between psychic disposition and aim, or between an identification and an object, or as a return of an aim upon itself is still to operate within the heterosexualizing norm and its teleological explanations. Foucault calls this kind of explanation into question, however, through an explanatory inversion which establishes sexuality as a regulatory regime that dissimulates itself by setting up the category of 'sex' as a quasi-naturalistic fictive unity. Exposed as a fiction, the body becomes a site for unregulated pleasures, sensations, practices, convergences and refigurations of masculine and feminine such that the naturalizing status of those terms is called radically into question.

Hence, the task for Foucault is not to claim the category of invert or of homosexual and to rework that term to signify something less pathological, mistaken, or deviant. The task is to call into question the explanatory gesture that requires a true identity and, hence, a mistaken one as well. If diagnostic discourse would make of Foucault an 'invert', then he will invert the very logic that makes something like 'inversion' possible. And he will do this by inverting the relation between sex and sexuality. This is an intensification and redoubling of inversion, one that is perhaps mobilized by the diagnosis but that has as its effect the disruption of the very vocabulary of diagnosis and cure, true and mistaken identity. This is as if to say: 'Yes, an invert, but I will show you what inversion can do; I can invert and subvert the categories of identity such that you will no longer be able to call me that and know what it is you mean'.

[. . .]

NOTES

1. See Michel Foucault, *The History of Sexuality, Volume 1: An Introduction*, trans. Robert Hurley (New York: Pantheon, 1978, pp. 85–91. This text was originally published as *La Volonté de savoir* (Paris: Editions Gallimard, 1976).
2. 'It is through sex', Foucault writes, '– in fact an imaginary point determined by the deployment of sexuality – that each individual has to pass in order to have access to his own intelligibility (seeing that it is both the hidden aspect and the generative principle of meaning), to the whole of his body (since it is a real and threatened part of it, while symbolically constituting the whole), to his identity (since it joins the force of a drive to the singularity of a history)' (1:155–6).
3. In this sense, the category of sex constitutes and regulates what will and will not be an intelligible and recognizable human existence, what will and will not be a citizen capable of rights or speech, an individual protected by law against violence or injury.

    The political question for Foucault, and for those of us who read him now, is *not* whether 'improperly sexed' beings should or should not be treated fairly or with justice or with tolerance. The question is whether, if improperly sexed, such a being can even be a being, a human being, a subject, one whom the law can condone or condemn. For Foucault has outlined a region that is, as it were, outside of the purview of the law, one that excludes certain kinds of improperly sexed beings from the very category of the human subject. The journals of Herculine Barbin, the hermaphrodite (ed. Michel Foucault, *Herculine Barbin, Being the Recently Discovered Memoirs of a Nineteenth-Century Hermaphrodite*, trans. Richard MacDougall (New York: Colophon, 1980)), demonstrate the violence of the law that would legislate identity on a body that resists it. But Herculine is to some extent a *figure* for a sexual ambiguity or inconsistency that emerges at the site of bodies and that contests the category of subject and its univocal or self-identical 'sex'.

4. This gives some clues to what a deconstructive critique of Foucault might look like.

5. If sexuality takes sex as its instrument and object, then sexuality is by definition more diffuse and less uniform than the category of sex; through the category of sex, sexuality performs a kind of self-reduction. Sexuality will always exceed sex, even as sex sets itself up as a category that accounts for sexuality *in toto* by posturing as its primary cause. In order to claim that one is a given sex, a certain radical reduction must take place, for 'sex' functions to describe not only certain relatively stable biological or anatomical traits but also an activity, what one does, and a state of mind or psychic disposition. The ambiguities of the term are temporarily overcome when 'sex' is understood as the biological basis for a psychic disposition, which then manifests itself in a set of acts. In this sense, the category of 'sex' functions to establish a fictive causality among these dimensions of bodily existence, so that to be female is to be disposed sexually in a certain way, namely, heterosexually, and to be positioned within sexual exchange such that the biological and psychic dimensions of 'sex' are consummated, integrated, and demonstrated. On the one hand, the category of sex works to blur the distinctions among biology, psychic reality, and sexual practice, for sex is all of these things, even as it proceeds through a certain force of teleology to relate each of these terms. But once the teleology is disrupted, shown to be disruptible, then the very discreteness of terms like biology and psyche becomes contestable. For if sex proves no longer to be as encompassing as it seems, then what in biology is 'sex', and what contests the univocity of that term, and where, if at all, is sex to be found in the psyche, if sex can no longer be placed within that heterosexualizing teleology? These terms become disjoined and internally destabilized when a biological female is perhaps psychically disposed in non-heterosexual ways or is positioned in sexual exchanges in ways that the categories of heterosexuality cannot quite describe. Then what Foucault has called 'the fictive unity of sex' is no longer secure. This disunity or disaggregation of 'sex' suggests that the category only works to the extent that it describes a hyperbolic heterosexuality, a normative heterosexuality, one that, in its idealized coherence, is uninhabitable by practising heterosexuals and as such is bound to oppress in its status as an impossible idealization. This is an idealization before which everyone is bound to fail and which of course is a failure, for clear political reasons, to be savored and safeguarded.

'WOMEN WORKERS AND CAPITALIST SCRIPTS: IDEOLOGIES OF DOMINATION, COMMON INTERESTS, AND THE POLITICS OF SOLIDARITY' BY CHANDRA TALPADE MOHANTY

At the time of writing, Chandra Talpade Mohanty is Professor of Women's Studies at Hamilton College, New York. She is well known for her work on feminist issues from a global perspective and with especial attention to cross-cultural and multicultural aspects of feminism and feminist theory. She is co-editor of the books *Feminist Genealogies, Colonial Legacies, Democratic Futures* (Routledge, 1997) and *Third World Women and the Politics of Feminism* (Indiana University Press, 1991). In this extract, she argues that global capitalism exploits women in particular ways and that it is necessary to rethink traditional theories of class conflict in order to take account of the ways in which the domination of women from the Third World takes place. Part of the motivation for this is to establish the ways in which this domination leads to shared experiences that can then become the basis for a trans-national solidarity that can form into organised movements of resistance.

'WOMEN WORKERS AND CAPITALIST SCRIPTS: IDEOLOGIES OF DOMINATION, COMMON INTERESTS, AND THE POLITICS OF SOLIDARITY' (1997)*

Chandra Talpade Mohanty

We dream that when we work hard, we'll be able to clothe our children decently, and still have a little time and money left for ourselves. And we dream that when we do as good as other people, we get treated the same, and that nobody puts us down because we are not like them. . . . Then we ask ourselves, 'How could we make these things come true?' And so far we've come up with only two possible answers: win the lottery, or organize. What can I say, except I have never been lucky with numbers. So tell

---

* From Chandra Talpade Mohanty, 'Women Workers and Capitalist Scripts: Ideologies of Domination, Common Interests, and the Politics of Solidarity', in M. Jacqui Alexander and Chandra Talpade Mohanty (eds), *Feminist Genealogies, Colonial Legacies, Democratic Futures* (New York: Routledge, 1997), pp. 3–8.

this in your book: tell them it may take time that people think they don't have, but they have to organize! . . . Because the only way to get a little measure of power over your own life is to do it collectively, with the support of other people who share your needs.

(Irma, a Filipina worker in the Silicon Valley, California)[1]

Irma's dreams of a decent life for her children and herself, her desire for equal treatment and dignity on the basis of the quality and merit of her work, her conviction that collective struggle is the means to 'get a little measure of power over your own life', succinctly capture the struggles of poor women workers in the global capitalist arena. In this essay, I want to focus on the exploitation of poor Third-World women, on their agency as workers, on the common interests of women workers based on an understanding of shared location and needs, and on the strategies/practices of organizing that are anchored in and lead to the transformation of the daily lives of women workers.

This has been an especially difficult essay to write – perhaps because the almost-total saturation of the processes of capitalist domination makes it hard to envision forms of feminist resistance which would make a real difference in the daily lives of poor women workers. However, as I began to sort through the actions, reflections, and analyses by and about women workers (or wage laborers) in the capitalist economy, I discovered the dignity of women workers' struggles in the face of overwhelming odds. From these struggles we can learn a great deal about processes of exploitation and domination as well as about autonomy and liberation.

A recent study tour to Tijuana, Mexico, organized by Mary Tong of the San Diego-based Support Committee for Maquiladora Workers, confirmed my belief in the radical possibilities of cross-border organizing, especially in the wake of NAFTA. Exchanging ideas, experiences, and strategies with Veronica Vasquez, a twenty-one-year-old Maquila worker fighting for her job, for better working conditions, and against sexual harassment, was as much of an inspiration as any in writing this essay. Veronica Vasquez, along with ninety-nine former employees of the Tijuana factory Exportadora Mano de Obra, S.A. de C.V., has filed an unprecedented lawsuit in Los Angeles, California, against the U.S owner of Exportadora, National O-Ring of Downey, demanding that it be forced to follow Mexican labor laws and provide workers with three months' back pay after shutting down company operations in Tijuana in November 1994. The courage, determination, and analytical clarity of these young Mexican women workers in launching the first case to test the legality of NAFTA suggest that in spite of the global saturation of processes of capitalist domination, 1995 was a moment of great possibility for building cross-border feminist solidarity.[2]

Over the years, I have been preoccupied with the limits as well as the possibilities of constructing feminist solidarities across national, racial, sexual, and class divides. Women's lives as workers, consumers, and citizens have changed radically with the triumphal rise of capitalism in the global arena. The common interests of capital (e.g., profit, accumulation, exploitation, etc.) are somewhat clear at this point. But how do we talk about poor Third-World women workers' interests, their agency, and their (in)visibility in so-called democratic processes? What are the possibilities for democratic citizenship for Third-World women workers in the contemporary capitalist economy? These are some of the questions driving this essay. I hope to clarify and analyze the location of Third-World women workers and their collective struggles in an attempt to generate ways to think about mobilization, organizing, and conscientization transnationally.

This essay extends the arguments I have made elsewhere regarding the location of Third-World women as workers in a global economy.[3] I write now, as I did then, from my own discontinuous locations: as a South Asian anti-capitalist feminist in the U S. committed to working on a truly liberatory feminist practice which theorizes and enacts the potential for a cross-cultural, international politics of solidarity; as a Third-World feminist teacher and activist for whom the psychic economy of 'home' and of 'work' has always been the space of contradiction and struggle; and as a woman whose middle-class struggles for self-definition and autonomy outside the definitions of daughter, wife, and mother mark an intellectual and political genealogy that led me to this particular analysis of Third-World women's work.

Here, I want to examine the analytical category of 'women's work', and to look at the historically specific *naturalization* of gender and race hierarchies through this category. An international division of labor is central to the establishment, consolidation, and maintenance of the current world order: global assembly lines are as much about the production of people as they are about 'providing jobs' or making profit. Thus, naturalized assumptions about *work* and the *worker* are crucial to understanding the sexual politics of global capitalism. I believe that the relation of local to global processes of colonization and exploitation, and the specification of a process of cultural and ideological homogenization across national borders, in part through the creation of the consumer as 'the' citizen under advanced capitalism, must be crucial aspects of any comparative feminist project. This definition of the citizen-consumer depends to a large degree on the definition and disciplining of producers/workers on whose backs the citizen-consumer gains legitimacy. It is the worker/producer side of this equation that I will address. Who are the workers that make the citizen-consumer possible? What role do sexual politics play in the ideological creation of this worker? How does global capitalism, in search of ever-increasing profits, utilize gender and racialized ideologies in crafting forms of women's work? And, does the social location of particular women as workers suggest the basis for common interests and potential solidarities across national borders?

As global capitalism develops and wage labor becomes the hegemonic form of organizing production and reproduction, class relations within and across national borders have become more complex and less transparent.[4] Thus, issues of spatial economy – the manner by which capital utilizes particular spaces for differential production and the accumulation of capital and, in the process, transforms these spaces (and peoples) – gain fundamental importance for feminist analysis.[5] In the aftermath of feminist struggles around the right to work and the demand for equal pay, the boundaries between home/family and work are no longer seen as inviolable (of course these boundaries were always fluid for poor and working-class women). Women are (and have always been) in the workforce, and we are here to stay. In this essay, I offer an analysis of certain historical and ideological transformations of gender, capital, and work across the borders of nation-states,[6] and, in the process, develop a way of thinking about the common interests of Third-World women workers, and in particular about questions of agency and the transformation of consciousness.

Drawing specifically on case studies of the incorporation of Third-World women into a global division of labor at different geographical ends of the new world order, I argue for a historically delineated category of 'women's work' as an example of a productive and necessary basis for feminist cross-cultural analysis.[7] The idea I am interested in invoking here is not 'the work that women do' or even the occupations that they/we happen to be concentrated in, but rather the ideological construction of jobs and tasks in terms of notions of appropriate femininity, domesticity, (hetero)sexuality, and racial and cultural stereotypes. I am interested in mapping these operations of capitalism across different divides, in tracing the naturalization of capitalist processes, ideologies, and values through the way women's work is *constitutively* defined – in this case, in terms of gender and racial parameters. One of the questions I explore pertains to the way gender identity (defined in domestic, heterosexual, familial terms) structures the nature of the work women are allowed to perform or precludes women from being 'workers' altogether.

While I base the details of my analysis in geographically anchored case studies, I am suggesting a comparative methodology which moves beyond the case-study approach and illuminates global processes which inflect and draw upon indigenous hierarchies, ideologies, and forms of exploitation to consolidate new modes of colonization. The local and the global are indeed connected through parallel, contradictory, and sometimes converging relations of rule which position women in different and similar locations as workers.[8] I agree with feminists who argue that class struggle, narrowly defined, can no longer be the only basis for solidarity among women workers. The fact of being women with particular racial, ethnic, cultural, sexual, and geographical histories has everything to do with our definitions and identities as workers. A number of feminists have analyzed the division between production and reproduction, and the construction of ideologies of womanhood in terms of public/private spheres. Here, I want to highlight (1) the persistence of patriarchal definitions of womanhood in the arena of wage labor; (2) the versatility and specificity of capitalist exploitative processes providing the basis for thinking about potential common interests and solidarity between Third-World women workers; and (3) the challenges for collective organizing in a context where traditional union methods (based on the idea of the class interests of the male worker) are inadequate as strategies for empowerment.

If, as I suggest, the logic of a world order characterized by a transnational economy involves the active construction and dissemination of an image of the 'Third-World/racialized, or marginalized woman worker' that draws on indigenous histories of gender and race inequalities, and if this worker's identity is coded in patriarchal terms which define her in relation to men and the heterosexual, conjugal family unit, then the model of class conflict between capitalists and workers needs to be recrafted in terms of the interests (and perhaps identities) of Third-World women workers. Patriarchal ideologies, which sometimes pit women against men within and outside the home, infuse the material realities of the lives of Third-World women workers, making it imperative to reconceptualize the way we think about working-class interests and strategies for organizing. Thus, while this is not an argument for just recognizing the 'common experiences' of Third-World women workers, it *is* an argument for recognizing (concrete, not abstract) 'common interests' and the potential bases of cross-national solidarity – a common context of struggle. In addition, while I choose to focus on the 'Third-World' woman worker, my argument holds for white women workers who are also racialized in similar ways. The argument then is about a *process* of gender and race domination, rather than about the *content* of 'Third World'. Making Third-World women workers visible in this gender, race, class formation involves engaging a capitalist script of subordination and exploitation. But it also leads to thinking about the possibilities of emancipatory action on the basis of the reconceptualization of Third-World women as agents rather than victims.

But why even use 'Third World', a somewhat problematic term which many now consider outdated? And why make an argument which privileges 'the social location, experiences, and identities of Third-World women workers, as opposed to any other group of workers, male or female? Certainly, there are problems with the term 'Third World'. It is inadequate in comprehensively characterizing the economic, political, racial, and cultural differences *within* the borders of Third-World nations. But in comparison with other similar formulations like 'North/South' and 'advanced/underdeveloped nations', 'Third World' retains a certain heuristic value and explanatory specificity in relation to the inheritance of colonialism and contemporary neocolonial economic and geopolitical processes that the other formulations lack.[9]

In response to the second question, I would argue that at this time in the development and operation of a 'new' world order, Third-World women workers (defined in this context as both women from the geographical Third World and immigrant and indigenous women of color in the U.S. and Western Europe) occupy a specific social location in the international division of labor which *illuminates* and *explains* crucial features of the capitalist processes of exploitation and domination. These are features of the social world that are usually obfuscated or mystified in discourses about the 'progress' and 'development' (e.g., the creation of jobs for poor, Third-World women as the marker of economic and social advancement) that is assumed to 'naturally' accompany the triumphal rise of global capitalism. I do not claim to explain *all* the relevant features of the social world or to offer a *comprehensive* analysis of capitalist processes of recolonization. However, I am suggesting that Third-World women workers have a potential identity in common, an identity as *workers* in a particular division of labor at this historical moment. And I believe that exploring and analyzing this potential commonality across geographical and cultural divides provides both a way of reading and understanding the world and an explanation of the consolidation of inequities of gender, race, class, and (hetero)sexuality, which are necessary to envision and enact transnational feminist solidarity.[10]

The argument that multinationals position and exploit women workers in certain ways does not originate with me. I want to suggest, however, that in interconnecting and comparing some of these case studies, a larger theoretical argument can be made about the category of women's work, specifically about the Third-World woman as worker, at this particular historical moment. I think this intersection of gender and work, where the very definition of work draws upon and reconstructs notions of masculinity, femininity, and sexuality, offers a basis of cross-cultural comparison and analysis which is grounded in the concrete realities of women's lives. I am not suggesting that this basis for comparison exhausts the *totality* of women's experience cross-culturally. In other words, because similar ideological constructions of 'women's work' make cross-cultural analysis possible, this does not automatically mean women's lives are the *same*, but rather that they are *comparable*. I argue for a notion of political solidarity and common interests, defined as a community or collectivity among women workers across class, race, and national boundaries which is based on shared material interests and identity and common ways of reading the world. This idea of political solidarity in the context of the incorporation of Third-World women into a global economy offers a basis for cross-cultural comparison and analysis which is grounded in history and social location rather than in an ahistorical notion of culture or experience. I am making a choice here to focus on and analyze the *continuities* in the experiences, histories, and strategies of survival of these particular workers. But this does not mean that differences and discontinuities in experience do not exist or that they are insignificant. The focus on continuities is a *strategic* one – it makes possible a way of reading the operation of capital from a location (that of Third-World women workers) which, while forming the bedrock of a certain kind of global exploitation of labor, remains somewhat invisible and undertheorized.

[. . .]

NOTES

1. See Karen Hossfeld, 'United States: Why Aren't High-Tech Workers Organised?', in Women Working Worldwide, eds, *Common Interests: Women Organising in Global Electronics* (London: Tavistock), pp. 33–52, esp. pp. 50–1.

2. See 'Tijuanans Sue in L. A. after Their Maquiladora Is Closed', by Sandra DriShle, in *The San Diego Union-Tribune*, Friday, December 16, 1994. The Support Committee for Maquiladora Workers promotes cross-border organizing against corporate impunity. This is a San Diego-based volunteer effort of unionists, community activists, and others to assist workers in building autonomous organizations and facilitating ties between Mexican and U.S. workers. The Committee, which is coordinated by Mary Tong, also sees its task as educating U.S. citizens about the realities of life, work, and efforts for change among maquiladora workers. For more information, write to the Support Committee at 3909 Centre Street, #210, San Diego, CA 92103.

3. See my essay, 'Cartographies of Struggle: Third World Women and the Politics of Feminism', in Mohanty, Russo and Torres, eds, *Third World Women and the Politics of Feminism* (Bloomington: Indiana University Press, 1991), especially p. 39, where I identified five provisional historical, political, and discursive junctures for understanding Third-World feminist politics: 'decolonization and national liberation movements in the third world, the consolidation of white, liberal capitalist patriarchies in Euro-America, the operation of multinational capital within a global economy, . . . anthropology as an example of a discourse of dominance and self-reflexivity, . . . (and) storytelling or autobiography (the practice of writing) as a discourse of oppositional consciousness and agency'. This essay represents a continuation of one part of this project: the operation of multinational capital and the location of poor Third-World women workers.

4. See the excellent analysis in Teresa L. Amott and Julie A. Matthaei, *Race, Gender and Work: A Multicultural Economic History of Women in the United States* (Boston: South End Press, 1991), esp. pp. 22–3.

5. See Bagguley, Mark-Lawson, Shapiro, Urry, Walby and Warde, *Restructuring: Place, Class and Gender* (London: Sage Publications, 1990).

6. Joan Smith has argued, in a similar vein, for the usefulness of a world-systems-theory approach (seeing the various economic and social hierarchies and national divisions around the globe as part of a singular systematic division of labor, with multiple parts, rather than as plural and autonomous national systems) which incorporates the notion of the 'household' as integral to understanding the profoundly gendered character of this systematic division of labor. While her analysis is useful in historicizing and analyzing the idea of the household as the constellation of relationships that makes the transfer of wealth possible across age, gender, class, and national lines, the ideologies of masculinity, femininity, and heterosexuality that are internal to the concept of the household are left curiously intact in her analysis – as are differences in understandings of the household in different cultures. In addition, the impact of domesticating ideologies in the sphere of production, in constructions of 'women's work' are also not addressed in Smith's analysis. While I find this version of the world-systems approach useful, my own analysis attempts a different series of connections and theorizations. See Joan Smith, 'The Creation of the World We Know: The World Economy and the Re-creation of Gendered Identities', in V. Moghadam, ed., *Identity Politics and Women: Cultural Reassertions in International Perspective* (Boulder: Westview Press, 1994), pp. 27–41.

7. The case studies I analyze are: Maria Mies, *The Lacemakers of Narsapur, Indian Housewives Produce for the World Market* (London: Zed Press, 1982); Naomi Katz and David Kemnitzer, 'Fast Forward: the Internationalization of the Silicon Valley', in June Nash and M. P. Fernandez-Kelly, *Women, Men, and the International*

Division of Labor (Albany: SUNY Press, 1983), pp. 273–331; Katz and Kemnitzer, 'Women and Work in the Silicon Valley', in Karen Brodkin Sacks and D. Remy (eds). *My Troubles Are Going to Have Trouble with Me: Everyday Trials and Triumphs of Women Workers* (New Brunswick, N.J.: Rutgers University Press, 1984), pp. 193–208; and Karen J. Hossfeld, 'Their Logic Against Them; Contradictions in Sex, Race, and Class in the Silicon Valley', in Kathryn Ward, ed., *Women Workers and Global Restructuring* (Ithaca: Cornell University Press, 1990), pp. 149–78. I also draw on case studies of Black women workers in the British context in Sallie Westwood and Parminder Bhachu, eds, *Enterprising Women* (New York: Routledge, 1988).

8. See my discussion of 'relations of rule' in 'Cartographies'. There has been an immense amount of excellent feminist scholarship on women and work and women and multinationals in the last decade. In fact, it is this scholarship which makes my argument possible. Without the analytic and political insights and analyses of scholars like Aihwa Ong, Maria Patricia Fernandez-Kelly, Lourdes Beneria and Martha Roldan, Maria Mies, Swasti Mitter, and Sallie Westwood, among others, my attempt to understand the stitch together the lives and struggles of women workers in different geographical spaces would be sharply limited. This essay builds on arguments offered by some of these scholars, while attempting to move beyond particular cases to an integrated analysis which is not the same as the world-systems model. See especially Nash and Fernandez-Kelly, *Women, Men and the International Division of Labor*; Ward, ed., *Women Workers and Global Restructuring*; *Review of Radical Political Economics* vol. 23, no. 3–4 (Fall/Winter 1991), special issue on 'Women in the International Economy'; Harriet Bradley, *Men's Work Women's Work* (Minneapolis: University of Minnesota Press, 1989); Lynne Brydon and Sylvia Chant, *Women in the Third World: Gender Issues in Rural and Urban Areas* (New Brunswick, N.J.: Rutgers University Press, 1989).

9. See Ella Shohat and Robert Stam, *Unthinking Eurocentrism: Multiculturalism and the Media* (London and New York: Routledge, 1994), esp. pp. 25–7. In a discussion of the analytic and political problems involved in using terms like 'Third World', Shohat and Stam draw attention to the adoption of 'third world' at the 1955 Bandung Conference of 'non-aligned' African and Asian nations, an adoption which was premised on the solidarity of these nations and the anticolonial struggles in Vietnam and Algeria. This is the genealogy of the term that I choose to invoke here.

10. My understanding and appreciation of the links between location, experience, and social identity in political and intellectual matters grows out of numerous discussions with Satya Mohanty. See especially his essay, 'Colonial Legacies, Multicultural Futures: Relativism, Objectivity, and the Challenge of Otherness', in *PMLA* (January 1995), 108–17.

'WELFARE AND CITIZENSHIP' BY GWENDOLYN MINK

At the time of writing, Gwendolyn Mink is Professor of Women's Studies at Smith College, Northampton, Massachusetts. She is a distinguished author, winning the Victoria Schuck Book Award from the American Political Science Association for the best book on women and politics for her 1995 work *The Wages of Motherhood: Inequality in the Welfare State, 1917–1942* (Cornell University Press). She has also been active in campaigns around the reform of welfare provision, particularly as these affect women. From 1995 to 1997, she co-chaired the Women's Committee of 100, which is described as 'a group of feminist academics, professionals, and activists who are concerned with the relationship between women, economic survival, and the work of care-giving' (see http://www.welfare2002.org/). The focus of Mink's research has been the way in which economic and welfare issues specifically affect and discriminate against women. Among numerous works, she has co-edited *The Readers' Companion to U.S. Women's History* (Houghton-Mifflin, 1998), edited *Whose Welfare?* (Cornell University Press, 1999) and written *Old Labor and New Immigrants in American Political Development* (Cornell University Press, 1986) and *Hostile Environment: The Political Betrayal of Sexually Harassed Women* (Cornell University Press, 2000). The extract below is from her 1998 book *Welfare's End*. In it, she examines the links between citizenship and welfare, arguing that inequalities undermine the universality of citizenship rights and showing how social rights to welfare support are subject to the fickle whim of political will. She suggests that welfare itself should be seen not as a mere entitlement but as a right, since it makes possible the exercise of the other political rights.

'WELFARE AND CITIZENSHIP' (1998)*

Gwendolyn Mink

Citizenship is the web of relationships between the individual and the state, relationships that incur both rights and obligations. In our constitutional democracy, the basic rights of citizenship are political. Citizenship confers such political rights as suffrage and such obligations as jury duty. These rights and

---

* From Gwendolyn Mink, *Welfare's End* (Ithaca, NY: Cornell University Press, 1998), pp. 9–20.

obligations are not directly reciprocal: the right to vote does not oblige us to do so, for example, any more than the obligation to jury duty gives us the right to be selected to serve. Our strongest obligations are enforced by law: accordingly, men's duty to contribute to the national defense has been enforced by military conscription. But many of our obligations are wholly ethical: we enter into public service or participate in community life because we are supposed to, not because we are required to. Perhaps the most coherent enumeration of the ethical and legal obligations of citizenship is contained in the oath of naturalization – with which only immigrant citizens ever become familiar.

If some of our obligations are codified in scattered statutes and others are simply implied by the political culture, our rights are explicitly enumerated in the Constitution or have been definitively located in its penumbras by the Supreme Court. We enjoy most political rights not because we earned them or because they are our moral due, but because a democratic political community bestows political rights on citizens as a condition of its own existence. In theory, political rights are universal: we do not each have to prove we deserve the right to vote or to speak or to be fairly tried. Because political rights are universal, we are theoretically equal as citizens.

Not all individuals have always been considered citizens, however. Under slave law, African Americans were chattel rather than persons; with the *Dred Scott* decision, African Americans, both enslaved and free, were declared ineligible for citizenship.[1] According to the naturalization law of 1790, only whites could become naturalized citizens. A change in the law in 1870 admitted Africans to naturalization, but Asian immigrants remained barred from naturalization – and hence from citizenship – until 1952. For the native-born and naturalized, restrictions on citizenship were relaxed, in theory, when the Fifteenth Amendment conferred political rights on male citizens of all races in 1870. However, political practice withheld political rights from most African Americans and many Mexican Americans until the 1960s. Meanwhile, the Supreme Court explained in 1875 that women were not citizens in any sense that implied rights of political participation.[2] Although women won the right to participate in elections in 1920, they were denied collateral rights and obligations of citizenship (for example, jury duty) well into the 1970s and continue to be excluded from certain citizenship obligations even at the twentieth century's end (for example, draft registration, and Army combat duty). As a result of these varied exclusions from and distinctions within citizenship, full citizenship has been categorical rather than universal throughout most of US history, with rights inhering in the racial, cultural, and gender status of individuals rather than in the individual as such.

Many rights that we ordinarily refer to as civil rights and liberties flow from the formal procedural and participatory guarantees of citizenship. Since the 1930s, rights that most directly affect the integrity of democratic processes have received special recognition and protection, most notably the rights to speak, associate, and assemble.[3] Also in the 1930s, the Supreme Court began to question the categorical distribution of rights, such as the right to counsel and the right to own property.[4] By the 1950s, the Court had declared 'that the constitution of the United States . . . forbids, so far as civil and political rights are concerned, discrimination by the general government'.[5] This assertion opened the way to the review and revision of legislation that created distinctions among individuals, particularly distinctions that disabled claims to full citizenship. Among the civil rights receiving heightened judicial protection were the right to marry (or not to) and the right to procreate (or not to).[6]

Beginning in the 1960s, certain rights deemed fundamental to democratic life became available to everyone: the right to counsel (1963); voting rights (1965); the right to be tried by a jury of one's peers (1976). But this universalizing of political rights did not guarantee citizen equality. To universalize rights is to vest everyone with the same rights, to erase categorical distinctions. Even as political distinctions disappear, however, social inequalities differentiate citizen capacities to exercise rights. A homeless person has no address and cannot register to vote; a hungry person may not have the time to devote to her own political education; an illiterate person cannot read her ballot and therefore cannot cast it. Because homelessness, hunger, illiteracy, and other social conditions encroach on political rights, most serious democracies have recognized that the transition from categorical to universal citizenship requires mitigating social inequality. Policies that allay unequal social conditions include provisions guaranteeing the basic economic security of citizens. These provisions comprise social rights – primordial claims to those social supports that enable one to live and to participate in the political community. The United States has not offered generous social supports to its citizens, but it has provided for minimal subsistence (a safety net) to cushion different categories of need.

Most political rights are grounded in the Constitution and only with great difficulty can be denied. The Supreme Court occasionally has insisted, moreover, that certain constitutional guarantees must be secured through social provision: in *Gideon v. Wainwright*, for example, the Court ordered government to furnish indigent criminal defendants with counsel, arguing that the fundamental right to counsel was meaningless for defendants who could not afford to pay for an attorney.[7] Most social rights, however, derive not from the Constitution but from claims endorsed by political majorities through the legislative process. Though they cannot be denied so long as majorities support them, social rights are hostage to shifting political winds. In US policy parlance we call legislated social rights 'entitlements' and situate them along a continuum of claims running from privileges to constitutional guarantees.[8]

Although social rights are weaker than political rights, the full and universal exercise of political rights pivots on their availability. Like political rights, social rights are conceptually universal as they guarantee everyone their right to a subsistence sufficient to ensure survival and to facilitate independent participation in the life of the community. But where political rights *assume* equality among the individuals who possess them, social rights *enable* equality by countervailing inequalities among individuals. Because inequalities are various, most social rights become targeted entitlements in practice. We may all have the same right to vote regardless of social station, but we are entitled to different social benefits depending on what our needs are and what our contributions have been. The elderly receive retirement benefits, for example, while the sick poor receive Medicaid and laid-off workers receive unemployment insurance. Thus entitlements are categorical, but have the effect of universalizing the political rights of citizenship.

The specific content of most social entitlements varies with the needs and circumstances of individuals, and so the strength of specific entitlements often depends on what we think of the people claiming them. The strongest entitlements – those most difficult to deny – are those we link to sweat and to sacrifice. The veteran, for example, is said to deserve his GI benefits because military service entails risks to life and limb. The worker is said to have earned his old-age pension through paid employment and taxes. The concept of earned benefits rests on the fiction that individuals get back from the benefits system only what they paid in, and no more. But even the most popular social benefits are structured to provide in part according to need and so are not strictly tied to the beneficiary's degree of contribution.[9] For example, the average social security beneficiary who retired at age sixty-five in 1995 would get back all the taxes she contributed to the social security system within three and a half years.[10] Although 'earned' social security benefits eventually become 'welfare' for retired workers, we do not begrudge the elderly their pensions. Rather, we believe that retired workers have paid for their benefits at least metaphorically, through lifelong attachment to the labor market.

The idea that certain benefits are earned appeals to the ethic of contract, expressing the view that government owes the individual his benefit in exchange for services rendered. If recipients of putatively contractual benefits are the first among citizens of the welfare state, the most vulnerable and unequal citizens have been those who need their benefits and who receive them as a gratuity from government rather than as their due. Income support for needy citizens tends to be stingier and more begrudging than for citizens who are believed to have paid for it.[11] Hence, for example, even though mothers in the survivors' insurance system and mothers in the welfare system are all mothers parenting alone, a widowed mother whose husband paid social security taxes receives a survivors' stipend for herself and her children four times greater than the average monthly welfare grant received by divorced or never-married mothers and their children.[12]

Both discursively and structurally, welfare – economic assistance to poor single mothers and their children – affirmed rather than repaired inequality. During the 1960s and early 1970s, the national welfare rights movement fought to secure rights for welfare participants – the right to move to another state, for example, as well as the right to a fair hearing. Welfare rights litigation made headway beginning in 1968: following the Supreme Court's announcement in

King v. Smith that state welfare rules must conform to the national statutory purpose of welfare, a single set of national criteria determined poor families' eligibility.[13] And following the Supreme Court's decision in *Shapiro v. Thompson* that welfare residency requirements compromised poor families' 'basic right' to travel, mothers who received welfare were afforded certain constitutional protections.[14] In these respects, rights of national citizenship were extended to poor single mothers. Yet even during this period of widening rights within welfare, racism, sexism, and moral stigma poisoned poor single mothers' right *to* welfare. Moreover, the structure of welfare distinguished poor single mothers from other recipients of social entitlements. While payment levels for widowed mothers and their children in the survivors' insurance system are nationally determined and uniform, for example, welfare benefit levels have been controlled by the states. Hence, even before the Personal Responsibility Act, the degree of support available to a mother and her children depended on where they resided: for example, 1995 cash payments in Mississippi were $120 per month for a family of three, while in Connecticut they were more than $600.[15]

Historically, benefits for those who most need them have been most fragile – most susceptible to political attack. This is why, despite their posturing against the welfare state as a whole, the Republicans in the 104th Congress singled out economic assistance for poor single mothers and their children for repeal. Calling recipients 'lazy' and their children 'illegitimate', welfare reformers played to the view that welfare lies outside the social contract. Ridiculing welfare as a payment to women who do not work, they made the welfare entitlement very easy to deny.

In rejecting poor single mothers' social claim to economic assistance, welfare reformers did not end welfare absolutely but rather restricted its availability through time limits and rules for participation. Many of the rules for participation are burdens that government cannot impose on citizens directly: for example, government cannot pressure a woman directly to choose abortion any more than it can pressure her directly to choose childbirth.[16] Nor can government force an individual into a particular job – except through military conscription – especially if that job is unpaid.

Since one mission of the Personal Responsibility Act is precisely to pressure women's rights by regulating how poor mothers exercise them, it may not withstand constitutional scrutiny.[17] From the standpoint of liberty that would be good news. However, in the absence of a recognized right to welfare, constitutionally suspicious welfare policy may be succeeded by no welfare policy at all. This would be devastating for equal citizenship. So it is important to connect the recovery of poor mothers' rights *within* welfare to their right *to receive* welfare in the first place.

To some extent we can derive a right to welfare through constitutional reasoning: a socially provided income guarantee is (or ought to be) a condition of reproductive, marital, family, and vocational rights, as well as a matter of equal protection. Ultimately, however, the claim to a welfare right is a political one, for we lack a strong jurisprudential tradition binding economic provision to constitutional guarantees: the Court generally does not require government to subsidize the exercise of a right (say, reproductive choice) even though without a subsidy (Medicaid funding) a person may not be able to exercise her right (for example, choose abortion).[18] In fact, the Court emphatically rejects the claim that government bears affirmative obligations to support fundamental rights, arguing that 'the Due Process Clauses . . . confer no affirmative right to governmental aid, even where such aid may be necessary to secure life, liberty, or property interests of which the government itself may not deprive the individual'.[19] Nor does the Court hold government constitutionally responsible to provide for the economic security of its citizens.

Notwithstanding these judicial restraints on what it compels, however, the Constitution does permit us to imagine different ways to enforce its meaning legislatively: the Fourteenth Amendment gives Congress the responsibility to enact laws that enforce its provisions, including its clause promising 'equal protection of the law'.[20] More to the point, the Constitution permits us to defend rights with remedies, including social supports without which the rights of some citizens would either erode or disappear.

The equality clause of the Fourteenth Amendment is the wellspring of doctrine and policy universalizing citizenship. Beginning in the 1970s, the Supreme Court brought women within equality's purview, deriving from the promise of equal treatment the basic civil rights of women. The Court has generally declined to require equal treatment where women are differently positioned from men: for example, in a decision that still stands, the Court in 1974 ruled that discrimination against pregnant women workers is not discrimination based on gender, and thus not prohibited by the equal protection clause (*Geduldig v. Aiello* 417 U.S. 484). Similarly, in 1981 the Court upheld a statutory rape law under which only girls could be victims (*Michael M. v. Superior Court of Sonoma County* 450 U.S. 464). Such exceptions to equal treatment often have impaired women's equality.

However, the Court also has occasionally noticed that equality may sometimes require treating women and men differently by vesting women with rights or benefits that are uniquely their own. Thus Justice O'Connor argued after reconsidering *Roe v. Wade* that 'the liberty of the woman is at stake in a sense unique to the human condition and so unique to the law. . . . The destiny of the woman must be shaped to a large extent on her own conception of her spiritual imperatives and her place in society.'[21] The Court has likewise acknowledged that at the conjuncture of biology and gender may reside inequalities that only remedies gauged to women's circumstances can repair.[22] For example, upholding California's job security guarantee for women workers who take pregnancy leave, the Court noted that the goal of the gender-specific disability protection 'is to guarantee women the basic right to participate fully and equally in the workforce, without denying them the fundamental right to full participation in family life'.[23] Drawing a distinction between gender-sensitive enabling rights and gender-prescriptive restrictions, the Court also has cautioned: 'But such classifications may not be used, as they once were . . . to create or perpetuate the legal, social, and economic inferiority of women'.[24]

Gendered rights are tricky business, as the differential treatment of women in law and policy has too often meant our unequal treatment. Moreover, policies or rights derived for the generic woman risk defining the experiences and needs of particular groups of women as the experiences and needs of all. They further risk prescribing or ascribing roles and choices to women who may rather eschew them. That said, I think too many inequalities flow from ignoring women's various gender-based needs and dilemmas. These inequalities find an excuse in difference, handicap women in private and public relations with men, and command conformity to white male rules as the price of women's civic and social incorporation.

But we don't need to claim rights for women only. We can draw from women's diverse gendered experiences to design policies that correct inequalities attached to those experiences. We can write such gender-sensitive laws in gender-neutral language – as parental leave policy is written, for example, and as welfare policy was from 1935 to 1996. We can consciously avoid assuming or requiring that *all* women conform to a single gender role, and avoid obligating *only* women to perform that role. But we cannot cure inequality where it is most gendered – in sexual, reproductive, and family relations – without addressing the ways in which that inequality directly and disproportionately burdens women.

One such inequality is the economic disfranchisement of mothers who are their children's care-givers. Mothers who work inside the home raising children are deprived of fair remuneration for their labor, and thus of the means for independence, because we do not impute economic value to the work they do. In marriages, mothers who work inside the home surrender their economic personhood to husbands and occupy the legal status of dependent. Their lack of independent economic resources – earnings – skews power relations in the family: some mothers may feel tethered to husbands because they could not survive the economic consequences of leaving them. Single mothers bear the costs of economic disfranchisement most acutely, for they must accept destitution as a condition of caring for their children. Unpaid and disdained, they are expected to forswear child-raising for full-time wage-earning. Mothers who work inside the home caring for children, then, are disproportionately dependent on men if married and disproportionately poor, if not. These private inequalities have public effects, foreclosing such mothers' independent citizenship.

We should not think of welfare as a subsidy for dependence; nor should we think of it as an income substitute for the wage earned by breadwinners – fathers – in the labor market. Rather, we should reconceive welfare as the income *owed* to persons who work inside the home caring for, nurturing, and

595

protecting children. As it has been for sixty years, welfare should be available to solo care-giving parents of either sex. But though sex-blind, welfare cannot be gender-neutral, for it should assign economic value to a role mostly performed by women: care-giving. Thus conceived, welfare would enhance equality by compensating solo care-giving mothers for the work they do and extending to them the work-based social rights of citizenship.

As a social right, welfare must remedy material as well as gender conditions that impede equality – that stratify citizenship. Accordingly, while welfare should establish the principle that all family care-giving is work, it should support that work in a way that redistributes income security toward the most vulnerable family care-givers. Mothers who need to leave marriages or who are already single and poor are most at risk of exploitation and destitution because they must both care and provide for their children. Welfare should redress this inequality, thereby guarding the rights and promoting the independence of mothers who must parent alone. Meanwhile, the availability of welfare for single care-givers would enhance equality in marriage: giving married mothers the means to exit marriages, welfare would give them a choice to remain, as well.

As an income for poor single care-givers and as a safety net for all care-givers who might find themselves alone and poor, welfare is a prerequisite for equality in the family, in the labor market, and in the state. As such, welfare should be a right, not a gratuity – a claim backed by law and courts that should be irresistible, or at least very hard to deny. We can locate a welfare right in the penumbras of other rights. In one sense, it is a right upon which other rights, such as reproductive choice, depend. But welfare is also a right unto itself: under the Thirteenth and Fourteenth Amendments, everyone has the right to be paid for their labor.

[. . .]

NOTES

1. *Dred Scott v. Sandford* 19 How (60 U.S.) 393 (1857).
2. *Minor v. Happersett* 88 U.S. 162, 11 L. Ed. 627 (1875).
3. *Palko v. Connecticut* 302 U.S. 319 (1937) discussed the scheme of fundamental rights and asked of government action, 'Does it violate those fundamental principles of liberty and justice which lie at the base of all our civil and political institutions?'
4. *United States v. Carolene Products* 304 U.S. 144 (1938), note 4, planted the seed for modern Fourteenth Amendment jurisprudence. In this footnote, Justice Harlan Stone suggested that courts might apply special scrutiny in cases affecting fundamental rights or where legislation singles out racial, national, or religious minorities.
5. *Bolling v. Sharpe* 347 U.S. 497 (1954).
6. *Loving v. Virginia* 388 U.S. 1 (1967) found that 'under our Constitution, the freedom to marry, or not marry . . . resides with the individual and cannot be infringed by the State.' *Skinner v. Oklahoma* 316 U.S. 535 struck down the compulsory sterilization of certain classes of felons as a discriminatory violation of 'the right to have offspring.' *Planned Parenthood of Southeastern Pennsylvania v. Casey*

112 S Ct 2705 (1992) upheld a woman's right to terminate pregnancy as an aspect of her right to chart her own destiny and make her own place in society.

7. *Gideon v. Wainwright* 372 U.S. 335 (1965).

8. Theodore J. Rowl, conversation with author.

9. *Flemming v. Nestor* 363 U.S. 603, 608–609 (1960); *Weinberger v. Wiesenfeld* 420 U.S. 636 (1975).

10. Robert D. Hershey, Jr., 'Misunderstanding Social Security,' *New York Times*, August 20, 1995.

11. See, e.g., *Jefferson v. Hackney* 406 U.S. 535, 575 (1972). Justice Thurgood Marshall noted in his dissent that Texas had funded welfare at a lower level than other social benefits because it is politically unpopular, because a stigma uniquely attaches to welfare recipients, and because a large proportion of welfare recipients are people of color.

12. In 1993, the average monthly benefit for a widowed mother was $445, and for each surviving child, $443, subject to a family benefit limit. Where the spouse died at age forty and had earned the national average wage, the monthly family benefit limit was $1,527. U.S. House of Representatives, Committee on Ways and Means, *1994 Green Book: Overview of Entitlement Programs* (Washington, D.C., 1994), pp. 4, 37. A wage-earner insured under the social security system who died at age forty in 1995 left his widow and children a maximum family benefit of $1,362 per month if he earned $20,000 annually. See Congressional Research Service, *1995 Guide to Social Security and Medicare* (Washington, D.C., 1994), p. 30; Social Security Administration, *Social Security handbook*, 12th ed. (Washington, D.C., 1995). The average monthly welfare benefit in 1993 was $367.

13. *King v. Smith* stated that welfare must be provided to all eligible persons.

14. *Shapiro v. Thompson* 394 U.S. 618 (1969) held that Connecticut's residency requirements were unconstitutional discrimination and violated the right to travel; *Goldberg v. Kelly* 397 U.S. 254 (1970) found welfare a 'statutory entitlement,' triggering due process protections for recipients in their relations with welfare agencies.

15. *Dandridge v. Williams* 397 U.S. 471 (1970) upheld Maryland's family benefit limit and thus rejected the claim that individuals have a right to a particular or equal amount of cash payment. 'Tough-love Index,' *New York Times*, December 8, 1996.

16. See Kathleen M. Sullivan, 'Unconstitutional Conditions,' *Harvard Law Review* 102, no. 7 (May 1989. 1413–1506. On welfare reform and reproductive liberty, see Catherine R. Albiston and Laura Beth Nielsen, 'Welfare Queens and Other Fairy Tales: Welfare Reform and Unconstitutional Reproductive Controls,' *Harvard Law Journal* 38, no. 3 (Summer 1995): 473–519.

17. In addition to probable rights violations contained in the new welfare policy is its questionable claim of a federal police power governing family matters. See *United States v. Lopez* 115 S. Ct. 1624 (1995), narrowly typing Congress's power to regulate to those activities that directly affect interstate commerce and 'withholding from Congress a plenary police power.' The Court rejected the federal government's 'national productivity' reasoning, according to which 'Congress could regulate any activity that it found was related to the economic productivity of individual citizens: family law (including marriage, divorce, and child custody), for example'; the Court argued further that 'If we were to accept the Government's arguments, we are hard-pressed to posit any activity by an individual that Congress is without power to regulate.'

18. *Harris v. McRae* 448 U.S. 297 (1980).

19. *Webster v. Reproductive Health Services* 492 U.S. 490, 507 (1989), reiterated in *Rust v. Sullivan* 500 U.S. 173, 201 (1991).

20. Robin West, *Progressive Constitutionalism* (Durham, N.C., 1994) especially chapters 1–3, discovers affirmative guarantees in the Fourteenth Amendment from its legislative history and argues that Congress has broad responsibilities to enforce those guarantees.

21. *Permitted Parenthood of Southeastern Pennsylvania v. Casey* 112 S. Ct. 2791 (1992).
22. Sex classifications may be used to compensate women 'for particular economic disabilities [they have] suffered' (*Califano v. Webster* 430 U.S. 313, 320 [1977]) and to 'promote equal employment opportunity' (*California Federal Savings & Loan Association v. Guerra* 479 U.S. 272, 289 [1987]).
23. Justice Thurgood Marshall for the Court, quoting from a sponsor of the Pregnancy Discrimination Act, *CalFed v. Guerra*, 289.
24. *United States v. Virginia et al.* no 94–1942 (1996).

SECTION 4: QUESTIONS FOR DISCUSSION

- Do you agree that affirmative action/positive discrimination can, as Iris Young argues, 'compensate for the dominance of one set of cultural attributes'?
- What is the difference between an individual human right and a collective or group right?
- What similarities and differences are there in the approach to the practical and policy-orientated political theory advocated by Modood and Favell and the engaged radical democratic theory of Smith?
- What are the benefits and difficulties of properly incorporating an empirical sensibility into normative political theorising?
- Is there a strong overlap between some of the arguments relating to multiculturalism and the radical democracy advocated by Smith?
- What is distinctive in Butler's theorisation of the constitution of categories of sex, gender and sexuality? What are the political stakes in such theorisation?
- How can we comprehend the links between gender, race, class and sexuality in the organisation of state structures and policies?
- What aspects of the philosophical themes presented by Suzuki, Khomeini and Mao strike you as most different from Western styles of thinking? What strikes you as most similar?
- What is recognisably Marxist about Mao's argument? Do any elements strike you as particularly non-Marxist?
- Can religion and democratic politics ever be reconciled?

SECTION 4: FURTHER READING

There is a vast literature on multiculturalism, much of it coming from disciplines other than political theory (such as cultural studies, literary theory, history and so on). From the point of view of political theory, it would be worth following up on the writers featured here and consulting Kymlicka's *Multicultural Citizenship: A Liberal Theory of Minority Rights* (Oxford University Press, 1995) and Parekh's *Rethinking Multiculturalism: Cultural Diversity and Political Theory* (Macmillan, 2000). It would also be a good idea to look at Amy Gutmann (ed.), *Multiculturalism and the Politics of Recognition* (Princeton University Press, 1994), which includes Charles **Taylor**'s important essay on the subject. For a critique of multiculturalism on the grounds of egalitarianism, see Brian **Barry**'s *Culture and Equality* (Polity Press, 2001). There has also been considerable debate about the measure of complement and conflict between feminism and multiculturalism. For a feminist critique, see *Is Multiculturalism Bad for Women?* by Susan Moller Okin, Joshua Cohen, Matthew Howard and Martha Nussbaum (Princeton University Press, 1999). For more on the complex politics of this, consult work by both Modood and Favell, including the volume edited by Modood, *The Politics of Multiculturalism in the New Europe: Racism, Identity and Community* (Zed Books, 1997), and Favell's *The Politics of Belonging: Migrants and Minorities in Contemporary Europe* (Ashgate, 1999).

Readers wishing to expand their knowledge on non-Western forms of thought might start with Leaman's work, including *A Brief Introduction to Islamic Philosophy* (Polity Press, 1999) and *Introduction to Classical Islamic Philosophy* (Cambridge University Press, 2001). For background on the Iranian context of Khomeini, consult E. Abrahamian, *Iran Between Two Revolutions*

(Princeton University Press, 1982) and S. Amir Arjomand, *The Turban for the Crown: The Islamic Revolution in Iran* (Oxford University Press, 1998). For more detail on the system, try A. Schirazi, *The Constitution of Iran: Politics and the State in the Islamic Republic of Iran* (I. B. Tauris, 1997). For a more general study of politics and ideas in the region, see S. Zubaida, *Islam, The People and the State: Political Ideas and Movements in the Middle East* (I. B. Tauris, 1993). For further study of Islamic political ideas, you can consult Amir Arjomand, *Authority and Political Culture in Shi'ism* (1988), A. Enayat, *Modern Islamic Political Thought* (1982). For Khomeini specifically, try E. Abrahamian, *Khomeinism* (London, 1993). Mao's selected writings are vast and are all published by Lawrence and Wishart. A recent big but readable biography is *Mao: A Life* by Philip Short (Henry Holt and Co., 2000).

The topics presented in Smith's chapter are many and varied. Much of the reading suggested in relation to other chapters (on feminism, ecologism and poststructuralism) would be helpful for further study. It would also be worthwhile consulting other works by the authors presented, such as Mink's *The Wages of Motherhood: Inequality in the Welfare State, 1917–1942* (Cornell University Press, 1995) and the edited volume *Whose Welfare?* (Cornell University Press, 1999). Wider-ranging investigation into the issues of welfare, equality, race, class and gender might include some of the following: Esther Chow, Doris Wilkinson and Maxine Baca Zinn (eds), *Race, Class and Gender: Common Bonds, Different Voices* (Sage, 1996); Sandra Harding and Uma Narayan (eds), *Border Crossings: Multicultural and Postcolonial Feminist Challenges to Philosophy* (Indiana University Press, 1998); and Michael Awkward, *Negotiating Difference: Race, Gender, and the Politics of Positionality* (University of Chicago Press, 1995). Within left-wing debates relating to poststructuralist and radical democratic conceptions, see Judith Butler and Joan Scott (eds), *Feminists Theorize the Political* (Routledge, 1992). For a critique of the politics of recognition that advocates more attention to matters of income inequality, see Nancy Fraser's *Justice Interruptus: Critical Reflections on the 'Post-socialist' Condition* (Routledge, 1997). Also relevant to the issues raised by Smith is Linda Singer (ed.), *Erotic Welfare: Sexual Theory and Politics in the Age of Epidemic*, edited posthumously by Judith Butler and M. MacGrogan (Routledge, 1993). On the issue of discrimination and control in welfare, see C. Jones and T. Novak, *Poverty, Welfare and the Disciplinary State* (Routledge, 1999), which examines the authoritarianism of recent social policy.

BIBLIOGRAPHY

Aiken, William (1992) 'Human Rights in an Ecological Era', *Environmental Values*, 1.3: 191–203.

Althusser, Louis (1971) 'Ideology and Ideological State Apparatuses (Notes towards an Investigation)', in L. Althusser, *Lenin and Philosophy and other Essays*, New York: Monthly Review Press.

Arendt, Hannah (1953) 'Understanding and Politics', *Partisan Review*, 20: 4.

Arendt, Hannah (1973) *The Origins of Totalitarianism*, 4th edn, New York: Harcourt Brace Jovanovich.

Aughey, Arthur (1992) 'The Character of Conservatism', in Arthur Aughey, Greta Jones and W. T. Riches, *The Conservative Political Tradition in Britain and the United States*, London: Pinter.

Austin, J. L. (1975 [1962]) *How to Do Things with Words*, ed. J. O. Urmson and Marina Sbisa, 2nd edn, Oxford: Clarendon Press.

Bacchi, C. (1990) *Same Difference: Feminism and Sexual Difference*, London: Allen and Unwin.

Bagehot, Walter (1905) *The English Constitution*, London: Kegan Paul, Trench, Trubner.

Ball, Terence, James Farr and Russell L. Hanson (eds) (1989) *Political Innovation and Conceptual Change*, Cambridge: Cambridge University Press.

Barker, Philip (1998) *Michel Foucault: An Introduction*, Edinburgh: Edinburgh University Press.

Barrett, M. (1980) *Women's Oppression Today*, London: Verso.

Barry, B. (2001) *Culture and Equality*, Cambridge, MA: Harvard University Press; Cambridge: Polity.

Barthes, Roland (1977) *Image–Music–Text*, trans. S. Heath, London: Fontana.

Baylis, John and Steve Smith (eds) (2001) *The Globalization of World Politics*, Oxford: Clarendon.

Beiner, R. (1996) 'What Liberalism Means', *Social Philosophy and Policy*, 13 (1): 190–206.

Beiner, R. and W. Norman (eds) (2000) *Canadian Political Philosophy*, Oxford: Oxford University Press.

Bell, Daniel (1960) *The End of Ideology: On the Exhaustion of Political Ideas in the Fifties*, New York: Free Press.

Bell, Daniel (1993) *Communitarianism and its Critics*, Oxford: Clarendon Press.

Bellamy, R. (1992) *Liberalism and Modern Society: An Historical Argument*, Cambridge: Polity.

Benhabib, S. (1992) *Situating the Self: Gender, Community and Post-modernism in Contemporary Ethics*, New York: Routledge.

Benton, Ted (1993) *Natural Relations: Ecology, Animal Rights and Social Justice*, London: Verso.

Berlin, Isaiah (1962) 'Does Political Theory Still Exist?', in Peter Laslett and W. G. Runciman (eds), *Philosophy, Politics and Society*, 2nd series, Oxford: Basil Blackwell, pp. 1–33.

Bradley, F. H. (1968 [1874]) *The Presuppositions of Critical History*, ed. Lionel Rubinoff, Donn Mills, Ontario: J. M. Dent.

Bramwell, Anna (1989) *Ecology in the 20th Century: A History*, New Haven, CT: Yale University Press.

Burke, Edmund (1990 [1791]) 'An Appeal from the New to the Old Whigs, in Consequence of Some Late Discussions in Parliament, Relative to the Reflections on the French Revolution', in Robert Eccleshall, *English Conservatism Since the Restoration: An Introduction and Anthology*, London: Unwin Hyman, pp. 71–4.

Butler, Judith (1990) *Gender Trouble: Feminism and the Subversion of Identity*, London: Routledge.

Butler, Judith (1993) *Bodies that Matter: On the Discursive Limits of Sex*, London: Routledge.

Butler, Judith and Joan Scott (eds) (1992) *Feminists Theorize the Political*, London: Routledge.

Butterfield, Herbert (1931) *The Whig Interpretation of History*, London: G. Bell and Sons.

Caney, S. (1992) 'Liberalism and Communitarianism: A Misconceived Debate', *Political Studies*, 40: 273–90.

Carens, J. (2000) *Culture, Citizenship and Community*, Oxford: Oxford University Press.

Carver, Terrell (1981) *Engels*, Oxford: Oxford University Press.

Carver, Terrell (1982) *Marx's Social Theory*, Oxford: Oxford University Press.

Carver, Terrell (1983) *Marx and Engels: The Intellectual Relationship*, Brighton: Harvester/Wheatsheaf.

Carver, Terrell (2003 forthcoming) 'Marx and Marxism', in *The Cambridge History of Science*, Volume 7: *The Modern Social and Behavioral Sciences*, ed. Theodore Porter and Dorothy Ross, New York: Cambridge University Press.

Castles, S. and A. Davidson (2000) *Citizenship and Migration: Globalization and the Politics of Belonging*, London: Macmillan.

Chodorow, N. (1978) *The Reproduction of Mothering: Psychoanalysis and the Sociology of Gender*, Berkeley, CA: University of California Press.

Chong, Dennis (2000) *Rational Lives: Norms and Values in Politics and Society*, Chicago, IL: University of Chicago Press.

Cixous, Hélène with Catherine Clément (1986 [1975]) *The Newly Born Woman*, trans. B. Wing, Minneapolis, MN: University of Minnesota Press.

Cobban, Alfred (1953) 'The Decline of Political Theory', *Political Science Quarterly*, 68.2: 321–37.

Cohen, G. A. (1978), *Karl Marx's Theory of History: A Defence*, Oxford: Clarendon Press.

Collingwood, R. G. (1939) *An Autobiography*, Oxford: Oxford University Press.

Collingwood, R. G. (1946) *The Idea of History*, Oxford: Clarendon Press.

Connolly, William E. (1991) *Identity/Difference: Democratic Negotiations of Political Paradox*, New York: Cornell University Press.

Crenshaw, Kimberlé (1992) 'Whose Story Is It Anyway? Feminist and Antiracist Appropriations of Anita Hill', in T. Morrison (ed.), *Race-ing Justice, En-gendering Power: Essays on Anita Hill, Clarence Thomas and the Construction of Social Reality*, New York: Pantheon.

Dahl, Robert A. (1958) 'Political Theory: Truth or Consequences', *World Politics*, 11: 89–102.

Deleuze, Gilles (1983) *Nietzsche and Philosophy*, trans. H. Tomlinson, New York: Columbia University Press.

Deleuze, Gilles (1994 [1968]) *Difference and Repetition*, trans. P. Patton, New York: Columbia University Press.

Deleuze, Gilles and Felix Guattari (1983 [1972]) *Anti-Oedipus*, trans. R. Hurley, M. Seem and H. R. Lane, Minneapolis, MN: University of Minnesota Press.

Deleuze, Gilles and Felix Guattari (1987 [1980]) *A Thousand Plateaus*, trans. B. Massumi, Minneapolis, MN: University of Minnesota Press.

D'Entrèves, M. P. (1990) 'Communitarianism and the Question of Tolerance', *Journal of Social Philosophy*, 21 (1): 77–89.

Derrida, Jacques (1976 [1967]) *Of Grammatology*, trans. G. Spivak, Baltimore, MD: Johns Hopkins University Press.

Derrida, Jacques (1982 [1972]) *Margins – Of Philosophy*, trans. A. Bass, Chicago, IL: University of Chicago Press.

Derrida, Jacques (1988) *Limited Inc.*, Evanston, IL: Northwestern University Press.

Derrida, Jacques (1994 [1993]) *Spectres of Marx: The State of Debt, the Work of Mourning and the New International*, trans. P. Kamuf, London: Routledge.

De-Shalit, Avner (2000) *The Environment: Between Theory and Practice*, Oxford: Oxford University Press.

DiStefano, C. (1991) *Configurations of Masculinity: A Feminist Perspective*, Ithaca, NY: Cornell University Press.

Dobson, Andrew (2000), *Green Political Thought*, 3rd edn, London: Routledge.

Dowding, Keith (2001) 'There Must Be End to Confusion: Policy Networks, Intellectual Fatigue, and the Need for Political Science Methods Courses in British Universities', *Political Studies*, 49.1: 89–105.

Dryzek, John (1987) *Rational Ecology: Environment and Political Economy*, Oxford: Blackwell.

Dryzek, John (1992) 'Ecology and Discursive Democracy: Beyond Liberal Capitalism and the Administrative State', *Capitalism, Nature, Socialism*, 10: 18–42.

Dunn, John (1969) *The Political Thought of John Locke*, Cambridge: Cambridge University Press.

Dunn, John (1990) 'What is Living and What is Dead in the Political Thought of John Locke?', in John Dunn, *Interpreting Political Responsibility*, Cambridge: Polity, pp. 9–25.

Dunn, John (1996) 'The History of Political Theory', in John Dunn *The History of Political Theory and Other Essays*, Cambridge: Cambridge University Press, pp. 11–38.

Dworkin, R. (1977) *Taking Rights Seriously*, London: Duckworth.

Easton, David (1953) *The Political System*, New York: Alfred A. Knopf.

Eisenstein, Zillah (1979) *Capitalist Patriarchy and the Case for Socialist Feminism*, New York: Monthly Review Press.

Eliot, T. S. (1964) *Knowledge and Experience in the Philosophy of F. H. Bradley*, New York: Columbia University Press.

Elster, J. (1992) *Local Justice: How Institutions Allocate Scarce Goods and Necessary Burdens*, Cambridge: Cambridge University Press.

Etzioni, A. (1995) *The Spirit of Community: Rights, Responsibilities and the Communitarian Agenda*, London: Fontana.

Etzioni, A. (1997) *The New Golden Rule: Community and Morality in a Democratic Society*, London: Profile Books.

Fausto-Sterling, Anne (1993) 'The Five Sexes: Why Male and Female Are Not Enough', *The Sciences* (March/April): 20–4.

Favell, A. (2001) *Philosophies of Integration: Immigration and the Idea of Citizenship in France and Britain*, 2nd edn, London: Palgrave.

Ferry, J.-M. (1992) 'La pertinence du postnationel', in J. Lenoble and N. Dewandre, *L'Europe au soir des siècles*, Paris: Seuil.

Foucault, Michel (1977 [1975]) *Discipline and Punish: The Birth of the Prison*, trans. A. Sheridan, Harmondsworth: Penguin.

Foucault, Michel (1978 [1976]) *The History of Sexuality, Vol. 1: An Introduction*, trans. R. Hurley, London: Penguin.

Foucault, Michel (1980) *Power/Knowledge: Selected Interviews and Other Writings 1972–1977*, trans. C. Gordon, L. Marshall, J. Mepham and K. Soper, London: Harvester Wheatsheaf.

Fraser, N. (1998) 'Sex, Lies and the Public Sphere: Reflections on the Confirmation of Clarence Thomas', in J. B. Landes (ed.), *Feminism, the Public and the Private*, Oxford: Oxford University Press.

Frazer, E. and N. Lacey (1993) *The Politics of Community: A Feminist Critique of the Liberal-Communitarian Debate*, Hemel Hempstead: Harvester Wheatsheaf.

Freeden, Michael (1996) *Ideologies and Political Theory: A Conceptual Approach*, Oxford: Clarendon Press.

Friedman, J. (1994) 'The Politics of Communitarianism', *Critical Review*, 8 (1): 297–339.

Fukuyama, Francis (1992) *The End of History and the Last Man*, London: Hamish Hamilton.

Fuss, D. (1989) *Essentially Speaking: Feminism, Nature and Difference*, London: Routledge.

Gadamer, Hans-Georg (1989) *Truth and Method*, trans. and ed. Garrett Barden and John Cumming, 2nd edn, New York: Crossroad (transl. from *Wahrheit und Methode*, 2nd edn, Tübingen: J. C. B. Mohr (Paul Siebeck)).

Galston, W. (1991) *Liberal Purposes: Goods Diversity and Virtue in the Liberal State*, Cambridge: Cambridge University Press.

Gamble, Andrew (1988) *The Free Economy and the Strong State: The Politics of Thatcherism*, Basingstoke: Macmillan.

Giddens, Anthony (1990) *The Consequences of Modernity*, Cambridge: Polity.

Giddens, Anthony (1994) *Beyond Left and Right*, Cambridge: Polity.

Giddens, Anthony (1996) *In Defence of Sociology*, Cambridge: Polity.

Giddens, Anthony (1999) *Runaway World: How Globalisation is Reshaping Our Lives*, London: Profile.

Gilligan, C. (1982) *In a Different Voice: Psychological Theory and Women's Development*, Cambridge, MA: Harvard University Press.

Gilroy, P. (1987) *There Ain't No Black in the Union Jack*, London: Heinemann.

Gilroy, P. (1993) *The Black Atlantic*, London: Verso.

Gilroy, P. (2000) *Between Camps*, London: Penguin.

Goodin, R. (1995) *Utilitarianism as a Public Philosophy*, Cambridge: Cambridge University Press.

Gray, J. (1995a) *Enlightenment's Wake: Politics and Culture at the Close of the Modern Age*, London: Routledge.

Gray, John (1995b) 'Agonistic Liberalism', in E. F. Paul et al. (eds), *Contemporary Political and Social Philosophy*, Cambridge: Cambridge University Press, pp. 111–35.

Gray, John (1996) *After Social Democracy: Politics, Capitalism and the Common Life*, London: Demos.

Gray, John (1998) *False Dawn: The Delusions of Global Capitalism*, London: Granta.

Grosz, Elizabeth (1994) *Volatile Bodies: Toward a Corporeal Feminism*, Bloomington, IN: Indiana University Press.

Grugel, Jean (2002) *Democratization: A Critical Introduction*, Basingstoke: Palgrave.

Guattari, Felix (1984 [1977]) *Molecular Revolution*, trans. R. Sheed, London: Penguin.

Gutmann, A. (1985) 'Communitarian Critics of Liberalism', *Philosophy and Public Affairs*, 14.

Gutmann, A. (ed.) (1994) *Multiculturalism and the Politics of Recognition*, Princeton, NJ: Princeton University Press.

Habermas, J. (1992) 'Citizenship and National Identity: Some Reflections on the Future of Europe', *Praxis International*, 12.1: 1–19.

Habermas, Jürgen (1984 [1981]) *The Theory of Communicative Action, Vol. 1: Reason and the Rationalization of Society*, trans. T. McCarthy, London: Heinemann.

Habermas, Jürgen (1987 [1981]), *The Theory of Communicative Action, Vol. 2: A Critique of Functionalist Reason*, trans. T. McCarthy, Cambridge: Polity.

Hall, Stuart (1988) *The Hard Road to Renewal: Thatcherism and the Crisis of the Left*, London: Verso.

Hall, Stuart (1992) 'New Ethnicities', in J. Donald and A. Rattansi (eds), *'Race', Culture and Difference*, London: Sage.

Hall, Stuart (2000) 'Conclusion: The Multi-cultural Question', in B. Hesse (ed.), *Un/settled Multiculturalisms*, London: Zed Books.

Halperin, David M. (1995) *Saint Foucault: Towards a Gay Historiography*, Oxford: Oxford University Press.

Hardin, Garrett (1968) 'The Tragedy of the Commons', *Science*, 162: 1,243–8.

Hardt, Michael (1993) *Gilles Deleuze: An Apprenticeship in Philosophy*, London: UCL Press.

Hawkes, Terence (1977) *Structuralism and Semiotics*, London: Routledge.

Hayek, Friedrich von (1944) *The Road to Serfdom*, London: Routledge.

Hayek, Friedrich A. (1960), *The Constitution of Liberty*, London: Routledge and Kegan Paul.

Hayward, Tim (1995) *Ecological Thought: An Introduction*, Cambridge: Polity Press.

Hayward, Tim (1998) *Political Theory and Ecological Values*, Cambridge: Polity Press.

Hegel, G. W. F. (1991) *Elements of the Philosophy of Right*, Cambridge: Cambridge University Press.

Held, D. (1996) *Democracy and the Global Order: From the Modern State to Cosmopolitan Governance*, Cambridge: Polity.

Held, David (1999) *Global Transformations: Politics, Economics and Culture*, Oxford: Polity.

Held, David and Anthony McGrew (eds) (2000) *The Global Transformations Reader: An Introduction to the Globalization Debate*, Cambridge: Polity.

Hitchens, P. (1999) *The Abolition of Britain*, London: Quartet.

Holland, Alan (1992) 'Editorial', *Environmental Values*, 1.

hooks, bell (1984) *Feminist Theory: From Margin to Center*, Boston, MA: South End Press.

Hoover, Kenneth and Raymond Plant (1989) *Conservative Capitalism in Britain and the United States: A Critical Appraisal*, London: Routledge.

Horkheimer, Max and Theodor Adorno (1973 [1947]) *Dialectic of Enlightenment*, London: Allen Lane.

Huntington, Samuel (1996) *The Clash of Civilizations and the Remaking of World Order*, New York: Simon and Schuster.

Irigaray, Luce (1985a [1974]) *Speculum of the Other Woman*, trans. G. Gill, New York: Cornell University Press.

Irigaray, Luce (1985b [1977]) *This Sex Which Is Not One*, trans. C. Porter and C. Burke, New York: Cornell University Press.

Kant, Immanuel (1996a) [essays 1783–98]) *Practical Philosophy*, trans. M. J. Gregor, Cambridge: Cambridge University Press.

Kant, Immanuel (1996b) *Political Writings*, ed. Hans Reiss, Cambridge: Cambridge University Press.

Kastoryano, R. (ed.) (1998) *Quelle identité pour l'Europe? Le multicultur-alisme à l'épreuve*, Paris: Presses de Science Po.

Kenny, M. (1991) 'Community in the Work of Raymond Williams in the Fifties and Sixties', *Politics*, 11 (2): 14–19.

Koopmans, R. and P. Statham (eds) (2000) *Challenging Immigration and Ethnic Relations Politics*, Oxford: Oxford University Press.

Kristeva, Julia (1984 [1974]), *Revolution in Poetic Language*, trans. M. Waller, New York: Columbia University Press.

Kristeva, Julia (1986) *The Kristeva Reader*, ed. Toril Moi, Oxford: Basil Blackwell (repr. 1996).

Kristol, I. (1996) 'Pornography, Obscenity, and the Case for Censorship', in M. Gerson and J. Q. Wilson (eds), *The Essential Neo-Conservative Reader*, Reading, MA: Addison-Wesley (first published in *The New York Times Magazine*, 1971).

Kukathas, C. (1996) 'Liberalism, Communitarianism, and Political Community', in E. F. Paul, F. D. Miller Jr and J. Paul (eds), *The Communitarian Challenge to Liberalism*, Cambridge: Cambridge University Press.

Kymlicka, W. (1989) *Liberalism, Community and Culture*, Oxford: Clarendon.

Kymlicka, W. (1995) *Multicultural Citizenship: A Liberal Theory of Minority Rights*, Oxford: Oxford University Press.

Kymlicka, W. (1998) 'Introduction: An Emerging Consensus?', *Ethical Theory and Moral Practice*, special edition on 'Nationalism, multiculturalism and liberal democracy', 1(2): 143–57.

Kymlicka, W. (2000) 'Nation-building and minority rights: comparing West and East', *Journal of Ethnic and Migration Studies*, 26(2): 183–212.

Laclau, Ernesto (1996) *Emancipations*, London: Verso.

Laclau, Ernesto and Chantal Mouffe (1985) *Hegemony and Socialist Strategy: Towards a Radical Democratic Politics*, London: Verso.

Landes, J. B. (ed.) (1998) *Feminism, the Public and the Private*, Oxford: Oxford University Press.

Larmore, C. (1987) *Patterns of Moral Complexity*, Cambridge: Cambridge University Press.

Latour, Bruno (1999) 'Ein Ding ist Ein Thing: A (Philosophical) Platform for a Left (European) Party, *Soundings*, 12: 12–25.

Levin, Michael (1989) *Marx, Engels and Liberal Democracy*, Basingstoke: Macmillan.

Lévi-Strauss, Claude (1981 [1971]) *The Naked Man: Introduction to a Science of Mythology*, trans. John and Doreen Weightman, London: Jonathan Cape.

Light, Andrew and Eric Katz (eds) (1996) *Environmental Pragmatism*, London: Routledge.

Lopes, Anne and Gary Roth (2000) *Men's Feminism: August Bebel and the German Socialist Movement*, Amherst, NY: Humanity Books.

Lovenduski, J. and V. Randall (1993) *Contemporary Feminist Politics*, Oxford: Oxford University Press.

Lukes, Steven (1974) *Power: A Radical View*, London: Macmillan.

Lyotard, Jean-François (1984 [1979]) *The Postmodern Condition: A Report on Knowledge*, trans. B. Massumi and G. Bennington, Manchester: Manchester University Press; Minneapolis, MN: University of Minnesota Press.

Lyotard, Jean-François (1993 [1974]), *Libidinal Economy*, trans. I. H. Grant, London: Athlone.

MacIntyre, Alasdair (1985) *After Virtue: A Study in Moral Theory*, London: Duckworth.

MacIntyre, A. (1988) *Whose Justice? Which Rationality?*, London: Duckworth.

Mannheim, Karl (1976 [1936]) *Ideology and Utopia: An Introduction to the Sociology of Knowledge*, London: Routledge.

Marsh, David and Martin J. Smith (2001) 'There is More than One Way to Do Political Science: On Different Ways to Study Policy Networks', *Political Studies*, 49(3): 528–41.

Martin, James (1998) *Gramsci's Political Analysis: A Critical Introduction*, Basingstoke: Macmillan.

Marx, Karl (1977) *Selected Writings*, ed. David McLellan, Oxford: Oxford University Press.

Mason, A. (2000) 'Communitarianism and its Legacy', in Noel O'Sullivan (ed.), *Political Theory in Transition*, London: Routledge.

Mill, J. S. (1989 [1869]) *On Liberty, with The Subjection of Women and Chapters on Socialism*, ed. S. Collini, Cambridge: Cambridge University Press.

Modood, T. (1998) 'Anti-essentialism, Multiculturalism and the "Recognition" of Religious Minorities', *Journal of Political Philosophy*, 6 (4); repr. in W. Kymlicka and W. Norman (eds), *Citizenship in Diverse Societies*, Oxford: Oxford University Press.

Modood, T. (2001) 'The Place of Muslims in British Secular Multiculturalism', in N. AlSayyad and M. Castells (eds), *Muslim Europe*, New York: Lexington Books.

Mouffe, Chantal (1993) *The Return of the Political*, London: Verso.

Mulhall, S. and A. Swift (1992) *Liberals and Communitarians*, Oxford: Blackwell.

Naess, Arne (1989) *Ecology, Community and Lifestyle*, Cambridge: Cambridge University Press.

Nash, K. (1998) 'Beyond Liberalism? Feminist Theories of Democracy', in V. Randall and G. Waylen (eds), *Gender, Politics and the State*, London: Routledge.

Nietzsche, Friedrich (1969) *On the Genealogy of Morals*, New York: Vintage Books.

Noddings, N. (1984) *Caring: A Feminine Approach to Ethics and Moral Education*, Berkeley, CA: University of California Press.

Oakeshott, Michael (1981) *Rationalism in Politics and Other Essays*, London: Methuen.

Oakeshott, Michael (1983) *On History and Other Essays*, Oxford: Blackwell.

Okin, S. (1991) 'Gender, the Public and the Private', in D. Held (ed.), *Political Theory Today*, Cambridge: Polity.

O'Sullivan, Noel (1976) *Conservatism*, London: J. M. Dent.

Parekh, B. (2000) *Rethinking Multiculturalism: Cultural Diversity and Political Theory*, London: Macmillan.

Pateman, C. (1989) *The Disorder of Women*, Cambridge: Polity.

Phillips, A. (1991) *Engendering Democracy*, Cambridge: Polity.

Phillips, A. (1992) 'Universal Pretensions in Political Thought' in M. Barrett and A. Phillips (eds), *Destabilizing Theory: Contemporary Feminist Debates*, Cambridge: Polity.

Phillips, A. (1995) *The Politics of Presence*, Oxford: Clarendon Press.

Phillips, A. (1999) *Which Equalities Matter?*, Cambridge: Polity.

Plant, R. (1991) 'Community', in D. Miller (ed.), *The Blackwell Encyclopaedia of Political Thought*, Cambridge, MA and Oxford: Blackwell.

Pocock, J. G. A. (1989) *Politics, Language and Time*, 2nd edn, Chicago, IL: University of Chicago Press.

Rabinow, Paul (1984) 'Introduction', in Paul Rabinow (ed.), *The Foucault Reader*, New York: Pantheon Books.

Rajchman, John (ed.) (1995) *The Identity in Question*, London: Routledge.

Rawls, John (1971) *A Theory of Justice*, Cambridge, MA: Harvard University Press.

Rawls, John (1996) *Political Liberalism*, New York: Columbia University Press.

Rawls, John (1999) *The Law of Peoples*, Cambridge, MA: Harvard University Press.

Raz, J. (1986) *The Morality of Freedom*, Oxford: Clarendon.

Rodgers, D. T. (1996) 'Republicanism: The Career of a Concept', *Journal of American History*, 79 (1): 11–38.

Rossiter, Clinton (1962) *Conservatism in America: The Thankless Persuasion*, New York: Random House.

Rousseau, J.-J. (1974 [1762]) *Émile*, New York: Everyman.

Rowbotham, Sheila, Lynne Segal and Hilary Wainwright (1981) *Beyond the Fragments: Feminism and the Making of Socialism*, Boston, MA: Alyson.

Said, Edward W. (1978) *Orientalism*, London: Penguin.

Said, Edward W. (1994) *Culture and Imperialism*, London: Vintage.

Sandel, M. (1982) *Liberalism and the Limits of Justice*, Cambridge: Cambridge University Press.

Sandel, M. (1984) 'The Procedural Republic and the Unencumbered Self', *Political Theory*, 12 (1): 81–96.

Sandel, M. (1996) *Democracy's Discontent: America in Search of a Public Philosophy*, Cambridge, MA and London: Belknap Press of Harvard University Press.

Sandoval, Chela (1990) 'Feminism and Racism: A Report on the 1981 National Women's Studies Association Conference', in G. Anzaldúa (ed.), *Making Face, Making Soul = Haciendo Caras: Creative and Critical Perspectives By Women of Color*, San Francisco, CA: Aunt Lute Foundation Books.

Sargent, Lydia (ed.) (1986) *The Unhappy Marriage of Marxism and Feminism: A Debate of Class and Patriarchy*, Boston, MA: South End Press.

Saussure, Ferdinand de (1960 [1916]) *Course in General Linguistics*, trans. W. Baskin, London: Peter Owen.

Schrift, Alan (1995) *Nietzsche's French Legacy: A Genealogy of Post-structuralism*, London: Routledge.

Scott, Joan W. (1990) 'Deconstructing Equality-Versus-Difference: Or, the Uses of Poststructuralist Theory for Feminism' in M. Hirsch and E. Fox Keller (eds), *Conflicts in Feminism*, London: Routledge.

Scruton, Roger (1984) *The Meaning of Conservatism*, Basingstoke: Macmillan.

Scruton, Roger (ed.) (1991) *Conservative Texts: An Anthology*, Basingstoke: Macmillan.

Selznick, P. (1994) *The Moral Commonwealth: Social Theory and the Promise of Community*, Berkeley, CA and Oxford: University of California Press.

Shanley, M. (1989) *Feminism, Marriage and the Law in Victorian Britain 1850–95*, London: I. B. Taurus.

Shiva, Vandana (1989) *Staying Alive: Women, Ecology and Development*, London: Zed Books.

Shklar, Judith (1957) *After Utopia: The Decline of Political Faith*, Princeton, NJ: Princeton University Press.

Skinner, Quentin (1988a [1969]), 'Meaning and Understanding in the History of Ideas', *History and Theory*, 8: 3–53, repr. in James Tully (ed.), *Meaning and Context: Quentin Skinner and His Critics*, Princeton, NJ: Princeton University Press, pp. 29–67.

Skinner, Quentin (1988b), 'A Reply to my Critics', in James Tully (ed.), *Meaning and Context: Quentin Skinner and His Critics*, Princeton, NJ: Princeton University Press, pp. 231–88.

Skinner, Q. (1998) *Liberty Before Liberalism*, Cambridge: Cambridge University Press.

Smith, Anna Marie (1998) *Laclau and Mouffe: The Radical Democratic Imaginary*, London: Routledge.

Steger, Manfred (1997) *The Quest for Evolutionary Socialism: Edward Bernstein and Social Democracy*, Cambridge: Cambridge University Press.

Strauss, Leo (1957) 'What Is Political Philosophy?', *Journal of Politics*, 19 (August): 343–68.

Strauss, Leo (1970) 'The New Political Science', in William F. Buckley Jr (ed.), *American Conservative Thought in the Twentieth Century*, Indianapolis, IN: Bobbs-Merrill Education Publishing.

Strong, Tracy B. (1983) 'Nihilism and Political Theory', in John S. Nelson (ed.), *What Should Political Theory Be Now?*, Albany, New York: State University of New York Press, pp. 243–63.

Tam, H. (1998) *Communitarianism: A New Agenda for Politics and Citizenship*, Basingstoke: Macmillan.

Taylor, C. (1985) 'What is Human Agency?', in *Human Agency and Language: Philosophical Papers Vol. 1*, Cambridge: Cambridge University Press.

Taylor, C. (1992) *Sources of the Self*, Cambridge, MA: Harvard University Press.

Taylor, C. (1994) 'The Politics of Recognition', in A. Gutmann (ed.) *Multiculturalism and the Politics of Recognition*, pp. 25–74.

Tuck, Richard (1991) 'History of Political Thought', in Peter Burke (ed.), *New Perspectives on Historical Writing*, Cambridge: Polity.

Tully, James (ed.) (1988) *Meaning and Context: Quentin Skinner and His Critics*, Princeton, NJ: Princeton University Press.

United States Department of Labor Office of Policy Planning and Research

(1965) *The Negro Family: The Case for National Action*, Washington, DC: Government Printing Office.

Wall, Derek (1990) *Getting There: Steps to a Green Society*, London: Green Print.

Walzer, M. (1983) *Spheres of Justice: A Defence of Pluralism and Equality*, Oxford: Robertson.

Walzer, Michael (ed.) (1995) *Toward a Global Civil Society*, Oxford: Berghahn Books.

Weber, Max (1946a) 'Politics as a Vocation', in H. H. Gerth and C. Wright Mills (eds), *From Max Weber: Essays in Sociology*, New York: Oxford University Press, pp. 77–128.

Weber, Max (1946b) 'Science as a Vocation', in H. H. Gerth and C. Wright Mills (eds), *From Max Weber: Essays in Sociology*, New York: Oxford University Press, pp. 129–54.

Weber, Max (1958) *The Protestant Ethic and the Spirit of Capitalism*, trans. Talcott Parsons, New York: Charles Scribner's Sons.

Weldon, T. D. (1956) 'Political Principles', in Peter Laslett (ed.), *Philosophy, Politics and Society, 1st series*, Oxford: Basil Blackwell, pp. 22–34.

Wilson, J. Q. (1993) *The Moral Sense*, New York: The Free Press.

Wilson, J. Q. and G. L. Kelling (1996), 'Broken Windows: The Police and Neighborhood Safety', in M. Gerson and J. Q. Wilson (eds), *The Essential Neo-Conservative Reader*, Reading, MA: Addison-Wesley (first published in *The Atlantic Monthly*, 1982).

Wittgenstein, Ludwig (1988 [1953]), *Philosophical Investigations*, trans. G. E. M. Anscombe, 3rd edn, Oxford: Blackwell.

Wolin, Sheldon S. (1969) 'Political Theory as a Vocation', *American Political Science Review*, 63 (4).

Wootton, David (1984) 'Preface', in David Wootton (ed.), *Divine Right and Democracy*, London: Penguin, pp. 9–19.

World Commission on Environment and Development (1987) *Our Common Future*, Oxford: Oxford University Press.

Young, I. M. (1990) *Justice and the Politics of Difference*, Princeton, NJ: Princeton University Press.

Žižek, Slavoj (1997) 'Multiculturalism, Or, the Cultural Logic of Multinational Capitalism', *New Left Review*, 225 (September–October): 28–51.

GLOSSARY

Abiotic. Literally 'not living'. When used of aspects of the environment, it refers to those that are non-living such as light, temperature, gases and so forth.

Adorno, Theodor. German (neo)-Marxist philosopher (1903–69). Adorno was a member of the Frankfurt Institute for Social Research, known as the Frankfurt School, which developed a blend of philosophical Marxism, Freudian psycho-analytic theory and sociological criticism. The Institute relocated from Nazi Germany to Zurich in 1934, and to the USA in 1938. *Dialectic of Enlighten-ment*, co-written with Max Horkheimer in 1947, argued that Enlightenment reason, rather than emancipating humanity, had extended domination because it promoted 'instrumental rationality', reason orientated towards the attain-ment of ends and which facilitated control of nature and of human beings. It also developed a critique of the 'culture industry' (modern forms of entertain-ment including popular song, cinema and, later, television) which Adorno saw as pacifying, wedding individuals to a social system that repressed individual-ity. Later, Adorno advanced a critique of 'identity thinking' by which he meant that way of explaining (and experiencing) the world in terms of identities between things (i.e. that one thing is like another at some level), erasing partic-ularity in the name of that which is universal. Such identity thinking can be related to the world of commodity capitalism which presupposes that there is a category of value underlying all things and constituting a level of equivalence between them. His influence (acknowledged or not) is wide and deep, and he was a rare, philosophical, poetic and political personality. See also **Critical Theory, Horkheimer, Habermas, Frankfurt School** and the introductory book

---

by Martin Jay, *Adorno* (Fontana, 1984). Hauke Brunkhorst, *Adorno and Critical Theory* (University of Wales Press, 1999), provides a short, interesting recent interpretation. See also *Adorno: A Critical Reader*, edited by Nigel C. Gibson and Andrew Rubin (Blackwell, 2001).

Alterity. This term means 'otherness' but implies a sense of 'alternative'. The alterity of another is not simply an otherness separated from me by an unbridgeable gulf but an alternative to my identity. In this sense, it is possible for me to experience my own alterity (something for which many people will pay good money).

Althusser, Louis. French philosopher of Marxism (1918–90). Althusser has been, indirectly, one of the most influential political thinkers of the twentieth century. He attempted to develop a rigorous philosophical Marxism, establishing the concepts and methods that made it a unique and superior science. In the form of structuralist Marxism, this was seen by supporters as providing a sure foundation for Marxism but by detractors, such as **E. P. Thompson**, as overly elaborate, theoretically obscure and itself a repressive system of thinking. In *Reading Capital* (New Left Books, 1968), Althusser and colleagues developed a strategy of reading philosophical works by establishing the underlying conceptual structures that animate them. In an important late essay, 'Ideology and Ideological State Apparatuses', Althusser argued that ideology does not simply mask reality from us but constitutes it in a particular way, a theory that has been very important for numerous critical analysts (see also Chapter 12). Though his structuralism was supplanted by poststructuralism, the latter was a movement to which Althusser gave much inspiration. He has currently been moderately revived in some circles of North American literary theory and also by the leading contemporary philosopher Slavoj Žižek. For more, see the critical *Althusser's Marxism* by Alex Callinicos (Pluto Press, 1976), the thoughtful and careful *Althusser: The Detour of Theory* by Gregory Elliott (Verso, 1987) and the helpful *Althusser: A Critical Reader* edited by Gregory Elliott (Blackwell, 1994). The famous essay on ideology can be found in Louis Althusser, *Lenin and Philosophy and Other Essays* (New Left Books, 1971).

Amish. Religious sect, largely based in North America. 'Sooner or later', writes Brian Barry, 'all political theorists who address the rights of illiberal communities to run their own affairs without interference feel called upon to say something about the Old Order Amish in North America' (Barry, 2001: 176). The Amish are part of the Anabaptist sect of Protestantism and hold to a very traditional, conservative and fundamentalist theology. They live simple lives rejecting the inventions of the contemporary world, preferring a puritan, agricultural life to the hedonistic, industrial one the rest of us enjoy so much. The Amish are of interest to North American political thought because they have successfully won exemptions from otherwise universal statutes such as those requiring permissions for land use, the wearing of hard hats on construction sites, registration of midwives and so forth and, most significantly, a 1972 Supreme Court judgement (*Wisconsin vs Yoder*) exempting them from the requirement that children be sent to high school up to graduation. The Amish became extremely well known after their representation in Peter Weir's 1985 film *Witness* starring Harrison Ford. The area of Pennsylvania in which the film was set is now a successful tourist attraction, and many Amish souvenirs can be purchased there.

Analytical philosophy. A philosophical style (particularly associated with the work of Bertrand Russell, G. E. Moore and Gottlieb Frege) essentially concerned with logic and the possibility of making legitimate, clear and verifiable propositions about the world. For analytical philosophy, religious, aesthetic and ethical statements are meaningless metaphysics, and the task of philosophy is to ensure we do not stray from the path of logical righteousness.

Anti-essentialism. A way of thinking or analysing that does not presume things can be understood through their reduction to a fixed, universal or trans-historical element or essence that makes up their core. For anti-essentialists, essentialism suppresses the appreciation of variation.

Anti-foundationalism. Philosophical attitude. Anti-foundationalists argue that it is not necessary (and in fact may be a trap) for theory to seek some point of origin or baseline from which it can proceed. Critics of this position argue that without a foundation there can be no secure truth-claims and that anti-foundationalism is thus equivalent to relativism. An example of an anti-foundationalist thinker is the North American philosopher Richard Rorty (see Chapter 4), who urges us to break with the notion that philosophy is concerned with developing a form of knowledge that exactly mirrors the world of nature, and sees philosophy as a pragmatic activity in which concepts should be judged not by how true they are but by how much use they are in helping us do whatever it was we wanted to do when we started thinking.

Aristotle. Classical Greek philosopher (384–322 BC). Alongside his teacher Plato, Aristotle is one of the founders of the Western philosophical tradition. Where Plato is associated with metaphysical speculation, Aristotle is often regarded as the developer of an early sort of science in that he sought systematically to investigate many aspects of the natural world. He wrote works on logic and analytics, on physics and on phenomena such as weather and comets. In politics, his most important work is *The Politics*, which attempts to be a systematic investigation into the nature of political association, and his *Nicomachean Ethics*, which examines, among other topics, the question of virtue (subsequently influential on the medieval theologian Thomas Aquinas and the contemporary philosopher **MacIntyre**).

Austin, J. L. British philosopher specialising in the study of ordinary language (1911–60). Emerging from the currents of English thought associated with the analytical tradition, and later logical positivism, a group of Oxford philosophers in the 1950s turned their attention to the ordinary usage of language on the grounds that a close study of it could reveal much about the nature of experience. Austin was an exemplar of this school. His idea of linguistic performatives – actions where saying you are doing a thing is the same as doing it (such as saying 'I promise') – has influenced some recent poststructuralists (of whom Austin would surely have disapproved). His work is beguilingly simple and often quite funny. See *How to Do Things with Words* (Oxford University Press, 1975) and *Philosophical Papers* (Oxford University Press, 1979), in which the essays on pretending and on excuses are particular fun.

Autonomia. Italian radical movement of the 1970s. Born of the widespread political unrest of 1968, the Autonomia movement was committed to autonomous struggle independent of organised Marxist, communist and trade-union movements. Philosophically, the Autonomists reversed the general way in which the left has conceived of the relation of the working class to capitalism, arguing that it is capital which mutates in order to struggle against the workers, who must continually be co-opted. The best-known autonomist theorist is Antonio Negri, who in 1979 was arrested by the Italian police and charged with the notorious murder (allegedly by the Red Brigades) of Aldo Moro, leader of the Christian Democrat Party. Negri was acquitted but still imprisoned on charges of involvement in terror. He has always maintained his innocence, and at the time of writing he is in prison in Italy, having returned from exile in France in 1997. He is now rather famous, having written, with Michael Hardt, a big book called *Empire* (Harvard University Press, 2000).

Autonomy. From the Ancient Greek, meaning 'the law of one's self'. This concept is absolutely central to modern liberalism. For Kant, to take an example, if the individual is to be a moral agent he must also be autonomous, otherwise he would not be able to follow the moral law out of choice but under duress (in which case it wouldn't be a moral act). This usage in relation to individual autonomy is to be distinguished from a more general usage when referring to institutions or levels of government. In the specific sense given to it by Kant, we should understand that autonomy was a creation of modernity and enlightenment (and perhaps also of Kant).

Barry, Brian. British political philosopher. At the time of writing, Barry is Professor of Political Science at Columbia University in New York. He is a political philosopher in the (broadly defined) Anglo-American liberal normative tradition, particularly notable for a style that can most judiciously be described as pugnacious. Recently he has attacked liberal philosophers of multiculturalism for what he regards as confused thinking and for attaching too much importance to matters of 'culture' and not enough to problems of equality. In his view, multiculturalism militates against a solidaristic conception of political life and so undermines liberal egalitarianism which, if properly understood and acted upon, would resolve the sorts of problems multiculturalists think they are dealing with (see his book *Culture and Equality*, Harvard University Press, 2001).

Beauvoir, Simone de. French philosopher, feminist and novelist (1908–86). Strongly associated with the existentialist movement in post-war France (and partner to Jean-Paul Sartre, its leading guru), de Beauvoir explored the nature of meaning and existence in her philosophical writing and in her novels (such as *The Mandarins*, 1954). Her most famous work of politically orientated thinking is *The Second Sex* (1949), which explored the position of women in subordination to men and in search of meaning in a world defined against them.

Behaviourism. As a method in philosophy, social science and especially psychology, behaviourism argues that all that should be studied is behaviour itself and not anything that we might infer as lying behind that behaviour. B. F. Skinner extended this to the argument that behaviour is to be explained by reference to various kinds of external stimuli and not by appeal to the inward consciousness of the actors. We should look at how behaviour is learned in our environment and conditioned by rewards and punishments. Extended to politics, this means that policy should be geared towards creating the conditions that will produce the desired outcome (though where that comes from is another matter).

Bernstein, Eduard. German social democrat and political leader (1850–1932). Associated with 'revisionist' Marxism, Bernstein argued that class conflict was not always inevitable and that capitalism would not collapse, and consequently advocated a 'parliamentary' road to socialism. Influenced by neo-Kantian forms of thought, he became what we might call an 'ethical socialist' (similar to Fabianism in Britain). He was a member of the Reichstag (the German legislature) and served in government with the SPD in 1919, continuing his 'parliamentary' career as a strident opponent of Nazism. A key work is *Evolutionary Socialism: A Criticism and Affirmation* (1899).

Biotic. Living. When used of the environment, it refers to those parts of it that are living, or have to do with living organisms. See **abiotic**.

Bodhisattva. A kind of Buddhist saint. A bodhisattva is a Buddhist who has attained enlightenment and may reach Nirvana (heaven) but chooses not to in order to help others.

Bradley, Francis Herbert. British philosopher (1846–1924). Bradley was a central member of the philosophical school known as British Idealism which was very influential in the UK at the end of the nineteenth century (before it was overtaken by analytical philosophy and logical positivism). Bradley was an important influence on the poet T. S. Eliot and on philosophers of history such R. G. Collingwood, bringing into the English way of thinking the approach of German hermeneutics, a sceptical attitude to the records of the past and a sense of the need to get into the frame of thinking of those who wrote them. Those interested in finding out more about British Idealism are directed to David Boucher (ed.), *The British Idealists* (Cambridge University Press, 1997), which contains a good introduction and a range of writings from many of the leading figures including Bradley.

British Sex Discrimination Act. Passed into law in 1976, this landmark act outlawed employment discrimination on the grounds of gender. It meant that if a person feels they were not able to obtain a particular job because of prejudice against them on the grounds of their being male or female, they can take a case to an industrial tribunal and, if the case is upheld, be awarded damages.

Buddhism. Indian religious system founded in the fifth century BC by Siddharta Gautama – Buddha, or 'the enlightened one'. The Buddhist sees him- or herself as linked with the lives of all other creatures and to future and past incarnations. This holism and interconnectedness mean that Buddhist philosophies often preach a strong sense of social solidarity and moral obligation to others: all things are equal, and life is sacred.

Burke, Edmund. Irish-British conservative political theorist (1729–97). Burke was the 'founder' of modern conservative thought. His most famous work, *Reflections on the Revolution in France*, was written in 1790 in the form of a response to those people in England sympathetic to the French Revolution and considering its emulation. Burke challenged the revolution on the grounds that the attempt to apply rational principles to society could only ever end in failure because society is not itself a rational order and no individual could ever come up with a complete system for its organisation. Burke described society as a slowly evolving organic community (famously declaring society 'a contract . . . between . . . those who are living, those who are dead and those who are yet to be born') and stressed the importance of natural 'prejudice', those customs, habits and assumptions that a people share and which thus enable society to function. This book is the best starting point for those new to Burke. There are a number of editions, but the one published in 1987 by Cambridge University Press with an introduction by J. G. A. Pocock is probably the best. You can also consult Ian Harris (ed.), *Burke: Pre-Revolutionary Writings* (Cambridge University Press, 1993).

Butterfield, Sir Herbert. British historian (1900–79). A leading historian (of Christianity and science among other topics) and also a writer on historiography (ideas about how history should be studied and understood), Butterfield is now well remembered for his book *The Whig Interpretation of History* (W. W. Norton, 1965 [1931]). He argued that many scholars of English history had a tendency 'to write on the side of Protestants and Whigs, to praise revolutions provided they have been successful, to emphasize certain principles of progress in the past and to produce a story which is the ratification if not the glorification of the present'. This was to make unjustifiable inferences from the study of history, to organise it in terms of a story of progress that was not warranted, using it to justify the present (in that history was shown to have led necessarily to English parliamentary democracy), and to make moral judgements on the characters of the past in as much as they were on the winning, good side or losing, bad side.

Carter, Jimmy. 39th President of the USA (b. 1924). Carter, Governor of Georgia in 1970, was elected President in 1976, serving for one term. His tenure was notable for foreign-policy successes such as the signing of peace accords between Israel and Egypt in 1979, arms-limitation treaties with the Soviet Union and the establishment of full diplomatic relations with China. Less successful domestically, he failed to reform welfare or health insurance, and an innovative energy policy (designed to limit dependence on fossil fuels) was also defeated. In 1979, hostages were taken at the US Embassy in Iran (see **Iranian Revolution**), and a rescue attempt ended in disaster, adding to the image of a weak President. In 1980, he lost the election to Ronald **Reagan**.

Chodorow, Nancy. North American psychoanalytic feminist. At the time of writing, she is Professor of Sociology at Berkeley, University of California. Chodorow's primary influence stems from her book *The Reproduction of Mothering* (University of California Press, 1978), which argued that gender identity is formed within family relationships: girls identify themselves in terms of their relationship with their mother, while boys define themselves against her, and so gender roles are reproduced.

Cicero, Marcus Tullus. Roman orator, consul and political writer (106–43 BC). In addition to texts on oratory, Cicero is notable for writing *De Re Publica* (The Republic) and *De Legibus* (The Laws). The former considers the way in which the Roman republic should be run, touching on the nature of justice and the ideal statesman, and advocating a form of open kingship as the best form of rule. The latter offers the laws of that republic.

Civil-rights movement. The broad movement campaigning for the full recognition of the rights of African Americans from the 1950s through to the 1970s, led by figures such as Rev. Dr Martin Luther King. Key moments include the

Supreme Court ruling in *Brown vs Board of Education of Topeka Kansas*, that ruled the segregation of education into white and black unconstitutional; the bus boycott organised in Montgomery, Alabama, in 1955 as a result of the famous refusal of Rosa Parkes (a middle-aged black woman) to give up her seat on a bus to a white man; sit-ins at diners where black customers were refused entry; riots by whites in reaction to the integration of schools; and the passing of the Voting Rights Act in 1965 to ensure that states did not hinder the right of African Americans to register and then vote. The whole civil-rights period was one of great convulsion for the USA, especially in the Southern states, and a good case can be made that it still casts a shadow of ideological and cultural division across present-day America.

Cixous, Hélène. French feminist, literary theorist and novelist. At the time of writing, she is based at the University of Paris VIII. Cixous has been particularly interested in theorising writing and in the possibilities of what she terms an *écriture féminine*: a form of writing that breaks with the masculine-centred domination of language and which explores the experience of multiplicity which she also finds to be part of the experience of being a woman. She describes it as that which will 'always surpass the discourse that regulates the phallocentric system: it does and will take place in areas other than those subordinated to philosophical-theoretical domination. It will be conceived of only by subjects who are breakers of automatisms, by peripheral figures that no authority can ever subjugate' (see 'The Laugh of the Medusa', in *Signs*, 1976).

Confucius. Chinese philosopher (551–479 BC). The most significant of all figures in Chinese philosophy, perhaps in Chinese history. His sayings and some dialogues, collected in the Analects, provide a moral and political system of great scope. In the second century AD, during the Han dynasty, Confucianism became something like a national ideology of China, and spread throughout Asia. The Analects are aphoristic in nature, but their central claim can perhaps be (rather crudely) summarised as that one should cultivate a feeling of love (which means something like concern and respect, or ethical depth) that is appropriate for others around us. Love, then, is also a kind of discipline (in both senses of that term). According to Confucius, one cultivates this through adherence to societal codes of behaviour. For Westerners, this might suggest that Confucianism advocates social conformity (but it may just mean a recognition of the fact that spiritual growth depends on proper relations with others and cannot be attained independent of them). When it comes to politics, Confucius advocated a ruler who 'governs with morality, as if he were the Northern Star, staying in his position, surrounded by all other planets'. The ruler has to be exemplary, and his people should follow him. Social order rests on each performing the role that is theirs and not another. Confucius is being revived in contemporary China.

Critical Theory. Form of Marxist theorising associated with the Frankfurt School. Sometimes, literary critics refer to any analysis of literature that is not confined to the practical analysis of the qualities of a text as critical theory. In social and political thought, Critical Theory was the conscious construction of thinkers associated with the Frankfurt School of Social Research such as **Adorno, Horkheimer,** Marcuse and, in the subsequent generation, **Jürgen Habermas.** In general, the aim of Critical Theory is the construction of a theory of the totality (one that relates the parts of society to each other rather than treating them as isolated elements) – and that is critical because it explicitly takes the view that the point of understanding the world is so as to be able to change it. As such, theory has to be dynamic, reflecting upon its own concepts and categories and aware of its own location in history and in a particular social formation. The early Critical Theorists analysed systems of domination or control in modern society and were heavily critical of 'instrumental rationality', the restriction of reason to that which enables the control of the world (including other people), and which they associated with capitalism. They were thus very critical of positivist and empiricist methods of social science. Subsequently, **Jürgen Habermas** inherited the mantle of critical theory. His work has been devoted to a reconstruction of the capacity of reason to help order human affairs. He argues that instrumental rationality is one form of reason that has been allowed to dominate over communicative reason (which is orientated towards understanding) and critical reason (which works for emancipation). On this basis, Habermas has developed an influential theory of deliberative democracy. See also David Held: *An Introduction to Critical Theory: Horkheimer to Habermas* (Hutchinson, 1980); Martin Jay, *The Dialectical Imagination: A History of the Frankfurt School and the Institute of Social Research, 1923–1950* (University of California Press, 1973); Frankfurt Institute for Social Research, *Aspects of Sociology* (Heinemann Educational, 1973).

Cultural Revolution. Movement initiated in China by Mao Tze Tung in 1966. Mao became leader of the People's Republic of China on its creation (after civil war) on 1 October 1949. The attempt at rapid modernisation of the country led to economic crises and much starvation, weakening Mao's power. The Cultural Revolution was an ideological fightback entailing the mass mobilisation of young people against their leaders in the state bureaucracy on the grounds that the latter were becoming an entrenched hierarchy akin to that found in the Soviet Union. There was also an attack on party functionaries, intellectuals and even schoolteachers, many of whom were forced to work as peasants while arts and culture were circumscribed, schools closed and students urged to join the Red Army. The Cultural Revolution lasted until Mao's death in 1976, an event which precipitated the arrest of China's then leaders.

Darwin, Charles. British naturalist (1809–82). Darwin developed the theory of evolution, but perhaps he should more accurately be called the theorist of natural selection. The core of Darwin's argument was that species flourish through their possession of characteristics that suit them to the environment in which they find themselves. Thus, nature will 'select' for survival those best suited to the natural world around them. The cultural, social, philosophical, psychological and political ramifications of Darwinism have been, and are, immense. It challenged the idea that mankind's development is solely a result of God's endeavour and put humans back into the environment from which the churches had, presumptuously, removed them. The mutation Social Darwinism held that societal evolution followed the same principles as the natural kind, a view manifested in a number of different political forms including racist and elitist theories prepared to see the 'weaker' of the human species replaced by the 'superior' (most obviously manifested in eugenics, the attempt to engineer the breeding of the population which was considered by early twentieth-century thinkers of all persuasions but discredited after the horror of Nazism). Biological thinking still influences political theory, most recently through a more sophisticated 'sociobiology' and evolutionary psychology (attempting to explain human behaviours by reference to the longer-term evolutionary needs of the species). In the USA, the teaching of Darwinism in schools has been a politically significant issue. Christian fundamentalists reject it as ungodly and insist on teaching creation theory (the idea that God created everything in six days) in science class or on the prevention of the teaching of evolutionary theory in schools. In 1999, the Board of Education in Kansas decided to remove evolution from its list of necessary subjects. The issue thus touches on constitutional concerns about the relation of church and state, and it has also forced the state to make an adjudication (which it does not want to) as to the epistemological status of Darwinism.

Deconstruction. Form of thought or analysis associated with the philosopher **Jacques Derrida**. It is a method of reading philosophical (or other) texts that shows how they achieve coherence only at the expense of dependence on that which they disavow. For example, if I write a survey of contemporary political thought and declare at the start that I will not look at any Marxism, there is a sense in which my text will be founded precisely on this exclusion, making Marxism essential to the structuring of my text despite my never considering it. Deconstruction is used as a critique of key philosophical concepts (but also political and everyday ones), showing how they are sustained by excluding something which is subsequently denigrated (see also *Différance*).

Deep ecologism. A term developed to distinguish between positions within the broader green movement. As Tim Hayward shows in Chapter 8 of this book, some writers advocate a distinction between environmentalism and more radical ecologism. The distinction has also been made in terms of light and dark (or deep) greens, and thus deep ecologism refers to the radical or fundamental strands within ecological thinking. Deep ecologists put general ecological concerns above the specific concerns of humanity.

Deleuze, Gilles. French philosopher (1925–95). A key figure in the range of philosophies lumped together under the label 'French poststructuralism'. To sum up the Deleuzian project, we might say that it aims to replace all philosophies predicated on a notion of what 'is' with one based on what 'can be'. Deleuze urged not the construction of theoretical edifices but the establishment of new connections between things and the construction of new ways of being, doing and thinking; a philosophy that starts from the multiple and diferentiated rather than the singular and identical (see also **Guattari** and Chapter 9). There is quite a Deleuze industry at the moment. Since the work can easily appear off-puttingly strange to the uninitiated, a good place to start might be the essay by Paul Patton, 'Deleuze and Guattari's Political Philosophy', in *Political Theory: Tradition and Diversity*, edited by Andrew Vincent (Cambridge University Press, 1997), followed by Philip Goodchild, *Deleuze and Guattari: An Introduction to the Politics of Desire* (Sage, 1996). The bolder can try *Deleuze and the Political* by Paul Patton (Routledge, 2000) or the important Keith Ansell-Pearson, *Germinal Life: The Difference and Repetition of Deleuze* (Routledge, 1999). John Rajchman's *The Deleuze Connections* (MIT, 2000) communicates some of the dynamism and excitement of Deleuze, but ultimately the reader should just plunge in to the original texts.

Deontological. A kind of moral theory that focuses on duty or obligation (such as that of Kant). The word derives from the Greek *deon* meaning necessary or necessity. Put simply, in deontological moral theory, the rightness of an action stems from the extent to which it is done in accordance with the formal rules of conduct and thus out of a sense of duty. This is the opposite of theories that focus on the outcomes of actions (i.e. consequentialist theories such as utilitarianism).

Derrida, Jacques. French Algerian philosopher (b. 1930). One of the most (in)famous philosophers of recent times and a great influence on many, his philosophy is not easy to summarise. Derrida forces us to read philosophical texts very closely, to look at their construction and the way that apparently rationally arranged concepts depend on the exclusion of certain things such that they depend on that which they disavow. Derrida is a creative and poetic philosopher with a strong sense of the tradition of Western metaphysics within which we think. Though a critic of this metaphysics, he knows that we cannot simply walk away from it and that we have a fidelity to the tradition that enables us to speak. But it is our duty to move beyond it and not treat it as frozen and immobile (see also Chapter 9, **Deconstruction**, and *Différance*). A useful introduction (though it has its own view) is Christina Howell's *Derrida: Deconstruction from Phenomenology to Ethics* (Polity, 1999). Simon Critchley's *The Ethics of Deconstruction: Derrida and Levinas* (Edinburgh University Press, 1999) is a sensitive analysis and a work of philosophy in its own right. *Jacques Derrida* by Geoffrey Bennington and Jacques Derrida (University of

Chicago Press, 1993) combines an exegesis of the philosophy (on the top half of the page) with autobiographical writings by Derrida (on the bottom half of the page). A good starting point for Derrida's own writing is the short interviews in *Positions* (University of Chicago Press, 1981).

Descartes, René. European philosopher (1596–1650). Descartes' philosophical work marked a major transformation in Western philosophy – the shift from medieval scholastic philosophy to modern rationalism and the embrace of the new science as a form of knowledge at least on a par with religious knowledge. He is famous for, in his *Meditations* and *Discourse on Method*, developing a new method of ascertaining truth based on internal reflection. Descartes decided to doubt everything, even his own senses. He might perhaps be dreaming, or a demon might be misleading him. He continued this procedure until he had doubted everything and was left only with the fact that something was doing the doubting of its existence. At this point, he hit on the realisation that what must exist was that which was thinking: I think, therefore I am. From there he reconstructed thought, showing how it was possible to have knowledge of the world. Descartes is credited by some with having thus invented the idea of the individual 'subject' understood as an isolated mind, separate from its body, abstracted from nature and from others. However, that is a little too simple, and there is more to Descartes (and to concepts of the subject) than that.

Dewey, John. North American philosopher of pragmatism (1859–1952). Dewey rejected traditional approaches to the theory of knowledge, arguing that, rather than think of truth as that which accurately reflects reality, we should look for propositions that help us live and solve actual problems in the real world of human action. Because he based his work on the claim that evaluation was essentially practical, he was able to reformulate metaphysics in an anti-foundational direction (since, if the criterion is usefulness, you do not need a prior ontological foundation). Interestingly, this led him to an empirical metaphysics in which we understand the way we experience the world in terms of our practical relationship with it. This is different to the general tendency of Western metaphysics to divide the world into (superficial) 'appearance' and (underlying) reality. For Dewey, philosophy has no special relationship to knowledge or truth. It follows that ethics is a practical matter concerned with how to deal with the world, and politically he advocated a conception of democracy in which we are all active inquirers into how to live joyous and creative lives (an activity best undertaken as a common project). In his time, Dewey was a respected public intellectual and a particular influence on theories of education. He is still a very important part of the US canon of thinkers but rather less well known in the UK and continental Europe (see Matthew Festenstein, *Pragmatism and Political Theory: From Dewey to Rorty*, University of Chicago Press, 1997).

Diachronic. The study of things as they change across time. It is usually used of linguistic analysis and contrasted with the **synchronic** study of things.

Dialectical materialism. This term is sometimes used to describe the philosophical method of Marx. Hegel understood history as dialectical. The ideas or philosophy of one period are confronted by their negation, by contradictions, with which they must reconcile. This reconciliation results not in the defeat of one system of ideas by another but in their synthesis into a new one which in turn will have to be, in the same way, dialectically transformed. In Hegel, this is focused on the conceptions of the world which for him have a certain primacy. Marx, in the words of Engels, found Hegel standing on his head and turned him the right way up. That is to say, he employed the dialectical method to understand history, but instead of the movement of ideas he looked at the movement of the material organisation of society (how it produced that which it needed to continue being a society, i.e. food, shelter, wealth and so on). Hence dialectical *materialism* is often (and more happily) referred to as historical materialism.

Différance. Term used by Derrida in his philosophical writings. This word relies on a textual pun in French such that the words meaning 'difference' and 'deferral' become blurred. For Derrida, a linguistic system is based on relations of difference so that the stability of meaning afforded to a term depends on its differentiation from other terms. Meaning does not reside in a term but in the overall system of terms: it is thus always deferred and a final settlement is never reached (see also **Derrida** and **Deconstruction**).

Difference. Philosophy and politics since the 1960s have increasingly emphasised difference over sameness but in a number of ways that ought to be distinguished. On the one hand, it can refer to a general interest in the ways in which people are varied in aims, desires and conceptions of the good. Thus an interest in difference is a response to the increasing pluralism or diversity of our societies but also an attempt to reconstruct thinking. Feminist and anti-racist critiques have shown how political thought makes assumptions about the universality of human beings or human nature that are disguised particularisms and that exclude, for example, women, non-Western peoples and so on. Thinkers of 'difference' attempt to incorporate a recognition of this variety without reducing it to a universalised concept of human nature. On the other hand, the term is used in, broadly speaking, poststructuralist philosophies where it stems from the structuralist interest in the shaping of linguistic and cultural systems through a system of relations based on the difference of terms. The two approaches to difference are related, but their conflation is not, in the end, helpful.

Distributive justice. 'Justice' is one of the most contested words in the whole of Western political philosophy, even though that tradition begins with a consideration of the meaning of justice (see Plato's *Republic*). Increasingly, philosophers recognise that there are different types or aspects of justice, one of which is justice in terms of the distribution of resources or wealth. This can be contrasted with theories of justice centred on rights, individual freedom or, increasingly, on recognition. The point to theories of distributive justice is that they presume that to give to some will necessarily mean to take from others. Hence they concern themselves with what people justly deserve but also with what can justly be taken from them.

Diwali. The Hindu festival of lights. Celebrated in the late autumn, it symbolises the triumph of spiritual righteousness over the darkness. More specifically, it celebrates the return of Lord Rama to his kingdom after a period of exile. Celebrants decorate their houses, give out sweets and light lamps. The Christian equivalent is Candlemas.

Dual systems theory. One of the problems feminist theory has faced is that of relating the oppression of women as women (patriarchy) with other aspects of oppression, especially that which derives from economic or class power. Some argue that patriarchy derives from a more fundamental class oppression while others argue that sexism is primary and makes class-based exploitation possible. Dual systems theory attempts to show that there are distinct systems of exploitation and oppression operating relatively autonomously from each other though sometimes interacting. Although this debate has, to some extent, been relegated to the past, it is still of importance and relevance. See Zillah Eisenstein, *Capitalist Patriarchy and the Case for Socialist Feminism* (Monthly Review Press, 1979); Michelle Barrett, *Women's Oppression Today: The Marxist/ Feminist Encounter* (Verso, 1988); Sylvia Walby, *Theorising Patriarchy* (Blackwell, 1990).

Du Bois, W. E. B. African American scholar, writer and activist (1877–1963). A co-founder of the National Association for the Advancement of Coloured People (NAACP), organiser of the Pan-African Congress and crusading writer, Du Bois is one of the leading figures not only in African American history but in US history in general. His work made known the experiences of the African American people and sought to develop political and social strategies for their development. Those unfamiliar with him are advised to go straight to his *The Souls of Black Folk*. The Norton Critical edition (edited by Henry Louis Gates Jr and Terri Hume Oliver) contains a number of useful contextualising pieces and a good introduction.

Dworkin, Ronald. North American legal and political philosopher. At the time of writing, he is Professor of Jurisprudence at Oxford and a professor in the law school at NYU. Working within the liberal tradition of legal and political theory, Dworkin attempts to clarify our political and legal principles. He is strongly opposed to anti-foundationalism and scepticism, seeking an objective basis for our judgements in the practical and defensible reason he regards as the heart of legal processes. See *Taking Rights Seriously* (Duckworth, 1977); *Law's Empire* (Fontana, 1986); *Freedom's Law: The Moral Reading of the American Constitution* (Harvard University Press, 1996); *Sovereign Virtue: The Theory and Practice of Equality* (Harvard University Press, 2000).

Eco-anarchism. A combination of ecological thinking and anarchism that sometimes claims to have roots in the writings of the Russian anarchist Peter Kropotkin (1842–1921). In essence, it argues that these two ideologies naturally go together and one requires the other. The domination of people by the state and of nature by capitalists are part of the same process, and both must be smashed (see, for example, work by, and debates about, Murray Bookchin as well as Chapter 8).

Eco-feminism. A political outlook that sees the demands of ecologism and the women's movement as linked. Often exponents argue that the domination of man over woman and of man over nature are linked and that the destruction of sexism is at one with the destruction of policies that harm the environment. Masculinity makes both nature and woman 'other' and exploits them (see Maria Mies and Vandana Shiva, *Eco-Feminism* (Zed Books, 1993) and Chapter 8).

Elster, Jon. Rational choice theorist. At the time of writing, he is Robert K. Merton Professor of Social Sciences in the Department of Political Science at Columbia University in New York and an exponent of something called rational choice Marxism which combines a Marxist approach to social analysis with the insights of **rational choice theory**. This is an important perspective in the methodology of social science, the influence of which should not be underestimated; see Jon Elster (ed.), *Rational Choice Theory* (Blackwell, 1986).

Engels, Friedrich. German philosopher (1820–95). Engels was a long-term collaborator of Karl Marx, and co-wrote some of their most important works. He came from a wealthy family and spent much of his life financially supporting Marx. When working in his father's mills in Manchester, he wrote the landmark *Condition of the Working Classes in England* (first published in 1845), a stark account of the exploitation and poor treatment of the workers. His most notable works of Marxist thinking are probably *Anti-Duhring* (1878) and *The Origin of the Family, Private Property and the State* (1884), at one time an important source for socialist/Marxist feminists. When Marx died, Engels edited and translated much of his work including Volume 2 of *Capital*, and collated Marx's notes to produce Volume 3. There is still debate among Marx scholars as to the extent to which Engels shaped or altered Marx's works, and some regard him as having presented a science-fixated and deterministic Marx. See Chapter 3.

Enlightenment. This is the term given to the long movement of intellectual, cultural and artistic transformation that overtook Europe in the eighteenth century. Central to it was the conviction that human reason could be applied to the problems of science and society more successfully than fidelity to the traditional authorities of both church and state. In Kant's famous words, it meant the liberation of humanity from its 'self-incurred immaturity', and its maxim was 'the courage to use your own reason'. Enlightenment was closely linked to the challenge to absolutist and monarchical government. Subsequently, critics have charged Enlightenment with having a dark side, entailing the subordination of the world to man's 'instrumental reason' (see **Adorno, Critical Theory** and **Frankfurt School**). Postmodernism is also often understood as an attempt to criticise or move beyond Enlightenment.

Equal protection clause. The equal protection clause is part of the fourteenth amendment to the United States Constitution. It prohibits states from denying to any person equal protection under the law. This thus protects people on the grounds of sex or race from discrimination. It was important in relation to the civil-rights movement.

Equal Treatment Directive. Passed by what was then called the European Economic Community (now the EU) in 1976, this guaranteed equal treatment for men and women when seeking employment or training and in working conditions and so on.

Essentialism. General term used, usually critically, to describe theories or analyses that proceed on the basis of a belief that there is an essence to the thing being studied; an aspect or element that is constant across all particular cases. For example, an 'essentialist' theory of gender might hold that across all other variations there is something of women that is always the same and something else that makes men essentially the same regardless of other differences (which can be treated as superficial or inessential).

European Union. The Second World War persuaded many in Europe that some form of intergovernmental cooperation was desirable, if only to bind European nations together and prevent the recurrence of war. Since that time, Europe has seen the slow emergence, through many mutations, of intergovernmental agreements and bodies. Under current arrangements, states that are members of the EU delegate certain powers to central bodies which are supposed to oversee the interests of the Union as a whole while members retain national sovereignty. The central institutions of the EU are the European Parliament (made up of members elected across the Union), the Council (which represents the individual member states) and the Commission (made up of people appointed by the council with the approval of the Parliament and which acts as a kind of cabinet or executive). Around this are a European Court of Justice (overseeing EU law) and the European Central Bank (of particular importance since the EU, minus the UK and Denmark, adopted a single currency at the start of 2001). The EU is a unique political arrangement though far from universally loved, and attitudes to it are one of the central sources of division across European states. However, in the future it will undoubtedly be of immense importance in global politics, especially as membership expands into Eastern Europe. See, among many others, Desmond Dinan, *Ever Closer Union: An Introduction to European Integration* (Macmillan, 1999).

Evolution. See **Darwin.**

Fausto-Sterling, Anne. North American biologist. At the time of writing, Fausto-Sterling is Professor of Biology and Women's Studies in the Division of Biology and Medicine in the Department of Molecular and Cell Biology at Brown University. In addition to her biological studies on genetics, reproduction and development, she has written critiques of the way in which assumptions about gender shape biological research. As a scientific voice arguing that sexuality and gender are social/cultural constructions, she has been of importance to feminist and other radical social scientists. She has paid particular attention to the treatment of babies born 'intersexed' or of indeterminate gender, advocating that we recognise the existence of five sexes: male, female, 'herms' (hermaphrodites, people born with both a testes and an ovary), 'merms' (born with testes and some female genitalia) and 'ferms' (born with ovaries combined with some male genitalia). See *Myths of Gender: Biological Theories of Women and Men* (Basic Books, 1992) and *Sexing the Body: Gender Politics and the Construction of Sexuality* (Basic Books, 2000).

Foundationalism. The view that all philosophy (and hence all knowledge or argument) must proceed from a secure foundation that must be established first. Technically, a foundationalist belief is one that is self-justifying – without need for any further beliefs to ground its own justification, although the contemporary theoretical use of the term is slightly more permissive. The particular foundation may vary, but examples would include the metaphysics of forms found in Plato, the rationalism developed by Descartes or the experimentalism of contemporary science and exemplified in philosophical form by someone such as Karl Popper. See also **anti-foundationalism.**

Founding fathers. In 1757, the thirteen original states of the USA (excluding Rhode Island) appointed delegates to attend a constitutional convention in Philadelphia with the purpose of revising the Articles of Confederation into a new Constitution for the new state. Fifty-five attended, but only thirty-nine signed the Constitution that resulted and was later ratified by the individual states. These are regarded as the founding fathers of the United States, and political and legal discussion in the USA sometimes turns on assertions as to what they intended in their design.

Fourier, Charles. French socialist theorist (1772–1837). A critic of the effects of industrialisation, Fourier founded a utopian community designed to achieve harmony of the human passions. People did what they pleased and lived communally, the idea being that the community would self-regulate because of their harmonised interests. Through this experiment, and his writings, he was a significant influence on the European socialist movement (including Marx despite the latter's dismissal of him as merely utopian).

Frankfurt School. Group of neo-Marxist social theorists and philosophers based at the Frankfurt Institute for Social Research founded in 1923. See **Critical Theory, Adorno** and **Horkheimer.**

Free rider problem. Associated with rational choice theory, the free rider problem draws attention to a genuine difficulty when dealing with public goods. Essentially, the idea is that people will, if they can, try to avoid contributing to something if they know that someone else will bear the cost, and therefore those who may be willing to bear the cost may not do so because they don't want to support free riders. Straightforward examples are when people living in separate flats share some common space such as a kitchen. With no clear ownership of the space, who is responsible for looking after it, cleaning it and so forth? The free rider problem states that there is a disincentive since each will rely on another person taking responsibility, but those who might won't because they don't want to carry the free rider.

Freud, Sigmund. Founder of psychoanalysis (1856–1939). Freud towers over the twentieth century. He developed the idea that the unconscious motivated all sorts of human action and behaviour without the conscious part of our minds knowing it. Repressing our taboo desires led to neurosis which could be understood as the stifled attempt of the unconscious to speak. **Psychoanalysis** became a massive movement stimulating interest in the unconscious (especially for artists) and motivating the continuing 'obsession' with sexuality. While psychoanalysis as a medical movement is much frowned upon these days, there is no doubt that as a writer about the human condition Freud transformed the way we think about ourselves. Freud was linked with Marxism by members of the **Frankfurt School,** and numerous contemporary theorists (especially those associated with poststructuralism) draw on themes derived from Freud.

Genealogy. Method of historical study and analysis 'developed' by Nietzsche and latterly revived and implemented by Foucault. It entails studying history not as the unfolding of a pre-given logic nor as the emergence of higher stages of civilisation but as the spread of different sorts of concept or practice, related like a family but originating in singular acts of power or domination. The method is critical in that it shows the historical roots of present phenomena we take for granted or imagine to be natural (see Chapters 1 and 9).

Gilligan, Carol. North American feminist theorist. At the time of writing, she is Patricia Alberg Graham Professor of Gender Studies in the Harvard Graduate School for Education. Gilligan became well known for her work *In a Different Voice* (Harvard University Press, 1982) that aimed to show how men and women develop moral arguments, and perceive moral issues, in fundamentally different ways. Where men emphasise individual rights and moral rules in making judgements, women, she argued, emphasise a wider context of relationships, advancing judgements on the basis of what will help sustain those relationships. These arguments have influenced psychology, feminism and moral theory, while they have inspired some political theorists to develop an 'ethics of care' where the central moral principle is not what is 'right' but what will be in the interests of the people for whom we care, thus stressing responsibilities towards others rather than the rights of ourselves. See Chapter 7 and Selma Sevenhuijsen, *Citizenship and the Ethics of Care: Feminist Considerations on Justice, Morality, and Politics* (Routledge, 1998).

Gilroy, Paul. British sociologist. At the time of writing, he is Professor of African American Studies and Sociology in the African American Studies Department at Yale. Gilroy's theories and analyses of the relationship between black culture, popular culture and politics have been influential in sociology and cultural studies. His work deconstructs collective identities while not denying them as experiences. He stresses that these are constructed on the terrain of cultural practice and that we can build hybrid forms that move us beyond the confines of race thinking. See, for example, *Against Race: Imagining Political Culture Beyond the Color Line* (Harvard University Press, 2000).

Godwin, William. British writer, philosopher and political anarchist/utopian (1756–1836). An inspiration to the later British romantics (the younger Coleridge, Wordsworth and others), Godwin argued that governments, in order to keep power, maintained their populations in ignorance but that the spread of reason would lead to a refusal to submit to such unjustified authority. He also advanced ideas that would later reappear as utilitarianism and stressed the importance of maximising happiness. See his *Enquiry Concerning Political Justice* (various editions).

Gramsci, Antonio. Italian Marxist political theorist (1891–1937). One of the most influential of Western Marxist thinkers, Gramsci helped to found (and for a time led) the Italian Communist Party. In 1926, he was arrested by Mussolini's

Fascist authorities and put in prison, where he died in 1937. There he produced a vast range of notes and essays (known as the Prison Writings) which, when published in English in the early 1970s, were regarded as highly important within the field of what would become Cultural Studies. Gramsci's importance lies in his reconfiguration of Marxism as an open political philosophy, rather than a system where the economy determines all social relations. He emphasised the importance of political intervention and ideological struggle. Particularly important is his concept of 'hegemony' or leadership. He argued that a ruling group or class will also lead in the 'intellectual and moral' realms. The task of radicals lay in becoming persuasive and taking back control of the intellectual and moral realms. For many Western radicals, these ideas helped in the formulation of a cultural politics that took place outside the state fighting the battle for ideas, hearts and minds. See *Selections from the Prison Notebooks* (Lawrence and Wishart, 1971) or, among others, James Martin, *Gramsci's Political Analysis: A Critical Introduction* (Macmillan, 1998).

Green, Thomas Hill. British philosopher (1836–82). Green was a leading figure in British idealism and a great influence on the teaching of political philosophy in Britain. He is important as a theorist of Liberalism because he developed an approach distinct from that of utilitarianism by not basing everything on individualism and recognising that people are members of social groups with shared norms and activities. Individuals are embedded in relationships that give them responsibilities for, and duties towards, each other. In short, Green sought to combine individualism and community, without sacrificing either. He is thus of relevance to contemporary communitarianism. For more, see David Boucher (ed.), *The British Idealists* (Cambridge University Press, 1997).

Guattari, Felix. French intellectual and psychoanalyst. Guattari is best known for his collaboration with Gilles Deleuze; but see also Gary Genosko (ed.), *The Guattari Reader* (Blackwell, 1996).

Habermas, Jürgen. German philosopher associated with Critical Theory. From the generation after **Horkheimer** and **Adorno**, Habermas has inherited the mantle of **Critical Theory**. He is particularly important for having focused on the normative foundations of Critical Theory, developing the idea that there is a distinctive form of rationality called communicative rationality (that supplements instrumental rationality) and that from this we may derive a benchmark against which to assess the procedures by which decisions are taken (see **ideal speech situation**). His has been a wide-ranging career touching on many areas of philosophical and political inquiry, and he has also been involved in public political debates in Germany. He is well known for (in distinction to postmodernists and to some of his **Frankfurt School** predecessors) wanting to rescue the project of modernity or Enlightenment, regarding it as incomplete rather than corrupt. There are so many books by and about him; but try Thomas

McCarthy, *The Critical Theory of Jürgen Habermas* (Polity, 1984) and, for a study that puts Habermas in the context of mainstream debates in liberal political theory, see Shane O'Neill, *Impartiality in Context: Grounding Justice in a Pluralist World* (State University of New York Press, 1997).

Halal. Arabic word for 'lawful' or 'permitted'. It is commonly used to refer to foods which have been prepared in the manner required by Islamic religious practice. For meat to be halal, the animal must have been killed while conscious. This has led to conflict when practised in states with laws on animal welfare that require the creatures to be stunned before slaughter. Exemptions to such rules have been granted to Muslims, and these are an example of the practice of multi-culturalism. The Jewish equivalent to halal is kosher, and Jews have also been granted such legal exemptions.

Hall, Stuart. Caribbean-born British social and cultural theorist. At the time of writing, he is Emeritus Professor of Sociology at the Open University in Britain. Hall has been a major influence on parts of the British left, particularly through his analyses of the New Right and Thatcherism in Britain in the 1980s. For his work at the Birmingham Centre for Contemporary Cultural Studies in the 1970s and 1980s, he is regarded as the founder of Cultural Studies. His combination of interests (political, cultural and theoretical) inspired a generation, and some regard his writings on cultural politics, race and ethnicity as visionary. See David Morley and Kuan-Hsing Chen (eds), *Stuart Hall: Critical Dialogues in Cultural Studies* (Routledge, 1996).

Hayek, Friedrich August von. Austrian political and economic philosopher (1899–1992). Hayek's economics represented the principal alternative to those of Keynes. He stressed the role of the market in assigning value to goods and strongly opposed all state planning, which, he argued, would lead to totalitarianism. He was awarded the Nobel Prize for economics in 1974. See his *The Road to Serfdom* (Ark Publications, 1986) and, for critical comment, Andrew Gamble, *Hayek: The Iron Cage of Liberty* (Polity, 1996).

Hegel, G. W. F. German philosopher (1770–1831). One of the most significant and influential of all Western philosophers, Hegel is often seen as the great enlightenment alternative to Kant. His philosophy is impossible to summarise; but, in contrast to Kant's formalistic approach to the abstract moral law, Hegel's philosophy is rooted in history and community. A philosophical idealist, he understood history to be the unfolding of the Absolute Idea or Spirit, a dialectical process by which the individual, and the species, came to know and realise him- or itself. In his political theory, he saw the modern state as the realisation of man's rationality and freedom, the synthesis of private, family and public, civil life, within which ethical life could prosper. Hegel was a great influence on Marx despite Marx's thoroughgoing criticism of Hegelianism. Two useful but different introductions are Shlomo Avineri, *Hegel's Theory of the Modern State* (Cambridge University Press, 1972) and Raymond Plant, *Hegel: An Introduction* (Blackwell, 1983).

Heidegger, Martin. German philosopher (1889–1976). Associated with the major twentieth-century philosophical movements of existentialism and phenomenology, Heidegger and his mammoth philosophical project cannot be summarised here. He attempted to rethink the entirety of Western metaphysical thought, which he regarded as leading the West into nihilism. Its central error, he argued, was a forgetting of being, the question of what it is 'to be'. Our philosophy, Heidegger said, was based on unthinking assumptions about humanity, nature and existence – and he was particularly critical of the way in which our conceptions of man as an active subject operating on a passive objectified nature had led to technological domination. Heidegger became (and still is) a controversial figure because of his support for the Nazi Party in the 1930s (and its support for him), though the extent to which these political views derived from his philosophy is a difficult matter to resolve. In his later work, he turned to poetic language as affording a possibility of refuge or shelter from the errors of modern life. George Steiner's *Heidegger* (Fontana, 1978) is dense but ultimately comprehensible, while the collection of Heidegger's essays *Poetry, Language, Thought* (Harper and Row, 1971) communicates the sensibility behind his later ruminations.

Hermeneutics. Literally, this word means interpretation or explanation. It was first used in a more technical sense to name the science of historical biblical interpretation. It has since given its name to a philosophical school of social science that distinguishes itself from methodologies aping the natural sciences. Hermeneutics regards human activity as intrinsically meaningful, so that to understand it one must try to interpret the meanings actions have for those undertaking them while accepting that we too are embedded in our own tradition (or horizon) of meaning. See the discussion of Gadamer in Chapter 1.

Hill, Anita. In 1991, African American **Clarence Thomas** was nominated to the Supreme Court of the United States by George Bush senior. Thomas looked likely to be approved by the Senate until Anita Hill, a former assistant, came forward alleging serious sexual harassment. The hearings turned into a rather nasty spectacle, polarising US political and social opinion.

Hobbes, Thomas. English political theorist and philosopher (1588–1679). Hobbes is one of the giants in the history of political thought. He has this special place not only because of an impressive rhetorical style but also for being one of the first to try and develop a materialistic (rather than theistic) foundation for a theory of political order, and for developing a theory of political obligation and legitimacy on the basis of a social contract. In Hobbes' theory, we all agree to obey the absolute law of the state, the Leviathan, because it is in our interest to do so, in order to avoid the horror of the pre-political state of nature which is a war of all against all. A good short student introduction is Richard Tuck, *Hobbes* (Oxford University Press, 1989).

Hobhouse, Leonard Trelawny. British political philosopher (1864–1929). Most notable as a thinker of 'new' liberalism (also associated with **T. H. Green**), Hobhouse tried to balance out individual liberty with a recognition of the necessary social context of human development and thus the need for some element of commonality in political organisation. He thus saw that the state had a role in promoting the good of the individual and the community. His work has been revived of late by those looking for a 'third way' between individualism and collectivism, right and left. For more, see Michael Freeden, *The New Liberalism: An Ideology of Social Reform* (Clarendon Press, 1978).

Horkheimer, Max. German social and political theorist (1895–1973). He was a director of the Institute of Social Research in Frankfurt and a founder of **Critical Theory**. See also **Adorno** and the important essay by Horkheimer, 'Traditional and Critical Theory', in Max Horkheimer, *Critical Theory: Selected Essays* (Seabury Press, 1972).

Humanism. The meaning attached to this word or concept can vary depending on who is using it (or when in history it is being used), and the student is advised to be careful. One meaning is that associated with the Renaissance. Here, it refers to a focus on secular pursuits and secular knowledge as stimulated by the Renaissance emphasis on the new science and new arts. Humanism can also refer to a general way of thinking that places human beings and their intrinsic worth at the centre of ethics and which is thus distinguished from theistic (or god-centred) views of the world. It is a sort of moral atheism. A third usage is more derogatory. Here, humanism represents that outlook on the world which places human beings at the centre, with the individual as the source of all meaning and value. This sort of humanism is usually criticised by poststructuralists such as Foucault or Derrida, who, when being anti-humanist, are not being anti-human but are voicing disagreement with the placing of individuals at the centre of all knowledge and thought.

Hume, David. Scottish philosopher (1711–76). Hume is one of the most strident exponents of empiricism. He argued that ultimately all knowledge can only come from the direct experience of our senses (as opposed to being generated from within our minds by pure reason). He pushed this rather far into a quite radical scepticism. In a famous example, Hume argued that just because we see a billiard ball move when another hits it, our experience of this event does not justify our conclusion that the first ball caused the second ball to move, nor that this will always happen when the balls strike each other. Rather, he argued, we hold beliefs because of our habitual association of them, and we have a habit of combining experiences in our imagination and then believing our fabrications. Hume moved this into moral philosophy arguing that morality comes not from reason but from our feelings of sympathy when we think about or see other people. Although there is no ultimate rational basis to our moral views, custom and sensation do give us strongly held beliefs that may well be shared. It follows that there is no rational justification for political institutions, but they can be defended on the basis of what works well given the circumstances. Hume's views were a great influence on what would become known as consequentialist moral thinking (associated with some strands of liberalism), but they are also related to a scepticism and traditionalism that crop up in both conservatism and pragmatism.

Hybridity. A hybrid is something that is made up of a mixture of two or more distinct things. It used to apply primarily to genetics and particularly plants. It has more recently come to be used by cultural and literary theorists wishing to draw attention to the impure and hybrid nature of culture (as opposed to those who believe in the purity of cultures, who are sometimes known as fascists).

Ideal speech situation. Concept associated with the later philosophy of **Habermas**. Emerging from **Critical Theory**, **Habermas** sought to re-establish a basis for forms of reason other than the instrumental one that was challenged by critical theorists. He argued that there were other types of rationality including 'communicative rationality', the rationality that governs our attempts to reach understanding through dialogue. Implicit in the act of communication, he argues, are four 'validity claims': that what we are saying is meaningful, true, justified and sincere. These are implied in speech, if not actually always met, and it should be possible for speakers to verify or prove that they are at work in any particular exchange. But they are often not met because of things that distort communicative encounters such as the intrusion of instrumental rationality, which is reason orientated towards achieving particular ends rather than understanding. A situation in which all four validity claims could be rationally adhered to and justified, and in which speech would therefore be 'undistorted', is that towards which we should aim in our political deliberations – an ideal speech situation in which all that wins is the force of the better argument. This ideal, though it may be unattainable, can, Habermas avers, take on the force of a 'regulative ideal' and normative principle.

Idealism. In philosophy, this refers to the metaphysical claim that the only things which really or ultimately exist are ideas or mental constructs. In political thought, the forms of idealism that have been most important are those of Plato, Kant and Hegel. For Plato, the only things that really exist are the ideal forms of which the world is an inferior representation, and the rulers should be those who seek knowledge of these eternal truths. For Kant, we can only know the world through fixed categories that make possible our cognition, so knowing the world 'in itself' is impossible but the very presence of these categories permits the formation of a 'transcendental' idealism which can be the basis for a practical reason providing a moral foundation. For Hegel, history can be understood as the unfolding of reason in the world such that the rational and the real will coincide. The rational is thus given priority over the real. The reverse of idealism is materialism, which runs the risk of abandoning the search for ultimate truths in its quest to become attuned to the flux of matter but has the advantage of not being so easily susceptible to the charge that it is nonsense.

Identity. An innocent-looking but fiendishly tricky concept. The word derives from Latin, its roots implying something like the quality of being the same but also of being so repeatedly. Hence identity denotes the condition of being the same over a period of time. We now use it to refer to our specific personality: that which makes us identifiable and unique, is always part of us and cannot be tampered with without violating us. In a world where everything is changing quite rapidly, it is hard always to be the same, and so it gets difficult to recognise any identity, even when we are looking at ourselves. In such a situation, where identity is uncertain, it may become political.

Identity politics. Forms of politics based on the demand that an identity be recognised, be accommodated to or form the basis of a collective movement of some kind. Usually (for historical reasons), these are distinguished from class-based politics and nationalist movements (unless that of a minority and especially if lacking a territory) even though these were clearly also politics linked to identity. Rather, the term usually refers to movements built around gender, ethnicity, sexuality and so on where the demand is as much for realisation and acceptance of difference as it is for inclusion in the whole. Often the campaigns associated with identity politics demand the right to have and express the identity in question.

Incommensurable/Incommensurability. Things that are incommensurable with each other are incomparable: there is no basis or common property by which they can be compared. The term has been used in social theory emerging from currents of linguistic philosophy and, latterly, poststructuralist philosophy and is often used to suggest that differing 'language games' or claims made within different cultural frameworks are incommensurable.

International Monetary Fund. This body was created at Bretton Woods, where, in July 1944, towards the end of the Second World War, Allied and associated nations met to form global financial institutions that would prevent the sorts of damaging crises of the 1930s that had led to the war. In the 1930s, a common response to economic difficulty had been to devalue currency (making domestic goods cheaper and exports dearer) or to engage in other practices to restrict the inflow of goods. When others retaliated by doing the same, global trade ground to a halt, leaving everyone screwed. The purpose of the IMF was, with monies lent to it by each member state, to assist in preventing this occurrence by loaning currency to nations at difficult times, thus removing the need for devaluation (and allowing exchange rates to stay pretty much fixed). When the dollar came off the gold standard in 1971 and currencies began to float freely, the role of the IMF changed. It became a major lender, particularly to the developing world. In order to secure its loans, the IMF began investigating and regulating the use of the money it lent, tying loans and the structure of debt repayments to the meeting of certain conditions – mostly those that made developing economies conform to models of free-market economics. This has led to great criticism of the IMF from those who see it as effectively shaping poor economies to suit the interests of more powerful ones.

Interpellation. A concept developed by Louis **Althusser** in his influential essay on 'Ideology and Ideological State Apparatuses'. Althusser argued that ideology does not simply mystify or obscure the truth but constitutes our imaginary relationship to the world by calling/forcing us to adopt a particular social identity. The word literally means an official summons (with shades of 'interposing' or 'demanding'). It certainly suggests an imperative of some sort, which, for Althusser, was the point. See also the discussion in Chapter 12.

Iranian Revolution. The country of Iran (once the centre of the great Persian empire) is central to the Middle East, bordering the Caspian Sea, the Gulf, Iraq, Pakistan, Afghanistan and a number of former republics of the Soviet Union. In the 1920s, a secular nationalist Riza Khan (Riza Shah) took power and sought to modernise the country, but his Westernisation angered many. He banned the wearing of traditional and religious clothes, trying to force Western dress on people, and was not averse to using police brutality to impose his will. He was forced to abdicate in 1941 and during the Second World War Iran was occupied by Soviet and Allied forces. After the war, a popular nationalist movement took power, but it was overthrown in 1953 by a US/CIA-sponsored coup installing Riza Khan's son as a military-backed dictator or Shah. Though troubled politically, as a client state of the USA Iran had access to finance, and the economy developed (the country became something of a playground for rich Westerners). In the 1970s, economic problems, combined with the cultural dislocation of Westernisation and the repression of secular dissent by the Shah, led to the rise in power of Islam. Trouble spread, and massacres of protestors by state troops followed. The religious leader Ayatollah Khomeini (who had led opposition to the Shah in the early 1960s) emerged as leader of the protestors. With massive demonstrations under way (as many as 4,000,000 people on the streets of Tehran), the Shah fled Iran in January 1979. Khomeini returned from exile in France in February and began to set up a new government. On 11–12

February, rebels took police stations, government buildings and the royal palace. This was an almost unique revolution involving millions of people and not just a small cadre leading a coup. After a referendum, on 1 April 1979 Iran was declared an Islamic republic. It had a mixed constitutional system but with ultimate authority given to a spiritual ruler – Khomeini. In November 1979, radicals hostile to pro-Western and secular elements seized the US Embassy in Tehran, taking hostages and demanding the return of the Shah from America so he might face justice. The hostage crisis lasted for over a year, during which time Washington froze Iranian assets and cut Iran off diplomatically (which is perhaps what the radicals always intended). Despite a vicious conflict with neighbouring Iraq, Iran has been a stable, non-Western Islamic republic and did not collapse with the death of Khomeini in 1989. However, there are political tensions in the state between the hard-line clerics and those wanting reform and greater democracy.

Irigaray, Luce. Belgian-born 'French' feminist theorist. An activist and campaigner, she is best known for work on the ethics and politics of sexual difference. Patriarchal culture, she argues, renders women unknowable and unrepresentable. In her psychoanalytically influenced work, Irigaray conceives the political challenge for feminism not as that of enabling women to enter the patriarchal culture but as the construction of an alternative symbolic order, based not on the phallic 'lack' of woman but on the presence of her own different sexuality. For introductory material to Irigaray (and others), try Toril Moi, *Sexual/Textual Politics: Feminist Literary Theory* (Methuen, 1985) and Toril Moi (ed.), *French Feminist Thought: A Reader* (Blackwell, 1987).

Iteration. Repetition. In mathematics, this term refers to the repetition of a cycle of operations in order to get closer and closer to the intended outcome. The term has been used by poststructuralists to describe the nature of language and meaning. Since meaning is not inherent in the word or thing named, stability of reference can only come from the repeated usage of the word in regularised contexts. This has been expanded by **Derrida**, for example, and used by Judith Butler to describe sexed identity in that it is the (apparently stable) outcome of processes that are continually repeated. The difference between the philosophical and mathematical uses is, of course, that for the former there is no final answer whereas in the latter there is (sometimes).

Jurisprudence. The philosophy or science of law. This is important to political theory because, in states with a written constitution (such as the USA), the law comes above the decisions of politics, and the judiciary has a powerful role in deciding what actions are and are not constitutional. In the USA, many political developments take place in the courts. As a result, a philosophy of law is essential to political philosophy.

Justice. The definition of this term has been one of the endeavours of political theory since its inception. Plato's *Republic* (written in approximately 490 BC) begins with (and is partially structured by) the question of what justice is. Different political theories and ideologies define justice differently (this is one of the main things that makes them different theories) just as they consider the ways of achieving justice in numerous different ways (through redistribution, recognition and so on). Some theorists have attempted to develop a perspective suggesting that justice may have multiple forms. The term is so important and so contested that this short comment really cannot do it justice.

Kant, Immanuel. German philosopher (1724–1804). Kant is one of the most influential philosophers of all time. Although he was not always recognised as central to political theory, he has long been understood as the central philosopher of enlightenment. Kant's philosophical project aimed to reach a new accommodation between the twin poles of scepticism and total rationalism. He achieved this through a 'Copernican revolution' in which he reversed the focus of philosophy, arguing that the human mind is not blank but perceives the world through necessary categories of experience (such as space and time). We do have knowledge of things 'out there', but that knowledge is made possible and shaped by the perceptual apparatus of our minds such that the 'things in themselves' (as they would be without our mental apparatus) are not accessible to us. Kant's intention was to create a philosophy that would not collapse into claims that we only know what is in our heads but that could also preserve a space for our innate reason. Because of this innate capacity for reason, it is possible for people to formulate their own purposes and to exercise their will in making decisions. Thus it is possible for them to act according to rational, practical, moral principles provided that they have the freedom or autonomy to do so. Kant thus tried to give to politics and political theory a moral basis with the principle that people should be treated as ends in themselves and not as any sort of means to an end. The legal state should attempt to follow this maxim and act as a support to people, who should act on it if they are able to exercise, freely, their own 'good will'. The state should therefore be a republic, which is central to the attainment of peace between states (since republics will not want to go to war, unlike absolutist states that are prepared to use subjects as the means to the end of expansion). With this latter argument, Kant has become an important figure in some schools of contemporary international relations in addition to the immeasurable influence he has had on almost all forms of liberal thinking up to the present day.

Kristeva, Julia. Bulgarian-born 'French' feminist theorist. Combining psychoanalysis, semiotics and linguistics, Julia Kristeva has developed her own kind of feminist literary and political theory. Her work has helped focus the attention of social science on the body, urging us to place greater emphasis on the maternal (as opposed to paternal) in the shaping of our subjectivity.

Consequently, she has stressed the poor resources Western culture has when it comes to representing motherhood. Kristeva has also analysed the phenomenon of 'abjection'. Identity (collective or individual) is maintained, she argues, through the exclusion of particular others that are construed as a threat. In particular, the maternal body has been so abjected since our dependence on it, as children, is understood to threaten our solid identity: it is only by breaking with the mother's body that we become 'individuals'; but this turns the female body into an object about which we are ambivalent, both desiring and fearing it. Kristeva stresses a feminism that seeks to bring identity and difference into relationship and to reconsider the 'maternal semiotic', a freer form of meaning making that precedes the rigidities of the conventional symbolic order. Kristeva has been more influential in literary than in political theory; but this may be changing. See Toril Moi (ed.), *The Kristeva Reader* (Blackwell, 1986) and also her introductory book *Sexual/Textual Politics: Feminist Literary Theory* (Methuen, 1985).

Kuhn, Thomas. American philosopher and historian of science (1922–96). Kuhn is most famous for his 1962 book *The Structure of Scientific Revolutions* in which he argued that the development of science has not been a smooth process of progressive evolution but rather one marked by sudden changes in the fundamental organising principles of scientific thinking that Kuhn called 'paradigm-shifts'. Most of the time, scientists operate on the basis of conventional assumptions, pushing any anomalous findings that challenge them to one side. However, as the anomalies pile up, 'normal science' gives way to 'revolutionary science' and precipitates an overall shift in thinking. This implies that scientific knowledge has a non-objective basis and opens the way for a sociology of scientific knowledge but also, as many critics aver, to relativism. Kuhn's book was very influential and made the word 'paradigm' famous.

Labriola, Antonio. Italian Marxist (1843–1904). Regarded as the 'father' of Italian Marxism, Labriola was the first translator of the Communist Manifesto into that language and active in the formation of an Italian workers' party. He was an influence on the next generation of Italian Marxists such as Gramsci.

l'affaire foulard. In French, a 'foulard' is a scarf, but in this context it refers specifically to the headscarf or 'hijab' worn by Muslim girls, which, in 1989, became extremely controversial when worn to school. As a result, schoolteachers refused to teach. For more information, see the discussion in the extract by Bhikhu Parekh (Chapter 10).

Laissez-faire. Literally (from the French), it means 'let-do'. The term is usually used to refer to an economic doctrine (though one that spreads into politics more generally) which urges the state not to interfere in individual economic actions and to leave free enterprise to work by itself.

Langue. **The underlying structure of language.** This term was used by the influential Swiss linguist Ferdinand de **Saussure** in his *Course on General Linguistics* published in 1916. He wanted to distinguish between an actual act of speech or meaning-making (the saying or writing of something) and the implicit or underlying structure of language and meaning that made the expression possible, calling the former *parole* and the latter *langue*. Only *langue* could be the proper object of a science of linguistics.

Laslett, Peter. British historian of political thought (1915–2001). Sometimes associated with the Cambridge School (though he was their senior), Laslett collated and edited the works of key early modern political thinkers such as Sir Robert Filmer and John Locke. In placing their thought in its historical context, he inspired later figures such as Quentin Skinner. In the 1960s, Laslett turned to the statistical analysis of social structures, studying population and family structure in pre-modern England.

Legalists. A school of Ancient Chinese political philosophy. Where Confucius believed in a kind of natural order and hierarchy, the Legalists regarded humanity as greedy, selfish and unruly. They therefore required an absolute law, applied to all, that would be above any ruler, and that would impose order. Legalist principles were applied to China in the late third century BC under Qin, the first emperor, who ruled from 221–206 BC. Perhaps because of his Legalism he unified China, but under his rule books were banned, dissent was punished and people were forced into labour that was regarded as socially useful and productive (so, not into philosophy). This period of rule was, perhaps unsurprisingly, short-lived; but, in standardising Chinese culture, it shaped the China to come, and one can perhaps see here themes and practices that have reappeared in Chinese political culture over the centuries.

Leibniz, Gottfried Wilhelm von. German philosopher, mathematician, historian and jurist (1646–1716). Leibniz (a contemporary of **Spinoza** and Isaac Newton) developed a rationalist philosophy based on the idea of a pre-established harmony that he hoped might reconcile rationalism with theology. One of the most significant things he did was invent calculus, the basis for modern mathematics. He was revived in the nineteenth and twentieth centuries, and Bertrand Russell admired him greatly. Parts of his work have also been appropriated by **Deleuze**.

Lenin, Vladimir Ilyich Ulyanov. Revolutionary leader and political theorist (1870–1924). Lenin is a legendary and controversial historical figure. As leader of the Bolsheviks in the Russian Revolution of 1917, he is regarded both as a strategist of genius and as a ruthless operator. Whatever the disputes about his legacy (and one's answer to the question of whether or not Stalinism would have come about had he lived longer), there is no doubt that Lenin is a towering figure and a notable political thinker. His importance in this latter respect lies in the way in which he adapted Marxism to the imperatives of bringing about revolution in a 'backward' country. After him, there would be not only Marxism but also Marxism-Leninism. For example, in the pamphlet *What is to be Done* (written in 1902), Lenin argued that the working class alone will develop only a 'trade-union consciousness' and that it requires a 'vanguard' party to bring about revolution and to lead the working class to fulfilment of its true historical role. Also important is his theory of imperialism, which he understood as the outcome of monopoly-finance capitalism seeking super-profits from colonialism. As an introduction to his thought, see Neil Harding, *Leninism* (Macmillan, 1996). Left for dead by the collapse of the Soviet Union in 1989, Lenin has recently been revived by those in search of inspiration for radical opponents of global capitalism. See the collection of Lenin's writings edited by Slavoj Zizek, *Revolution at the Gates* (Verso, 2002).

Lévi-Strauss, Claude. Belgian-born 'French' social anthropologist and theorist. (b. 1908). Lévi-Strauss is understood by many to be the founder of the method of social analysis known as structuralism. Drawing on the structural linguistics of Ferdinand de **Saussure**, he developed a way of analysing cultures in terms of their underlying structural organisation rather than their surface appearance, examining the relations between things rather than the things themselves. For example, what is important in the arrangement of the seats at the high table for a wedding reception is not who is sitting in any particular place but the relationship of their seat to the others (which assigns each a particular place in the hierarchy and a symbolic role in the ceremonies). Particularly influential were Lévi-Strauss' interpretations of myths and his argument that fundamental 'binary oppositions' shape all culture (such as raw-cooked, nature-culture, animal-human). In showing that these structures shaped 'primitive' cultures as well as the 'advanced' societies of the West, Lévi-Strauss was opposing the ethnocentrism that animated much early anthropological study and showing that traditional cultures had their own validity. Understanding this sort of structuralism is an important prelude to understanding poststructuralism. For more, see John Sturrock, *Structuralism* (Fontana, 1993) and John Sturrock (ed.), *Structuralism and Since: From Lévi-Strauss to Derrida* (Oxford University Press, 1979).

Libertarian(ism). The idea that the state has no (or minimal) legitimacy when it interferes in the actions of individuals in any way. Mostly a twentieth-century political movement, it can be traced back to earlier currents if one includes anarchists as libertarians (but libertarians tend to be of the political right and hostile to the egalitarian anti-legal instincts of anarchists). In essence, libertarians regard the state as properly having only the responsibility for enforcing the law and fighting wars. They also believe in laissez-faire capitalism and support the right to property (which the state should protect).

Libidinal economies. The libido, a term popularised by **Freud**, refers to our instinctual (especially sexual) energy. The word 'economy' derives from Ancient Greek for the laws of the household, referring to the management and organisation of domestic life. It is this sense of management or organisation that matters in the generalisation of the term but also the newer notion that economics involves exchange of some sort. Thus, in using the term 'libidinal economy', recent theorists (such as **Lyotard**) imply that (sexual) instincts and energies are organised, circulate and get invested or reinvested, in a way analogous to the financial economy. It is this system of investment and exchange that they make into an object of study and may see as the definitive feature of a social order.

Locke, John. English philosopher (1632–1704). One of the giants of philosophy in general, Locke is also crucial to the history of political thought. His early liberal doctrines still shape debate today. Epistemologically, he was an empiricist arguing against claims that we possess certain innate ideas, instead describing our mind as a *tabula rasa* (blank slate) onto which are left the impressions of experiences from which alone we can gain knowledge. Central to his political theory are the famous *Two Treatises on Government*. The first of these demolishes the argument of Sir Robert Filmer that the monarch has a divine right to rule because he is descended from Adam. The second develops an argument for natural law and natural right and for a form of government based on rational foundations. Locke argues that political authority can only be founded on the consent of the governed. They so consent because it is rational to institute a mechanism for the protection of rights. As such, the justification of government is that it is in the interests of the people. By the same token, if government works against the interests of the people, then it is unjust and can be challenged. Locke's work was therefore a philosophical justification of the English Revolution and of parliamentary government against the defenders of the absolute right to rule of the Crown. He also wrote about the importance of religious toleration and the need for the state to eschew judgement in matters of faith (and in this the Constitution of the United States is a very Lockean political document). See, among so many others, John Dunn, *The Political Thought of John Locke: An Historical Account of the Argument of the 'Two Treatises on Government'* (Cambridge University Press, 1969).

Lukács, Georg. Hungarian Marxist philosopher, writer and literary critic (1885–1971). Lukács was quite an influence on European Marxist thinking in the twentieth century. He developed an influential (Hegelian-leaning) theory of alienation and also a theory of artistic production that linked artistic history to the history of class struggle. His key work is *History and Class Consciousness* (1923).

Lukes, Steven. British social theorist. At the time of writing, he is a Professor at the European University in Florence, Italy. He is best known for his so-called 'radical' theory of power. Lukes criticised social theories of power for reducing it to the actions of individuals and for not paying sufficient attention to collective or organisational actions that could not be reduced to individual activity. He argued that we needed to see how power could shape individual desires and prevent people from seeing their own 'real objective interests'. See his *Power: A Radical View* (Macmillan, 1974).

Lyotard, Jean-François. French philosopher (1924–98). One of a number of left-wing French philosophers mobilised by the crisis in Algeria and by the events of 1968, Lyotard is best known in the English-speaking world as a philosopher of postmodernism, which he defined in headline terms as 'incredulity towards metanarratives' (1984, xxiv) and for his analyses of art and aesthetics. He is perhaps most relevant to political thought when developing his concept of the 'differend'. Because, according to Lyotard, we speak within different language games or genres, conflicts can arise in that people will not understand what others are saying even when the terms are the same. This can lead to a kind of violence in which one party is simply silenced. Lyotard's ethical views urge us to listen out to this silence, to seek that which cannot be represented. For a better explanation, try James Williams, *Lyotard and the Political* (Routledge, 2000).

Machiavelli, Niccolò. Florentine political theorist and historian (1469–1527). Everybody knows about Machiavelli because his name has become a label for scheming and power-hungry political operators. This derives from his short book *The Prince* in which Machiavelli advised Lorenzo de Medici on how to get and retain power through the use of all manner of wiles. But there is more to him than this, and Machiavelli is a deeply suggestive thinker. He is notable for having founded a 'new' method of political theory based on historical analysis of political acts and for developing a theory of republican government. He was not at all the defender of despotism that he is still believed to be. See the short introduction by Quentin Skinner, *Machiavelli* (Oxford University Press, 1981).

MacIntyre, Alasdair. North American moral philosopher. At the time of writing, he is Senior Research Professor of Philosophy at Notre Dame. Influenced by both Marxism and Christianity, MacIntyre has been mistakenly associated with the rise of communitarian political philosophy, although he joins its practitioners in criticising the corrosive effects on morality of liberal individualism. However, MacIntyre's argument is broader than that. He suggests that our moral language has fallen into chaos and our moral preferences reduced to expressions of feeling or emotion with no rational justification. The enlightenment project of justifying morality was doomed to fail because it lacked the breadth of the older Catholic-Aristotelian theology for which ethics was the study of how man could realise his essential nature, attaining rational happiness. In conceiving of the individual as an authoritative rational moral agent, enlightenment (i.e. Kantian) thinking removed him from a communal context, so emptying moral discussion of its real meaning, reducing it to mere utilitarianism. It is only in a communal context that a person can have a role and relations with others to whom they are accountable, and this makes it possible for people to conceive of the kinds of virtue or excellence they should cultivate. One way to understand this argument is to note how often, in moral argument, we say that people 'want this', or 'desire that' and then argue over whether or not they have the right to it. We discuss rather less the extent to which the want itself is a good one established in a good way. Under Macintyre's influence, we might say that it doesn't matter whether x has the right to an abortion or not. The important question is whether having an abortion is a good thing to do. MacIntyre's arguments have been influential but also controversial, understood by some to advocate a conservative authoritarian politics. However, in posing a framework of morality that exposes the partiality of the liberal framework we tend to take for granted, MacIntyre has the advantage of certainly being interesting and challenging. See his *A Short History of Ethics* (Routledge, 1967) and *After Virtue: A Study in Moral Theory* (Duckworth, 1985) as well as Chapter 6.

Madison, James. US political philosopher and politician (1751–1836). A key figure in the Constitutional Convention of 1787 that produced the Constitution of the USA and later a founder of the Republican Party as well as the fourth President of the USA (1809–17). As a theorist, he is important for his contributions to *The Federalist*, the collection of essays that defended the American Constitution and that were co-produced with Alexander Hamilton and John Jay. Madison was an advocate of a republican system of government, explaining and defending the separation of powers and the mixed constitution. For some, this has led to a system of government so well designed to prevent unwise governmental action that it prevents governmental action as such (inducing the kinds of covert action that so mark US governmental activity, especially in foreign affairs).

Mandela, Nelson. South African civil-rights campaign leader. Mandela was one of a number of people active in the African National Congress campaigning (and prepared to use violence) against the South African regime that enshrined minority white power and subordinated the majority non-white population through a system of apartheid (keeping the 'races' entirely separate). Imprisoned in 1962, he became a globally recognised symbol of the struggle for freedom and equality in South Africa and, indeed, the world. Released in 1990 to worldwide acclaim, he became the President of the ANC, pivotal in the final change of the South African system, and then President of South Africa. He was awarded the Nobel Peace Prize in 1993.

Marx, Karl. German philosopher, social scientist, economist and political activist (1818–83). Probably the most influential political thinker of all time, though the legacy of Marxism is still unclear. The regimes instituted in his name were ignominious and their passing largely unmourned; but he has also been, and continues to be, an inspiration for people struggling against exploitation and oppression. Marxism is still a vibrant if much-contested body of thought indispensable to social science. Indeed, some Marxist arguments are so widely accepted that people do not know that Marx gave birth to them. Much current Marx scholarship seeks to recover his legacy free from the damage done to it by others, while there is still much to be said by Marxists about the workings of capitalism in the era of 'globalisation'. See Chapter 5.

May 1968. The year 1968 was one of social and radical political unrest (particularly among the young) across the Western world and beyond. In the USA, regular student demonstrations against the Vietnam War led to violent clashes with the police. There were also riots sparked off by issues of race and civil rights. In April 1968, Martin Luther King was assassinated, and in June so was Robert Kennedy. In August, at the Democratic Convention in Chicago, 'Yippie' student activists and police clashed to brutal effect. In the UK, there were also clashes at anti-war demonstrations, and many students staged sit-ins at their universities. Meanwhile, in Czechoslovakia (at that time part of the communist Eastern Bloc of nations), the government began to liberalise and become openly critical of the Soviet Union. It was invaded by Warsaw Pact troops in August. There were scenes of unrest and protest from Mexico to Europe but with most strength in France, where, in May, widespread demonstrations and street actions by students sparked off sympathetic strikes by workers. The situation was such that President de Gaulle fled Paris in fear. The overall mood of radicalism and revolutionary spirit left an indelible mark on many. In France, a whole generation of philosophers was understood to be associated with 'May '68' and its radical opposition both to the capitalist state and to the Stalinism of the French Communist Party. Philosophers such as **Lyotard, Deleuze, Derrida** and others are sometimes referred to as 'soixante-huitards' ('68ers).

Metanarratives. Term used to describe grand theories and philosophies that attempt to explain everything about society and history. Such would include both Marxism and the liberal notion of historical progress and other theories that aspire to universalism. The term is most often used critically by those opposed to the narratives in question (usually, but not exclusively, postmodernists).

Methodological individualism. The perspective in social science that social phenomena should be explained in terms of the individual actions of people and not by reference to some underlying structure. As such, it is very much a rejection of Marxist approaches.

Mill, John Stuart. English philosopher and political economist (1806–73). One of England's most important political philosophers and a central figure in the history of liberal thinking. His work was wide-ranging, covering logic, political economy, a critique of the utilitarianism of his father James Mill and early advocacy of the rights of women. His short text *On Liberty* is a powerful expression of the importance of personal freedom. Mill wanted to maintain the 'antagonism of opinions' in society against both state incursion and the 'tyranny' of common opinion. He made famous his 'one very simple principle': that nobody had any right to curtail the actions of another except in self-defence. Instead, he promoted 'experiments in living' so that we might all be helped to find the best way to live. Although he advocated a policy of weighted voting (giving more votes to the better educated and more able), which seems to us now a clearly elitist position, Mill should be understood as a believer in the perfectability of human beings and in their capacity for development and improvement. It was to assist this that he advocated elitist measures rather than because of a commitment to the rule of the 'best'. With this belief, Mill's liberalism can certainly be differentiated from the cruder utilitarianism and libertarianism that are popular today.

Modernity. This most unsatisfactory term is used by sociologists, social theorists and social scientists to refer to the shift from 'traditional' societies (presumed to be small-scale, rural, agricultural and dominated by superstition) to modern ones (presumed to be larger in scale, industrial, urban and dominated by rationality). Obviously this is a huge generalisation which has meant that actually defining the concept of modernity has become a central (perhaps the only) project of Western sociology. One might say that such a consciousness of living in a period that is in need of definition is a hallmark of modernity.

More, Thomas. English Renaissance man, lawyer, politician, theologian, writer and martyr (1478–1535). Lord Chancellor to King Henry VIII, More attacked Protestantism (writing works against Luther) and defended the Church, but fell out with Henry when he refused to sanction the king's divorce from Catherine of Aragon and did not attend the coronation of Anne Boleyn. Becoming associated with those who opposed Henry's break with the church in Rome, More was accused of treason, imprisoned in the Tower of London and beheaded on 6 July 1535. He was made a saint by Pope Pius XI in 1935. His interest for political thought stems primarily from his short work *Utopia* (a word he invented and which in Latin means 'no place'). In it, he imagined an ideal society on a remote island in which the people lived a frugal, communal (some say communistic) existence with minimal interest in material possessions.

Morris, William. British artist and socialist utopian (1834–96). Often regarded as a romantic, Morris, when not producing his own artistic work, wrote about the dehumanising nature of industrial work, which destroyed what he saw as the creative and pleasurable aspects of labour. He also wrote a utopian text called *News from Nowhere* and was an inspiration for many sections of the twentieth-century British New Left. Much can be learned about our time by reflecting on the fact that Morris is now best known for designing wallpaper.

New Labour. The Labour Party in Britain was formed in 1900 in order to provide representation in Parliament for the labour movement (the trade unions and socialist societies). In 1994, Tony Blair was elected its leader. He continued and extended a series of reforms designed both to make the party more electable and to draw it away from its roots in the labour movement and in traditional post-war socialist policies. Reforming also the image and marketing of the party, he led the strategy of calling the party 'New' Labour, a name which though not official has all but stuck. Tony Blair was elected Prime Minister of the UK in 1997 and re-elected in 2001.

Nichiren. Thirteenth-century Japanese Buddhist (1222–82). Nichiren was an important figure in the spread of Buddhism and in the clarification of its philosophy. He lived at a time of political and military turmoil when Japan was threatened by Mongol invasion, and argued that Japan's leaders should take steps to unify the Buddhist religion (thus bringing about stability, peace and prosperity) by promoting one form of it (the Lotus Sutra) over others (such as Zen).

Nietzsche, Friedrich. German philosopher (1844–1900). Nietzsche is more difficult to summarise than any other philosopher of note. Much of the meaning of his work is contained in its expression – a heady mix of aphorism, provocation, daring argumentation and poetic meandering. The project of his work (if it can be called that) was a kind of call to arms for a new type of human being who might transcend the decadence and nihilism of Western culture which, according to Nietzsche, was based on a 'slave morality' in which being was defined by the very oppression it claimed to denounce or transcend. Currently, the most influential aspect of Nietzsche's work is his theory of power, which he regarded as a force that constituted (as we might now say) social relations, a constant presence striving for its expression. Where most political thinkers today seek to contain or limit power, Nietzsche urges us to expand and celebrate it, for the increase of power is the feeling of joy and the celebration of life. This has particularly influenced thinkers such as Foucault. For a beginner's guide to Nietzsche and politics, see Keith Ansell-Pearson, *Introduction to Nietzsche as Political Thinker: The Perfect Nihilist* (Cambridge University Press, 1994). The works themselves have to be read if one is to get a sense of their passion and frightening beauty. The Cambridge edition of *Nietzsche: 'On the Genealogy of Morality' and Other Writings* edited by Ansell-Pearson (1994) is very well done, but *Human, All Too Human* or *Twilight of the Idols* are perhaps more immediately exciting and dizzying in their virtuosity.

Nomadology. This term is associated with the thought of **Deleuze** and **Guattari** and particularly their attempt to create a philosophy of movement, action and becoming as opposed to one of stasis, containment and being. Nomadic thought, as the name suggests, is always moving on, creating and defying as it does so. See their little book *Nomadology* (Semiotext(e), 1986), which is an extract from their big book *A Thousand Plateaus: Capitalism and Schizophrenia* (University of Minnesota Press, 1987). See also Chapter 9.

Normative. Political theories that are normative aim to provide a prescriptive standard for conduct – to provide norms of behaviour or procedure.

Nozick, Robert. North American political philosopher associated with laissez-faire and libertarian thought (1938–2002). Nozick's breakthrough work was *Anarchy, State, and Utopia* (1974), regarded by many as the great challenge to Rawls' *A Theory of Justice*. This book gave primacy to the rights of the individual and advocated a minimal state. However, it was not simply a conservative apologia for laissez-faire economics, since he went all the way and defended individual rights that conservatives might object to (such as those pertaining to lifestyle). His later work tackled philosophical questions of a broader nature.

Ontology/ontological. Ontology is that form of metaphysical philosophy that deals with the nature or essence of being. As such, it is often used in a rather loose way to refer to something like 'first principles'. To ask after the ontology of a particular political theory is to ask how it conceives of the fundamental nature or essence of being. As such, one can often find that what underlies conflict or argument between rival political positions is a hidden clash of ontologies (fundamentally differing conceptions of the nature of being).

Orientalism. This concept was developed by the literary and critical theorist Edward Said. He argued that, in writing about the 'East', Western analysts tended to treat the region as if it were all one unified and exotic phenomenon. Furthermore, such analyses generated forms of knowledge of use in controlling and dominating the regions in question. Hence the Orient was objectified and seen as something in need of taming and managing. It was defined not in its own terms but in the terms given to it by Western scholars. This matters now because Orientalist forms of thought continue to shape scholarship, analysis and policy towards the Middle East and the Arabic peoples which are premised on the implicit assumption that 'they' are a problem and their main problem is that they are not like 'us'. Said's concept of Orientalism is central to the area of literary and cultural studies known as postcolonialism.

Original position. A conceptual (though some might say literary) device deployed by the political philosopher John Rawls in his book *A Theory of Justice*. It is similar in purpose to the pre-political 'state of nature' imagined by early modern and modern political theorists so that they could formulate an idea about how and why people form a political association in the first place. Rawls' aim is not to establish the grounds for political obligation but to work out what form of social organisation and distribution of rights and resources would be just. He asks us to imagine ourselves in a pre-political position behind a 'veil of ignorance' such that we do not know what sort of people we might be in society (male, female, rich, poor, talented and so on). All we know is that we are self-interested rational actors out to maximise our personal benefit. What sort of social system could we agree on if in this position? Rawls' argument (to cut a very long story short) is that we would choose a course of action that would allow some to do well out of social arrangements but also ensure that none would do really badly. This means we would endorse, firstly, a fundamental equality of rights to liberty and, secondly, what Rawls calls the 'difference prin-ciple'. This states that inequalities will be such that they benefit the worst off and, if attached to particular social positions, then these will be open to all fairly and equally. This latter principle effectively justifies some sort of gentle system of redistribution of wealth through progressive taxation (where the richer are taxed a little more than the poor). Rawls has been one of the most important of recent philosophers in the Anglo-American tradition and incredibly influential. His arguments are mostly directed at the liberal tradition, especially utilitarian-ism, which he criticises because it may lead, in the name of greatest happiness for the greatest number, to the systematic exclusion of a minority.

Overdetermined. Althusserian concept derived from psychoanalysis. Put simply, it means multi-causal. For **Freud**, the images in dreams derive from our unconscious, but the analytic process is complicated because a particular image may be caused by a number of different internal conflicts, not all of which can be established. The picture is complicated even more by the fact that one symptom may trigger others or convert previous traumas into the source of a neurosis. **Althusser** took over the term and applied it in his Marxist analysis of society to suggest that certain phenomena may not be explicable by reference to one fundamental contradiction in society (such as class conflict) and that areas of weakness in a social formation are overdetermined (they occur where a number of conflicts converge or where in concert they cause other things to become sources of conflict or contradiction). The concept allowed Althusser to break away from a Marxism focused solely on class conflict and to develop a more complex theory of social determination.

Overlapping consensus. A concept central to the later arguments of John Rawls. One of the central problems for contemporary liberalism is how to maintain the notion that the liberal state is neutral when it comes to the idea of the good life that citizens hold (i.e. that it does not try to make citizens live their lives in particular ways but leaves them to decide what is the right and best way to be) when: (1) society is becoming more diverse, and different ideas of the good come into conflict, (2) the state is thus asked to adjudicate over questions of the good, and (3) liberalism has been challenged by some critics for actually being a particular notion of the good and (4) has faced the related criticism that it undermines the communal basis of life in which notions of the good are formed. Rawls has claimed that his philosophy of justice as fairness is not a substantive view of the good life, not what he calls a 'comprehensive doctrine' (i.e. one that pronounces on all aspects of life). It is a political not metaphysical conception, he argues, in that it comments only on the basic structure of society. What a theory has to do, he says, is build on the site where different conceptions of the good life, different 'comprehensive doctrines', converge. This is the point of overlapping consensus.

Owen, Robert. British utopian socialist (1771–1858). Originally an industrialist managing cotton mills, Owen was appalled at the long hours and harsh conditions of the workers (especially the children). Convinced that environment shaped character, he thought that if one could organise the right sort of community the best character would follow. In addition to expounding this idea (and participating in the emergence of the co-operative and trade-union movement), he set up experiments in such communal living, notably at New Lanark in Scotland and later at New Harmony in Indiana, USA. He was also an active advocate of the reform of working conditions.

Pahlavi regime. Another name for the period of Iranian political history stemming from the accession to power of Riza Khan in 1921 up to the **Iranian Revolution** in 1979. Pahlavi was the family name of the dynasty.

Parole. **Term used in the linguistic theory of Ferdinand de Saussure.** Saussure's intention was to develop a theory of language as a closed system of differences. The structured system underlies and makes possible any actual use of speech. The structure is known as *langue* and the actual utterance which is dependent on it is *parole*.

Particularism. The opposite of universalism. Where moral universalists are concerned with principles that apply regardless of context, particularists stress the opposite: the irreducible contexts of moral actions or decisions. The term can also refer to those focused on cultural and historical specificity in the understanding of social or political action rather than on the search for generalisable laws.

Performative. Performative utterances as defined by **J. L. Austin** are those in which the saying of a thing is also the doing of it (as in 'I promise' or 'I do' when getting married). The conditions for such statements (and for their success) are much analysed by Austin. The notion has been redeveloped recently by, for example, Judith Butler.

Plato. Greek philosopher (427–347 BC). Plato is probably the second most famous of all philosophers, the most famous being Socrates, about whom we know anything primarily because of the writings of Plato. With good reason, Plato is understood to be the founder of Western philosophy. One of the central aims of his works is to define philosophy (as the search for true knowledge and virtue) against the activities of poets, sophists and so on. His primary political work is also one of his most important philosophically: the *Republic* in which he advocates rule by a philosophical elite inclined towards the truth of the universe.

Pocock, J. G. A. New Zealand/British historian of political thought. Associated in part with the Cambridge School, and founder of the Folger Centre for the History of British Political Thought, he has written a number of important studies on the history and the language of political thought.

Positivism. Philosophical approach. For positivists, the only proper data for philosophical (or any other analysis) are empirical observations which can be subjected to rigorous analysis in order to establish the fixed laws that underlie them. As such, positivism entails a certain scientific attitude. It is associated with the 'founder' of sociology, August Comte and later with the Logical Positivism of the Vienna circle of philosophers, mathematicians and scientists. In political thought today, many (perhaps most) would describe themselves as **postpositivists**, though this refers to a variety of positions.

Postcolonialism. A general movement within cultural and literary theory that focuses on the relationship between colonialism and culture and its impact after colonialism. It is hard to summarise, but stems from the view that colonial countries defined their subject populations in certain ways (in some cases inventing the nations they ruled). These definitions (that made possible colonial administrations and bureaucracies) were, naturally, produced from the point of view of the colonial occupier. In many instances, they provided the very terms and tools with which the subjugated populations would come to understand themselves and assert their independence; but this often left a legacy after colonialism, as the people liberated from colonial rule had still to liberate itself from colonial culture. Postcolonialism theorises the ways in which the culture of former colonies (and of the former colonisers) is shaped by this negotiation. A particularly important theorist here is Edward Said, who developed the concept of **Orientalism.**

Postpositivism. This term describes a number of theories of science and philosophies of knowledge that came about after the critique of the positivist approach (according to which the findings of science were directly and unproblematically related to reality and presumed to describe laws in action in the real world). Postpositivists stress, to varying degrees, the extent to which the laws we ascribe to the world around us are our own constructions.

Power/knowledge. Term used by Foucault to denote the linkage of operations of power with forms of knowledge such that power operates through knowledge and knowledge is a form taken by power.

Pragmatism. Philosophical movement. For pragmatists, to assess the truth of some claim we should look not to its inward rationality but to its practical efficacy. It has precedents but was brought together in the nineteenth century by US thinkers such as Charles Peirce, John Dewey and William James (although they produced slightly different versions of it). The leading contemporary exponent is Rorty. For a readable introduction, see William James' *Pragmatism* (various editions).

Psychoanalysis. The medical/philosophical movement effectively founded by Sigmund **Freud** that emphasises the workings of the unconscious mind and its hidden influence on our conscious actions. For Freud, our repressed desires and instinctual drives manifest themselves in unconscious actions that surreptitiously express our true wishes. One of the most influential of all twentieth-century theories, the impact of psychoanalysis on our culture is immeasurable, despite the controversy surrounding many of its claims. Its influence on politics and political theory has been extensive but indirect. Psychoanalytic theories have influenced governmental approaches to propaganda and population-management, while in the intellectual world they have entered into cultural analyses that see in our wider (especially popular) culture expressions of a kind of societal unconscious.

Public sphere. According to Habermas, this is 'first of all a realm of our social life in which something approaching public opinion can be formed . . . A proportion of the public sphere comes into being in every conversation in which private individuals assemble to form a public body.' The term thus denotes that aspect of social life in which people gather to discuss their society, politics and so forth. The idea of a public sphere is associated with enlightenment thinking in that, for Kant, public life, and the expression of views within the public sphere, were crucial to the life of a democratic republic and to the development of reason. A central question for political thought today is whether or not there can be a public sphere in societies that are large, complex and dominated by a privately owned mass entertainment media. In his early work, Habermas argued that we have ceased to be a 'culture-debating' society and have become a 'culture-consuming' one, while the public sphere has been reduced to a realm of opinion-management and public relations. There is also a broader and looser use of the term in relation to the **public–private distinction.**

Public–private distinction. Many hold that a central feature of liberal thought is its distinction between a public realm (where people meet, trade, argue and organise, and in which they are subject to law and obligation) and a private realm (the domestic or family household) where they are in charge of themselves. The distinction has been criticised heavily by feminist theorists, who have shown how it is gendered. Public life has been a preserve of male equals, while the private sphere is a domain of male domination over women and children. Because actions in the domestic sphere were private and not political, it was necessary for women to assert the political aspects of domestic relations which often involved the control and abuse of women. For example, courts were, for a long time, reluctant to recognise a crime of domestic abuse, and it was not until 1991 that a crime of rape in marriage was recognised in British law. See Jean Bethke Elshtain, *Public Man, Private Woman: Women in Social and Political Thought* (Princeton University Press, 1981); Susan Moller Okin, 'Gender, the Public, and the Private', in Anne Phillips (ed.), *Feminism and Politics* (Oxford University Press, 1998); and Joan B. Landes (ed.), *Feminism, the Public and the Private* (Oxford University Press, 1998). See also Chapter 7.

Punjabi. One of the family of languages making up the Indo-Iranian subfield. The Punjab is a region in the north of India and was one of the centres of the ancient Indus civilisation from which Europeans are believed to have come. Occupied by the British in the nineteenth century, it was partitioned in 1947, one half being in Pakistan and mostly Muslim, the other half with a large Sikh population but also some Hindus. The area has continued to be a site of ethnoreligious tension between Sikhs and Hindus.

Quebec/Quebecois. Province of Canada. Canada is a confederate state made up of ten provinces and three territories. The eastern province of Quebec is French-speaking and has a French-orientated culture distinct from that of the rest of the country. This has presented a political problem for years, since a sizeable number of Quebecois desire some form of independence. The original Canadian constitution recognised the division and made the state officially bilingual, but in 1974 the province was made entirely French-speaking. The most serious event in the conflict between Quebec and the rest of Canada occurred in 1970 when separatist terrorists kidnapped a British diplomat and the Quebec Minister of Labour, killing the latter. When nationalists took power in the provincial parliament in 1976, they downgraded English-speaking and caused a movement of such speakers out of the province. In the 1980s, a number of referenda on secession were narrowly defeated and there was much constitutional disputation. In the 1990s, Quebec was recognised by the parliament to possess a distinct culture, and since that time outright support for the separatists has fallen. The whole phenomenon stands as a central example of the multicultural society, of the problems and possibilities of different peoples living under one regime.

Queer studies. University/intellectual movement studying all aspects of the gay lifestyle, experience and developing recognition of the queer aspect to all social activities/societies.

Raj. Deriving from the Sanskrit for 'king' in Hindi, the word means 'rule' or 'reign'. It is specifically used to describe the period of British dominion over India from 1757 to 1947.

Rational choice theory. A methodological school of social science. Rational choice theory adapts the techniques of economic analysis to form a social theory. Basically, it assumes that people act rationally in self-interested ways that are intended to maximise their utility (i.e. they weigh up the costs and benefits of courses of action and choose the one that will benefit them most). Other theorists have started from similar individualist premises and with the assumption of purposeful, rational behaviour (**Weber**, for example). What distinguishes rational choice theory is that it takes this to be the sole or primary form of social behaviour and that it is applicable to all spheres of social action. It is fundamentalist in its presumption of **methodological individualism** – the idea that social action is ultimately the end result of various individual actions and that, in this sense, structure does not exist. The attraction is that it is possible to use the theory to build up mathematically modelled and testable hypotheses of social behaviour. But, to do so, it is necessary to convert all actions into a calculable form. A particular problem for rational choice theory has been that of collective action. Rational choice theorists try to explain this by reference to the actions of individuals, though it is not clear it can explain how such groups form in the first place. That said, it is probably the most widely employed method in political science and is of inestimable importance in shaping contemporary government, politics and culture in general. It is also capable of greater subtlety than this summary allows. See (among many works) James S. Coleman and Thomas J. Fararo (eds), *Rational Choice Theory: Advocacy and Critique* (Sage, 1992) and Dennis Chong, *Rational Lives: Norms and Values in Politics and Society* (University of Chicago Press, 2000).

Reagan, Ronald (b. 1911). Successful film actor, one-time president of the Screen Actors' Guild, Governor of California for two terms and finally the fortieth President of the USA (from 1981–9). The Reagan era is important, for it marked a sharp shift away from sympathy for state intervention into society or economy to improve the welfare of citizens, complementing the policies of Margaret Thatcher in the United Kingdom. Under Reagan, taxes (personal but especially corporate) were cut, and welfare spending was cut but defence spending rocketed as part of the Reagan plan of 'Peace Through Strength' during the Cold War. During his presidency, significant advances were made in US–Soviet relations. Supporters of Reagan argue that his tenure brought pride back to America, reformed the national finances and brought prosperity to all. Critics say that it left the nation with record budget deficits, increased inequality and greater power over government for corporations.

Realism. Simply put, realism is the view that there is a real world which exists and can be described in terms that are independent of our mental processes of apprehending it (in other words, that scientific findings express the truth in an uncomplicated fashion). Some see this as 'naive' realism. A more modified version goes under the name of Critical Realism. All of this is not to be confused with realism in international relations, which is the view that to understand the actions of states one should just be realistic and accept that they are all out for what they can get.

Reformation. A religious movement of sixteenth-century Europe, and of inestimable significance, the Reformation can be said (for those who like drama) to have begun on 31 October 1527 when the monk and theologian Martin Luther nailed his '95 Theses' to the door of the cathedral in Wittenberg, Germany. Naturally, in truth, the Reformation has much earlier roots in a variety of forms of religious dissent and in the cultural shifts of Renaissance humanism. Luther's missive invited debate on various aspects of Church practice and doctrine but in particular challenged the giving of indulgences (exemptions from punishment for sins) which were, at the time, subject to much abuse and often granted in return for financial and other favours. In short, Luther attacked what he saw as the corruption of the Roman Church and denied the absolute authority of the papacy. Subsequently, Calvin developed this Protestant theology, emphasising justification through faith and not works, and stressing the inherently sinful nature of mankind which could only be redeemed through absolute faith in Christ and fidelity to the word of God. The Reformation swept across Europe, transforming religious practice and introducing in a new way the perennial problem of the relation between civil and ecclesiastical authority. Ultimately, it led to the ending of the power of the Catholic Church in a number of European countries and in turn to a cultural transformation that, if **Weber** is to be believed, laid the basis for capitalism and industrialisation.

Relativism. Various things get given the label 'relativism', and it is important to be careful and to distinguish between **different uses.** One form of moral relativism simply argues that societies produce moralities that are shaped by the times and circumstances of that society. In other words, any particular morality is relative to the society that produces it. Sometimes, usually by critics, this is construed as the argument that all moralities are as good as any other or equally valid. There is also epistemological relativism, which can be divided into the interesting proposition that forms of knowledge and truth are conditioned by the societies in which they are developed and the straw man that asserts that any idea of the truth is as good as any other. Relativism is to be contrasted with moral or epistemological absolutisms that assert the fixed truth or morality usually discovered because the proponent has access to God.

Republicanism. The opposite of monarchism. In a republic, government is by all the people and not just by one person. Because republicanism has usually been born of opposition to monarchies or other forms of despotism, it is also associated with concepts of liberty and citizenship (since being a citizen is the opposite of being a subject of a king). Republicanism was a widespread political philosophy and actuality in the classical world, most notably in Rome. It was revived in the later Middle Ages initially in the form of city states, most famously Florence. Despite its attachment to liberty and citizenship, however, Republicanism is to be distinguished from Liberalism. The main difference between these two positions is that republican thinkers usually argue that the people must be virtuous citizens if the republic is not to collapse into tyranny or decadence: they must themselves pursue the common good of the republic and not their own interests and must be prepared to be active in and to defend their republic. Thus republics tend to have a strong collective doctrine, something which liberal states, officially, eschew. Republican ideas influenced the shaping of the American constitution and the ideals of the French Revolution. Today, liberal ideals of freedom as a private possession distinguished by the absence of restraints predominate, and the republican vision of freedom as a civic position experienced in public is held by Arendt, toyed with by **Skinner** and occasionally advanced as a solution to the crisis of contemporary political culture.

Résumé. In British English, a résumé is known as a curriculum vitae (c.v.).

Rousseau, Jean-Jacques. French political philosopher (1712–78). Rousseau has a well-earned place in the canon of legendary political theorists, for his fraught character as well as his bold thinking. His most famous work is *The Social Contract*, in which he sought to answer the question of how naturally free man could submit to being ruled by the laws of others. His answer was that one could only submit to laws that had been made by oneself. It was thus necessary for the state to be a republic in which all participated in the framing of laws which were based on the 'general will' of the community. He was a Romantic attached to nature, and prone to celebrate the natural condition of man as one in which, untainted by the vicissitudes and pretensions of society, humans existed as 'noble savages'. He influenced both Kant and Marx but has been decried as the philosopher of totalitarianism for his argument that, in order to realise the necessity of submitting only to the general will, people could be 'forced to be free'.

Saussure, Ferdinand de. Swiss theorist of linguistics (1857–1913). Saussure is chiefly famous for his *Course on General Linguistics* (Fontana, 1974) delivered to his students, who subsequently reconstructed it for publication after his death. In the course, his aim was to establish the scientific basis for the objective study of language. He argued that we should look at the underlying structure of language (which he called *langue*) since this makes possible the actual utterances (*parole*) we make. The system or structure of language was understood by him as one established through the differential relations of the terms.

There is no intrinsic connection between the word 'dog' (or 'chien', or 'Hund') and the things we refer to with these terms (these sounds or black marks on pages). They are signifiers that conjure up the concept of 'dog' in our minds. They function as meaningful terms because they are part of a system and are different to other words (such as 'cat' or 'log'). This approach to language as a system of differences with a kind of autonomy from the real world influenced the later structuralist anthropology of Claude **Lévi-Strauss** and generations of cultural theorists. As a short introduction, see Jonathan Culler, *Saussure* (Fontana, 1976).

Sears case. One of the longest-running of legal cases taken by the US Equal Employment Opportunity Commission was against Sears Roebuck, a large chain of clothing stores in the USA. Basing its case on statistical evidence, the EEOC alleged that the company was against hiring women in management and sales positions. The case drew academic attention for a lot of obvious reasons but also because some of the evidence given in defence was presented by female academics who claimed that the statistics revealed only that men and women have different attitudes and behaviours and so, naturally, would choose different sorts of career. See Ruth Milkman (1986), 'Women's History and the Sears Case', *Feminist Studies* 12 (2): 375–400.

Skinner, Quentin. English historian of political thought. Skinner came to prominence as the key figure in the development of a new approach to the history of political thought based on study of the language and using this to investigate the contextualised intentions of writers of key works of political thought. The best introduction to this important approach can be found in *Meaning and Context: Quentin Skinner and his Critics* edited by James Tully (Polity, 1988). See also Chapter 2 and the extract by John Dunn.

Smith, Adam. Scottish philosopher and political economist (1723–90). Smith is known as the founder of classical political economy, and his economic and moral philosophy (part of a broader movement known as the Scottish Enlightenment) have recently been revived in the context of economic doctrine in the USA and the UK. It is important, therefore, that we understand it properly. In *The Wealth of Nations*, he showed how the pursuit of self-interest could lead to public benefit if undertaken in the context of free and competitive markets. An 'invisible hand' guided the totality of exchanges such that, at the end, everything would balance out and each get what they wanted. This notion of private greed leading to public gain has been used to justify a return to the doctrine of free markets over the intervention of states in the management of economy and society. But the revivalists tend to emphasise a notion of the rational actor that Smith would not have shared, and he also paid due attention to the underlying institutional and cultural structures needed for freedom and the market to flourish.

Spinoza, Baruch. European philosopher (1632–77). Spinoza carries the rare distinction of having managed to be excommunicated not only from the Jewish faith but from the Christian one also. Writing at the time when Europe was in transition from medieval thinking to **Enlightenment**, Spinoza's is one of the most remarkable of all the rationalist metaphysical schemas. In *The Ethics*, he employed a geometrical method to derive what he saw as a complete and logical description of the universe premised on the notion that God and nature are the same thing. This pantheism caused him to be labelled both an atheist (for its materialism) and, later, a 'god-intoxicated' man. He was also a supporter of republicanism in the Dutch state where he lived for most of his later life. Spinoza was a significant influence on Marxist thinkers such as **Althusser**.

State of nature. The concept of a state of nature was widely used in early modern and modern political thought (**Hobbes, Locke** and **Rousseau** most notably) as a device for explaining the origins of political obligation. This entailed imagining what natural man would be like (man without the benefits of society) and extrapolating from it the reasons why persons would come together to alienate some degree of their individual power through a social contract with each other. Different theorists conceive of the state of nature differently and thus, naturally, reach different conclusions.

Strauss, Leo. German-born North American political philosopher (1899–1973). Leo Strauss was a kind of conservative, the main animating principle of whose philosophy was that the moral crisis of our times (nihilism essentially) should force us back to the philosophy of the ancients and especially to Plato, whom we should read in search of timeless truths rather than in a historicist fashion. For Strauss, everything went wrong with Machiavelli (i.e. modern republicanism) when human will became the source of moral guidance. It put humanity and culture above the nature to which only the true philosopher is open. However, this true philosopher, because he is open to nature, will come into conflict with the political order which is precisely defined by its opposition to nature. Strauss was quite an influence on American political thought in that he turned attention back to the classics and because his students have carried his conservatism on into the academy and the wider culture (including government). See Shadia B. Drury, *Leo Strauss and the American Right* (Macmillan, 1997).

Structuralism. Theory of language and culture. Structuralism examines the underlying structures that make possible linguistic statements or cultural formations. It is associated most with the work of **Ferdinand de Saussure** and **Claude Lévi-Strauss.**

Subject. The concept of the subject has become central to contemporary social and cultural thought. By subject is meant the 'individual' or 'self', but not in a straightforward way. Nor is it a synonym for identity (although this can be a closely related concept). Rather, the concept of subject refers us to a series of particular configurations of what (or who) a self or an identity is. A self becomes a subject by grasping itself in certain ways. We might grasp at a sense of ourselves via recourse to a notion of human nature (of what is essential to the human subject); but many contemporary critical theories emphasise their discontinuity with concepts of human nature, instead understanding the subject as a construct of some kind rather than an essence that precedes historical or cultural influence. It follows that there can be a history of subjectivity in that humans have not at all times and in all places exercised or achieved consciousness of self in the same way. Such a history is, in large part, not a history of the subject but of the discourses, the cognitive frameworks (such as those of human nature), through which subjectivity is made graspable, experienced and acted upon. It is a short step then to investigating how power (or ideology) 'encourages' us to conceive of our subjectivity in particular ways that may serve the interests of some part of society.

Synchronic. The opposite of diachronic. To study things synchronically is to study them in their static, structural dimension, without regard to their historical or temporal aspect.

Syncretic. The merging of different forms. This term may refer to beliefs (particularly religious) or cultural practices in general. It suggests the combination of elements in ways that still preserve something of their individual flavour rather than their absolute recombination into something completely new.

Tao/Taoism/Taoist. Eastern system of thought and/or religion. Tao (or Dao) literally means 'the way'. The philosophy of Taoism is associated with a contemporary of Confucius called Lao Tzu (or Laozi).

Taylor, Charles. Canadian philosopher and political theorist. At the time of writing, he is Emeritus Professor in the Department of Philosophy at McGill University in the Quebec province of Canada. Taylor is associated with communitarianism and with multiculturalism. Philosophically, he is influenced by Hegel and has revived Hegelian concepts relating to the realisation of the self in a communal context and, crucially, of the need for recognition from others. These he has applied in a sensitive way to political questions. See his *Sources of the Self: The Making of Modern Identity* (Harvard University Press, 1989) and Amy Gutmann (ed.), *Multiculturalism and 'The Politics of Recognition'* (Princeton University Press, 1992).

Thatcher, Margaret. British Prime Minister, 1979–90 (b. 1925). The Thatcher years in Britain were a time of great political change and trauma. For her supporters, Thatcher transformed the country, returned its lost pride, removed the threat of socialism embodied in the trade unions and won the Cold War. To her detractors, she was an autocratic ruler who needlessly created painful levels of unemployment and promoted an aggressive and selfish individualism. During her tenure in Downing Street, she was a close ally of Ronald **Reagan.**

Thomas, Clarence. In 1991, a vacancy arose on the bench of the Supreme Court of the United States, and President George Bush nominated the African American Clarence Thomas. He replaced another African American, Justice Marshall, who had overseen many progressive judgements on desegregation. But Thomas was well known as a political conservative and opponent of affirmative action and abortion. Despite this opposition, Thomas looked likely to be confirmed by the Senate until **Anita Hill,** a law professor at the University of Oklahoma, accused Thomas of sexual harassment when she had worked for him some years earlier. She alleged that he had repeatedly discussed sexual matters with her including the content of pornographic films he had seen. In defence, Thomas raised issues of race and prejudicial assumptions about the sexuality of black men. Events spiralled into a frenzy of allegations and denials and a bitter hearing touching on sensitive issues of race, sexuality, gender and discrimination. The event publicised sexual harassment at work and polarised opinion. Thomas was confirmed by the Senate and is now a Supreme Court judge.

Thompson, E. P. British (English) Marxist historian, radical activist and peace campaigner (1924–93). Thompson was a great influence on a tradition of British historical study that, while motivated by political and Marxist concerns, rejected the high theory of continental Marxism. In his essay 'The Poverty of Theory', Thompson launched a sharp polemic against **Althusser** and the historians influenced by him who sought large theories of society and history and eschewed attention to the doings and sayings of the working class themselves, who Thompson, in a famous phrase, wished to save from 'the enormous condescension of posterity'. Founder of a number of important journals (including *New Left Review*), Thompson was crucial to the construction of a tradition of English dissent that began with Blake and **Morris,** a project taken up by a generation of English radical historians. An advocate of 'socialist humanism', he was also a tireless protester against nuclear weapons, and some have argued that his contribution will be judged by history to have been crucial to the ending of the Cold War.

Tokimune, Hojo. Thirteenth-century Japanese military leader and regent (1268–84). Tokimune became regent at the age of just 18. He led the army in the repelling of Kublai Khan and the Mongol invaders. As a notable leader who repelled foreigners from Japanese lands, he can, for some, have a strong mythic significance. A large-scale television drama about him was made and shown on Japanese television in 2001. He is discussed in the reading by Suzuki found as part of Chapter 11.

Tradition. The way we do stuff. The word derives from the Latin meaning 'to transmit, to deliver'. This sums up tradition well, since it refers to that which has been delivered to us by our forebears. To do things in the traditional way is to do them the way we have always done them, the way that was passed on to us. As such, tradition can often seem intrinsically inimical to political theorising in as much as the latter activity is usually embarked upon in order to find a way of doing things that is better than the one we are doing now or, at least, to find a way of criticising the way things are presently done. For this reason, advocates of tradition as a political principle (conservatives) usually claim to be opposed to political theory. In general, though, political theory has to pay great attention to tradition since it is both the product of one (or more) traditions and any attempt to affect or alter political arrangements needs to take account of the actual traditions of people. Indeed, as **Weber** pointed out, tradition can be understood as one of the major sources of authority – acts and practices can be powerfully justified by an appeal to tradition which makes it something the political activist is wise to attempt to manipulate if he or she can. Strange as it may seem, tradition is likely to become more, not less, important in twenty-first-century politics. Contemporary forms of social life are so fast-moving and subjected to such rapid transformation (what is fashionable one day is not the next, and settled ways of life are disrupted, even destroyed by, social and technological change) that people in search of stability may seek to cling to tradition, which, defended in the traditional way, may justly be called fundamentalism.

Tully, James. Professor in the Department of Political Science at the University of Victoria in Canada. Building on the work of people such as **Wittgenstein, Skinner** and Foucault, he has advocated and developed a critical analysis of democracy that he hopes will allow us (through historical understanding) to make sense of the language games of politics and thus think them better.

Universalism. That which is universal applies always regardless of time or place. If I say that acquisitiveness is a universal feature of human beings, then I am saying you will find it in all people throughout history and regardless of their culture and background. Thinking universally also means abstracting away from the specifics of particular situations. For example, it may be that the acquisitiveness of human beings to which I wish to draw attention takes different forms in different epochs or cultures, but in thinking in a universalistic way I am trying to draw away from these particularities. As such, universalism is important for political theories that wish to be objective in the sense of not being rooted in historically or culturally specific frameworks or merely subjective suppositions. Universalism is thus held to be 'a good thing' by those who want their theories to be seen as rational and grounded but 'a bad thing' by those who think that the particular contexts are important and that losing sight of them could be damaging (see also **Communitarianism, Identity politics** and Chapter 9). Critics of universalism, it should be noted, do not simply reject it but rather argue that those who believe themselves universal are really advocating an unrecognised particularity.

Utilitarianism. Form of political theorising particularly associated with nineteenth-century liberals such as Jeremy Bentham and still absolutely central to debates within Anglo-American liberal theory. In essence, utilitarianism is based on the argument that social and political arrangements should aim to maximise utility. Utility literally means usefulness – to appreciate things because of this usefulness is to be distinguished from appreciating them because of their ornament or beauty or indeed precisely because of their lack of usefulness (as some aesthetes might advocate). In other words, things are wanted in as much as they are useful to achieve some end; the notion of utility always implies use for some end. For Bentham, the aim of human life was pleasure or happiness. He thus set out to understand the world in terms of how useful things were in attaining happiness. This is to be distinguished from other kinds of liberal theorising (particularly that of Kant) in that it is most interested in the consequence of an action where Kant might be more interested in its motivations or intentions. The central principle of utilitarianism is that social arrangements should seek to establish the greatest possible happiness for the greatest number. By means of his 'felicific calculus', Bentham hoped to be able to measure happiness. The problems of utilitarianism are obvious (and well described by an advocate, J. S. Mill): not everyone derives happiness from the same things, and happiness is not merely the presence of pleasure and absence of pain. The view of human nature taken by utilitarianism is perhaps too individualistic (as communitarians might point out) and too narrow. But such quibbles have not stopped something like utilitarianism from essentially shaping the principles of contemporary economics – though in this field, naturally, it is shorn of all social dimensions.

Veil of ignorance. In Rawls' thought experiment regarding the **original position**, we are also supposed to imagine ourselves behind a veil of ignorance such that we do not know what sort of social being we might be. As such, we cannot bank on being one of a privileged class. This is an important step in Rawls' argument and assists in his deriving the difference principle.

Vietnam. Small country at the far end of South-East Asia. In 1858, after long domination by China, the French began military action to colonise Vietnam, assuming full control in 1883. During the Second World War, the Japanese took over. When Japan surrendered, Chinese and British forces both entered the country, but on 16 August 1945 the Viet Minh (a revolutionary anti-colonial group linked to the Indo-Chinese Communist Party) launched a revolutionary offensive, taking control of the capital within days. There were negotiations with the French for independence; but relations soured, and the French began bombing in 1946. A long guerrilla struggle for independence followed, culminating in the division of the country into North (under communist rule) and South in 1954. By 1961, the USA was committing troops to the region in order to challenge Northern attempts to take control of the South. This developed into a long period of nasty (often jungle-based) war with widespread casualties. The USA withdrew on 20 April 1975. The region fell into horrendous conflict involving Laos and Cambodia (which had been sucked into the war by the incursions of both US and Vietnamese forces) which became notorious for the vast death toll of the 'killing fields' when the country was led by Pol Pot and the Khmer Rouge. Greatly affected by the unravelling of the Soviet Union, by the end of the 1990s Vietnam was attempting serious economic reform and mending relations with other nations including China. The impact of the war on the region was, in the long term, catastrophic, and it also had great effects upon US politics, dividing the country and shaping perception of the role of the USA in world politics.

Walzer, Michael. North American political philosopher. At the time of writing, he is a Professor in the Institute for Advanced Study at Princeton. He is often associated with communitarianism, a philosophical label that does not do justice to his range of interests and arguments. He is particularly famous for his argument that in any society there are different worlds or spheres within which different standards of justice hold. So, in the cultural sphere of life, there should be diversity. In the economic, we should strive for the best ways of generating wealth efficiently, while in the welfare sphere we should honour solidarity. In each sphere, this is an important principle; but it could not be applied across all spheres. See *Spheres of Justice* (Basic Books, 1983) and *On Toleration* (Yale University Press, 1997).

Weber, Max. German sociologist (1864–1920). Weber towers over Western social thought and is properly regarded as one of the founders of sociological thinking. His work represents the major intellectual alternative to Marxist theories of society. The range of things he wrote about is so large that it cannot be summarised in a short comment such as this. His famous works include *The Protestant Ethic and the Spirit of Capitalism* which argued that the injunctions of Protestantism (especially Calvinism) to abstain from physical pleasures, to work hard and methodically, laid the basis for the spirit of capitalist accumulation and reinvestment. This was important in that it did not reduce the importance of ideas and motivational structures but linked them to history and economy. Weber went on to analyse the predominance of instrumental rationality in Western society (the deployment of reason in order to attain certain ends, a very influential concept), forms of authority in modern society, the overall impact of a process of rationalisation/demystification, and the growth of bureaucracy. Sometimes regarded as the bourgeois opposition to Marx,

Weber was much more than that. His approach to politics was premised on the sense that political values could not be rooted in reason or in history and that society must be organised to mediate between contending conceptions. This is liberalism; but its **anti-foundational** nature has made Weber a renewable resource for current generations of political thinkers. See also Chapter 1.

Wittgenstein, Ludwig. Austrian-born but British-based philosopher (1889–1951). Wittgenstein began as part of the **analytical** school of philosophy, producing the *Tractatus Logico-Philosophicus*, a landmark work that attempted to specify what could and could not meaningfully be proposed in language. In later work, especially the *Philosophical Investigations*, he appeared to revise his earlier views, adopting instead the influential argument that there is a multiplicity of what he called 'language games': forms of talk that have their own rules and set moves such that communication between them may not be, strictly speaking, possible. His argument that a language game was also a form of life opened the connection between this view and social science as argued, not uncontroversially, by Peter Winch in *The Idea of a Social Science* (Routledge, 1958). Wittgenstein's provocative semi-aphoristic way of writing, in addition to his undoubted imaginative genius and romantically erratic character, have made him into one of the great philosophical figures of the twentieth century.

Wollstonecraft, Mary. English political philosopher (1759–97). One of the most significant figures in the (pre)history of feminism. *A Vindication of the Rights of Women*, published in 1792 not only argued for the granting of full rights to women but also examined womanhood as an experience, advocating the recognition of an essentially genderless essence. Married to William Godwin, she is an important figure from the radical and romantic strand of British leftism. Their daughter Mary Shelley, is famous for writing *Frankenstein*.

World Bank. In July 1944 (as the Second World War was coming to a close and the Allies seemed certain to win), delegates of forty-four nations met at Bretton Woods in New Hampshire. Their purpose was to found global economic institutions to match the global political ones such as the United Nations. The two main ones were the **International Monetary Fund** and the Bank for International Reconstruction and Development, or World Bank. The purpose of the latter was to assist in the provision of loans (the actual money mostly coming from private banks) to countries undergoing reconstruction, beginning with the European countries destroyed by wars and moving on to developing countries. Since the crises in the economy in the 1970s, many have seen the bank as a hard player in world economics, tying its loans to strict requirements for economic restructuring and acting more in the interest of the creditor banks than the developing economies. By the 1980s, the debt of the poorest countries seemed to be spiralling out of control, the payments were almost impossible to meet, and to many the bank began to look more like a loan shark.

Yale School. Yale is, of course, a leading American university in Connecticut. There is not, strictly speaking, a Yale School; but, in the context used in this book, it refers to the influential group of scholars centred on the journal *Yale French Studies*, founded in 1948, which was a major conduit for the introduction of French theory into the world of US literary theory. It is important that such work entered the USA through this route as, arguably, it has coloured its reception.

COPYRIGHT ACKNOWLEDGEMENTS

Political edited by Judith Butler and Joan W. Scott. Reproduced by permission of Taylor and Francis, Inc./Routledge, Inc., http://www.routledge-ny.com

25. *Green Political Thought, 3rd Edition* by Andrew Dobson. Routledge, 2000. Reprinted with permission of Taylor & Francis Ltd.

26. *Green Political Theory* by Robert Goodin, Cambridge: Polity Press, 1992. Reprinted with permission of Blackwell Publishing.

27. *Staying Alive* by Vandana Shiva, London: Zed Books, 1989. Reproduced by permission of Zed Books.

28. *The Return of the Political* by Chantal Mouffe, London: Verso 1993, reproduced by permission.

29. 'The Purity of Politics' reprinted by permission of Sage Publications Ltd from 'A Critique of Pure Politics' by W. E. Connolly in *Philosophy and Social Criticism*, Volume 23 (5).

30. Copyright © 1990 from 'Conclusion: From Parody to Politics' by Judith Butler in *Gender Trouble: Feminism and the Subversion of Identity* edited by Judith Butler. Reproduced by permission of Taylor and Francis, Inc./Routledge, Inc., http://www.routledge-ny.com

31. © Will Kymlicka 1995. Reprinted from *Multicultural Citizenship: A Liberal Theory of Minority Rights* by Will Kymlicka (1995) by permission of Oxford University Press.

32. Young, Iris: *Justice and the Politics of Difference*. Copyright © 1990 by Princeton University Press. Reprinted by permission of Princeton University Press.

33. Bhikhu Parekh, *Rethinking Multiculturalism*, 2000, Macmillan. Reproduced with permission of Palgrave Macmillan. Reprinted by permission of the publisher from *Rethinking Multiculturalism: Culture Diversity and Political Theory* by Bhikhu Parckh, pp. 165–168, 286–292, 249–254, Cambridge, MA: Harvard University Press, Copyright © 2000 by Bhikhu Parekh.

34. Suzuki, D. T.: *Zen and Japanese Culture*. Copyright © 1959 by Princeton University Press. Reprinted by permission of Princeton University Press.

35. 'On Practice' from *Selected Works of Mao Tse-Tung* Volume 1 by Mao Tse-Tung. Lawrence and Wishart, 1954.

36. 'The Necessity for Islamic Government' from *Islam and Revolution* by Imam Khomeini, Mizan Press, 1981, translated by Hamid Algar, reproduced by permission.

37. *Discourses of Sexuality: From Aristotle to AIDS* by Donna C. Stanton, Editor, Ann Arbor: The University of Michigan Press, 1993, reproduced by permission.

38. Chandra Talpade Mohanty, 'Women Workers and Capitalist Scripts: Ideologies of Domination, Common Interests and the Politics of Solidarity'. Copyright 1997 from *Feminist Genealogies, Colonial Legacies, Democratic Futures* by M. Jacqui Alexander and Chandra Talpade Mohanty (eds). Reproduced by permission of Routledge, Inc., part of The Taylor and Francis Group.

39. Reprinted from Gwendolyn Mink: *Welfare's End*. Copyright © 1998 by Cornell University. Used by permission of the publisher, Cornell University Press.

INDEX